Gay San Francisco: Eyewitness Drummer

Awards

National Leather Association Nonfiction Best Book Award
ForeWord Magazine Book of the Year Award
Independent Publisher Book Award
San Francisco Book Festival Award

Critics' Quotes, Author and Book Credentials

• **Jeanne Barney, First and Founding Los Angeles Editor in Chief of** *Drummer*: "For those of us who were there inventing *Drummer* three decades ago, Fritscher serves up a thoroughly researched and well-written account of a particular era in gay history, reporting on what may well have been 'The Golden Age of Leather' and of *Drummer*...*Gay San Francisco* is an historical resource for those who want to know How Things Used to Be, as well as a nostalgic look back for those of us who were ourselves eyewitness participants. I invite you all to join us in this extraordinary walk down memory lane."

• **John F. Karr,** *Bay Area Reporter*: "Veteran author Jack Fritscher is an anarchist of gay sexual prose, the man who invented the South of Market prose style (as well as its magazines...).... Fritscher writes with sweat and wit."

• **San Francisco** *Chronicle*: "Jack Fritscher reads gloriously!"

• **Samuel Streit, Director, Special Collections, Brown University**: "....*Gay San Francisco* is a remarkable history of a remarkable time in a remarkable place, combining contemporary documents, photographs and reportage with a first-hand and first-rate memoir that brings an unforgettable era back to life...."

• **Planetout.com:** Fritscher is "the ground-breaking editor of *Drummer* magazine."

• **Willie Walker, GLBT Historical Society**, San Francisco: "Jack Fritscher is a prolific writer who since the late sixties has helped document the gay world and the changes it has undergone."

• **Catherine Johnson-Roehr, Curator of Art, Artifacts, and Photographs, The Kinsey Institute for Research in Sex, Gender, and Reproduction, Indiana University**: "Those of us who are concerned with the preservation of GLBT history are very fortunate that Jack Fritscher has such a remarkable memory for the people, places, and pivotal events that he has witnessed over his lifetime. His long association with

Drummer in San Francisco placed him at the center of the revolution, and *Gay San Francisco* is filled with significant details from those years."

• **Mark Thompson,** editor emeritus, *The Advocate,* author of *Leatherfolk*: "What a good thing Fritscher has done in *Gay San Francisco*...This is an invaluable testament that will be useful for decades to come."

• **Joseph W. Bean,** former **editor of** *Drummer* and **executive director, Leather Archives & Museum**, Chicago, abridged from *Leather Times: News from the Leather Archives & Museum*: "When it came to creating an issue of *Drummer*, no one did it better than Jack Fritscher. He began reinterpreting popular culture in a leather context. With perfect pitch, he wrote with zest, energy, cynicism, sarcasm, respect, and awareness working out the blend of secret brotherhood and popular culture, guiding leathermen's hearts and minds. He had the skills, talent, and lifestyle experience needed. He could juxtapose God, gonads, and drooling desire. Fritscher's method was perfect for who we were and for the time. He grabbed us and we learned to think in his 'language.' He wrote with style, intelligence, and urgency. He changed as we changed in finding ourselves. I owe Fritscher a lot, starting with my adult sexual vocabulary. When I became editor of *Drummer* and an upcoming issue was at an impasse, publisher Tony DeBlase often counseled: 'Do a Fritscher!'"

• **Geoff Mains**, author, *Urban Aboriginals*, in *The Advocate*: "Jack Fritscher writes wonderful books...careful writing...a world of insight."

• **Jim Stewart, Department Head emeritus, Social Sciences & History Dept., Chicago Public Library**: "Jack Fritscher as 'eyewitness' in *Gay San Francisco* is kin to Christopher Isherwood as 'camera' in his *Berlin Stories*. Climbing the scaffolding of the chapter-and-verse structure of *Drummer*, he unfurls a rainbow flag of narrative about the foreign country of our gay past, and of its citizens and denizens, living, lost, dead, or forgotten."

• **Jim Van Buskirk, Program Manager, James C. Hormel Gay & Lesbian Center, San Francisco Public Library**: "*Gay San Francisco* offers a uniquely personal perspective on the history and culture of one of San Francisco's previously under-documented underground communities—the masculine-identified."

• **David Perry,** *The Advocate*: "Jack Fritscher—himself something of an icon—didn't invent the Castro [and Folsom]. He just made it mythical...heady, erotic, comic....If one can learn American history from the novels of Gore Vidal, one can learn gay American history from *Some Dance to Remember* [the '*Drummer* novel' excerpted in *Drummer*]....Graphically elegant style."

• **Marilyn Jaye Lewis**, founder, **Erotic Authors Association**: "*Gay San Francisco* is an essential document in the 'Gay Enlightenment' culled from the pages of *Drummer* ...Fritscher empowers the Truth of those times by enabling history to tell itself."

- **Richard Labonté**, critic and founder, **A Different Light Bookstores, BooksToWatchOutFor.com**: "Fritscher's *Gay San Francisco* account reads true to me...rewarding...I relish his...story being told."

- **Harold Cox**, publisher, ***Checkmate* Magazine**: "There were two great *Drummer* editors: Jeanne Barney and Jack Fritscher...Gay San Francisco is an essential acquisition for every GLBT collection."

- **Chuck Renslow**, founder, Chicago **Leather Archives & Museum** and International Mr Leather (IML): "*Drummer* was a map of leather culture; Fritscher and his book are unabashed and uninhibited tour guides."

- **Justin Spring**, author, ***Samuel Steward: A Biography***: "Fritscher has basically done all the research work that most academics won't do—thus ensuring that historians, critics, and anthropologists will cut and paste with delight in the years to come."

- **Larry Townsend**, author, ***The Leatherman's Handbook*** and ***Drummer* columnist**: "Fritscher is the master of gay writing. He made 1977-1980 the Golden Age of *Drummer*, formulating entire issues, and then contributing writing and photography for 17 years through three owners."

- **Calamusbooks.com**: "Fritscher's *Drummer* in its early issues back in the late 1970s, was a terrific contribution to the erotic literature of gay men."

- **Steven Saylor (Aaron Travis)**, author, *Slaves of the Empire*, **fiction editor of *Drummer***, reviewing Fritscher's collected *Drummer* writing: "There's enough ghettoized angst to keep the Manhattan literati wired for months..."

- **David Stein**, founder, **GMSMA**: "Fritscher, one of the great *Drummer* editors, seems to have been everywhere and done everyone during the 'good old days' of leather culture... Fritscher is the editor most responsible for making *Drummer* what it became. His aim was to reflect changes in gay culture even as they were occurring."

- **Niall Richardson**, lecturer, Film and Media Studies, **University of Sussex, UK, author,** *The Queer Cinema of Derek Jarman*: "...a fascinating insight into gay culture of the 1970s. Containing a wealth of original writing from one of the most important gay magazines, *Gay San Francisco: Eyewitness Drummer* chronicles an exciting era in gay history which saw the formation of leather culture and the active de-sissyfication of gay culture: factors which have shaped contemporary gay identification. Varied and compelling....a genuine enthusiasm for gay popular culture."

- **Mira Schwirtz**, *San Francisco Review of Books*: "Fritscher is not shy....He plants himself squarely at the book's center...as star witness, sociologist, and critic [of the] charmed circle Fritscher shared with [his bi-coastal lover] Mapplethorpe....Fritscher's study of popular culture forms the core of the book, *Mapplethorpe* [originally published in *Drummer*], as it did the setting of his memoir-novel titled *Some Dance to Remember* [excerpted in *Drummer*]...a personal, passionate memoir...a vulnerable look at a relationship with an artist, his work, and celebrity....*Mapplethorpe* is a portrait of the artists as young men."

• **Tim Barrus, editor of *Drummer***: "In the 1970s, there were two gay writers' jobs in San Francisco. Randy Shilts had one at the *Chronicle*, and Jack Fritscher had the other at *Drummer*. Without Jack, there would be no *Drummer*."

• **Michael Bronski, *Gay Community News*, Boston**: Fritscher's collected *Drummer* features and fiction are "graphic, explicit...and unabashedly romantic in a truer sense than are most books [magazines] aimed at gay audiences....[The anthology, *Corporal in Charge*, is a] collection of [Fritscher's *Drummer*] pieces which deal with individual consciousness. Like Genet's work, Fritscher's [*Drummer* writings] are essentially masturbatory fantasies...about the actual fantasy of romance...and gay men love to read about romance."

• **Dave Rhodes**, founding publisher, **The Leather Journal**: "There is no written account of Old Guard leather. Fritscher's detailing of the *Drummer* Boom in *Gay San Francisco* is unparalleled, and we need it."

• **Rick Storer**, Executive Director, **Leather Archives & Museum**: "Fritscher is uniquely positioned as the creator of *Drummer* content, as a practitioner of *Drummer* content, and as an observer of *Drummer* culture. With insight and eroticism, he is the sole source for this thoroughly enjoyable erotic laydown of leather history."

• **David Van Leer**, professor, **Lesbian and Gay Studies, University of California, Davis**, and author of *The Queening of America*: "Fritscher is a key player in the masculinity of homosexuality...Must reading for those who want to know more about their past and those who simply want to relive the days when it was fun to be gay. *Gay San Francisco* is history for GLBT people who want to know the diversity of our gay roots."

• **Eric Rofes**, Associate Professor of Education, **Humboldt State University**, author, *Dry Bones Breath: Gay Men Creating Post-AIDS Identities and Cultures*: "For my university class '**Gay Men's Urban Cultures: San Francisco in the 1970s and Today**,' Jack Fritscher's astounding novel *Some Dance to Remember* is required course reading."

• **Charles Casillo**, *New York Native*: "Fritscher is intelligent, perceptive, sensitive, articulate—and a good writer."

• **Ron Suresha**, author, **Bears on Bears**: "Fritscher brings a loving ear, erotic eye, and lyric voice to American Gay Popular culture, and is an archivist active in researching, recording, and preserving the heritage of gay history."

• **Joan Levin,** *Library Journal:* "Fritscher's brutally frank memoir of his ex-lover, confidante, and colleague, drawn from the author's personal documents, seeks to strip away the notoriety surrounding the defiant photographer Robert Mapplethorpe....In *Mapplethorpe*, [first excerpted in *Drummer*, 1978] Fritscher graphically portrays the masculine subculture of the homosexual community....Recommended for popular culture collections."

• **Q,** *Philadelphia Gay News*: "Jack Fritscher is a master of gay prose pornography, a rarity in our...video-oriented culture.... The manner in which he manipulates language, sensuality, feeling, nuance, style, atmosphere, and even one's visual sense...is enough to guarantee this book [of *Drummer* stories, *Corporal in Charge*] sensational status for many, many years."

• **Kit Christopher**, creative director, **Stroke magazine**: "...veteran writer Fritscher's fine prose has induced many soiled bed sheets over the years, and his style has set a standard in the industry."

• **John Rowberry, editor of** *Drummer*: "The subject matter [of Fritscher's *Drummer* writing] is as varied as Fritscher's imagination, which seems endless and totally without remorse. What may really surprise you is that amid the graphic descriptions...there are actually ideas here."

• *Torso* **Magazine**: In his *Drummer* work, "Fritscher writes funny, descriptive and on-target essays...Fritscher is positively riveting"

• **Owen Keehnen,** *Honcho* **Magazine**: "Fritscher is an interesting man, a solid and intriguing blend of theory and knowledge."

• **Alexander Renault,** *Pornographic Pulsar*: "Fritscher is dedicated to the preservation and continuation of gay cultural studies and the expansion of its horizons."

• **Leif Waters,** *Bear* **Magazine**: "Fritscher is unlike any other chronicler of masculine perversion. His stories are...about growth, limits, expansion of the mind..."

• **Virginia Sink,** *The Tribune*, **Oklahoma City**: "Fritscher is a polished writer, editing his work to the bone..."

• **Nancy Sundstrom,** *ForeWord* **magazine**, "Fritscher is epicentric to gay literature...he is first and foremost an extraordinary American writer. He deserves a broad-based audience because his powerful and original voice rings in one's head long after the book has been completed."

GAY SAN FRANCISCO: EYEWITNESS *DRUMMER*

A Memoir of the
Sex, Art, Salon,
Pop Culture War,
and Gay History of
Drummer Magazine
The Titanic 1970s to 1999

Volume 1

Jack Fritscher, Ph.D.
Founding San Francisco
Editor in Chief of *Drummer*

Collected and Edited by Mark Hemry

A Narrative Timeline, Analysis, and Archive of Art,
Sex, Erotica, Obscenity, Homophobia, Identity Politics,
the Culture War, and the Salon around *Drummer* Magazine

Based on internal evidence in *Drummer* magazine,
and in journals, diaries, letters, photographs,
interviews, recordings, magazines, and newspapers
in the Collection of Jack Fritscher and Mark Hemry

Palm Drive Publishing ™
San Francisco

Copyright ©2008 Jack Fritscher
All rights are reserved by the author. Except for brief passages quoted in newspaper, magazine, radio, television, internet review, or other electronic media, or academic paper, no part of this book may be reproduced or transmitted in any form or by any means, electronic or mechanical, including photocopy, recording, web posting, or any information storage-and-retrieval system now known or to be invented, without permission in writing from the publisher.

For author history and for historical research www.JackFritscher.com

Cover and book design by Mark Hemry. Cover photography by Mark Hemry.

Published by Palm Drive Publishing, San Francisco
Email: publisher@PalmDrivePublishing.com

This memoir is a product of the author's recollections and is thus rendered as a subjective accounting of events that occurred in his life. This is a memoir book of humor, comedy, and satire meant to refract the author's eyewitness experience of what might otherwise be objective history. While all of this written "oral history" may be true, none of it may be. It must be emphasized that the text and allegations are provisional. With the first pages written in 1977, this is the first history to begin the difficult documentation of *Drummer* magazine. The text, the lists, the quotations, the illustrations, the credits for the illustrations, and the annotated bibliography in this "work in progress" are as thoroughly fact-checked as possible from internal evidence in *Drummer* itself, as well as, where possible, from journals, diaries, letters, photographs, interviews, recordings, magazines, and newspapers found in the personal collection of the Jack Fritscher and Mark Hemry GLBT Archive. Text and photographs may or may not be true and accurate, and do not reflect the sexual orientation of persons mentioned or depicted therein. The opinions, views, and allegations expressed are those of the author, or of the individual writers and speakers quoted, who themselves, in turn, do not represent the views or opinions of the author or the editor or the publisher; these opinions, views, and allegations may differ substantially from the opinion, views, and allegations of those who are referenced as personalities in this historical survey. The author, regretting any misrepresentation or misinformation or violation of copyright, apologizes; and he encourages documented corrections for future editions be sent to the publisher. Any person who is mentioned in these pages, or is an eyewitness to this history, or is a copyright owner, or is somehow concerned, is invited to correct or add or subtract from this book by contacting the publisher@PalmDrivePublishing.com

WARNING: Sexually Explicit Content
This book of words and illustrations contains explicit sexual material which may be offensive to some readers or viewers. You must be 18 years or older to read this book. By opening this book, you acknowledge that you are 18 years or older. All persons who appear in any visual depiction of actual sexual conduct appearing or otherwise contained in this adult book and adult site were over the age of eighteen years at the time of the creation of such depictions. Some of the aforementioned depictions appearing or otherwise included in this book contain only visual depictions of actual sexually explicit conduct made before July 3, 1995, and, as such, are exempt from the requirements set forth in 18 U.S.C. 2257 and C.F.R. 75. With regard to the remaining depictions of actual sexual conduct appearing or otherwise contained in this adult book or at this adult site, the records required pursuant to 18 U.S.C. 2257 and C.F.R. 75 are kept by the custodian of records of Palm Drive Publishing whose address is 2755 Blucher 95472.

Library of Congress Control Number: 2008920734
Fritscher, Jack 1939-
Gay San Francisco: Eyewitness Drummer, Volume 1 / Jack Fritscher
p.cm
ISBN 978-1-890834-38-8
1. Biography/Autobiography, 2. Personal Memoirs, 3. Homosexuality, 4. Masculinity, 5. Gay and Lesbian Studies, 6. Gay Studies (Gay Men), 7. Popular Culture, 8. Editors, Journalists, Publishers, 9. Sadomasochism, 10. American Literature—20th Century. 11. Feminism

First Printing 2008
10 9 8 7 6 5 4 3
www.PalmDrivePublishing.com

How to Use This Text in the Printed Book and on the Internet

Initiated in 1977, this is the first history to begin the documentation of *Drummer* magazine. This book may be read as a narrative stream beginning with page one and continuing to the end. However, for both the fun of browsing and the ease of research, the book is designed with an index, and may be opened and entered on almost any page. Because each section is written to stand alone, what sometimes may seem like repetition is instead a refrain and rephrasing of a statement or a theme. The reader, who must be his or her own best critic, can turn the text like a chunk of Labrador spar to see the facets.

Responsibility and Transparency in This Book

For thirty years this book has been a work in progress. I was not paid, nor was I given grants, nor lunch, nor sex to write this book, nor do I expect much if any commercial return for the joy and labor required to fill in some big blanks in previously ignored and censored gay history. No agent or corporate publishers enforced spin, revisionism, or censorship. Asking the readers' indulgence, I assert that in my opining content and style, what is accurate is mine; what is inaccurate is also mine, and will be revised in future editions. What is here written is the eyewitness documentary and the oral history I have transparently offered for years to GLBT ethnographers. As a gay community service, my goal is to offer *Gay San Francisco: Eyewitness Drummer* as the first GLBT book to be published simultaneously both as a low-cost-plus trade paperback, and as a free research document on the Internet. Visit www.JackFritscher.com

This Book Is Rated NC-17

An NC-17 rated book is one that is too adult for children 17 and under. NC-17 does not mean "obscene" or "pornographic" in the common or legal meaning of those words, and should not be construed as a negative judgment in any sense. The rating simply signals that the content is appropriate only for an adult audience. An NC-17 rating can be based on sex, violence, aberrational behavior, drug use, or any other element too advanced for minors.

Research Materials

All research materials including publications, personal journals, letters, audio and video recordings, art, artifacts, photographs, and graphics are from the Jack Fritscher and Mark Hemry GLBT History Collection. Every reasonable effort has been made to acknowledge all copyright holders. Any errors or omissions that may have occurred are inadvertent, and anyone with any copyright queries is invited to write to the publisher, so that full acknowledgment may be included in subsequent editions of this work.

Authorship

Except for the signed introductions, Jack Fritscher is the author of all the writing in this book.

Dedication

Gay San Francisco: Eyewitness Drummer

How the Boys in the Band Played On!

Gay San Francisco is dedicated to the following essential contributors to *Drummer* magazine: Jeanne Barney, Robert Mapplethorpe, A. Jay (Al Shapiro), David Sparrow, Larry Townsend, Robert Opel, Chuck Arnett, Phil Andros (Samuel Steward), Fred Halsted, Val Martin, Old Reliable (David Hurles), Jim Stewart, Rex, Tom Hinde, Lou Thomas, Mikal Bales, Wakefield Poole, Patrick Califia, Gene Weber, Bob Zygarlicki, Max Morales, Steven Saylor, John Preston, Richard Hamilton, M.D., Anthony F. DeBlase, Andrew Charles, Tim Barrus, JimEd Thompson, J. D. Slater, Mark Thompson, The Hun, Mason Powell, Robert Davolt, Ronald Johnson, Mr. Marcus Hernandez, Skipper Davis, Mark I. Chester, Efren Ramirez, Ed Menerth, Guy Baldwin, Ken Lackey, Joseph W. Bean, and John H. Embry

Special dedication and thanks
to my stoic editor Mark Hemry
without whose remarkable diligence over thirty years
this material would have been
impossible to collect, analyze, and present

With gratitude to
Jeanne Barney,
Jim Stewart, Dick Kriegmont,
Michael Williams, Justin Spring,
Trent Dunphy, Bob Mainardi,
Chuck Renslow, Rick Storer,
and Mark Thompson

The Sexual Revolution of the Titanic 1970s

Epigraphs

...men everywhere,
Jazz...
Booze...
Life...
Joy everywhere...
—"(Oh, It's Heaven) Nowadays,"
John Kander and Fred Ebb,
Chicago (1975)
Chicago opened on Broadway
the same June 1975 that *Drummer* debuted.

Whoever did not live in the years neighboring the revolution
does not know what the pleasure of living means.
—Charles Maurice de Talleyrand

Bliss was it that dawn to be alive,
but to be young was very heaven.
—William Wordsworth, *The Prelude* (1805)

To me this part of the city always seemed joyful
but now is just horror and nothing more.
—Pier Paolo Pasolini,
"The Search for a Home," *Roman Poems*

Contents

Introductions
Mark Hemry: *Drummer*'s Institutional Memory ... 1
Joseph W. Bean: Nobody Did It Better ... 7
Tim Barrus: My Glittering Hotel ... 13
Jim Stewart: History Descending a Staircase ... 19
Harold Cox: Coaching *Drummer* ... 27
David Hurles: A Thousand Light Years Ago ... 33
Edward Lucie-Smith: Jack Fritscher's American Men ... 43
david stein: *Drummer*-ing up the Zeitgeist ... 57
Alexander Renault: Vanguard ... 65
Larry Townsend: The Golden Age of *Drummer* ... 77

Author's Foreword ... 83
Author's Summary Timeline ... 121

Jack Fritscher's Road to *Drummer*
James Dean: Magnificent Failure ... 133
The Untimely Death of J. Cristobal ... 149
The Church Mid-Decade and the Negro ... 159
Chicago 7 ... 179
Leather *Dolce Vita* ... 189
Porno, Ergo Sum ... 207
Homomasculinity: Queer Keywords ... 231

***Drummer* 14 (April 1977)**
Men South of Market ... 261

***Drummer* 15 (May 1977)**
Stunning Omission ... 295
Cock Casting ... 303
Durk Parker ... 309

***Drummer* 16 (June 1977)**
Tom Hinde Portfolio ... 315
Johnny Gets His Hair Cut ... 347

***Drummer* 18 (August 1977)**
The Leatherneck ... 355

Drummer 19 (December 1977)

Leather Christmas 1977	373
Astrologic *Capricorn*	395
El Paso Wrecking Corp.	407
Steve Reeves' Screen Test	413
Star Trick	423
The Mineshaft	447
Gifting	493

Drummer 20 (January 1978)

Crimes Against Nature 1977	503
Gay Jock Sports	531
Dune Body	573
Pissing in the Wind	579
Astrologic *Aquarius*	593
Toward an Understanding of *Salo*	601
Gay Source: A Catalog for Men	625
CMC Carnival	631
Night Flight 1977	647
Timeline Bibliography	661
Index	689

Poster, *Rashomon*. Discerning readers of this droll *Gay San Francisco* memoir of the living, the DOA, and the MIA may appreciate the drop-dead minimalist tag line of *Rashomon*: "One dead body. Two [eye]witnesses. Three accounts. Four versions." Jack Fritscher: "In the midst of allegations, truth lies."

Drummer's Institutional Memory
Mark Hemry, Editor

"The past is a foreign country..."
—L. P. Hartley, *The Go-Between*

"What happened in 1977 could fill a book.
We hired A. Jay's friend
Jack Fritscher as editor in chief..."
—John Embry, founding publisher of *Drummer*,
Drummer 188 (September 1995), 20th Anniversary Issue

- The *Drummer* Salon: A Gathering of the Right People in the Right Place at the Right Time
- Leather Heritage, History, Legacy, and Narrative Timeline
- *Drummer*'s Institutional Memory: Robert Mapplethorpe and Edward Lucie-Smith
- *Rashomon* and *The Alexandria Quartet*

Jack Fritscher, the founding San Francisco editor in chief of *Drummer* magazine, met John Embry, the founding Los Angeles publisher, in March 1977, and worked with him, and observed him, during nearly thirty years, including three years as editor in chief and for twenty years after their *Drummer* partnership, writing for Embry's twenty-first-century magazines *Manifest Reader*, *Manhood Rituals*, and *Super MR*.

In 1986, as Anthony F. DeBlase was purchasing *Drummer* from Embry, he asked Fritscher to return as editor in chief. As an alternative, Fritscher continued to contribute writing, photographs, and issue themes to *Drummer*, even after DeBlase sold the magazine in 1992 to Martijn Bakker, the publisher from Amsterdam who shut *Drummer* down in 1999.

Only two people were editor in chief of *Drummer*: Jeanne Barney and Jack Fritscher.

I myself have been an eyewitness of Fritscher and *Drummer* since 1979. In fact, I met Fritscher at the precise moment in May 1979 when he had edited half the *Drummer* issues in existence.

Fritscher was the marquee editor in chief of *Drummer* for thirty-two intense and seminal months: March 1977 to December 31, 1979. During this formative time, he edited and signed *Drummer* 19-30 as well as his unsigned hybrid issues *Drummer* 14-18, and 31-33, plus his special extra issue of New York art, *Son of Drummer* (September 1978). He kept steady through the *sturm und drang* of all three owner-publishers: John Embry, Anthony F. DeBlase, and Martijn Bakker. Fritscher was *Drummer*'s most frequent contributing writer and photographer for 65 of the 214 issues during three publishers over 24 years

Embry hired Fritscher conceptually as the "founding San Francisco editor in chief of *Drummer*."

By "founding San Francisco editor in chief," Embry, who was new to the city, meant the deeply established Fritscher was to be his San Francisco talent scout discovering and recruiting a new group of contributors, ideas, and themes for *Drummer* orphaned in LA. The legendary Sam Steward, who was an intimate in the charmed circle around Gertrude Stein and Alice B. Toklas, dubbed the 1970s group Fritscher collected as "The *Drummer* Salon."

Fritscher is the historian of *Drummer*'s institutional memory.

During those 24 years of Fritscher's surveillance of *Drummer* as editor in chief, writer, and photographer, the three publishers' feuds with each other—each with his blacklist—destroyed the very institutional memory of *Drummer*. Out of the cabals and brawls, Fritscher was the one, single, longtime, and very inside eyewitness left standing.

Over 24 years, he observed *Drummer* for 2.5 times longer than John Embry, the founding owner and publisher who worked with *Drummer* for only 11 years, and fought with it for 14 years. DeBlase toyed with *Drummer* for 6 years; Bakker killed *Drummer* in an assisted suicide that took 6 years.

Arts critic John F. Karr wrote in the *Bay Area Reporter*, June 27, 1985: "Fritscher invented the South of Market prose style and its magazines which would not be the same without him."

Planetout.com defined Fritscher as "the groundbreaking editor of *Drummer* magazine."

The Gay and Lesbian Historical Society mentioned: "Fritscher is the prolific author who since the late sixties has helped document the gay world and the changes it has undergone."

Memory may fragment with time; but Fritscher's germinal reflection restores the institutional memory timeline of *Drummer*

Introduction: *Drummer*'s Institutional Memory

with dates, and more importantly with the streaming flow of life, feeling, and blood with which he connects the dots of incident, calendar, clock, and personalities into a useful reminiscence of a lost civilization. His eyewitness testimony is supported by internal evidence from an array of public and private archived documents.

Spoken by a pioneer-participant, this *Gay San Francisco: Eyewitness Drummer* text is oral history written down for remembrance. It is a personal memoir ricocheting off Gertrude Stein's *Everybody's Autobiography*. Fritscher insists, "There are several other autobiographical eyewitness stories to be told about *Drummer* by others from their own experience. I can't tell them all; I don't know them all; but I welcome them all."

As a teenager, he was impressed by L. P. Hartley's 1953 novel *The Go-Between*. Hartley was schooled at Oxford where Fritscher studied briefly. As a tenured associate professor teaching university classes titled Creative Writing, American Literature, and Esthetics of Cinema, he lectured on the screen play of *The Go-Between* (1970) written by Harold Pinter and directed by Joseph Losey who had been blacklisted as a Communist by the House Un-American Activities Committee. "That HUAC witch hunt, that opening salvo of the culture war," he says, "was run by Republican Senator Joseph McCarthy who was the progenitor of Jesse Helms who crucified Robert Mapplethorpe, and of Carl Rove and the neocons kneeling on their right-wing prayer rugs."

Hartley's famous first line in both his book and the Pinter-Losey film of *The Go-Between* is: "The past is a foreign country; they did things differently there." Having kept a journal since he was seventeen in early 1957, Fritscher in 1970 began writing entries of the "foreign gay past" as it happened before it was past and while it was not foreign to him as eyewitness. These entries were integral to his signature novel, the 1990 Lambda Literary Award Finalist, *Some Dance to Remember: A Memoir-Novel of San Francisco 1970-1982*. As a humanist, he wrote his essentialist "opening line": "In the end he could not deny his human heart."

In 1988, he began his *Drummer* 133 "Pentimento" salute to his bicoastal lover Robert Mapplethorpe: "The pre-AIDS past of the 1970s has become a strange country. We lived life differently a dozen years ago."

What of the past is written in Fritscher's *Eyewitness Drummer* history is not a fiction. He allows, however, that its "truth is, of course, *Rashomon*. In that 1950 film, director Akira Kurosawa told the same story from four points of view."

As a college student who graduated in 1961, Fritscher also idolized *The Alexandria Quartet* written by Lawrence Durrell between 1957 and 1960.

"Durrell wrote one story," Fritscher says, "told from four different points of view. He exhibits the human degrees of relativity—the six degrees of separation. He dramatizes how his four characters can experience the same thing and come away with contradictory truths. *The Alexandria Quartet* adds a quantum time-folding twist to *Rashomon*. Besides each Durrell character having his or her own point of view, each over time is changing his or her point of view. How very like us survivors of the Titanic 70s after the iceberg of HIV."

In August 1963, while waiting near a military hospital for his first nephew to be born in Washington, DC, Fritscher re-read *The Alexandria Quartet* in Alexandria, Virginia.

"Bull Rider Mark Hemry," Gay Rodeo, Reno, 1979. Photograph by Jack Fritscher. ©Jack Fritscher

"It was one Alexandria," he said, "of the several which Durrell recommended as ideal places to read his *Quartet*."

Fritscher completed the four books, *Justine, Balthazar, Mountolive*, and *Clea* before and after participating in Martin Luther King, Jr.'s "I Have a Dream" March on Washington.

On July 31, 1990, *The Advocate* published a review of *Some Dance to Remember*. Reviewer David Perry cheered the sweep and scope of that memoir-novel. I quote it here because Perry's description of that book aptly describes the scope of *Gay San Francisco: Eyewitness Drummer*.

> For 562 pages, the 51-year-old author lays out stories from what he calls the Castro's Golden Age (1970-1982) in the recently released novel, *Some Dance to Remember*. Heady, erotic, comic, and often boggling for the sheer weight of information it contains, Fritscher's novel is the first comprehensive fictional chronicle of the best of times bleeding into the worst.

Introduction: *Drummer*'s Institutional Memory

Gay San Francisco: Eyewitness Drummer is a kind of oral history told by a *seanachie* who repeats bits that reveal more with each telling. (A *seanachie* is an Irish storyteller, a keeper of the village tales.) Fritscher, a wordsmith with ancestral blood roots in Ireland, knows his way around a story.

Gay San Francisco: Eyewitness Drummer is *Some Dance to Remember* with real people.

In 1992, when Fritscher was writing his historical memoir of life with his bicoastal lover, Robert Mapplethorpe, the British critic Edward Lucie-Smith told him that it was unfortunate that Mapplethorpe had never written a monograph explaining what he was trying to do in his photography. Edward Lucie-Smith told Fritscher, "In that is a lesson about your own involvement as a writer and a photographer in *Drummer* and in gay culture."

—Mark Hemry, editor

Youth needs the wisdom of the established, and the established need the energy of the young. The present usually takes a dim view of the past. This attitude is attractive to the naive who often think that the whole wide world began the day they first noticed it. Sometimes, too, people with some mileage wrongly dismiss the younger because the young weren't present at the past.

—Jack Fritscher, Introduction to Larry Townsend's *The Leatherman's Handbook*

**American Editor:
From Prof to Pop—From University to Diversity
(What People Like)[100]**

In the Prague Spring of 1968 with student revolutions sweeping the world, university professor Jack Fritscher was a founding member of the American Popular Culture Association that was invented to introduce diversity to American Studies, and he was one of the first contributors to the *Journal of Popular Culture*. In July 1978, he added to the masthead of *Drummer* 23 the high-concept tag line, "The American Review of Gay Popular Culture." When asked why a tenured academic would become involved with *Drummer*, Fritscher emailed:

> Why did I choose to throw in my lot with *Drummer* in 1977? Because in pre-Stonewall 1968, I realized the potential

transgressive value of gay publishing. Gay pop culture was coming out of the closet in the 1960s the way Black culture and Beat culture had come out in the 1950s. Pop culture is what ordinary people like. I figured attention must be paid.

As an eyewitness, I was a tenured and openly gay professor, and I announced to editors of academic journals that I was available with dual credentials as both a cultural arts critic and an erotic participant to document our 1960s gay culture. With people like Bella Abzug, I toured as a speaker in college-campus lecture series, and wrote essays (such as "Originality in *The Boys in the Band*") for the newly founded *Journal of Popular Culture* edited by PCA founder Ray Browne. His Popular Culture Press at Bowling Green University contracted in 1969 to publish my *Popular Witchcraft: Straight from the Witch's Mouth* which was the first book to discuss gay magic and leather ritual.

Soon enough, along came Stonewall and the Titanic 1970s with gay liberation and *Drummer* begging for air pressure, content, self-discovery, and identity.

I groomed *Drummer* to reflect the readers who identified themselves and what they liked in thousands of their personals ads. The perfect demographic. *Drummer* was the people's magazine, at least among a million masculine-identified leatherfolk worldwide.

In its mission statement (www.msu.edu/~tjpc/), *The Journal of Popular Culture* has articulated concepts that help explain the reader-reflexive, grass-roots, and *erotica verite* principles of the first-person, dialog-driven, documentary scenes that Fritscher as analytical editor in chief and New Journalism author introduced into *Drummer*, into his popular culture memoir-novel *Some Dance to Remember*, and into *Gay San Francisco: Eyewitness Drummer*.

The popular culture movement was founded on the principle that the perspectives and experiences of common folk offer compelling insights into the social world. The fabric of human social life is not merely the art deemed worthy to hang in museums, the books that have won literary prizes or been named "classics," or the religious and social ceremonies carried out by societies' elite. *The Journal of Popular Culture* continues to break down the barriers between so-called "low" and "high" culture and focuses on filling in the gaps a neglect of popular culture has left in our understanding of the workings of society.

Nobody Did It Better
by Joseph W. Bean

Lines in appreciation of Jack Fritscher
as he appeared in *Drummer* magazine

Jack Fritscher \'jak-'friche®\ prop. noun—no plural poss. [Unique coinage, more at homomasculine]. 1. Legendary 20th to 21st Century homocultural figure said to have war-painted himself with the splatter from strafing pop cultural icons and gay pseudo-leather cults with sweat-and cum-scented rounds fired from unimaginable heights at what he viewed as bastions of slow-moving and therefore false imagination below. 2. Variant view: mythical writer whose stream of sanity blew away posers, especially those clad in chaps or leather clothing, while attracting a following as he wrote his heart out into "ho-sex, mo-sex leathersex" reality, creating in his one lifetime an entire non-virtual world of both steam and substance.

Drummer had a long run from June 1975 to its 214th issue dated April 1999. Along the way, the magazine frankly created a good many writers, but it served a more important function for some writers. It gave them a forum where they were free to say what was most on their hearts and minds, what stirred them most powerfully in their guts and groins, and what got them off most perfectly. In those nearly 24 years, few writers took more complete advantage of the special soap-box that was *Drummer* magazine than Jack Fritscher. And very few were as well equipped as Fritscher to benefit the very particular readers of *Drummer*. He had not only the skills and talents, but the lifestyle and experience needed. In fact, maybe no one was better supplied with passions worth exposing to the half-formed world of leathersex for that matter. For volume (both much-ness and loudness) and frequency (both pitch and often-ness) and for both voracity and for veracity...for memorable texts and inescapable even cataclysmic juxtapositions of God and gonads, sweet perfection and drooling desire, nobody did it better. In the entire history of *Drummer* and its many spin-offs, "brother" publications and imitators, and in his own books and periodicals, Fritscher was creating a unique leathersex universe to which—even now—only a handful of writers have made any additional "direct deposits."

In one tumbling, fully-conscious stream of truth after another, Fritscher left us *Drummer* readers numb and spent and happy to have been run-over so gloriously. He seldom spoke when shouting would be tolerated and never explained when exuberant telling would get the job done. He grabbed us with his language and his style and, without stopping to ask how we liked to be fucked, just rammed it in and pleased himself, which is just what we'd have asked for if we had the courage and self-confidence to do that.

Leathermen were just steps out of the super-cultural closet when *Drummer* came along. A decade before, or less, they were nearly invisible, and meant to stay that way. Being invisible to the world had a certain positive value, maybe. Being invisible to each other at the distance of a city or two was not so good—damned inconvenient, really. Being invisible to the fresh meat that was seeking hungry users and abusers and brothers and Dads, mentors, re-inventors, bike riders to buddy with and buddies to fuck with... well, frankly, *that* kind of being invisible was intolerable. Even though there were other magazines from time to time—none for long, but always something else—*Drummer* was a necessity. The new Technicolor reality springing up from the gone-gray flats of gay social nothingness needed to be named and defined and cheered and kicked in the butt.

For all of that, the naming and defining for sure, the cheering when absolutely necessary and the kicking in the butt any time at all (thank you), again, nobody did it better than Jack Fritscher.

Fritscher's straight fiction and features were published years before Larry Townsend, but Townsend in the leather genre hit print first with a publisher to whom Fritscher would not sell his own book manuscripts such as 1969's *I Am Curious (Leather)* because the publisher demanded ownership of the author's copyright. Both Townsend and Fritscher published significant books in 1972: Townsend's *The Leatherman's Handbook* and Fritscher's *Popular Witchcraft* with its academic analysis of magic ritual in leather culture.

Townsend, a different kind of writer from stylist Fritscher, was doing his own thing, plus a couple of other things. He was entertaining and Fritscher was too, but Townsend was also a lot about scientifically proving what we were and what we did. His column—along with Bill Ward's *Drum* cartoon—was among the longest running features in *Drummer*, and they both were sources of great bar-talk and cocktail conversation. All

Introduction: Nobody Did It Better

good; in fact, these things were very good, but it was culture shock when the vainglorious bonfires of leather "political correctness" ignited around Fritscher's contributions. While one circle of leathermen demanded to know, "How could he say *that*?" another would be shocked into asking, "Did you see *how* he said that?"

I don't know about other readers, but Fritscher was an unexpected shock for me when he appeared in *Drummer*. I didn't really notice the byline on the piece about the Leatherneck bar (*Drummer* 18) before I saw his name as editor in chief in *Drummer* 19. I was not thinking of writing for *Drummer* myself, not by a long shot. Even though I did a lot of writing for *Drummer*, I didn't do any of it for another ten years. Hey, it was just about the time of my thirtieth birthday that I saw this new Fritscher phenomenon in print, and my opinion was that the guys who were doing this magazine were gods—ageless and eternal if not omniscient. How could I have known that Jack Fritscher was only eight years and one day older. He was on fire and I was on track to be a late-bloomer (as a writer about all this "jazz"), I guess. But, maybe eight years would have seemed a lot *then*.

In any case, back in the spring of 1977, Fritscher was on a mission which others would attempt to join, but only he could perform, pursue, posterize, and perfect with such zest and energy. He began reinterpreting popular culture in a leather context. This could have been done a million ways, and many famous writers and artists before and since have done something like it, but Fritscher's method was perfect for who we were and for the time. What's more, since we learned from Fritscher to think in his "language" (as much as that can be done by anyone other than the man himself), we "naturally" realized that his views were our views, his discoveries our truths. And, to make his dominance perfect, he changed as we changed and kept up with the times in a peculiar, all-Fritscher way that didn't involve any unnecessary trendiness.

The recipe for the emerging leatherman's point of view is not something that can ever be entirely clear, but the list of ingredients had to include cynicism and sarcasm along with respect and broad awareness. A special flavor of humor was a requirement, and Fritscher put his finger on the right one after *Drummer* had thumbed across humorous options unsuccessfully for nearly 20 issues. There had to be a degree of separation, even superiority, without the slightest touch of smug condescension. Once this blend of secret brotherhood and popular culture was worked out, we all knew better than we thought we ever could just who we were and where in the Big Picture to "find ourselves."

In fictions and fetish features and editorials, *Drummer* under Fritscher's guidance became the leatherman's mind as well as his heart—-

without letting go of his sex for a second—and it defied us to be more or different or otherwise. This was all very good for everyone, particularly a youngish guy who believed that the leather-clad men you could find in *Drummer* were a separate and special creation, on a higher order than *homo sapiens sapiens*. That's me thinking that, until a few Fritscher features drew pictures in which I could see myself without even straining. Then, just to keep me in my place after all, he'd come along with something like the *Drummer* 23 editorial where, in effect, *Drummer* claimed its place in the world and demanded that the readers notice the magazine was hung bigger than we were and had balls like we only dreamed of.

"Just you mention *Drummer* in a roomful of guys," Fritscher wrote, "and you'll get a heavy feedback of attitude. They either love us or hate us. They either understand us (meaning themselves) or they refuse to understand us (again, meaning themselves)." That's balls! And, not surprisingly, the editorial began by asking "where's *Drummer* get the leather balls to…" and ended with the honest answer that the readers who kept buying the magazine gave those who produced it the balls to do it as hard as they did and, in every other way, just as they did.

I don't know that the truth of the moment is really in that. For me, and I suspect a lot of others, it was impossible to see myself as a provider of chutzpah. I was being fed and encouraged, not consumed or reflected… but then I saw it, thanks to that editorial: There was a breed of leathermen—Val Martin and Fred Halsted and Joey Yale and Durk Dehner and the rest, art director Al "A. Jay" Shapiro and editor/writer Jack Fritscher among them—who were the source of all this ballsy machismo. And, closer to my home, there was a less plugged-in tribe—myself included—who were being lifted and flown, like little kids being "airplaned" in circles by their Dads. Fritscher was the Braveheart, the Shaka Zulu, the Kamehameha, the battle-crier who did *not* say something never before said or thought but, instead, gave voice to a thing never before made clear enough to rally around and to pass along to strangers in print.

The style and intelligence and urgency of Fritscher's message were his own, but the message itself was the one leathermen wanted (or, just as often definitely didn't want) disseminated. The essential content of what he was saying in "his" issues of *Drummer* (19 through 30 and his hybrid issues 14-18, 31, 32, 33) and in his other work and, as a contributor, in later issues of *Drummer* changed naturally because we changed, but the essential nature of it, the thing that made it Fritscher, never changed.

By the time I went to work at *Drummer*, 100 issues after the last one Fritscher edited, he really was a god of leather, an unimpeachable and unassailable solitaire whose very name had developed a meaning. "What

Introduction: Nobody Did It Better

do you want done with the 'Leather Lifestyles' theme you announced for *Drummer* 132?" I asked my boss, *Drummer* publisher Tony DeBlase.

"Go all the way with it," he answered, apparently leaving me unsure of what he meant. "You know," he added, "do a Fritscher!" Yes, I knew. In fact, either the topic was unyielding or I was unable. It didn't work that time. Subject after subject thereafter, the concept kept being "do a Fritscher" on it. Brown leather (*Drummer* 134) fell far short of that goal; leathersex and spirituality (*Drummer* 136) almost made it; bears (*Drummer* 140) got pretty close; spandex (*Drummer* 141) felt like a success. We really did a Fritscher on that "kinky softwear" as we called the form-accentuating garments. Edge play (*Drummer* 148) felt even more fully Fritscher-ed, but none of the issues I worked on were sufficiently Fritscher-ed except the ones put on that footing by the one and only *original* Jack Fritscher.

The now infamous "Remembrance of Sleaze Past" issue (*Drummer* 139) has to be the best of that lot and, if I remember correctly that idea either came from Fritscher or from DeBlase in conversation with Fritscher!

I owe Jack a lot, starting with my adult sexual vocabulary, and maybe including whatever success I have had writing and speaking of leathersex. I might never have done any of it at all if I had not been inspired, encouraged and kicked in the butt every step of the way. And, for all that, I can assure you, nobody did it better than Jack Fritscher.

Joseph W. Bean is the bricoleur editor of *Drummer* issues 133-161 who kept *Drummer* alive in the aftermath of the Loma Prieta earthquake that

destroyed the *Drummer* office in 1989. His writing and his erotic art have appeared in dozens of magazines from *Drummer* and *SandMutopia Guardian* to *The Advocate*. Besides *Drummer*, he has served as the editor of the magazines *Mach*, *DungeonMaster*, *International Leatherman*, *Powerplay*, *Bear*, and *Foreskin Quarterly*. In 1990, he spun his magazine *Tough Customers* from the long-running "Tough Customers" column that Jack Fritscher had invented as a Christmas present to readers in *Drummer* 25 (December 1978). He also served as the executive director of the Leather Archives and Museum in Chicago in whose magazine *Leather Times* #1 (2007) this article "Nobody Did It Better" was first published. His many books include *Leathersex Shadows: The Art of Joseph Bean*, *The Master's Manual: A Handbook of Erotic Dominance* (with Jack Rinella), and *International Mr. Leather: 25 Years of Champions* (2004). He lives and writes in Hawaii.

Previous page. Cover. *International Mr. Leather: 25 Years of Champions*. Above. *The Leather Times*. Used with permission of Chuck Renslow and the Leather Archives & Museum.

My Glittering Hotel
by Tim Barrus

I have never even once referred to *Drummer* magazine as a publication.

Drummer was and is and will always be my glittering hotel.

It was a place. It was where I lived. It was where the most extraordinary men walked into my life. It was a fantasy. It was reality. It was where I lost my mind and nearly my life. It was about the drugs. It was about the sex. It was about the leather. It was rock and roll gone lost in the chaos of a dark music so dark you, too, became naked in the shadows. It was work. It was sweat. It was a place inundated, crowded, and haunted by ghosts.

Both the living and the dead. Ghosts.

I do not dare even dream the dreams of those nights anymore. I cannot go back. I don't think I could survive another stint at my glittering hotel.

Scott O'Hara walks into my office unannounced: "Let's walk naked down Market Street with NAMBLA at the parade."

"Okay."

Mark I. Chester walks into my office unannounced. Sits down. Puts head between his knees: "They're driving me insane."

"Okay."

TR Witomski walks into my office unannounced: "I hate it you got this job as editor."

"Okay."

Jim Wigler walks into my office unannounced: "You will never be organized. It's not possible."

"Okay."

Scott Taylor walks into my office unannounced: "I'll set myself on fire if you'll take the photographs."

"Okay."

Coulter Thomas walks into my office unannounced: "I have a new tattoo of a snake emerging from my rectum. Would you like to see it."

"Okay."

Australian cowboy walks into my office unannounced: "I've come all the way from Australia to see you. I'm staying with you for the next three months."

"Okay. Here's the key."

Jack Fritscher walks into my office.

He hugs me. Hug is the wrong word. He holds me. Tight.

This does not happen quite like this at Other Magazines. This happened at *Drummer* daily.

What magazine.

I learned a lot while there. Mainly these were things I didn't want to know. Like my limitations. I didn't want to think back then that I had any. I do.

Drugs. You couldn't keep the drug dealers out of my office. I didn't exactly want to. They all had free samples and I sampled. Like a smorgasbord.

I knew I had a proclivity for the stuff. What I didn't know then but know now is that I am more than capable of going (jumping) overboard and it's a very fast ship that leaves you drowning in a very big sea.

I was treading water. At *Drummer*.

I very much needed someone to hold me. Tight. Jack Fritscher did. I wonder if he even remembers.

At that point in my life (I have grown quite accustomed to this and am today indifferent to it) I had never been hated as much as I was hated at *Drummer*. Today, hating me is so passé. *Drummer* was my entree into a life of crime.

You couldn't win. It was not unlike being imprisoned in a small room with twenty interior designers. No matter what you do with the furniture, someone somewhere was going to bitch.

Drummer was a letting go of every single moral injunction you ever had. *Drummer* was the Attorney General's Commission on Pornography. You figure.

There was no holding all the loose ends of these contradictions together. There were two jobs in San Francisco back then for gay writers, and Randy Shilts had one of them.

I had the other. Which had once been Jack's.

I was the front desk of my glittering hotel.

At the end, I had totally disintegrated.

I can't talk about what working at *Drummer* meant for other people. I can only speak for myself. I didn't even like *Drummer*. I loved *Mach*. Billy Bowers and I hung a naked blond boy upside down on a black cross and we hung the cross from a tree and took photographs of Brian Neal trying to breath between screams for us to take him down. The cross sort of swinging gently in the wind.

Mach published those photographs. I liked *Mach*. But *Drummer* came with the package.

I put my photograph in there as a "model" and sold myself as a whore. I made more money as a whore than I did as an editor.

Introduction: My Glittering Hotel

In the final analysis, drugs are not free forever.

When I think about the number of times I almost overdosed back then, it leaves me breathless. Today, I am quite aware of my own mortality. Drugs are the past.

Hello, my name is Tim Barrus and I'm a junkiebitchwhore.

Recovery was a year on the shores of Lake Michigan. After *Drummer*. Staring into sunset after sunset.

"I wrote a novel," Jack said.

I wanted to run.

Not another novel. Every bitch with a credit card and leather chaps South of Market had written a novel. I had read thousands of them.

Jack knew that look. "No, really, it's good."

It was.

Some Dance To Remember was more than good. "Does he know what he's done," Elizabeth Gershman asked me. "It's a historical document. Really, a piece of American history."

"I think he knows what he's done," I said. "The question is what will you do with it."

She published it.

I blame myself. I put Jack into bed with Knights Press.

Remember that big sea with the drowning and the treading water. Publishing companies tread water and drown regularly. Publishing companies are why writers need drugs.

We see time. Ships in the night. Shadows passing.

I'm living at Mariano Lake on the Navajo Reservation. I'm writing (remember that life of crime). I'm fucking poor.

No. Really, really, really, really poor. The thing about living among the Navajo is that they're poor, too. It is the norm. It is not unusual. Publishing stories in *Advocate Men* as Nasdijj was not a living. Publishing as Nasdijj for Random House was a living. But let us not go there.

How poor was poor.

I was stealing food from dumpsters at elementary schools. Poor is pizza crust some first grader did not eat.

A check arrived in the mail.

There was a note attached. "Eat," it said.

How Jack Fritscher even knew where I was shall be one of the great mysteries of my life. That check lasted a very long time. I could even go to Safeway.

I don't know what Other People see when they see Jack. I knew of him long before I met him. Without Jack, there would be no *Drummer*. No my glittering hotel. Whenever I see Jack in my head, I go completely psychic.

That was the thing about my glittering hotel. If you were open to dancing with the thing, you learned something about the power of the visions it would lend your life. Once you have them, they do not fade away. They will hurt you good, baby, all the way to the fucking grave.

Coulter and the snake.

Scott and the boys.

Jack Fritscher like a ghost who had made us all.

That was when I started seeing Jack as a Holy Man. Yes, a Holy Man. A man who had studied for the priesthood.

But here's the thing.

A man who had studied for the priesthood and who then transcended it.

I don't see Jack in leather.

Beyond ritual, I see Jack in monk's robes. Jack is like a monk to me. Someone who represents the thing at ground level. Someone who doesn't consult scripture, he lives it.

You will meet only a couple of people like this in your or any lifetime. There is a word for what Jack is. That word is spelled a-u-t-h-e-n-t-i-c.

Jack had set my stage. *Drummer* was where I started to listen to the voices. In me.

Call it psychotic. Or whatever you want. I've been called everything else. It doesn't mean anything. What was meaningful to me beyond the glittering dramas that were played out with such staggering force at my glittering hotel, if you could transcend the details, you would see another world.

Jack had transcended it. His writing and his person had transcended *Drummer*. He had the ability to hear Other People's voices (which is why he is twenty times the writer I am) and here's the thing: he could respond to them.

Maybe it was just a hug to Jack. I would not know. I know this: it saved me.

Beyond *Drummer*, what Jack gave me was transcendence. It was no theory. It left his body with that hug and entered mine. It has pushed me along this journey in ways Jack could never know.

Some dance in my glittering hotel with grace. My memory is a razor blade of blood. They are mostly gone now. But they were here and we danced and we connected and we gave voice to a history of what does amount to change.

So many people, many of them now haunt me, many of them wondrous, walked into that office. For one thing or another. My glittering hotel is still crowded with the likes of dancing ghosts. Remembering them is so painful, it is almost more than I can do. I loved them.

Introduction: My Glittering Hotel 17

But not one of them ever held me.

With one important exception. How many men do you know strong enough and self-aware enough to fathom you might need holding. Then and there. No waiting around for the appropriate time. No bullshit. You need to be held in that moment and someone walks into your life who sees not only right through you, but beyond you into what you need. Not as a writer. Not as a boy-editor. Not as an artist. Not as an opportunist. Not as a poet. Not as a gay anything. But as a human being. *Drummer* was the loss of everything. For me.

With one huge exception. The man is a sculptor. He has pounded out the likes of us in sometimes horrifying detail. He knows us. He hears us. He sees us. He sees through us. He can smell us a mile away. Sometimes what he knows is that we are not as invulnerable as we pretend we are.

In many ways, he is still holding me.

His name is Jack.

Tim Barrus, who was editor of *Drummer* issues 117-121 in 1988, is the controversial author of many novels including *Genocide* (1988), *To Indigo Dust* (1992), and—writing as his channeled identifier the Native-American Nasdijj—*The Blood Runs Like a River through My Dreams* (2001), *The Boy and His Dog Are Sleeping* (2003), and *Geronimo's Bones: A Memoir of My Brother and Me* (2005). He was the subject of a major article by Andrew Chaikivsky in *Esquire* (May 2006). His fiction also appeared in *Drummer* issues 67, 72, and 77. He was the founder of the 1980s "LeatherLit Movement" in San Francisco. As chief editor at Knights Press in 1988, he acquired and directed the first publication of Jack Fritscher's *Some Dance to Remember: A Memoir-Novel of San Francisco 1970-1982*. Married to Tina Giovanni, Tim Barrus is a filmmaker who lives and works in Paris.

History Descending a Staircase: The Enchanted Cargo of the Freighter SS *Jack Fritscher*

by Jim Stewart, Department Head, Emeritus,
Social Sciences & History Dept., Chicago Public Library,
and Photographer and Founder,
Keyhole Studios, SoMa, San Francisco

History can be a bitch. It can taunt you. It can seduce you. It can entice you down that dark narrow passage of time with the glimpse of a firm butt framed in open-ass chaps. In San Francisco, South of Market, it suddenly turns the corner and disappears into the midnight fog of a long-forgotten Ringold Alley. You see it again. History's bold building blocks loom large like the shoulders of a Duchamps construction worker in hard-hat and wife-beater shirt who erects scaffolding on Folsom Street. You climb its stairs into the fourth dimension of the time-lapsing past. Your eyes say your heart once yearned for bad-ass boys in leather motorcycle jackets.

In the 1970s, we loved the Eagles' *Hotel California* where "you can check in but you can never leave." We loved Streisand and Redford in *The Way We Were*. We loved Harold Pinter's film, *The Go-Between*, and its author L.P. Hartley announcing: "The past is a foreign country; they do things differently there."

"We can never sever our links with the past," Ludwik Fleck wrote in his work on the origin of the modern concept of syphilis (*Genesis and Development of a Scientific Fact*, University of Chicago Press, 1979, p. 20). At one time, syphilis was thought to be punishment for sexual sins. Lest we laugh at our ancestors, we must remember that AIDS continues to be viewed by many in a similar light. Gay puritans, for instance, in the 1980s concocted the reactionary myth that the 1970s was a sick decade whose behavior caused disease.

The gay past is a sexual past, and that precise *eros* complicates the telling of the "people's gay history." That past is a country foreign to the institutions that house history. Book publishers and academic journals rightfully fear censorship. Universities and library collections, as well as the National Endowment for the Arts, are protective of their government funding. The next generation of writers and historians is often biased by politics, gender, race, and the prevailing *zeitgeist*. *Drummer*—the first GLBT magazine to fight the culture war—should not be seen as an erotic embarrassment of pre-historic male-driven sex. Exclusionary puritan history should not pin a huge Scarlet Letter on *Drummer*'s chest.

Fleck suggested that all links to our past "survive in accepted concepts [*accepted* being the operative discriminatory word]...in everyday life as well as in...language and...institutions." Any concept or way of viewing things and ideas, Fleck argued, does not spring fully grown, like Venus from the sea, but rather is determined by its "ancestors." The "proto-ideas" (such as found in the gay roots of *Drummer* and its salon) on which contemporary ideas are built, he maintained, must not be "taken out of their chronological context, because they correspond to a different thought collective and a different thought style...one their originators certainly considered [in their day]...to be correct." (Ibid, p. 25). In precisely this way does Fritscher in *Gay San Francisco* try to resurrect chronological context of *Drummer*'s ancestral and proto-ideas.

Fleck also maintained that each "thought collective" is developed within a discipline by a Vanguard, usually working within a specific situation—such as the first post-Stonewall generation of liberated gay men creating the demotic *Drummer* and living in the SoMa subculture. This first-wave proto-activity by the Vanguard is then followed by the second-wave "official community" that determines the "official canon" of the discipline. Fritscher is in the unique position of being both a Vanguard participant and a surviving analyst of the Vanguard.

Unfortunately for gay history, as the 1970s became the 1980s, AIDS and the gender wars virtually destroyed the first-wave proto-activity of the Vanguard pioneers, and enabled the second-wave to commit that fallacy of logic that because something follows something, the thing it follows caused it.

The main body, Fleck argued, "adjusts its advance according to reports received from the Vanguard, but maintains a certain independence." In short, *Drummer* existed in a creative reciprocity with its readers and reported actual gay life as lived. Readers independently chose to construct their behavior accordingly. Another stage is reached when the idea becomes "everyday popular knowledge," and "the fact [for instance, the *Drummer* leather lifestyle] becomes incarnated as an immediately perceptible object of reality." (Ibid, pp. 124-5). Throughout its life (1975-1999) *Drummer* was a pop-culture perfect circle that, distinct from other magazines, actually created the global leather lifestyle that it reported on. Readers followed its descriptions (not prescriptions) and sent in personal requests and personal ads that shaped the upcoming issues.

Introduction: History Descending a Staircase 21

The whole process of Vanguard leadership (the *Drummer* creators) and independent critical thinking about that *avant garde* (of *Drummer* creators) is constantly in flux. It is interesting to note how totally *Drummer* was accepted by its readers into their lives for the last quarter of the twentieth century, but that *Drummer* Vanguard and all it represents of male-identified homosexuality has yet to be accepted into the canon of almost-pan-sexual and "official" GLBT history that, ironically, prides itself on every other kind of diversity and inclusion.

The culture war over the right to self-fashion gender identity, which once was *intermural* between heterosexuals and homosexuals, has become *intramural* among gay people. This is precisely when "history can be a bitch," because some thought collectives operate within specific "thought styles" (*denkstils*), and the "thought styles" tend to "ethnically cleanse" what they don't like about the thought collectives of the Vanguard.

It appears that correct "thought styles," which come after the edgy Vanguard, are much slower to change than are the thought collectives of the Vanguard that created the history that must be analyzed.

Group "thought styles" are much broader in reach than is an individual *avant garde* artist or entity, and the "thought style" can encompass whole cultures, such as Euro-cultures, Afro-cultures, Native American cultures, and, one could argue, modern and postmodern gay cultures. The twenty-first-century record of twentieth-century masculine-identified men must not be diminished. Its authentic twentieth-century Vanguard roots must not be excluded from the "thought styles" of GLBT history.

Jack Fritscher and the creative cadre of homomasculine-identified men he brought together under the *Drummer* salon are that Vanguard in twentieth-century gay history. It is a Vanguard whose analysis could help educate the *denkkollektiv* of GLBT history to look beyond what is currently considered politically correct to a broader view of what the "people's gay history," in fact, encompasses.

The embarrassing separatist habit—the bad intellectual and academic habit—of excluding masculine-identified gay men or the art and literature of homomasculinity from the canon of gay history is analogous to expunging field slaves from a history of slavery, or lesbians from a history of women. Fritscher, not just in *Gay San Francisco: Eyewitness Drummer*, but in his entire oeuvre of books and articles and photographs and videos, invites everyone into the tent even while he tries to tell the hidden history of the homomasculine Vanguard of *Drummer* that was read by thousands of people per month. He writes in *Gay San Francisco* that "the history of leather should be open to all analysts the way the pages of 1970s

Drummer were open to all." The *Drummer* Salon, Fritscher continues, was "inclusive" not "exclusive."

The student of history should be cognizant of the paradigm or construct within which such a study takes place. Like the "thought collective," the paradigm can shift in an historically short time span.

An examination of the "history" of the "Gay Liberation Movement" in the United States, for example, can be examined within the paradigm of the "birth of a movement," the "hegemony of a movement," the "meeting of cultures," or other constructs. Whatever the paradigm, there is bound to occur a shifting in the thought collective within the paradigm. This flux in the thought collective can often act as a smoke screen to suggest a shift in the paradigm. Although there may be either an emphasis on what Arthur Schlesinger, Jr. in *The Disuniting of America* terms "exculpatory" (i.e., "top-dog") history, or "compensatory" (i.e., "underdog") history, this does not necessarily indicate a shift in the paradigm. (NY: Norton, 1992, pp. 48-49).

Jack Fritscher, constructing the *denkkollektiv* memoir of *Gay San Francisco: Eyewitness Drummer*, is a tour guide to the "foreign country" of the past, providing his readers with a look at South of Market, San Francisco, before it was SoMa, before it became prime real estate, even before it was shabby chic, and condo rich. South of Market was once a light-industrial skid row where bad-ass boys in leather motorcycle jackets hung out in clouds of popper, ether, smoke, and sweat. SoMa was the post-Beat bohemian section of the City to which the airlines would not deliver lost luggage after dark. I know. I lived there then. I was the carpenter who customized Robert Opel's storefront into Fey-Way Gallery. I constructed the inside of the Leatherneck bar. I took photographs. I worked for the publisher of *Drummer*. I took notes for my *Clementina Street Tales*. For years, I was an eyewitness in that strange country, South of Market, when we did things differently.

Jack Fritscher as "eyewitness" in *Gay San Francisco* is kin to Christopher Isherwood as "camera" in his *Berlin Stories*. Climbing the scaffolding of the chapter-and-verse structure of *Drummer*, he unfurls a rainbow flag of narrative about the foreign country of our gay past, and of its citizens and denizens, living, lost, dead, or forgotten.

As editor in chief of *Drummer*, he helped the fledgling Los Angeles publication be born-again in the 1970s freedom of San Francisco. *Drummer* had fled north, followed by its publisher John Embry, to escape trumped-up slavery charges from the Los Angeles Police Department. Under Jack's tutelage *Drummer* became a voice for homomasculine men, art, and literature. He did not invent them; he encouraged them. This media attention attracted a group of gay, masculine-identified artists,

Introduction: History Descending a Staircase   23

graphic designers, cartoonists, writers, and photographers. The fraternity grew and began to flex its muscle in what Sam Steward, legendary pioneer of gay leather writing dubbed "The *Drummer* Salon."

In an instantly symbiotic relationship, *Drummer* under Fritscher publicized the South of Market leather community that by its nature was otherwise evanescent. Mapplethorpe in Manhattan knew the value of the SoMa art scene. Seeking *entre*, he introduced himself to editor Fritscher who connected him to nearly every leather person Mapplethorpe met or photographed in San Francisco, including poet Thom Gunn; serial-killer victim Larry Hunt; Jerry Paderski (face turned away, sitting butt backwards on a toilet bowl in a Tenderloin hotel); and founder of the Janus Society, Cynthia Slater. The SoMa demimonde frequented performance leather bars like Ron Johnson's No Name, David Delay's Ambush, and Allan Lowery's Leatherneck. The crowd surged for two years through Robert Opel's Fey-Way gallery where he was soon murdered. It included artists Chuck Arnett, Tom Hinde, and A. Jay/Al Shapiro; photographers David Hurles, David Sparrow and Jack Fritscher, and myself and a host of others, who all worked together for mutual support of our art, our creative ideas, ourselves, because it was fun. We were a leather Bloomsbury of masculine-identified male artists. We often lived together at the same addresses. We drove each other's cars and trucks and motorcycles. We worked with each other and for each other. We exchanged art work. We alerted each other to what hot esoteric foreign films were screening at the Strand, the Lumiere, and the Roxie. We picked up our tools and built playrooms in our homes and in our bars. We exchanged ideas and partied together. And, yes, we sometimes had sex together.

Drummer was our Vanguard collective diary, our traveling art show, our sexual politics, our snapshot album, our unfolding autobiography of the way we were. *Drummer* published Al Shapiro's graphic novel, *Harry Chess*, and Shapiro painted the murals for the walls of the Leatherneck bar on Folsom Street. Jack wrote about the Leatherneck. I photographed it. *Drummer* published his article with my pictures. Men went to that bar, went home with a buddy, and acted out what they had read in *Drummer*, and the next month they found themselves reflected in *Drummer*. In the Vanguard, Fritscher wrote about cigars as a fetish, and the next month the first cigars appeared in bars. This was our bohemia. It was 1970s San Francisco, South of Market.

Fritscher also allowed his readers to view this world through his friends and fellow travelers. He not only talked the talk; he walked the walk. I know. I was there. The night I got my head shaved at the Slot, that infamous bathhouse on Folsom Street, he was there. I have photos to prove it. He applied dozens of clip-clothes pins to my torso and removed them all in a flash of epiphany. It was a rush I passed along again and again to other men in that long lost leather community South of Market. "As high as passions, fun, creativity, and sex always surged around *Drummer*, it was not the worst of times," Fritscher writes in *Gay San Francisco*, "but the best..."

As in the study of Native American culture, there are a couple of obstacles for some historians delving into the study of homomasculinity. One is the concept of the cosmos. In the study of both, the historian must not only engage in time travel but must—existentially—also be able to view the order of the universe from a different angle. Back in the day, the order of the cosmos looked far different through a bohemian-homomasculine "SoMa70s" lens than it does through a latter-day feminist lens or a bourgeois hetero lens. *Drummer* itself viewed the universe from a different underground-undersea angle, and Fritscher's "periscope up" through both *Drummer* and *Gay San Francisco* is the lens whose cross hairs accurately target that angle we, or at least I, saw. Though forgotten, ignored, or denied by some, that angle through that lens is for this Stewart more than *auld lang syne*.

Another obstacle faced by many historians is the method of record keeping. (Fritscher has famously been a diarist and a journalist and an archivist of graphics, letters, and taped interviews for years.) Authenticity of experience is placed on the written primary document which is frequently venerated as an icon. When documentation is something other than written, other steps must be taken to verify its authenticity. Discussing the oral testimony of Native Americans, Daniel Richter argued, "Oral genres," and here one might include the Old Testament and its campfire tales, "require unfeigned belief in the immutability of the message in the same way that written scholarly genres require implicit confidence in the accuracy of footnotes—as a validation of the historian's authority to interpret the past." (*"Who's Written History?" William and Mary Quarterly* 50:2, April 1993: 385.) Hertha Dawn Wong, in *Sending My Heart Back Across the Years: Tradition and Innovation in Native American Autobiography*, proposes that not only oral tradition, but also songs, chants, clothing and other remnants of the past are legitimate fields to be mined for historical information. (NY: Oxford University Press, 1992.)

Fritscher, who earned his academic credentials with his 1968 PhD, long ago earned the authority to mine and interpret the leather past because of his role in editing *Drummer*, and in writing his historical novel-memoir, *Some Dance to Remember*. When I first met him in 1974, he had written four books and had been writing for the *Journal of Popular Culture* since 1968. He knows what he is doing; and, almost as an object lesson to some GLBT historians, it seems that everywhere possible in *Gay San Francisco*, he cites sources to support his text.

Even before the beginning of the 1970s, he was aware that our athletic night-trips in bars and baths and barracks were like the wild treks big-game adventurers once made into uncharted continents from where they would bring back exotic and enchanted cargo. Even in the heat of fuck, he once told me decades ago that someday he expected that all of us in the 70s would be tales told in bedrooms around the world. What no one planned on was the mass death by plague of so many storytellers and photographers who could have kept the true brilliance of the 1970s alive. So with his books of fiction and nonfiction, we can sit on the ground and tell the sad stories of the death of kings, and their enchanted sex lives that were surprisingly artful and personal during a revolution of the species that may never come again.

Jack Fritscher, who taught university film courses in the same city where I was the manager of a commercial movie theater, frequently references Japanese director Akira Kurosawa's 1950 film *Rashomon* in which the viewer sees a rape and murder through the eyes of four different participants. Each account is different.

As an eyewitness-analyst, Fritscher is the first to warn that conflicting eyewitness accounts of an incident may prevent its "truth" from being known; that is why he, an eyewitness, has interviewed and cross-examined so many other eyewitnesses to testify before the jury of his readers.

Rashomon has become a catch-word for the difficulty of verifying what "really" happened. Seemingly conflicting accounts only make the event multifaceted. It's much like viewing a cubist painting by Picasso, or an all-angles painting by Duchamps. In *Gay San Francisco: Eyewitness Drummer*, Fritscher writes a multi-faceted "autobiography of us" that could be called *History Descending a Staircase*.

Mystic chords of memory echo through the fog trailing the freighter SS *Jack Fritscher* as it steams in under the Golden Gate Bridge that appears significantly on the cover of *Some Dance to Remember*. That freighter is laden with enchanted cargo from a foreign country: the Past. Brawny seamen appear on deck. When it docks, be there. That's an order.

Jim Stewart (b. 1942) was for many years the department head of the Social Sciences and History Department at the Chicago Public Library. Previously, in 1976 he was one of the first artists in San Francisco to move South of Market to Clementina Street where he was a key force in the creative epiphanies of the SoMa art scene with friends such as Chuck Arnett, Robert Opel, Camille O'Grady, and David Hurles. While managing a commercial movie theater, he had met Jack Fritscher in 1973 and lived in Fritscher's home for six months after moving to San Francisco in 1975. As a working carpenter in 1977, he built the interior of the legendary Fey-Way Gallery where Opel mainlined formerly closeted gay art in the space where he was murdered in 1979. As a working photographer, Stewart founded Keyhole Studios in 1976, and his strong black-and-white images of Folsom Street sexuality often appeared in SoMa exhibitions and in *Drummer* (beginning as early as *Drummer* 14, May 1977). For several seasons, he worked as a manager for various San Francisco leather venues, such as the Leatherneck bar, and for years he managed the bar and retail store owned by the *Drummer* publisher. He grew up on a farm in Mason County, Michigan, and has lived in the San Francisco Bay Area (including the Russian River), Chicago, and other Third Coast locations. As a photographer, he focused on leather culture, and as a writer, he has concentrated on historical topics and research methods. In addition to poetry, he is currently writing a murder mystery set along Michigan's West Shore, as well as a series of interconnecting stories about 1970s life in SoMa titled *Clementina Tales*. He lives in a nineteenth-century farm house that has been in his family for more than a hundred years.

"Jim Stewart," Golden Gate Park, 1976. Auto-photograph by Jim Stewart. ©Jim Stewart. Used with permission.

Coaching *Drummer*:
How Jack Fritscher Survived Every Owner, Publisher, and Editor
by Harold E. Cox, Ph.D.

The history of *Drummer* is closely tied to the liberation history of masculine-identified gay male sex in the United States and there is no one alive today better qualified to write this history than Jack Fritscher. Associated with the legendary magazine as editor, writer, and photographer for some twenty-plus years, Fritscher is the keeper of the institutional memory of *Drummer*. In the confusion that followed the Stonewall Riot in New York, it was clear to Fritscher that the macho male community was a different breed from the drag queens of the Village, the two groups having stylistically little in common beyond basic same-sex drives. While the fight for freedom may have been the same for both (or perhaps not—you decide), the route to be traveled to gender identity was far different. This difference was explained to me some years ago by an observer who had watched the police and the drag queens fight for a while, decided that the screaming was boring, and went down to the Trucks for some *real* action.

Jack Fritscher, born in the 1930s, recognized through boyhood epiphanies that masculine erotic culture was rooted in the heroic military men of World War II. As a teenager seeing magazines and movies, he responded to the alienated veterans' banding into the motorcycle gangs which evolved with their male-male rituals in the 1950s and 1960s. This was something new because prior to WWII, traditional S&M relations were—and still are—hide bound in the set formulas of Victorian English "games." Our modern macho male colors are black leather, blue denim, and prison orange. The modern "Victorian" gays following Oscar Wilde tend more to lavender and pinks. Think Shiites and Sunnis.

The roots of gay male S&M in America are to be found in the weekend sex games played by rugged young military men in the sand dunes at Virginia Beach during the 1940s, a time when the immediate vicinity contained the largest aggregation in the world of soldiers, sailors, air corps, and Marines who mustered out and disseminated throughout the US. In his war stories and military photography in *Drummer*, editor in chief Fritscher knew that *Drummer*'s 1970s demographic was readers who grew up during WWII in erotic awe of soldiers who were their fathers, uncles, brothers, and the older "boy next door."

Having been recruited as a deputy sheriff for the City and County of San Francisco, Jack Fritscher had the lust to focus on military themes and cops and prisons and brigs and cowboys and sports to bring out of the closet idealized man-to-man relationships so that those theretofore straight identities could cross-over into gay man-to-man sex games. Because of the Vietnam War which lasted until the first issue of *Drummer* in 1975, he was careful to glorify not war but the same kind of soldierly camaraderie found celebrated in Walt Whitman. In the virulently anti-war culture of the 1970s, he dared make it okay to wear uniforms for sexual role play. As *Drummer* publisher Tony DeBlase pointed out, Fritscher recognized that the *Drummer* base was interested in bikes and leather as only the first of many metaphors and fetishes of the kind of masculinity Fritscher was creating in his monthly training manual.

Personally, Jack Fritscher was a major influence on my emergence into the world of gay male S&M. Born in the hills of Virginia in the early 1930s, I was not aware of my homosexual tendencies until I was in my early twenties. I knew something wasn't quite in sync with the world around me and I definitely knew I liked to tie men up, but that was as far as it went. Living in Appalachia, I sought others with similar drives in urban publications ranging from *Justice Weekly* to *The Advocate*, but it was not until 1975 when I encountered *Drummer* that I felt I was on the right emotional track. The first *Drummer* I read was interesting, but not interesting enough to hold my attention. Then Fritscher appeared on the scene and refocused the magazine. The impact on me is a personal and professional history which I have yet to put on paper.

Some day perhaps I'll add my eyewitness to his.

Fritscher, whom I never met personally until the 1990s, influenced me from afar in other ways. One of his missions was to clarify the mysteries of gay S&M to those seekers who wished to play but didn't know how to start. He published articles (e.g.: bondage) on technique, safety practices, and other practical information for the benefit of the uninitiated. When he left the editorship of *Drummer* which in the 1980s deflated into a leather contest magazine, the mission of covering technical matters passed on, for the most part, to *Dungeonmaster*, of which I became editor in the late 1980s. Fritscher's influence encouraged me when I wrote my own cross-over article on adapting military interrogations to S&M play for the first issue of *Dungeonmaster*.

When *Dungeonmaster* went into decline, I and my partner, Bob Reite, established *Checkmate* that Fritscher volunteered to support with his *Drummer*-style writing and photography which we published. Like

Introduction: Coaching *Drummer*   29

Drummer, Checkmate was killed by the Internet after our ten-year run. Without Fritscher blazing the trail to opening up S&M writing about masculine games and leather psychology, it is likely that none of these monthly chronicles about leather S&M would have happened, and neither DeBlase's *Dungeonmaster* or our *Checkmate* would have ever existed.

Fritscher's *Gay San Francisco: Eyewitness Drummer* history is written in typical full-frontal Fritscher format: pull no punches, evade no problems, and take no prisoners. No one should think that some of what he has written about *Drummer*'s history simply represents the squabblings of a dysfunctional family of perverts trying against all odds to put out the world's first leather magazine.

It is my professional observation, as a university history professor, that *Gay San Francisco* is the history of a period of masculine sexual liberation in which there was a seminal change in the manner in which males dealt with questions of their own new identities and their sexual relationships with other men for which new rules had to be defined and new games played.

Nearly a hundred years previously, when slaves were emancipated after the Civil War and given the vote, Blacks, led by Stephen Douglass, opposed the granting of civil rights to women, presumably because they feared that more rights for women would mean fewer rights for them. When Victoria Woodhull Claflin became the first woman to run for president in 1872 and battled against the anti-obscenity laws of the day, she was strongly opposed by more conservative women who considered her advocacy of free love to be immoral.

Every leader in a moment of drastic change will encounter those who can't lead, won't follow, and don't get out of the way. Fritscher was never deterred.

He is one of the last original activist writers of the culture war that began in the 1970s. His intimate *Drummer* history—a kind of autobiography of all of us in leather—should be read by anyone who seeks a deeper understanding of the masculine-identified sexual revolution.

There were, of course, hundreds of great people who contributed to *Drummer*, but Fritscher drove *Drummer*. He wrote *Drummer*. He coached *Drummer*. He chronicled *Drummer*. He outlasted every other editor and owner and publisher. As editor, writer, and photographer, he was *Drummer*'s main contributor through nearly seventy issues of the magazine's twenty-four year run.

What would our leather community be like today if he had continued, not just as a contributor, but as editor in chief of *Drummer* after New Year's Eve 1979 became the 1980s.

Harold Cox is professor of history at Wilkes University and the eminence gris of S&M who is the founding editor and owner of *Checkmate* magazine into which he incorporated *DungeonMaster*, a magazine begun by the second publisher of *Drummer*, Anthony F. DeBlase. A leather player since the 1950s, Harold Cox, with Bob Reite, has created, besides *Checkmate*, two legendary institutions within leather culture. He is the founder and owner of the international S&M rendezvous, the Delta Run, held annually in the woods of Pennsylvania. He is also the *primus inter pares* founder of the 1990s New York leather bar, the Lure. His writing ranges from reportage about "reality-based power-exchange S&M" to the history of electric street railroading: *The Fairmount Park Trolley: A Unique Philadelphia Experiment* (1970).

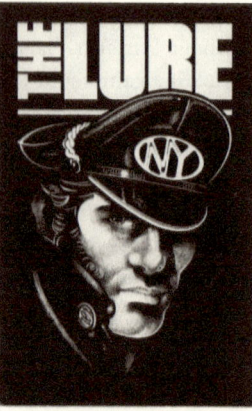

Lure poster by Rex. Used with permission.

"Harold Cox and Bob Reite, Alcatraz," San Francisco, 1995. Photograph by Jack Fritscher. ©Jack Fritscher

Introduction: Coaching *Drummer* 31

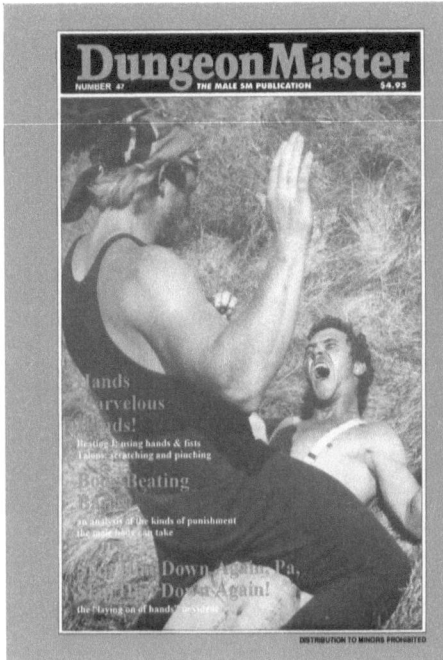

Fritscher enlarged and cultivated the *Drummer* salon and its homomasculine esthetic beyond even *Drummer* itself. Publisher Anthony DeBlase, having sold *Drummer*, featured Fritscher's photography on covers of his "Virtual *Drummer*" magazine, *DungeonMaster*. See *Dungeon-Master* 47 (January 1994). *Checkmate* magazine publisher Harold Cox, having purchased *DungeonMaster* continued Fritscher's writing and photography exemplified by the cover of *Checkmate* 18 *Incorporating DungeonMaster* (February 1997). Two photographs by Jack Fritscher. @Jack Fritscher. Covers used with permission.

A Thousand Light Years Ago: *Drummer*
by David Hurles, Old Reliable

> He haunted the sleazy grind houses on Market Street. Blacks smoked. Mexicans sat singly in blue watchcaps. Unstoppable cocksuckers roamed the balconies. His feet stuck to the floor... He paid to intensify reality in images so big and bright even the blind could see.
> — *Some Dance to Remember: A Memoir-Novel of San Francisco 1970-1982,* Jack Fritscher

> ....On Market Street in dewy San Francisco, from Seventh Street to the magazine store at Powell, as they stand perhaps in the drizzle, fugitive spirits will respond to that now faint message soon to become *drummingly* insistent [italics added]
> — *City of Night* (Part Four), John Rechy (1963)

"What a man knows at fifty is incommunicable to a man of twenty," said Adlai Stevenson. If he had won the 1956 presidential election, the 1960s, 1970s, and 1980s would have surely looked different to those who were part of those times. In their recall they are also changed from the times we know we lived through, because we have lived more, and the layers of time change the texture of our recall. We are faithful to those years, knowing they will never come around again, still not quite convinced there were such times. Time toys with us. At twenty a man might think he can see fifty in the distance, but there is no possible way to suspect what lands he will pass through on the way to fifty. Most twenty-year-olds eventually reach fifty, or worse, wondering how they got there so impossibly fast, question both the math and the justice of the situation.

HURLES IN THE CITY, A BOY

I was nineteen the year *City of Night* aroused me with incredible stories I could only hope were true. The next summer, in 1964, *Life* magazine tightened the knot in my stomach with its expose of gay life in the big cities, in San Francisco. Right before my eyes, two pages wide, was a dark photo of a place called the Tool Box, men in leather silhouetted before a huge wall mural of other men in leather, the work of Chuck Arnett. In the summer of 1965, sharing the drive with a stranger, Ohio vanished in a rear-view mirror. In Berkeley I turned twenty-one. In San Francisco I grew up. In the same summer, Jack Fritscher also arrived at the edge of the world, and became another cell in the rapidly growing body of gay men. Every day there were new arrivals, men who braved the prairies and mountains, in search of a place to call home, to be with their own kind. Untold numbers of sex refugees, of gay immigrants, reached the end of the rainbow with no money, and no one to call. But San Francisco welcomed them all. The earlier arrivals helped provide comfort and sustenance to those who followed. The only agenda was brotherhood and sharing, peace and love.

What followed were fifteen years of sexual freedom, sexual anarchy, sexual invention and redefinition. It was exciting. Corporal Works of Mercy were the order of the day. Practices and relationships heretofore the province of only a few, now exposed to the light of day, attracted and connected men who had at some time thought that they were the "only one." But for subversive sex to open up, expand, be shared, it needed someone with the loyalty and passion of a monk to search out, record and describe it, write about it, to make it accessible to the uninitiated.

In 1975 I was living in an ancient three-unit building on Clementina Street, south of Market Street, in a cheap apartment directly above Chuck Arnett. Chuck was a gentle soul in a seductive body, totally unashamed of his passion for heavy-duty sex. Although I saw his well-deserved popularity, and heard through the floor boards his remarkable sexual stamina, I wasn't aware, at the time, that Chuck Arnett had created the testosterone generating mural I had seen in *Life* a decade earlier. Industrial artist Jim Sterling lived a few doors away. Photographer Jim Stewart hosted parties (and photo exhibitions) in his flat directly across the street. Creative, sexually intense, hot players increasingly populated the low-rent South of Market area.

The unseen hand of dignified, hypnotic, and enthusiastically brutal sexual buccaneer Jim Stewart instinctively and surely guided me toward his longtime friend, Jack Fritscher. At the time, the young men who were summoned, then seduced, by the pariah pastel city, also assumed the weight and duty of mutual assistance, each looking out for all; in this place, whether it was popular hallucination or something more cosmic, the 1960s continued right on through the better part of the 1970s. Coming to San Francisco was rarely something that was decided upon; it was a necessity, a force, a duty, a blessing, and out of our hands. When Jim Stewart and Jack Fritscher headed west from Michigan, coming to live together in San Francisco, they left their individual elsewhere's behind them; like me, they came because they had to come.

A TRIBE OF MEN...HORNY MEN

It must have been a similar raw force that led Jim to bring Jack and myself together. It had to be done, and so he did it. I soon appreciated that Jack knew, and was known by, a large and diverse ensemble of people. His interests were courageously wide-ranging, and completely sincere. He was determined to understand all of the pieces of this new cultural puzzle we found ourselves in, and by assembling the many pieces to see what it was that the pieces were working to form. It was a time when free and readily available sex, in infinite variety sometimes anonymous but more often not, defined the day. Sex was everywhere, really and truly everywhere, and you could have as much as you could handle.

In this place and time, Jack was as eager a reveler as everyone, but he was more than a participant in this throbbing crowd scene. With sex everywhere, many people blissfully thought no further than the next, soon to be realized, orgasm. Jack, however, also recognized uncommon, unknown, or "new" variations beyond the traditional man-to-man "naked sweat and grunt," and sensed that these other sexually charged interactions were rich and significant. Jack undertook the weighty task of seeking out often secret and unspoken aspects of manly sexual excess, obsession, and activity; he was driven to make sense of it all, and intellectually willing and able to explain it in a judgmental-free manner, thus opening the doors to other men who needed a little push, or a pull, to open themselves up.

It would be immodest for me to claim that I ever planned to become a student of men, or sex, or human nature. My awareness developed in parallel to my work. I regard my own experiences as the product of having lived a very lucky life. Jack, on the other hand, spent many disciplined years in universities, learning and teaching. In the end, we have each become student and scholar of the same tribe, but with the wonderful advantage of perspective drawn from opposite poles. For both of us, calling became a vocation. As members of a subculture, in a special time and place, we each were provided an opportunity to observe aspects of our own culture and various sub-cultural fringes, from the inside and the outside. We each chose to trust the integrity of the unguided voices of other men who we determined knew the truth, and who would describe the truth to us.

In 1975, *Drummer* was launched in Los Angeles. But before it had time to define itself, find its voice, fate intervened. A gay bar fund-raiser, tongue in cheek calling itself a "Slave Auction," was raided by the LAPD who with "straight" face announced that they had acted in the interest of freeing the slaves from their bondage. Among the hundred or so arrested that day was *Drummer* publisher John Embry. Righteously angry, he left Los Angeles as soon as he could, and moved to San Francisco, bringing the promising magazine, and his now fiercely populist political activism with him.

Tucked away in our minds are memories of moments that we can't even remember forgetting, memories that long ago escaped the bondage of effortless recall, but which come again, bright and loud and full of life, when summoned by a chance sequence of words. Jack, in midnight phone calls that cut through the thick bright white San Francisco night fog, cautiously weighed the opportunities and consequences that might lie ahead. Becoming editor of such a magazine carried with it the potential to be a life-changing event, a county fair midway littered with landmines. Wearing the ringmaster's top hat would require him to surrender a large measure of personal security, and to commit his reputation to the climate of another season. His decision was never driven by dollars and cents. With a leap of faith, he gambled that he would be afforded the freedom to cultivate Embry's undeveloped *Drummer* with thoughts heretofore unspoken, opening up for many, the more often than not unseen leather brotherhood — its past and its present — for the future.

A very few erotically exclusive groups had started to find their own voice, most specifically wrestling, which had come together both regionally and nationwide. There was also some action in underwear and water-sports. Jack used *Drummer* to celebrate a multitude of out-of-the-ordinary, unusual, pursuits in the process de-stigmatizing many activities, which opened them up to others who previously may have only dreamed of being included. Jack created a midway where even the most marginal act could have an audience, and everyone could be entertained. Those with some religious or political aversion to cigar-smoking midget Argentinean amputees, or bearded behemoths, or even sleazy, sweaty, tattooed carnies...well, they could either welcome the occasion to widen their outlook, or move on to another booth in this panoramic midway, to continue the pursuit of their own special kewpie doll.

DRUMMER MEETS OLD RELIABLE

In my idiosyncratic manner, I resisted actually meeting Jack face to face, for many months. All the while, however, we engaged in a thought-provoking and wide-ranging telephone conversation that moved forward, several hours each night every night (and that continued for years after

Introduction: A Thousand Light Years Ago

we met). So the time finally came that I met Jack in person, with the quite natural result that our friendship, and our ongoing deliberations, observations, and points of view blossomed. Looking back, I may have appeared to be a greater fount of wisdom than I actually was. Jack, however, was an idea man, and I gave him resonance and reverberation. A favorable consequence of our collaboration was the recurrent appearance of my own modest photographs (and sometimes words) displayed by Jack in *Drummer*, exhibited in manner I might not have considered or dared.

It became clear, once I had finally met Jack face to face, that he had an insatiable interest in what I had done or collected, starting with my earliest work, nude photos and slides taken in 1968. In the intervening eight years or so I had done some Super-8 filming, and for several years I had been making audio recordings of men having sex, or talking about it. Video was still a few years away. The audiotapes were, and remain, enormously significant. They are an oral history of what was still a silent era. The speakers are primarily the disenfranchised, hustlers, ex-cons, outcasts of one sort or another. In an atmosphere absent of pressure, alone and speaking their thoughts out loud, the most startling things were often revealed. Many of the audios continue many stops beyond frightening. My ears perked up! With photos, what started out as random projects started to unify into something entirely different than I had initially foreseen.

To keep this long story short, Jack flattered me, and that encouraged me. Even though I had been working as a photographer since 1968, and was able to provide for myself in this manner, however modestly, I didn't get much respect. If a magazine mentioned me at all, it was almost certain to be in a negative light. Nevertheless, I was eating regularly, and didn't feel a mandate to change my style or the subjects I cared about. By the time I met Jack, I had already been arrested, tailed, subpoenaed, lied to, betrayed, cheated and ignored, and I bore some scar tissue, so to speak. Jack, unlike many others, was enthused by what I showed him. Once he became editor of *Drummer*, he tirelessly promoted my photos and tapes, and on several occasions invited me to contribute an article or review.

I recall Jack bringing his friend Robert Mapplethorpe over to meet me, before he was touched by fame. I was especially delighted when he asked to buy some black-and-white prints of a favorite Old Reliable model, Mongoose. I declined any payment, rewarded instead by the pleasure of sharing the joy these photos obviously brought him.

While Jack may have had to drag me kicking and screaming into the world, I never doubted that I was being dragged, at least, in the right direction.

A "FAGGOT'S" SECRETS ARE TOLD: THE *DRUMMER* SALON

More significantly, having drawn me out into the larger world, I became something of an accomplice, collaborator, and ally. I could time and again recognize in *Drummer* the best moments of our trips, and tricks, and travels in the night. The details weren't offered as gossip, however, but as part of a larger erotic epic, presented without gratuitous first person pronouns, or names. *Drummer* wasn't about Jack, or myself, or his many, many friends and contacts. It was, in fact, a means of leveling the playing field. If I had sex with dangerous, heavily tattooed cigar-smoking ex-cons, who slapped and choked me while calling me "faggot" and threatening me (and more, for a very modest fee), *Drummer* was there to let other guys with the same interest in on the game, judgment free. Not everyone's cup of tea, but somewhere this honest revelation would prompt a lot of other men to blissfully walk around stiff-legged for days on end.

Jack wrote a roman a clef about San Francisco in the 70s called *Some Dance To Remember*, which is in many ways "the *Drummer* novel." Woven into the intimate, documentary fiction style of the book, are moments and stories from my own life as an avant-garde artist existing near the perilous edge that Jack found suitable to progress the encompassing narrative. I was pleased to recognize aspects of my life, true even when unflattering, reflected back to me from the character of porn mogul, Solly Blue. In *Some Dance*, where things born of truth are retold as fiction, it is a reasonable speculation that *Some Dance's* fictional magazine, *Maneuvers*, opens a window into some true moments and times between the covers of the real *Drummer*. As witness to the actual march of time, and like an Uncle who watched the novel develop even through the awkward years, I confidently suggest that no other book, fiction or nonfiction, not even Armistead Maupin, has sorted out, packaged up, and then delivered back the 70s era of gay, and sexual, liberation in San Francisco, with greater dramatic detail, historic accuracy, or sensitivity for the time itself.

SMOKIN' A J WITH DA' BAD BOYS:
CHRISMAS AT FRITSCHER'S

Memories overflow and fill the room as I recall just a few of our exploits. One Christmas day gathered at Jack's home, I was accompanied by a tall bank robber (a recent pen pal who had written scorching sexual promises), just hours off the Greyhound, paroled from Walla Walla State Pen the prior day. I was very keyed up, eager to commence the blistering encounters pledged in his letters, to submit myself to the frenzied physical aggression,

Introduction: A Thousand Light Years Ago

muscle, and vigor of this strong young man who had been starved of sexual liberty for so long, prepared to stare at his angry face, and face his antisocial rage, focused to burn a hole through my body, ready already, not pleased by delay! In fact, with the presents open around the tree and bread broken, each person at Jack's home was anxious for the sweet desert of a good joint and the familiar embrace of an unfamiliar male body, to meld with one's own, to finalize the holiday with the bliss and ecstasy that holidays would seem to command and deserve. Jack also had plans laid out to celebrate the smells and tastes of the day with another throbbing side of brute. Nevertheless, with a scholar's determination (and maybe some brandy or a joint), he patiently made my bank robber the center of attention, encouraging him to educate us about his area of expertise, about sex behind bars. Happy, fed, and joyful, those assembled finally dispersed into the fog-bound white night to rendezvous with our individual physical, or metaphysical, closure of the day.

On every possible occasion Jack and I went, sometimes with others, to the Golden Gloves, as well as to the pro fights (usually featuring lustrous lightweight Latino hopefuls, all of who looked good enough to eat without washing first), when they still had Friday night fight cards at the Civic Center Auditorium. Greg Varney, a Golden Gloves trainer, explained to us the ins and outs of the teen amateur sluggers, and got us as close as we could get to the worldly wise young brawlers. We would leave sprayed with blood, spit, and sweat; but we left with new schooling, too, plus material for a month's worth of vivid wet dreams. Jack wrote a "Gay Sports" article about boxing for *Drummer* as well as a Golden Gloves article about Varney whom he dubbed "Noodles Romanov." [See *Drummer* 20 (January 1978) and *Drummer* 29 (May 1979).] Much the same dream infusion could be said about the amateur bodybuilding contests that Jack managed to discover and film in out-of the-way high-school gyms and East Bay Masonic Lodge halls. These were very "straight" affairs loaded with sexual tension, and we were moles, intermingling to observe a hidden culture.

Within my bedroom (and despite the exasperation of his longtime lover David Sparrow) Jack examined the planes and curves of many muscular hustlers, along with the chasms and gorges of their minds. Some were my gift to him; others probably qualified as Research and Development for *Drummer*. I was accustomed to the nuances and signals of my thugs, but Jack dove headfirst into the shallow end with some of the most treacherous and unpredictable brutes, yet always came through with a (sometimes shaky) smile, and having learned and experienced new things.

IN THE SWEATY PITS OF THE PEN

If I might look back from perhaps thirty-five years, I will always treasure one particular adventure Jack twisted my hesitant elbow hard enough to convince me I'd be a raging fool to pass up. The occasion was a six-hour tour inside San Quentin, broken up into very small groups, with convicts as our extremely friendly and intimate tour guides. Jack, who knew everybody, knew someone who knew someone who could get us into prison. Included was a basic dinner meal in the main dining hall, convicts, guards, guns and all. To even get in to prison, however, we were required to release the State of California of all liability for our safety, and we were notified that in the event that we were to be taken hostage, we would not be bargained for; a thorough strip search was then required before we could finally pass through the main gate. What a night to remember! The prison system was comparatively peaceful then (and a lot less crowded than it has now become), and nothing was hidden from us...it was an Open House! As we went along, Jack memorized every detail, and with his keen eye he directed my own sight to unwelcoming, but overwhelming, sights I might have otherwise missed. (Actually, he alerted me to quite a number of exceptionally pleasing sights, too, like a convict tongue wagging its way through a small hole in a steel door. Jack observed that we were like French royals touring the Bastille before the Revolution.) We were inside a dream, maybe it was a nightmare, but the cool part was that we got instant parole, so we could leave later that same night, smuggling out with us thousands of mental pictures, sights, smells, and feelings, of heaven and hell, and an ample supply of muscular, sweaty, tattooed, temporarily unavailable miscreants, to recall for a long, long time.

These escapades, and hundreds more, filtered, translated, explained, and celebrated, all found their way into *Drummer* as in Jack's article about our adventure, "Prison Blues." [*Drummer* 21 (March 1978)] As much as the gay popular culture of the period could be examined, explained or codified, it was done in the pages of *Drummer*. It was in those pages that the actual facts of contemporary gay men's lives, and the sexual truth of a sexual time were recorded. *Drummer* was a journal, a guidebook, and an open invitation. Time has shown that the risks Jack took were worth taking, as curious subscribers became committed loyalists, rather than turning away. Jack could thrust directly to the heart of the hardon, and didn't need to be coaxed, either. Sometimes he pushed the magazine defensively ahead of him; other times he stood protectively in front of it, but always he wrote for *Drummer*, and his frequent, unique photographic layouts for *Drummer* filled thought-spaces between his words, right up to

Introduction: A Thousand Light Years Ago

the very end, in 1999, of *Drummer*, and yesterday's millennium. *Drummer* was a minute in time for Jack the observer, Jack the teacher, Jack the sexual adventurer, and, most of all, for Jack the journalist. He ranged far beyond *Drummer*. *Drummer* did not define him. He defined *Drummer*.

David Hurles is the legendary photographer and video artist Old Reliable famous for his trademark street hustlers and ex-cons. In Washington, DC, he began his photographic career with Guild Press in whose defense he testified as both model and photographer in one of the most important obscenity trials of the 1960s. In the post-Stonewall migrations, he moved his low-rent atelier to San Francisco's Tenderloin where like a bohemian painter he cast his romantic manwhores from the streets, the Zee Hotel, and the Old Crow bar. Starting up one of the first gay mail-order companies in 1971, he created a niche for his photographs and erotic audiotapes of verbal abuse by rough trade. In 1976 when he met Jack Fritscher, he was filming in the difficult Super-8 format used by his mentor and longtime friend Bob Mizer of Athletic Model Guild. His homomasculine photographs frightened gay magazine publishers whose rude dismissals caused him to retreat until Fritscher persuaded him that *Drummer* needed him. With photos published as Old Reliable in *Drummer* 20 (January 1978), he was introduced in "Prison Blues" in *Drummer* 21 (March 1978) as an artist—whose personality provided the basis for the fictitious pornographer who steals the show in Fritscher's *Some Dance to Remember: A Memoir-Novel of San Francisco 1970-1982*. He also shot

"David Hurles (Old Reliable)," Fritscher-Hemry House, 1981. Photograph by Jack Fritscher. ©Jack Fritscher

many covers and centerfolds for *Man2Man Quarterly* (1980-1982). Old Reliable, collected by Robert Mapplethorpe and Sam Wagstaff, is a singular eye within American popular culture: thousands of his photographs have appeared in dozens of gay magazines, and his videos have sold more than a million copies. He earned fortunes and lost them and earned them again. In 2005, the artist Rex edited the coffee-table book *Speeding: The Old Reliable Photos of David Hurles*. On October 19, 2007, film director John Waters made a pilgrimage to visit Old Reliable because, John Waters said, Old Reliable was both a "guilty pleasure" and an important influence in his own life and films. Pals with Gore Vidal, David Hurles lives in Hollywood.

Jack Fritscher's American Men
by Edward Lucie-Smith

Jack Fritscher has been many things: tenured university professor, novelist, writer of short stories, biographer, magazine editor, maker of more than two hundred erotic videos, chronicler and critic of American pop culture — also (as this book demonstrates) skilled photographer. Many of these activities have been linked to an exploration of eroticism, which is, for Fritscher, an arena of masculine-identified sexuality. His approach is twofold. On the one hand he is the formally trained critic and ethnologist, curious about all aspects of human behaviour. On the other, he is the writer-artist dramatizing a personal vision — the vision expressed for example in his ambitious novel, *Some Dance to Remember*. There, as here in these photographs, his focus is on what he calls "homomasculinity" — less the act of sex itself, more a complete state of being.

He sees in the very male males who attract him — bodybuilders, cowboys, cops, men in various kinds of sports gear, men wearing military uniform — ritualized totems of the potent American Dream, taken from his own dream visions, as well as from the dreams of the intense cult following whose tastes he has recorded and reflected for many years on page and screen. He believes that, just as some women now legitimately investigate their own gender, so too many men have become increasingly curious about their own gender identification. In his view, true homomasculinity, far from cancelling out the female principle, offers the valid gender balance of male animus that the female anima demands and deserves. He notes that there is in male-to-male sex an underlying current of violence — that sexual relationships between grown-up men, the bulls of the herd, often veer towards displays of brute strength, and even beyond this, to episodes of direct physical competition. He also perceives that this kind of physical competition, these outbursts of destructive energy, are all intrinsic to the nature of American life — part and parcel of what was once, and not so very long ago, a lawless frontier society.

Though Fritscher was in fact one of the early generation of social humanists working on various frontiers of the American conscience — the Civil Rights Movement (beginning in 1961), the Peace Movement (1965), Gay Liberation (1967), these perceptions, feelings and preferences have increasingly tended to get him into hot water with the "politically correct." The politically correct point of view is that feelings of the kind he reflects may, regrettably, exist, but ought not to be represented. Failure to represent such things will eventually, so current doctrine has it, lead to the abolition of what is deplored. There is a sad irony in the fact that the "gay" world, the realm of the queer or homosexual, has no sooner achieved recognition and to a certain extent legitimate status, than it begins to designate forbidden areas within its own territory. Fritscher's images may be all the more threatening to a certain type of gay puritan because we immediately understand that to him they are familiar territory, not things encountered for the first time and recorded chiefly because they seem bizarre and startling. The late Robert Mapplethorpe once said that there was nothing shown in his own photographs that he hadn't done himself. Fritscher can say the same, though with a subtly different nuance. A reminder of this is the more relevant because Fritscher and Mapplethorpe were once so closely linked personally, not only as friends but as lovers, protagonists in a stormy bicoastal affair conducted just at the *noir* moment when Mapplethorpe was rising to the first peak of his reputation. It was Fritscher who commissioned Mapplethorpe to produce his first magazine cover, and who at the same time introduced him to the West Coast leather scene. This cover was done in 1977 for the San Francisco-based leather magazine *Drummer*, which Fritscher was then editing. Fritscher not only drew the design for it, but provided the model, Elliot Siegal, who then became a frequent model for Mapplethorpe.

Knowing this, one might look at Fritscher's photographs expecting to find some trace of Mapplethorpe's influence, though his own early photographic images were published when he was just eighteen, twenty years before he and Mapplethorpe encountered one another. In fact their approach is very different. Mapplethorpe's most typical photographs are calculated, coolly staged, Deco artifacts where the subjects become objects, deprived of nearly all personality, frozen by the icy stare of the lens. Fritscher's work is, by contrast, informal, candid, a product of the desire to seize and fix some epiphany, some magic moment, rather than to construct a particular pattern which already pre-exists in the photographer's imagination. Some images are the result of Fritscher's involvement with gay magazines and with video. These portray men who one time or another have been gay icons, and often show them at their most overtly sexual. Thus, there is a fine series of nudes of Donnie Russo, the ultra-macho star of a whole series of recent erotic videos, among them four made by Fritscher himself in collaboration with his partner Mark Hemry. Russo has a sexual electricity. Fritscher speaks of Russo's "priapism"—which accounts for his impacting still photographs as well as video. Photographing this phenomenon (the kind of fully independent personality Mapplethorpe usually seems to have avoided in his sexually

Introduction: *Jack Fritscher's American Men* 45

oriented work) Fritscher seems to regard himself, not as someone who is imposing a stereotype, but as a collaborator with his subject. They are working together, one behind the camera, and one in front of it, to focus a particular set of qualities and characteristics, and give them their full effect. The same can be said of another photograph, which is a full-length nude of Val Martin, star of the mid-70s S&M classic, *Born to Raise Hell*. "We're all motor-driven hacks compared with Robert as a photographer," Fritscher has said, "but at least I'm not going to end up photographing lilies and leaves because I'm afraid, as Robert grew to be, of having somebody look back at me from the other side of the lens."

Many of his photographs, in fact, are true candids, shot in public places, where the model or subject's sexual preference remains deliberately indeterminate. Fritscher often shoots on location, from the hip, and on the run. "I dare to stalk public events," he claims, "lying in wait for that magic moment when some man in a crowd looks directly at my raised camera and focuses on my lens with a "look," a precise narrowing of the eyes, a look of bonding, superiority, surrender, even contempt. Any passion will do! Sexual inferences are drawn only because of my attitudes, as expressed in the photographs, and because of my gender. If I signed a woman's name to these images they would be regarded very differently." With Fritscher there is in fact no absolutely impermeable barrier between reality and erotic fantasy. There are certain kinds of activity which obsess him—bodybuilding, weightlifting, boxing, wrestling—because they seem to sum up the essence of masculinity, and also because they allow free rein to the kind of male narcissism which attracts him. He is always aware that the voyeur, in this case the man with the still camera or the video camera, often fulfills the needs of the one who is observed, that the transaction, far from being one sided, is fully reciprocal. He feels that many of the photographs taken in these circumstances—those of bodybuilders posing in contests or on the boardwalk at Venice Beach are just as erotically charged as those which are more overtly sexual. Even more charged, he might claim, because the relationship between the one who views and the one who is viewed is more complex and ambiguous than it is in circumstances where the sexual element is fully spelt out.

Fritscher admits, however, that the men he stalks in public invariably carry with them a strong sexual aura—and that this is the very aura which he is also trying to project when he photographs models in his studio. A case in point is the image of celebrated American bodybuilder Chris Duffy wearing a tartan necktie. Here the model, far from being unaware of the camera, is working in collaboration with the photographer to project a particular image of himself. Even here, however, there are things the model cannot fully know. From start to finish of a shoot of this type, Fritscher is trying to peel away the masks his subject wears. The masculine self is revealed as well as the carefully constructed masculine image which both reinforces and partly conceals it. This unveiled process of co-creation is especially evident in Fritscher's photographs of his long-time collaborator, the multi-titled bodybuilder Jim Enger. Enger takes on many guises—he is seen laughing disarmingly, but also as the straight Mr. Iron Man which he was on the physique contest stage. Fritscher here, as in much of his work, both fictional and photographic, exerts a certain suspension of disbelief from the reader or viewer. There is a narrative present, but is it real or is it made up? Another case in point, but this time coming from the other, or "documentary" direction, is the superb image of a shirtless cowboy climbing a fence. Is this pure documentary, or posed erotic choreography? One's imagination is led by the startled look on the face of the young man behind and to the left of the subject.

The narrative element in the photographs is reinforced in some cases by the fact that many were originally shot as stills during video features cast and directed by Fritscher, and produced and distributed by Mark Hemry, for their boutique studio, Palm Drive Video, founded in 1984. Some scenes are obvious fantasies, but the images nevertheless remain portraits to the same extent as the fantasy shots of celebrities made by Annie Leibowitz. They look, just as Leibowitz's portraits do, in two directions: towards the fantasies of the subjects themselves, and towards the expectations (therefore also the fantasies) of the audience. Examples are the goggled truck mechanic in "Hand Gun," the cowboy in "Last Cigar," with hangman's noose around his neck, and the prison bondage, and medical fantasies. These resemble Leibowitz's work, but also have a kinship with the operatic extremism of Joel-Peter Witkin. In photographs of this type one is conscious that the line is blurred between fact and fiction, just as it is in Truman Capote's "faction," *In Cold Blood*, and in Woody Allen's film, *Zelig*. On occasion, the boundary between art and life dissolves altogether. "Bound and Hooded," taken in August 1979, is a vérité play shot of Larry Hunt, obviously made with the model's consent and cooperation. Hunt later modelled formally for Robert Mapplethorpe. Later, in the 1980s, he was abducted from a Los Angeles leather bar. His fate was deduced from a single relic: a human jawbone, identifiable from dental records, which turned up long after his disappearance in Griffith Park in L.A. Fritscher's photograph perhaps prophesies some aspects of fate regarding the vulnerability of the subject, but artists are hardly causally responsible for any coincidence of murderous events which take place after their images were made.

In a broader sense, the fact/fiction blur is one of the most important aspects of Fritscher's work, and part of his truly original contribution to gay photography. With him, there is no absolutely impermeable barrier between asexual reality and erotic fantasy. There are pictures here where there is no specific element of sexual display not even of the rather generalized sort which can be found in images of bodybuilders posing for the camera. Examples are the power-lifter, a competitor in the Police Olympics, or the men in a kilt throwing the hammer. Here the element of collaboration with the photographer may be presumed to be missing. The image is, in each case, the product of a single, fortunate never-to-be-repeated moment. It tells us nothing about the sexuality of the subject, but much about the image-maker's own reactions to the world which surrounds him — the things he is attuned to, and is likely to notice and record. In "Butch: Hell's Angels," for instance, Fritscher makes masculinity itself a fetish. There are pictures which revel in the ordinary sweat of life which is, by some twist of photographic magic, made special and extraordinary. Fritscher's eye constantly perceives the world erotically. Guided by that eye, his camera picks out the ripe erotic sub-text which might otherwise remain unnoticed.

This, therefore, can be thought of as a book whose images are held together by an argument, or rather by a whole series of arguments, expressed through images rather than through words, about the nature of masculinity, and of male sexuality, within the wider framework of American society. It is, for example, about the way in which men present themselves sexually to the camera when they know they are being observed. Over the years, a whole series of conventions have been created, which are used when women present themselves in this fashion. The tendency in gay male photography has often been to adapt these for use with the male body — hence innumerable versions of the *Playgirl* male nude, languorous and passively provocative. Fritscher knows that this pictorial grammar runs contrary to his purposes. He knows, too, that poses and pictorial conventions taken over from Greco-Roman statuary, beloved by quite a number of photographers working in this field, have a distancing effect, when what he wants to give is the *closeness* of the male, the scent and presence of masculinity, like a hunter stumbling upon a tiger in its jungle lair. There are photographs here which go well beyond the boundaries of established conventions of male eroticism — frames captured from the flux of time, single never-to-be-repeated moments: a boxer taking a punch, a young father who drove his car off the road, a biker bloodied in a skid. Again, such photos tell us nothing about the sexuality of the subject, but much about the image-maker, especially when placed within this particular context. It is Fritscher's overall vision which makes them erotically charged.

"My portraits," Fritscher once wrote, "define a certain kind of man in stasis and motion, in joy and pain, in the mutuality of sports and sex. Each is a single frame from an otherwise invisible movie. These are traditionally masculine men. Period. If one insists on politics, they are culturally traditional men surviving gender abuse in an age that trashes the legitimate male ethos. Found mostly on the streets, at construction sites, and at athletic events, these men — that is, their images — are presented without apology to provide comfort and joy to men and women who prefer masculine men in the best sense where power is not power over others, but is power in the disciplined control of oneself. Let me be quite clear. None of these images is pornographic. Pornography is wanting to control the object. Erotic art is loving the subject you want to behold, not possess. I'm very clear with these guys about keeping things pure. Few of these men actually 'posed' for the camera. Even when they were fully aware of its presence, they maintained their integrity without acting. That is precisely what I strive for. These are simply men, hopefully archetypic, celebrating masculine rites — of sport or sensuality, often mano-a-mano, offering themselves declaratively as athletes, adventurers, icons, saints, victims, survivors, and heroes, with the frailties and strengths to which all humans, regardless of gender, are heir."

His work is not about men having sex with other men. It is about men exhibiting a sense of their masculine selves. Just for a moment, they are releasing the full power of their masculine natures. For Fritscher, a born observer and (as perhaps he would admit) a born voyeur, these images are irrefutable evidence of things which are latent in most men, and which, when the right moment comes, can be made to imprint themselves indelibly on a photographic negative, for everyone to see.

Edward Lucie-Smith is a British writer, poet, art critic, photographer, curator, and author of international exhibition catalogues who has served in the Royal Air Force (RAF) and as a member of the art and literature panels of the Arts Council of Great Britain. Known from his broadcasting on the BBC and for his more than one hundred books on art, he is the world's most prolific and best-selling writer on art, art history, and sexuality and art. His major books may be represented by *Movements in Art Since 1945*, *Sexuality in Western Art*, *20th Century Latin American Art*, *Ars Erotica*, and *Race, Sex, and Gender*. His photography, as published in his solo coffee-table book, *Flesh and Stone*, is currently in exhibitions around the world, and his book of poems, *Changing Shape*, was published in 2002. In 2006, the Tom of Finland Foundation acknowledged him as writer and photographer with its "Lifetime Achievement Award." During

Introduction: *Jack Fritscher's American Men* 49

his forays to the United States, where he frequently resides in the New Mexico salon of painter Delmas Howe, he has written the introductory essays to two homomasculine photography books, Chris Nelson's *The Bear Cult* (1992) and *Jack Fritscher's American Men* (1996) from which the introduction is reprinted. In 1992, he was interviewed as an eyewitness by Jack Fritscher for the book *Mapplethorpe: Assault with a Deadly Camera*. Living internationally on planes, between galleries and lecture halls in Boston and Beirut, Dubai and Beijing, he calls London home.

"Edward Lucie-Smith," Fritscher-Hemry House, 2001. Photograph by Jack Fritscher. ©Jack Fritscher.

| Eyewitness Illustration | Three book covers of Lucie-Smith titles: *Flesh & Stone*, *Race, Sex and Gender*, and *Sexuality in Western Art*. |

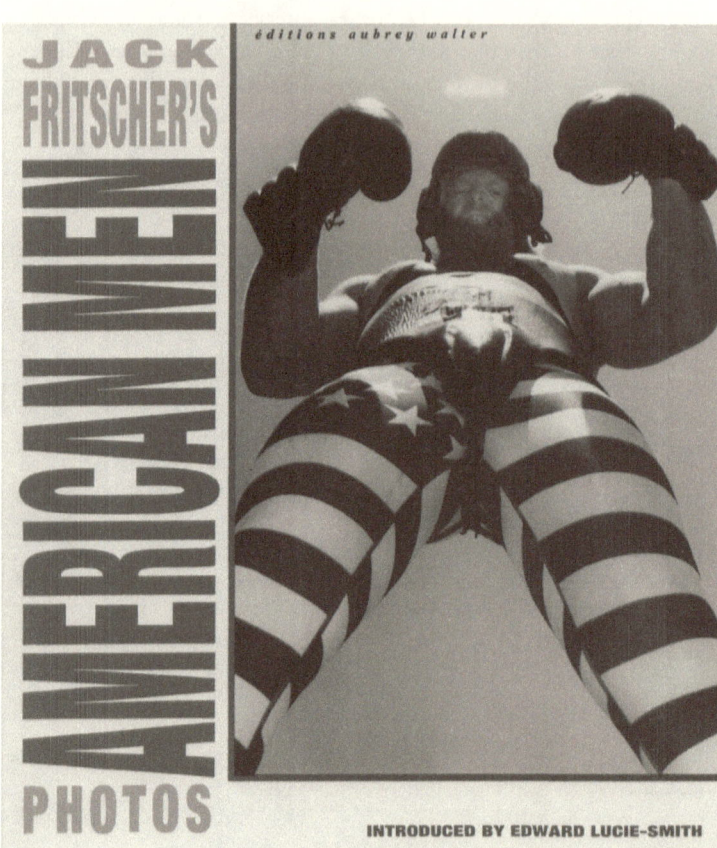

Cover, *Jack Fritscher's American Men*, 55 photographs, 1995, Gay Men's Press, London. The collection in *American Men* reveals Fritscher's depth-perception of *Drummer*. The British publisher originally planned to print a full-color cover dramatizing the model "Goliath" in his red-and-white wrestling tights against the blue sky, wearing boxing gear to characterize American aggression astride the world. In the 1990s when former *Drummer* editor Joseph W. Bean, and Alex Wagner, were editors creating various "Virtual *Drummer*" magazines at Brush Creek Media, they did justice to the original color of this photograph on the cover of *Powerplay* 10 (May 1996). One of Fritscher's most frequent models over a period of twelve years, "Goliath" also appeared twice in *Drummer* 140 (June 1990), as the centerfold in *Drummer* 148 (April 1991), and, favorited, on the cover of *Drummer* publisher Anthony DeBlase's "Virtual *Drummer*," *DungeonMaster* 47 (January 1994), and Harold Cox's *Checkmate Incorporating DungeonMaster* 18 (February 1997). Photograph by Jack Fritscher. ©Jack Fritscher

"Donnie Russo," Palm Drive Video, 1993. Jack Fritscher shot three feature videos of Donnie Russo and photographed him as "I, Priapus" for *American Men* as well as for the cover and centerfold of *Drummer* 170 (December 1993), for the cover of the first issue of Dave Rhodes' spinoff magazine from *The Leather Journal*, *Eagle* (July 1996), and for Scott O'Hara's *Steam* magazine (1996). Photograph by Jack Fritscher. ©Jack Fritscher

"Mickey Squires, Roadside Diner,'" Palm Drive Video, 1992. Jack Fritscher shot Colt model Mickey Squires (Richard Bernstein) in a Palm Drive Video feature, and posed him for this *American Men* photograph at the San Francisco home of Bob Cato who was sent to prison for crashing his van into the taxi carrying elderly actresses Mary Martin and Janet Gaynor. In the zero degrees of incestuous separation in eyewitness Fritscher's *Drummer* salon, Squires was also lensed in Super-8 footage by LA photographer and bodybuilding champion Jim Enger who in the mid-1970s (before Enger partnered with Fritscher) was the partner of the wildly famous Colt model and former LAPD cop Clint Lockner who several times co-starred in front of a camera with Squires. Mickey Squires was a favorite cover and centerfold in *Drummer* publications and in magazines imitating *Drummer*. Photograph by Jack Fritscher. ©Jack Fritscher

Introduction: *Jack Fritscher's American Men* 53

"Chris Duffy aka Bull Stanton," Palm Drive Video, 1995. Jack Fritscher and Mark Hemry used three cameras filming international bodybuilding superstar Chris Duffy in the video feature, *Sunset Bull*. In a series of photographs, Jack Fritscher shot Chris Duffy for *American Men*, for the three covers of *Thrust* (November 1996), *International Leatherman* (March 1997), and *Bear* 62 (September 2000), and for the cover of the third edition of *Corporal in Charge of Taking Care of Captain O'Malley and Other Stories* (2000). Former *Drummer* publisher John Embry also chose eight of the Fritscher shots of Chris Duffy for interior display in his "Virtual *Drummer*" magazine *Manhood Rituals* 2 (1998), and *Manhood Rituals* 3 (1999). Photograph by Jack Fritscher. ©Jack Fritscher

"Steve Thrasher," Palm Drive Video, 1987. Jack Fritscher photographed the straight construction worker, actually named Steve Thrasher, for two video features. Thrasher was an ongoing favorite of Fritscher who shot him for two photographs in *American Men* and for the cover of *Drummer* publisher Anthony DeBlase's *DungeonMaster* 47 (January 1994), as well as for the cover of the James Purdy novel, *Empty Rooms*. In the salon around *Drummer*, Anthony DeBlase who became publisher of *Drummer* on August 22, 1986, retained Fritscher as an ongoing advisor and contributor listed on the masthead. Photograph by Jack Fritscher. ©Jack Fritscher

Introduction: *Jack Fritscher's American Men* 55

"Road Warrior: Bob Hayn," Palm Drive Video, 1987. Published in *American Men* and as one of a portfolio of potential *Drummer* covers. Photograph by Jack Fritscher. ©Jack Fritscher

"Steve Thrasher," Palm Drive Video, 1987. Cover photograph of Steve Thrasher cast as the Appalachian "Renderer" for the Gay Men's Press British edition of James Purdy's novel *Empty Rooms* which dying director Derek Jarman had planned to film. Photograph by Jack Fritscher. ©Jack Fritscher

"Mike Jacob," Palm Drive Video, 1995. Shot during the filming of *My Nephew, My Lover* at Palm Drive Video. Mike Jacob of Germany appeared in Fritscher photographs in Joseph W. Bean's book *International Mr. Leather: 25 Years of Champions* published by the Leather Archives & Museum, Chicago, and in *American Men*. Photograph by Jack Fritscher. ©Jack Fritscher. When Fritscher began importing national and international leather culture into *Drummer*, he chose Chuck Renslow's Chicago leather values over Los Angeles leather-bar culture where publisher John Embry had started up *Drummer*.

Drummer-ing up the Zeitgeist
by david stein

As editor in chief and principal feature writer of *Drummer* during the critical early years of 1977-79 (*Drummer* 19-30, plus ghost-editor of *Drummer* 14-18, 31, 32, 33), Jack Fritscher was both chronicler and instigator of what he was the first to call gay America's "Second Coming Out." The first coming out is when a guy discovers that what gets his dick hard and makes it shoot is, well, *dick*. The second coming out is when he moves beyond dick and ass to discover ("total body sensuality," as Jack called it, which leads to a desire "to play and to please itself in true S and M (Sensuality and Mutuality) with other men."

During the nearly quarter century of *Drummer*'s run, the ruthless logic of that desire, colliding with the even more ruthless imperatives of post-industrial capitalism, enabled leathersex to spread for better or worse from the back alleys and waterfront dives of America to its shopping malls, theaters, campuses, living rooms, and Internet chat rooms. Practices that seemed thrillingly *outré* when the magazine began are now considered suitable for jokes on prime-time sitcoms. What was still a cottage industry of individual craftsmen making custom leather-wear and unique "toys" back then has become serious business today, employing thousands of people and generating many millions of dollars in revenues. A community that was virtually invisible to "civilians" before Stonewall has spilled so far out of the closet that we've become the latest target for the religious extremists who seek to shut down our ever-larger events and ever-glitzier meeting places.

The butt end of the 1970s laid the foundations for the leather population/popularity explosion to come, and Jack's *Drummer* was a big part of that pop-culture process. In the ensuing decades after Jack, often recycling Jack, *Drummer*'s publishers and editors kept trying to harness and direct the waves of New Leather (both men and ideas) that kept pouring into the scene, with decreasing success, until finally the magazine was left behind by the dot-com generation at the turn of the new century.

LEATHER AS A STATE OF MIND

To write about the new state of sexuality writers had to corral concepts. Before I coined the phrase "Safe, Sane, and Consensual" in the 1980s,

Jack had re-defined S&M as "Sensuality and Mutuality" (1972) and had coined the word *homomasculinity* (1978). We needed new vocabulary to write about our new attitudes, our new identities, and our new way of expressing sex that till then dared not speak its name. Tom Lehrer sang "When correctly viewed, everything is lewd," and it was Jack, more than anyone else, who taught us that leather is as much a state of mind as a piece of clothing. Many of the ideas, terms, fantasies, and practices that leathermen and other masculine queers take for granted today (tit play, Daddies, prison sex, raunch scenes, bondage as meditation, cigar sex, gut-punching, rubber sex, sports-gear fetishes, pain as ecstatic release, and much more) can be traced back to Jack's writing and photographs published in *Drummer* during the years Jack edited it and provided much of the content himself, or else to articles he wrote or suggested after Tony DeBlase brought him back as a frequent contributor starting in *Drummer* 100 (October 1986). Jack didn't invent any of these practices and fetishes which he debuted, but his bravura writing and inspired editing helped fix them in the minds of two generations of perverts.

Jack understood early on that the brain is the largest and most important sex organ, and he kept telling us so both directly and indirectly. Nearly always writing in the first person, he showed us by example that the best way to enjoy an unfamiliar or off-putting scene is to dive in head first, imagination wide open, and judgments locked down. Get a man's head in the right place, and his dick and balls will follow.

Much of Jack's writing, both fiction and nonfiction, turns on the courage it takes for a man to accept his need and desire (occasional for some of us, practically constitutional for others) to bottom out, to go down, to just give in and accept what ever another man chooses to throw at him. Jack likes to write about tough, strong, masculine men who know what they want and are ready to take it (in either sense of taking it). His bottoms aren't wimps or wusses but every bit as tough as his tops, which certainly makes switching roles a lot more practical!

THE RISE OF THE BUTCH BOTTOM

The mainstreaming of leathersex could not have happened without Jack's masculinization of the bottom side of homosexuality. One of the reasons leathersex was able to fly under the radar for so long was that the public image of the gay male was so tightly (and wrongly) linked with effeminacy. Butch guys could get away with anything because they could always "pass." But in the 1970s it all changed; the "butch bottom" arose and increasingly demanded the respect that had hitherto been accorded exclusively to tops and straights.

Introduction: *Drummer*-ing up the Zeitgeist 59

Up-and-coming American fags-in-training of my generation learned the great lesson that even if we started out as sissies, we didn't have to stay sissies just because we liked cock. We might push paper or curl hair at work, but afterward we could go to the gym and lift weights till we had the kind of bodies we'd always envied. Or we could at least dress like it. A more masculine style became the norm throughout the gay subculture.

Drummer both reflected and promoted this development, and no one—except maybe Tom of Finland—did more to cement it in gay-male consciousness than Jack Fritscher. His play, *Corporal in Charge of Taking Care of Captain O'Malley,* which first appeared in *Drummer* 22 and *Drummer* 23 (May and July 1978), hit us with an unforgettable one-two punch to the groin and the psyche. In place of the classic polarity of butch and femme, or he-man and punk/twink (still visible in early *Drummer* itself in such role models as Fred Halsted and Joey Yale), *Corporal in Charge* gave us butch and super-butch.

Not even being called a "cunt" (a label the character rejects) can shake the Marine Corporal's sense of himself as a *man* in love with serving and servicing another man like himself—superior precisely because he has *more* of the same qualities present in the man on the bottom.

In the coming decades, *more of the same* would become the new paradigm for homomasculine sexuality.

REFLECTIONS IN MIRRORED SHADES

Jack knew what he was doing. It was no accident, or joke, that he added the tag, "American Review of Gay Popular Culture" above the masthead in *Drummer* 23. His aim was to reflect changes in gay culture even as they were occurring, by reflecting the lives of *Drummer*'s readers back to them, creating a feedback loop that would reinforce the already existing trends toward a more masculine style and a more experimental, all-embracing sensuality. His much-imitated creation of "Tough Customers" (*Drummer* 25, December 1978), in which the readers themselves became the porn stars, is only one of the devices he employed to this end.

Jack's landmark features reporting on such establishments as the Mineshaft (*Drummer* 19), the Catacombs (*Drummer* 23), the Quarters (*Drummer* 24), and the Academy Training Center (*Drummer* 145) can he viewed in the same light. His super-heated prose and photos fueled their legends, yes, but at the same time he demystified them, making them seem less distant and inaccessible. He actively challenged readers (especially in the Training Center piece) to do what he did, master their fears and fulfill their fantasies by checking the facilities out in person. Jack had no truck with the conventional porn-mag "Look, but don't touch" attitude. Instead, his siren call was, "See what can be yours, if you have the balls to reach out and grab it."

But along with reports on such unquestionably "popular" phenomena as jock sports (*Drummer* 19), punk rock (*Drummer* 21), and rodeo (*Drummer* 26), Jack didn't hesitate to make detours into the precincts of "high culture." No, he didn't review opera, but he did write one of the smartest pieces ever on Pasolini's difficult film, *Salo* (*Drummer* 20); he urged readers to take Pasolini's cautionary politics as seriously as his art. And if Jack's greatest discovery, Robert Mapplethorpe, eventually became one of the most widely known (if least understood) artists in the world, other enthusiasms of his, like the filmmaker Derek Jarman (review of *Sebastiane*) and the photographer Arthur Tress (four poems accompanying a gallery feature in *Drummer* 30), remain relatively esoteric delights to this day. But Jack wrote about them—and Mapplethorpe and the artist Rex (both in his "New York art" issue, *Son of Drummer*, 1978)—without a trace of condescension, as if every *Drummer* reader would just naturally care as much about their work as he did.

PRACTICAL ALCHEMY

Bondage, a theme close to my own heart, is something Jack returned to several times in *Drummer* and elsewhere (particularly his own later zine, *Man2Man*). He wrote about this fetish or practice more perceptively than anyone before or, probably, since. "Bondage: Blest Be the Tie That Binds" (*Drummer* 24, September 1978, the Mapplethorpe cover issue) is an interview with a New York City bondage master. Like many of Jack's best pieces, it's illustrated mainly with photos he himself shot for the article (using the name of his then longtime lover, David Sparrow, who co-owned the camera given to him as a birthday gift by Jack). His other illustrations are several of his appropriate "found" images, like a San Francisco Ballet photo of a male dancer suspended from ropes tied to his limbs and flying in a body harness. Whether this is, as Jack claims, the first feature to analyze bondage in the gay press or not, it was the first to come to my attention that not only turned me on but made me *think* about why.

So much of Jack's bondage article is quotable, better not to start; and anyhow you have the whole thing in this book. Whether the ideas sprang from Jack (with his years-long background in the spiritual disciplines of the Catholic priesthood), or from his interview subject, or emerged in the interplay between them, here is the *ur*-text for the now commonplace notion that rigid, immobile bondage is a form of meditation, a way of stilling the mind, and thus releasing it, and thereby the body as well, from everyday cares and tensions. You'll also find the idea, not surprising given Jack's overall catechism of leather, that bondage promotes whole-body sensuality instead of genital-centered sexuality. Then there are the ideas that you entrust yourself to the bondage master's care, giving yourself to him, and he gives you back to yourself, unharmed but not unchanged, at the end. And that he takes you on a trip and returns you safely again. It's all there, explicitly or implicitly.

Another, rather curious theme pops out if you quickly scan through Jack's *Drummer* bibliography; the man had a recurrent case of the blues. There's "Prison Blues" (*Drummer* 21), "Cigar Blues" (*Drummer* 22), "Castro Street Blues" (*Drummer* 24), "Tit Torture Blues" (*Drummer* 30), "Foreskin Prison Blues" (*Drummer* 186), and his wonderful short novel *I am Curious (Leather)* aka *Leather Blues*. Maybe it was just a catchy tag word; or maybe he was riffing like a jazz stylist on a theme trying to signal something about how to read them? Maybe he meant us to infer that in these pieces, especially, he was *testifying*, telling us truths that might be painful to hear? Or, as a reporter, enabling others to testify *through* him? But *Drummer*'s about S&M, right? Pain is pleasure, right? So it's all really about pleasure, right? Yeah, right; *not*.

As a masochist of long standing myself, allow me to testify that the pain is *real*, and the greatest endorphin rush in the world doesn't make it any less real. It just helps you accept it, embrace it, and transmute it into an equally real pleasure. Jack discovered sadomasochists are practical alchemists, and he figured if we can transmute raw pain into ecstasy, then by God, we can pretty much transmute anything into anything we want. Whatever fetish he chose to write about, in the end it came down to some form of alchemy, just as he wrote about leather magic and leather ritual in his book, *Popular Witchcraft*, written at the same time as *Leather Blues* (during 1968-1972) and published at the same time as Larry Townsend's *The Leatherman's Handbook*. How boring it would be if a cigar had to stay *just* a cigar!

THE *AUTHENTICITY* FETISH

Like most fetishists, however, Jack is obsessed with "authenticity." And like a great many highly introspective intellectuals, including Henry David Thoreau who is quoted on nearly every masthead of *Drummer*, he tends to locate human authenticity in the *un*reflective, the "natural man" untainted by societal repression and superficiality. (See especially his "authenticity" editorial, "Getting Off," in *Drummer* 24.) That may explain his fascination not only with such iconic figures as athletes, cowboys, cops, and soldiers, but also with such less bourgeois characters as convicts, hustlers, outlaw bikers, and rednecks. Throw in his reportage of his readers' desires (not necessarily his) for every sort of sweaty raunch, from headcheese to snot, not excluding piss, spit, and a below-stairs whiff of forbidden scat, and it would seem *Drummer* gave its readers what at the time they wanted, what the French call *nostalgia pour la boue,* or *nostalgia for the mud.* That phrase can refer either to the dirt of a peasant village or the mud-choked gutters of an urban slum, depending on which one you, or your ancestors, crawled out of to reach a state of gentility or bourgeois comfort that may define liberated gay culture.

Jack re-incarnated this "nostalgia against the bourgeois" by making a fetish of blue-collar men as a class, their masculine way of being, their clothing and their pursuits. He glamorized "Tough Customers." Within a forty-year spread in gay history (1930s-1970s), Jack uses this *nostalgia pour la boue* in the same literary way that Christopher Isherwood colorizes his own personal slumming with Sally Bowles and Otto Nowak in *The Berlin Stories.* Both insert the outsider authors and their middle-class readers into proletarian life in a way most vividly illustrated in *Drummer* by Jack's other discovery, Old Reliable, who thrilled *Drummer* readers with his extremely authentic *boue* photographs of young, dangerous, gay-for-play ex-cons, street hustlers, boxers, and AWOL military who live outside gay culture, and stretch the parameter of my axiom, "Safe, Sane, and Consensual." Jack also commissioned, cast, and designed the anti-piss-elegant Robert Mapplethorpe photograph *de la boue* "Authentic Biker for Hire" for *Drummer* 24, the same issue that showcased Old Reliable's photography in the interview, "In Hot Blood: Ex-Cons - We Abuse Fags."

Is such nostalgia a bad thing? Not necessarily, and perhaps only when it's in bad faith (indulged in, say, while being hypocritically denied, like a homophobic Republican politician arrested for sucking cock in a bus station toilet), or taken to a self-destructive excess. In Jack's case, it seems clear that his literary nostalgia for the mud is, in some ways, a response to the self-ghettoizing tendencies of an all too "self-conscious" American urban faggotry. Countering that gay skintight narcissism, he's nostalgic — romantic even, as the critic Michael Bronski says — for our collective memory of the "ideal world of male otherness" outside the gay ghetto, a blue-collar Eden of rodeo and motorcycles and soldiery he conjures repeatedly in his *Drummer* fiction and novels, where men can be physically intimate with other men without labeling what they're doing, a world of "best buds," "partners," and "teammates" who "stand by" each other without question.

"Good as Gay Lib is," Jack wrote in his provocative editorial in the *nostalgia pour la boue* issue of *Drummer* 24, "the total gay lifestyle as it has been commercialized means that gay men basically screw around only

Introduction: *Drummer*-ing up the Zeitgeist

with other gay men. Gone are the pre-Lib days when a gay guy adventured out to find a straight male to ball with." Of course, by now that world is pretty much gone forever; it's hard to imagine a het man anywhere in America today who *wouldn't* be self-conscious about gestures and come-ons that might be thought queer. But at the same time, today's young queers are even less patient with the limitations of the gay ghetto than Jack was back in the 1970s. So when uptight leatherfolk of a certain age feel affronted by the anything-goes attitudes of "post-gay" queer twenty-somethings, guess which ones are following in Jack's bootsteps?

POLYMORPHOUS PERVERSITY

Although Jack is only a few years my senior, he clearly got started with this sex stuff a lot sooner, and no doubt had fewer inhibitions to begin with. Reading Jack's *Drummer* articles, essays, stories, and poems as they appeared, and seeing the photos accompanying them, opened my eyes (and many others!) not only to what was being done in the burgeoning gay leather scene, but also to how much more *could* be done if we had the courage and imagination. Reacquainting myself with the pieces collected in this book was a treat, because so much in them is still as fresh, smart, sexy, and insightful today as when they were first published. If they're new to you, be prepared for a wild ride. But relax—you're in good hands.

---

david stein is the much-published author of *Carried Away: An S&M Romance*, a novel enthusiastically reviewed by Laura Antoniou, Patrick Califia, and Joseph W. Bean in 2002. His writing has appeared in such magazines as *Drummer*, *International Leatherman*, and *Bound and Gagged* as well as in anthologies such as Mark Thompson's *Leatherfolk: Radical Sex, People, Politics, and Practice* (1991), and Joseph W. Bean's *Horsemen: Leathersex Short Fiction* (1997). In 1980, he was cofounder of Gay Male S&M Activists (GMSMA) and was founding editor of its historic newsletter in which he published Jack Fritscher's essay, "Toward a Masculinist M/O: Why Bondage?" from *Man2Man Quarterly* #7 (1981). He is author of the ongoing online *History of Our Leather-S/M Fetish Sub-Culture and Communities*, and is a frequent columnist for the group, Masters and Slaves Together (MasT). As an acclaimed practitioner, he coined the S&M keyword mantra, "Safe, Sane, Consensual," and has famously appeared in quintessential bondage photographs from Inferno. He lives in Manhattan.

Vanguard
by Alexander Renault

"An artist does not reflect himself in his art
as much as he provides a mirror
for the readers and viewers to see themselves."
–Jack Fritscher

Thumbnail (2003): Jack Fritscher is an enigma of grand proportions, and one of the most respected and controversial writers of his versatile generation which includes John Rechy, Edmund White, Anne Rice, William Carney, Felice Picano, Allan Gurganus, Dorothy Allison, Armistead Maupin, Larry Kramer, Rita Mae Brown, and Andrew Halloran.

You cultural "completists" who like reading lists and comparable books, check out these comps. In memoirs in the shape of novels, Edmund White's *A Boy's Own Story* and Felice Picano's *Ambidextrous: The Secret Lives of Children* compare to Fritscher's *What They Did to the Kid: Confessions of an Altar Boy*; additionally, White's *Loss within Loss: Artists in the Age of Aids* compares to Fritscher's *Mapplethorpe: Assault with a Deadly Camera*; Anne Rice's *Interview with the Vampire* compares with his *Popular Witchcraft: Straight from the Witch's Mouth*; John Rechy's *Numbers* and William Carney's *The Real Thing* compare with his *Leather Blues* plus his *Drummer* magazine writing which fills five separate volumes of his fiction books, including *Corporal in Charge* and *Rainbow County*; Armistead Maupin's *Tales of the City*, Larry Kramer's *Faggots,* and Andrew Halloran's *Dancer from the Dance* compare with his *Some Dance to Remember: A Novel of Gay Liberation in San Francisco 1970-1982*; Allan Gurganus' *Oldest Living Confederate Widow*, Dorothy Allison's *Trash*, and Rita Mae Brown's *Rubyfruit Jungle* compare with his *Geography of Women* as well as with his *Sweet Embraceable You: Coffee-House Stories*.

All these authors have lived interesting lives, but it is rare to find an artist who has lived a life so filled with operatic opposing forces, but then, San Francisco writer Fritscher, who shares a birthday with Lillian Hellman, is a Gemini, moon in Leo, with Scorpio Rising. From 1953-1963, he was schooled in the Latin, Greek, British, and American classics in the prestigious Vatican seminary, the Pontifical College Josephinum, and is actually an ordained exorcist possessing all the minor orders of the Catholic priesthood.

He received his doctorate in American Literature from Loyola University, Chicago, where with the cooperation of Tennessee Williams he wrote his dissertation, *Love and Death in Tennessee Williams*. Moving into academia, where he hung with the poet Thom Gunn, he became a tenured university professor while hanging out with the likes of Andy Warhol, Mario Amaya, Robert Mapplethorpe, George Dureau, Sam Steward (Phil Andros), Edward Lucie-Smith, as well as Picasso biographer, John Richardson, and the High Priest of the Church of Satan, Anton LaVey, whom he featured in his book, *Popular Witchcraft*.

From the mid-1960s, he combined the strange bedfellows of academic discourse, mainstream literature, pop culture, sexual politics, witchcraft, erotic photography, and the world of gay male pornography on page and on screen. He is the founding San Francisco editor in chief of the legendary *Drummer* magazine in which his work appeared for 25 years and which he used as background for his signature novel, *Some Dance to Remember*.

As author of a dozen books and writer-director of more than 150 gay documentary and erotic videos, he works and lives near the Golden Gate Bridge with his domestic lover of nearly 30 years, Mark Hemry, where *Pornographic Pulsar* chased him down for a few gems to share with his readers, viewers, fans, and detractors, as well as LGBT studies mavens.

Pornographic Pulsar: During the interview Fritscher came across as sweet but unshakable, charismatic and full of opinions, but not opinionated, even though my job was to ask him to opine. I did not find myself experiencing my usual anxiety at interviewing brilliant academics. As anyone who knows me will attest, I have a love-hate relationship with the world of academia and it is interesting to note that Fritscher seems to be the exception to every rule of its jargon and pomposity.

One hates to trip on one's own clown shoes, but fools rush in! You cannot imagine my embarrassment when I realized I had been mispronouncing his former lover's name, "Mapplethorpe," through the first half of our chat. (The first syllable is pronounced like the tree, not like "grapple.") Oh, well. He never pointed it out. He simply pronounced it correctly. Actually, I was just glad I understood most of what he was talking about. There is simply nothing worse than being in over one's head without a life jacket during an interview with someone whose literary work has been explored by so many other journalists and critics (and men jerking off) who may have a far better insight into the interview subject than I do.

Introduction: Vanguard

In an interview with the critic, John F. Karr, from *The Bay Area Reporter* in June 1989, Fritscher described himself as "an iconoclastic visual artist." He certainly began in a time of artistic frenzy, the 60s and 70s, standing in a crowd that included the Gay Golden Age of John Waters and Divine, the Cockettes, Sylvester, David Bowie, Lou Reed, and Andy Warhol. Yet he has never had to go out of his way to prove himself because his ideas and writing and photography are unique across the genres because they speak for themselves, and he has always stood out among his peers without effort—in fact, without trying to do so, as he is rather reticent and reclusive.

As Winnie the Pooh once said, it is best to start at the beginning.

Jack was born John Joseph Fritscher on June 20, 1939. A fellow Gemini, he entered the world during the noon hour on the summer solstice, the brightest light of the year's longest day. In high school, he was the senior-class reporter and author of the all-male musical comedy, *Continental Caper*, 1959. He translated religious texts from German for American publication between 1960 and 1966. More than twenty of his early short stories and features, many of them coded gay stories and articles, were published in unsuspecting Catholic magazines. Teaching university journalism and literature beginning in 1964, he was that generation of professors who introduced a fourth genre to literary interpretation, "film interpretation," which was added to fiction, drama, and poetry.

Fritscher received his B.A. in Philosophy and English (1961) followed by graduate work in Aquinian Theology (1963) at the Pontifical College Josephinum in Columbus, Ohio. During that conformist Catholic time, he started his school's first student magazine, aggressively called *Pulse*, which had the priest in charge pounding on his desk in fury. He spent the very early civil-rights summers of 1961 and 1962 as a "worker priest" on Chicago's South Side in the heart of the ghetto at 63rd and Cottage Grove where he worked directly in the African-American community with the legendary radical, Saul Alinsky.

In 1966, he received his master's degree in English from Loyola University with his thesis, *When Malory Met Arthur: Sex and Magic in Camelot*. In May 1967, he came out formally regretting he had the year before told Tennessee Williams that Williams could not, mmm, depend on his kindness. In February, 1968, he completed his doctorate in American Literature/Creative Writing and Journalism, and took off for swinging London's Carnaby Street, as well as Paris, Madrid, and Amsterdam which all were in the throes of student revolution in the streets—from which he did not shy away.

In 1969, he signed a contract for his nonfiction book, *Popular Witchcraft: Straight from the Witch's Mouth*, which he wrote in San Francisco in the Castro where coincidentally Anne Rice was also living. They both knew the same witches, ghouls, ritualists, and vampires. Fritscher's nonfiction interviews with gay witches and Satanists was published in 1972. Anne Rice's fictional *Interview with the Vampire* came out in 1976. Both authors distilled the essence of that very psychic time in gay history.

In the 1970s, Fritscher received a National Endowment for the Arts grant to record audio interviews with his friend, the veteran writer, Sam Steward (aka Phil Andros) who told his life story including his times with Gertrude Stein, Alice B. Toklas, Thornton Wilder, and James Purdy for whose novel, *Narrow Rooms*, Fritscher shot the cover (GMP, London). In the mid-70s, Fritscher became the founding San Francisco editor of *Drummer* magazine which he made infamous. He is the original "Mr. Drummer" in the real sense of that title because by the time *Drummer* ceased publication at the end of 1999, his writing and photographs had appeared in 62 of *Drummer*'s 200 issues over twenty-five years, making him the author most published in *Drummer*.

He is currently working on a book which is kind of *The Best of Drummer*, an anthology of writing from the international magazine's torrid history. Who knew that one day a men's progressive gay skin magazine would become a historical document? Fritscher did. Actually, some of the *Drummer* material appears in *Corporal in Charge and Other Stories* (1984) — the first collection of *Drummer* stories — and in *Jacked: The Best of Jack Fritscher*, published by Alyson Press (2002) and nominated by the Erotic Authors Association (2003) as the best anthology written by one author. He is also currently nominated by the Erotic Authors Association for a Lifetime Achievement Award. [Editor's note: granted 2007]

Fritscher is dedicated to the preservation and continuation of gay cultural studies and the expansions of its horizons. He believes that there are some important facets of gay culture, including the "homomasculinist" subcultures of leather, muscle, fetish, daddies, and bears which need to be fully documented as part of gay history. In the mid-70s in *Drummer* he coined the word *homomasculine* to address the most neglected species in the gay zoo: the masculine-identified homosexual.

He says he is not himself a masculinist or a feminist, because, inclusive of both terms, he is a humanist. (Some people, trapped in gender politics, he says, don't rise to that concept.) He is also currently concerned about the political "repackaging" of the gay community, and how our culture and media have hi-jacked the "gay edge" only to sell it back to us in a new, corporate form. For years he has stood foursquare against the "politically correct" whom he terms fundamentalist Puritans who, born out of failed Marxism, actually hate art, sex, and the transcendentals of truth, beauty, and goodness.

A compelling and sexually unapologetic author, he once stated in *The Burning Pen*, "I confess. I breathe in experience. I exhale fiction. Feeling, emotion, is the oxygen of my fictive voice." You know an erotica writer has struck an intense stride by authoring a play called *Corporal In Charge of Taking Care of Captain O'Malley*. That story is such a *good* one that iconic publisher Winston Leyland included *Corporal in Charge* as the only play in his historic 1990 anthology, *Gay Roots*.

So powerful is Fritscher's fiction, critic Nancy Sundstrom wrote in *Independent Publisher* in 1998:

> Fritscher is undoubtedly a masterful writer of gay fiction, but he is first and foremost an extraordinary American writer. He deserves a broad-based audience because his powerful and original voice rings in one's head long after the book has been completed.

Fritscher has written critically acclaimed novels including *Leather Blues* which first appeared as the pioneer gay novel, *I Am Curious (Leather)*, written in 1969 and published in 1972; *Some Dance to Remember*, the epic novel which *The Advocate* called the "gay *Gone with the Wind*"; *The Geography of Women: A Romantic Lesbian Comedy*; and the novel which CNN noticed in its top 100 books, *What They Did to the Kid: Confessions of an Altar Boy* for which he won several literary awards including "Story Teller of the Year."

As in Hollywood, numbers often show how deep roots go in gay culture. In 30 years in adult entertainment, his books have sold more than 110,000 copies; his 150 videos, shot in the US and Europe for several companies including his own production company www.PalmDriveVideo.com have sold 250,000 copies; and his writing in thirty gay magazines (some like *Drummer* with a press run of 42,000 copies every month) have literally reached millions of readers. A thousand of his photographs have appeared in gay pop-culture magazines like *Honcho*, *Bear*, *Leather Man*, *Powerplay*, and *Thrust*, as well as in three high-end art books from England such as *Adam: The Male Figure in Art* and *Ars Erotica: An Arousing History of Erotic Art*, as well as the coffee-table book, *Jack Fritscher's American Men* published by Editions Aubrey Walters at Gay Men's Press (GMP), London. His on-screen production credential comes from the Hollywood Film Institute. Two of his videos regarding the photographer, George Dureau, are in the permanent collection of the Maison Europeene de la Photographie, Paris.

In the earlier San Francisco days of what Fritscher named the "Titanic 1970s," Fritscher met Robert Mapplethorpe who later tragically died of AIDS in 1989, at age 42. Noting the brilliance of Mapplethorpe's photography, *Drummer* editor in chief Fritscher hired him to do a cover which was Mapplethorpe's first magazine cover assignment (*Drummer* 24, September 1978). They became lovers and Fritscher went on write the biography, *Mapplethorpe: Assault With A Deadly Camera, A Pop Culture Memoir, An Outlaw Reminiscence..*.

Fritscher's book was the first biography of the controversial artist and photographer ever published, beating out Patricia Morrisroe's "horrified straight-woman" Mapplethorpe biography. In the typical fever of a Gemini, Fritscher wrote the final-final version of his erotic memoir of his ex-lover and confidante in only ninety days, because he included writing he had done about Mapplethorpe over the years. Adding other voices to make a chorus beyond his own voice keening, Fritscher included his interviews of other Mapplethorpe friends and heavy-weights such as Robert Opel, Camille O'Grady, George Dureau, Holly Solomon, Edward Lucie-Smith, and Joel-Peter Witkin. (Fritscher has taken gorgeous photos of Robert Opel's muse, the singer and poet, Camille O'Grady.)

His *Mapplethorpe* book went on to become a critically acclaimed piece of gay American history while Morrisroe's sophomoric, middle-American-esque attempt bombed. Morrisroe had interviewed Fritscher for five hours (recorded on the phone) and sent a note praising his information. When she found out years later that Fritscher was writing another kind of Mapplethorpe book that looked to her like insider competition, she denounced Fritscher as "The King of Sleaze" because he had then recently written a gay-culture historical piece in *Drummer* titled "Remembrance of Sleaze Past" to nail down historically what sex had actually been like before fluid exchange became problematical. Morrisroe so misread the "reverse code" of gay language she did not realize that "sleaze" is a sexual compliment.

A read of Morrisroe's prudish biography makes it painfully obvious that she does not understand—and actually seems to loathe—the gay subculture which she claims shocked her beyond comprehension while researching Mapplethorpe's life. I guess no one ever told Patty Morrisroe that the Number One Rule For Writers is *only write what you know*, babe. The poor bitch didn't understand that in the inversion of the gay world, *sleaze* is considered a good thing. She is the perfect example of what Fritscher means about the corporate "repackaging of the gay community." The corporate Random House published Morrisroe's book which was reviewed by the corporate *Vanity Fair* which is not surprising because the head of Random House at that time was married to the head of *Vanity Fair*. Where Morrisroe freaked over Mapplethorpe's Satanism, exorcist Fritscher, author of *Popular Witchcraft* and friend of Anton LaVey, truly

Introduction: Vanguard

understood and encouraged in his lover Mapplethorpe the heady mix of Catholicism and Satanism inherent in much very potent gay art; for instance, Mapplethorpe's most Satanic and scatalogical photos graced a new edition of the poet Rimbaud's *A Season in Hell*.

Charles Winnic, Ph.D., Professor of sociology at City University of New York, writes of *Mapplethorpe: Assault with a Deadly Camera*:

> Jack Fritscher's memoir is a marvelous recreation of an epoch, an art, and a man. Mapplethorpe was a...romantic figure who did more to liberate popular taste than any other artist.... Fritscher is the perfect interpreter of Mapplethorpe, and his beautifully written book helps us to understand how an apolitical photographer became so politically potent a culture symbol.

Like many great writers, Fritscher knows himself well and has clearly developed tremendous confidence. His knowledge of human sexuality runs deep, both from academic study and hands-on experience with the 13,000 veterans of the gay liberation wars to whom he dedicated *Some Dance to Remember*, which is an autobiographical novel that is also very much the autobiography of San Francisco, 1970-1982. Fritscher's tales of the City are a bit more realistic, and certainly more historical, than Armistead Maupin's *Tales of the City* for which Fritscher has an Irish storyteller's respect. Maupin has said he himself writes to capture people's hearts, not their sex; Fritscher says he aims for both, and for their intellects. (The resounding opening line of *Some Dance* is "In the end, he could not deny his human heart.) Asked about his own dual role as author and historian, he writes,

> Perhaps I am a unique hybrid: I am personally leather and a pioneer "action figure" (according to *Drummer* cartoonist A. Jay) in leather culture as well as a scholar-historian of gay male leather culture. But I am not part of the establishment Leather Reich of "Mother-May-I S/M." In my *Porno Manifesto*, art for art's sake may go beyond the pale of consent.

Fritscher is also a pop-culture scholar and expert on cinema and television, and has published numerous articles. In his pioneering 1972 media book, *Television Today*, a chapter titled "Americanned Creativity" goes:

> For TV now, the Commercial Sell is the Frankenstein that creates our buffered, not-so-glad-wrapped, gotta-have-

a-gimmick Americanned culture. Whenever business lays its hands on art, art suffers the slings and arrows of outrageous fortunehunters. If business exists to supply the demand, business must often create the demand. Advertisers tell us what they think we need; what they want us to demand, so they can supply it. In the following blank, enter your nominee for the most worthless product ever plugged as a necessity: _____ .

Upon seeing that blank line, I first thought of feminine deodorant spray, diet soda, Fox News, and the National Republican Convention.

Fritscher is an uncanny swami — well, he is a witch! — whose instincts and life experiences have made him an extremely prophetic social critic. About the 1990s, he stated to John F. Karr in *The Bay Area Reporter* in 1989:

> I think in the 90s we're going to see a resurgence of gays in the media, especially as the AIDS cases explode, and we serve as the model for the world on how to deal with this.... So instead of *The Golden Girls* dropping their gay butler, you'll see gay people returning to [visibility on] the tube. And I think that will allow gay erotica to grow on a level of above-ground commercial television and video.

Fritscher also predicted that we would see a wider range of gay characters both on television *and* in films in the 1990s. *Philadelphia, The Bird Cage, Beautiful Thing, The Incredibly True Adventure of Two Girls In Love,* and *In and Out* were each a box office success. Multiple gay characters hit the television scene and gave us *Will and Grace, Roseanne, Queer as Folk,* and HBO's *Six Feet Under*. His instincts for media analysis were right on. Gay culture has started to swim more toward the mainstream although only *Queer as Folk* and *Six Feet Under* avoid desaturation of gays and dare feature homosexual characters who actually have sex. *Queer as Folk* works the diversity of gay characters, while on *Six Feet Under* the characters lean more distinctly to homomasculinity.

Fritscher was likewise correct about the incredible mobilization of the gay community in the 1990s to battle AIDS. Grossly and inhumanely over-inflated medication costs, and our abilities to adjust our sexual behaviors have been, for the most part, successful. Unfortunately, according to most recent reports, gay men are backsliding again in regard to safer sex practices but that is another dangerously spicy enchilada entirely. Fritscher was quoted in the magazine, *Continuum* (November 1996), by the Canadian author, Ian Young, who wrote an article titled "The AIDS Cult and Its Seroconverts." Fritscher said: "Purposely, some twenty-something boys, who have never known a sex life without AIDS, fatalistically expose themselves to HIV as a test of ritual manhood." That's not what Fritscher means about homomasculinity.

Also, gay erotica has grown in slow fits and starts over the past 34 years since Stonewall in 1969. In the early 1980s, a long fifteen years after Stonewall, Gay Sunshine Press became the first real book publisher of gay literature. In the 1970s, gay publishing was not books, but was magazines—the kind where Fritscher drove the content and style. Multiple gay book publishers, magazines, and journals have since risen closer to the surface of the straight mainstream's bookstores and consciousness. Telling people you write erotica these days is not met with the sneers and patronizing derision of years past.

Gay porn, which took off in the 70s, also took off like a rocket in the 1990s. In a time when gay people were streaming out of their closets and fears of HIV were keeping more people at home with their VCRs, baby oil, and remote control, both professional and amateur gay sex videos flourished. Fritscher waxes whimsical: "So many more people watch videos than read books that I have joked with some guys who buy my books: 'Don't try to stick this in your VCR.'"

Fritscher who shot the original video, *Gut Punchers*, rarely pulls punches. He told John F. Karr during an interview that AIDS has changed and challenged gay men's sexuality, resulting in an increase in nontraditional sex practices and its uses for increased sexual creativity. He notes that gay porn videos are increasingly made by individual artists who are directors casting real guys who may not be porn stars but are certainly no amateurs when it comes to having sex the way actual gay men do. These indie video companies, he says, excel over the larger West Hollywood companies that grind out videos that do not reflect the viewer the way that independent video does with indie artists like Old Reliable who was early on another Fritscher discovery in the pages of *Drummer*. When asked, Fritscher answers:

> Where's video going? It's going to be more fetish oriented, because sex is not only your dick and your butt. The point is to let them have a good time, and also diverge from just thinking about sucking dick and fucking ass. And censorship? That influence of the Meese Commission still rolls along under the principle that if somebody abuses something, you have to take it away. But the abuse of a thing doesn't take away the use of the thing. You can take that principle and put that on every adult video.

Prohibition doesn't work. So we're going to see more gay films from independent artists.

Fritscher has predicted some sweeping changes in the face of the continuing AIDS crisis and its effect upon gay pornography. He grasps the extremely important psychology of the porn consumer and the need for producers of porn to adjust to the changes in demand. One of the most vibrant characters in *Some Dance to Remember* is the video-porn mogul Solly Blue who reveals what real gay sex on tape was like in the 70s. Fritscher—always the analyst connecting the dots—points out that in 1982, the VCR and HIV hit at the same time. Rather than cruising the bars, many gay men began staying home watching gay videos. He writes:

> And [a higher production of gay porn] will change the sexuality of gay men. I think art should primarily entertain; but if it's art, it will change you. Gayness gets you into places you wouldn't get into as just a [straight] person. And a lot of gay boys miss that point if they think the bar style is the only way to be. That sounds like I'm crusading, and I'm not at all. I'm just offering an alternative [to bars].

Kicking shit in the 21st century, these days Fritscher voices his concerns about the genre of gay literature. As a trained cultural analyst, he is critical of the "gay writing genre" and all of its traps. He seems to be always pushing for something better from gay artists and writers. Fritscher comments in 2001's *The Burning Pen: Sex Writers On Sex Writing* (edited by M. Christian): "Look at the lesbigay magazines. Most of the illustrations look like the drawings of mental patients. Most of the models, pro or amateur, have dead faces. Much lesbigay writing reads the same: mental and dead. Humorless. Lesbigay narrative is largely unimaginative." He told me, "Gay writing has to be more than the 'coming-out novel' and the 'AIDS novel.' Lesbigay writing should begin to cover lesbigay people in terms of the great themes of the whole range of the human condition, because—ta-DA—we are human first and lesbigay second."

Chatting it up with Jack Fritscher on a Sunday afternoon was an enchanting experience that was, at times, both unsettling and delightful. I have been warned over and over again to write in the third person, to stick to relevant information only, and not to bring too much of my own personality, biases, and opinions to my writing. Apparently, this is especially true in regard to interviewing.

Introduction: Vanguard

Of course, this is what many academics might tell you. In my case, that academic is my partner, Robert. He loves to point out any *faux pas* in my writing because he cannot help it—he is an academic. I usually just tell him to piss off.

The first Fritscher characteristic to strike me was his voice. With brilliance often comes an ostentatious air, those sometimes overly professional (read: defensive), articulate (read: I rule the planet), and aggressive (read: poor social skills) traits that make for a challenging interview. Anticipating the possibility of this combination makes my emergency Ativan supply beckon to me from the medicine cabinet. Take me, it says, and relax into the moment. It turned out that I needed no pharmaceutical kick whatsoever because Fritscher, who seems assertive but neither ostentatious or defensive, nearly charmed the pants (literally) off me.

This interview came at an unplanned moment when Fritscher and I connected between a ridiculous array of problems and obligations. Both of our mothers were ailing; our domestic partners needed special attention (Fritscher's is recovering from knee replacement surgery); and I quite frankly grew afraid that Fritscher might change his mind before I dipped into the resources of his worldly mind with my ladle. Yes, Robert, my love, you are right. That is a pretty hideous analogy but it stays.

To begin on a more carnal note (and why not, really?), Fritscher is a deadly combination of three alternate elements, opposing the three I had initially feared, all seemingly orchestrated by the Goddess to completely unnerve me. First, his physical appearance is strong in a sexual-authority-figure kind of way. (He finished at #11 on the San Francisco Sheriff's Exam in 1976.) And second, he has a voice that would be a perfect match for an old boyfriend of mine from Philly, still affectionately referred to as "Philadelphia Joe." It is almost like a deep purr, a melodic confidence rarely found except perhaps when you hit the jackpot calling a 900 line (not that I have done such as thing because, man, those expensive minutes add up so goddamn quickly). Fritscher knows pillow talk.

Last, I have never been a huge Marilyn Monroe fan, but I do share at least one trait with her. We are two Geminis wowed by the raw sexual power of intelligence. Marilyn went after writer Arthur Miller whose most famous play was about witchcraft. Hmmm. And Mapplethorpe liked Fritscher because, Mapplethorpe said, "We have intelligent sex." Hmmm, again. This may not be the most professional statement I will ever make, but I am willing to admit that Fritscher warmed my cockles a degree or two.

[The entire interview can be read at www.JackFritscher.com]

Alexander Renault is the pen name of the young writer Nicholas Hornack who was killed in a car crash in February 2006. As a journalist, he wrote many reviews and interviews for his online magazine, *Pornographic Pulsar,* featuring writers such as Patricia Nell Warren who co-opted the words, *front runner;* Jack Fritscher who coined the word, *homomasculinity*; and Mark Simpson, "the Skinhead Oscar Wilde" who coined the word, *metrosexual.* He conceptualized and edited the anthology, *Walking Higher: Gay Men Write about the Deaths of Their Mothers* (2004), and wrote the books, *Soul Kiss: The Confessions of a Homoerotic Vampire* (2004), *Queerer Than You Think: Post-Millennial Bodies, Sex, and Porn* (2004), and *Forbidden Tricks* (2005). He was a columnist for *Fusion* magazine in Savannah, and for Marilyn Jaye Lewis's Erotic Authors Association, and for the Velvet Mafia and beefyboyz.com. At the time of his death, according to his personal correspondence with Jack Fritscher, he was beginning a Master's Degree in Creative Nonfiction Writing overseen by Norman Mailer at Wilkes University in Pennsylvania where he intended to write his travelogue memoir, *A Damn Yankee in Savannah.* His "Vanguard: An Interview with Jack Fritscher" was published in *Pornographic Pulsar* (April 2003) and in Stevie "Chazda" Burns' *Voracity Beat* webzine in Germany. As planned by Nicholas Hornack, the introduction to that interview—albeit unable to be updated—is re-printed in *Gay San Francisco* as he originally wrote it.

Who Lit up the "Lit" of the Golden Age of *Drummer*?
by Larry Townsend

When *Drummer* was founded in 1975, publisher John Embry was nearing fifty; editor in chief Jeanne Barney was thirtysomething; Jack Fritscher was thirty-six; and I was forty-five. My personal eyewitness of *Drummer*'s invention began when I met John Embry in 1972 when I was president of Homophile Effort for Legal Protection (H.E.L.P.), Inc. in Los Angeles. John had just returned from Hawaii where he had lived for several years selling advertising. He immediately became so interested in H.E.L.P. that I gladly handed over to him the production of our newsletter. A couple years later when he succeeded me as president of the organization, he tried to change our *H.E.L.P. Newsletter* into a less political and more leather-social newspaper that he called *H.E.L.P. Drummer*.

Its tabloid format looked like Dick Saunders' 1960s *Frontier Bulletin Gazette*, like Dick Michaels' 1970s *The Advocate*, and like the *Bay Area Reporter* in San Francisco. John's hybrid ran for several issues, but it never really worked because John wanted a real leather magazine, and this was not always politically compatible with our group's organizational purposes. At that time, when gay liberation was still fighting in the trenches against forces like the LAPD, H.E.L.P. was basically involved in protecting gay men from entrapment, and with paying bail after arrests. H.E.L.P. had the largest membership of any secular gay group in Los Angeles. Only Ray Broshears' Metropolitan Community Church had more members.

John stepped down from the H.E.L.P. leadership and from editing *H.E.L.P.Drummer* so he could start up the slick magazine format dedicated to the kind of leather content that up to then had only been done in onesies and twosies—and never monthly—by publishers like Bob Mizer with *Physique Pictorial* at AMG in LA, and Chuck Renslow with *Raw* at Kris Studio in Chicago. (In 1972, there was also a one-time leather photography magazine produced out of San Francisco called *Whipcrack* that Jack Fritscher had produced.) John asked several people including myself, Jeanne Barney, Fred Halsted, and Robert Opel to come in with him. (Jeanne wrote for the original *The Advocate* penning her column "Smoke from Jeanne's Lamp.") I declined because I am mainly known as a novelist and I did not want to involve myself with a monthly publication stressed by a due date every thirty days. I had experienced that kind of pressure, on a much smaller scale, with the *H.E.L.P. Newsletter*.

So John embarked on his new venture with (to me) an unlikely assortment of people. ('Nuff said on that score.) Still, despite any number of problems, he got the magazine off the ground and seemed to be doing well with its mail-order and subscriptions until, when *Drummer* was not quite a year old, he decided to host a charity "Slave Auction" in April 1976. This was almost the end of *Drummer,* because the LAPD raided the event, "freed the slaves," and afterward hassled John and the tiny *Drummer* staff so badly that by February 1977 John fled to San Francisco where he hired Jack Fritscher as editor in chief.

I could write a novel on this publishing and arrest drama, but during those five years from 1975 to 1980, John and I were on bad terms and I was not privy to every detail due to the love-hate relationship that has always dogged John's and my friendship. My estrangement from John kept me aloof from *Drummer*, which, thankfully kept me from attending his "Slave Auction" where I would have been arrested along with John himself, his lover Mario Simon, Fred Halsted, Val Martin, and forty others. The only top *Drummer* personality not arrested was Bob Opel who so much loved being arrested that on other occasions he mooned LAPD Chief Ed Davis and streaked Elizabeth Taylor at the Academy Awards. My longtime friend Jeanne Barney was the only woman present at the great arrest. As the cops were hauling her off to jail one of them asked if she was a real woman, to which she made her classic response: "Of course I'm a real woman; if I were a drag, I'd have bigger tits."

During the several months after the "Slave Auction," the LAPD harassed the *Drummer* staff—tailing them on foot and in cars, tapping their phones, and raiding the tiny *Drummer* office allegedly (according to the search warrant) to find and confiscate copies of the straight porn film, *Behind the Green Door*. They never found anything, but they managed to totally disrupt the magazine's production to say nothing of terrorizing the few employees who were brave enough to stick it out. Attorney Al Gordon, a mutual friend of John's and mine was defending them against all of this, but he told me how frustrating it was to have the LAPD and the district attorney's office constantly seeking some new way to inconvenience John and his mail-order business. That was of concern to me because of my own mail-order business selling my books. At the urging of several of his friends, John decided to relocate outside the repressive jurisdiction of the Los Angeles authorities who constantly raided leather bars and outlawed theater screenings of gay films by *Drummer* contributors Fred Halsted (*LA Plays Itself, Sextool*) and Terry LeGrand and Roger Earl (*Born to Raise Hell*).

Introduction: Who Lit up the Golden Age of *Drummer*?

I remember it was over a period of months, maybe February to May 1977, that John—minus his LA staff—fled with van load after van load to the freedom of the City by the Bay. He took his personality with him, and, as some have alleged, his LA "style"—maybe fueled with anger over being arrested and "exiled"—made his acceptance in laid-back San Francisco problematic. He needed a local envoy and editor who could recruit for him a new talent pool for *Drummer*. When John hired Al Shapiro as art director, Al suggested John interview his friend Jack Fritscher who had twenty years of magazine experience. The three of them transformed LA *Drummer* into San Francisco *Drummer* which by some alchemy made the magazine international.

Then bad luck hit. Within eighteen months, John was struck with colon cancer that took him out for months and, for a second time, almost killed *Drummer*. Was there a psychosomatic cause from the stress of the arrests, the harassment, the move, the sheer pressure of monthly publishing? It was here that Jack Fritscher rode to the rescue—the proverbial hero in the white hat (and black leather chaps). As editor in chief, his uncompromising drive to produce a magazine by, for, and about masculine leathermen built perfectly on, and enlarged, John Embry's original conception. (Only two people were titled "editor in chief" of *Drummer*: Jeanne Barney and Jack Fritscher. All the rest were titled "editor" only.) In March 1977, Fritscher began working behind the scenes as a producer drumming up talent and topics for *Drummer* beginning in issues 14 or 15 and ghost-editing *Drummer* 18 before coming out as editor in chief, I remember, with the Christmas issue, *Drummer* 19.

As a writer and observer, I agree that the period 1977 to 1980 when Jack Fritscher was editor was the "Golden Age" of *Drummer*. My opinion might seem gratuitous or coincidental until a person studies the 1970s issues, like *Drummer* 21, in which Jack wrote so many articles and shot so many cover photographs, centerfolds, and interior photo spreads. In addition, he turned his circle of friends, like Robert Mapplethorpe and Old Reliable and a renewed Robert Opel, into the *Drummer* talent pool Embry had hired Jack to recruit. Jack was not a fan of the "camp" in LA *Drummer*, particularly John's cartoon balloons pasted on sex pictures. Jack, like the *Drummer* readership who complained in Letters to the Editor, declared the gender-fuck cover of the "Cycle Sluts" on *Drummer* 9 as the worst *Drummer* cover ever. Dumping camp, and widening the demographic of leather, Jack introduced "theme" issues like bondage, prisons, rough trade, and fetishes like cigars. "If, for instance," Jack once told a leather audience at a reading, "the 1964 Beatles and the 1967 Beatles were analogous to *Drummer* magazine, LA *Drummer* would have been the teen-hit singles on the album, *Meet the Beatles,* and San Francisco

Drummer would have been the high-concept album, *Sgt. Pepper.*" When Embry was ill and absent, Fritscher not only shouldered the load, he and, I think, Al Shapiro, pushed out even further the envelope of *Drummer*.

Drummer moved from its first LA popularity into being sold all across the country by subscription and in some leather stores. I remember in 1979 when I was doing a reading and signing my novels at A Different Light in Silver Lake, the store manager Richard Labonté told me he had tripled his *Drummer* order during Fritscher's tenure as editor. Despite this amazing success, few readers knew the problems inside *Drummer* ranging from John's extended illness to money problems with distributors and censorship caused by do-gooders like Anita Bryant and John Briggs that curtailed sales in retail outlets. I can't speak for all the *Drummer* contributors I knew in LA, but Jeanne and Fred Halsted and, I think, Ed Franklin, had quit John Embry because of creative differences and business ethics differences. Halsted started his own magazine called *Package*.

In 1978, I drove to San Francisco and met Jack for the first time face to face. We had talked on the phone and I certainly knew his writing. He took me to his favorite Italian restaurant called the Haystack on 24th Street near Castro Street where we compared notes and he asked me to consider writing for *Drummer* even though he warned me of what I knew: that John Embry was very lax in paying the talent. Because of the old tension between John Embry and me, I held off until the 1980s when I first began contributing to *Drummer* in trade for advertising rather than money.

Unlike Jack and John, I was never "a *Drummer* writer." I am a novelist whose novels were often excerpted in *Drummer* and a columnist published for a dozen years in *Drummer* before I sold my "Leather Notebook" column to *Honcho*. I was outside the inner orbit even after John and I buried the hatchet after his illness in 1980. I never pushed *Drummer* the way Jack pushed it and formulated concepts for entire issues. His writing, as well as the direction he gave other contributors, pushed *Drummer* through its initial leather-only phase into an era of many fetishes and into masculinity.

Readers (including myself) found his changes so gradual, and so natural it was hard to imagine his upgrades were not all part of John's original grand scheme. In other words, I feel that Jack's work in keeping *Drummer* alive and interjecting his own ideas into it advanced John's initial conceptions beyond its original scope.

What Jack accomplished was, in effect, the expansion of the vision John had tried to achieve—and which circumstances had prevented John from doing. Under Jack Fritscher's guidance, *Drummer* became one of the important icons of San Francisco's Golden 70s. When Jack and John parted company over financial matters, John never once regretted the changes Jack wrought or the writings he wrote. In fact, after Jack left *Drummer*, John frequently reprised many of Jack's themes and fetishes in *Drummer* and in his post-*Drummer* magazines like *MR* where he asked Jack for reprint permission.

Timeline detectives may note that while John owned *Drummer* for eleven years, Jack Fritscher wrote and photographed for *Drummer* for seventeen years through three owners. Jack's last issue for John Embry was 32 or 33, and he returned after John sold *Drummer* with issue 98, and continued contributing to the end, appearing in something like nearly seventy issues.

Fritscher, like me, also really cannot be defined or limited as "a *Drummer* writer." While I think that as interesting and occasionally as brilliant as Jack's writings were within the covers of *Drummer*, he has produced a far more significant body of writing and photography on his own in gay and straight publishing. He is a writer who is a stylist, and his style defines him. He brushed his signature style onto the blank pages of *Drummer* and into his *Drummer* novel *Some Dance to Remember*. It's there the way it is in his first S&M novel written in 1969, *I Am Curious (Leather)*. He tried to make *Drummer* literary and sexy, and he worked under pressure of deadlines which is the thing I told John Embry at the start of *Drummer* I would not do.

Over the years, many *Drummer* editors would call Jack and say there was a hole in the next issue and could he write them a cover feature article in four days. His style is grace under pressure. In his books like the wild and dirty biography, *Mapplethorpe: Assault with a Deadly Camera*, I see the fingerprints of his *Drummer* experience because he often composes in single sentence paragraphs to keep the reader's eye going down the column of print. So, in essence, I think we have to recognize that the glory years of golden sexuality, especially in San Francisco, coincided with the Golden Age of *Drummer*, and this was largely due to the hard work and extraordinary talents of Jack Fritscher who, crediting all the contributors, told me if it takes a village to raise a child, it took all us village people to fill *Drummer*.

Larry Townsend (born 1930) is the pseudonymous author of dozens of books including *Run Little Leather Boy* (1970) and *The Leatherman's Handbook* (1972) at pioneer erotic presses such as Greenleaf Classics and the Other Traveler imprint of Olympia Press. Growing up as a teenager of Swiss-German extraction in Los Angeles a few houses from Noel Coward and Irene Dunne, he ate cookies with his neighbor Laura Hope Crews who was Aunt Pittypat in *Gone with the Wind*. He attended the prestigious Peddie School, and was stationed as Staff Sergeant in charge of NCOIC Operations of Air Intelligence Squadrons for nearly five years with the US Air Force in Germany (1950-1954). Completing his tour of duty, he entered into the 1950s underground of the LA leather scene where he and Montgomery Clift shared a lover. With his degree in industrial psychology from UCLA (1957), he worked in the private sector and as a probation officer with the Forestry Service. He began his pioneering activism in the politics of gay liberation in the early 1960s. In 1972, as president of the Homophile Effort for Legal Protection which had been founded in 1969 to defend gays during and after arrests, he introduced John Embry to the *H.E.L.P. Newsletter*, the forebear of *Drummer* (1975). Fearing shoddy gay business practices, he cautioned Embry not to allow H.E.L.P. to fall into bankruptcy. As the longtime friend of Jeanne Barney, who was the founding Los Angeles editor in chief of *Drummer*, he is an essential eyewitness of the drama and salon around *Drummer* in which his novels were frequently excerpted. His signature "Leather Notebook" column appeared in *Drummer* for twelve years beginning in 1980.

"Larry Townsend," Fritscher-Hemry House, June 16, 1995. Photograph by Jack Fritscher. ©Jack Fritscher

Foreword
by the Author

SOME DANCE TO REMEMBER.
SOME DON'T.
Toward an Autobiography of *Drummer* Magazine

"Of course I have no right whatsoever to write down the truth about my life, involving as it naturally does the lives of so many other people, but I do so urged by a necessity of truth-telling, because there is no living soul who knows the complete truth; here, may be one who knows a section; and, there, one who knows another section; but to the whole picture not one is initiated."
—Vita Sackville-West, *Portrait of a Marriage*

LET'S START AT THE VERY BEGINNING...

MY ZERO DEGREES OF SEPARATION
(MAP INCLUDED)

Allegedly.

In the vertigo of memory, I write these eyewitness objective notes and subjective opinions *allegedly*, because I can only analyze events, manuscripts, and how we people all *seemed* together, and not the true hearts of persons.

As I said to Proust nibbling on his *madeleine*, "How pungent is the smell of old magazines."

Drummer is the Rosetta Stone of leather heritage.

Drummer published its first issue June 1975.

What happened next depends on whom you ask.

Before history defaults to fable, I choose to write down my oral eyewitness testimony.

Readers might try to understand the huge task of writing history that includes the melodrama of one's own life lived in the first post-Stonewall decade of gay publishing and gay life.

The Titanic 1970s were the Gay Belle Epoque of the newly possible.

"The first rule of Fight Club is not to talk about Fight Club."
—Chuck Palahniuk

"The worst thing homosexuality can do is rob you of your identity by becoming your identity."
—Jack Fritscher

I was a witness to my time.
As a pioneer participant, I was there.
As a collector, I stored the evidence.
As an author, I wrote within that time.
As a trained scholar, I am an analyst of that time.
As a humanist, I never drank the Kool-Aid of the politically correct dogmatists whose views and diktats were always at odds with the lives of most gay people.
As a survivor, I am sharing—which is what survivors do.
As I near seventy years of age, this is one last chance to tell this untold story of the part I played in the euphoria. I must disclose that when I was five years old my kindergarten teacher, Mrs. Deitwig, wrote on my report card during the war in 1944: "Jackie is a very verbal little boy with a tendency to tattle." Is that revelation naked enough?

This is *Rashomon*. This is *The Alexandria Quartet*. And it is autobiography. Is it also an autobiography of *Drummer*?

This is my experience. This lion in winter does not intend to beard any other lions in winter. The closer eyewitness pioneers get to the end the more we remember of the beginning.

I must thank the first publisher of *Drummer,* John Embry, who hired me as editor in chief, because without him I would have been less motivated to give my deposition in this eyewitness testimony were it not for his "visions and revisions and tricky takes and mistakes" about who did what to whom in the streaming history of *Drummer.*

Embry wrote about himself in *Manifest Reader* 33: "Like any survivor, I have gotten to the stage where I can tell you that being one isn't nearly everything it's cracked up to be."

For years, Embry has been writing an autobiographical book titled, *Epilogue*. I hope that this, my version of leather history at *Drummer,* might be interpolated with Embry's in order to keep balance on the tightrope of memory. I recommend his *Epilogue* memoir which has not yet been published except in part in very provocative fragments in *Drummer* 2

(August 1975), and in two of Embry's post-*Drummer* magazines, *Manifest Reader* 26 (1995), and *Super MR* 5 (January 2000).

I am an exorcist properly ordained by the Catholic Church, but I wish to be devil's advocate, not for Embry or myself, or for our shifting points of view, but, if it is possible, for the truth of canonizing gay history.

In fact, on August 11, 2006, I sent Embry an email asking for permission to reprint two excerpts from his *Epilogue* as his own eyewitness testimony in this series of books. On October 17, he telephoned, thanked me for the floral arrangement I had sent him from Ixia, the drop-dead shop in the Castro, and, suddenly, in our conversation which was not about this book, gave oral permission for the reprint requested three months earlier. His representative excerpt from his *Epilogue* is included in the *Gay San Francisco: Eyewitness Drummer* volume titled *The Drummer Salon*.

For objective correlative throughout this memoir, I have tried fairly to include and quote other eyewitnesses, including John Embry who plays the part of the perfect antagonist. I wanted *Drummer* to exude San Francisco underground aura; he wanted it to have LA mass appeal.

What of my analysis is too intuitional or too nuanced to be proven, I offer "allegedly."

Where it may be wrong, I offer apology as well as correction in future editions.

The rest, I swear, is true—even though I am the first to say that new revelations in my own memory and archives constantly pop up to support or dislocate previous testimony which I then change to the accuracy of the evidence.

This is not revisionism; this is first-hand eyewitness memoir.

I can't be neutral, but I can try to be fair.

About *Drummer* history...

> ...I think I'll here...tell it, if I may.
> And, therefore, every gentle soul, I pray
> That for God's love you'll hold not what I say
> Evilly meant, but that I must rehearse,
> All their tales, the better and the worse,
> Or else prove false to some of my design.
> —Geoffrey Chaucer, "The Miller's Tale,"
> *The Canterbury Tales*

A documentary such as this is good history when the origami of memory unfolds to ever-more specific perspectives wherein the events of a timeline are supported by human feeling backed with cold evidence.

Former *Drummer* editor, Joseph Bean, wrote to me on July 15, 2002:

> I think that if your introductory histories in *Eyewitness Drummer* are huge compared to the articles they attach to, that's great. It is the nature of history to be huge by comparison to the once simple event described. Think of the massive volume of historical reflection, analysis, etc. written about any given moment or action in the human past. Moments have consequence. Those moments in *Drummer* and in the Leather Community are of great consequence. It makes complete sense that it takes far more words to describe a river decades later than it took to stand in the flow at the time, and say it's just this cold and only as deep as this.

MEMORY: NOT ALL ALONE IN THE MOONLIGHT

In a *pentimento*, made literary by Lillian Hellman with whom *Drummer* and I share June 20 as a midsummer's eve birthday, a painter at his canvas scrapes his way through layers of color and line and texture to reveal hidden pictures underneath which may or may not be a better truth.

Nearly everything alleged in this *pentimento* of *Drummer*, in fact, in this whole series of books, is based on my archived documents, nearly a thousand hours of my taped interviews of others, and my personal journals, photography, videography, and Super-8 films as eyewitness of late twentieth-century life as we lived it.

My friend Samuel Steward, a model record-keeper, was a great help to Dr. Alfred Kinsey researching the history of sexuality. Steward gave Kinsey grist for the Kinsey Institute studies: his high-school sex stories, 1950s sex photos and 1960s Polaroids, records of all his tricks, erotic journals of tattooing, artwork, and his two early closeted books, the short-fiction collection *Pan and the Firebird* and the novel *Angels on the Bough*. Sam wrote in *Chapters from an Autobiography*, page 98:

> Later...at their request, I sent the Institute *all* of the Phil Andros novels I had produced, together *with a bibliography locating the hundred and fifty stories I had written for European and other magazines, and all the ephemera and reproduced artwork I had done.* [Italics added]

Just so. Some of my work is also archived at the Kinsey Institute where my photography is in the permanent collection. My annotated bibliography collecting my writing and photography spread throughout *Drummer* may serve others building a complete bibliography of everyone's work in *Drummer*. Its intimate recall may be of help in a general timeline of gay history and leather culture. My leather heritage work aims to support my premise that gays are a developing nation: a fourth-world culture of eros whose history, intellect, and roots will not be denied.

Various other scholars and historians have told and retold various stories of leather history in San Francisco. Some of the stories are true. Some are lies. Some are errors. Some are cautionary fables. Some are incorrectly sanctified by repetition. No offense is meant, but who of those people was ever inside the eyewitness loop of leather anchored in the 1970s salon centered around *Drummer* where it was "zero degrees of separation"? Who of them was an eyewitness listed as "Contributor" over a span of nearly twenty-five years?

Nevertheless, the history of leather should be open to all analysts the way the pages of 1970s *Drummer* were open to all. In fact, "the *Drummer* Salon," as Sam Steward dubbed my magazine crowd, was inclusive unlike, for instance, the exclusive Violet Quill book club in Manhattan in the 1980s.

Drummer with all its hundreds of voices (writers, and readers writing personals) and eyes (cameras and graphic artists) was an inclusive, but transient, culture eagerly inviting everyone into the open tent.

That's what made *Drummer* culture unique.

It took a village to fill an issue.

It took the village people to act it out.

Drummer was a center of a whole cultural phenomenon....and its editor Jack Fritscher is a prolific writer who since the late sixties has helped document the gay world and the changes it has undergone.... if queer people do not preserve our own history, most of it will simply disappear.

—Willie Walker, founder, GLBT Historical Society (1985); Board of Directors, San Francisco Lesbian and Gay History Project (1982); quote from "Periodically Obscene," October 2002

The legacy of *Drummer* has many sides and to ignore one or the other because it is untidy is to subtract from the total.

—Robert Davolt, the last editor of *Drummer*, interviewed by Joe Gallagher at leatherweb.com

Having arrived in San Francisco the first time in August 1961, I experienced personally, sexually, and esthetically the growth of Folsom Street culture in many ways: streets, bars, baths, backrooms, clubs, restaurants, galleries, and theaters. On March 13, 1976, my one-act comedy *Coming Attractions* was the first gay play written in San Francisco about contemporary San Francisco and produced in San Francisco. It opened South of Market at the SIR Center Theater (Society for Individual Rights) presented by Michael Lewis and the Yonkers Theater Production Company, famous for its *Hello Dolly* (1975). The double-bill also featured Lanford Wilson's *The Madness of Lady Bright*. The plays were noticed by the San Francisco *Chronicle* and were headlined on the cover of the *Bay Area Reporter* (BAR), Volume 6, Number 5, March 4, 1976.

(*Coming Attractions* was the first appearance of my female character Kweenasheba aka Kweenie who plays a major role as the "Sharon McKnight" cabaret chanteuse "Queen of the Castro" in *Some Dance to Remember*.)

The same spring 1976, the buzz around San Francisco was that a newspaper centered on Folsom Street life was about to begin publication and be distributed free in the South of Market bars and restaurants. It was to be called *The Bridge*, but despite it being a great idea it never took off because, at the same time, San Francisco leather men began to hear of *Drummer* in Los Angeles. By the time *Drummer* began its slow six-month move to San Francisco in February 1977, the idea of *The Bridge* had collapsed.

From my eyewitness recall, the San Francisco leather community early on—even with the vanilla *Bar Area Reporter* and *Vector* magazine starting up—had a need for a dedicated newspaper or magazine when *Drummer* blew into town. Having worked in magazine editing and writing for twenty years at that time, I sensed support was there not only in potential readers but in a talent base eager to be tapped to fill the pages of a leather publication.

LIFE NEED NOT UNRAVEL EVEN AS IT UNFOLDS

Gay history is a medium distorted by decades of irony, gender politics, and disease. The time has come for forward thinking about the leather past in San Francisco which was way more than what most first-wave GLBT historians have so far written, for instance, about what ultimately proved to be the *reductive* archetypes of "the Catacombs" and "the Society of Janus."

For years I was a participant in both clubs. I loved the Catacombs' founder Steve McEachern whom I hired to work for me as my personal transcriber at *Drummer*. I played with Janus' founder Cynthia Slater who had an affair with my straight brother, and for a time almost became my sister-in-law. Cynthia seemed worth introducing to my bicoastal lover Robert Mapplethorpe because she was an instant classic in the new identity category of "leather woman." In the stroboscopic zero degrees of a woman descending a staircase in an incestuous salon, "Fritscher's *Mapplethorpe* shot Janus' *Slater* at *McEachern*'s Catacombs."

In the same zero degrees, California *Drummer* magazine (1975) created itself on the Philadelphia magazine *Drum* (1964-1969); and the San Francisco Society of Janus modeled itself on the Philadelphia Janus Society. That Janus begat *Drum*. When Philadelphia Janus split in a civil war over lesbian and gender issues, Clark Polak took control of Janus and founded the male-oriented *Drum* which premiered the first panels of future *Drummer* art director Allen J. Shapiro's satiric cartoon strip *Harry Chess*. Polak shut down *Drum* when the government accused him of mailing obscene materials. Driven out of business, he may have become embittered because when the gifted young David Hurles (who in 1976 became my longtime friend whose talent I immediately embraced and whose star I would raise in the 1977-1979 *Drummer* salon) pilgrimaged in 1969 to meet Polak, Polak—perhaps overwhelmed by the singular vision of the not-yet-famous "Old Reliable"—savaged Hurles' portfolio. Hurles, sweet-tempered enough to be undeterred, flew off to Washington, D. C., to enter the cosmos of erotic media working with the legendary physique publisher Dr. Herman Lynn Womack who welcomed Hurles as model, apprentice, photographer, and friend working at Guild Press, and testifying in court defending Womack against the government's bourgeois charge that erotic models are by definition exploited adults. Where Polak had been persecuted, Hurles and Womack won the case and pioneered the legal road that allowed *Drummer* to be invented in June 1975. Aspects of the lesbigay civil war over gender and internecine rivalries are dramatized in *Some Dance to Remember*, Reel 2, Scene 15, "Queers against Gays."

Some leather historians might re-calibrate their perspective regarding the Catacombs and the Society of Janus. Leather culture was a social force far bigger than either important but tiny private venue. It is reductive for historians looking the wrong way through time's telescope to try to retrofit either group into more than each was at the time. Most leather people in 1970s San Francisco were never personally invited to, nor had anything to do with, either. The Catacombs was an elite group.

The Society of Janus was a private group. Both had "requirements" and "codes." It was easier to get into the clannish Mineshaft or the privileged Studio 54 than it was to get into the Catacombs. Over the years, no more than a floating total of 200-300 of us played at the Catacombs. The intimate Janus membership grew even smaller with schism over issues ranging from gender to consent. Witness the famous Society of Janus gender drama when my longtime friend, the Catholic leather priest, the Reverend Jim Kane, bolted out the door, never to return. Earlier, I had written about him under a pseudonym I created for him, Frank Cross, in "The Janus Society," *Drummer* 27 (February 1979), pages 14-22.

In the separating leatherstream culture of the late 1970s, the distaff theorists Gayle Rubin (b. 1949) and Pat Califia (b. 1954), reached into *The Story of O* and founded the lesbian-feminist S&M Samois (punning the identity, C'est moi?) collective (1978-1983) as a kind of response to the Catacombs and Janus and to the way each had marginalized itself through inclusions and exclusions around fisting, gender, and power exchanges.

Insofar as religion threads its agenda through homosexuality, it is neat balance to Catholicism and Judaism to mention that Pat Califia arrived on scene simultaneously with the 1970s "Mormon Mafia" imported from Salt Lake to LA by Robert I. McQueen, the Mormon editor of *The Advocate*, because David Goodstein, the Jewish owner of *The Advocate* preferred what he termed "the Mormon work ethic." Goodstein also popularized the phrase "Mormon Mafia." (I mentioned Califia by name and as a Mormon in an homage in *Some Dance to Remember: A Memoir-Novel of San Francisco 1970-1982*, Reel 3, Sequence 3.) Open-hearted diversity allowed the immortal changeling Califia, once a Mormon female, to write an advice column for non-Mormon gay males in *The Advocate*, 1981-1991. In December 1979, *The Advocate* 238 showcased then Pat, now Patrick, Califia authoring "A Secret Side of Lesbian Sexuality" which connected to *Drummer* through Samois, the Janus Society, and the Catacombs.

On my birthday, June 20, 1984, Pat Califia, a decade before transitioning FTM, generously connected the dots from me to *Drummer* in her "Dear Jack" letter in which she, "very excited," thanked me for sending her the complete eight-issue run of my *Man2Man Quarterly* which she had specifically requested, and to which I had added for her historical archives a complete run of my San Francisco tabloid, *The California Action Guide* (1982). Coming from Califia, a salonista around both *The Advocate* and *Drummer*, it was birthday cake indeed to read "You are one of the finest gay porn writers around...you write a 'dirty-talking' story better than anybody else I know." Commenting on my magazines themselves, analyst Califia confided with a personal sentiment I treasure: "In every single publication you've produced...something...hits me right between the eyes." (Fellow-academic Patrick Califia and I also share the fact that we both have BDSM books that have been seized by Canadian customs in a dragnet chronicled in *The New Yorker*, October 3, 1994.) With the 1984 startup of her *The Power Exchange, A Newsleather for Women*, Pat, perhaps feeling isolated in Richmond Hill, New York, generously signed off her long June 20 letter with: "...if it wasn't for your work, I'd feel impoverished. There were a lot of times when...a Jack Fritscher story renewed my optimism....I'd like to put you on the comp list for the *Newsleather*."

Of course, her words pleased me as much as did her return to live and work in San Francisco, appearing in a back-to-back reading with me at Karen Mendelsohn's September 1989 QSM Conference; speaking during Leather Week 1993 with Robin Sweeney, April Miller, Nicola Ginzler, and Lydia Steptoe at venues as outre as the men's sex club, Eros; and entertaining at the Women's Building Benefit for the Spanner Defense Fund, with music by Gayle Rubin.

Supporting inclusive camaraderie, on December 26, 2001, I mailed Patrick Califia a copy of one of my new Palm Drive Video leather documentaries about the Folsom Street Fair; and, because we have been so frequently connected through the years, I invited him to write an historical essay for *Gay San Francisco: Eyewitness Drummer*. Early on, Califia had exhibited the drive and talent that would make her the San Francisco editor of *The Advocate*; so in the byzantine drama when I was exiting *Drummer* in late 1979, I proposed to *Drummer* art director Al Shapiro (who was negotiating between publisher Embry and me) that Califia follow me as editor of *Drummer*, because I thought she authored a good calling card in her article, "A Secret Side of Lesbian Sexuality" in *The Advocate* #238, December 1979 (!). However, I had no power, and gender separatism on every side scotched the concept which was further trampled by the Machiavellian John Rowberry who would have knifed Eve Harrington to get himself temporarily hired as "assignment editor" of *Drummer* 31 to *Drummer* 39 for the year 1980 during which no actual "editor in chief" was hired to replace me.

So, torching myths, and inviting Califia into the *Gay San Francisco* tent in 2001, I had my reasons precisely connected to the history of my editorial direction of *Drummer*. We've had our, our...six degrees of relationship? exchanging Solstice and Beltane greeting cards...how many decades now? She with her Mormon SLC BDSM FTM, and I with my Catholic stories of homomasculine Platonism, muscle worship, and shapeshifting Irish she/he's.

One might say: Fritscher and Califia both began in sex and set about intellectually changing S&M.

In one of Patrick Califia's books, I don't recall which one, he dubbed me a "prophet of homomasculinity" which is the clarion keyword defining that men can self-fashion their own identity as legitimately as can women. (I may be a bit apostolic, but a prophet?)

On April 18, 1991, Pat Califia sent me the final draft of her essay for the Mark Thompson *Leatherfolk* anthology which also included my *Drummer* article on Folsom Street's "Artist Chuck Arnett." Her piece was titled "Mr. Benson Doesn't Live Here Anymore," and she thought I might like to see the pre-pub copy because, she wrote, I "was one of the few people who will know what I'm talking about." (I had done the final "polish edit," and had serialized, *Mr. Benson* in *Drummer*.)

In an earlier *Drummer* connection, on May 16, 1979, Pat Califia had written personally to me, at my home address, as editor in chief of *Drummer* regarding "the dimensions of gay male fantasies about women [in *Drummer*]" in her proposed story about "a female top fist-fucking a male bottom" with what I dubbed the "O. Henry twist" in that at the end the bottom discovers the top's gender. She also thanked me for addressing her concerns over my inclusive "Society of Janus" feature in *Drummer* 27 (February 1979), and she included some of her S&M poetry and her lesbian-masochist story, "Jessie," for my consideration.

At the same moment vis a vis women and *Drummer*, I was conferring with Society of Janus founder Cynthia Slater, who was dating my straight brother, about her straight-female BDSM story, "Discovery," which she dedicated to our mutual pals, the Catholic leather priest, Jim Kane, and his lover, the former pro-football player, Ike Barnes, and to John Pfleiderer, the S&M male escort, who was her straight top.

Unfortunately, in the autumn of 1979 during San Francisco's nervous breakdown over anti-gay assassination at City Hall, gay riot in the streets, and gay murder South of Market, *Drummer* itself was in chaos; the publisher had been ill and AWOL with cancer; I was not being paid; and I began withdrawing my authorial input prior to my editorial exit on December 31, 1979.

The upshot was that, having been the first author and editor to mention women inside *Drummer*, I was unable to continue my experimental evolution toward a gender-blind magazine because in the office chaos I could not fight the publisher who, perhaps because he had hired a woman to be the first LA editor of *Drummer*, seemed, well, perhaps reactionary in his keeping *Drummer* for men only. (He denounced that first strong female editor in *Drummer* 30, June 1979, page 38.) That, I think was one of his (not *Drummer*'s) missteps, because, as the names of women here entwined exhibits, there existed, at least before the tsunami of feminist-driven separatism, a huge talent pool and demographic that *Drummer* might have tapped.

When the lesbigay civil war over gender broke out during the Titanic 1970s, *Drummer* was affected as much as the rest of the GLBT community. Because females turned from males, *Drummer*, abandoned by feminist identity politics for what it was not, turned to homomasculine identity "esthetics and erotics" to define what it was, and to answer to the demand of the demographic of masculine-identified men who had no magazine and no media representation.

It "was a whiter shade of" beyond the "pale."

Califia in her person fashioning himself, and I as an author-editor driving *Drummer,* both chose to virilize ourselves.

And "the crowd called out for more."

We all live in a world so foreign no straight tourists bother. That's why our kind will always be forever marginal with never a presidential candidate of our own.

In *Drummer* 31 (September 1979), I published a letter to the editor sent by Samois (presumably Rubin and Califia) in response to my Society of Janus feature in *Drummer* 27 (February 1979). I titled the letter "Things That Go Bump in the Night." Samois based in Berkeley seemed intent on keeping its membership separate from Janus based in San Francisco:

> "[The Society of Janus]...was an informative and well-written article....however...Samois...is an independent organization, which does not have, and never has had any official connection with the Society of Janus. There is some overlap of membership and this may have been partly responsible for the error. Several of Samois' founding members were and still are members of Janus. Apparently, even within Janus there is some confusion about this matter...."

Along with this letter, Samois sent its "Handkerchief Color Code for Lesbians." In a bid to acknowledge in 1979 the emerging presence of leather women who did not really break the Leather Ceiling until the 1980s, I printed the Lesbian Hanky Code with Samois' letter on page 79 of *Drummer* 31. My pro-active "Janus Society" feature and the publication of this Samois letter were the first gestures toward women made in the pages of *Drummer*.

After my exit as editor in chief on December 31, 1979, my initial gender-tuned steps in *Drummer* evaporated because of a rising civil war of gender separatism, and because women, in founding their own feminist magazines, made *Drummer* ever more masculinist—although *Drummer* was never ever separatist.

In fact, between 1987-1990, nearly every issue of *Drummer* addressed the "civil wars" in the leather community which I had dramatized in *Some Dance to Remember*. (I've always been more "Cowboy Up!" than "Kumbaya.") Sadly, AIDS-era publisher DeBlase tried to please everyone and broker some civility and make a buck. His misguided "kumbaya pages" ate up precious column inches that should have been filled with *Drummer*'s famous erotic writing. The gender war, not the earthquake, was the main reason DeBlase's *Drummer* tanked, sales fell, and he had to sell.

In *Drummer* 100 (August 1987), eyewitness Judy Tallwing McCarthy, International Ms. Leather 1987, lamented the "uncivil war" in her guest editorial calling astutely for unity rather than separatism. In *Drummer* 107 (August 1987), page 7, eyewitness Dane Leathers aka Mike Leathers, who was on the *Drummer* staff for a dozen years, wrote: "Educational organizations such as GMSMA [Gay Men's SM Activists] and [the] Janus Society...tend to attract groupies and petty power-junkies more than stable teachers."

In *Drummer* 133 (September 1989), page 32, Sal Vittore wrote an editorial calling for unity in the leather community: "What's going on here? Is it now to be you're gay, but you're not gay enough?"

That interested me because that is the charge most often leveled against me by vanilla queens—that I am not "gay enough." Leather columnist Mr. Marcus and others in the gay press have written about that as irony. In the same *Drummer* 133, page 33, Paul Martin published a flyer purportedly distributed at the Michigan Womyn's Music Festival by a group called "Seps [Separatists] Against Sadomasochism." Martin responded: "I won't go into the issue of Lesbian Separatism here. Suffice it to say that stupidity knows no gender."

In *Drummer* 134 (October 1989), managing editor Joseph W. Bean wrote a two-page editorial, pages 4-5, refuting the anti-leather book *After the Ball: How America Will Conquer Its Fear and Hatred of Gays in the 90s*. Written by two allegedly homophobic gay men, Marshall Kirk and Hunter Madsen, *After the Ball* was a mainstream queer book that proposed that the leather community should disappear. So virulent was the Kirk-Hunter attack that Bean editorialized a "Know Your Enemy" campaign against the book a year later in *Drummer* 144 (November 1990).

Drummer 138 (March 1990) was a satirical issue. The reader had to flip it upside down and backwards, literally, to open the "front cover" of the post-earthquake Naugahyde magazine *Dummer*. My initial proposal had been to title it *Dumber* as a parody of the movie *Dumb and Dumber*. The editorial by "Pipistrelle" aka "Fledermaus" aka DeBlase satirized the dichotomies of the gender civil war as a kind of theater of the absurd:

> San Francisco says one thing and Los Angeles disagrees...Establishment gay men say that it does not properly conform to tradition and leather women refuse to participate until there is a full and complete financial accounting....
>
> In the rainbow arena, deep breathing is required.
>
> In all diversity, there is a principle at work over which the "thought police" have no moral right to the politically correct control they wish to enforce in life or encode in revisionist history.

Every human being has analytical thoughts and personal feelings, for example, about race, but those thoughts and feelings are *racial* not *racist*. Race feelings don't become *racist* until a person's actions discriminate against another person.

The same is true of thoughts and feelings *versus* actions around gender. In addition to the Seven Deadly Sins, one might add the sins of racism and sexism.

It is through such territory that self-fashioning gay identity struggles to achieve a delicate balance. It is necessary to know this to address *Drummer*. Trying to dramatize this moral difficulty in gay culture, I purposely wrote *Some Dance to Remember*. Amidst its comedy and satire, the book was also a "tell-all expose" of the "politically correct civil war" over "heterophobia," "gay sexism," and "gay fascism" that drove some gender bigots crazy.

For instance, instead of hating gay males, some myopic genderistas might acknowledge that the 1970s decade of gay liberation, at least in San Francisco, was kick-started by young gay male pioneers who, as the first wave of sex immigrants emerging from the Stonewall closet, created the Titanic 70s out of whole cloth. *Drummer* itself was a document of immigrant self-assertion. Gay liberation of the 1970s wasn't dominated by gay white males; it was simply populated with GWMs who dared come out first.

In the early to mid-1970s, gay males struggled—and had to struggle—with growing their own identity and unity first before activating that identity and unity to support other diversities. By 1979, an army of gay males, who were hardly sexist or racist, opened up the Gay Parade to a new theme of "Diversity," as advertised in my edit of a press release I prepared for *Drummer* 30 (June 1979), page 86.

The 1979 Gay Freedom Day Parade & Celebration
Sunday, June 24, 1979

Diversity...

...the right to be different...to live your own way...to follow a "different drummer..." These rights are what the annual Gay Freedom Day Parade and Celebration are all about.

When we march in support of others' right to adopt different modes of speech, dress, sexuality, and self-expression, we are supporting our own right to be different.

When we celebrate the home we have found in this city, we also celebrate the tremendous value we derive in our lives from the diversity that IS San Francisco.

This year marks the 10th anniversary of the Stonewall Rebellion, the beginning of the end of second-class citizenship for gay men and women everywhere.

We will march to support gay men and women here, and throughout the world, who look to this event, more than any other, as evidence that our numbers are plentiful and that our movement is strong.

We will march to remind politicians, in this election year, that votes are not to be won at our expense, and that harassment of any part of our community will be met with the resistance of our entire community.

We will all be there, celebrating the joy and full self-expression we experience in our sexuality...celebrating our cultural contributions...celebrating with music, color, sun, and dancing in the streets.

Join us.

Even more then than now, the rate of uncloseting oneself and freeing oneself varied vastly according to culture and gender: whites tended to come out before Blacks and Hispanics, males tended to come out before females. There was no All-American Boy clothing store on Castro Street before gay males arrived. Presence creates culture signified by commerce. Genderistas might note that gay men could not back then support women who were not present. It is not ingenuous to posit that in the 1970s, *Drummer* did not publish female creatives, even when Jeanne Barney was editor in chief, because, as far as she remembers and I know, no women submitted material. Before the arrival of Cynthia Slater, Pat Califia, Camille O'Grady, and Gayle Rubin, gay men's acquaintance with "women in leather" began with Ann-Margret in *Kitten with a Whip* (1964) and ended with *Ilsa: She-Wolf of the SS* (1975).

My first mention of women in *Drummer* was at the time *avant garde* in my feature "Leather Christmas" which I wrote for the first issue I edited under my byline, *Drummer* 19 (December 1977). (I produced words and images for *Drummer* issues 14 to 18 and for the special issue, *Son of Drummer*, and ghost-edited *Drummer* 18, *Drummer* 31, 32, and 33.)

Even though proprietor McEachern sometimes rented to female groups on separate nights, the Catacombs was a gentlemen's club that "invited a few women"—specifically, Cynthia Slater. Janus was an educational support group whose bisexual females "invited some sympathetic gay, straight, and bisexual men" who, of course, all turned out to be gay and competing to pick up the straight men the women supposedly attracted.

Those self-defined profiles made the Catacombs and Janus historical, but not representative of mainstream leather history which in the pioneer 1970s was only beginning its wide-stream identity evolution:

1) toward its first immediate self-fashioning masculine identity;

2) toward the new wave of pop-culture S&M in advertising, fashion, and the arts; and

3) toward the next wave of gender immigration of the 1980s when men died and women migrated in to nurse and nurture queer culture.

AIDS enabled omni-gendered opportunists to inject their own virus. HIV was the Trojan Horse that prepared the way for the galloping Marxist *coup* whose political correctness started the gay civil war that turned the joyous "gay liberation" of the 1970s into the divisive "gay politics" of the 1980s. This coup was driven by gay-left-wing fundamentalists kneeling on their politically correct prayer rugs arrogantly demanding compulsory egalitarianism. It was sanctified by Foucault who, because he was not conventionally good-looking, confused sex with power.

I saw the best minds of my generation destroyed by political correctness.

Arts analyst Jane Kramer in *The New Yorker* named these troublemakers "the storm troopers of political correctness." (October 8, 2007, page 49)

One day the "divisive far-out-wing GLBT conspiracy" may renounce its hateful heresy of declaring male-identified homosexuality anathema. In one generation, those gays disrespecting homomasculinity have become so Marxist and Fascist that if they could travel back to the future of their more liberated youth, they would denounce themselves for what they have become: saboteurs of an integrated and inclusive gay gestalt.

Drummer and its inclusive salon was *the* hub interpreting leather popular culture. *Drummer*, according to the San Francisco GLBT Historical Society was — in the most important assessment in this book — "the center of a whole cultural phenomenon."

Drummer was epicentric to leather culture for what happened then and for what happened later.

Leather, like homosexuality itself, is a hologram. I might say, "You see it; but when you reach out to touch it, your hand closes empty around the projection of what your eye tells you is there."

Our leather history has no more memory than the remembrance we give it.

And all our leather memoirs are epic.

Question Marx?
Socrates: It Takes a Village to Raise a Question?

Is there in the younger politically correct crowd a kind of gay-moral disapproval, a kind of Puritan uptightness, and a jealous ageism as if they are angry that their forebears stole a march on them? Is theirs a petulance about a party missed that rebels against the generation of us who in the first decade after Stonewall invented gay life while celebrating our psychological liberation like the fauns, satyrs, angels, imps, and gods that the sex, music, and drugs revealed we were in our new world of faerie?

DEATH AT THE FIRST CASTRO STREET FAIR,
AUGUST 18, 1974

The gay world lies somewhere between the Wild West and Chaos.

For instance, in 1970 in San Francisco, long before there was a *Drummer*, my lover David Sparrow and I posed as two leather players in a couple hundred black-and-white photos for the first leather magazine published in San Francisco, *Whipcrack*. Intending it as a one-issue one-off, we helped create that slick, large-format magazine with photographer Walt Jebe, David's employer, who owned Jebe's Camera, 4117 20th Street. Jebe's Camera, founded in the 1960s, was the first camera shop to hire gay clerks and develop gay sex photos in the Castro. The straight Jebe had been in business ten years before *arriviste* Harvey Milk immigrated and opened his own Castro Camera shop a couple doors away, around the corner on the main drag at 575 Castro Street.

If eyewitness truth be sorted, the hyper-zealous Milk was considered rather a jokey camp on cool Castro Street where he was liked okay as a sexual immigrant, but not well liked as a political carpetbagger, because he was Manhattanizing laid-back San Francisco. He wasn't particularly cool. He was a New Yorker telling "The City That Knows How" what to do in his "Milk Forum" column in the *Bay Area Reporter*. In the 1970s, *Manhattanization* was a very bad word. He was elected because he was gay, not because he was "Harvey Milk." It was not personal. The 1970s was a period of rapid population growth in California, the Bay Area, and San Francisco. The horde of new gay immigrants, five minutes or five months in the City, knowing little of local San Francisco politics, voted on one issue in the way campus towns fear the temporary student population will turn out to change local laws and then leave the town holding the bag. Beyond even Harvey's control, he was swept up in a symbolic role in ritual politics. The convergence of his times, not his life, propelled him. His latter-day sainthood came through a martyrdom that could have happened to anyone playing the role of gay supervisor. It was his bad fortune that "Tonight the role of gay supervisor will be played by Harvey Milk." Even in death, the urban-legend jokes continued: the mourning crowd on the party boat, spreading his ashes at sea, deciding instead to snort lines of Harvey.

There are other instances of eyewitness events no other historian has mentioned: on Sunday, August 18, 1974, at the first Castro Street Fair—exactly at the corner of 18th and Castro—a gunman who had opened fire on the huge crowd was shot dead at my feet by a San Francisco cop as reported the next day when David Sparrow and I appeared in the right half of the tragic "death photo" on the front page of the August 19, 1974, *San Francisco Chronicle*.

Reporter Kevin Wallace wrote:

> A shotgun blast from a crowded sidewalk....Police Officer Arnold Strite [rushing with gun drawn and knocking David and me down], finding two shopkeepers trying to grapple with the man with the shotgun, shoved his revolver against the young

man's rib cage and told him to drop the shotgun. Instead, a second shotgun discharge ripped into the nearby pavement, sending ricocheting pellets into the shoulders of two women in the surrounding crowd—and Police Officer Arnold Strite fired his .357 Magnum. ©*San Francisco Chronicle*

Ironically, Harvey Milk had invented that first street fair because he wanted to register 20,000 gay voters. Instead, suddenly, like a foreshadowing in Greek tragedy, suddenly that summer, death, *gravitas*—suddenly death by gun—became possible in our liberated golden dream time when we dreamed the happy dreams of urban aboriginals before the political and religious poachers arrived with their culture war swinging too far right and too far left.

In this way, newspaper clippings, and my handwritten diary entries, crept into my eyewitness journals which created the *mise en scene* of both *Drummer* and *Some Dance to Remember: A Memoir-Novel of San Francisco 1970-1982.*

That autobiographical front-page "death photo" is a measure of the zero degrees of gunfire in all this gonzo eyewitness testimony.

I was there.

Dodging bullets.

PIONEER PARTICIPANT CREDENTIALS: HIRING ON TO *DRUMMER*

In March 1977, when Embry offered me the job of editor in chief of *Drummer*, I was otherwise employed—twice-over. Educated for eleven years for the Catholic priesthood (1953-1963), with a Ph.D. from Loyola University of Chicago (1968), and a California lifetime teaching credential for university lecturing, and working in a permanent position as a full-time writer managing the marketing and proposals department of Kaiser Engineers, I had also on March 7, 1977, placed eleventh among 1,200 straight and gay men and women when I qualified as a "Class 8304 Deputy Sheriff" for the City and County of San Francisco, and was offered a deputy's job which I had three opportunities to accept or decline. I had nearly twenty years' experience writing for magazines and had already written five published books [*What They Did to the Kid: Confessions of an Altar Boy* (written 1965); *Love and Death in Tennessee Williams* (1967); *I Am Curious (Leather)* aka *Leather Blues* (1968-69); *Television Today* (1971); and *Popular Witchcraft: Straight from the Witch's Mouth* (1972)] and was in the midst of writing what has been called my

"signature novel" *Some Dance to Remember* which I had begun in 1970 and completed in 1984.
    Priest. Professor. Writer. Sheriff. Editor.
    I had lots of choices.
    Q. So why *Drummer*? Why did I choose to throw in my lot with *Drummer* in 1977?
    A. Because in pre-Stonewall 1968 I saw the transgressive value of gay publishing. Gay pop culture had come out of the closet in the 1960s the way Black culture and Beat culture had come out in the 1950s. I figured attention must be paid. At the Second Annual Meeting of the American Studies Association, October 30, 1969, I presented my paper, "Popular Culture in Tennessee Williams." Immediately thereafter, when approached by Ray Browne who was one of the founders of the American Popular Culture Association (1968), I jumped on the opportunity to document our gay popular subculture by writing gay-themed essays in the newly founded *Journal of Popular Culture*, and in writing the nonfiction book *Popular Witchcraft: Straight from the Witch's Mouth* (1972; 2005). Soon enough, along came *Drummer* begging for content and identity.

    In the dual roles of 1) pioneer-participant, and as 2) historian-analyst commenting on that participation, I have been writing this eyewitness history for around forty years, but I am not clinging to a floating deck chair from the "Titanic 70s."

    I have had a long and rewarding personal and literary life and photographic career before, during, and after *Drummer*.

    Nevertheless, in a way, this memoir is my last will and testament about *Drummer* made in response to queer historian Dusk Darkling who once asked me to describe "a typical day during the 1970s in the *Drummer* office."

    As high as passions, fun, creativity, and sex always surged around *Drummer*, it was not the worst of times, but the best, as the innocent first-class party-people in the Titanic 70s cruised on not knowing that ahead lay the iceberg of HIV.

In a drag-dominated GLBT culture of sissyhood entitled by feminism, I edited, wrote, and photographed for the gay men's homomasculine adventure magazine *Drummer*...

Masturbation Is Magical Thinking

What I did to virilize *Drummer* was add realism to the magical thinking of *Drummer* readers who wanted a magazine that made the frontiers of newly liberated sex seem possible, accessible, and boundless. What they wanted they saw in the media image of themselves come alive in my *verite* pages reflecting what they really did at night.

Drummer reported the lifestyle it generated.

WHERE THE BOYS ARE:
A Manifesto of Equality
Addressed to GLBT Historians, Journalists, Academics, and Fiction Writers

Compton's Cafeteria, Stonewall, and the *Drummer* "Slave Auction"

When revisionists writing their "new histories" come to historic moments of gay riots and gay resistance such as the Compton's Cafeteria rebellion (San Francisco, 1966) or the Stonewall riot (New York, 1969), the tradition of "gay urban legend" is to fantasize that drag queens and hustlers and transgenders led the charge the way that some people insist that witches historically were feminist leaders rather than victims caught in a trap. (See *Popular Witchcraft: Straight from the Witch's Mouth*.) What is consistent in these GLBT urban legends is that masculine-identified gay men are deleted.

The suspects who create this revisionist slant are most often the journalists who need a hook, or at least a hooker, to give their stories flamboyant local color in the way that *Priscilla, Queen of the Desert* would be a generic road-trip movie were it not about drag queens.

Masculine-identified gay men are as difficult to dramatize emotionally as are heteromasculine straight men. Ask Oliver Stone who stumbled with his homomasculine love story *Alexander* (2004). In *The Advocate* (February 28, 2007), Stone said his premise for the love between Alexander and Hephaistion and Bogaos was that "With the passing of sperm was the passing of wisdom, literally, so that's why the older man always took on the young man, to pass on his wisdom." In *Drummer* 132 (August 1989), Mark C. Blazek's story "To Show That I'm a Man" began with a quote of secret wisdom from Aldous Huxley's *Brave New World*:

> "Do you mean to say that you wanted to be hit with that whip?" ...the young man made a sign of affirmation. "For the sake of the pueblo—and to make the rain come and the corn grow. And to please Pookong and Jesus. And to show that I can bear pain...Yes," and his voice took on a new resonance.... "To show that I'm a man."

Most journalists and most novelists, overly perplexed in a feminist-acute culture, reduce masculine men to villainous abusers, romantic ciphers, and action figures. Or worse, they make them invisible as Tennessee Williams' absent father in *The Glass Menagerie*: he worked for the phone company and fell in love with long distance.

This is why Annie Proulx, Diana Ossana, and Larry McMurtry were so brilliant with *Brokeback Mountain*. Actors Heath Ledger and Jake Gyllenhaal played masculine men with nary a hint of drag; and their performances quivered with a fresh sexuality and humanity in the cold mountain air. There is a camp infinity between *Brokeback Mountain* (2005) and *City Slickers* (1991), the other gay cowboy movie in which Jake Gyllenhaal appeared.

That element of the "human male force" is missing in most every historical narrative of gay rebellion. In truth, that archetypal force has rarely been dramatized in gay literature because of politics and because of the perceived inherent difficulty in dramatizing two men in love. Long before *Brokeback Mountain*, there was its predecessor, that other edgy homomasculine film, *Midnight Cowboy* (1969.)

I have argued this same gender point regarding polarity witchcraft that some wiccan traditionalists mistakenly demand requires a man and a woman. My research, best exemplified by Aleister Crowley, is that polarity magic can be practiced by two people of the same gender who discover subtler polarities between their physical and spiritual selves.

A case in point is the drag-free *Some Dance to Remember*. Both leading men are masculine, which means that each character had to be defined by subtleties of characterization other than the easy deus-ex-machina polarities of male-female and butch-sissy gender differences that dramatize most love stories.

Some reviewers, victims of speed-reading too many gay books, wanted one of the pair of men in *Some Dance* to be draggy, or camp, or, at the very least, gayer, because that kind of comic relief and dramatic shorthand is the norm that plays to the groundlings where camp is easily pitched.

One reason that the reporting about the riots at Compton's Cafeteria and of Stonewall are drag-intense is that when a journalist or scholar goes trolling for post-factum interviews, drag queens are as willing to be interviewed as the eager Lady Chablis in *Midnight in the Garden of Good and Evil*.

In the same way, hustlers who sell sex for cash are extremely willing to "tell you what you want to hear" for cash.

Masculine men, on the whole, are more taciturn, more invisible and harder to find, and once found, tend to a human-male reticence that is not "for sale" and does not lead to a particularly colorful interview.

This hardly helps the heat-seeking journalist or the queer historian such as Martin Duberman or the queer theorist such as Eve Kosofsky Sedgwick.

For instance, regarding the masculine-identified *Drummer* "Slave Auction" busted in LA in 1976, no journalist created any instant legend. No one rioted. Defense funds were quietly raised. As there were no drag queens to spin for color, *The Advocate* retreated to the opposite sensationalism quoting the lurid LAPD police report about "slaves and nipples" because *The Advocate* had a grudge against unsavory men in leather. In its coverage, *The Advocate* carefully never mentioned Embry or *Drummer*. The *Drummer* arrests, widely covered in the straight press, went un-championed in the gay press because the incident shattered "the received stereotype of gay oppression" with a new gay archetype: homomasculinity came out of the closet.

That night of April 10, 1976, everything changed: it was homomasculine men who were abused by heteromasculine cops. Not a drag queen in sight. The *mise en scene* was muscular Kabuki scripted by Mishima who had launched the leather decade of the 1970s with his manifesto and ritual suicide on November 25, 1970. As if it were one of the initiation sacraments such as Baptism or Confirmation, the "Slave Auction" arrest was the acting out of one of the primal themes constant in *Drummer*: masculine gay men involved with masculine straight men.

Unto itself, that night was erotically brilliant, even though no one had then what few have now: the tropes or the chops to handle this newly uncloseted archetypal way to be a manly homosexual.

Annie Proulx knew this.

She applied her insight to *Brokeback Mountain*.

Michael Bronski knew this.

He wrote his seminal article, "S/M: The New Romance," *Gay Community News* (Boston), Volume 2, Number 30 (1984), examining the emergence of the trope of courtly love in homomasculine romance in Sam Steward's Phil Andros stories, in John Preston's *Mr. Benson* (1979), and in Jack Fritscher's *Leather Blues* (1969) and *Corporal in Charge of Taking Care of Captain O'Malley* (1984).

Drummer editor Joseph Bean knew this. In a recorded conversation in June, 1997, he told me that in his youth, not yet intuiting the possibility of homomasculinity, he had invested in effeminate gay culture because acting out "sissiness" was the only behavior he knew. Part of our chat exemplifies the two polar views:

> Fritscher: I never went through that [an effeminate coming out] because in Chicago in the 1960s even before I knew fully the range of what homosexuality was, I knew to go to the Gold Coast and not one of the other bars, because I knew men went to the Gold Coast.
> Bean: That's the difference between us in our youth. You thought of yourself as a man...
> Fritscher: ...liking other men. And I knew I'd find...
> Bean: I thought of them as men, and thought they wouldn't want me around, because they're men. Why would they want me around?
> Fritscher: Because they like other men around.
> Bean: But I didn't think of me as a man.
> Fritscher: You didn't? But there's nothing effeminate about you.
> Bean: But I tried desperately to be effeminate. I was terribly unsuccessful. But I really tried, because, I thought, there are men and then there are people who like men, and I was one

of the people who liked men. It didn't occur to me...

Fritscher: But that's thinking like a heterosexual.

Bean: I was raised among heterosexuals and adopted their view.

Fritscher: But, see, homosexuality, the "homo" part means "the same," like, you like the same thing you are.

Bean: I didn't get that till I matured.

Is homomasculinity a new meme of gay natural selection? It's as if masculine-identified homosexuals have come out as a brand-new gender requiring, among other gay-culture mutations, a bricolage of gay identity that breaks the traditional frames of acculturated effeminacy. The Darwinian *Drummer*, for instance, always served as a virtual gay *Origin of the Species* for leathermen, bears, and other evolutionary homomasculine identities. For instance, *Bear* magazine required the DNA of its ancestors, *Drummer* and *Man2Man Quarterly*.

Before, during, and after *Drummer*, I have been an eyewitness-participant as well as a critic-analyst of this kind of journalistic thinking and this kind of local-color choice. When I decided to write a short story about 1960s gay liberation, I chose to write a campy drag-queen comedy titled "Stonewall, June 27, 1969, 11 PM" rather than a leatherman story about the *Drummer* "Slave Auction" which no author has yet fictionalized on page or screen.

As a further eyewitness, let me add Tony Tavarossi who is as important to gay liberation history in San Francisco as his contemporary, the drag-queen politician Jose Sarria. The homomasculine entrepreneur Tony Tavarossi was my longtime friend and sex playmate from 1970 to 1981.

No one else knows what I reveal here for the first time: he nicknamed himself "Tony"; his birth name was Elloyd Tavarossi, and he was born December 17, 1933; he died of AIDS July 12, 1981, two days after the epic fire that destroyed the Barracks bath on Folsom Street, putting an end to the Titanic 1970s.

Tony Tavarossi was a native San Franciscan who came out at the age of twelve under the tables in the curtained booths of the South China Café at 18th and Castro streets. He was a "walking oral historian" who in his own personal history set in motion a "domino effect" in gay liberation history:
1. Tony Tavarossi founded San Francisco's first bike bar or leather bar, the Why Not? (1960), where
2. he was himself arrested for propositioning an undercover cop, thus closing the Why Not? in a raid that was a rehearsal for
3. the police raid on the Tay-Bush Inn (1961) which emboldened
4. Chuck Arnett to hire Tony Tavarossi in opening the legendary Tool Box bar (1961) which, as a symbol of masculine mutiny, fortified the gay resolve to
5. found the Tavern Guild (1962) to protect gay citizens from harassment by the San Francisco Police Department.

Tony Tavarossi told me explicitly that the Compton's Cafeteria scene in 1966 was a riot led by a mixed crowd of Levi's-wearing leathermen, straight-trade hustlers (many of them ex-GI's from World War II and Korea), and tough drag queens.

What gay-ghetto journalists forget is that all three groups—aged forty and younger at that time—were men born in the 1920s, 1930s, and early 1940s. Underneath the butch boys sausaged into Levi's 501s and the drag queens swimming laps in Chanel Number 5, the Compton's Cafeteria crowd were seasoned combat veterans of three then recent wars: World War II, Korea, and Vietnam.

As Tony Tavarossi said, it is a truism of the bar business, as it was true of Compton's Cafeteria as a late-night hang-out, that for the most part, drag queens and male hustlers follow the money. They have a vested interest in hanging out where the boys are, where the men are, because that's where the wallets are.

Journalists love "appearance and reality" the way historians love a "good story."

In *And the Band Played On*, Randy Shilts—and I knew and worked with Randy Shilts—so loved the "hook" of Patient Zero that he tilted the HIV truth, not into a lie, but into the legend that, I think, immorally demonized the fun-loving flight attendant Gaetan Dugas into some kind of Typhoid Mary. In short, Shilts succumbed to a storyteller's temptation: he narrowed down the huge AIDS story in the same way journalists simplify and dramatize the seventeen-year-old drag Sylvia Rivera as the "hook" at the anonymous Stonewall Rebellion.

In just such an endless stream of personalization of an historical moment, the writer Edmund White, like Woody Allen's omnipresent character in *Zelig*, claims he was part of the Stonewall Riots; so do hundreds, if not thousands, of others, who were also, of course, at Woodstock eight weeks later! The review-proof White and the others may have turned up on the second night but that's not original-recipe Stonewall. It's all wannabe sons of Christopher Isherwood screaming the mantra about 1930s Berlin: "I Am a Camera!" Of course, you are, darling; sit down and have a martini, so literary devices can be separated from reality.

Such fly-on-the-wall point-of-view coverage makes great copy; it makes human interest; it's a chance for a post-factum photo op; it makes a movie; it builds careers; it wins GLBT awards. But it's not truth. It's worse: it's not quite the truth, but it seems true enough until the sniff test.

Perhaps journalists over-characterize drag queens as "ultra-tough real men" because that definition is one way to rebut and deconstruct the straight homophobic prejudice that "all gay men want to be women" and thus, in the straight mind, are as deserving of abuse as are "women who don't fight back."

In a GLBT society constantly bragging about inclusion, GLBT journalists, historians, and novelists might start liberating their perceptions of the reality-TV *mise en scene* before their very eyes.

It's necessary for authors to correct and square off the lists of simpleminded threes: "The riot was fought by drag queens, hustlers, and transgenders."

This may be true of some gay riot some place, but all gay riots everywhere forever had no gay male representation?

Foreword   109

WHAT WAS IT LIKE EDITING *DRUMMER* FOR THREE YEARS FROM MARCH 1977 TO DECEMBER 31, 1979?

Eyewitness historian Mark Thompson, one of the important former editors of *The Advocate*, reminded me with a wonderful objective correlative of what kind of "hysteria" gay life in San Francisco was up against during the high time I was editor in chief of *Drummer*.

Mark Thompson, separating facts and legends, is writing both a screenplay and an analytical biography of author and photographer Robert Opel, the first "star" created by *Drummer*. Thompson is the author of several books including *Gay Spirit: Myth and Meaning* (1987) and the seminal anthology, *Leatherfolk: Radical Sex, People, Politics, and Practice* (1991). His article "Black Leather Wings: The Radical Faeries Host a Leather Gathering" appeared in *Drummer* 136 (January 1990), pages 6-8, with seven photographs by Thompson, pages 66-69.

On May 30, 2001, Mark Thompson wrote:

Dear Jack,
    It was good speaking recently. Thanks for agreeing to see me on Friday, June 15. I really look forward to catching up...and...to discuss the Robert Opel [murder] case [at Fey-Way Gallery, South of Market, July 8, 1979].
    What was your relationship to Opel? Did you know him well, or mainly in the context of his gallery?
    What was your view of the man? Do you have any insight into the personal factors that may—or may not—have contributed to his demise?
    You once mentioned to me that you had met a man (at a party, I believe) who claimed he knew who was behind the murder. Can you remember what he said? Was it a police conspiracy? A hit job by a rival drug dealer? Maybe a combination of both? There were a lot of hysterical rumors floating around after Robert's death. [Opel had famously streaked the live telecast of the 1974 Academy Award Oscar show when David Niven and Elizabeth Taylor were at the microphone.] Can you remember other theories or views about the circumstances relating to his murder?
    The autumn of 1978 through the summer of 1979 [precisely when I was editing and writing *Drummer*] was a very volatile time for San Francisco: [the] Jonestown [Massacre committed by San Francisco gay messiah Jim Jones], the Moscone-Milk assassinations, Dan White's trial and subsequent City Hall riot,

and then the Opel murder. What is your perspective of that period? It seemed like the end of an era. Why and how did these tragic events follow so closely and what impact did they ultimately have on...the gay community?

Finally, I would enjoy hearing about where you are today concerning the past. Do you entertain fond memories, regrets, sadness—or a bit of each? Are there lessons for today's generation from what transpired in the past?....

All best wishes,
Mark [Thompson]
©Mark Thompson. Used with permission.

In the zero degrees of separation, the soigne party in question was a cocktail benefit sponsored on Sunday, March 4, 1990, by *Drummer* owners Anthony DeBlase and Andrew Charles, and *Drummer* editor Joseph W. Bean at the San Francisco home of advertising and circulation manager John Ferrari. (See John Ferrari, *Drummer* 115, April 1988, page 94; *Drummer* 145, masthead.) The purpose was to raise travel cash for International Mr. Leather, Guy Baldwin, a *Drummer* columnist and a psychotherapist who had appeared in Jim Wigler photographs in *Drummer* 128 (May 1989), page 30, and on the cover and in the centerfold of *Drummer* 132 (August 1989), and in *Drummer* 139 (May 1990), page 58. With an RSVP invitation suggesting the dress code of "formal leathers, dress uniform, or black tie," the *creme de leather* crowd was that year's quintessence of the drop-dead salon around *Drummer*. Behind the charade of that party, who was doing what to whom, and what was the truth of that salon?

(For *Rashomon* details in this *Gay San Francisco: Eyewitness Drummer*, see the volume titled *The Drummer Salon*.)

"SPEAK LOW WHEN YOU SPEAK LOVE"

Marlon Brando's film *The Wild One* (1953) exposed leather culture and shaped *Drummer* in a good way.

John Ford's film *The Man Who Shot Liberty Valence* (1962) forecast leather history in a bad way.

When the unruly biker Brando is asked, "What are you rebelling against?" He snaps back: "Whatcha got?"

When the reporters conspire about how they should report the truth about the man who supposedly shot Liberty Valence, revisionism wins when one says: "When the legend becomes fact, print the legend."

Some messengers should be killed.

Some seigneurial "historians" should stop quoting crap.

Revisionism is a cover up that is the worst kind of journalism, the worst kind of history, and the worst kind of lie.

Before the Titanic 1970s and the era of *Drummer* pass into the hands of historians, it is time to blow the whistle.

It is time for extrapolations and disinformation and agenda to stop.

Legend is gossip and lies.

Fact always trumps legend.

Truth is a boner.

415/346-4747

JACK FRITSCHER
Editor

1730 DIVISADERO / SAN FRANCISCO, CALIFORNIA 94115

Top: "Jack Fritscher, Golden Gate Park," 1976. Photograph by David Sparrow. ©Jack Fritscher. Middle: "David Sparrow and Jack Fritscher: Honeymoon Album," with alternative shots in *American Men*, Fritscher-Sparrow House, Kalamazoo, Michigan, 1969. Auto-Photograph by Sparrow and Fritscher. ©Jack Fritscher. "David Sparrow Solo," Fritscher-Sparrow House, San Francisco, 1974. Photograph by Jack Fritscher. ©Jack Fritscher. Bottom: "Jack Fritscher, 19th and Castro Street," Jim Kane-Ike Barnes House, 1972. Photograph by David Sparrow. ©Jack Fritscher. During his fiftieth year in publishing, Fritscher was awarded a "Lifetime Achievement Award 2007" from the national Erotic Authors Association founded by Marilyn Jaye Lewis.

Foreword 113

Top: "Jack Fritscher and Steve Saunders," Davisburg, Michigan, 1968. Auto-Photograph by Jack Fritscher. ©Jack Fritscher. Middle: "Jack Fritscher, *Whipcrack*," set of *Whipcrack* magazine photo shoot, 19th and Castro, 1970. Photograph by Walter Jebe. Bottom: "David Sparrow and Jack Fritscher, *Whipcrack*," *Whipcrack* photo shoot, 19th and Castro, 1970. Photograph by Walter Jebe. ©Walter Jebe. Used with permission.

Top: "Jack Fritscher, Castro Street," 1970. Photograph by David Sparrow. ©Jack Fritscher. Bottom left and right: "Castro Theater Marquee, Castro Street Fair 1975," and "Crowd at Market and Castro Streets: Castro Street Fair 1975." Photographs by Jack Fritscher. ©Jack Fritscher

Foreword

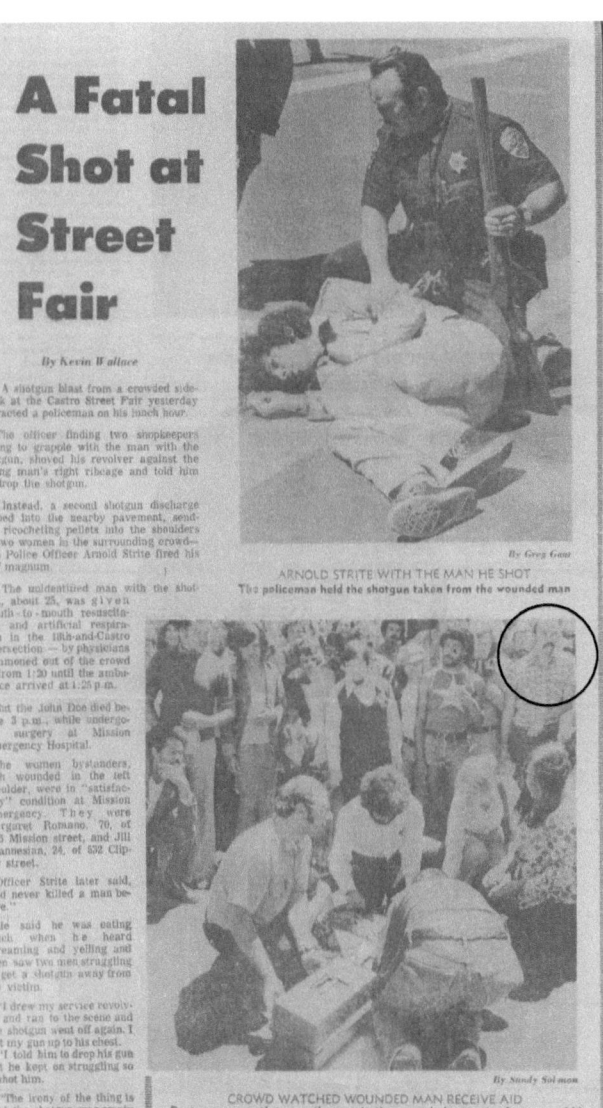

"Death at the First Castro Street Fair," August 18, 1974. *San Francisco Chronicle*, August 19, 1974. Lensed within the intersection of 18th and Castro, this front-page news photograph is essential to *Gay San Francisco* insofar as it documents and symbolizes the literal role of Jack Fritscher (circled) as an historical eyewitness of GLBT culture. ©*San Francisco Chronicle*

Top: "Thom Morrison and Jack Fritscher, Election Day, November 1979." The editor in chief of *Drummer* campaigning at corner of 18th and Castro for Dianne Feinstein who plays a walk-on in *Some Dance to Remember: A Memoir-Novel of San Francisco 1970-1982*. Photograph by David Sparrow. ©Jack Fritscher. Bottom: "Jack Fritscher and Jim Kane, Gay Rally 1972." Longtime companions from 1968, Fritscher and Catholic priest Jim Kane, San Francisco Civic Center plaza, June 1972. Fritscher was a monthly columnist for editor Kane's *Dateline Colorado*, the newspaper for the Catholic diocese of Colorado Springs. When Fritscher became editor in chief of *Drummer*, he profiled Jim Kane in "The Janus Society," *Drummer* 27 (February 1979). Photograph by David Sparrow. ©Jack Fritscher

Diversity…

… the right to be different … to live your own way … to follow a "different drummer …." These rights are what the annual Gay Freedom Day Parade and Celebration are all about.

When we march in support of others' rights to adopt different modes of speech, dress, sexuality, and self-expression, we are supporting our own right to be different.

When we celebrate the home we have found in this city, we also celebrate the tremendous value we derive in our lives from the diversity that IS San Francisco.

This year marks the 10th anniversary of the Stonewall Rebellion, the beginning of the end of second-class citizenship for gay men and women everywhere.

We will march to support gay men and women here, and throughout the world, who look to this event, more than any other, as evidence that our numbers are plentiful and that our movement is strong.

We will march to remind local politicians, in this election year, that votes are not to be won at our expense, and that harassment of any part of our community will be met with the resistance of our entire community.

We will all be there, celebrating the joy and full self-expression we experience in our sexuality … celebrating our cultural contributions … celebrating with music, color, sun, and dancing in the streets.

Join us.

The 1979 Gay Freedom Day Parade & Celebration Sunday, June 24, 1979

'Diversity" proclamation published by editor in chief Fritscher in *Drummer* 30 (June 1979).

Top: "*Drummer* art director A. Jay (Al Shapiro) and *Drummer* editor in chief Jack Fritscher," Fey-Way Studios, Friday, May 26, 1978. Publicity kit photograph by Efren Ramirez. ©Efren Ramirez. Published with permission from the Al Shapiro-Dick Kriegmont Archives. Bottom: "Jack Fritscher and Andrew Charles," Mr. *Drummer* Contest 1988, the Galleria, San Francisco. Friends since 1969, Fritscher was a judge of Mr. *Drummer* 1988, and Andrew Charles was the Chicago psychiatrist who in 1986 bought *Drummer* magazine for his lover, the writer Anthony DeBlase, who became the publisher of *Drummer* until 1992. Photograph by Mark Hemry. ©Mark Hemry

Foreword

Three players key to the founding of *Drummer* magazine. "Jack Fritscher, Jeanne Barney, and Larry Townsend," Dorothy Chandler Pavilion, Los Angeles, January 10, 2007. Photograph by Mark Hemry. ©Mark Hemry

Front and back covers of *Mapplethorpe: Assault with a Deadly Camera*, the erotic biography of bicoastal lovers Robert Mapplethorpe and Jack Fritscher who gave Mapplethorpe his first magazine cover, *Drummer* 24 (September 1978), and wrote the first article on Mapplethorpe in the gay press for the "New York Art" special issue, *Son of Drummer*. Front cover photograph of Mapplethorpe by George Dureau. ©George Dureau. Back cover photograph of Fritscher and Mapplethorpe by Rink. ©Rink

Captions: Eyewitness documentation of the existence of graphics providing internal evidence supporting Jack Fritscher's text are located in the Jack Fritscher and Mark Hemry GLBT History collection. Out of respect for issues of copyright, model releases, permissions, and privacy, some graphics are not available for publication at this time, but can be shown by appointment.

Eyewitness Illustration: Poster for Kenneth Anger's *Scorpio Rising*.

Eyewitness Illustration: Two drawings of legendary founding icon of Folsom Street, Tony Tavarossi, who was intimate friends with Fritscher for eleven years from 1970 to his death (1981) which Fritscher dramatized in the memoir-novel *Some Dance to Remember*. Top: Flash drawing, large watercolor, created in the Ambush bar by Lou Rudolph, 1975, Tavarossi on left. ©Lou Rudolph. Bottom: Pencil sketch limned in the Barracks baths by Chuck Arnett (1972) ©Chuck Arnett. Both drawings were gifts from Tavarossi to Fritscher.

Eyewitness Illustration: Drawing. "Jeanne Barney, Founding LA *Drummer* Editor in Chief," drawing by Chuck Arnett (1975). ©Chuck Arnett. In the salon around *Drummer*, Arnett was the house artist. His leggy drawing of Jeanne Barney is revealed for the first time in *Gay San Francisco: Eyewitness Drummer*. From the collection of Jeanne Barney.

Eyewitness Illustration: Book cover. *Sun and Steel*. Grove Press, 1970. "The Leather Decade" of the 1970s began with the ritual harakiri of writer and leatherman Yukio Mishima November 25, 1970, and ended with the burning of the Barracks baths, July 10, 1981, as first word of "gay cancer" spread.

Summary Timeline

Drummer
Quick Timeline & Cast of Characters
(The Evolution of Leather)

- Name Game: Who's Who and Not Who
- Key Timeline: 14 Turning Points of *Drummer*
- 3 Publishers
- 2 Editors in Chief, Some Other Editors, and an Art Director

A List of Frequently Confused Names
Sorted for Convenience

- Mark Hemry, editor of this series of books, *Gay San Francisco: Eyewitness Drummer*
- John Henry Embry, first publisher of *Drummer*
- Don Embinder, publisher of *Blueboy* magazine
- Jim Enger, bodybuilder icon 1970s, Fritscher companion
- Kenneth Anger, magus and leather filmmaker, *Scorpio Rising*
- John Rowberry, editor (never editor in chief) beginning in *Drummer* 40 through 86
- Robert Opel, Academy Award streaker, Fey-Way Gallery founder, and murdered *Drummer* photographer and writer
- Robert Mapplethorpe, photographer, Fritscher companion
- Sam Steward aka Phil Andros aka Phil Sparrow, legendary forebear of gay male writing and leather culture: intimate of Gertrude Stein and Alice B. Toklas, Chuck Renslow, Dom Orejudos, and Fritscher
- Jim Stewart, photographer, Fritscher housemate, early SoMa insider
- David Andrew Sparrow, Fritscher domestic partner (1969-1979; gay marriage by Catholic priest Jim Kane in Manhattan, May 7, 1972); his name bylines *Drummer* photography shot by Sparrow-Fritscher together

Hemry is not Embry; there is no "Mark Hembry." Robert Mapplethorpe is not Robert Opel; there is no "Robert Opelthorpe."

THE EVOLUTION OF LEATHER

BEGINNING AND ENDING THE LEATHER DECADE: THE 1970s

- September 30, 1970: The Presidential Commission on Obscenity and Pornography releases its 646-page report recommending that all sexually explicit movies, books, and magazines should be legalized
- November 25, 1970: The Leather Decade of the 1970s begins with the harakiri of Yukio Mishima, writer and soldier, who eroticised leather, uniforms, bodybuilding, edge play, and homomasculinity
- July 10, 1981: The Leather Decade ends with the burning of the Barracks Baths and Tony Tavarossi's July 12 death from a mystery disease at San Francisco General Hospital

DRUMMER KEY TIMELINE: 14 TURNING POINTS
WHEN, WHERE, AND WHY WHO AND WHAT CHANGED

1. June 20, 1975. *Drummer* 1 premieres edited by Jeanne Barney and published by John Embry

2. April 10, 1976. Great "Slave Auction" raid and arrests by gay-bashing LAPD in tactical "Operation Emancipation" run by Police Chief Ed Davis, 65 officers, one helicopter, one bus, and 40 victims

3. December 1976. Editor in chief Jeanne Barney exits original-concept LA *Drummer* after completing *Drummer* 11 and parts of 12 and 13

4. February-October 1977. *Drummer* makes desultory move from LA to San Francisco; *Drummer* 12 (February 1977) is first hybrid issue with both LA and San Francisco addresses on masthead

5. March 1977. Embry hires Allen J. Shapiro (A. Jay) as art director and Jack Fritscher as editor in chief to change LA *Drummer* into San Francisco *Drummer*; beginning after *Drummer* 18 (August 1977), which Fritscher ghost-edited, *Drummer* takes four-month publishing hiatus, absent from

the news stands and starting up again when Fritscher debuts his first issue, *Drummer* 19 (December 1977); the most representative, intense, archetypal, and perfect issue of *Drummer* in writing and graphic content is *Drummer* 21 (March 1978); Fritscher edits *Drummer* for three years: 32 months; Shapiro designs *Drummer* for 34 months

6. Winter 1978-Spring 1979. During Embry's cancer surgery and absence, Shapiro and Fritscher further remodel and refresh *Drummer*; Fritscher refashions leather as the focal point of a broader masculine-identified magazine reflecting its readers' actual gender identity in the personal ads where *masculine* and *masculinity* are the most repeated keywords; Anthony DeBlase acknowledges: "Embry was the main person responsible for...allowing it [*Drummer* while he was absent] to be modified [by Shapiro and Fritscher]." (*Drummer* 188, September 1995, page 19)

> For a year, a fog of depression and paranoia hangs over San Francisco and *Drummer*, both freaked out by the double-whammy of the Jonestown Massacre on November 18, 1978, and the assassination of Milk and Moscone on November 27, 1978. The mass suicide by Kool-Aid of 900 persons, mostly San Franciscans, at the People's Temple in Guyana was committed by former San Francisco Housing Board member, Jim Jones, who earlier had been arrested for masturbating and hitting on an undercover LAPD officer in the men's room of the West Lake Theater in LA; Jones was instrumental in electing Mayor Moscone to office. Jones and Moscone died nine days apart.

7. June 1979. Embry reveals his "Blacklist" in *Drummer* 30 attacking Jeanne Barney; the shadow list begins with Police Chief Ed Davis and continues with anyone uncontrollable by Embry who does not seem to like being held accountable by eyewitnesses

8. July 8, 1979. The assassin-like murder of *Drummer* writer and photographer Robert Opel in his South of Market Fey-Way Gallery follows Jonestown and Milk-Moscone killings by six months, and causes a new kind of gay hysteria in bars, baths, bistros, and the *Drummer* office

9. August to December 31, 1979. Shapiro and Fritscher exit together taking the *Drummer* salon of talent such as Robert Mapplethorpe, thus

ending what Embry and others term the "classic 1970s *Drummer*"; Fritscher is the second and last editor in chief of *Drummer*; thirteen months after Fritscher exits, John Rowberry becomes editor with *Drummer* 40 (January 1981) to *Drummer* 86 (January 1986)

10. 1982. "HIV and VCR." Virus and video change everything in editorial content of writing and photography; under Embry-Rowberry, *Drummer* becomes a leathery *People* magazine, featuring porn stars and Mr. *Drummer* leather-contest models

11. August 22, 1986. Embry sells *Drummer* to Anthony F. DeBlase and Andrew Charles, Desmodus Inc., whose first issue is *Drummer* 99; DeBlase and Charles take victory lap in special issue *Drummer* 100; Fritscher says, "DeBlase bought *Drummer* to save it from Embry." DeBlase and Embry greet each other in *Drummer* 98 and immediately begin civil war in their various publications: *Manifest Reader*, *Drummer* 107, *Drummer* 120.

- AIDS-era owner DeBlase acts up: increasing with each issue from *Drummer* 100, with *Drummer* 150—e.g.: "Dykes for Madonna!"—being one of the worst of the nagging, preachy, camp issues, DeBlase mistakenly devotes even more pages to congenial leather contestants and, worse, he turns *Drummer* from jerkoff erotica into a whiney self-help examination of conscience over leather identity, gender, sobriety, and "how-to" articles in the magazine that had succeeded in the 1970s because its premise was based on the presumption that the readers, in fact, already knew "how to."
- In their feud, salesman Embry must have cackled as the increasingly papal DeBlase murders his own business by encouraging his staff to publish didactic articles preaching to the politically correct leather choir. Subscriptions and sales of *Drummer* plummet.
- Once famous for writing about fisting with a punch, *Drummer* becomes irrelevant outside San Francisco-NY-and-LA to national readers wanting erotica rather than gay politics and leather mysticism. Rendered impotent, the erotic magazine is going out of business, and DeBlase is seeking an exit strategy when, like a lucky *deus ex machina* (for DeBlase), the earth shakes.

12. October 17, 1989. Loma Prieta earthquake destroys *Drummer* offices giving DeBlase an excuse to offer the floundering *Drummer* for sale in

Summary Timeline

Drummer 140 (June 1990) with a more desperate full-page pitch, "*Drummer* Is for Sale," in *Drummer* 150 (September 1991), page 4

13. September 1992. Dutch businessman Martijn Bakker buys *Drummer* and, beginning with *Drummer* 159, mistakenly Europeanizes *Drummer* whose secret of success is that it is a quintessentially American magazine of gay and leather popular culture; Bakker re-titles *Drummer* as *International Drummer*

14. 1996. Internet arrives and causes slow death of 20th-century gay magazines; *Drummer* 214 is the final issue (April 1999); Bakker officially closes the *Drummer* business on September 30, 1999

EYEWITNESS: *DRUMMER* TIMELINE & SCORE CARD
3 OWNER/PUBLISHERS + 1 CONTRIBUTOR

1. John Henry Embry, Publisher: 11 years, 1975-1986, issues 1-98
"Much of the 116 issues that followed the first 100 didn't have all that much to recommend it [*sic*]." —John Embry

2. Anthony DeBlase and Andrew Charles, AIDS-era Publishers: 6 years, 1986-1992, issues 99-158
"We were fools to buy *Drummer*." —Andrew Charles

3. Martijn Bakker, Publisher: 6 years, 1992-1999, issues 159-214
"The Dutchman was the sole killer of *Drummer* and all it stood for." —Mister Marcus

4. Jack Fritscher, Contributor: 17 years, 1977-1995; founding San Francisco editor in chief, March 1977-December 31, 1979; *Drummer*'s most frequent contributor in 65 issues, often with several contributions to each issue; only editor to shoot *Drummer* covers
"*Drummer* was a home, and a home run." —Jack Fritscher

> "Jack Fritscher is...the man who invented the South of Market prose style as well as its magazines which have never been the same without him."
> —John F. Karr, *Bay Area Reporter*, June 27, 1985

3 SAN FRANCISCO VERSIONS OF *DRUMMER* SORTED BY 3 OFFICE ADDRESSES

1. "California Street *Drummer*" *Drummer* 12 - *Drummer* 18: 311 California Street (Embry's first office in the prestigious Robert Dollar Building), San Francisco, on masthead.

2. "Divisadero Street *Drummer*" *Drummer* 19 - *Drummer* 31: 1730 Divisadero Street (a down-at-heel Victorian), San Francisco, on masthead; "Divisadero *Drummer*" is the *Drummer* edited by Jack Fritscher (14-17, plus ghost-editor of *Drummer* 18, *Drummer* 31, 32, and 33).

3. "Harriet Street *Drummer*" *Drummer* 32- following: 15 Harriet Street (a dump over a garage), San Francisco, on masthead; later, offices on Folsom Street followed by Natoma Street and Shipley Street.

"EDITOR IN CHIEF" TITLE FOR BARNEY AND FRITSCHER ONLY

1. Jeanne Barney: *Drummer* 1 - *Drummer* 11 + hybrid issues *Drummer* 12, *Drummer* 13; outspoken founding LA editor in chief of *Drummer* (1975), and columnist, "Smoke from Jeannie's Lamp"; editor of *Dateline: The NewsMagazine of Gay America* (1976); Leather Awards Humanitarian of the Year (1976); the only woman arrested by the LAPD at the *Drummer* "Slave Auction" and main contact for follow-up print and television news coverage; eyewitness to *Drummer* history through association since 1973 with founding publisher John Embry and to leather history since 1972 through Larry Townsend.

2. Jack Fritscher: *Drummer* 19 - *Drummer* 30, *Son of Drummer*, + hybrid issues *Drummer* 14-18 and *Drummer* 31-33; Fritscher and Shapiro refashion *Drummer* while covering publisher Embry's long absences as he seemed to fall ill in 1978 and during his Spring 1979 cancer surgery and recuperation. See Embry's "thank you note" in "Getting Off," *Drummer* 30, 4th Anniversary Issue, June 1979. Anthony DeBlase in *Drummer* 100: "With *Drummer* 19 Jack Fritscher came upon the scene [where he had been producing behind the scenes since *Drummer* 14, ghost-editing *Drummer* 18]. Under Jack's direction SM per se became less prominent, and rough and raunchy sexuality often written by Jack himself became the main theme."

Summary Timeline 127

SOME OTHER "EDITORS" & "ASSIGNMENT EDITORS"

1. "Robert Payne" aka John Embry. Following Fritscher's 1970s identity-driven *Drummer* exploring the new "gender" of gay masculinity with its many foci, Embry reductively focused *Drummer* on the leather-pageant contest, Mr. *Drummer*.

2. John W. Rowberry. Following Fritscher, Rowberry was never "editor in chief" of *Drummer*; Rowberry had arrived from LA looking for work after quitting as the night porter at the Ramada Inn on Santa Monica Boulevard in WeHo; Rowberry was listed as "assignment editor" from *Drummer* 31 through *Drummer* 39, and finally—thirteen months after Fritscher's exit—as "editor" beginning in *Drummer* 40. Changing *Drummer* from Fritscher's 1970s reader-reflexive *verite* magazine of masculine culture, Rowberry reductively focused *Drummer* on genitality, on Mr. *Drummer* leather contests, and on video stars. After Rowberry exited *Drummer*, Embry turned on him and wrote in *Manifest Reader* (1997), page 79, that Rowberry was "no authority on the type of action" that Embry's readers preferred. Some years after Rowberry's death on December 4, 1993, founding Los Angeles editor in chief Jeanne Barney wrote: "I found Rowberry to be a good writer (when I edited him), but based on his editorial skills in magazines where he had sole editorial responsibilities, well, to be frank, he sucked."

3. Tim Barrus. Provocative associate editor for only five issues, with publisher Anthony DeBlase, wrote his first fiery editorial in *Drummer* 117 (June 1988), page 4; earlier his fiction had appeared in Embry's *Drummer* 67, 72, and 77. He also appeared unnamed in a photograph with and by Mark I. Chester in *Drummer* 138, page 24. In *Drummer* 122 (October 1988), a presidential election year, publisher DeBlase noted on page 4:

> Barrus Resigns. I regret having to announce that Tim Barrus has resigned as Associate Editor. I was quite pleased with many of the improvements he had made in the magazine and with many of his plans for the future. However, he became quite concerned about Justice Department persecution of publishers of erotica and decided to sever his relationship with Desmodus Inc.

4. Joseph W. Bean. Editor (*Drummer* 133 - *Drummer* 158 + hybrid issues *Drummer* 159 - *Drummer* 161) with editorial coordinator Marcus-Jay Wonacott; in the process of exiting, Bean's name does not appear on the masthead of ill-fated *Drummer* 161 (March 1993) which was allegedly

mostly shredded and not distributed because of legal action over *Drummer*'s copyright violation of the World Wrestling Federation word, *Wrestlemania*; Bean, however, aids DeBlase's exit and maintains continuity through the sale of *Drummer* to Martijn Bakker; Bean was the "earthquake editor" who kept *Drummer* alive in 1989-1990; see Bean's "The Day the Earth Did Not Stand Still" in *Drummer* 135 (December 1989).

5. Robert Davolt. Operations manager, 1997, under Dutch publisher Martijn Bakker who hired him as an American manager with *Drummer* 209; Davolt titled himself both "editor" and "publisher"; in those straw positions, he managed to produce a total of only six issues of the "monthly" *Drummer* between April 1998 and April 1999 when *Drummer* went out of business with *Drummer* 214. Davolt became an accomplice in the killing of *Drummer*, the magazine, by spending all his energy on Mr. *Drummer*, the contest, where he could indulge his weakness for playing the social lion on his coast-to-coast grand tours producing the contest. Traveling on an expense account wrung from the struggling magazine, Davolt reduced *Drummer* to nothing more than the Mr. *Drummer* contest and video ads.

FOUNDING SAN FRANCISCO ART DIRECTOR

Al Shapiro aka A. Jay: *Drummer* 17 - *Drummer* 32; publisher Anthony DeBlase in *Drummer* 100 (October 1986) wrote that Fritscher's discovery "David Hurles' Old Reliable photos and A. Jay's drawings characterized this era....and A. Jay's illustrations for stories and ads had exactly the right look for Jack Fritscher's version of *Drummer*."

DRUMMER TRIVIA

- *Drummer* 1 and *Drummer* 2 were "closet" issues, with no names on masthead
- *Drummer* 4 - *Drummer* 12: no Thoreau "marching quote" on masthead

    What rollicking fun...to reopen old friendships and even some ancient hostilities of that golden age. To be a by-stander to those vibrant talents and hear again those voices.... Can you imagine the pleasure in being able to put one's arms around some of those people, just like you maybe should have done back then when they were still around and available?
    —John Embry, *Manifest Reader* 33 (1997), page 5

Ten years earlier, in *Drummer* 107 (August 1987), page 91, running through *Drummer* 116 (May 1988), page 82, John Embry, having sold his megaphone that was *Drummer*, placed a classified ad seeking what I term "eyewitness *Drummer* participants" from the 1970s for a book he was pitching for his Alternate Publishing. At the height of the AIDS plague, he knew of my completed book *Some Dance to Remember: A Memoir-Novel of San Francisco 1970-1982*. Even though Embry's "eyewitness" book never happened, his instincts were correct. His *Drummer* "Wanted" ad paralleled my own years of preservation and reconstruction of the Golden Age of Leather in *Some Dance to Remember* (written during 1970-1984) and *Mapplethorpe: Assault with a Deadly Camera* (written during 1979-1993).

WANTED
THE GOLDEN AGE OF FOLSOM

We are looking for input into a collection of the phenomena that was South of Market. The men, the experiences, the fact and the fiction, the legends and the graphics. Tell us your memories of those years for the most important leather volume ever. To be published by Alternate Publishing [John Embry], PO Box 42009. San Francisco, CA 94142-2009. Artists, Photographers, Writers may call (707) 869-0945 for more details.

"*DRUMMER* PAID THE BILLS" FOR ITS POOR SIBLINGS

In his latter-day magazine *Super MR* 5 (2000), page 39, publisher Embry, at the sundown of his publishing career, finally confessed in print what *Drummer*'s army of unpaid and underpaid writers, artists, photographers, and staff without benefits always suspected.

Drummer was a cash cow milked to support sibling magazines owned by Embry, to prop up his annual Mr. *Drummer* contests, and to float his assorted ventures in mail order and—it was alleged—personal real estate.

In the nearly three years that I was editor in chief, *Drummer* had, according to Embry, a press run of 42,000 copies. A million people had bought and read some issue of 1970s *Drummer* by the end of my editorship with *Drummer* 33, December 31, 1979.

I did the math; I asked to be paid; I exited, mostly unpaid, to begin the 1980s afresh.

If only the income from *Drummer* had been spent on properly paying the talented gayfolk who created it.

If only the profit had been used to upgrade the production of *Drummer* by printing it on better paper that didn't feel like rag stock soaking up the photographs like inkblots.

History will not look kindly on the corners cut at *Drummer*.

Embry finally admitted with some transparency in *Super MR* (2000) page 39:

> *Drummer*'s steady growth made it possible for much experimentation, including [other magazines like] *Alternate, Mach, FQ* [*Foreskin Quarterly*], *Manifest*, and all the annuals [e.g.: *Son of Drummer*] that followed. None of our publishing lost money, some made more than others, of course. But it was *Drummer* that paid the bills and gave us the opportunity to increase and expand.

"Homosexuality in America" written by Paul Welch with photographs by William Eppridge, *Life* magazine, June 26, 1964. Pop-culture analyst Jack Fritscher, who experienced the *Life* issue as a twenty-five-year-old eyewitness subscriber in 1964, was the first historian to point out this seminal issue of *Life* magazine as a benchmark in the gender-identity history of gay culture. (*Life* emphasized the civil war between masculine-identified gays and female-identified gays.) His clarion point, now a canonical reference to many, was made in his heirloom "Rear-View Mirror" history column in *Drummer* 134 (October 1989). ©*Life*

Fritscher created themes to anchor and develop
the following 21 issues of *Drummer*
and it was the first time each theme
was published in *Drummer*

- *Drummer* 20 (January 1978): Gay Sports
- *Drummer* 21 (March 1978): Prison
- *Drummer* 22 (May 1978): Cigars
- *Drummer* 23 (July 1978): Underground Sex: Gay Pop Culture — The Catacombs
- *Drummer* 24 (September 1978): Authenticity, Mapplethorpe, and Bondage
- *Son of Drummer* (September 1978): New York Art — Rex and Mapplethorpe
- *Drummer* 25 (December 1978: Leather Identity — Homomasculinity
- *Drummer* 26 (January 1979): Cowboys and Performance Art
- *Drummer* 27 (February 1979): Gay Film and the Society of Janus
- *Drummer* 28 (April 1979): Gyms and Prisons
- *Drummer* 29 (May 1979): Dangerous Sex, Boxing, and Blue-Collar Men
- *Drummer* 30 (June 1979): Nipples and Arthur Tress Photography
- *Drummer* 31 (September 1979): Spit and Other Erotic Bodily Functions
- *Drummer* 118 (July 1988): Rubber (Keith Ardent)
- *Drummer* 119 (also dated July 1988): Bears
- *Drummer* 124 (December 1988): Bodybuilders and "the *Drummer* Novel," *Some Dance to Remember: A Memoir-Novel of San Francisco 1970-1982*
- *Drummer* 133 (September 1989): Mapplethorpe and Censorship
- *Drummer* 134 (October 1989): Brown Leather
- *Drummer* 138 (March 1990): Satirical Upside-Down Earthquake Issue of *Drummer* titled *"Dummer": A Unique Drummer Semi-Publication*
- *Drummer* 139 (*May 1990): Remembrance of Sleaze Past in the Titanic 1970s
- *Drummer* 170 (December 1993): Russomania — Shooting Porn

James Dean: Magnificent Failure

> Written in 1960 and revised in September 1961, this feature essay was published in *Preview: The Family Entertainment Guide*, June 1962.
> I. Author's Eyewitness Historical-Context Introduction written July 29, 2007
> II. The feature article as published in *Preview: The Family Entertainment Guide*, June 1962
> III. Eyewitness Illustrations

I. Author's Eyewitness Historical-Context Introduction written July 29, 2007

<blockquote>
Revealing the Iconography of *Drummer*:
When James Dean Met Marlon Brando,
Heath Ledger, and Jake Gyllenhaal

Marlon Brando: "Stella!"
James Dean: "You're tearing me apart."
Jake Gyllenhaal to Heath Ledger:
"I wish I knew how to quit you."
</blockquote>

As soon as we teenagers invented and liberated our tortured selves in the pop culture of the deadly dull 1950s, my leather bomber jacket morphed in meaning from "play clothing" to teen symbol. I was swept up by the movie *Blackboard Jungle* (1955) and its theme song, Bill Haley's "Rock around the Clock," which was played every ten minutes on the radio because no other white rock-n-roll songs yet existed. At the same instant, I found my first lover in James Dean, in his jackets, his motorcycle, his face, his attitude, his *verite*. When he was killed at age twenty-four on September 30, 1955, I was sixteen, a junior in high school, and stricken with grief.

Even though I was in the Catholic seminary and was a sexually pure boy, art and literature and movies cancelled my chances of being parochial. (In 2007, it is more difficult to come out as a progressive Catholic than it is to come out as gay.) I knew that James Dean was who we all were inside. That struggling universal identity was one of his secrets. He died young and found eternal life on film. Looking at him, seduced by his charisma, we discovered sex worship while we ate popcorn and went rocketing on in a rising perfect storm of popular culture that eventually led me to *Drummer*.

In 1956, I bought the paperback, *James Dean, A Biography*, written by his roommate, William Bast, whose unspoken clues and cues told me to read between the lines.

At the same time I wrapped a brown-paper bag around Walt Whitman's *Leaves of Grass*, a book praised in my high-school literature class, even though we had been cautioned by the priests not to read it because parts of it were impure.

With flashlight under my blanket covers, I was also reading Grace Metalious' sensational bestseller, *Peyton Place* (1956). I knew what Betty Anderson did to Rodney Harrington.

Those books were about a liberated life I was longing to have. In the pressure cooker of the conformist 1950s, we were reading in code the books that would liberate us in the 1960s.

On television in 1956, I watched TV news footage of the Hungarian Revolt as students marched through the streets of Budapest, and I wondered why we couldn't do that.

I never recovered from the 1955 death of James Dean any more than I have recovered from the 1963 death of Jack Kennedy. Distraught over JFK, I left the Catholic seminary three weeks after he was killed. I should have left on the Friday, September 30, 1955, when Dean died. Both men, aged twenty-four and forty-six, imprinted me and my teen-beatnik generation which grew to be the first generation of gay liberation and the first generation of *Drummer* readers.

By the time James Dean crashed his Porsche Spyder at sunset east of Paso Robles, California, he had appeared on Broadway as a gay Arab hustler in Andre Gide's *The Immoralist* (1954); and he had made three films in one year: *East of Eden* (1955) from the novel by John Steinbeck, *Rebel Without a Cause* (1955) from the screenplay by legendary director Nicholas Ray, and *Giant* (1956) from the novel by Edna Ferber, the keenest lesbian of the fabled Algonquin Club. While the publicity-savvy Warner Brothers rushed the postmortem premiere of *Rebel* into theaters, the studio withheld *Giant* from screens for a whole year "out of respect" for Jimmy, watching Dean fever spread from teenager to teenager. We worshiped him the way Sal Mineo worshiped him even more than Natalie Wood wanted him with all her heart on-screen and off. It was not lost on

James Dean

me that the gay Mineo's character was named Plato, and James Dean was his Ideal.

James Dean was masculine; he was blond; he was hot; he was California; he was American; he was gay.

I wanted James Dean. I wanted to be him.

I never wanted Marlon Brando.

In ways emblematic of the times, Marlon Brando was James Dean, or some said, Dean was Brando: Brando had done a screen test for *Rebel Without a Cause*; both attended the Actor's Studio; both rode motorcycles; both uncloseted a new kind of hyper-masculine sexuality; both became icons in gay leather culture.

By the late 1970s when *Drummer* was a bestseller on news stands all across America, James Dean had grown so iconic in queer memory that Bette Midler in *The Rose* (1979) was desperately seeking out blond men who were ghosts of the James Dean poster that hung in her garage. (Still obsessed a decade after directing *The Rose*, Mark Rydell directed the 2001 bio film, *James Dean*.) In 1981, a coven of gay divas—Cher, Karen Black, Kathy Bates, and Sandy Dennis—all playing disciples of Dean, starred in the Robert Altman play and film, *Come Back to the Five and Dime, Jimmy Dean, Jimmy Dean* (1982). See my review of the erotic archetype of Dean in *The Rose* in the Virtual *Drummer, Man2Man Quarterly* #1 (October 1980), page 13.

Dean and Brando made leather culture and *Drummer* inevitable. The outlaw rebellion common to both Brando's *The Wild One* (1953) and Dean's *Rebel Without a Cause* liberated masculine gay men in the same r/evolution as Betty Friedan liberated women with *The Feminine Mystique* (1963) changing sexuality in the 1960s leading to the Stonewall Rebellion (1969), with a through-line threading Kenneth Anger's *Scorpio Rising* (1964), and John Rechy's *City of Night* (1963) and *The Sexual Outlaw* (1977).

In *Drummer* 16 (June 1977), there is an interview with John Rechy who in the 1950s as an LA hustler groomed himself after the fashion of James Dean who had been a sometime hustler in LA on Santa Monica Boulevard and in New York on 42nd Street. In his writing, Rechy has such high esteem for Dean, I suspect he hung out at Googie's coffee shop on Sunset Strip where Dean was a post-midnight habitue with the insomniac goth crowd that included Vampira, the camp TV hostess of horror films. Had Dean lived, and if Hollywood had wanted to film *City of*

Night, Dean, as Rechy's hustler, would have been as perfectly conflicted in his own way as Jon Voight was in *Midnight Cowboy* (1969), the John Schlesinger film based on gay author James Leo Herlihy's 1965 novel.

Brando and Dean fused into one archetypal leather image repeated a thousand times in irresistible 1950s "juvenile delinquent" photographs from Chuck Renslow and Etienne's Kris Studio in Chicago and from Bob Mizer's Athletic Model Guild in LA. The names of the characters Dean played all sounded like AMG porn stars: Cal Trask in *East of Eden*, Jim Stark in *Rebel*, and Jett Rink in *Giant*.

On Folsom Street in San Francisco, artist Mike Caffee sculpted his famous *Leather David* statue (1966) for Fe-Be's bar, but its leather jacket and cap were from Brando, and its existential slouch was pure, patented James Dean. In 1970, I bought a Caffee *Leather David* from Fe-Be's for $125. Research Mike Caffee, the statue, and leather heritage in *Popular Witchcraft: Straight from the Witch's Mouth*.

If Dean had not been seven years younger than Brando, Tennessee Williams might have had some interesting choices casting his leading men who were considered peers by their mutual Actor's Studio director, Elia Kazan. Dean was born too late, but perfect, for *The Glass Menagerie* (1945) and was counter-intuitively ideal for *A Streetcar Named Desire* (1948), and was dead too soon for *Cat on a Hot Tin Roof* (1955). As a lifelong critic writing on Tennessee Williams, I have noted that very often the actors cast in Williams' plays are too old for the roles. What James Dean could have brought to Tennessee Williams' *Suddenly Last Summer* and *Sweet Bird of Youth*! Research Tennessee Williams: jackfritscher.com.

In the 1950s, I was a gay boy who—same as everyone else—did not know what being a "masculine gay" was, and I could not let go of Jimmy Dean because I wanted to be like him. I wanted to be the kind of man he was.

He so absorbed me into him that I began writing anguished teenage-boy fiction like "The Odyssey of Bobby Joad" and "Father and Son" which the Catholic press seemed happy to publish because the stories safely reflected teenage angst. In August 1957, as soon as I turned eighteen, I flew to New York for my first visit to Manhattan to track Dean's haunts on 42nd Street, on West 68th Street #19 where he had sublet, and in the Village on Christopher Street at the Theater de Lys where he had appeared on stage. That didn't take much time so I was soon catching folk singers in Washington Square Park and beat poets in coffee houses, and I was buying books on yoga and physique magazines, and dying my hair red. I was too young to know gay bars existed.

Homosexuality always pushes into the future those who listen which is why fundamentalists hate it and the change it causes. I was fifteen years

James Dean

ahead of Lou Reed who got "me" right when he wrote his 1972 song, "Walk on the Wild Side": "Jackie is just speeding away—thought she was James Dean for a day." On August 14, 1957, having returned from Manhattan, I wrote an anguished eyewitness beatnik poem about the world, Greenwich Village, and James Dean titled, "Cry! The Young Hunters," which is re-printed as background gay *juvenilia* for "gay roots nostalgia" in this series after my *Drummer* article, "Leather Christmas 1977."

I was mad for James Dean, and wrote a feature article about him when I turned twenty-one in 1960; but I was a seminarian, and the priest-censor told me (cryptically) that my article was inappropriate and that no Catholic magazine would publish it.

For the next twelve months, I practiced what I had learned from the book written by James Dean's roommate, William Bast. Having learned to read between the lines, I taught myself how to write between the lines.

And I succeeded, even though I had to keep the closet door closed. My passion for him surfaced in my article, "James Dean: Magnificent Failure," published in the Catholic *Preview: The Family Entertainment Guide* (June 1962). But there was a price. I had to closet my idolatry of him and revise the title of the article with the oxymoron angle, "Magnificent Failure." In my spin, I had to open with disclaiming sentiments that evaporate as the article goes on. As a very young man, my theme was identity and cult. As a twenty-year-old I wrote about the legend of Dean overtaking the person he was; that was the exact premise I posited thirty years later writing my erotic bio about my lover Mapplethorpe when postmortem scandals and fame erased what a sweet person he had been before he died too young.

In truth, James Dean imprinted a generation and me archetypally. Fully coming out of my closet during the mid-1960s, I exploded and wrote my young leather-biker novel, *I Am Curious (Leather)* aka *Leather Blues* (1969). I frankly "imagined" my *mise en scene* on James Dean and his fuck-you attitude. In a weird coincidence signifying nothing, three days after I completed the final draft of that manuscript, I was nearly killed in a terrible car crash when rammed by a Checker cab that destroyed my vehicle with me buckled inside on August 9, 1969, at the same hour the Manson Family was murdering movie star Sharon Tate and four others including stylist Jay Sebring who designed the hair for the film *Spartacus* and opened the first "salon for men" in San Francisco in 1969. Urban legend rumored that the once-married Sebring was gay and into leather because of items allegedly found in the trunk of his car parked outside the murder house.

With the headlines the next morning, the culture-shaking Manson Family became part of my book, *Popular Witchcraft*, (1972) which I had begun writing three months before. A chapter of *I Am Curious (Leather)*, based on James Dean's leaving home, and on our bomber-jackets, was serialized in *Son of Drummer* (September 1978), and was announced as "the new *Drummer* novel."

When I began shaping the psychological input of *Drummer* in 1977, James Dean (hot and dead), even more than the obvious Brando (old and fat), flowed into my concept of a homomasculine ideal for *Drummer* in fiction, features, and photography.

In the pop-art 1960s and 1970s, huge black-and-white photo posters of James Dean hung like icons on the walls of leather bars like Keller's in New York and Chuck Arnett's Tool Box in San Francisco. On Folsom Street, the Ramrod bar in those pre-VCR years switched on its 16mm movie projector every Wednesday night to build a crowd, and frequently screened reels from all three of James Dean's films, as well as Mel Brooks' "Springtime for Hitler" sequences from *The Producers* (1968).

In *Giant* (filmed in 1955), the chain-smoking cowboy Dean invented the "Marlboro Cowboy" that came to dominate 1960s American advertising. Before James Dean, the Marlboro Man, created by Leo Burnett in 1954, was not necessarily a cowboy. Post-Dean in *Giant*, Marlboro Country, fetishizing itself, became nothing but saddles, boots, yellow slickers, riding gloves, cowboy hats, and bunkhouses. The Marlboro Man so infused American ideas of masculinity that I folded that sensibility into 1970s *Drummer* to queer Marlboro's man-to-man sex appeal, and to ground *Drummer* so that it would not be light in its loafers. Just as the world loved the Marlboro Man, gay men internationally loved the open-faced American masculinity of *Drummer* which, with its leather and cowboy lifestyle, was not like all the other effeminate and campy gay magazines.

The most reviled issue of *Drummer* was first publisher John Embry's "Cycle Sluts" drag cover and contents of *Drummer* 9 (October 1976) which readers wrote they never wanted to see again. The second publisher Anthony DeBlase, pressured by political correctness, and desperate to sell the *Drummer* business, made a similar anti-erotic misstep leading to the death of *Drummer* when he printed "Dykes for Madonna" in *Drummer* 150 (September 1991). His mistake of switching icons Dean and Brando for Madonna in his nagging, preachy, and camp issue created an uproar, alienated core readers, and put off potential American buyers.

As if in proof of *Drummer* gestating the Marlboro male *isolato* image, Dean's laconic smoking cowboy in *Giant*, with his rifle slung across his shoulders, filtered through gay lore and surfaced as the prototype for actors Jake Gyllenhaal and Heath Ledger (especially) in *Brokeback Mountain* (2005).

James Dean

Jack Twist was James Dean.

As an insight into the pervasive pop-culture influence of *Drummer*, it is worth noting that long before Annie Proulx ever spun the yarn for her sensitive Edna Ferber-esque short story for *The New Yorker* (1997), the archetype, plot, and characters of that cowboy love story had appeared in a dozen testosterone versions during twenty-four years in *Drummer*.

Dean died iconic, a misunderstood good boy, like an anguished Peter Pan who people judged was a victim of his life in the fast lane.

In other words, Dean was like a good middle-class boy who thinks he fits in until interior voices tell him he doesn't, and outsiders try to shame him with guilt.

James Dean died a rebel forever. That's what queers are. It takes an act of rebellion, an act of revolution to come out of the closet, and then—the sucker punch!—not get sucked down into gay culture where a lifestyle is not a life.

If readers thought I brought "something special" to the leather culture of *Drummer*, it was, maybe, simply that quintessence of liberated masculine-identified gay male I saw in the rebellious fuck-you stare of James Dean.

Because of his face that had validated a generation of young men, I changed the face of *Drummer* during my three years as editor in chief and validated the new generation of homomasculine men

- with my pen writing about our authentic leather scene and not about camp,
- with my own camera shooting real people who were players one could meet in real life, and
- with my grassroots *Drummer* Outreach to readers to participate in my gonzo journalism by sending in photos of their accessible selves for features like my "Tough Customers" so that *Drummer* was not filled only with the faces and bodies of don't-touch-me models.

If I hadn't struggled against all odds to write about a man like James Dean, I might not have become muscular enough to write *Drummer*.

Back in the 1950s when, as a teenager, I had to read between the lines, and then learned to write between the lines, I ached for the day I would write lines that were out, honest, *verite*, masculine, and erotic.

That's how James Dean fitted me up for *Drummer*.

He was identity.

He was desire.

He was a hot dangerous image a careful driver sees approaching in a rear-view mirror.

Speeding forward at 125 mph in his silver Porsche convertible, James Dean hovered in the back of the heads of *Drummer* readers in the 1970s.

II. The feature article as published in *Preview: The Family Entertainment Guide*, June 1962

**In a short, tragic career,
brooding James Dean unknowingly toyed
with the emotions of a generation and
even after death held their misguided loyalty.
Fortunately, the years have erased
this adulation for one who was,
in truth, no more than a...**

Magnificent Failure
by Jack Fritscher writing as John J. Fritscher

Near seven years his name has lived on three short years of limelit life. Valentino could not die and Byron will be seen forever at Missolonghi. Yet in the ruins of abrupt tragedy, when his searching was not ended, there was frozen in last season's generation the memory of the sweet lost pains of adolescence and the old times that are forever gone.

In September, 1955, when James Dean sped to his death in California's fertile Salinas Valley, Warner Bros. calculated and shook its collective head at the loss. The first crush of mail was indignant, almost hysterically resentful, piqued with premature death. Then the letters slowed to a trickle and Hollywood recognized the chilling calm that leads to obscurity. Yet in December there was a surprising increase; January delivered 3,000 letters; and by summer, 1956, the studio was averaging 7,000 letters a month with payment enclosed for photographs of James Byron Dean.

The for-once-amazed press agentry was stymied by the gratuitous flood of mail. From mouth to mouth spread the personal commitment to his memory, the adulation, the rumors. Through the high schools and junior colleges of the nation the secret whispered that Jimmy Dean was not dead, that he was horribly disfigured, temporarily insane, hidden away. The public demanded the whole truth about the young actor who lived and died almost between the blinks of a weary world's eye.

From city to city vulgar stage shows promised the ectoplasmic return of James Dean in person, on stage. A sculptured head sold out nationally at thirty dollars a likeness. Magazines entirely devoted to Dean vended hundreds of thousands of copies. His two released motion pictures were requested and rebooked across the country. Columbia Records pressed an extended play album of tortured painful music from the soundtracks of his pictures. A Forest record entitled *His Name Was Dean* sold 25,000 copies the first week of release.

What had begun spontaneously was perverted by calculation. The money changers were marching through hysteria.

Warner Bros., rolling with the punches, decided to hold the last Dean movie in reserve with release postponed "out of respect for a fine actor's memory." It was a gamble, shelving momentarily Edna Ferber's *Giant*, holding back the completed performances of big-box-office Elizabeth Taylor and Rock Hudson; but it was also an ace in the hole. Everyone knew Jimmy Dean had completed his last scene as Jett Rink only three days before his death.

Fourteen months after the accident, with excitement at a fever pitch, Warners released director George Stevens' *Giant* which in the ensuing weeks won seven major Academy Award nominations, not the least meaningful of which was the posthumous nomination given James Dean for the best performance by an actor. With full integrity, but wounding loyalists' hearts, Yul Brynner went on to win that coveted 1956 Oscar for his performance in *The King and I*. It had been Dean's last chance.

Against the glutted background of such neon ballyhoo, it is easy to miss the personality of the twenty-four-year-old youth who, unknowing, toyed psychologically with the emotions of a generation. James Dean was a magnificent failure.

Tragedy stalked Dean's life and the shadows were always with him, driving him, tormenting him. "My mother died on me when I was nine years old," he cried melodramatically in a studio tantrum. "What does she expect me to do? Do it all by myself?"

From childhood he blamed himself for Mildred Dean's death by cancer and in blaming himself alternately loved and hated her the more for the pain he remembered in her face, for her enervating abandonment of him.

There was nothing in his life with his Uncle Marcus and Aunt Ortense to explain the moodiness, the brooding among the coffins in the Fairmont, Indiana, general store. His environment had been normal enough, adjustable; but Mildred had dreamed great unfulfilled dreams for herself and when they had not worked for her, perhaps they would work for Jimmy. They had to; they must.

James Byron Dean. The *James* was plain for Indiana; but the *Byron* was for Mildred. In Fairmont, there was no time for himself, troubled among the constant ghosts of his mother, plotting ways to repay her for dying. Existentially he did not know who he was or what he was, crippled, force-molded by the hope and wild dreams of his farm-girl mother.

The years in Indiana, portending no future, James Dean went to California, in 1950, to see his father; but the myths are tangled with the truth. Few knew him well; none knew him long. The devotees of such things can relate what stations there are.

In audition, the discerning Elia Kazan saw in the turbulent young student from U.C.L.A. the deep feeling and raw communication that translates a particular actor into a portrayal. Dean won the role of Steinbeck's tortured Cal Trask in *East of Eden*. The critics acclaimed his performance precisely because over the crags of tragedy his portrayal came to grips with truly human problems, something Jimmy Dean could not manage in real life.

Now he was on the way—with the gnawing emptiness still there. He received excellent reviews in the Broadway play, *See the Jaguar*, but the show itself closed within a week. Yet a niche seemed to be opening for his life. "Acting," he said, "is the greatest. Every town has its successful lawyers, but how many successful actors has it got? The first time I found out acting was as big a challenge as law, I flipped."

But the twenty-two-year-old actor could not reverse the equation. He gave life to characters in scripts, but the celluloid solutions gave him no peace in return. The title of his second picture, *Rebel Without a Cause*, fitted him well. Tormented genius? Angry man? Sullen, ill-tempered, snapping back at the acclaim given his artistry, he was despite the euphemisms of the magazines, an emotionally stunted misfit.

About his life there was nothing pretty. He did not drink, but he smoked too much, slept too little, drove too fast. He was running at a pace that would not let him see where he had been or where he was going. It was tragic when his $7,000 Porsche Spyder plowed into a Ford driven by a Salinas farmer. Mildred Dean had always wanted to protect him from farmers.

Any psychologist can explain idolization. Cult is a question of identity and in the case of James Dean adolescence found its Self, its personification.

Always emotionally immature, he was the heroic example of rebellion to adolescents experiencing normal emotional disturbances at the proper age. He rebelled against conformity and he not only got away with it, he got rich at it.

And there was insurance. He was solid. He was dead. His cycle was complete. There was no danger that once the investment of identification had been made he would desert his promises and fly to the adult society that youth imagines so callously wanting.

Identification enables one to regain an object that has been lost; in identifying with a loved person who has died or from whom one has been separated, the lost person's expressiveness becomes reincarnated as an incorporated feature of one's personality.

James Dean was dead; he had this appeal of lost tragedy and it found complementary expression in the varying degrees of sympathetic imitation characteristic of his prep-school followers. They subconsciously resolved he had not died in vain. A little of his struggle, a little of him, was living in them.

Everyone knew, even in the furor of 1956, that he had been hardly better than he should have been, that his inappropriate aggressiveness had repelled all but two close friends; but few paid ardent attention to his personal life. What had had important influence, what had been seen by millions, was the film image he had projected.

Sympathy was given him in *East of Eden*; identification with him was made in the searching nobility of *Rebel Without a Cause*; and the laurels of emotive versatility were paid him for *Giant*. Whatever James Dean was as a person, as an actor he was an artist eliciting an artist's due.

In the face of young legends, the phenomenon of James Dean has paled slowly and it has paled inevitably. The youngsters of seven years ago have outgrown the need for the expressive example of the boy who could not outgrow the tangles of his maternally dominated life; and now these young adults, content like the slowly-aging and little-increasing sets of Garland and Sinatra fans, are not rejecting and forgetting the James Dean of their nonage.

He is recalled with a wistful smile and a dash of pity; for his whole anguished life is a commemorative symbol of unresolved maturity's most temporarily endless period.

Another generation will have another lord; but those who remember like to think this was a little different, that he sparked a minute of truth, that for one brief shining moment when he was needed, James Dean was someone good and someone very special.

The secret of the spontaneity was that despite everything, despite all his personal shortcomings, his lost nobility flickered in empathy with every gangling kid whoever stood alone and aching on the threshold of the world. He seemed to understand the misunderstood.

In 1957, a partially fictionalized biography ended quintessentially: "Do not judge me as James Byron Dean. I am the man you dreamed me to be. I am the parts I played throughout my meager yesterdays. I am the young and the lonely and the lost. I will remain a part of every one of you who knew of me."

Even in life he was more spirit than flesh.

Anticipating *Drummer* and the Gay Press

In 1956 in high school at the Pontifical College Josephinum, I began as a sixteen-year-old book-review editor for *The Josephinum Review*, and was the high-school senior reporter for the stodgy *Pravda* student publication, *The Ad Rem*. In 1960, I started up an alternative, but officially tolerated, college magazine which — referencing the "Body Electric" — I titled *Pulse*. The attitude and objectives and inter-activity in my introductory editorial (read: manifesto!) in the first issue, Halloween 1960, could just as well have been my first editorial in *Drummer* in 1977.

In 1960, I was militant against the apathy and passivity of seminarians who — stultified in the boring and conformist 1950s we had just exited — were not yet awake to the fact that Jack Kennedy signaled something as new for the American 1960s as Stonewall signaled for the gay 1970s. As a crusading college magazine editor, I was kept under strict surveillance by priests and was very nearly expelled for radical ideas. The disciplinarian Reverend Alfred E. Camp, called me into his office after my first issue, pounded his desk with his fist as hard as he could, and exploded with the line, "I am the editor of this magazine." I thought he was hallucinating. I had known him when he was a seminarian, and he remained a cunt even after his ordination to the priesthood.

As editor at the dawn of the 1960s, I called for social activism among the largely passive student body, and my stories in *Pulse* contained camp writing like:

> She acted strangely, as vampires will. Come to think of it, I did only see her at night. As I imagine it now, it does seem to detract from the romance of it all; she, lying there in her cold little tomb the whole day long, an extra-dry martini in one hand, Balzac in the other....I saw them drive a stake through her heart. "Good Lord, man, what are you doing?" I cried just making

the scene. "Well," he said, "I'm not giving her a facial, that's for surenik."

My writing—a clue to my character—was the beginning of the Catholic Church threatening me for coloring outside the lines. Many of my fellow seminarians—like the future "Prince of the Church" Bernard Cardinal Law dragging his persona and his kveeny entourage around the campus—seemed hungry for the status of the priesthood: life in a parish rectory staffed by cook and housekeeper; golf with rich parishioners at their country club; and Buicks!

I wanted to be like the romantic French worker priests who lived among their poor parishioners, fought for workers' rights, and earned their own keep. Pope Pius XII condemned the worker priests for being too close to Communism; he said nothing about the parish priests who were too close to capitalism.

In a certain underground resistance of "forbidden books and authors," I was sometimes able to read *The Catholic Worker* newspaper edited by the ardent, progressive, and saintly Catholic journalist Dorothy Day (1897-1980). (My mother's maiden name was *Day*.)

In January 1960, I was twenty years old. In two years, I would be living in the Negro slums of Chicago's South Side, and working for civil rights with leftist organizer Saul Alinsky and his grassroots "The Woodlawn Organization" (TWO).

Not quite knowing that DNA was about to throw the curve ball of homosexuality into my young life, I was four years from finding gay sex in 1964 at Chicago's twenty-four-story Lawson YMCA—where descending the staircase from the nude sunroof down past the cubicle rooms to the basement pool was like performing the gay-waiter title number in that year's biggest Broadway hit, *Hello Dolly!*

Before the delicious deluge of the Swinging 60s, I wrote this editorial in what would become my editorial style in *Drummer*:

Pulse Magazine, Editorial, First Issue, Halloween 1960,

Trick or Treat the *Pulse* you now feel is yours.

Here is your first issue of "College *Mad*," a bouillon potpourri of college life. It is frankly an experiment, an expedition into the recesses of the student scene: the serious, the absurd, the off-beat, the up-beat.

It is intended as a sampling and taste of current opinions, preferences, and trends. It purports to be a review of creative student craftsmanship and as such welcomes all manuscripts, ideas, and contributions of whatever kind.

The format is expansive and dynamic enough to include a new, fresh approach in each issue. Published once a quarter, the May segment will be issued as a college yearbook [because we didn't have one].

The purpose is entertainment; the policy is truth, rarely varnished and often raw. Suggestions, gripes, letters to the editor, complaints? Drop them off anonymously. No names will be used—in fact, the anonymity is half the fun and all the freedom of saying what you have to say in a place where you will be heard.

The title *Pulse* is an exclamatory reaction to the general acrotism of the college students. Nine out of ten collegians have a ring in the nose. [No one could have predicted that the metaphor would years later transgress into into a fashion accessory.] But that servility can be broken.

Lastly, this issue is not perfect. We hope each succeeding one will be better as you make it known what you want: more about politics? Monsters? Philosophy? Liturgy? Fellow students?

"We stand on the edge of a New Frontier. Give us your voice, your hand...."

Address all correspondence: The Editor, Suite 233.

═══

James Dean 147

III. Eyewitness Illustrations

Catholic Preview of Entertainment (June 1962) published Fritscher's closeted feature, "James Dean: Magnificent Failure."

 Captions: Eyewitness documentation of the existence of graphics providing internal evidence supporting Jack Fritscher's text are located in the Jack Fritscher and Mark Hemry GLBT History collection. Out of respect for issues of copyright, model releases, permissions, and privacy, some graphics are not available for publication at this time, but can be shown by appointment.

| Eyewitness Illustration | Book cover. *James Dean, A Biography* by William Bast, New York: Ballantine Books, 1956. Having had William Bast's closeted biography of his life with James Dean on his bookshelf in the 1950s, Fritscher abandoned Bast's pre-Stonewall timidity when he wrote his own frank erotic biography of his life with photographer Robert Mapplethorpe titled *Mapplethorpe: Assault with a Deadly Camera.* |

| Eyewitness Illustration | Two book covers. *A Street Car Named Desire* by Tennessee Williams, Signet, 1951. *One Arm and Other Stories* by Tennessee Williams, New Directions, 1954. Having written academia's first doctoral dissertation on Tennessee Williams (1967), Fritscher continued to reference Williams' influence on homomasculine leather culture in Williams' scripts and casting, and made Tennessee Williams part of the theatrical subtext and ritual iconography of *Drummer: A Streetcar Named Desire, Suddenly Last Summer,* "One Arm," and "Desire and the Black Masseur." |

The Untimely Death of J. Cristobal

> Written in April 1963, this short story was published in respected magazine of the Dominican Order, *The Torch*, Volume XLVIII, Number 2, February 1964.
> I. Author's Eyewitness Historical Context written July 25, 2004
> II. The short story as published in *The Torch*, Volume XLVIII, Number 2, February 1964
> III. Eyewitness Illustrations

I. Author's Eyewitness Historical Context written July 25, 2004

I wrote this story while an innocent boy-seminarian at the Pontifical College Josephinum where from age fourteen to twenty-four I had to listen every day at lunch to gory-detailed readings from *The Roman Martyrology* in which Roman soldiers ripped the nipples off Saint Agnes with red hot iron pincers; during other lunches, Roman soldiers who had converted to Christianity were whipped by pagan Roman soldiers who tied them up naked and laid them out on frozen lakes until they died or recanted as one did, "but died anyway in a bath of tepid water." Why, the nudity alone to a fourteen-year-old boy was hotter than the gladiators and martyrs in the Colosseum in *Quo Vadis?*

Thus impressed, I exited the Josephinum forever on December 15, 1963, as this "J. Cristobal" story was about to go to press. In early 1963, I had designed this S&M noir story as an homage to Hemingway's Spanish stories and to the New Testament reportage of Veronica and her veil (the camera), the death of Christ with his mother as witness, and Judas's betrayal of a man-to-man kiss.

I showed the final typed draft of this story to seminarian David Fellhauer who had recently been my "potty pal"—that was the term—when we had shared the same bathroom connecting our two rooms. We had been friends for ten years since we were fourteen. Alphabetical seating in the classroom had thrown us together as Fellhauer, Fritscher, etc., and I, who had never even heard words such as *queer*, had fixated on the back of his straight neck and the burr of his flattop and his handsome Texas profile, and I hid mash notes in his Latin book signed "The Phantom." Omigod. We were both fourteen; but as freshmen in 1953, he was already mature, and shaving, and he smoked even though it was against the rules, and he was great pals with our other classmate from Texas, the muscular Carl Poirot who had a tattoo that none of us nicer boys ever spoke about. I had no concept of sex; I only wanted "to be like them."

So in April 1963, I told him that the "J. Cristobal" story had been sent by a freelance author to *The Josephinum Review*, and that I was supposed to edit it, and what did he think of it. He said he thought the story was written by a homosexual sadist. (I didn't even know that such a category existed!) He was kind enough not to let on if he thought I was the author, but I was secretly delighted to know I had company out in the big world.

Since 1990, David Fellhauer has been the Catholic bishop of Victoria, Texas, and, while he has otherwise been a magnificent prelate, he has allegedly admitted that he made an administrative mistake in handling the diocesan re-assignment of a priest suspected of molestation of minors. If he pegged me by reading four typed pages of fiction in 1963, how did he, reading massive legal documents, miss what he should have done in Texas in 1993? But then, he did nothing about me.

I was, even as a boy ingenue who played football and basketball and softball, not perceived as homosexual because a queer in our seminary training was defined as "a man who comes up to you in a bus station, and you kick him in the groin." That is an exact quote (1955) from the Dean of Discipline, the Reverend George Kempker, USMC, who told of his nights keeping watch as chaplain in WWII barracks where young Catholic soldiers slept with both hands outside the blankets, fingers wrapped in their rosaries. Because the mostly farm-boy seminarians had no keyword for an ordinary gay boy, some of the more astute kidded me about being a writer and a bon vivant. Was that code? What kind of popularity was it when high-school boys and then college seminarians invited me to the woods several times a week to struggle in what we called slow-motion movie wrestling in jeans and T-shirts with no sex involved? Once, at seventeen, I noticed one of my favorite wrestling partners had a hardon in his jeans, and without mentioning why, I told him we could never wrestle again. All he said was, "It's your fault." I didn't get it; his hardon was his own doing; his mortal sin came from something unspoken inside him, not from me in my clueless chastity. And then he said, "You're so pretty you should be a girl." My fist bloodied his nose.

When David Fellhauer wrote to me in the 1960s, he addressed me as "Dear Worldly Jack." At the same post-seminary time—say, 11/6/68, a certain wonderful Jim Pogue in Chicago was writing me thank-you letters addressed: "Beloved Catamite! Glorious Ganymede! Voluptuous Whore!"

The Untimely Death of J. Cristobal

The polarity was perfect for this Gemini.

For biographical purposes, the two quotes following, may be useful expository sketches at the beginning of this series of books.

My college graduation yearbook (1961) characterized "John Fritscher" with the artsy profile:

> This young knave about campus has been involved in muchly [*sic*, current slang] as co-author of Glee Club Show 1959...Choir 3 and 4. *Josephinum Review* staff, stage crew...likes stereo soundtracks, Georges Rouault, horrible puns, and has a secret ambition to live in Greenwich Village...often seen hatching new "insanities" for public consumption....has a Puritan conscience but the will of a Nietzsche; would dive off the 30-story bell tower into a damp hankie for a laugh.

Sixteen years before, my kindergarten teacher inked in on my report card (1944-1945):

> Jackie...converses well.... has definite ideas and is not afraid to express them... Very expressive... Tells experiences very fluently.... Good balance in giving and taking and can be assertive.... Shows ability to solve problems.... Does good art work.... skips well.... shows interest in trying to sing a tune which is an improvement. Also loves stories.... In spontaneity, he is independent.... Stands up for his rights.... Is inclined to tattle..... He should do well in first grade.

In the on-going tattling department, some other bishops and one cardinal who were my schoolmates include Bishop William Skylstad (current president of the United States Conference of Catholic Bishops), Bishop X [my good straight friend whose name is deleted], and Bernard Cardinal Law who was infamous for his molestation cover-ups in Boston. After Bernie Law gave his sworn deposition in Massachusetts, playwright Michael Murphy adapted Law's words to expose the nature of "sins of omission" in *Sin: A Cardinal Deposed* which, as a drama, was positively reviewed in *Variety*, June 28-July 11, 2004. As for Bernie Law, the Pope swiftly swept him off to Rome and installed him in a palace as a protected Prince of the Church, safe from future testimony in the US.

That back story said, my S&M-y noir tale of "J. Cristobal" had to be approved by papal censors before I was allowed to mail it to an assortment of editors in the Catholic press. Perhaps they enjoyed it.

II. The short story as published in *The Torch*, Volume XLVIII, Number 2, February 1964

The Untimely Death of J. Cristobal
by Jack Fritscher writing as John J. Fritscher

"You did not read about it in the North American papers, *señor*. What is such a man in such a little country that you should read about him? To you it is all the same. And to us. But this time to me it was different, *señor. Si, muy diferente.*"

In the Rio bar, the dark little man with the rheumy eyes sat across from me, elbows and eager arms on the table, gesturing, never resting. His gabardine shirt was wrinkled from the heat and beads of sweat diffracted the hotel light across his low forehead. He did not quite fill the slack folds of his dirty Panama suit.

"It was in the Spring of last year the revolution failed. He had not wanted to lead us, but his father had the promise of him. That was his first mistake—that he did not have it to heart in him. But we did not know it then. And many do not know it even now.

"When we took and gave him the republic and the former *Presidente*, he accepted the one and exiled the other. His second mistake. He should have had him lawfully tried and shot him then, even as a year later the evil one returned and killed him. But he could kill nothing needlessly. He had not really the *cojones* even for the bull ring.

"In that year life was good but everyone wanted it better. How much can a man do in a few months? He was a *General* not a god." His shoulders shrugged in disbelief at what he was to say and the wine glass trembled before his lips. "And then, one night the *Presidente* came back across the frontier and down the mountains to the Capital. Before dawn the main regiments were his and the fighting and rioting was over by lunch. In the evening they danced in the streets. Their feet paid no more mind to what had come to pass than did their heads. Who is the strongest, he should rule them. Until his strength begins to pinch their feet.

"The next day, *señor*, there was a grand trial in the sports arena and there he was condemned to die as befitted a traitor who was part-Indian from the hills. While the fiesta went on above, he was delivered to the common soldiers' quarters in the locker rooms below. And they did not treat him kindly. After he was dead I saw close up the marks on his body. But he was not so fortunate as to die from their beating.

"I am not so sure what happened to him the rest of the day. I think, perhaps, he was interrogated much the same as we all were."

I filled his glass again, looking the while into those dark eyes that pleaded for me to see their secrets without his telling me. But I wanted to hear him out, even at the late hour. He sighed and sank back into his chair. For a long while he did not speak.

"The next day was declared another fiesta and early in the morning a bull was let loose in the streets. The brave young men tried to hang their ladies' scarves on his horns. Three of them were gored and one the devil crushed to death against a wall. Nothing was low-key that day and blood-lust ran high.

"The bull was killed, *señor*, torn apart by the mob, in front of the police garrison. And the timing was perfect. Before they could even think on what they had done, the *prisonero* was dragged into the street with two of his cabinet ministers. The one did not look half-alive even then. They were hitched like stupid oxen to the former *General*'s official car and made to drag it through the jammed streets.

"There were words on the car that should have made the women turn away in shame. But they did not. Wherever they passed, on their descent to the plain outside the city there was music and laughter and young men spitting and shouting *General! General!* And when the procession had gone, they turned back to their women. It was not every day such a greedy one meets the peoples' justice they said.

But one there was one who did not spit at him. She stood behind the mob lining the streets. The *General* did not see her, but I heard she was there. It was from her that he drew his Indian blood that excused all this. She was alone because, as I said, the *General*'s father had been killed by the *Presidente* and the *General* himself had never married. He did not even keep a woman. And many held even this against him.

"Halfway to the edge of the Capital, the cabinet minister, the one I thought to be dying, fell into the street. Lying there, he was missing, anyone could see, the fingers from his left hand. He must have died while they kicked him because they threw his body into the car...I can tell no more."

He stood up to leave and his chair fell backwards to the floor. "I am sorry." he said. "I should tell you this not at all. *Por favor*, excuse me."

"Please," I asked, "I must know the rest."

"No, *señor*."

"You can't expect to lead me on for a whole evening, then tell me nothing."

"I promised you nothing, *amigo*, but to share your bottle of wine. The wine is gone and it is late."

"You mean you made the story up?"

"*Ojala!* That do I wish." He held his hand to his head.

"Let me drive you to your place. My car's outside."

"*Si, señor amigo*. You take me home." He started out the door taking a bottle from the counter. I dropped a bill and followed him. Outside he had propped his knees up against the car's dash and was nursing the bottle like a playing child who already had his fill. I got in.

"You want to know quickly what happened next, *señor*? Finally, they killed him, you know, but not without the sideshow. Every circus must have its sideshow. Three blocks from where they killed his friend and left the Indian lady standing, a crazy woman with a camera stood out in the crowd, not four feet from him and took his dirty little picture. The *policia* could not catch her in the crowd and she got away in the side streets. She'll have a pretty time of it, I think, looking. She can put it on her bureau and dream dreams of him at night–if she likes bruises and blood and the rope burning around his neck and shoulders. The crowd, they laughed at her, but mostly at the stupid running police.

"But then, not laughing, out on the plain below the city, while it was still morning, they shot the other cabinet minister and threw his body down from the cliff. But the *General* was not to be so lucky.

"Out there on the plain in our summertime, nothing grows because of the wind and the burning sun. It grows so hot the very stones dry and crack into dust. To this place had they made them drag the car. And it was here they tied the *General* to the black Packard roof, with his arms outstretched to the side windows.

"No one but the police came close to the execution because of the heat. And even they left long before the man was dead."

"It is not a good story," I said.

"It is not finished," he answered. "That evening the *policia* returned and found him dead as they had planned. The car was set afire and plunged over the gorge. They hoped to destroy completely all trace of him. But in the fall, his body was wrenched loose and thrown clear of the car. Later some of his people found it and buried him. They say there was not so much as a drop of blood left in his body, the sun had dried it so horribly."

I was driving slowly now through the wreckage of the Rio slums.

"I will walk from here," he said.

I pulled over. "It must have been terrible for you, his friend," I said.

He got out, closed the door, and bent back through the window. "It is terrible, *señor*, but I was not his friend."

"How do you mean?"

"The *General* spent much on 'his people' as he called them. The Minister of the Treasury could not watch money wasted like so many melons at a fiesta. *Por favor*, I am quite drunk."

He started away from the car.

"You said about the Minister of the Treasury?" I asked through the window.

"*Si!*" he called back. "You must know by now, *señor*. It was I, I who told the *Presidente* what night to cross back down the mountains."

The swinging glass bottle glistened, moving away, catching small flashes of the lights of the tumbled down world. And I sat there till long after he disappeared through the twisted alleys of darkness.

III. Eyewitness Illustrations

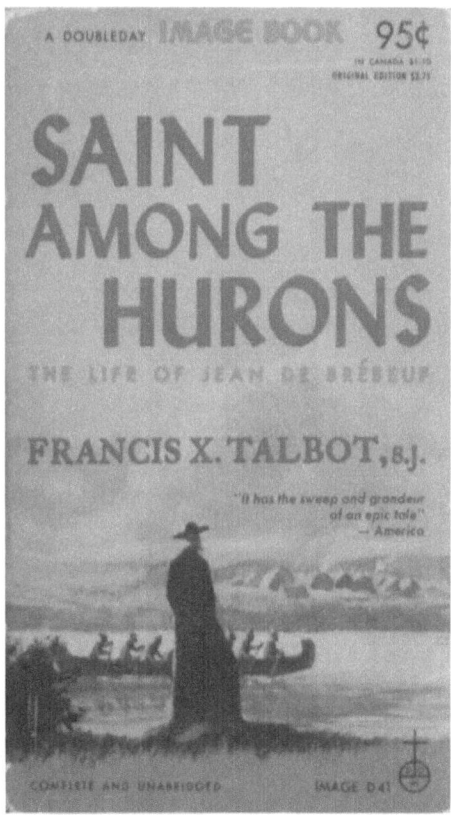

The weird DNA of leather culture. Under the Sign of the Cross dominating Western Civilization for two thousand years, the book of daily readings, *The Catholic Martyrology*, and other titles of saintly suffering, including the kidnap, whipping, and crucifixion of the nearly naked and muscular bearded Christ by uniformed soldiers of Fascist Rome, inspired generations of Catholic youth with vivid impressions of nudity, bondage, and sadomasochism. *Saint Among the Hurons* was a morose delectation about Native Americans torturing handsome French Jesuit priests naked in bondage. What a boy reads when he is fourteen marks him forever.

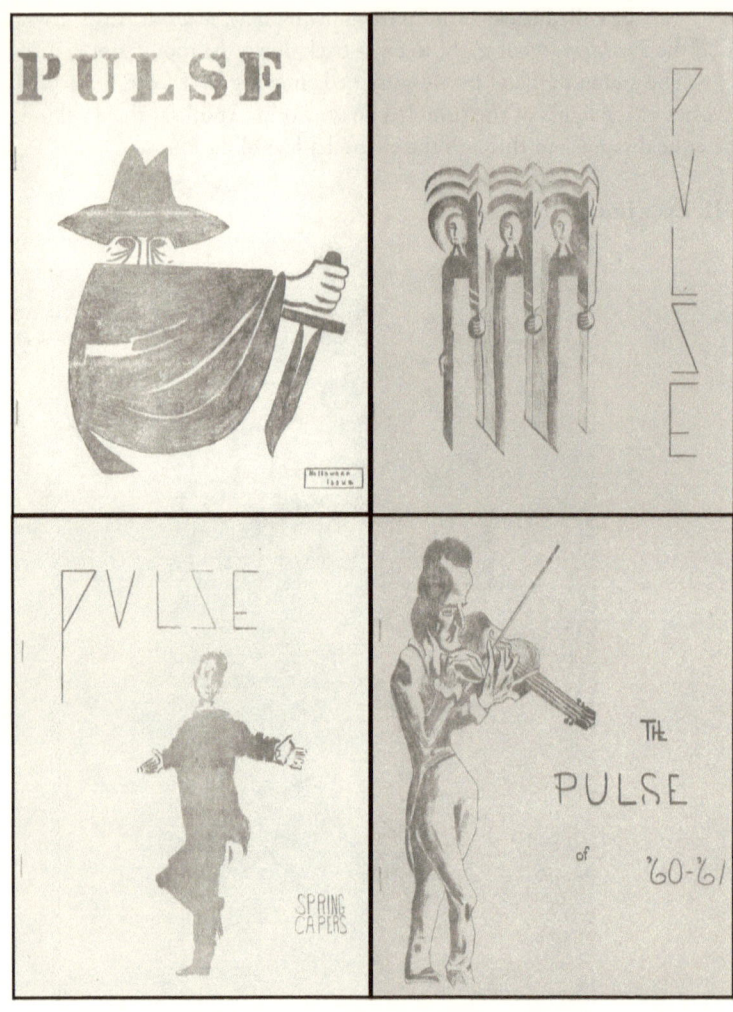

Editor Jack Fritscher, 20, started up the college magazine he dubbed *Pulse* at the Pontifical College Josephinum in 1960. The covers he designed, pre-dating Susan Sontag's definition of *camp* and Gilles Deleuze's *subtext*, almost outed themselves as screaming Rorschachs of the closeted life in the Catholic seminary. He was the only editor in chief of *Drummer* who also shot photographs for *Drummer* covers. *Pulse* covers ©Jack Fritscher.

The Untimely Death of J. Cristobal

Top: "Jack Fritscher, Seminarian," (second from left), ordained an exorcist by the Catholic Church, assists with the book in an ordination ritual conducted by the Pope's personal emissary, the Apostolic Delegate, Egidio Cardinal Vagnozzi, on the high altar at the Pontifical College Josephinum, 1962.

Bottom: *What They Did to the Kid: Confessions of an Altar Boy* (1965). One of Jack Fritscher's schoolmates for six years became Bernard Cardinal Law, infamous in Boston for his cover-up of the priest molestation scandals. The cover shown is the 2000 edition chosen by CNN among "The Top 100 You Are Reading."

The Church Mid-Decade and the Negro

> Written in Summer 1963, this essay was published in *The Torch*, Volume XLVIII, Number 1, February 1965.
> I-A. Author's Eyewitness Historical Context written October 21, 2001
> I-B. Author's Eyewitness Historical-Context Introduction written March 19, 1994
> II. The essay as published in *The Torch*, Volume XLVIII, Number 1, February 1965
> III. Eyewitness Illustrations

I-A. Author's Eyewitness Historical Context written October 21, 2001

Drummer Was Not Created from Nothing
Drummer and the DNA of Religious Iconography
Homosexuality Is a Religion

If I don't count the years (1949-1953) when I was a newspaper carrier for the *Peoria Journal Star*, for whom my father also worked as a branch manager, my career in publishing began in the Catholic press in 1957 under the direction of my mentor, the Reverend Leonard J. Fick, the editor of the long-running bi-weekly, *The Josephinum Review*. The *TJR* paid nothing to its volunteer staff—which was good training for writing for gay publishers who fail to pay. Starting as a proof reader and re-write editor on freelancers' submitted articles and stories, I also began writing book and film reviews.

In 1957-1958 when I was a seventeen-year-old high-school senior turning eighteen, I won a Quaker Oats writing contest, edited one book, sold two book reviews and three short stories and hauled in for the year an astonishing $90.50 which in today's dollars would be $2,443.50.

I moved on to social-justice feature articles such as the migrant worker article, "The Bitter Harvest," with Alice Ogle (*The Josephinum Review*, May 24, 1961) and my own "Objectives of the Second Vatican Council" (*TJR*, October 10, 1962). As a companion feature pre-dating my solo article, "The Church, Mid-Century and the Negro," my longtime straight friend, Frank E. Fortkamp, and I wrote about our civil rights experiences working together on the Chicago South Side in "Bringing Christ to Woodlawn: The Story of Last Summer's Most Ambitious, Large-Scale, Parish Census Project in the United States" (*TJR*, October 23, 1963). [This was the same neighborhood worked in the same way by Barack Obama in his own youth twenty-five years later: we shared the same mentor in the social organizer Saul Alinsky. —JF, 2008]

In a lighter entertainment vein, my short fiction published in *The Josephinum Review*, beginning when I was a teenager, was only nominally Catholic, and rather cynical—even mocking as one could be in those innocent days, verging on camp—in holiday stories such as "Timothy and the Shamrocks" (3/12/58), "Juicy Fruit Was Down That Day" (11/12/58), the anti-Valentine's story, "The Good-Timing Pinkhams of Chowder Lane" (2/13/63), and "It Came upon a Midnight, Dear" (ironically published 12/25/63, ten days after my final exit from the Josephinum).

Because *The Josephinum Review* paid $5 per story and article, I much preferred other Catholic rags such as *The Torch* that paid $18 per story for my tales spun out of my torrid Catholic vision of social justice: the closeted "The Odyssey of Bobby Joad" (08/61), the filial "Father and Son" (08/63), the Latino "The Untimely Death of J. Cristobal" (02/64), and the racial "Nobody Knows What Sorrow" (12/64).

As early as 1958, Leonard Fick connected me professionally to the publisher of his books, the Newman Press, in Westminster, MD. I loved the work, pretended I was in a Greenwich Village garret, and refused to consider that Newman Press was a sweat shop. For $50 per volume, I proofed, copy edited, rewrote, and re-translated several books written by German theologians such as the three-volume, 1500-page, *The Law of Christ* by Bernard Haring. I took my reward indirectly. When W. C. Fields was asked if he read the Bible, he responded he did—looking for loopholes. In a similar way, during the liberationist climate of Vatican II, I felt free in my editing and translating for Newman to loosen up some of the stringent German texts of moral theology to make life easier for real-life American Catholics.

The Catholic press has always been as provocative a niche as any other subculture's including the GLBT press.

My career as a Catholic writer reached toward worldly glamour with my very closeted features, "James Dean: Magnificent Failure," in *Catholic Preview of Entertainment* (06/62), and "*Darling*! What to Do at a Dirty Movie," *Today* magazine (05/66).

A Letter from the Some-Things-Never-Change Department

Catholic Preview of Entertainment Magazine
Catholic Periodicals, Inc.
Seminary Hill
Carmel, New York

July 23, 1962

Dear Mr. Fritscher,

Please excuse this delay in answering your letter of July 12 regarding copies and payment for your article, "James Dean: Magnificent Failure." But, I was on a one week vacation and upon returning I was struck with, of all the things, the mumps!

Nevertheless, I am sending, under separate cover, six copies of the June issue of "Catholic Preview" to your Willow Lane address.

I submitted a bill for $60, on April 9, to Mr. Saunders, the publisher. Although I have absolutely no authority in the financial end of this magazine—only Mr. Saunders has—I am more than embarrassed over the neglect shown you. I will inform him, most strongly, of this oversight, since I still feel that your piece was one of the best examples of writing ever carried by this publication. He is on vacation at the moment but will return on July 30.

Sincerely,
Robert Papierowicz
Executive Editor

Oh, and then there was that huge two-page—accidentally "beefcake-glamour"—photo-spread I wrote and photographed about a chaste seminarian's last days before ordination which seemed much like a groom's before his wedding. As I would for *Drummer* fifteen years later, I produced, wrote, and photographed "The Long Last Days Before the Priesthood: A Story for School's End."

It was a nostalgic piece for *The Josephinum Review* (05/22/63) published the week the pope's apostolic delegate arrived to conduct ordinations.

Naturally, as if I were producing a USMC recruiting layout, I picked the hottest and manliest of the twenty-five-year-olds being ordained. He was a southern blond, built and hairy. My camera gave me authority over him. He took my direction and he photographed handsomely, posing in priestly vestments, swathed in clouds of incense, and holding bell, book, and candle, as well as in a woods petting an adoring dog, and, of course, in a plaid bathrobe, and in Speedos sunk neck-deep in a rippling swimming pool that rendered his body surreal. I made the shoot so like a manly recruiting commercial for the priesthood, everyone involved let me get away with everything. The photos illustrated the long poem I wrote for the text. It was gay Catholic soft-core pornography. I can't imagine they didn't know what I was doing. The interaction was so eye-opening to me that seven months later I left the seminary to dedicate myself to turning such subliminals into overt homosexual text and photographs.

In 1969 and 1970, the Roman Catholic priest James Kane, who was also my longtime sex partner known as the leather priest Jim Kane, began publishing my socially progressive feature column in his monthly newspaper, *Dateline Colorado*. Also, in 1970, I noticed that Kevin Axe, one of my schoolmates from our eleven years at the Pontifical College Josephinum, had become editor of *Today* magazine that had published my Julie Christie and Dirk Bogarde *"Darling"* feature in 1966. I pitched him the idea of my writing solo an entire issue aimed at high-school kids needing to know how to interpret TV images and archetypes critically in a media-saturated age. He paid me $500 for the book-length *Television Today*, Volume 26, No. 2, February 1971. My source for my article on the literary interpretation of soap operas was Frank Olson, the New York lighting director who took me onto the set of *The Secret Storm* where he had a long and distinguished career. In the zero degrees of separation, I had known Olson for years because he was the longtime domestic lover of my longtime sex partner, Don Morrison, and together they were partners in the Anvil leather bar and were longstanding friends of my other Manhattan sex pal, Lou Thomas, the co-founder of Colt Studio and the founder of Target Studio.

This was the leather salon, and how it worked, long before I brought these guys into my *Drummer* salon.

While all my writing in *Drummer* and in my novels and short fiction is "Catholic" in the way that Woody Allen's films are "Jewish," my career as a Catholic author peaked with my 1965 novel, *What They Did to the Kid: Confessions of an Altar Boy*, which on its reprint in 2002 won an Indie Publishing Award as best novel of the year, and CNN named it "One of the 100 Novels You Are Reading."

The Church Mid-Decade and the Negro

It is my eyewitness observation, based on internal evidence, that *Drummer* was a kind of "Catholic" magazine in its strict observance of S&M borne out of western civilization's ingestion of the S&M of the Old and New Testaments, of *The Roman Martyrology*, and of the history of sculpture and painting representing great themes of Greek and Roman mythology that morphed into Christian theology, especially in the depictions of Christianity's dramatic moments of the passion and death of Christ. The Crucifixion is one of the main images, if not the chief image, of western art through the twentieth century, and it, and other images of heroic and saintly suffering at the top-hands of SPQR fascist authority, appeared variously in *Drummer* in writing, photographs, and drawings transmogrified into BDSM play. A literal example is the story, "Crucifixion Derby," written by Allen Eagles, illustrated by the Hun, and published in *Drummer*'s brother magazine, *Mach* 13 (November 1987).

As a gay man aware of my own unspoken civil rights in 1963, I wrote this essay, "The Church Mid-Decade and the Negro," to document my identity and feelings insofar as Black culture upended my bourgeois view of my self and opened up my queer view of my self. I might never have become a gay activist in the late 60s if I had not been a progressive Catholic activist for civil rights in the early 1960s. When I was twenty-four, I wrote this essay about my experiences when I was twenty-two and twenty-three in 1962 and 1963.

What happened to me living full time inside the African-American community at 63rd and Cottage Grove streets in Chicago, and what happened to me tutored by the Reverend Martin O'Farrell and the peerless Saul Alinsky, changed me forever. On philosophical reasons that had nothing to do with sexuality, the experience woke me up enough to justify my abandoning my eleven-year investment in the priesthood. The very act of exiting the Roman Catholic seminary in December 1963, uncloseted me sexually as recounted in *What They Did to the Kid*. I saw, and see, little difference between Black freedom's cultural expression and gay freedom's expression. I was born shameless; and without guilt, I exited the Catholic sex closet full of wonder.

In terms of iconography and worship, I have never experienced an existential disconnect between Catholicism and homosexuality. At that level, whatever the pope says has no effect because—unless the pope is speaking *ex cathedra* (formally) on matters of faith and morals—he is simply one of many theologians debating faith and morals. This is especially true as the glacial Church progresses in slow retreat from the medieval to the modern, changing its canon laws and theological understanding of eating fish on Friday, the who's who of saints, Limbo, cremation, condoms to prevent HIV, and even abortion which is permitted—progressive theologians insist—when the child is an unjust aggressor in the woman's body because of rape or incest. With all its absolutes and its condemnation of relativism, the Church evolves relatively, for instance, in condemning modern capital punishment which was once the main tool of the Inquisition run by the Church to punish progressive thinkers branded as heretics. Galileo, the heliocentrist, was lucky to have escaped alive. If these changes signify anything, they mean that Rome's vision of homosexuality was, is, and will be changing in the modernization of sexuality that will inevitably occur in Church teaching. If the priest molestation and child abuse scandals are anything, they are a wake-up call for the Church to update its understanding of sexuality and to bring it into the 21st century.

Politically, esthetically and erotically, I know that without Catholicism I could never have lived some of the rich rituals of S&M published both in *Drummer* and in some of the more sublime sex scenes, particularly the "crucifixion" of the bodybuilder, in *Some Dance to Remember*, Reel 3, Scene 7. Catholicism proved also to be a key to understanding the reactionary infrastructure of American witchcraft and Satanism in my research for *Popular Witchcraft* (1972; new edition 2005).

This essay written when I was twenty-three and completed when I was twenty-four, is Exhibit A of the kind of participatory journalism that always interested me, and that I specialized in at *Drummer*. When I was fourteen, I figured a writer had to live it up to write it down. I also knew that if anything interesting was going to happen to me, I had to make it happen. I exited the seminary twenty-three days after the assassination of my idealized lover, my dear Jack, in Dallas. November 22 ruined everything way more fundamentally than either Pearl Harbor or 9/11. By the time this essay was published in 1965, I was well on my way out of the closet and into the leather culture of Chicago, New York, and San Francisco.

In 1964, fresh out of the Josephinum and beginning graduate work at Loyola University in Chicago, my mentor, the Very Reverend Monsignor Leonard J. Fick continued to stand by me as he had since we first met in 1953. In a letter dated September 6, 1964, he who always typed sent me a handwritten note:

> Dear John, Here in the uplands of Missouri [where he visited his family in the summer], without benefit of typewriter, I shall only—by way of an interim reply to your recent communication—say that I have forwarded my appraisal to Loyola, and that I am sure the fellowship will be yours. I know nobody [underscored] more qualified. Best wishes, Leonard J. Fick.

Recalling him makes me well up with a deep and abiding human love. He was my Mr. Chips. This celibate and pure intellectual who had no children fathered me as writer from 1953 at age fourteen when he took me under his chaste wing and nurtured me as a student and assistant editor for eleven years. Only twice did he scold me. The first time was in an English class when I turned in a short story and he said in front of all the boys, "This is an excellent story; but because it does not fulfill the requirements of the assignment, it earns only a 92." The second time was when I split an infinitive, something no one did in the 1950s! I was mortified, and, even today, with grammar so changed and styles so relaxed, I find it a hard thing "to really do."

In 1975, and in 1977, while I was editing *Drummer*, Leonard J. Fick, twice requested me to consider returning to the Pontifical College Josephinum to teach writing and literature.

I could not travel back in time.

But I was carrying the past into the present.

To me, homosexuality is the Old Religion predating even the Druids, and certainly predating Judaism, Christianity, Islam, and Buddhism.

Gay people need a "text"—something to wave in the air like a Bible, a Koran, a grimoire. Why have we not learned from others? In the 1950s, Magus Gerald Gardiner in Britain dared declare witchcraft a religion and secured government protection. If we simply define and declare that homosexuality is a religion, then we become protected by the U. S. Constitution in the same way that Wiccans and Latter-Day Saints and born-again Protestant store-front fundamentalists and Scientologists are now protected because each declared it was a religion. All revealed religions had to announce their identity. There was a time when humans lived quite happily before there was any Judaism, any Christianity, and any Islam. Sourcing itself from inside human nature, homosexuality is not a revealed religion; it is an intuitive spirituality that grows out of human nature. For further reading, consider again the religious themes in *Some Dance to Remember*, and explicit arguments in *Popular Witchcraft: Straight from the Witch's Mouth*, second edition, 2005.

Editor's Note: In 2006, Matt and Andrej Koymasky wrote in *The Living Room - Gay Biographies*:

Themes and rituals of Catholicism thread through his [Fritscher's] fiction and nonfiction from the incarnational *Some Dance to Remember* to the passion and death of *Mapplethorpe: Assault with a Deadly Camera*. His formal training in philosophy, theology, literature, and criticism is the architecture of his sweeping historical work on witchcraft, the drama of Tennessee Williams, the photography of Robert Mapplethorpe, and the popular culture of homosexuality. His photography is a succession of heroic and suffering images from *The Roman Martyrology of the Saints*. www.andrejkoymasky.com, retrieved October 31, 2001

I-B. Author's Eyewitness Historical-Context Introduction written March 19, 1994

Tutored by the legendary father of community organizing, Saul Alinsky (1909-1972), I was among sixteen Catholic seminarians who in the summers of 1962 and 1963 worked with The Woodlawn Organization (TWO) out of Holy Cross Parish on the South Side of Chicago near the El stop at 63rd and Cottage Grove. I was an impressionable age twenty-three and twenty-four those summers I volunteered to help make a census of Blacks newly arrived in Chicago. At that time of the Vatican Council, the Catholic Church under Pope John XXIII was wide open to change, and the ideal—my personal ideal—was that of the French Worker priests who lived among the people, supported themselves, and did not live in a parish house with servants.

Wearing the proper "civil-rights uniform" of the time (black chinos, short-sleeved white shirt, button-down collar and tie), we smiling white boys went door to door in every tenement on every floor of every high-rise and carved-up house through the vast urban blocks of Holy Cross parish. To minimize any possible hostility, we steered politely clear of the Blackstone Rangers who were the indigenous street gang looking out for the good of the neighborhood. By 1968, the Blackstone Rangers worked against the infamous political machine of the "Fascist" Mayor Daley, which, of course, was one more straw that made him so angry that he unleashed his Chicago Police into the famous police riot at the Democratic Convention in 1968. So, in a way, the Blackstone Rangers were one of the many resistance fighters who led to the gay resistance at the Stonewall Riot in 1969, because we all learned something at the Democratic Convention. (From 1964-1967, whenever there was an election in Chicago, I volunteered as a poll watcher to "keep the dead from voting too many times.")

In the 1960s whirl of those wild days in civil rights, we seminarians literally marched with Martin Luther King, Jr. for a sit-in at the office of Mayor Daley who had us all carried out bodily by cops. I wasn't gay yet, but, ah, those hot cops! Perhaps this first-person feature essay from another time is the best way to illustrate the kind of street credentials I took into 1960s civil rights and 1970s gay liberation.

The Church Mid-Decade and the Negro

Civil rights activism was one of the experiences that I brought to the table at *Drummer*. When John Preston and other leatherfolk told me about their own work in Black civil rights in the 1960s, it proved that the Gay Power crusade for our own civil rights grew out of many GLBT people's experience working for the upside of Black Power within the African-American community.

Of eyewitness note: Around our table one hot summer evening, the fifty-something Saul Alinsky was holding his regular court and welcome sway, beguiling us boys with his stories and philosophy. He was very droll in telling us about his first encounters with Catholics. He said he was shocked when the first convent of nuns he organized gave him a novena card that offered up to God, in Saul's name, "300 Masses, 1,200 rosaries, and 20,000 ejaculations." He laughed remembering the face of the no-nonsense nun who explained that in Catholicism an *ejaculation* means a very short prayer such as "Sacred Heart of Jesus, have mercy." Into our virgin-pure adolescent ears, he was pouring his glistening subversive humor.

I loved Saul Alinsky as a brain who liberated me from everything I was before I met him.

The worst mistake of many that the Catholic Church ever made was sending us innocent boys off into such worldly, cynical, and saintly company. I think hardly more than one of the sixteen of us seminarians was later ordained a priest. Alinsky and the interracial experience itself taught us there was truth in the then popular song, "Moon River." There was "such a lot of world to see."

Research this same TWO history in Woodlawn as experienced and as written by my friend since boyhood and my colleague those two summers: the straight (Catholic and then Episcopal) priest, Frank E. Fortkamp, "Bringing Christ to Woodlawn: The Story of Last Summer's Most Ambitious, Large-scale, Parish Census Project in the United States," *The Josephinum Review*, October 23, 1963.

These Chicago activist summers were portrayed fictively in my gay "novel of the closet," *What They Did to the Kid: Confessions of an Altar Boy* (1965); *Kid* is a prequel to *Some Dance to Remember: A Memoir-Novel of San Francisco, 1970-1982*; the protagonist and supporting characters have the same names in *Kid* as they do in *Some Dance*.

When I wrote this feature article while a seminarian at the Pontifical College Josephinum in the summer of 1963, I did not quite know I was six months away from returning to Chicago to begin my career as a graduate student earning my doctorate at Loyola University of Chicago (1967). It took the death of the open-hearted and ecumenical Pope John XXIII on June 3, 1963, and the assassination of John F. Kennedy on November

22, 1963, to slap me fully awake. The briefly liberal world tilted on its axis; flat-world conservatives took over the Church and the American government, and we young ran into the streets waving James Baldwin's brand-new book, *The Fire Next Time*, and shouting, "Fire!"

"Do I really want to be integrated into a burning house?" James Baldwin asked.

As I headed forward to teach on a burning university campus beginning in 1965, I also carried his bipolar novel, *Giovanni's Room*, because Baldwin mixed questions of race and sex in a way that intrigued me personally as the gay liberation of the 1960s sparked into flame, and we homophiles seemed finally, free at last, to call ourselves *gay*.

It was, at that time, correct to use the word *Negro*.

II. **The essay as published in *The Torch*, Volume XLVIII, Number 1 (February 1965), The Official Publication of the Third Order of Saint Dominic, Reverend Francis N. Wendell, editor, 141 East 65th Street, New York, 10021**

The Church Mid-Decade and the Negro
by Jack Fritscher writing as John J. Fritscher

I am white, twenty-four, the son of a salesman's middle-class family. Despite the Civil Rights Bill I still live in the *de facto* segregated suburbs of a Midwestern city over 125,000 population. I am a student for the priesthood and I have sat on the floor of Chicago Mayor Daley's office. For the heat of the last two summers [1962 and 1963], I have been in Chicago. I have lived with the Negroes on Chicago's South Side. And since my return from the Black Belt many of my parents' friends tolerate me with the cool regard or the heated remarks sacred only to the memory of Benedict Arnold.

I am told by them that if they're prejudiced, then I am just as prejudiced—but the other way. If it seems that way to them, then I am sorry that I have not been clearer, kinder in expressing why I walked alone for the first time through a colored neighborhood. Why I wore a roman collar door to door and talked for hours to people living in unspeakable conditions. Why I marched and why I sat-in.

Like everyone else I've always seen and heard what I wanted to see and hear. But this time I tried to walk with my eyes wide open. I wanted

The Church Mid-Decade and the Negro

to find if really it was true what is said: that by negligence and silence, I and my comfortable neighbors and the Church I intend to serve all my life are somehow accessories before God to the injustices committed against Negroes.

I'd read that Mayor Daley had said ghettos do not exist in Chicago. I thought they did, but figured I could be wrong. And I *was* wrong if a thirty-two per cent male unemployment rate, subhuman housing, and vice and crime (all restricted in one neighborhood tighter than any zoning commission ever dreamed) are not symptoms of a ghetto existence.

One can prove anything by selecting examples, and in my first week in the area I could have verified any of the worst stories anyone has ever heard about slums and sin and other human beings. I could have lined them up: the junkies, the prostitutes, the alcoholics, the deviates, and the good people sunk despairingly deep in the vicious circle of their circumstances.

A walk down any street, a climb up any stairwell proves that we have not abolished slavery. We have perfected it. Before, a master at least had to feed and house his slave to protect his initial investment. Since Emancipation there is no purchasing, no investment to guard, and the master-society has been free to hire and fire, to use and abuse according to its own whim, and the needs of the "slave" be hanged. So what if he gets sick, killed, is ignorant and discriminated against. There's always more where he came from.

And precisely because there are more where he came from, the Negro in 1964 has reached at least a landing lit by outside legal light on his way up the cellar steps. But he started on that climb long before this mid-decade. The Negro has worked for freedom since the very first day of his captivity. Passive resistance is as old as the Plantation.

And by your mint julep if you don't think breakin' massa's new plow, forgettin' how to ruin massa's cotton gin, and havin' some ol' kind of mysterious misery every time massa needed something pronto wasn't passive resistance in its most primitive form, then think again.

But this resistance historically got bad publicity. It birthed, nursed, and weaned the full blown Negro stereotype that today is thankfully being laid to rest. My whole time on the South Side I did not hear one single wide-eyed chorus of "Summertime" or see one tap dancing bootblack or eat any Aunt Jemima pancakes. Instead, I saw individuals, people who basically were no different from the white society in which I had always lived. People who would have been the same were it not for discrimination and its ugly brood of children.

If I say Negroes are like this or like that, someone will always say, "Well I know one that isn't." Then let me say that Americans are like this or Catholics are like that and everyone knows I don't mean each and every American or Catholic, but rather the majority.

In the course of our work in Chicago's Woodlawn, we sixteen seminarians met and talked to more than a great majority of the forty thousand people in the neighborhood. We found the sensational all right: the characters right out of the novels of Richard Wright and James Baldwin. But more importantly, we found the people called *Negro*.

We found the good ordinary people trying to live ordinary family lives in a circle of appalling circumstances. We went door to door in hundreds of six-family dwellings inhabited by up to fourteen families. And we talked. And *how* we talked. If nothing else, we established communication with some of those people locked behind their tenement doors. We were Catholic priests to them, but we were also the first social contact many of them had made in the community. Since the area's entire population shifts about every three years, the neighborhood is a constant flux of new addresses. Many are Southern Negroes new to the city. Their adjustment from their former rural or small-town way-of-life is not easily made. Many of them do not known their neighbor across the hall, much less where the local church is, who the doctor is, whom to see for social help. And for as many who sit bitterly in their one-room walk-ups because the North is not the Promised Land, there are more who are attending night classes at local schools, more who recognize the difficulties in their neighborhood, more are worried to death over their children's future.

And here with the children is the impelling force driving the Negro to seek his rights. He wants education for his children so that applications for decent jobs can be made by qualified Negro applicants, so that life can be lived with some dignity of profession. He doesn't want his children to slide back into the morass that has stalled the Negro for centuries. Up to this past summer he was finding it more and more difficult to tell nine-year-old Suzie she couldn't go to this or that movie theater because she is Black; and more and more easy to explain to her why she must go with her father to a freedom march ("Because you're a human being, honey, and you have a right to live like one."), knowing full well that her participation in the demonstration would be awakening in her the social consciousness of a whole new generation.

The Civil Rights Bill has boosted the Negro's hopes and responsibilities enormously.

The Negro puts a different value on children than does our white "control-conscious" society. Perhaps because he has fewer other distractions his focus is electrically on the worth and future of his children as social entities. Even the names common among Negroes, outlines of the most famous heroes of American history from Washington to Lincoln to

Roosevelt and now John Kennedy, are clues to the aspirations American Negro parents dream for their children.

But why were we in Woodlawn? Negroes asked us that and we asked ourselves and each other. Monsignor John J. Egan, director of the Chicago Archdiocesan Conservation Council, answered us quite succinctly one July evening: "The religious institution which remains aloof from its neighborhood and whose administrators do not involve themselves with the aspirations, causes, and organizations of the neighborhood, is, by virtue of its symbolic role, denying God in that neighborhood."

With those fighting words no one wants to quarrel, least of all the pastor of Woodlawn's Holy Cross Parish, Father Martin Farrell. He it was who invited us to the South Side. He needed a large force to canvass his shifting parish population quickly. And he thought seminarians might jump at the chance to people the somewhat dry pages of their theology textbooks with real experience.

So we set out, frankly frightened at first, to teach and to learn. Ultimately we were there for a spiritual reason, to bring souls to Christ in the Church. But we quickly found that is done in a very concrete way.

The culture of many large northern cities has been largely shaped by Roman Catholics and their institutions. And Chicago is no exception. (Woodlawn itself had been Irish Catholic.) Thus with a basically Catholic spirit somewhat dominant in the city's social consciousness, one judges there can be little serious tackling of the still existing problems of segregation and discrimination if Catholics and Catholic parishes do not earnestly tackle them.

That was our place to begin, or rather to enter what Father Farrell had long before begun. That was how we came to sit on the Mayor's floor with four hundred Negro demonstrators, how we came to march in the NAACP's July 4th parade to Grant Park. This we could understand having heard often that you can't preach the gospel to an empty stomach.

Father Farrell's instrument for community improvement is the nonsectarian group, The Woodlawn Organization, in whose circle he has been a leader since its beginning. TWO has been called by sociologist advisor to Cardinal Montini (now Pope Paul VI), Saul Alinsky, "the most effective community organization of Negroes in America."

But besides TWO which pressures slum landlords, fights for neighborhood urban renewal on a local level, and crusades for all the justice lacking in everything from job discrimination to unequal education, Father Farrell has thrown his own parochial resources into the fray. In answer to the parents' concern for their children's education, he has opened his school to all area children, Catholic or not. And here our task took specific form: to flood the teeming neighborhood with literature about the "Sisters' School"; to spread information about the adult instruction classes; to awaken in the neighborhood conscience the fact that the Church is there, doing more than watching, actually caring what happens to their bodies and minds as well as their souls.

It is evident the Church simply cannot afford to miss the boat in the current social revolution and so lose the American Negro. The Church cannot afford to repeat the maneuvers made during the eighteenth-century Industrial Revolution when her slowness lost her the European working class. The Church either opens to the Negro now or never.

It's all very well and good to have one of the neighborhood status symbols be the children's attendance at the Sisters' School. (A status symbol and more because the children receive, besides the regular curriculum, a highly valued "training in goodness"—as the character formation is popularly called.) And it's also well and good that the Church draw in converts through its classes and its civic and social prominence in the community; that it help the mothers and fathers of families obtain all the rights owed to them and their children; that buses chartered for demonstrations leave from the Church door. It is well and good that this clamor after Rights is preached from the pulpit of the Catholic Church; but more than this, the Negro sitting in the pews hears that with every right comes a corresponding duty. Duty too he must discover. Duty too he must seek and fulfill to become an integral member of society.

The honor given by Negroes this summer to John Kennedy can compare only with the love given last summer to another John, the Twenty-third, whose picture, cut from magazines and torn from newspapers, was conspicuous in apartment after apartment, Catholic and non-Catholic. The Pontiff's name, in those first months after his death, was spoken with boundless admiration. And rightly so. For only the April before the summer he died had he said in *Pacem in Terris*: "...The conviction that all men are equal by reason of their natural dignity has been generally accepted. Hence racial discrimination can in no way be justified at least doctrinally or in theory. And this is of fundamental importance and significance for the formation of human society...For, if a man becomes conscious of his rights, he must become equally aware of his duties. Thus *he who possesses certain rights has likewise the duty to claim those rights as marks of his dignity, while all others have the obligation to acknowledge those rights and respect them.*" (Italics added)

The American Negro has heard the late head of the Catholic Church, the Vicar of Christ, saying such things on radio and television, in newspapers and in some Catholic pulpits. The ground is plowed for the Church. The seed is there. It must be nurtured carefully in the next months and coming years. For the Catholic Church, as a body already present in

The Church Mid-Decade and the Negro

society, can help through education and social action the implementation of the Civil Rights Bill and thus hasten the day when rats and hate and hunger no longer distract men from the care of their souls.

Because this social revolution will continue until justice is righted, I want my parents' friends to understand what is happening. I want everyone to know that every time a Negro minister is dragged down courthouse steps, Christ is dragged again; that every time a Negro girl is killed in a senseless Sunday School bombing, Christ is killed again; that subhuman housing, substandard education, all the devices and implements of racial hatred and prejudice have as their victim not a race or a mere cultural minority. They have as their victim Christ.

I want them all to know that my generation of Chaneys and Goodmans and Schwerners is in a state of revolution, and certain values once held can no longer be supported by antiquated law or outdated custom, by private agreement or public indifference. Already the barber in the shopping center near my home can no longer insist to me after a casual question that he will never cut a Negro's hair. Discrimination has always been immoral. Now it is illegal as well.

I want my good Catholic friends, even the ones who attend study clubs and Holy Name and Altar-Rosary, to know something that I found out about them, about the ones who say they have nothing against Negroes but don't want any next door. They say they know they are prejudiced, but they can't help it. But when they talk about it, it's clear they're not anti-Negro because Negroes have dark skins. Their prejudice is against filth and poverty and laziness and vice. These are what they hate. Not Negroes. And when these otherwise good people finally make this distinction, they see that discrimination in jobs and education has bred the poverty all must war against. They see that poverty breeds defeat and dirt and hopelessness and sin in whatever group it enters. It is then they see that it is not the victim, the Negro, that they hate. But rather it is the cause and the cancer itself, the denial of human dignity and rights implicit in discrimination, that they despise. And this practicing Catholics need to know for a right conscience; for prejudice, no matter how it is sliced, is sinful.

Christ was the world's greatest rebel. Christianity is the religion of revolution. And the Church in these days of ecumenical renewal is out to establish beachheads. Revolutions are not new to the Church and she knows how to handle them. The Church, founded in upheaval, has seen too much growth come from upheaval to cast any movement off lightly.

Every nation that ever rose and fell, collapsed because people who forgot how to suffer and sacrifice themselves for justice weakened its moral fiber. Today the American Negro character stands purified by centuries of patient suffering. Full integration has legally come. The racially incestuous barriers of cultures and ideas and blood will be melted away. And as the Negro is accepted into the society of American business and politics and religion and art, the very strength he brings to the transfusion, especially if guided by the social-moral doctrines of solid Christianity, well be for our country and our world the bringing in of a new hope.

III. Eyewitness Illustrations

The Church Mid-Decade and the Negro 175

Sequencing the genome of the gay press: How the early marginal gay press of *Drummer* grew out of the specific underground press of the Catholic press. Three short stories by Jack Fritscher, beginning as a teenager, published in the national biweekly *The Josephinum Review* between 1958 and 1963 when Fritscher left the closet of the Catholic priesthood for a life in Chicago.

Opposite page. "63rd and Cottage Grove, Chicago, 1963," three photographs. How "gay rights" evolved as "civil rights." In summers 1962 and 1963, Jack Fritscher, like many other gay people, was active in civil rights, marching with Martin Luther King, Jr., schooled by Saul Alinsky, and being carried bodily out of Mayor Richard Daley's office, while living and working in the ghetto at 63rd and Cottage Grove, Chicago. Pictured at the El stop corner that Black Muslims claimed as their own until a *detente cordiale* is Fritscher's fellow seminarian and longtime straight friend (since 1953), Frank E. Fortkamp, Episcopal vicar of Brunswick, MD (2007). Fritscher detailed this experience in his article "Church Mid-Decade" 1965.

As a prelude to the kind of photography layouts Jack Fritscher created for *Drummer*, the two photographs pictured are part of his photo feature "The Long, Last Days Before the Priesthood: A Story of School's End" which Fritscher wrote and photographed for *The Josephinum Review* (May 22, 1963). When he cast a real seminarian in his photographs, Fritscher chose a straight man who was as masculine, blond, and bear-like as the men who would later surface in his homomasculine photography in *Drummer*. Photographs by Jack Fritscher. ©Jack Fritscher

The Church Mid-Decade and the Negro 177

"Jack Fritscher and Roger Radloff," 1961. Fritscher and Radloff were longtime nonsexual friends and roommates at the Pontifical College Josephinum where Fritscher was the editor of the college paper, *Pulse*, as well as writer and editor for *The Josephinum Review*. In 1991, the Reverend Roger Radloff, a Jungian psychiatrist and priest in Miami, died of [Catholic obituary quote] "the dread disease of cancer" [unquote], after being—in the wider salon—a client of Fritscher's friend, David Hurles, whose Old Reliable studio specialized in photos and videos of rough trade. Photograph taken with Jack Fritscher's camera handed to a friend. ©Jack Fritscher.

 Captions: Eyewitness documentation of the existence of graphics providing internal evidence supporting Jack Fritscher's text are located in the Jack Fritscher and Mark Hemry GLBT History collection. Out of respect for issues of copyright, model releases, permissions, and privacy, some graphics are not available for publication at this time, but can be shown by appointment.

| Eyewitness Illustration | Photograph. "Jack Fritscher and Robert Mapplethorpe Entwined," Stompers Gallery, New York, 1979. Photographer as yet unknown. |

"Down at the River," 1959. Photograph by Jack Fritscher. ©1959, 2008 Jack Fritscher. "At age 20, in summer 1959, living in an innocent pre-verbal and pre-gay dream of the Platonic Ideal of homomasculinity, I composed and photographed my best straight friend since childhood in a blond-muscle shot that Chuck Renslow, Etienne, and Bob Mizer could have immediately published on the covers of *Mars, Triumph*, and *Physique Pictorial*, and that I could have published on the cover of the "Gay Jock Sports" issue *Drummer* 20 (January 1978). My quintessential 50-year-old photograph pegs me for what I am and for what my writing and photography are all about." —Jack Fritscher

Chicago 7

> Written February 1970 and published in *Dateline: Colorado*, March 1970.
> I. Author's Eyewitness Historical Context written December 12, 2001
> II. The feature essay as published in *Dateline: Colorado*, March 1970
> III. Eyewitness Illustrations

I. Author's Eyewitness Historical-Context Introduction written December 12, 2001

How the Police Riot at the 1968 Democratic Convention Facilitated the 1969 Stonewall Rebellion

Years before *Drummer*, the 1960s alerted us to resist fascism and its police enforcers by using the newspapers and magazines to promote art, freedom of expression and sexual rights which all add up to our inalienable rights to life, liberty, and the pursuit of happiness decreed in the Declaration of Independence. Having freedom of speech at rallies, freedom of the press in gay publications, and freedom to assemble peaceably in gay bars and baths are freedoms guaranteed by the First Amendment to the Constitution. As a professor in a university culture made volcanic by anti-Vietnam activism and a gay culture revolutionized by Stonewall, I wrote this "Chicago Seven" essay in February 1970 and it was published in March 1970 as an installment of my on-going media column for the monthly newspaper, *Dateline: Colorado*, Colorado Springs, edited by Reverend James Kane who was also the leather-priest Jim Kane who was several times featured in photographs in *Drummer*.

During that time of social revolution, one might observe, that editor Kane's publishing of my columns on art, media, and politics was a subversive contribution to the traditional Catholic press made by me, a seminarian, who was once almost a priest, and him, a priest who was on the verge of leaving the priesthood. As it was, Jim Kane and I were vacationing together and sleeping together having sex in an affair that lasted from 1968-1973, and in a friendship that crumbled but did not dissolve until 1989 when he was afflicted with senior dementia.

This article proposes taxing churches to fund art, and mentions gay bashing. As a longtime activist for social justice, civil rights, and peace, I need to explain that the Catholic press was once quite progressive before it was corrupted by the fundamentalism sweeping the planet in the 21st century. The same is true of the gay press which was progressive in its first years in the 1970s before being hijacked by politically correct fundamentalist conservatives in the 1980s.

For my "Chicago Seven" article, my original typed manuscript exists with edit marks made in red ink by Jim Kane who returned the original to me with copies of the published column which also exists. [Editor's note: See other columns on "media" written by Jack Fritscher and published in *Dateline Colorado*, edited by Jim Kane, at www.JackFritscher.com.]

The Chicago Seven were put on trial (September 24, 1969) for inciting a riot at the 1968 Democratic Convention in Chicago. Four of the "Chicago Seven" were Abbie Hoffman, Tom Hayden, Rennie Davis, and Jerry Rubin, with the side-wise participation of Allen Ginsberg, William Burroughs, Timothy Leary, Phil Ochs, and Judy Collins. The riot had, in fact, been caused by the police who opened the hostilities by moving in against guru Ginsberg and his gay followers in Lincoln Park, 11 PM, Sunday, August 25, the eve of the Convention. A year before Stonewall in New York, the fags in Chicago fought back. Both cop-riot and hippie-resistance spread out of Lincoln Park as captured in Haskell Wexler's dramatic film shot as *cinema verite* during the confrontations, *Medium Cool* (1969). The iron-fisted conservative fascist Mayor Richard Daley, confronted by the hippie Yippie gay protest, detailed nearly 25,000 police, soldiers, and National Guard who overshot their mark and began clubbing and gassing the rather bourgeois Convention crowd—live, on television, to the chant of "The Whole World Is Watching." Inside the Convention, at the same time, August 28, 1968, CBS News correspondent Dan Rather was slugged in the stomach on the Convention floor shouting, "Get your hands off me," causing CBS News anchor Walter Cronkite to say live on TV: "It looks like you have some thugs down there, Dan." Proving thirty-five years later in 2005 that "1984" goes on forever, similar thugs saw to Dan Rather's firing from CBS News because of—it was "reported"—his anti-Bush "reporting" during the 2004 presidential election.

In his *Palimpsest*, Gore Vidal explained that eventually the Chicago courts, rejecting that the 1968 bloodbath was a hippie riot, called this a "police riot"—that is, a riot caused by the police who beat and bloodied hippies and convention delegates and news reporters and anyone—male or female, young or old, black or white, gay or straight—opposed to the war. "The police," Vidal wrote, "were unselective in their porcine fury, and so, for once, they got a moderately bad press." (Page 211) Vidal's use of the word *porcine* is a polite way of writing that the police were loudly called *pigs* in Chicago.

Because the international press turned on the cops, because of the new awareness of live media coverage, and because of the chant to the media cameras "The Whole World Is Watching," this 1968 people's rebellion against the police was the activist model for the Stonewall rebellion ten months later in New York.

Without anti-war defiance of the cops in Chicago in August 1968, Stonewall might not have happened in Greenwich Village in June 1969.

In the zero degrees of separation and participation, I was living during this time of social trauma in and around Chicago. I wrote this article during the media frenzy of the "Chicago Seven" trial which ended February 20, 1970, eight days before this article was published after a last-minute edit update.

In such a climate of big-government fascism, I witnessed gay liberation rise up as an avatar of personal freedom.

If freedom to do what you want with your body is the ultimate political act, then *Drummer* was a sexual declaration of independence.

My social activism in Chicago, where I earned my doctorate at Loyola University (1968), began in 1961 when I lived on the South Side at 63rd and Cottage Grove working with the Woodlawn Organization at Holy Cross Parish, organized by the Reverend Martin Farrell, guided by Saul Alinsky and the NAACP, and marching—on one unforgettable occasion—with Martin Luther King, Jr. to a sit-in at Mayor Daley's office where each of us was literally carried out bodily by the Chicago police. See the articles, "Bringing Christ to Woodlawn" by Frank E. Fortkamp (*The Josephinum Review*, October 23, 1963) and "The Church Mid-Decade and the Negro" by Jack Fritscher (*The Torch*, Volume 58, February 1965, New York).

Some years later, another contributor to the gay press, John Preston, revealed he too had been working in the civil rights of race relations before he entered gay publishing. That, of course, was logical, because so many who became part of the GLBT civil rights movement were graduates of the struggle for Black civil rights.

II. The feature essay as published in *Dateline: Colorado*, March 1970, James Kane (Jim Kane), Editor

Art, Politics, and Revolution:
You are in the midst of the 2nd American Revolution

Chicago 7

Dateline Colorado Editor's Note [Jim Kane]: Dr. Fritscher writes in a serious vein this month about the interaction of art with our new rough-and-tumble American society. He here gives candid opinions on the secularizing, revolutionary world parents can expect for their children.

No matter what your opinion of the "Chicago Seven" trial, one fact is unmistakably clear. The arts, especially film, are of immense import to our revolutionary times. This came personally clear to me on New Year's afternoon, 1970.

It was a cold and gray day, a bad way to begin the new decade in Chicago. The political climate was even more depressing than the weather. Constantin Costa-Gavras' film *Z* had opened a few days earlier. Word-of-mouth said *Z* was good. I called some friends and took off.

I'll not soon forget that beginning of this year sitting next to Abbie Hoffman watching him watching *Z*. I had the sick feeling the film was about Abbie, and I wanted to ask Anita, his wife, if she felt that, too. Seven weeks later, another of the "Chicago Seven," Tom Hayden, husband of actress-activist Jane Fonda, stood in a Middle-America courtroom saying on his day of sentencing that he felt as if he were a character in *Z*. It was no accident that at the same time as the trial, a film was in town to comment on the difference between politics and justice.

Now *Z* has five Academy Award nominations and five of the "Chicago Seven" have maximum prison sentences. [With nominations for Best Picture, Best Director, Best Adapted Screenplay, Best Editing, and Best Foreign Film, the anti-fascist *Z* went on to win the 1970 Oscar for Best Foreign Film, and remains remarkably relevant to the American politics of George W. Bush. —JF]

CHICAGO: THAT BOGGLIN' TOWN

Chicago at best is a strange, artless place. Southern Blacks moving North don't move to Chicago. They move to 63rd and Cottage Grove in Chicago.

Displaced Southern Whites locate around Belmont or Argyle in Chicago and prey nights on the homosexuals cruising solitary in middle Lincoln Park. "The Patch," an Irish gang that grows out of the Catholic basketball courts up around Loyola Avenue, is neither as feisty nor as infamous as the militant Afro-American "Blackstone Rangers," but the Patch spawns more police vocations than any other gang in Chicago.

The "People's Park" at Halsted and Armitage is rocks since its neighborhood sponsor was murdered late last summer. He and his wife were killed while a friend of mine [the 2007 MacArthur Fellowship "Genius Award" writer, Stuart Dybek] sat studying late and deep next door. The next morning the detectives wondered why he had heard nothing; and he looked out on the play-yard swings of the children with the dead parents and said again, no, he had heard nothing.

The Spanish-American "Young Lords" gang continues making into a daycare center the local Protestant church emptied by the changing neighborhood. The Coven, a diabolical rock music group, can be reached c/o Dunwich, 25 East Chestnut, Chicago.

WITCH (*W*omen's *I*nternational *T*errorist *C*onspiracy from *H*ell) has its main national headquarters for the Women's Liberation Front in Chicago. And the blue-and-white cop cars are everywhere, sudden and tough, keeping all these parts and pieces in tight control.

ENTERTAINMENT'S PLACE IN A BURNING SOCIETY

No matter what the fine line between police protection and police state, the Chicago fact is clear that the city's population is divided. Some support the police as protection against the lawless; others say the police themselves are the lawless. Fear and over-reaction are the tunes they're fiddling in the city that has once already burned.

One side or the other over-reacted outside the Hilton Hotel during the 1968 Democratic Convention as the riot and the police beating of innocent conventioneers was televised live to the hippie chant "The Whole World Is Watching." Since then, more and more dissatisfied ordinary people have been dropping out. Haskell Wexler's beautiful *Medium Cool*—a film about how art might explain a riotous society—could not find an audience in Chicago where Wexler famously filmed it in Lincoln Park during the police riot at the Democratic Convention.

The *Chicago Sun-Times* liberal film critic, Roger Ebert, gave Wexler's film four reviews trying to hype it as a must-see. As a socially responsible critic, Ebert knows how art can clarify a confusing social situation. But he knows the double frustration of the artist in Chicago even better. "Reviewing a frothy piece of entertainment," Ebert said, "is a futile enterprise on the day when William Kunstler was sent to jail for four years and seven days."

Art in Chicago has hardly fared well. The movies are censored by the Chicago Film Board, a group of ladies whose Kabuki-like credentials are (no kidding) that they are widows of machine-politicians. The Aardvark Cinematheque, an experimental film emporium in Chicago's hip Old Town, was severely obstructed in its inception by Film Board censorship objections which interestingly were always over-ruled, after weeks of tension and fighting, by a higher appeals board of psychologists, professors, and artists who seemed to speak for more liberal Chicagoans.

If the Broadway musical *Hair* [which in each major city had a new edition] is representative of commercial theater now playing in Chicago, then "Chicago *Hair*"—unlike "New York *Hair*" or "LA *Hair*—is stripped of social-comment dialogue, because local satirical references that might be incendiary or revolutionary or sexual have been forbidden.

"Chicago *Hair*" sings pre-censored set lyrics and ad-libs little satire. Only the poster "DIAL-A-BEATING: PO-5-1515"—sneaked into a mob scene—makes any reference to the Chicago police by giving the fuzz' phone number. Art is obviously having a hard time in the city the kids call "Prague West."

TAX ART; EXEMPT CHURCHES

Chicago's head like Chicago's location is central Mid-America, without the extremities of either Coast. So it's no wonder art can barely survive in this U.S. "Central America." Acting out of 300 years of repressive Founding-Father Calvinism, the United States Government continues to tax art and exempt churches.

This tax inequity ignores the radical connection between art and religion: that both once performed the same function. They both mean to sort out man's relationship with other men and all men's relationship to their universe.

Something new is afoot. Even politically Catholic Chicago is paring back its piety. So much property tax revenue has been lost to the city that legislation was passed so that religious orders are now restricted from buying any more old non-taxable mansions on North Sheridan Road, two and three blocks south of Loyola university on Lake Michigan.

The city prefers—instead of ten tax-exempt Jesuits living in gilded-age splendor—that plush residential high rises (highly taxable) replace the razed manses so that 3,000 taxpayers can stack up 26-stories on a lot formerly occupied by a family of seven.

NIXON AND THE ARTS

Chicago is typical of the tax ground that institutional religion is losing just this side of professional atheist Madelyn Murray O'Hare. This past year, in fact, as Chicago took frown at its multiple religious exemptions, the "Chicago International Film Festival" was declared, at long last, tax-exempt to insure its artful survival.

While a move in the right direction, this art-exemption is roughly equivalent to President Nixon appropriating $35 million this year to promote culture. This entire annual cost—$35 million—is spent every ten hours by the United States in Vietnam.

Up to this year, the most the U.S. spent annually on the arts was $20 million. This is a global scandal when nearly every other government makes provision to sustain cultural activities through the arts and humanities. Not through militarism and violence, but through the arts does a nation preserve and promote its heritage of civilization.

PARENTS, KIDS, AND REVOLUTION

Despite the fact it's fashionable to knock Chicago, this appraisal is only accidentally fashionable.

The "Chicago Seven," free on bond during their trial, are preparing a film of their exploits. They'll act it themselves in the streets where-it-happened-with-the-original-cast. They will film their own *Z* in a city so uptight it's surprising the Film Censor Board let *Z* and its political message ever be screened.

I suspect the board didn't realize the underlying implications of *Z*, a French film made in Algeria about Greece—and about the Chicago-like society that spreads the fascist control of censorship across America. The point is the Seven, like *Z*'s director, Constantin Costa-Gavras, are turning to art to make the score they couldn't make in the Mid-American streets and Mid-American courts.

Maybe art can make sense out of disordered human reality. If so, then America's social reality is certainly disordered enough to give art a try. The possibility, at least, is enough that our short shrift of the popular arts ought to make us nationally embarrassed.

Half the kids in our primary schools won't finish high school. One-third of the kids who make it to high school won't graduate. If so few Americans finish even lower-level education, then the informal education provided through the open-minded arts seems a likely avenue into their unfilled minds.

Everyone sees some TV, some movies, some magazines and newspapers. The point here is: the popular arts of our popular culture can be more meaningful than frothy fluff and nonsense.

A PERSONAL NOTE

Maybe this week's column is too defensive, but if more parents with their children would look somewhere for some social answers about what it is to be human in our crazy society, then maybe I won't be tear-gassed again as I was last Wednesday while lecturing before 200 teachers at a "Teachers of English" convocation at Western Michigan University. The students blamed the police and the police the students, and all we teachers stood arm-in-arm outside at the entrances to the building to keep the two sides apart. [The campus riot that day was the largest and most violent in Western's history.]

When society squares off against itself, and the peace of art loses out to the violence of politics, I blame education and cities that fall short in encouraging *art* communication. That's a short-circuit which society can't afford. Tear gas is frightening in a crowd where twelve-thousand dollars' worth of damage is done. And we can all expect more of this from people and police alike before the Second American Revolution is over.

I'm still looking for an alternative to the coming violence.

[Editor's note: Fritscher's intuitive conclusion was prophetic. On May 4, 1970, approximately seventy days after this article was published, the National Guard fired their army rifles on a peace demonstration at Kent State University, killing four and wounding nine.]

III. Eyewitness Illustrations

Detail from a page of "Impeach Nixon" stamps, early 1970s.

Top: "Police Riot, Lincoln Park, Chicago, 1968." Two photographs shot in color of a redheaded protester, August 28, 1968, in the crowd surging through Lincoln Park during the Democratic National Convention. The Police Riot at the Democratic Convention caused citizens to fight back in the streets, and this, in turn, emboldened homosexuals ten months later to fight back against the NYPD at the Stonewall Rebellion, June 1969. Bottom: The Reverend Jim Kane photographed in Colorado Springs for his 1970 Christmas card at a time when exchanging personally made gay Christmas greetings was the custom not yet undone by political correctness. Photographs by Jack Fritscher. ©Jack Fritscher.

FRITSCHER FEATURE ARTICLE

DATELINE COLORADO

Pueblo, Colorado FRIDAY, JANUARY 23, 1970 Volume 3, Number 4

Sel 1 Kol - Published in DATELINE COLORADO MARCH 1970 3/27

Z - Fritscher MARCH 1970

By Dr. John J. Fritscher

No matter what your opinion of the Chicago Seven Trial, one fact is unmistakeably clear. The arts, especially film, are of immense import to our revolutionary times. This came personally clear to me on New Year's afternoon, 1970. It was a cold and gray day, a bad way to begin the new decade in Chicago. The political climate was even more depressing than the weather. Costa-Garvas' film Z had opened a few days earlier. Word-of-mouth said Z was good. I called some friends and took off.

SEE ALSO PUBLISHED COLUMN ON "MEDIA" BY J. FRITSCHER IN

FRITSCHER NOTE: ALL THE RED-INK MARKS ARE MADE BY EDITOR JIM KANE

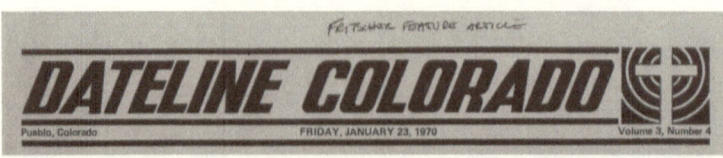

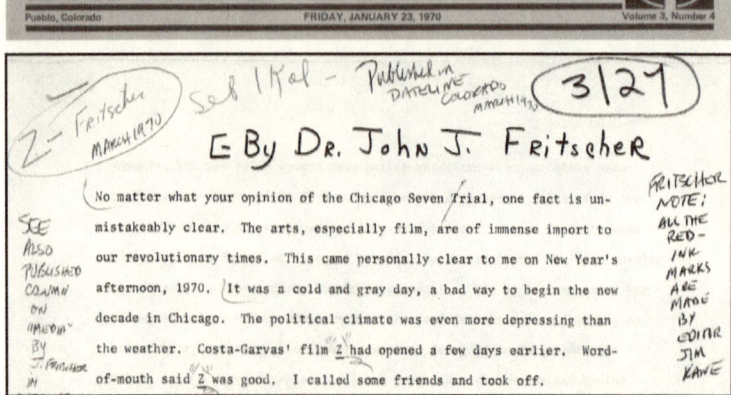

Manuscript copy for the "Chicago Seven Trial" from Jack Fritscher's manual Smith-Corona portable typewriter submitted to editor Jim Kane for Fritscher's monthly media column in *Dateline Colorado*. The hand-written editorial marks (in red) are Kane's.

The Eyes Have It

Movies & TV for the Catholic family

Not all 'G-rated' films are for the kiddies

Bullwinkle drips technicolor blood?

By Dr. John J. Fritscher

Dateline Colorado Friday March 27 1970

Popular culture--

By Dr. John J. Fritscher

You are in the midst of the 2nd American Revolution

A short story especially for this Christmas

All Job's Children

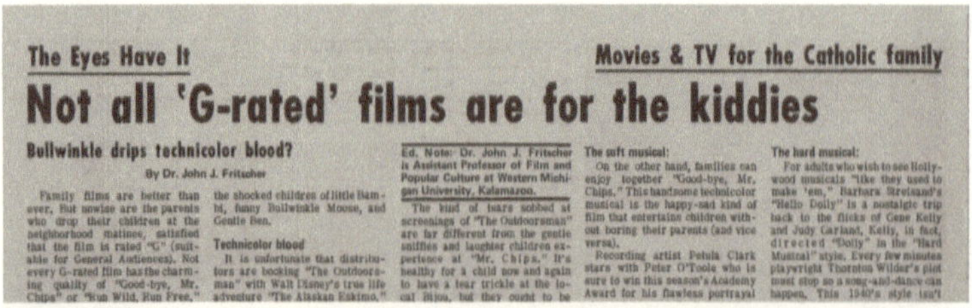

Three monthly column headlines and openings written in 1970 by Jack Fritscher for *Dateline Colorado* edited by leather priest Jim Kane.

Leather *Dolce Vita*, Pop Culture, & the Prime of Mr. Larry Townsend

> Written by Jack Fritscher during October 1996 and published as the "Introduction" to *The Leatherman's Handbook Silver Anniversary Edition* written by Larry Townsend, 1997; first edition of *The Leatherman's Handbook*, 1972.
> I. Author's Eyewitness Historical-Context Introduction written December 12, 1999
> II. The introductory essay as published in Larry Townsend, *The Leatherman's Handbook 25th Anniversary Edition*, Los Angeles: LT Publications, 1997
> III. Eyewitness Illustrations

I. Author's Eyewitness Historical-Context Introduction written December 12, 1999

If *Drummer* had not been dysfunctional all during 1997 and 1998 as it fell to its collapse this year with its last issue in April 1999, this historical essay about Larry Townsend, which was offered to the editors, might have been printed in *Drummer* in whole or in part.

Larry Townsend deserved this kind of full attention from *Drummer*. In 1972-1975, he had been a part of the group founding the LA newsletter, *H.E.L.P./Drummer*, which evolved into *Drummer* itself. (H.E.L.P. is the acronym for "Homophile Effort for Legal Protection.")

Author Townsend and publisher Embry, however, had certain disagreements, and Townsend kept his work out of *Drummer* for the first five years because, Townsend told me, he knew he'd "never be paid." There was little love lost between Townsend and Embry. They were both the same LA vintage; and they were both autocrat tycoons of mail order. Because they had similar post office-box addresses, Townsend told me that some customers thought they were the same mail-order company, and he grew tired of explaining to some of the disgruntled that they should complain to Embry because their business was with Embry.

And there was an eat-shit-and-die in LA moment.

In the first and only book review in the first issue of *Drummer* (June 1975), Embry—not loathe to use columnists as hand puppets—trashed Townsend's book, *Chains*. Reviewer "Cam Phillips" wrote: "the author [was] obviously confused"; "dull sex scenes"; "Townsend is not a 'good' writer in the sense that Christopher Isherwood and John Rechy are 'good' writers"; "he is weakest when dealing with his characters outside of the bedroom, or when he makes them open their mouths for anything other than sexual purposes"; and the cover which Townsend designed "promises an extremely heavy sexual book, but this is definitely not the case." (*Drummer* 1, page 13).

It was only in 1980 when mutual need caused the two strange bedfellows to kiss and make up. Embry, having alienated nearly all the talent base from the 1970s, needed his pages filled every thirty days, and Townsend needed a national platform to keep his name bill-boarded monthly to sell his novels mail order. Thus his advice column titled "Leather Notebook," written in trade for free advertising, became a regular *Drummer* feature from 1980 to 1992. This was a suitable fit because Townsend's 1972 *Leatherman's Handbook* had early on helped invent and form the "how-to" aspects of early 1970s leather behavior which he then popularized in mid-1980s *Drummer*. He was a leatherman whose vaunted top role in S&M propped up his credentials as writer. Larry has reminisced to me about his photo-studio dungeon where many a bound-and-gagged slave experienced S&M sessions feeling Larry's greatest "hits" while his stereo speakers boomed out tapes of the ominous, fervent hammer blows of Mahler's *Sixth* as well as his dark, terminal *Ninth*.

During my tenure as editor in chief of *Drummer* in the 1970s, I had concentrated on 1) gay literary quality in feature essays and fiction and drama, 2) the reflexive *verite* of gay pop culture as lived by the actual readers, and 3) themes of homomasculinity and wild sex.

I was all about 1970s sex vets: "Do It!"

Not about 1980s tyros: "How do I do it?"

In the 1970s, everyone seemed to know how.

Townsend is a clever man; he knew how to change with the times.

With the end of the Titanic 70s, and the rise of the HIV 80s, *Drummer* moved with the times to transpositions of 1970s sexuality into 1980s sociality: 1) practical columns, such as "Leather Notebook," on how to run a safe-sex and a consensual S&M scene; 2) in-house promotion photo spreads and centerfolds that focused on *Drummer* contest winners; and 3) an excessive interest in commercial videos as the dumbed-down mentality of television—via the Trojan Horse of the VCR—began to saturate written gay magazine culture—including *Drummer* itself—which video and the Internet eventually destroyed.

Leather *Dolce Vita* 191

(Historically, with the rise of video, both mail-order moguls, Townsend and Embry, were busy selling the hundred *Drummer*-style video features I directed and filmed for my own company, Palm Drive Video, which was showcased on *Drummer* covers and in centerfolds and monthly advertising. In a scalene triangle, we three seemed inextricably bound together by the gay mail order central to keeping *Drummer* alive.)

All generations of *Drummer* were valid. All issues of *Drummer* were valid. All the talent writing and creating *Drummer* was valid. That doesn't mean they were all equal as art, literature, erotica, and entertainment.

As much as the early *avant-garde Drummer* shaped the golden-age times of leatherfolk; the HIV-VCR times shaped *retro-garde Drummer*.

Riding these vicissitudes like the leatherman he is, my longtime friend, Larry Townsend, has done the most amazing act of gay survival: in a GLBT publishing culture famous for its flakiness, thievery, and outright human cruelty, he has remained functional, and his more than fifty productive years of non-stop writing are testament to his dedication to leather homosexuality and its popular vernacular literature.

Is there an award for that?

I'll create one here and now.

If anyone should be an "Honorary Mr. *Drummer*," it's "the Larry"; it's "the Townsend."

After Embry sold *Drummer* in 1986, author Townsend and publisher Embry parted ways.

Townsend's column continued on in *Drummer* under AIDS-era publisher Tony DeBlase until 1992 when Townsend switched his monthly column to Embry's longtime *bete noire*, *Honcho* magazine.

On March 4, 2006, the legendary Larry Townsend gave me permission to be the first journalist to print the following personal biographical information including the year of his birth: 1930. Of Swiss-German extraction, he served in the U. S. Air Force (1950-1954) as Staff Sergeant in charge of NCOIC Operations of Air Intelligence Squadrons in Germany. In 1957, he graduated UCLA with a B. A. in psychology, and has a PhD thesis pending at California State University, Los Angeles. He began his pioneering work in the politics of gay liberation in the early 1960s.

II. **The "Introduction" essay written by Jack Fritscher as published in Larry Townsend,** *The Leatherman's Handbook 25th Anniversary Edition*, **Los Angeles: LT Publications, 1997**

Introduction: *The Leatherman's Handbook*
The Controversial Best Seller

Leather *Dolce Vita*, Pop Culture, & the Prime of Mr. Larry Townsend

When principles collide with issues, principles win. *The Declaration of Independence* survives because it is a document of principle, not a document of issues current in 1776. Principle clarifies issues. Civil rights is a principle. Gay rights is an issue. Pursuit of issues *per se* causes political myopia. Abortion, suicide, and same-sex marriage are hot-button issues solved by the cool-button principle of free choice.

Give a person an issue and he will eat fire for a day; give a man a principle and he may think clearly for a lifetime. It takes common sense to raise a village. Common sense is precisely what professionally trained psychologist Larry Townsend offered the emerging world of leathermen in his original *Leatherman's Handbook*, 1972.

CONCEPT, CONQUERORS, & CAPTIVES

New Leather, as ancient as Eden when Lucifer pulled on a snake skin, presented the young Larry Townsend the same self-defining task Adam had in the Garden: naming nameless things. Leather is twice the love that had dare not speak its name, and an out-of-the-closet vocabulary had to be invented. *Leather* itself is a code word for domination and submission in the human condition. The Greeks and Romans often made names *pars pro toto* where part of something identified the whole—as in calling a man a "dick." So the word *leather* has come to symbolize more than its literal meaning which is skin, *toughened* skin.

Leather, as a concept, raises from the mists of pre-history, archetypes of conquerors and captives, masters and slaves, in literal and existential tableaux of sublime power and of human bondage. With the fall of barbarism and feudalism, and with the rise of enlightenment and democracy, humans evolved toward self-consciousness. Ask Freud. Ask Jung. Yet the psyche of many, even in this millennial new age of equality where no one is unworthy, remembers and requires the ancient rituals of the human past.

What scenes there be in ancient Greek theater—Ask Euripides—or in modern leather bars and postmodern leather play rooms, date back—whether or not the players acknowledge it—to the moment Eden fell and the knowledge of top and bottom entered the world: reciprocal concepts of power and no-power. That's why "Original Recipe Leather," the post WWII biker gangs, had power-structure names like "Hell's Angels" or "Satan's Slaves."

The universal human condition is masochism. Ask Aquinas, Boccaccio, Dante, and Milton. Ask Annie Lennox. Everybody's a misbehaving bottom looking for a top: sexual, political, theological, whatever. To paraphrase Monty Python's virtually Shakespearean take on what exactly is the distinguishing power of Topness in *The Holy Grail*: "You can tell the kings from the common people, because the kings are the ones not covered in shit." Even in the world of recreational sex, bottoms search for tops with their vernacular shit together so the top can, in all the coded roles of Master/Coach/Cop/Dad/DI/Trainer, work/beat the shit out of the bottom: get the bottom's shit/act together; and basically save/transfigure the bottom (who loves his passive-aggressive addiction to bottomness because he gets to be "bad" and exert his will on the top) from the graceless impotence of his unworthy self.

Leather as a playground perches on the cusp of human psychology. Ask De Sade. Ask Masoch. Ask Larry. By the time of the rip-roaring counter-culture of the 1960s, the specific word *leather*, transcending literal meaning as clothing, surfaced from the underground subculture redefined to mean a specific psycho-drama sex-style.

Leather, along with 60s peace, love, sex, drugs, and rock 'n' roll, arrived linguistically to name a way of being and becoming, of ritualizing and actualizing, of creation and recreation, of politicizing and marketing. Participant gonzo journalist, Larry Townsend, as both a psychologist and a leatherman, reported the debut as *Leather* stampeded out of the closet.

WARHOL, FOUCAULT, FETISH, & THE WORD MADE FLESH

Leather exploded into pop culture with the dark glamour of Hollywood, the Hell's Angels, and Andy Warhol's *Exploding Plastic Inevitable* featuring the Velvet Underground with Lou Reed singing, "Shiny Boots of Leather." At the same time, June 26, 1964, *Life* magazine, always breathlessly "Roman Catholic" about sadomasochism, featured a two-page worldwide alert on the Tool Box, not the first, but the first famous leather bar.

Compared to the Bimbeau Limbo of vanilla gay bars, the Leather Bar promised masculinity, the kind of masculine identification that has always lured homosexual men: straight, or straight-acting. Note that this Leather Declaration of Independence in *Life* was a full five years, almost to the day, before Stonewall: June 26, 1964, to June 29, 1969. Ask Abbott.

Ask Costello. Leather—barbaric, medieval, industrial—is from cow to linguistics, in truth, "the flesh become word."

Leather is the conjure amulet, the lo-tech talisman, the fetish to which a certain erotic drive attaches itself and through which a certain erotic desire commands its visible incarnation.

The word becomes flesh, and leather moves to a photographer's studio in New York, a doctor's office in San Francisco, or a bodybuilder's gym in Venice Beach. Literal leather skin, by the time leather moved to the typewriter of Larry Townsend, had become a psychologist's dream of a symbol for an outlaw lifestyle few wanted to acknowledge. Ask John Rechy.

In the mid-1960s, Larry Townsend was politically active in Los Angeles, the pop culture capital of the world where he was well aware of the leather culture popping up across the nation. By 1969, he was circulating his famous samizdat mimeographed sadomasochistic questionnaire through the circuit of leathermen. I dubbed it "The Leather List."

Townsend's was the job of the good reporter scouting the latest news of the newest liberation front during an astounding period in American culture. Remember, with the civil rights movement marrying the peace movement, the five years of war from the Summer of Love in 1967 to 1972 (when *The Leatherman's Handbook* was published), were the most rebellious civic episode in the U.S. twentieth century.

In November 1970, the world's premiere leather/uniform writer, Yukio Mishima, author of the must-read disciplinary *Sun and Steel*, accomplished the ultimate homomasculine S&M suicide-execution that rocked the literary world and freaked the gay leather culture.

Larry became absolutely necessary to arbitrate how leather was to behave this side of death. Twenty years later, in the 1980s, it fell to that freaky visitor to Folsom Street, the irrepressible French philosopher Foucault, "The S&M Poster Boy," to probe the human psyche far deeper. Foucault twisted S&M leather recreational sex into existential endgame about power.

But it was Larry Townsend who, "beating Foucault," introduced *Leather Vocabulary 101*. As a journalist he used his ear as a novelist to hear the voice of emerging leather and suggest certain standards of courtesy and behavior. He didn't invent codes of leather behavior; he searched at the grass roots level and introduced the leather underground to itself. Ask leather author William Carney.

Like everything else in life, leather takes time to come to conclusions about itself.

The Leatherman's Handbook was one of the first analytical mirrors held up to the masculine homosexual face.

Leather *Dolce Vita* 195

Leather liberated masculine love from the depressive drag stereotype.

Townsend helped define masculine-identified homosexuality in terms of the pop psychology that is the guywire of our media consciousness of self. Leather is a sock-to-the-jaw statement that, contrary to the straight stereotype, gay men are not *faux* females driven to dresses. Just as female drag had once been the town queer's way of signaling blowjobs to sailors, suddenly drag divided and alternated; and leather became the new semaphore advertising a new, open man-to-man sex encounter.

Leather was a welcome way out of the closet for masculine men who in larger numbers than anyone ever suspected thanked the gods that the New Leather Culture allowed them to do their Father's Act rather than their Mother's Act, and in doing their Father's Act to excel beyond the father.

The sign on the ceiling of the Tool Box said, "No Tennis Shoes," which nixed limp wrists, fluffy sweaters, and the passe code slang of the "Friends of Dorothy."

SAME WAVE-LENGTH, SAME TURF:
6 DEGREES OF LEATHER

Nothing happens in a vacuum. So parallel is the leather universe, that, in 1971, the year before the publication of *The Leatherman's Handbook,* I had no idea that "The Leather List" was anything but just another samizdat folk document circulated as jerk-off material, but informational enough that I quoted the anonymous questionnaire as a grass-roots source in my own nonfiction book, *Popular Witchcraft: Straight From the Witch's Mouth*, published at the same time as Larry's *Leatherman's Handbook* (1972).

This *Popular Witchcraft* was the first modern unclosteting, analysis, and mix of homosexuality, leather, and satanism.

In my own participatory research, I connected samples of 1960s leather-heritage DNA: Satanic S&M Black Masses in Greenwich Village, gay conjure-magic at Fe-Be's bar in San Francisco, and the rituals of the gay S&M coven called "The Order of the Sixth Martyr" in LA. I included quotes from William Carney's book, *The Real Thing* (1968), because Carney codified how-to-do and how-to-live the leather lifestyle. I've often thought that pioneer Carney in 1968 inspired pioneer Larry Townsend to begin his S&M survey published four years later. All of us participated in the same *zeitgeist*. Leather was "happening." [Author's note: Without knowing one another, several *Drummer* types were pursuing the same analysis of leather on a tight timeline: Carney's *The Real*

Thing (1968); my novel, *I Am Curious (Leather)* (1968) with my nonfiction book of interviews, *Popular Witchcraft* (1972); Sam Steward's *When in Rome Do* (1971); Townsend's *The Leatherman's Handbook* (1972); and Anne Rice, who in those years was sitting in the Castro writing *Interview with the Vampire* (1976) while I was sitting in the Castro writing *Popular Witchcraft* (1972).]

Larry was a fellow working-journalist in the midst of an extraordinary tribe of leatherfolk featuring a convergence of hands-on and heads-up "mediums" through whom leather homomasculinity articulated its modern self—to the continuing scorn, prejudice, and hatred from brainwashed homosexuals self-hating their own masculinity. That said, the seeming spontaneous outbreaks of gay culture in the 1960s were of major significance to academic models within the newly founded American Popular Culture Association where, generally, feminism is accepted and masculinism rejected.

IT TAKES A VILLAGE TO RAISE THE VILLAGE PEOPLE

Twenty-first-century leathermen might start highlighting their ancestral roots here. For instance, contemporary with Larry's research, underground filmmaker Kenneth Anger had been opening up cinema with his Cocteau-rooted leather classic, *Scorpio Rising* (1964) and its sequel *Lucifer Rising,* the print of which disappeared in the 1970s and, while reported to have been kept by Bobby Beausoleil of the Manson Family, was actually hidden for a time at the Berkeley home of *Drummer* author Sam Steward (friend of Gertrude and Alice), who wrote 1960s leather novels and stories under the pseudonym "Phil Andros." (Steward swore to me he had the film print at one time. Beausoleil, who remains in prison, denies ever taking *Lucifer Rising*.)

Auteur William Carney's daring 1968 epistolary novel, *The Real Thing*, brought the leather novel into serious hard cover and out of the leathery sweatshops of Evergreen Press to which Larry had sold *Run, Little Leather Boy*, and to which I would not sell for $100 my 1968 Chicago and Inferno leather novel, *I Am Curious (Leather)* aka *Leather Blues*.

In the nonverbal context of the Emergent Leather times, Chuck Arnett was painting Rorschach inkblot images of leathermen on the Lascaux walls of the Tool Box in San Francisco as Dom/Etienne had painted leather murals on the wall of the Gold Coast leather bar. In Chicago, Chuck Renslow, entrepreneur of the Gold Coast, had since the early 1950s run the manly and leathery Kris Photo Studio which featured seductively ominous photographs of muscular Polish-Catholic working-men culled from the streets and the Triumph gym Renslow managed. In this way,

Leather *Dolce Vita* 197

Renslow's ACLU-defended photography conditioned emerging gay men with a laser-straight masculinity that became archetypal totem and fetish for leathermen.

At the rear of the Gold Coast, leather pioneers, Bob Maddox and his lover Target Model Frank Goley, created Chicago's first leather shop, Male Hide Leathers. Few neo-leather historians remember that Illinois, where I grew up, was the first state to legalize homosexuality in 1961. Two years earlier, the Gold Coast leather bar had opened its doors. Thus freed up, Chicago leather society, inspired by photographer Renslow's Kris standard of masculinity, led the charge of the Leather Liberation Brigade.

Renslow's Chicago crew was as pivotal to the creation of the American leather archetype as was the early cartooning of the fine artist Tom of Finland, who was introduced to the United States by Bob Mizer via his LA-based *Physique Pictorial* magazine in 1957.

Bob Mizer with his Athletic Model Guild (AMG Studios 1945-1989) presented a rough-trade hustler version of straight tough young men that predated Renslow, matched the police-harassed Bruce of LA (without whom there'd be no Bruce Weber/Calvin Klein images), and inspired in 1970, out of the Guild Press, the genius photographer David "Old Reliable" Hurles with his S&M-tweaked delinquents. Associated with Chicago leather, centered at that time at Renslow's "Black Castle" house was the macho ballet star Dom Orejudos who was the leather S&M artist aka Etienne/Stephen, as well as the cop-lover, writer Sam Steward aka Phil Andros aka Phil Sparrow who had taught Chicago's ink-maven Cliff Raven how to tattoo leathermen. The "Leather List" questionnaire, circulating through the players in Chicago leather, was filled out and mailed to Los Angeles—that is, to Larry Townsend who collected them up, collated, tabulated, and made hay out of them.

In New York, photographer Jim French aka the artist Luger aka Rip Colt, co-founder of Colt Studio's Leather-Lite Look, in the late 60s split to the muscle beaches of California. His Colt partner, Lou Thomas, stayed with the New York Leather-Serious Look in developing his classic Target Studio and the Anvil Leather Bar with leathermen Frank Olson and super-top, the legendary Don Morrison, my longtime pal (1969-1975), who tutored and tortured only the *creme de* leather. Early on, I had the good fortune to model for Target and spent five years associating with Lou Thomas and his "take" on leather, before becoming bicoastal lover of Robert Mapplethorpe who in the early 1970s was collaging photographs of leathermen into high concept art that bloomed up and out of the gay ghetto and brought leather into the art world's mainstream. Manhattan "straight" magazine artist-illustrator, Steve Masters, imaginating muscular leathermen in painterly drawings killed himself when his wife found out about his second career. Masculine image input came from everywhere, and Larry's "Leather List" was read, re-typed, and mailed from Manhattan to Los Angeles.

In San Francisco, Harvey Milk opened a vanilla photo shop to compete with photographer Walt Jebe's leather-identified camera store on 19th Street in the Castro. In 1970, my lover of ten years, David Sparrow, and I posed duo for Jebe's leather photo magazine, *Whipcrack*, which predated *Drummer* by five years and provided a few more early gay images for the emerging leather analysts like Townsend and artists like Domino and Bill Ward. So it was that the leather cadre in Chicago and Manhattan gene-spliced the commercial leather genesis that was simultaneously combusting like wildfire in San Francisco and Los Angeles where Larry Townsend was busy working the leather pop-culture scene on the leather-bar and bike-run circuit at venues like the Black Pipe, Griff's, and Larry's (no relation to Townsend), with leather superstars like the respected British movie actor Peter Bromilow (*Camelot, The Railway Children*). Even in San Francisco and LA, curious leathermen filled out Larry's leather questionnaire and mailed it to Los Angeles.

LUST IN THE LEATHERAMA

Did the Roman Empire have gladiator bars? Ask Aaron Travis. Ask Steven Saylor. The original gay leather bar was an Italian-American invention inspired by the leather world's nicely capitalistic drive to make money. Ask the Mafia. Gay liberation, originally and in fact, was successfully and openly driven by gay capitalism much to the later chagrin of a successive generation of lesbigay Marxists with a taste for tuna casserole "fund-raisers" because they quit their day jobs. Sex, a recession-proof industry, always drives money. And vice versa. The Leather Bar had to be invented or all of us *etwas neues* leathermen—always seeking "something new"—would have been like Marlon Brando in the Ur-Leather movie, *The Wild One*, a biker *sans* biker bar. Sexmeister Tony Tavarossi (d. July 12, 1981) designed the basic leather bar as the 1950s became the 1960s: first in New York and then at the Why Not in San Francisco. The original decor has never needed improvement: black paint + red bulb = leather bar.

In Manhattan, leather begot Keller's and the Anvil where Jerry Torres, the star of the Maysles film documentary, *Grey Gardens*, took Jackie Kennedy Onassis.

Following faster than a speed trip was the very leather-identified club the Mineshaft, managed tongue-in-cheek by stand-up impresario Wally Wallace who in the 90s runs the Lure, another leather S&M venue

Leather *Dolce Vita* 199

connected to the premiere leather artist, Rex, who is Tom of Finland's Evil Twin.

Larry Townsend's *Leatherman's Handbook* was combination etiquette book and *Boy Scout Handbook* for the Mineshaft's epic nights of beautiful people where early motorcycle-inspired leather recombinated its functional concept as riding gear to include the farthest reaches of drug-driven S&M. To time-trip back to the sexual decor at the time of publication of *The Leatherman's Handbook,* throw onto a video monitor a copy of the William Friedkin film, *Cruising* (1980) which features actual leathermen of the 1970s period playing "atmosphere people." *Cruising* has always been controversial, because it's like the *X-Files* of being gay.

LEATHER, SEX, & GENDER:
DON'T LET THIS HAPPEN TO YOU

Everything rising out of the closets converged. Larry Townsend, a networked part of all he met, was well focused. He examined exactly how leather was kicking out from all the heretofore closeted places (military, prison, industry) where men enjoyed covert masculine contact that was very physical, very rough, and often very erotic, but not always sexual, and not ever female.

One can most assuredly agree with my pal Camille Paglia who says even homosexual men must observe women; but one can also agree with Katharine Hepburn who advised no more than, "Men and women should live next door and visit each other once in a while."

In 1964, Kenneth Marlowe had written a shocking non-fiction best seller titled *Mr. Madam.* Mr. Marlowe's virtual *Queen's Handbook* rather demanded the balance Mr. Townsend introduced in *The Leatherman's Handbook.*

Reference to gender of all kinds is suggested only to inform those "seeking offense" were no slight is meant, that at the start, in his initial field research, and laser-true even on its 25th anniversary, Townsend targeted a man's leather *Handbook* to a demographic of masculine-identified men before leather women and female bodybuilders were invented in American pop culture. While diverse others have read, enjoyed, and learned the basic leather tropes from the *Handbook*, the author's specific subject is homomasculinity and his operative audience is gay males.

Over the years, many women as well as many other-than-gay men, have quoted Townsend's man's *Handbook* as a leather primer, a clarificatory introduction into their own legitimate versions of leather culture. Hopefully, the diversity of all others who are not gay males—and who doesn't believe in women and female-identified homosexuals writing about and for women and female-identified homosexuals—will not hold a grudge ever in print or in their hearts against one of the earliest historic, agenda-free documents written by a man about men and for men.

THE CAUTIONER'S TALE

The Leatherman's Handbook, chock full of sexual entertainment and literary license to illustrate the wide psychology of leather, merits, by entertainment value, at least, status with Chaucer's travelers' handbook, *The Canterbury Tales*. Like New Journalist Hunter Thompson, author of *The Hell's Angels*, journalist-player Larry Townsend, the right reporter in the right place at the right time, did not invent leather culture, but he definitely caught the wave of a movement co-created by quite a few players, writers, photographers, and entrepreneurs who themselves were and are active and deeply established S&M leather masters and slaves whose influential names may not be known to a fresh new leatherboy who just fell off the turnip truck crossing the rough rails of the Millennium.

Masculine-identified leather artists of the visual, articulated by all the masculine-identified leather voices writing—including Townsend in 1972, helped motivate, and received validation in prompting, the American Psychiatric Association's removing homosexuality from its official list of mental disorders in 1974. This victory is a red-letter day in the black-and-blue History of Homosexuality.

The groundbreaking 1972 publication of Larry Townsend's *Leatherman's Handbook* is as remarkable a construct as Stonewall itself, because it was a declaration of independence for "anatomically correct" homomasculinity. Ask Martin Duberman. By June, 1976, Larry, with Robert Opel, reported the first leatherman's wedding and gay marriage between Tom Bertman and Fred Schultz at Griff's leather bar in LA. Townsend has always been a liberal voice advising common sense and progressive caution.

CREATING THE LEATHER GENRE

Larry, while writing his *Handbook*, which is more "etiquette book" and "encyclopedia" than "manifesto," was a celebrated political activist in Los Angeles with the Homophile Effort for Legal Protection, Inc., or H.E.L.P. This organization, lightly inspired by Henry David Thoreau, originated the newsprint paper, *H.E.L.P./Drummer,* in 1972. Larry Townsend was president of H.E.L.P. and his name appeared on the masthead of this "pre"-*Drummer* tabloid. At this early date, a major news article in

Leather *Dolce Vita*

H.E.L.P./Drummer, "We Weren't Born Yesterday," featured a 1971 Symposium on the importance of "preserving our considerable gay history."

Book reviews showcased Larry Townsend's *Run, Little Leather Boy*, its sequel *Run No More*, and *The Leatherman's Handbook*. Townsend was a gay pop culture phenomenon who held himself independent from the 1975 birth of the glossy magazine, *Drummer*, which I dubbed in 1978 "Leather's Publication of Record" and "The American Review of Gay Popular Culture" in *Drummer* 23. He didn't come aboard *Drummer* until 1980.

Cherchez le femme! A woman helped deliver *Drummer*. Ms. Jeanne Barney, according to Leather Patriarch Harold Cox, publisher of *Checkmate/Dungeonmaster*, was one of the two best editors *Drummer* ever had. Trouble—police-driven by then LA police chief Ed Davis—complicated the infighting causing *Drummer*'s founding partners split. Entrepreneur John Embry got custody of the infant *Drummer*, named himself publisher, and after the April 10, 1976, bust of his "Slave Auction," fled Los Angeles for San Francisco leaving behind such leather stars as filmmaker Fred Halsted, photographer and performance artist Robert Opel, and photographer/hustler JimEd (Master Tau) Thompson who in 1974 created *Gay Bondage* magazine and *Action Male* bondage magazine, the tutorials for Mikal Bales's Zeus bondage studio.

Drummer, once arrived in Mecca, quickly became leather's official voice to the world during the Golden Age of Liberation. Imitation is the sincerest form of flattery. Because Embry seemed peeved with and by Townsend, he also seemed rather pleased at Townsend's absence which might have imprinted *Drummer*. And miffed that he himself had not written *The Leatherman's Handbook*, claimjumper Embry—who was also trying to clone *The Advocate* by creating *The Alternate*—commissioned a clone of Larry's *Leatherman's Handbook* written by Bruce Werner and called *The New Leatherman's Guide* (*Drummer* 18, 1977). Embry followed this with *The Care and Training of the Male Slave* written by Embry himself aka Robert Payne. This kind of instant commercial imitation signaled the enthusiastic beginning of a pop culture genre: *how-to* and *self-improvement* books for leather players.

Larry Townsend, by talent really a novelist, achieved legendary status by founding this new leather genre of self-improvement through S&M. "Larry Townsend" became an instant Brand Name in leather popular culture. Embry himself, finally, could not resist publishing even more writing by Townsend in 1980s issues of *Drummer* where ultimately Townsend's monthly column, "Leather Notebook," appeared for twelve years.

Townsend's second regular column, "Ask Larry," on this Silver Anniversary of the *Handbook* is currently a regular feature in the international leather magazine *Honcho* edited by Doug McClemont. Larry's writing also appears in *Bound and Gagged* magazine and in the lists of Richard Kasak's Bad Boy Books as well as of Alyson Publications. *Ask Larry: The Collected Notebook*, the hard-core back-beat to *The Leatherman's Handbook*, was published by Masquerade Books in 1995.

TOWNSEND: PUBLISHER TO THE LEATHER AUTEURS

Larry Townsend, the person, and "Larry Townsend," the Brand Name, are a very viable pair. Larry remains, twenty-five years on, an active and very declarative public voice driving leather evolution in manners, mores, playing, and plague. He laughs, when he's not steaming mad, about resisting the lesbigay trend of political correctness that has nothing to do with masculine leathermen who prefer men masculine. Ask Stephen H. Miller. Larry is pro-men without being anti-women. So, he remains a favorite with both male and female leather audiences. Larry speaks often at seminars and reads with sense and sensibility at literary gatherings accompanied by his 90-pound Doberman Pinscher, "Mueller," who manages crowd control. He has written more than 26 books of fiction plus three nonfiction books. His 1997 novel, *Czar*, is an historical epic of literary S&M, and is a crowning achievement of his much-published life. Townsend is a contemporary writer, photographer, leather player, media personality, and businessman. As L. T. Publications he has himself produced more than 60 books and has published more than 55 gay writers of S&M leather literature.

OLD GUARD, NEW GUARD!
THE ONLY TRUE GUARD IS *AVANT GARDE*

However, no good deed goes unpunished. That's a basic tenet of S&M. So, naturally, on the progressive occasion of the 25th anniversary of *The Leatherman's Handbook*, it is necessary to weed out a certain hatefulness of rhetoric hurtful to the progress of leather and of homosexual activism itself. In a direct attack on Townsend, some "leatherish novice" recently coined the label "Old Guard" to discard the wisdom of deeply established writers, mentors, and teachers, and classic books such as *The Leatherman's Handbook*.

Shades of the Cultural Revolution in China where intellectuals and artists were murdered or exiled to remote work camps. That self-centered novice devised such exclusionist coinage as a separatist way of showboating his/her own generation as "New Guard." Shame on such "politically incorrect" ageists who should be slapped across the face (with a leather glove) the way hysterical twits in movies are always slapped to get a grip!

Actually, *The Leatherman's Handbook*, which has sold thousands of copies, thrives on this new brush-fire of controversy!

Youth needs the wisdom of the established, and the established need the energy of the young. The present usually takes a dim view of the past. This attitude is attractive to the naive who often think that the whole wide world began the day they first noticed it. Sometimes, too, people with some mileage wrongly dismiss the younger because the young weren't present at the past.

If people—for instance, artists, writers, leather players—are alive, working, and creating at the same time on the same clock and the same calendar, no matter what their individual ages, they are all contemporary, because they work in the "Culture of Here and Now."

Larry Townsend is as pertinent as the boy he beats, and the boy he beats is as pertinent as Larry Townsend.

If this principle attacks some dogmatist dragmatist's Inner Bette Davis, I make no apology for myself or for Larry, or for the very leathery Golden Age of the Titanic 70s whose celebratory sex-style has taken an unfair beating, as if "those ignorant leathermen at that decade's party" and not a virus caused the plague.

Once the plague is conquered, or at least controlled, the gay press will be driven to invent new material, and gay men will want their publishing jobs back. Before AIDS, the gay press featured news of tricycle races and show biz. Once the plague is controlled, will Tony Kushner be permitted to write the third act of *Angels in America*, or will he be dismissed as Old Guard, the way ACT UP discarded Larry Kramer, and OutWrite actually booed Edward Albee.

LEATHER *DESIDERATA*: PISSING ON TERRITORY

So, in the parallax view of 20/20 hindsight, what appears in *The Leatherman's Handbook* to be familiar, well, uh, "old guard" may in fact be very "new guard." What appears to be new may in fact, in this folk document, be familiar. So question what you know. Be your own best critic. Do penance and self-flagellation if you wish, but let no one unworthy teach you or top you.

Be skeptical of historical revisionists of any gender—especially the co-optations by post-AIDS non-males who, with unmitigated gall, fancy themselves saviorettes who will write the history of gay male culture and gay male leather culture as if Larry Townsend and fifty other living authors—and about 100 recently dead ones—haven't been writing this material, which is actually our group autobiography, for the last fifty years in fiction and nonfiction.

Ask Patricia Morrisroe. Be wary of wannabe artistes and stenographic historiennes who sacrilegiously and pompously invoke our dead whose history they claim to be "saving" from oblivion.

They actually think they're arriving in our life as if our life were abandoned and as if major talents have not kept full record of our life.

Sacre bleu!

I mean it's nice that foreign graduate students and tenure-hungry academics want to formulate leather on the head of a Prufrockian pin. True scholarship is, of course, welcome, even needed; but true scholars never make the actual "source people" and "source material" disappear so the scholar can appear to be the source.

That's theft of intellectual property.

This is not *ad hoc* or *ad hominem*. It's not even an issue. It's a principle

It's peculiar that every group has roots except white male faggot leathermen.

Ask Maya Angelou.

Why shouldn't this particular leather pop culture history be best told by the actual "author"-ities, the men who created it for males, lived it as males, and recorded it, not as separatists but as humanists. The sexual liberation fronts included everybody; gay men were just more immediately intense about succeeding.

All the male witness-authors, witness-photographers, and witness-artists who have been vastly creative and widely published for this last half a century have long done quite well mapping our leatherman's history. And, frankly, these deeply established writers don't appreciate the lesbigay *bandito* scholarship that literally steals facts, dates, names, vocabulary, and concepts from intellectual property that certain wannabe scholars then fail to acknowledge by so much as a footnote. (I am naming them in my will.)

Ask those semi-plagiarists who know who they are. You can always spot the usual suspects. They arrived post-1980 on the leather scene; they became first noticeably active at exactly the same time as AIDS; they write the trendspeak of political correctness; and they endlessly use the cliched rhetoric of queer studies—a language invented by academics who must publish or perish.

Despite such *faux* prophets in our midst, do seek your spirituality, mystical experiences, and transcendence, but not in gay magazines and leather literature—much of it written under the fundamentalist thumb of cultish egos and media money—published by straight males and edited by women for gay men. (Read the mastheads on magazines.)

Be somewhat sophisticated when seeking advice, because while homosexuality has been declared not a mental disorder, homosexuals themselves can still be mentally ill.

Even Larry would ask, should you really "Ask Larry"?

Don't let the horizon of your life be the skyline of Castro, SoMa, WeHo, SoHo, or Chelsea. For instance, when some certain—but certainly not all—leather "facilitators" get together to jerk each other off in public so they can spout S&M advice on anything, run away, little leather boy, as fast as you can—until you actually check out what might be their measurable credentials and actual biases.

Do you really want to sit at the feet of the Leather Bourgeoisie? Ask Brando: "The horror!" Check out the "facilitators" as carefully as you would a strange bondage Top.

If the talkers prove to be objectively credible, still remain your own best critic about anybody telling you anything. S&M leather is art. Unlike those bed-fellows, fundamentalist religious morality and fundamentalist lesbigay politics, it has no right or wrong way. Art transcends morality. You can "Ask Larry" as readers have for years, but...can you trust him? Uh! Trust, and the doubt about trust, razor-sharpen the double edge that makes leather fetish gear and S&M ritual play delicious.

Remember: there actually exist real live men who will tie you up and torture you until they cum!

I first applied the words *sensuality* and *mutuality* to S&M in print in 1972, but...can you trust the context of this Introduction? What if homosexuality exists for entertainment purposes only? Hey, that's the definition of recreational sex, which is a synonym for plain old *Lust*. Ask Larry. The playful sense of *The Leatherman's Handbook* keeps its principle of sexual titillation ahead of any humanoid issue.

You have to love a *Handbook* that is a guide to gay cannibalism! The author is the camp counselor telling scary, wonderful tales, mixed with just enough cautionary advice to encourage credibility, suspend disbelief, and give the audience goosebumps while imparting common sense for playing dangerous games.

LEATHER: TABOO AS STRONG AS TOTEM

As in the classic film *Casablanca*, sooner or later everyone comes to Rick's. Sooner or later everyone reads some classic Larry Townsend. The r/evolutionary discussion Larry opened up a quarter of a century ago about S&M continues, because Leather's taboo is as strong as Leather's totem. This kind of erotic narcotic gets readers' attention and keeps the players' interest. (The oldest living S&M leatherman still playing at the time of this writing is 92 years old, and, no, it's not Larry.)

Twenty-five years from now, *The Leatherman's Handbook* will be celebrated on its Fiftieth Anniversary in a collection published from the *oeuvre* of Larry Townsend. The future politics buzzing around Larry's *Handbook* will be even newer, shinier versions of jealousy, envy, calumny, and slander. The on-going never-ending tales of leather will have new chapters and new thrills and new cautions. But the crack of a whip will sound the same as it has since whip first touched flesh. In outer space, you cannot hear a scream. In the inner space of leather, the voices of innocence and the voices of experience will continue to whisper from the page...

III. Eyewitness Illustrations

"Larry Townsend and Jack Fritscher," Fritscher-Hemry House, June 16, 1995. Photograph by Mark Hemry. ©Mark Hemry

Porno, Ergo Sum: The Incredible Lightness of Being Male

> This literary monograph was written in April 2000 for the award-winning book *The Burning Pen: Sex Writers on Sex Writing*, an anthology collected by M. Christian, Alyson Books, November 2001. The text is the original unedited essay included to illustrate one of the ways *Drummer* was written.
> I. Author's Eyewitness Historical-Context Introduction written July 12, 2003
> II. The essay as published in *The Burning Pen: Sex Writers on Sex Writing*, collected by M. Christian, Alyson Books, November 2001
> III. Eyewitness Illustrations

I. Author's Eyewitness Historical-Context Introduction written July 12, 2003

Having earned an extremely useful double major in philosophy and literature, I titled this essay "Porno, Ergo Sum" as a satirical spin on Rene Descartes' *"Cogito, ergo sum. I think; therefore, I am."*

The premise of *The Burning Pen* anthology, published October 2001, was to investigate how writers create literary fiction which happens to be erotic. The samples of erotic writing quoted in the book represented bits from all the authors' works of fiction. In the original anthology, my essay was published in tandem with my World War II short story, "Wild Blue Yonder."

The contributors examining themselves in *The Burning Pen* were Laura Antoniou, Scott Brassart, Patrick Califia-Rice, M. Christian, Jack Fritscher, R. J. March, Leslea Newman, Felice Picano, Carol Queen, Shar Rednour, Thomas S. Roche, Simon Sheppard, Cecilia Tan, and Lucy Taylor.

II. The essay as published in *The Burning Pen: Sex Writers on Sex Writing*, collected by M. Christian, Alyson Books, November 2001

Porno, Ergo Sum: The Incredible Lightness of Being Male
(Why I Wrote, among Other Things, *Some Dance to Remember*)

Ask me no questions and I'll tell you no lies.

The British critic Edward Lucie-Smith told me that if my once-upon-a-time lover Robert Mapplethorpe had written a monograph on how and why he shot his photographs, the world would have had an invaluable insight into his work. Because Robert wrote nothing, his beautiful work stands on its own. Answering why and how I write my literary erotica is like skating a Figure 8 on an ice cube, naked. Anne Rice and I started out on Castro Street at the same time both writing books about the occult. From interviews, I wrote the nonfiction satanic history *Popular Witchcraft: Straight from the Witch's Mouth* (1972); she wrote the fictional *Interview with the Vampire* (1976). Both of us have double careers writing fiction and literary erotic fiction. Behind the mask of eros, we write literature. Erotica is literature with velocity. My writing is like thinking while cuming. I'm Gatsby's Daisy: "I write because men are so...so...beautiful," and because of the incredible lightness of being male.

Readers and critics feel my writing is autobiographical when it's only *verite*. In truth, from 1965 to the present, I've been downloading my personality into books, magazines, video features, and telephone tapes. Jeez, I have lived it up to write it down; but my work is no more autobiographical than the movie, *Platoon*, which director Oliver Stone said, "...is not about me, but if I had not been in Vietnam, I could not have written and directed such a film."

So it is with my signature novel, *Some Dance to Remember*, which is a gay history novel of the Golden Age of Liberation, 1970-1982, in San Francisco. *Some Dance*, full of real tales of the City, weaves its emotional and historical and erotic ropes around a specific group of people in a specific place at a specific time. My "quantum style" folds time, squeezes a dozen years into 562 pages so structured with Aristotelian unities and limned with stream-of-consciousness that readers willingly suspend their disbelief which is the aim of fiction. "Daddies" who were at the 1970s Gay Renaissance party write me that they make their "Boys" who missed the party read *Some Dance* to experience the High Water Mark to which gay culture once rose before plague and politics destroyed the most erotic decade in American history.

Born in 1939, the year after Thomas Wolfe (*Look Homeward, Angel*) died, I grew up as the other Tom Wolfe (*The Kandy-Kolored Tangerine-Flake Streamline Baby*) popularized gonzo journalism in which the writer must participate in the story. I came of age on the rhythms of James Joyce, Scott Fitzgerald, and Ernest Hemingway. I cried when at fifteen I first read Walt Whitman, forbidden at my high school as filthy erotic literature, and I wondered why the parts the teacher thought dirty seemed so achingly beautiful. I've been balancing Whitman with Rimbaud ever since. Some of my writing is erotic, *porno verite*, because Oscar Wilde was right as usual: "Nothing can cure the soul but the senses." Style sample:

> "In the end, he could not deny his human heart."
> —Opening sentence, a memoir-novel,
> *Some Dance to Remember*, 1990

I confess. I breathe in experience. I exhale fiction.

Feeling, emotion, is the oxygen of my fictive voice.

Stories for me begin as raw emotion felt, or a disembodied "voice" heard. As a humanist, who is neither a feminist nor a masculinist, I welcome all emotions as well as women's voices and men's voices which I channel.

As literary critic Michael Bronski points out, "In *Some Dance*, there are 9 plot lines and 15 major characters sweeping through the epic story of the rise and fall of everyone who was ever anyone." Those plot lines and characters are intricate to the way I write: avoiding sexual stereotype (Freud), going for erotic archetype (Jung). Slice-of-life stories rule, because that angle best matches our human lives lived in slices of time, emotion, and awareness.

Fiction should render the writer invisible behind strong story arcs, and layered characterizations, and strong dialog. Fiction actually "works" when the suspension of disbelief tips the reader into saying, "Aha! This is real. This happened. This is autobiography." Perhaps what is recognizable is my intention to try to reflect something universally human about "the autobiography of the reader's inner self." Readers of my erotic adventure-fiction want to know how I read their private sex journals, how I read their dirty minds, how I know what they did last summer. The storyteller is a trickster, a conjure man. Sex is only three degrees of separation.

At the baths, one time, a man whose tits were in my steely fingers, slipped down past my face, my cock, looking up at me, saying, "Do to me what you did to that guy in that story." I sent him on his way. My sex life is not a tour of my "Greatest Hits of Fritscher Friction Fiction," but erotic reputation is a pisser after more than thirty-five years in adult entertainment: literature and photography and video. With more than 8,000 pages in print, and around a thousand photographs in magazines from *Drummer* to *Bear* to *Unzipped* to *Honcho*, and more than 170 feature videos, I've been a busy boy living a wonderful life. My mantra is: "He who dies with the most column inches wins." That's a joke.

Personally, I *am* leather; I *am* wicca; I *am* bear fetish. But, in my literary poker hand, my "wild card" as "culture critic" trumps leather culture's Full House to top me; trumps satanic culture's four Aces of Spades to claim me; trumps bear-fetish culture's Hearts and Diamonds to seduce me.

I create erotic videos, but, maverick, neither join nor validate any adult director's guild or video corporation run by the Mafia. I am a unique hybrid: I am personally leather and a pioneer action-figure in leather culture as well as a scholar-historian of gay male leather culture, but not part of the establishment Leather Reich of "Mother-May-I S&M." In my *Porno Manifesto*, art for art's sake may go beyond the pale of consent as in this excerpt that pre-dates the murder of Matthew Shepard by almost thirty years. Style sample:

> The rest of that particular Wyoming night was the sort of history that never gets recorded, but's never forgot either: how three fairground fellows, all rodeo cowboys, paraded into the bar duded up...and started a punch-out with the barful of working cowboys in a brawl they could never win...The biggest one escaped when Arrow's dad kicked his ass through the bar window...The middle-size cowboy...revived fast when the barkeep dragged him across the floor to the john and shoved his face into the cold piss-water toilet. The third cowboy they dragged to the feedlot....A boot on the back of his neck shoved his face into a fresh steaming horse-pie. They pulled the shit-covered outsider to a railroad X-sign. Arrow watched them lift the drunken cowboy in his filthy satin shirt and torn jeans up against the railroad cross. They spreadeagled him to the four heavy-beamed wooden arms. He was roped tight and secure. The men passed around a bottle of whiskey. Arrow's dad handed the bottle to his son. Arrow raised the bottle to his lips and pulled a long burning swig. He could never forget that moment: looking at his father

who had led these men, tasting his first whiskey, feeling the pressure of his hardon in his jeans, seeing the crucified cowboy hanging on the railroad cross, helpless and drunk and howling at the full Wyoming moon low on the horizon behind him.

—Third-person omniscient point-of-view, scene from novel, *I Am Curious (Leather)*, written 1968, published 1972, and then partially published as a "*Drummer* novel" in *Son of Drummer*, 1978; serialized in whole under the title, *Leather Blues*, in *MAN2MAN Quarterly*, 1980-81; published as the novel, *Leather Blues* by Winston Leyland, Gay Sunshine Press, 1984.

Actually, critic John F. Karr, in the *Bay Area Reporter*, wrote, June 27, 1985, that beginning in 1972 with the first publication of my novella *Leather Blues* through my creating *Drummer* culture's heart, image, and style as *Drummer*'s founding San Francisco editor-in-chief: "Jack Fritscher is the man who invented the South-of-Market prose style (as well as its magazines which would never be the same without him)."

In the 1970s hardly anyone was writing, photographing, drawing erotica because they were all fucking. In the right place at the right time, I had twenty years of magazine and journalism experience in writing and photography, as well as ten years in leather and S&M, when I became editor of *Drummer*. Supply and demand. A nasty job, but somebody had to do it.

It was the dawn of gay culture. The times cast me as the hot boy editor...and, luckily, like "A Whiter Shade of Pale," the crowd called out for more. To put content, ethos, and style in those pages with everyone else out fucking and dancing, I had to fill that magazine cover to cover out of my own dick and brain inventing the first articles on cigars, tits, daddies, all the hot tickets that have become the usual "themes."

At one time in 1979, I had edited half the *Drummer* issues in existence.

In truth, I wrote two-year's worth of *Drummer*, a dozen issues (*Drummer* 19 through *Drummer* 33)—the thickest, juiciest, most original issues *Drummer* ever had—mostly at the baths, with pencil on yellow legal pads in small rooms painted black under a naked red light bulb.

Arriving at 8 PM, hard with anticipation of how the Barracks/the Slot/the Everard/the St. Mark's/wherever, would pick up by midnight, I mainlined (metaphor only) the anticipation of the action into the veins of my stories, feature articles, and interviews. I channeled the high energy of the sexual revolution at the baths into my erotic art (which is the other side of my "legit" literary writing).

My porno I write with my dick in one hand. Like the reader later falling into the story, I, the writer, must fall into the story while creating it. I must believe the fiction or the feature article ("Prison Blues," "Pumping Roger") to the degree my dick stays hard driving the words, just as the words ultimately must drive the dick of the reader into hardening, and cuming, in what I feel is the most interactive art in the world.

The ultimate porno review is a reader shooting his load.

Others may deny that, because they're gay Puritan Fundamentalists who swing "politically correct." I'm as fucking nice a BoBo (bourgeois bohemian) as you can get, but no one fucks with me—who successfully escaped the censorship of the Catholic Church and Vatican politics—when it comes to writing, photography, and videography. I am an indie artist.

What you read is what you get: no agenda; all entertainment. It's sexual truth, personal and raw, the kind you can't write if you suck off publishers, editors, workshops, museums, archives, or, worse, write for the failed Marxists in "politically-correct focus groups." Fuck 'em all. As Sondheim writes, and Streisand sings, in "Putting It Together," it's all about the work.

Porno is an act of aggression that tops the reader, making him go nucking futz making a party in his pants.

Erotic writing is so Fritscher-Rechy "outlaw," so much like shooting an "indie film" outside the studio system that the "proper" academic gay rags have yet to acknowledge the literary merits of the only real gay writing there is—erotica—in reviews or awards.

But God spare us from gay erotica becoming academically institutionalized. Teaching novels as assignments for class ruined the reading of fiction. College film courses assigning movies for term-paper critique destroyed the enjoyment of film.

The irony is that twenty years after erotic "outlaw writing" is written, the mainstream begins to suck it up into respectability. It's hard to be edgy; it's harder to remain edgy. For a good time, give me a heaven with wild fucking saints who aren't canonized.

Too bad the future of an art form lies in the prejudices of its audience. The straight press thinks I'm "gay." The gay press thinks I'm "erotic." (The San Francisco Gay and Lesbian Film Festival thinks my videos about homomasculine men are "not gay enough." Go figure.)

I'm professionally trained in literature. I know writing. Most gay writers who wannabe on the straight best-seller list are perpetually angry because the straight mainstream literary world judges "Gay" and "Lesbian" writing as just another genre like "Westerns," "Mysteries," and "Romances."

Porno, Ergo Sum

I witnessed the shameless 1997 Key West Writers conference when the President of the Writers association abruptly and indignantly ended the conference sending all of us—including the other writers in attendance, Tony Kushner, Edmund White, David Leavitt, Michael Bronski, agent Michael Denneny, and that sweet writer whose pseudonym is Andrew Holleran—out into the street. The topic was "Literature in the Age of AIDS."

We were kicked out and given the bum's rush not so much because the banshee Larry Kramer as usual went ballistic and ran screaming down the theater aisle and onto the stage, but because the readings and panel discussions had started to turn in the tropical heat from "lit'rature" to "erotica." Key West wanted us to talk about "AIDS as a Literary Genre." Instead, steamy, sweaty, promiscuous gay writing and culture got too icky to deal with when heretofore literary writers like David Bergman began to read their hidden erotica to the audience! And Michael Bronski and White confessed to masturbating to memories of sex with dead lovers! It was also not pretty when the gay writers turned on straight writer Ann Beattie who judged herself, perhaps aptly, saying she could not write about people with AIDS because she was not a person with AIDS. A fight broke out—"liberal gay New York Jews" versus "conservative straight Florida WASPs"—ostensibly over advocacy literature and politics; Sarah Shulman, Frank Rich, Kramer, and Kushner took on the straights and in a shocking move the straights closed down the uppity conference.

As a veteran of the attack on Mapplethorpe, I immediately assessed the writers' smackdown as one more skirmish in the culture war.

Face it. We'll always be driven into the streets like hated queers until the exclusionary gay literary establishment owns up to the reality that gay writing is quintessentially erotic, and therefore legitimate, because eros drives human nature—particularly gay human nature—the same way that erotica drives new technology: VCRs, DVDs, the Internet.

So much goes on behind the scenes of porno I could write a backstage musical.

Back in the 70s, I advertised my tutorial services in the pages of *Drummer* with a display ad called "Writer's Aid." Having been an associate professor teaching university journalism and literature for ten years, and needing other writers' work to fill *Drummer*, I took on, during those first years of gay lib, aspiring writers to tutor them in both creative writing and journalism of the erotic kind.

Two of my writing students were "Jack Prescott" and Anthony F. DeBlase. I counseled Prescott to take back to his real name, John Preston; and then, as editor of *Drummer*, I did the final rewrite on his raw manuscript, and published, *Mr. Benson*, from which draft Preston finally polished up the "unedited version" which was a mix of the two. Tony DeBlase, years later, actually paid money to buy the ailing *Drummer* and became its publisher.

Other 70s graduates of Writer's Aid include some wonderful current erotic writers who can reveal her/his/their own names *ad libitum*. So, actually, John F. Karr in the *Bay Area Reporter* (BAR) was right about my conscious nurturing of the South of Market leather fetish porn style.

Lesbigay conferences, hosted by historical-revisionist groupies, are full of certain gay authors of a certain age claiming they and their exclusive circles invented gay writing while all living in the same apartment building in Manhattan.

Fucking weird, man.

No one invented gay literature anymore than someone invented Irish literature or African-American literature or women's literature.

Yet we all participate. In 1999, helping gay literature come out of the closet, I contributed the title story to *Chasing Danny Boy* which was the first anthology of gay male Irish writing. Having immersed myself repeatedly in Dublin culture, I combined two ancient Irish myths collected by Lady Gregory with a stream-of-consciousness style that suits lives lived with orgasmic intensity. Style sample:

> In Dublin, the Banshee queen himself could well imagine the four lads from the punk band rolling in the fast-forward, slow-motion, and freeze-frame of the porno videos shelved in his rental shop. The hot wet mouths of those handsome handsome handsome swanlike boys lipping down slow then eager on jutting cocks spit wet tongued fucking pink butt yes like dogs taking every shape cum spurting on lips nose eye lashes stripped naked in the shed barn woods no no no yes linen sheets stained with shit dewlaps hot young sweat browning each other those four drip cum into me into you fuck into you fuck me oh yes wipe it on me eat it eat it swallow more more more fucking yes you and you and you those four lads ah ah ah.
>
> —Stream-of-consciousness orgy scene from "Chasing Danny Boy," the title story in the 1999 fiction anthology, *Chasing Danny Boy: Powerful Stories of Celtic Eros,* Finalist Best Gay and Lesbian Fiction, collected and edited by Mark Hemry.

Erotic content for me spins out of specific characters in a specific place at a specific time, so that the convergence of the quite "specific" nails a certain "universality" of human truth.

Some people think my Robert Mapplethorpe was a photographer when he was actually first an artist who was second a photographer. Never take this writer-editor-photographer-videographer, who was a founding member of the American Popular Culture Association in 1968, for anything less.

That pop-culture sensitivity and my education (which I earned, thanks to my working-class parents) trained me with a PhD in American literature and criticism, so that I was formally prepared, with my homework done, to take on gay culture's ignition at Stonewall and blast-off into the Titanic 70s for the cruise altitude of *Drummer*.

When the love that dare not speak its name began to scream, Golden Age writers' duty and necessity was to name those unspoken acts, facts, and people. Erotic writers are endlessly inventive creating infinite synonyms for sex organs and sex acts.

Actually, I had to determine for the 70s "Gay Culture Style Guide" that *cum* would be spelled "c-u-m" to match the Anglo-Saxon "f-u-c-k." and that *hardon* had no hyphen.

My name being "Jack" tuned my familiarity with the word *manjack*, as in "every manjack for himself." So I wrote a *portmanteau* word by planting the word *man* as a prefix as in "mancock." Oi and vay! Every imitator on the block has prefixed everything but the "mankitchen sink" into what is now a total cliche of "manporn." (Nothing's worse than jerking off to some writer's story and realizing he's imitating your style. Bummer.)

Pioneer writers had to create new vocabulary to spin/spin/spin queers from hated stereotype to heroic archetype.

Stereotypes can be down and dirty shorthand to create a quick villain; but heroes need to be archetypes.

I admit I write as a Platonist. Plato said that out there somewhere exists the Perfect Lover.

Quentin Crisp, who was not a Platonist, told me there was no such thing as the perfect tall, dark, and handsome Platonic Ideal.

I told Quentin, "Of course, there isn't. He's blond." Style sample:

> That first night when I first saw Kick, I recognized one of life's long shots at the Perfect Affirmation. He was a man. He had a man's strength and fragility, a man's grace and intensity, a man's joy, and a man's passion. He seemed my chance to celebrate the changes in me as growth. He was so fully a man, he was an Angel of Light. To him I could say nothing but *Yes*. One thing, you see, I know for sure: Nature very rarely puts it all together: looks, bearing, voice, appeal, smile, intelligence, artfulness, accomplishment, strength, kindness. That's what I

looked for all my life: the chance to say *Yes* to a man like that. I look in men for nothing more than that affirmative something that grabs you and won't let you look away. Maintaining my full self, to have some plenty to offer back in balance, I've looked for some man who fills in the appropriate existential blanks, for some man to be the way a man is supposed to be, for some man to keep on keeping on with, in all the evolving variations of friendship and fraternity, beyond the first night's encounter. I've looked for that to happen: to be able to say *Yes* inside myself when a good, clean glow of absolute trust settles over the world. Honest manliness is never half-revealed. When it's there, it's all right there in front of you. The hardest thing to be in the world today is a man....When Ryan first saw Kick, I dare say, his fantasy spanned a million years.

—Aria, "Archetype," from the novel, *Some Dance to Remember*, published by Elizabeth Gershman, Knight's Press, 1990; The Haworth Press, 2005.

Erotica is storytelling.
Erotica is pillow-talk.
Erotica is what you whisper into an ear to seduce.
Erotica is what you say in bed to bend your partner into three more inches.
Erotica is what you promise afterwards to make sure you get sex again.

If I may make a comment as one of the first and longest living gay writers/editors, lesbigay authors in the 21st century need to get their storytelling shit together. Lesbigay writing should be as good as straight writing, or better—especially if the *Queer Eye* minstrel fantasy is true that lesbigays have better taste than straights.

Look at the lesbigay magazines!

Most of the illustrations look like the drawings of mental patients.

Most of the models, pro or amateur, have dead faces.

Much lesbigay writing reads the same: mental and dead. Humorless.

Lesbigay erotic narrative is largely unimaginative: "I went to a bar, met a god who took me off on his bike, fucked me, and left me, but I'll never forget him, because he was my first time."

GLBT writers need to develop titles, story arcs, character back stories, dialog, points-of-view other than the "first person narrator," and certainly not one more "sensitive soul coming-of-age story" which deserves the "No More Wire Hangers Award"!

Just because writers' laptops print out instant-gratification columns—formatted to look like writing on a book page or a magazine page—doesn't mean that the writers need not go back over the first draft to polish it twenty times.

I started writing the 562 final pages of *Some Dance to Remember* in 1968 and finished it in 1982, with final edit in 1984, and publication in 1990. Be patient, but always keep focused. I could only write that novel as fast as history happened.

I knew this *Some Dance* diary of gay culture was a three-way love story told against the epic rise of gay lib, but I had no idea in 1978 that HIV would enter the novel the way the burning of Atlanta entered *Gone with the Wind* to which *Some Dance* has been compared, by, among others, *The Advocate,* as "the gay *Gone with the Wind.*"

(Originally in 1979, my whimsey was to title my gay *Gone with the Wind*: *Blown with the Wind*; but that was too satirical and precious.)

On the other hand in 1992 and 1993, dead-set-dedicated in more ways than one, I dared the psychic danger of writing my nonfiction memoir of my bicoastal lover, *Mapplethorpe: Assault with a Deadly Camera,* in ninety edgy days while over and over as loud as possible I played the soundtrack from *The Crying Game.* I wrote *Some Dance to Remember* listening to the Eagles' *Hotel California* (1976). This synthesis of music and writing received pop-culture confirmation in the "authors' circle of inspiration" when the playwright Tom Stoppard, screenwriter of *Shakespeare in Love* (1998), affirmed that he wrote his plays, *Arcadia* (1993), over the Rolling Stones' "You Can't Always Get What You Want," and *The Coast of Utopia* (2006) between listening repeatedly to the 1979 Pink Floyd track from *The Wall,* "Comfortably Numb." (*Vanity Fair,* November 2007, page 190-192)

Absolutely required reading for lesbigay writers: *The Writer's Journey: Mythic Structure for Storytellers and Screenwriters* by Christopher Vogler.

A trained cultural analyst, I mention this huge problem in gay storytelling, because such process analysis reveals the construct of what my erotica attempts. I'm tempestuously Irish (romantically independent) and Austrian (romantically aggressive), a Gemini born during the brightest hour of the longest day: noon hour on the summer solstice.

My first nonfiction book was about media and criticism: *Television Today* (1971). My second nonfiction book was about the occult, sex, and leather: *Popular Witchcraft: Straight from the Witch's Mouth* (1972). My third nonfiction was an erotic bio-memoir: *Mapplethorpe: Assault with a Deadly Camera* (1994). Patricia Morrisroe, the writer who attempted the horrible biography, *Mapplethorpe* (1995), named me, based on my journalism in *Drummer,* "The King of Sleaze," showing how shocking she—as a straight interloper—found gay-culture *verite* to be. Was Patsy pissed that my frankly honest *Mapplethorpe* memoir beat her puritanical Catholic school-girl biography into stores, and was the first book on Mapplethorpe ever published? (And I didn't inbreed in the corporate "incest" between Random House and *The New Yorker*!)

Anyway, this King of Sleaze thanks Ms. P. M. for her straight rant which in the inverted gay world is wonderful endorsement, actually, for quoting on covers of books with an exclamation point: ...a new erotic novel by "The King of Sleaze"! Style sample:

READER DISCRETION ADVISORY

This pop culture memoir contains sex, lies, greed, perversion, murder, deceit, infidelity, drugs, sex, immorality, scatology, ambition, sex, equivocation, character assassination, slander, blasphemy, aspersion, sex, betrayal, distortion, racism, ungodliness, sodomy–and that's just the critics of Mapplethorpe!

—First page, before title page of the erotic bio-memoir, *Mapplethorpe: Assault with a Deadly Camera*, published in hard cover by Hy Stierman, Hastings House, 1994

Educated in Catholic schools, I can't seem not to write "sexy." I try, but even my earliest stories, published in—believe it or not—Roman Catholic magazines—are erotic subliminally, written as they are about virgin-saints fighting impurity, martyrs suffering joyously under the sadistic hands in the Colosseum, and revolutionaries in Latin America nailed to the roofs of cars by the *policia* in my 1961 story, "The Untimely Death of J. Cristobal." (Get the coded name?)

My stories were "out" erotically before I was, in fact, before I knew that sex, or homosexuality even existed.

For a fictional memoir "take" on this, check out my first novel, the pre-quel to 1990's *Some Dance to Remember*, titled *What They Did to the Kid: Confessions of an Altar Boy* (1966). *Kid* is totally overheated eros told from *inside* "the closet," so it is a new kind of gay genre—a novel of the closet—that takes place before there is any coming-out story. *Kid* is, however, strictly in the tradition of mid-century novels such as Graham Greene's *The End of the Affair*.

When straight people ask me what I write, I say, "Men's adventure stories."

All my stories are relationship stories disguised as adventure stories ("Wild Blue Yonder"), comedy stories ("By Blonds Obsessed'), revenge stories ("The Lords of Leather," very Edgar Allen Poe), fetish stories ("Cigar Sarge," "K-9 Dog Dik," "Foreskin Blues"), war stories ("The

Porno, Ergo Sum

Shadow Soldiers"), leather stories ("S&M Ranch"), bear stories (the one-sentence, 3500-word "Three Bears in a Tub"), gym stories ("Father and Son Tag Team"), muscle stories ("Buzz Spaulding's Training Academy"), sci-fi stories ("Roughnight@sodom.cum" which won the Richard Labonté Different Light award for best title), and twinkie stories ("A Beach Boy Named Desire").

I write stories of the future ("Earthorse") and the past (*"Titanic,"* the gay version), as well as ethnic stories (the Irish "Chasing Danny Boy," the Native-American and German "Buckskin Foreskin," and the Latin "From Nada to Mañana").

Hell, I even write sapphic stories for straight magazines and lesbian novels (*The Geography of Women: A Romantic Comedy*) that win awards, despite being told by one prestigious reviewer at the *Harvard Gay and Lesbian Review*: "I know how to review your gay male porno, but I don't know how to review a man writing about women."

Duh. Such anti-humanist bigotry! Could he review *A Streetcar Named Desire*?

I'm known for helping editors out at the last minute when other writers don't meet the deadline. Editors beginning new magazines often invite me in to their first issue for good luck on the kickoff (*Skin, Just Men, Inches, Bear, Fetish Noir*, etc.).

To sustain a porno career, and a writing career, one must stretch, grow with the times, as in sometimes changing my byline to my web address "www.JackFritscher.com."

I'm famous for pastness, memoirs, but also hot on the latest novelty. I'm always trying to refresh the gray column inches of gay publishing, books and mags, with alternative erotic genres: plays ("Corporal in Charge of Taking Care of Captain O'Malley" which was the only gay play published in the Lammy Award canonical collection, *Gay Roots*) and screenplays (*Buck's Bunkhouse*), and features written in Internet e-style ("The Genome of Bear" for *Bear Classic 2000*, "The Genome of Leather" for "The Leather Magazine of Record," *Checkmate Magazine*).

I've written a ton of lesbian erotica for major straight publishers (Larry Flynt), because I'm a humanist, and not a slave to the failed Marxism of political correctness, and will defend to the death my pal Pat Califia's right to advise gay men about their penises.

Camille Paglia and I not long ago appeared together on a BBC Channel 4 TV program titled *Priapus Unsheathed* defending the penis as erotica for both women and men. These female/male gender-liaisons occur because writers are thinkers, analysts, and, maybe cultural weather vanes, as well as storytellers.

I write literary erotica, as bipolar as Anne Rice who is A N Roquelaure (all forms of sex), because it plays to a double audience: those interested in literature, and those interested in intelligent sex.

"My porno starts in your head and works its way down."

I like to be in America. Okay by me in America where box office maps pop culture. *Some Dance* has sold nearly 23,000 copies; *Mapplethorpe* in hard cover, 42,000; the other ten of my soft-to-hardcore books, 70,000. That's approximately 130,000 book copies, coupled with more than 250,000 units of my 130 erotic videos. Plus well over 500,000 copies of my *Drummer* issues in the 1970s.

That's major sales, and a rubdown with a velvet glove on the balls of a culture, especially when there's from one to a dozen places to jerk-off in each of those 980,000 units of book, magazine, and video entertainment. (Masturbation is the sexual pun in the name "Palm Drive.") That's say, conservatively, 4 million masturbatory loads out there in the dark, which is something to a Catholic boy who was raised to believe that masturbation is a mortal sin that condemns the masturbator to hell for all eternity.

Is that why I write? Christ meets Dionysius? Or do I just get off knowing every night that out there someone is wacking himself into a moment of sublime pleasure, his only joy after a day of a shitty job or of taking care of his elderly parents?

Sometimes tiny Stanislavski quirks sneak into the writing method: sometimes I get naked; sometimes I dress up in leather or sex gear; once upon a time I sometimes smoked a cigar, or sniffed popper because nothing clarifies erotica like amyl nitrite which in its purple haze turns Godzilla into God and the brain comes down with some little mantra, three or four words of essence, as valid as Gertie Stein's experimental writing, or Alice B's brownies—or so Gertrude's pal who became mine, Sam Steward, told me.

Art is a delicate balancing act: living in one's brain waves at alpha (14 cycles per second) in a beta-driven world (18 cycles per second). No one sane ever "does" writing; sane people make money. No one without the discipline of a monk and a Marine can do it.

The secret of art, of the art of writing, of porno, of literature, or of the art of literary erotica, is putting your butt in the chair, with all the notes on pieces of paper to cue the next paragraph, the dialog, the feeling. I write three pages every day, five if it feels good, but no more.

The spirit is willing, but the flesh is aged beef.

At five pages I begin to foreshorten. I stay hungry, eager, at three pages, so the next day the drive continues into the next three pages. Until a book is actually bound, until an article or story is actually in the publisher's hands, the writing is never over: visions, polishing, re-visions.

A person has to be very brave to write porno, and very secure to publish under their own name, because sooner or later "everything you say can and will be used against you."

For better or for worse, critics often mention my style. "Fritscher is a stylist." On a scale of 10, they love it or hate it. Mason Powell, known to me only by reputation, is the author of many books including the S&M classic, *The Brig* (serialized in *Drummer*, 1984), and the romantic-crime novel, *For the Love of a Green-Eyed Piano Player*. He is a San Francisco literary critic who wrote an unsolicited review of my fiction anthology, *Rainbow County and Other Stories* (1999):

> Book reviewers, almost as much as music critics, strive desperately for an original turn of phrase or image with which to imbue the prose which is their work and which, perforce, inevitably falls into a routine of tedium. One of the more overused descriptors which one encounters these days is that of "a unique voice." Yet with regard to Jack Fritscher I am forced to score and heat up that chestnut, for nobody, to the best of my knowledge, writes with anything closely approaching Fritscher's level of raw passion, poetry, and over the top sense of verbal drive.... Some writers fall naturally into either the medium of the novel or the short story, and I think perhaps Fritscher is at his best in the short story. That may be because of the white hot heat with which he sets word to paper. The novel requires some leisure, some pause to reflect; Fritscher is not contemplative, he is passionate, in your face, all over you. He is not Brahms, he is Edgar Varese, assaulting you with mind pictures and word stretches that may very well tear the membrane.
>
> Or maybe it is just that nobody can sustain the levels he reaches for more than the duration of a short story. In this collection of twenty works, both short stories and narrative poems, he goes the limit. All the icons for which he is famous are on display: the musclemen, the soldiers, the cowboys, the prisoners; but his takes on the icons are more intense, more extreme, than I think any other writer would care to set out.
>
> I am no novice when it comes to writing about sadomasochistic sex; it is a fascinating means of illuminating areas of human consciousness which cannot be lit with any other torch. But Fritscher goes way, way, beyond anything which I would seek to see. Be warned: there are stories in this book that are

too intense for me, stories that not only extend the envelope but put it through a shredder and set fire to it. If you are not up to sweating; sometimes with desire, sometimes with horror; then don't even try it! Fritscher is not a light weight, either in terms of subject matter or literary style.

If, however, you can stand the heat — if you are willing to go places in literary mode that you would likely never want to go in person — then Jack Fritscher is an ideal tour guide. Part James Joyce, part William Faulkner, and a whole lot more than the Marquis de Sade, I am forced to repeat the cliche: Jack Fritscher is a unique voice, and one who, if you are up to it, you should hear. The songs are steamy and scary, but God! Can this man sing! — ©1999 Mason Powell.

http://home.pon.net/rhinoceroslodge/reviews.htm
Retrieved July 12, 2003. Used with permission.

(I really should meet Mason Powell and take him to lunch anywhere he wants.)

Style for me is strong word choice, rhythmic phrases, colorful metaphor, filmic editing of space and time and memory, distinct objective dialog as well as the streaming-consciousness, the convoluted monolog of thought and conscience which reveals characters seen by themselves in contrast to how other characters see them.

"How Buddy Left Me," one of my favorite stories, is an example of strong word choice that turns a porno story into a love story. "Chasing Danny Boy" is full of rhythmic phrases born of the sex-rhythms of jerking off. "Titanic" spins on evergreen queer/queen metaphor: survival.

In the hold of *Titanic*, the second night of the ill-fated voyage, sex occurs. Style sample:

> Edward and the Stoker, two different classes of men, were as perfect an odds-on match as *Titanic* was for the North Atlantic.
>
> "When I beat you, young gentleman, sir...," the Stoker said. He appreciated Edward's cock and cockiness. "...You will stay with me for 24 focking hours below decks in the hold, in the boiler room, maybe even in chains in the brig, just so you see, young gentleman, how men like you make men like us live."
>
> Edward, ever the knightly aristocrat, picked up the gauntlet. He hated socialism and bolshevism....Edward either had to take the Stoker's 14-fat-inches down his throat, and, mind you, up his ass, or he had to spend a day and a night in the hold getting up

Porno, Ergo Sum

to the Stoker's "focking" speed, outdistancing his old sculling records, the way *Titanic*, slicing through the still, cold waters was outdistancing herself and her sister ship, *Olympic*.

The Stoker stripped naked to his boots. Edward shucked his clothes and shoes. A sailor started rapping a rhythmic tattoo on the iron railing in time to the rods pistoning the huge engines. The Stoker was a stroker, wrapping both big hands around his cock, squeezing out a third handful, vein-popping the bulbous mushroom head, its piss-slit dripping translucent 4-weight lube webs. His was a savage cock, primitive, animal, evolved somehow, from the mountain giants of Eastern Europe into a steel-hard, mechanized piston. The way his ox-driving ancestors wielded their barbarian swords, the Stoker aimed his ram at Edward like some unstoppable industrial weapon....The Stoker was the stuff of Edward's dreams.

—Orgy scene in the novella, *Titanic*, from the collection of 69 stories in 4 volumes, *Titanic: Forbidden Stories Hollywood Forgot*, 1999, first published in *Uncut Magazine*, September 1988, and *Mach Magazine #35*, March 1997.

Distinct objective dialog drives the two-man play or screenplay, "Corporal in Charge of Taking Care of Captain O'Malley," which first appeared in *Drummer* 22 and *Drummer* 23 (May and July 1978). How many porno writers bother to do dialog to catch the very rhythms of sex? This drama opens up the erotic back-story behind Walt Whitman's poem, "Oh, Captain, My Captain." Style sample:

> Captain O'Malley: Stick your tongue out so you can take the Captain's cum that's cuming out of his big dick.
> Corporal Powell: Ahhhgh! Yessir. Please, Sir.
> O'Malley: You keep that fuckin 'mouth open. You keep that fuckin' mouth open.
> Powell: Ahhh.
> O'Malley: Captain's gonna shoot a big load all over your fuckin' face...all over your fuckin' face. I'm gonna shoot a load all over your fuckin' face, Corporal. It's gettin' close...Big fuckin' load from the Captain's cock...I'm gonna shoot all over your fuckin' face.
> Powell: Oh, please, Sir. My God! Yessir! (With feeling) *Yessir!*

O'Malley: Your legs are quivering, Corporal.

Powell: Ahhhgh...I want, Sir....Please, Sir. Hurry and cum, Sir. Please, I'm ready.

O'Malley: Awright! Shoot that load. Shoot your fuckin' load.

Powell: Yessir!

O'Malley: C'mon, Corporal, shoot your fuckin' load. Shoot your fuckin' load. Captain's close. Captain's close...Oh, look at that cum cuming out!

Powell: Ahhhgh! Yes, ahh, yessir.

O'Malley: Look at that fuckin' cum. Ah, Corporal, cum's cuming out. (High cries of orgasm) Ohhaaaggh, there it comes. All over your fuckin' face, it's all over your fuckin' face, Corporal. It's in your fuckin' eyes.

Powell: I can't see. It's in my eyes.

O'Malley: Ow, your fuckin' mouth, your fuckin' chest, ahhh!

Powell: I can't see....It's burning my eyes...

O'Malley: The Captain shot a load. In your hair, Corporal.

Powell: Yessir.

O'Malley: You got cum in your hair.

Powell: Yessir. Ahhh.

O'Malley: The Captain wants to wipe your eyes, Corporal. (Post-orgasmic moans interspersed with dialogue) The Captain wants to hold you, Corporal.

Powell: Yessir.

O'Malley: The Captain want you to hold him.

Powell: Yessir. Ahhh. Captain. Ah, Captain. Just lay on top of me, Sir.

O'Malley: Big fuckin' Corporal to hold his Captain...

Powell: Yessir. Oh God. Layin' on top of me, Sir. This is really fine. Oh God. I needed that, Sir. This is really fine. Oh God. I had a rough day too, Sir...

O'Malley: Lick the rest of the cum out of the Captain's cock...

Powell: Yessir. Does the Captain have to piss, *Sir*?

> Close shot: CAPTAIN O'MALLEY's face grinning. Medium shot: slow motion. CAPTAIN O'MALLEY's semi-hard dick pisses heavy and golden down on CORPORAL POWELL who drinks fast. Gulping.
> Powell: OH, CAPTAIN! My Captain!
> O'MALLEY rubs his tight hairy belly. The piss splashes in slow motion, catching the back light, golden. Both men are laughing.
>
> —Final scene from "Corporal in Charge of Taking Care of Captain O'Malley" from the collection of 69 stories in 4 volumes, *Corporal in Charge and Other Stories;* first published in *Drummer,* May 1978; published in the canonical *Gay Roots: An Anthology of Gay History, Sex, Politics and Culture,* 1991

I used subjective streaming monolog plus carefully designed dialect spelling to tell the 3,500 word story, "Three Bears in a Tub," in one sentence that never takes a breath, yet is rather perfectly punctuated. The dialect is the same as the dialect designed for my first-person narrator in my lesbian novel of the American South in the 1950s, *The Geography of Women: A Romantic Comedy*. Style sample:

> Listen here, boy, there'll be no hibernatin till after I finish tellin you this bedtime story about Big Daddy when he was himself hardly more than a boy and he turned into a six-foot-five man and what he done to earn that reputation he got that famous summer on Bear Lake when the canoe overturned late around midnight and Big Daddy saw them two young hairy fishermen floppin like bears in the water next to drownin with their rubber boots suckin them down to the clear rock bottom and them able to stand just barely with their chin on the surface of the moonlit water…[omitting 5 pages]…and they was beggin Big Daddy to do with them what he wanted because he was their Big Daddy and they loved him so much and that's what Big Daddy wanted to hear so he saved them both by cuttin them out of their rubber waders so they floated to the surface of Bear Lake and Big Daddy took ahold of them by their hair and beards and nipples and dicks and buttholes and pulled both them boys into his rowboat where they sat the rest of the night laughin and drinkin and shoutin through their beards at the moon while stars glistened between them nipple to nipple with comets shootin flume tails from their dicks and they floated ever so happy on the still

surface of the water while the real constellation of the Bear rose and set over their heads and their fudgey fingers sticky from their buttholes were all entwined in the fur on their chest and the hair of their bellies and the carpet on their shoulders and the bush of their crotches and the hugeness of their beards and the curly sweep of the hair on their heads and they were all three of them so satisfied that the summer night smiled and half-asleep in each other's big furry arms, Griz and Cub and Big Daddy drifted slow across the mirror of stars to their dock on Bear Lake as if the rowboat knew their way home.

—"Three Bears in a Tub" from 69 stories in 4 volumes, *Titanic: Forbidden Stories Hollywood Forgot*, first published in *Bear Magazine Classic Annual 1999*, and in *Best Gay Erotica 2001*, as well as in Susie Bright's *Best American Erotica 2003*.

In this filmic age, I attempt stories vivid enough to jump directly from page to performance.

The Geography of Women and "Rainbow County" are virtual plays/screenplays ready for performance.

Like it or not in our culture, literary pages are validated by the screen, which is why I enjoy the high concept of turning my written fiction into porno videos, and vice versa, as in *Buck's Bunkhouse Discipline*.

The final test of writing is reading the text out loud. If as a writer I stumble, stutter, when reading the lines, something is wrong with the lines. Re-write. Find the rhythm of the words, of the sex, of the scene, and write that rhythm.

Faced with the huge difficulty of writing such a "confession" as this, I am tempted to retract the veracity of all these factual words, and turn fact into fiction, presented in a way that shows how reality is re-shaped by fiction, how autobiography turns to drama, how experience turns into entertainment. What follows is the erotic version of this preceding essay on writing. Style sample:

Not arrested, but picked up, questioned about what he did and how he did it, he told everything revealing nothing. On the table before him, the tips of his fingers, sensitive from years of typing, drummed the wood, impatient with the interrogation. From an ashtray, blue smoke from a half-twisted butt rose like incense at a seance toward the naked light bulb. *He breathed in experience.* He could feel the heat on his forehead. *He exhaled fiction.* Under the metal shade, the bulb hung like a burning pear, a scrotum, on a cord. He sat in the intense circle of light. He studied the detectives' movement in the darkness beyond the shade. His cock hardened untouched. He looked for the faces out there in the dark.

Other hands, other intentions, shuffled the evidence spread across the table, turning pages, trying to sort fiction from nonfiction, examining photographs, advancing videos frame by frame. He smirked. Excitement tweaked his nipples. Someone had tampered with the evidence: cum had spurted across his thousand photographs of naked men; more cum glued together the pages of his sixty-nine stories in four volumes; cum, mixed with sweat and tears, curled the pages of his 562-page ransom note he couldn't even dance to remember. *Everything you say can be held...against...hard against...fill-in-the-blank*, he figured.

At fourteen he had bet he could get away with murder. At first, all he needed to pull off the job were yellow legal pads, then a manual typewriter, then a Selectric, and finally a laptop. He moved on to cameras, black-and-white print film, 35mm transparencies (*mmm*, that first willing lifeguard on the beach in Chicago!), 8mm, Super-8, 16mm, video, digital, high-definition. He was an analyst. He lived it up to write it down. He was a part of all he met and *vice-versa verite*, baby. He nailed a warning above his bed: "Enter here to become a story told at night around the world." He could have sold space in his books and stories so eager were the accomplices wanting to be mentioned in code or in reality, desperate for him to write, "When the hero came into the bar, he walked by X who stood by the pinball machine."

He could have admitted to none, some, much, most, or all of the fiction that was truth that was fiction, but he didn't. His pen was mighty. He was a rich man with a big dick driving a fast car. As they had when he played football, everyone patted his ass. He always knew exactly what he was doing, who he was doing, when, where, and how he was doing it. His brain was his ultimate hardon. He had the last laugh.

— "Excerpt," unpublished work in progress

III. Eyewitness Illustrations

GAY WRITERS!

Sold any lately? Pro writer/editor/agent thoroughly critiques your poetry, fiction, articles, scripts! Erotic or straight. Novice writers also welcome. Send self-addressed stamped envelope for *very* reasonable rates and totally professional advice:

WRITER'S AID
4436 25th Street
San Francisco, CA 94114

Top: Fritscher's fifty-year writing career is a library stack of books documenting his work in the media of magazines, photography, and video. Bottom: With notice of his "Writer's Aid" running in *Drummer*, Jack Fritscher mentored many "Gay Writers" into the new genre of gay writing in the 1970s, the first decade after Stonewall, when magazines ruled gay culture ten years before the rise of GLBT book publishers in the mid-1980s. Among his clients was an unknown Chicago author named Anthony DeBlase who later purchased *Drummer* in 1986, became its publisher, and engaged Fritscher as an ongoing consultant on *Drummer*. Tutor Fritscher also counseled John Preston, and produced, edited, and serialized his *Mr. Benson* for *Drummer*.

Porno, Ergo Sum 229

Top: Business card for *Words*, 1975-1982, Jack Fritscher's business connecting and promoting the talents of the *Drummer* salon. Bottom: Cover, *Key West Literary Seminar: Literature in a Time of AIDS*. In January 1997, the straight Key West hosts abruptly disbanded the conference after unruly behavior on the theater stage by a ranting Larry Kramer and by panelists Tony Kushner and Sarah Schulman who "ganged up" on the delicate Key West author Ann Beattie for being rather much a straight white woman capitalist who didn't write enough about AIDS. In addition to eyewitness Fritscher who had returned to his fourth-row seat by walking down the aisle with the fire-breathing Kramer he had found working up to a tantrum in the men's room, also in attendance were keynote speaker Edmund White, Frank Rich, Michael Denneny, David Leavitt, and Michael Bronski.

Becoming visible men: American photographer Lou Thomas (right, with Gary Stone), published a photograph of himself on the cover of his 'zine *Boys in Leather* #1 (1964) as a "trial balloon" three years before he co-founded Colt Studio (1967) and his own Target Studio (1974). Masculine-identified artists Lou Thomas, Chuck Renslow, Etienne, A. Jay, Fred Halsted, Robert Mapplethorpe, and Jack Fritscher led the real-time leather players who created the photographs, writing, magazines, films, and books of early leather identity of homomasculinity emerging as a legitimate category from the revolving closet door set spinning by the Stonewall Rebellion of 1969. To strengthen and darken *Drummer* which was born blond in LA, Fritscher in San Francisco edited into *Drummer* a potent mix of Renslow and Etienne's Chicago leather values and Lou Thomas' New York leather scene. Lou Thomas shot many *Drummer* covers and centerfolds. *Boys in Leather #1*, featuring Lou Thomas as "Nick D'Arti," credited its photographs to Thomas' "Leather Photography, PO Box 352, New York," and was published by Elgin Products, Los Angeles, with the Elgin probably referencing the Elgin Marbles.

Homomasculinity:
Framing Keywords of Queer Popular Culture

> Written January-March 2005, this essay was published, and an abstract read by the author, at the Queer Keywords Conference, "The(e)ories: Advanced Seminars for Queer Research" Series, University College Dublin, Ireland, April 15, 2005.
> I. Author's Eyewitness Historical-Context Introduction written October 2, 2007
> II. The complete essay as published at the Queer Keywords Conference, "The(e)ories: Advanced Seminars for Queer Research" Series, University College of Dublin, Ireland, April 2005, which invited "the coiners of various homo-words to reflect on their neologisms, their cultural and societal significance, origins, contexts, political agendas, and so forth."
> III. Eyewitness Illustrations

I. Author's Eyewitness Historical-Context written October 2, 2007

Homo-Linguistics, Queer Identity, and Framing Homosexuality as a Religion

---

"You keep the language alive, you keep all of this alive."
—Loretta Kelsey, "the last person on Earth fluent in Elem Pomo, an 8,000-year-old Pomo Tribe language once spoken North of San Francisco"

"Language is not just a monument to knowledge, it's a monument to identity." —Leanne Hinton, Professor Emeritus, UC Berkeley, documenting Elem Pomo with Loretta Kelsey

—Kevin Fagan, "Only Living Elem Pomo Speaker Teaches So She Won't Be the Last," San Francisco *Chronicle*, SFGate.com, September 30, 2007

In 2005, because I was an historically documented coiner of "homo-words," I was invited to present this necessarily autobiographical paper on language, identity, and homosexuality in the series "The(e)ories: Advanced Seminars for Queer Research."

The "Queer Keywords" event was convened and directed by Michael O'Rourke and Noreen Giffney, Women's Studies, School of Social Justice, University College Dublin, Ireland, April 14-16, 2006.

Michael O'Rourke and Noreen Giffney are also Research Affiliates in the Centre for the Interdisciplinary Study of Sexuality and Gender in Europe at the University of Exeter, UK.

In concept and content, this "Homomasculinity" essay specifically answered the international invitation which Giffney and O'Rourke made to activist...

> ...coiners of various *homo-words* to reflect anecdotally on how and why they created their neologisms, their cultural and societal significance, origin, contexts, and agendas vis a vis the impulse to conceptualize, name, and label—particularly in the mass media of gay popular culture...with the idea of publishing a "Homoglossary"...

My essay on the linguistic ecology of *Drummer* posited that in order to write about the newly uncloseted homosexuality of the 1970s—the first decade after Stonewall, our suddenly liberated culture required a new vocabulary for authors reporting on the love that theretofore dare not speak. Breaking the silence of the closet, I coined the word *homomasculinity* in 1977 when I was editor in chief virilizing *Drummer* magazine in San Francisco and needed words to conceptualize the new way we were in our self-fashioning identities.

We were suddenly in our own new *La Dolce Vita*.

Necessity was the mother of invention.

In the way that Fellini created the new words *paparazzo* and *paparazzi* for his Roman film, I had to create new and useful words for San Francisco *Drummer*.

In this homo-word essay of transparent history, and in my germinal book, *Gay San Francisco: Eyewitness Drummer*, I am a protagonist as well as a priestling-scholar playing the part of Eusebius hot-linking the "canon tales" of *Drummer* and sorting, preserving, and quoting the leather history of *Drummer* that might otherwise have been lost.

Homomasculinity

Out of classical Greek and Latin roots, I grew the syllables of *homomasculinity* the way that Walt Whitman grew his linguistics in *Leaves of Grass*. The great "Gray (and Gay) Poet" Walt Whitman, a born homomasculinist, was peerless in designing gender-related language and rhetoric. Influenced by Plato's ideal of love, Whitman wrote, at the heart of *Leaves of Grass*, his Calamus poems singing of man-to-man love, often referred to as "the Calamus emotion."

Whitman's disciple, Allen Ginsberg, also a born homomasculinist who fetishized frank virility, worshiped his own circle of masculine straightish men including everyone's favorite endowed hustler, Neal Cassady; the handsome Jack Kerouac (who could be played on screen by look-alike Daniel Craig); and his longtime lover the not-quite-gay Peter Orlovsky. Nevertheless, the poet Ginsberg, whose personal sexuality acknowledged a new assertive kind of radical masculinity in lovers, did not coin for the Beats or for gay America any new word for the homomasculinity to which, in concept, he knelt.

Ginsberg's famous "blues," which I experienced with him when he landed in my lap in Kalamazoo, Michigan, was the source for the series of many of my *Drummer* articles titled variously, "Cigar Blues," Prison Blues," and "Castro Street Blues," capped with the novel, *Leather Blues*. At that time of the National Poetry Festival (1973) in nearby Allendale, Michigan, my sex-connection to Ginsberg was our mutual friend the poet, Thom Gunn, but Ginsberg's grooming (he was an appallingly unkempt Walt Whitman) and his horrible squeeze box got in the way. "Allen! Enough with the noise, already! I understand your masochistic *nostalgia de la boue*, but take a fuckin' bath!"

When the Beats gave way to the Hippies who gave way to the gays, I was impelled by the push of Stonewall and the rush of *Drummer* to coin several words to write my reportage, and that gonzo journalism—documented in the internationally known *Drummer*—led to an invitation to join the "Queer Keywords" conference.

Other participants in the "Queer Keywords" series included Richard Meyer, Associate Professor, Department of Art History, University of Southern California, author of *Outlaw Representation: Censorship and Homosexuality in Twentieth-Century American Art*; Robert McRuer, Associate Professor, Department of English, George Washington University, author of *Crip Theory: Cultural Signs of Queerness and Disability*; and Niall Richardson, Lecturer, University of Sussex, Falmer, Brighton, UK, author of *The Queer Cinema of Derek Jarman*, and, pertinently, "The Queer Activity of Extreme Male Bodybuilding: Gender Dissidence, Auto-Eroticism and Hysteria" in *Social Semiotics*, 14:1, 49-66, plus "Queer

Masculinity: The Representation of John Paul Pitoc's Body in *Trick*" in *Paragraph*, 26:1-2, March/July, 232-245.

II. The essay as published at the Queer Keywords Conference, "The(e)ories: Advanced Seminars for Queer Research" Series, University College of Dublin, Ireland, April 2005, which invited "the coiners of various homo-words to reflect on their neologisms, their cultural and societal significance, origins, contexts, political agendas, and so forth."

Homomasculinity:
Framing Keywords of Queer Popular Culture

Part I. Introduction: *The Mise en Scene* of Pop Culture
Part II. *Apologia Pro Vita Sua* (Sort a')

> "Good authors who once knew better words
> now only use four-letter words writing prose."
> —Cole Porter, "Anything Goes" (1934)

Part I. Introduction:
The *Mise en Scene* of Pop Culture, the 1960s, and Keystones in the Arch of the Stonewall;
A Survey of One Writer's Linguistic Journey through the Grotesque Odds of Publishing up to the Post-Factual Age of Bush

---

In London, on May 14, 1969, in a very cruisy movie theater in Piccadilly Circus, I asked a very hot sailor, "Are you 'top' or 'bottom'?" And he said, "You Americans. You label everything."

In or around Stonewall, June 28, 1969, gay character changed.

"In or around December 1910," Virginia Woolf famously wrote in 1924, "human character changed." The Bloomsbury Group re-keyed itself. In 1926, Ernest Hemingway's protagonist Jake Barnes in *The Sun Also Rises* virtually pukes in chapter three while Lady Brett Ashley parties with a festive group of Parisian gay men that Barnes—rendered speechless with Hemingway's homophobia—cannot name with a noun but can only refer to as *they* and *them* more than thirty times. In 1945, Raymond Williams returned from the war to Cambridge and found life had changed. "We no longer spoke the same language," he wrote in *Keywords: A Vocabulary of Culture and Society* (1983). Even as each 20th-century decade more or less accommodated homosexuality, the 1960s blew in on Stonewall by offering a perfect storm of liberation as elements converged through the media of popular culture wherein everything changed, if one applies Warhol, every fifteen minutes. In 1964, the trifecta of Mario Savio's Free Speech Movement at Berkeley, Kenneth Marlowe's best-selling *Mr. Madam*, and Susan Sontag's "Notes on 'Camp'" sounded the charge of the gay-keyword stampede out of Polari and into the streets.

In the revolutionary Prague Spring of 1968, after Martin Luther King was assassinated in April and protest riots of resistance broke out in sixty American cities, Robert Kennedy was killed in June, two days after Andy Warhol was shot by genderist Valerie Solanas. Word-slinger Mart Crowley's *The Boys in the Band* opened April 14 in New York and accurately outed fluent gay badinage into pop culture media. In August, when the Chicago police rioted with clubs beating activists at the Democratic Convention, the victims—surrounded in the streets—resisted and changed the politics of dominance by chanting to invoke the power of the international television cameras: "The whole world is watching."

In spring 1969, in Paris I listened to Serge Gainsbourg and Jane Birkin anointing 1969 sexually in their shocking duets, "69 Annee Erotique" and "Je T'aime Moi Non Plus." At the same moment, Gloria Steinem wrote her first feminist article, "After Black Power, Women's Liberation," the taboo-breaking *Midnight Cowboy* premiered May 25, and on the very "out" date of June 9, 1969, once-a-century "6/9/69 parties" were celebrated throughout the free world—which inaugurated the 1970s orgy fad. Driven by this tidal surge, eighteen days later, at the Stonewall Inn, as June 28 became June 29, the love that dare not speak its name began to shout underground vocabulary to the media, like some wild burlesque Berlitz teaching gayspeak as a foreign language.

Reporting the Stonewall uprising six hours after the first stone was cast, a reticent *New York Times* in ten short-shrift paragraphs used the word *homosexual* once and "young men" twice. The *New York Post* in five paragraphs used *homosexual* only once but actually dared quote the framing chant of "gay power." The *New York Daily News* tried to disarm the mutiny with the mocking, nelly, campy "Homo Nest Raided, Queen Bees Stinging Mad." In its Independence Day issue (July 3, 1969), *The Village Voice* nailed the gay *gravitas* with the headline feature "Gay Power Comes to Sheridan Square." On November 5, activists successfully picketed the *Los Angeles Times* for refusing to print the word *homosexual* in advertisements. By June 1970, thousands of gay militants—veterans of civil rights, women's lib, and peace movements—marched past news-media cameras with signs reading "Gay Pride" and "Gay Power" at the Christopher Street Liberation Day in Central Park. In my journal, I noted: gay character changed. That years-long journal grew into my love-letter book about the first Gay Renaissance, *Some Dance to Remember: A Memoir-Novel of San Francisco 1970-1982*.

> "Bliss was it that dawn to be alive,
> but to be young was heaven."
> —William Wordsworth, "The Prelude"

These events, outing gay speak, began the teach-in to make straight pop-culture bilingual. Just as in the early 1960s the Peace Movement and Civil Rights Movement debated their differences, then joined together for political strength, the best drag that queers ever did was cloaking gay liberation in the keywords of the civil rights movement. Revolutionary change drove the mood-swings during that "Stonewall summer" of America landing a man on the moon, of Charles Manson, of *Easy Rider*, of the Tet counteroffensive in Vietnam, and of Woodstock.

Five years before Stonewall, at the same instant that Sontag unleashed "Camp," *Life* magazine (June 26, 1964) framed the lifestyle of masculine-identified gay liberation in the feature article, "Homosexuality in America," with the lead lines: "A secret world grows open and bolder. Society is forced to look at it—and try to understand it." It was like sending an engraved invitation to San Francisco and started the migration of the gay nation west to the Left Coast. When Judy Garland, the ventriloquist of gay code whose funeral ignited the passions of Stonewall, sang "San Francisco" for the live concert *Judy at Carnegie Hall*, there can be heard—recorded for the first time, April 23, 1961—the group-cheering of gay men's voices. Like baby's first word, there was something so thrilling and uncloseted in that out-shout "finding the gay voice" that the quintessential framing poet of gay synonyms, Walt Whitman, would have recognized the united gay roar as part of his glorious "barbaric yawp."

"Coming out of the closet" is an act of immigration. First, the person coming out is forced to learn a new language of sex and identity. Second, coming out is fraught with all the framing and keying problems common to every other "immigrant *versus* host society" trying to establish a discourse. Both immigrant and host require path-breaking keywords each can accept. In a way, the acid-inflected morning after Stonewall was like the first visionary dawn in Eden when Adam's task was to name everything in sight.

In its whole history, San Francisco had never let "a stranger wait outside its Golden Gate," and especially not outside its Golden Gate YMCA. In the 1970s, San Francisco was suddenly teeming with thousands of gay refugees fleeing sexual, religious, and legal persecution. Other thousands arrived to carry on the 1960s hippie party of sex, drugs, and rock. Immigration's linguistic issues are often difficult, but, in the case of homosexuals, how were media to frame "sexual outlaws"? Even as San Francisco became gay Mecca, when the Ritch Street Baths caught fire very late one night in 1972, the morning *Chronicle* tapped code about the safe evacuation of hundreds of "slender young men in towels," because *gay* and *homosexual* were not fully "out" from the penumbra of libel.

Sex itself made the gay migration different from previous immigrants whose identity was keyed in race, nationality, and language. Sex and law and morality collided around labeling gay immigrants in ways that other immigrants, say, Irish or Jewish, defused alienation with cooking, music, and universal images of burgeoning pregnant family life—a trope now become a latter-day essential in the gay marriage crusade.

Language also relates, if anything can, the Black experience with the gay experience. Queer speak is as essential to gay identity as rap is to Black culture. Aside from all the controversies over "Ebonics" and Polari, the bilingual truth is that Blacks and gays both understand standard American English while speaking their own dialects not reciprocally understood by standard Americans. Actually, straight readers of gay fiction and nonfiction frequently mention that gay speak so eludes them they need a glossary or a gay interpreter named Bruce. Farther afield, fundamentalists see gays not as immigrants, but as colonists, whom they further reframe as terrorists, threatening their "family values" and their revenue source in the tax base for income and inheritance skewed against unmarried people. [1]

In the American culture war, eschatological TV preacher Jerry Falwell on September 14, 2001, blamed the events of 9/11 on his key litany of "homosexuals, abortionists, and the ACLU." (But, of course! Gays had practiced by destroying Sodom and Gomorrah, even as they gentrify all other cities.) The word *homophobia* had only climbed into the dictionary in 1972 with George Weinberg's book, *Society and the Healthy Homosexual*. In 1977, fundamentalist David A. Noebel wrote the book, *The Homosexual Revolution: End-Time Abomination*, which describes gay speak as "not in most people's frames of reference....Who would suspect that the homosexual sub-culture language contains over 12,000 terms used by homosexuals to identify themselves and their needs." Noebel fails to credit the value of his source, *The Queen's Vernacular*, even as he spins that jolly glossary against itself as if it were some evil Masonic incantation.

Fundamentalists obsessing over Bible words also obsess over gay language and judge, for instance, the triumphant word *pride* in "Gay Pride" as the "signature queer sin" among the seven deadly sins; for pride is vanity, the sin from which all other sins arise. ("Gay Pride/Power" is a riff, of course, on "Black Pride/Power.")

Ten years after Stonewall, on the night of May 21, 1979, thousands of San Francisco gays rushed on City Hall, attacked two squads of police, and set nine police cars afire. The "White Night Riot" ignited violently because a jury, believing the label "Twinkie Defense," gave a slap on the wrist to the assassin of Harvey Milk and Mayor George Moscone. Spinning off the snack food Twinkie, *Drummer* author Fred Halsted in 1975 had coined the terms *twink* and *twinkie* to define his boyish blond lover Joey Yale who typically represented a certain kind of young, hairless, and cream-filled gay youth. (I wrote three stories for the fiction anthology, *Twink: Stories of Gay Young Men*, Alyson Publications, 2001, and the opening definition of *twink* equates *cream* with *cum* which a twinkie is both full of and can be injected with.) The May 22 *San Francisco Chronicle* went beyond "slender young men" with the headline: "Gay Plea for Calm." These were no longer the amusing "friends of Dorothy." The 1950s and 1960s codes of self-defense had given way to 1970s rhetoric that the best defense is a good offense. As 1970s "gay liberation" rekeyed itself into 1980s "gay politics," fag tags turned linguistic helixes around 1) the politicalization represented in the rise of gay-and-lesbian studies and 2) the medicalization of terms around GRID (the specific blood libel of *Gay*-Related Immune Deficiency) and then around HIV which was the iceberg that struck the Titanic 1970s as the festive party was cruising on.

By 1983, AIDS vocabulary, particularly in the popular straight mind, virtually returned homosexuality — after only a decade off for good behavior — to its definition as a "disease" albeit not the "mental disorder" which had been abandoned by the American Psychiatric Association in 1973. The politically correct made a huge mistake in medicalizing 1970s behavior as the cause of AIDS. Their diktat is a *post-hoc-ergo-propter-hoc* fallacy. Truth be told: Some who felt left out of or who missed the 1970s celebration were simply jealous. It may have been cute to blame bell bottoms, disco, and bath houses, but a virus caused AIDS which was passed more by the sharing of needles among the A-List than by A-List sex acts. If HIV had never been invented, and if Marxist keywords had never been injected into the gay bloodstream, the 70s would be fondly remembered as a Gay Renaissance, the Golden Age of the First Decade of Gay Liberation, because the 70s were to sex what the enlightenment was to reason.

"Whoever did not live in the years
neighboring the revolution
does not know what the pleasure of living means."
— Charles Maurice de Talleyrand

The 1990s exploded academically around *queer*, but *queer* differentiation and revolt in pop culture predates even 1978 when a tagger spray-painted the ruined Falstaff Brewery in San Francisco with the armageddon graffiti, "Queers against Gays."[2] The minute that Bruce Rodgers published his 1973 thesaurus, *The Queens' Vernacular: A Gay Lexicon*, many masculine-identified gays judged his book a rather dangerous little dictionary of oppression because they were, as was Sontag, both drawn to camp and offended by it. In the straightstream media, *Time* magazine dared two very "out" latchkey covers: the gay-soldier shocker "I Am a Homosexual," September 8, 1975, featuring the sentence, "Like most subcultures, the homosexual world has its own language," and "How Gay Is Gay?" on April 23, 1979. The June 25, 1979, cover of *New York* magazine declared the headline promise to define "The Meaning of Gay."

The article "How Gay Is Gay" foreshadowed by twenty years President Clinton's re-framing oral/anal sex by declaring, "It all depends on what the definition of *is* is." The Southern Baptist Clinton, perhaps influenced by the Old Testament stricture against saying the name of "G-d," was also the defining censor of "g-y" and "homos-xuality" authoring "Don't Ask. Don't Tell."

Because masculinity in queer men is even more vexing than effeminacy in queer men, the rise of masculine-identified gay men took heteronormative men and women aback, causing mainstream magazines to run cover stories rethinking the nature of masculinity: e.g., "Masculinity: 60 Points of View," *Harper's Magazine*, July 1975.

The mantra of power is embedded in the book title of George Lakoff's *Don't Think of an Elephant: Know Your Values and Frame the Debate, The Essential Guide for Progressives*. Hi-jacking language is as easy as reframing *ego* as *self-esteem*. The Religious Right has reframed its off-center puritan fundamentalism by dropping the adjective *religious* for *faith-based*, and by grabbing hold of keywords like *family*, *values*, and *marriage* in coined phrases such as "heterosexuals hold the 'patent' on the word *marriage*."[3] Just so, because the American Psychiatric Association reframed *homosexuality*, and because gay activists reframed *gay lib* into the *gay politics* of civil rights, and because queers have extended — not narrowed — the definition of *family*, so might homosexuality reframe itself as a worldwide, "intuitive religion" predating the revealed religions of Judaism, Christianity, and Islam, in order to gain the protection that the United States Constitution extends to all religions. If Ron Hubbard got away with declaring Scientology a religion, why should homosexuality be any less sacred? Or any more taxed?

Verbally, the Stone Age literature of the Bible, which has an opinion about absolutely everything, was apparently made speechless by homosexuality which like feminism's primary goal separates sex from procreation. *Sodomite* seems geographical, and ignores Gomorrah, and has left law books confused about the definition of *sodomy*. "A man lying with another man as with a woman" is awkward in the way the German *Fernsehapparat*, "the far-seeing-apparatus," means a TV set. The Bible is hardly a dictionary, but its binary thumpers use it like the New Oxford even though Scripture's procreational chauvinism indicates that one half of a gay couple plays the woman which in truth would never enter the minds of two homomasculine men going at each other celebrating male essence and harvesting "manjuices." When two homomasculine men are fucking, neither is thinking about women anymore than two homofeminine women fucking on the *L Word* are thinking about men. Are there any keywords in Anglo-Saxon orgasm besides, *shit, fuck,* and *Oh, God*?

Most evangelicals—some of whom sincerely buy gay porno and gather in groups to study gay sins—have never actually seen gay sex except in DVDs that ape procreational sex insertion for the one reason that straight distributors insist gay producers include the heteronormative act of penetration in each feature. Actually, gay movies—not financed by straight mafias of whatever kind—fairly much reveal that sex for most gay men is less about anal penetration than it is about frottage, cocksucking, priapic worship, and mutual masturbation.

It does not require a degree in linguistics to figure out that the Bible, a misanthropic morass of ambiguity, has four thousand years of on-going translation issues that invalidate every single word in it. (The word *homosexuality* did not appear in the Bible until the Revised Standard Version of 1946.) Too bad the Bible text—which has had more massages than Hugh Hefner—is a "moral identity document" to people who have mostly never read any other book and who believe in private interpretation of the Scripture, but not in university classes teaching Literary Interpretation 101.

Actually, Christianity, in its original form as Catholicism and its pseudo-reformed version as Protestantism, is a "revealed religion" that has really little or no business interpreting the intuitive psychology of homosexuality which—and here is where queer culture can take Lakoff's *Elephant* advice and reframe the debate to gain constitutional freedom—is a "natural religion" more ancient than pagans and Druids. Gays worshiped at Stonehenge eons before Stonewall. Revealed religions

Homomasculinity

(Judaism, Christianity, Islam) and intuitive religions (nature-based like wicca, or homosexuality wherein erotic dreams conjure and envision true nature) don't speak the same language. Words also can be "natural" or "revealed."

This is key: In the revealed theocracy of Christianity the "word becomes flesh"; in the intuitive religion of homosexuality, "flesh becomes words." Queers squeeze flesh till it screams its new name, its new identity. ("I'm hairy, fat, and bald; I'm a *bear*.") Coined for *Popular Witchcraft*, the word and concept *homochristianity* was also explicitly dramatized in *Some Dance to Remember* where an erotic act of S&M crucifixion soars up the body, up the erections, and up out of the mouth of the protagonist who finds words for the essence of homosexual body worship based on the main image of western art: a heroic, muscular, nearly naked Jesus spreadeagled in bondage on the cross. What boy born gay does not feel the God Eros squeezing the God Christ's priapic body into transubstantiated erotica?

After the Greeks, the Jews, the Christians, Aquinas, and Shakespeare, why did it take till 1869 for the homomasculine (or maybe just anti-effete) Austrian Karoly Kertbeny, championing "the rights of man," to coin *homosexuality* in "love letters" to his unrequited "boyfriend" Karl Ulrichs?

If the sacred Walt Whitman, the best linguist ever at coining gay synonyms in his pansexual "bible" *Leaves of Grass*, had framed a specific word for his "Calamus" emotions, perhaps President Abraham Lincoln in the mid-1800s might have had a word for his "sleeping" in the same bed with the captain of his guards, and other men. Lacking any label, Lincoln's White House homosexuality simply evaporated.

Tennessee Williams often coded homosexuality for Broadway bluehairs as "something unspoken"—kind of "show-don't-tell"; e.g.: Neither Brick nor Maggie dares say *homosexual* in *Cat on a Hot Tin Roof*. In fact, Williams, America's greatest poetic dramatist, warned of the damaging psychology of keeping homosex unspoken in his perfectly hysterical fag aria, *Suddenly Last Summer*. *The Kinsey Report* (1948) introducing sex to the mainstream media proved that once a secret word becomes public it loses some of its private meaning. Familiarity subtracts fear, for instance, in the way that *Queer as Folk* and the minstrel-show, *Queer Eye for the Straight Guy*, re-coin *queer* into soap opera and consumerism.

George Rousseau has stated the necessity of naming because there is a reality to words and things, and, to elaborate on Rousseau, there is a magical, religious, transformative potency in verbal conjuration from *Hoc est enim corpus meum* to *hocus pocus* to "*Who's your daddy?*" Keywords such as *homomasculinity* are conjured as a kind of queer *abracadabra* that by coming into being identify the previously unspeakable unspoken. My liberationist idea of *Drummer* was to use words to seduce readers into daring to realize that, by the very trans-magical act of jerking off to the erotic contents of *Drummer*, they became informed and empowered to dare exit their masturbatory solitude and seek interaction with real live men. The greatest act of magic is the power of words to make a reader think, grin, imagine, and cum.

Gay literature is a body-driven genre in which keywords are invented in one palm-driving hand while the other hand types.

Ambidextrous verbal ability at keywording and "hiding in plain sight" is required especially when censorship causes eros to be coded as art and culture: for instance, gay physique magazines of the 1930s-1960s commonly justified their nude photos by declaring they were" intended only for artists who cannot afford live models." This agreed-upon lie about "artiness" has twisted the style of gay photography off its true north ever since; in the same way, this agreed-upon lie has affected the spelling of erotic keywords words to hide them in plain sight: *fug* and *come* instead of *fuck* and *cum*.

Living under the jail threat of Paragraph 175 in Germany, the proto-masculinist Adolf Brand edited his magazine, *Der Eigene*, whose keyword title he spun out of philosopher Max Stirner who had redefined *eigene* to mean "ownership of oneself." Lifestylist Brand, differing from gay-gene pioneer Magnus Hirschfeld, was championing the Greek virtue of ideal manhood for all males, and he would have understood the "Kinsey Six" scale. His *Der Eigene*, minus its militancy, was in many ways a direct ancestor of *Drummer*—with the important difference that *Drummer's* homomasculinity offered a democratic and Whitman-like identity to gay men, and was not at all like Brand's Nietzsche-like class structure of homosexuals dominating one another, and straight men, on the basis of perceived virility. Because *Der Eigene* was keyed on "the self" and on "man-to-man relations" in the manner of Sparta, *Der Eigene* (1896-1933) was hoist on its own petard and was destroyed by group-thinking Nazis insistent on procreation. Even the masculine homosexual Nazis thought the romantic Brand, who stood up against Nazi excesses such as book burning, went way too far claiming his Wandervogel masculine gay males were a Spartan ideal superior even to straight males and to effeminate gay males. Brand, who was an almost-Fascist life form preceding the inevitable evolution of equitable homomasculinity, retreated and married a woman and both were killed in an Allied bombing raid on the Tiergarten in Berlin in 1945. As a forebear of non-Fascist homomasculinity, he was one of those perhaps necessary genetic mutations who was a victim of his terrible, terrible times when the past was a foreign country where well-intentioned people did things differently, and war did not give them a grace period.

Gay literature has always been as flammable as faggots themselves. Up to the night of Stonewall, gay erotic fiction was often essentially a samizdat genre typed on feathery light onion-skin paper with one or two carbons beneath so that the one-handed typist, who also interpreted and changed the story (the way medieval monks "scratched out" the Bible), might send the copies (two to eight pages posted for three cents) on to friends who would themselves in a heightened sexual state retype, interpolate, and mail this chain of secret literature where gay plot, gay character, and especially primal gay language evolved in the hands and imaginations of its primary users. The "Tijuana Bibles" of these onion-skin samizdat stories are in a sense collective gay journals that are the roots of the public autobiography of gay men which first broke from the demimonde in the hectographed kitchen-table 'zines of the mid-twentieth century and then in the liberated gay magazines of the 1970s.[4]

The parallel to gay literature is the literature of witchcraft existing *subrosa* from ancient pre-pagan times. Sexual outlaws, like witches, tend not to publish their ideas and identities. In 1978, Mexican-American John Rechy shape-shifted language with his *Sexual Outlaw*; however, thirty years before, when British expatriate Harry Hay was founding the occult-named Mattachine Society with its neologue newsletter in Los Angeles in November 1950, British activist Gerald Gardner, arguing that witchcraft itself was the Old Religion, persuaded Britain to legalize witchcraft on June 22, 1951. Even on the cusp of victory, Gardner, the keeper of the keywords of cult and incantation, advised that *grimoires* stay handwritten and hidden so their pages, words, and spells could be set afire by oneself—if need be—before the neighbors with pitchforks and torches reached one's house.

Hay, himself the brilliant resurrectionist of what I call the "Old Religion of Gay Faerie," was less cautious about brandishing words. He dared publish more boldly; so he personally suffered as a gay man in 1954 at the hand of Senator Joseph McCarthy's House Un-American Activities' witch hunt run by the United States Senate. Thirty-five years later in a gay panic the same puritan Senate attacked photographer Robert Mapplethorpe as the synonymously deviant "homosexual, sadist, satanist, and child pornographer" whose guilt was proved by his portraits of liberated women like Susan Sarandon.

In 1969, gay pressure brought in a civil court suit from two very masculine-identified publishers, Chuck Renslow of Kris Studio in Chicago with support from Bob Mizer of Athletic Model Guild in Los Angeles, caused the U. S. Post Office to legalize full-frontal nudity. This single ruling regarding posting photographs through the mail ended censorship and made gay magazines—and thus "full-frontal gay vocabulary"—possible because while one picture was worth a thousand words, a thousand words quickly followed to amplify the photos.

Beginning in 1946, Bob Mizer (1922-1992), a reductive linguist with a fifty-year publishing career, had a very infamous keyword list of codes in his hugely popular magazine *Physique Pictorial*. His secret short hand of chicken-scratch primitive symbols told the sexuality of his models to his subscribers who had to request Mizer's "translation list" for deciphering the almost Lascaux symbols into words. In short, like the witchcraft grimoires before, the gay grimoires dared come forward from the subterra of underground outlaw culture into the straightstream of American pop culture.

Part II. *Apologia Pro Vita Sua* (Sort a')

Neologisms, Their Need, Genesis,
and Guide to the Past:
Homomasculinity, *Leather*, and *Bear*
with Attendant Cloned Words

Out of journalistic necessity,
I coined the word *homomasculinity*
so I could write about
the geography of men
at the existential 'XYY-Point'
where our male latitude
crosses our gay longitude

Stonewall was to gay liberation what talking pictures were to Hollywood. Suddenly in the 70s, gay magazines spoke! Gay culture found its voice. Gay mags were the first medium word-smithing uncoded gay popular culture—and, in a huge intellectual mistake, have been largely neglected by scholars. (Gay film was silent cinema until video cameras appeared in 1982; gay book publishers hardly appeared before the mid-to-late 1980s.) Coming out of a text-free tradition heretofore disguised coyly as physique photo booklets for "artists who cannot afford models," gay magazines such as the pioneer *Drummer* (first issue June 20, 1975) proclaimed something new: frontal nudity plus sexy captions, sex-narrative news articles, gonzo feature articles and interviews, and erotic fiction openly inviting masturbation.

To write is to conceptualize topic words for topic sentences to collapse huge concepts into one syllable for use by the writer and reader of academic and pop culture. In this instance, the uncloseting of butch queers was a striking reveal of homosexuality's most invisible population: the masculine-identified. Driving *Drummer*, I toyed with words on an abacus wire to make neologisms add up to something intelligent and hot—coining words that start in the reader's head and work their way down. I was a writer/editor/photographer into "the scene."

When the American Popular Culture Association (founded 1968) changed the character of American Studies by introducing diversity, race, sex, and gender, I immediately, as a charter member, penned gay-themed articles for the *Journal of Popular Culture* ("Gay Incest in *The Boys in the Band*") and wrote *Popular Witchcraft* (begun 1969; published 1972 by Citadel Press, and 2005 by University of Wisconsin Press), one of the first books for the Bowling Green University Popular Culture Press. Back then I was stuck with words like *homophile* and *invert* even as the 1968 pop-culture mandate was to examine culture as it happened rather than wait fifty years for historians to comment. Thus stuck as the Titanic 70s began, it was necessary to name, label, and conceptualize words that organized deviant identity, sexuality, and politics.

In terms of how on-the-spot coinages help us rethink the past, the GLBT Historical Society, San Francisco, kindly assessed that my writing "pioneering since the late sixties has helped document the gay world and the changes it has undergone." In my 1968 novel, *I Am Curious (Leather)*, written while I was a tenured university professor, an experienced biker teaches a young man (and therefore the pre-Stonewall reader, and then, when serialized in 1978, the *Drummer* reader) a list of primer words which clue him into S&M sex and define his innate behavior as a masculine man. (In 1989, Thomas E. Murray and Thomas R. Murrell surveyed S&M personals ads and listed 800 words coined by specific-use necessity in *The Language of Sadomasochism: A Glossary and Linguistic Analysis*.)

Because the neologisms and sex-narrative news features worked, the *Bay Area Reporter* observed that my 1970s "writing created the leather prose style and its magazines" meaning directly *Man2Man Quarterly*, the *California Action Guide*, and *Drummer* whose "groundbreaking editor," so mentioned PlanetOut.com, I had the good luck to be. (The "leather prose style" was my introducing, by spinning off Hunter Thompson, an erotic participatory element into journalistic news stories as well as Joycean wordplay and stream of consciousness into erotic fiction to make it "literary." Michael Bronski wrote that my participatory eyewitness style from the 1970s was about "ideas" and represented the then new wave of "masculine romance"[5] which, I find, was made new again by Annie

Proulx in her 1997 *New Yorker* short story, "Brokeback Mountain," and turned to box-office gold in the 2005 film, *Brokeback Mountain*, scripted by Diana Ossana and Larry McMurtry.)

As gonzo eyewitness in sex and art, particularly with my lover, Robert Mapplethorpe, all I knew was that our gay history would have no more memory than the remembrance we give it. Opposite the maxim that "Christ is the Word made flesh," my sex credo is: "Flesh becomes words." Robert Frost in his poem about building a stone wall says that we learn from our hands to our heads. The conundrum is that homosexuality is a hologram. You see it, but when you reach out to touch it, your physical hand closes empty around what you think is tangibly there. That very disconnect between head and hand invites coinage not only in pop culture but in men's studies which ought to approach males and masculinities parallel to feminist approaches to women, female identity, and femininities.

Over forty-five years, from Stonewall to the *fin de siecle*, at the ends of my fingers, experimental words appeared early on in the starting-gate books *What They Did to the Kid* (1965), *Love and Death in Tennessee Williams* (1967), the aforementioned *I Am Curious (Leather)* (1968), and *Popular Witchcraft: Straight from the Witch's Mouth* (1972). Some words were one-off poetic spontaneities: e.g., *cumshine*. Others were carefully crafted for repeated use: *homomasculinity*. Perhaps some future student of gay literature or queer theory (or whatever gay studies are called next generation) can sort through my *kama sutra* short stories and novels and biographies and academic essays to separate words that are merely stylistically buoyant from words that actually designed a concept and moved the gay conversation forward to a perspective helpful to rethinking the past.

By 1977 in *Drummer* and in the 1970-1982 journal drafts of *Some Dance to Remember* (memoir-novel completed 1984), the necessity of naming concepts entailed my coining the following:

- *homomasculinity, homomasculine, homomuscular*, as well as the reciprocal *homofemininity, heteromasculinity*, as well as *homochristianity*;
- slam-dunk spinoffs such as *heterophobia* (this unspoken virus infecting gay newspapers and blogs is never mentioned at self-defined "inclusive" queer conferences, is rarely admitted or studied, and deserves its own conference or issue in some academic journal);
- *perversatility* (a positive quality; from *perverse* + *versatility*);

- the prefix *man* (eg. *mansex*) — for which I rather apologize because its adaptation by others has made what was once fresh into something of a cliche;
- the suffix *stream* (e.g. *gaystream, leatherstream, bearstream*);
- *recreational sex, man2man, straight queens* (e.g., TV's *Frasier*); and
- the first use of the eponymous *bear* which like *leather* no one person invented *per se*;
- a gazillion new synonyms for *penis, sperm,* and *orgasm* because all neologisms had to be interactively surprising enough to keep the magazine reader cuming, and coming back;
- a new 1972 definition of S&M as "sensuality and mutuality" which led to *mutualist*;
- plus attempts at a gay style guide to standardize, according to the Anglo-Saxon rather than the French-Norman, the slippery erotic spellings of *hardon, cum/cuming,* etc.

When the once bright young thing Norman Mailer, who had spelled *fuck* as *fug* in his huge best-seller *The Naked and the Dead* (1948), was being lionized at a New York party, he was introduced to the diva Tallullah Bankhead who hissed, "Oh, darling! You're the young man who can't spell *fuck*."

The act of "Naming the Neologism," *homomasculinity,* an ennobling (rather than enabling) word born out of my re-conception of courtly love as found in Malory's *Le Morte d'Arthur*, was carefully designed to deflect from the word *sex* in the center of *homosexuality,* because that "neon centrality" reduced gays to sexual acts, so much so that straights (always uncomfortable with the word *sex* buried in any word) rather immediately preferred the alternative *gay* which scared neither the horses nor their children, because *gay* does not imply *sex*. In addition, *gay* is three letters brief—a keyword perfectly sized for headlines. Nevertheless, *homosexuality* as a construct suggested a classic utility worth building on, even if *homo* was often a pop epithet equal to *fag* and *queer*. (It is a gay linguistic theorem that epithets can be unhorsed and co-opted.) *Homo* is a root to cling to. After the fashion of Raymond Williams' *Key Words, homomasculinity* might be analyzed in the following genesis.

During my eleven years at the Pontifical College Josephinum where I was a schoolmate of Cardinal Bernard Law who became a media scandal in Boston for covering up molestation of minors by his priests, my eight years of Greek and Latin studies caused my lifting of *homo* as a prefix from the Greek meaning "the same" and not from the Latin noun meaning "man." (Priests began teaching me Latin and Greek as a freshman in high school, and what happens to a boy when he is fourteen marks him forever.) *Homomasculinity*, therefore, is as Williams mentions of the words he examined, one of those words that forces itself on our attention, because the problems of its meaning seem "inextricably bound up with the problems it was being used to discuss." This linguistic bondage of *meaning* and *problem* is the "good cholesterol" and the "bad cholesterol" of keywords.

Homomasculinity and its sibling words *leather* and *bear* (which are categories more than synonyms) were detached from *macho* and *butch* even before *macho* went straight and *butch* went lesbian. In the pop-culture genesis and use of *homomasculinity*, the word is an apolitical identity category of non-hegemonic masculinity that allows men's bodies to shape esthetic, erotic, and social vocabulary, delving behind the "Number One Keyword" used in gay personals ads to apply to the advertiser and to his quarry: *straight-acting*. Like it or not, the statistical truth — revealed by marketing and personals ads that do not lie — is that *straight-acting* is the main unit of erotic measure for many millions of gay men.

Homomasculinity, *leather*, and *bear* (all of which led to the Instamatic flash coinages of *daddy* and *boy* in *Drummer*) actually "flesh out" the masculine-identified diversity behind this enormous gay demand for "straight-acting" and "straight-appearing." Not to pull back the Wizard's emerald curtain, but it might be a revelation to point out that most bears are middle-class gay men who travel in packs to conventions and resorts, and that their middle-class "bear lust" romanticizing blue-collar working men is the same as the lust that the upper-crust has always had for working-class sexuality. (See the "T. S. Eliot" drawings of homomasculine artists Domino and Rex who celebrate "restless nights in one-night cheap hotels," toilets, and filling stations.)

Homomasculinity seeks the pure heart of the archetypal best that males do, not the stereotypical worst. *Homomasculinity* taken to extremes is *hyper-masculinity*. Once embodied in right-wing Hollywood cowboy John Wayne, that hyper-masculine exaggeration of an actual cowboy is the affected bowlegged walk, sneering southern drawl, and fetish gear of George W. Bush cloned like a "Gay Bill Doll" action figure in cowboy hats and flight suits on the deck of an aircraft carrier with his keywords "Mission Accomplished" painted on a banner three stories tall.

Homomasculinity, *leather*, and *bear*, firstly, are apolitical and archetypal expressions of the embodied masculine realities of gay men keyed to how male bodies have emerged within homosexuality — our bodies, our selves, our destiny — to celebrate (that is, *fetishize*) male secondary sex characteristics of body-hair patterns, moustache, beard, bone mass, weight, musculature, and voice as well as ageing (on into andropause and seniority), in a vocabulary of in-*corpor*-ated identity markers psychologically antidotal to the ever-young androgyne as well as to effeminate conventions, stereotypes, and fears. Secondly, these words, fixed at the time of their coining, provided the muscular vocabulary gay men needed as they rejected society's subjugation and dismissal that classified them as feminine, because as long as people think gays "want to be women," people will, using that key phrase, bash and abuse gays the way they victimize women, which is why gays' and women's causes are so similar, and can be linked to such mutual benefit.

In 1978, at age thirty-nine, I looked at the futurity of gay men in a feature interview with the thirty-seven-year-old pornstar legend Richard Locke in *Drummer* 24 (September 1978), and I wrote, conscious of our future history, "Years from now when you read this and you will read this, remember the way we were in 1978." The need for homomasculinity arose because Peter Pan cannot stop growing thicker, hairier, and older. So I thought to make a virtue of necessity—literally, *virtue*, from the Latin, *vir*, meaning *male*. Inspired by the then new Spanish film, *In Praise of Older Women* (1978), I introduced the *nouvelle* but reader-friendly phrase "In Praise of Older Men" into "Upcoming at *Drummer*" which became the special unnumbered issue *Drummer Daddies*, "In Search of Older Men." In that same *Drummer* 24, with its famous Mapplethorpe cover deconstructing the cliche of kveeny male beauty, my editorial, "Let Us Praise Fucking with Authentic Men," amplified the text and photos of grown men doing their dad's act not their mum's.

In 1969, my friend Al Shapiro (the artist A. Jay) had become art director of the self-defining *Queen's Quarterly*; by the mid-70s, he turned 180 degrees of separation from *QQ* and we began creating *Drummer* as a pro-active lifestyle magazine for masculine-identified guys. Thus ignited by my original coinages and high concepts in these early issues, *Drummer* then built—for the next twenty years of its existence—entire issues on homomasculine fetishes and themes of "dads" and "sons/boys" and "bears" and finally on "mountainmen." That word I introduced from my own twelve-years' buck-skinning re-enactment experience as a new fetish category in the huge "Bear Issue" of *Drummer* 119 (August 1988). I make a tiny nod to Richard Amory's pastoral *Song of the Loon* (book 1966; film 1970), his Fenimore Cooper leatherman, and his Native-American named "Bear-Who-Dreams." "Dick Amory," however, who spent too much time making a pseudo-sexy pen-name, blew the coming tide because he did bother to fetishize the word *bear*. So *bear* lay ignored, mostly because gay consciousness was too young and too skinny to need *bear*'s interpretive dance titled "The Old Man's Boy Grows Older." (Paging Matthew Bourne!)

Linguistic history is *Rashomon*, and editing and writing *Drummer* positioned me in the center flow of the leatherstream of diversified homomasculinity. In *Drummer* 20 (January 1978), I immediately widened the magazine with the first "gay sports" feature article, and in *Drummer* 23 (July 1978), added the key line to the masthead: "The American Review of Gay Popular Culture," and in that landmark *Drummer* 24 (September 1978), wrote a homomasculinist editorial celebrating "male authenticity" cited as important historically by Joseph W. Bean in *Leather Times* #1 (2007), the magazine of the Leather Archives and Museum. For the twenty-five years of *Drummer*'s existence, in 64 of its 214 issues, as *Drummer*'s most continuous contributor, I was dedicated to keeping the magazine both *verite* and "reader reflexive." For instance, no one person invented the word *bear* which was in common American straight use for "a non-threatening hairy, burly, jovial, blue-collar man's man" as well as in the name of the football team, the Chicago Bears, who fairly much sum up the heteromasculine blue-collar bear body type. As writer and editor, I helped turn the word *bear* specifically gay—that is, into a fetish item which means into a category of desire—insofar as I wrote the first ever feature article on bears, actually using *bear* as a keyword denoting category, identity, and commodity in the *California Action Guide* (November 1982). Pumping this first feature article about *bears*, I was also the first editor to put the word *bear* on a magazine cover (the same *CAG*, 11/82), under the banner headline, "Beyond Gay: Homomasculinity for the 80s! Why You're Not Gay Anymore!" with "Bears: Hair-Fetish Ranch" to announce the feature "Hair-Balling: Hair Fetish Confidential." The text directly connected *bear* and *homomasculinity* in the first paragraph.

Five years later, Richard Bulger founded *Bear* magazine (1987), and stated that my 'zine *Man2Man Quarterly* (1979-1982) had been his 'zine's model even as he wrote about his publishing mission, "There's another side to gay media: the side which *Drummer*, *RFD*, and the *Leather Journal*...capture. You can feel the homomasculinity in these publications, and I like that." (Bulger, *Bear Magazine*, Volume 2 #6, 1988, page 23.) When the photocopied small-format 'zine *Bear* was one year old, I had publicized its *bearstream* in the glossy large-format pages of *leatherstream Drummer* 119, the aforementioned issue of August 1988, in my essay that was the first bear feature article in *Drummer*: "How to Hunt Buckskin-Leather Mountain Men and Live among the Bears."

In those five years from my introducing *bear* to the moment Bulger created *Bear* magazine, as the gay look changed with the emaciation of AIDS, *bear* widened its original definition of "hairy body and/or beard" to include *avoirdupois* because, I think, weight seemed a marker of virus-free health. Again, flesh becomes word. *Time* magazine writer, Andrew Sullivan, declared himself a *bear* August 1, 2003, on Salon.com. In writing about the keyword *bear*, Sullivan rather much repeated Williams "inextricable" syndrome: "Every time I try and write a semi-serious sociological assessment of the bear phenomenon, I find myself erasing large amounts of text." That's because *bear* is a huge, receptive, inclusive, wonderful, humorous blank. In my "Foreword" to Les Wright's *Bear Book II* (2001), my definition of the incredible lightness of being bear had been: "The concept of bear is blank enough to absorb countless male identities and fantasies." In Ron Suresha's *Bears on Bears: Interviews and Discussions* (2002), I specified: "*Bear* is a concept so receptively blank that as a label it welcomes and absorbs all masculine fantasies, fetishes, identities, and body types. *Bear* is all inclusive."[6]

When publisher Anthony F. DeBlase, Ph.D., bought *Drummer*, he wrote an editorial in *Drummer* 100 (October 1986) acknowledging that my 1970s *Drummer* focused on *masculinity* and then on the subcategories of *leather*, *western*, and *fetishes*. *Leather* was the keyword for masculine bonding beginning in California with motorcycle-riding ex-soldiers after 1945 up through Marlon Brando's subversive hetero-seeming masculinity in *A Streetcar Named Desire* (1951) and homo-seeming masculinity in *The Wild One* (1953) which James Dean queered in his homoerotic coming-out film *Rebel without a Cause* (1955), and occult magus Kenneth Anger made startlingly homomasculine in his Christ-queering religious epic of gay leather ritual, *Scorpio Rising* (1963); this homo Christ worship became central sex act in *Some Dance to Remember*.

Leather defines a masculine way of being homosexual as in Larry Townsend's pioneering work, *The Leatherman's Handbook* (1972) for whose Silver Anniversary Edition (1997) I wrote an introduction:

> By the time of the rip-roaring counter-culture of the 60s, the specific word *leather*, transcending literal meaning as clothing, surfaced from the underground subculture redefined to mean a specific psycho-drama sex-style. *Leather*, along with 60s peace, love, sex, drugs, and rock-n-roll, arrived to name a way of being and becoming, of ritualizing and actualizing, of creation and recreation, of politicizing and marketing....*Leather*—barbaric, medieval, industrial—is the flesh become word. *Leather* is the conjure amulet....the fetish to which a certain erotic drive attaches itself and through which a certain erotic desire commands its visible incarnation....Foucault twisted S&M *leather*

recreational sex into...endgame....*Leather* liberated masculine love...and helped define masculine-identified homosexuality.[7]

Leather, with its gear and BDSM rituals provided grist and gristle for great copy and hot photos, but still seemed a bit specific and not inclusive of the wide market for *Drummer* which continued adding fetishized words such as *jock, muscleman, cowboy, blue-collar, chub, bear, cop,* and *uniform.* (I added a special column to publish readers' self-pictures titled "Tough Customers" beginning *Drummer* 25 (December 1978); that key phrase finally became its own magazine in the 1990s under editor Joseph W. Bean.) The predilection for these "action-hero key frames" arises partly from the linguistic and erotic fact that most of the 1960s-1970s gay lib generation were all "war babies," impressionable children who learned the gaydar of specific gender-tight language during World War II—while acutely aware of heroic absent daddies hypermasculinized in uniform and of "mannish" women doing "men's jobs" in factories and of "girly, womanly, female, feminine dames" (*South Pacific*) sexing up blue-collar male working gear. (I define *gaydar* as the 69th sense of multi-sensual queers.)

While I was editor, *Drummer*'s press run, according to publisher John Embry, was 42,000 monthly, with another 42,000 pass-along. Twelve issues in twelve months times 84,000 equals over one million readers per year which, in pop culture where mass box-office numbers mean something, shows how embedded the need for a widely inclusive homomasculine identity actually was. (*Drummer*'s 214 issues from 1975-1999 reached a virtual infinity of international readers; those 1970s issues sell for $150-$450 per collector's copy in New York.) In filling each issue with *homomasculine* buzzwords to keep the pages fresh, *Drummer* was a lifestyle teaching device. If I introduced *cigar* as a fetish word as I did in *Drummer* 22 (May 1978), thirty days later, men appeared smoking cigars in bars.

So *homomasculinity* first appeared as an attitude in late 70s use in *Drummer,* then as a word in *Man2Man Quarterly* (1979), and then in the *California Action Guide* (1982). Mark Hemry was my partner in founding the 'zine *Man2Man Quarterly* and the tabloid *California Action Guide* —both designed to go deeper than *Drummer* into the then emerging homomasculine culture of totems and taboos. Fifteen Warhol minutes after *Man2Man* came forward as a keyword title, long before numerals became common in gangsta and punk spelling, the phrase "man-to-man"—so internally defining and reciprocal—suddenly became a very vogue catch-phrase in gay magazines which had never before mentioned the "concept" or tried the "breakthrough concept" of marketing to gay men as men. Both *Drummer* and *Bear* tagged their personals ads as "man-to-man." I learned that phrase at my father's knee, and at school from Robert Burns' "A Man's a Man for A' [All] That." In 1795, during the Age of Enlightenment and on the eve of the French Revolution which led to our Gay Revolution in the 1970s, Burns wrote this inclusive poem of egalitarian social justice:

> Then let us pray that come it may
> (As come it will for a' that),
> That Sense and Worth o'er a' the earth,
> Shall bear the gree an a' that.
> For a' that, an a' that,
> It's coming yet for a' that,
> That man to man, the world, o'er
> Shall brithers be for a' that.

Gays spin everything for camp. I'll be the first to say the world is full of male impersonators of every kind. If satire of a concept is proof of its existence, I gladly point out homomasculinity's confirmation in the comic camp of the disco group "The Village People" who staged a commercial stereotype of the archetype singing "Macho Man," "In the Navy," and "YMCA." "The Village People" leatherman, Glenn Hughes, oftentimes partied with our *Drummer* salon who were also—late nights at the Slot Hotel and the Barracks bath on Folsom Street—fisting and fucking Foucault.

During the 1980s, I tub-thumped *homomasculinity*, importing it with my leatherstream fiction and nonfiction to the original *Bear* magazine as well as to the Mavety Corporation's younger, blonder magazines (*Uncut, Inches, Skinflicks, Just Men*) and Brush Creek Media magazines such as the new *Bear* magazine, *Powerplay*, and *Leatherman* which acknowledged in issue two that its title was taken from the name of a fictional magazine in *Some Dance to Remember*. After my artificially inseminating their pages with my turkey-baster seed words, the magazines themselves began to use the terms as did the readers in writing their personals ads. The true test of a word becoming key is when the readers start writing it in their personals ads. It also appeared as the specifically mentioned main theme in books such as *Some Dance to Remember* (1990, new edition 2005); *Corporal in Charge of Taking Care of Captain O'Malley* (1978; 1984; republished for its specific gay-speak as the homomasculinist one-act drama in the Lammy winning *Gay Roots*, Winston Leyland, 1991); *Titanic: Forbidden Stories Hollywood Forgot* (1999); *Chasing Danny Boy: Powerful Stories of Celtic Eros*, with Neil Jordan (1999); and *Tales from the Bear Cult: Bearotica for Your Inner Goldilocks* (2001).

By 1990, *homomasculinity* had jumped into gender studies' use within the bear movement in which Ron Suresha coined *ursomasculinity*; Les Wright, Ph.D., pioneering men's studies in ways similar to feminist approaches to women, female identities, and femininities furthered "homomasculinities" by studying "gay men identifying as men more than as gay" at his Nashoba Institute research site (bearhistory.com) and in his *Bear Book: Readings in the History and Evolution of a Gay Male Subculture* (1997), and *Bear Book II: Further Readings* (2001) with a timeline "Foreword" explaining how the word *bear* became a homomasculine construct; *homomasculinity* and *gaystream* were both used by documentarian Ron Suresha in his *Bears on Bears* which included his Q&A titled "Bearness's Beautiful Big Blank: Tracing the Genome of Ursomasculinity—An Interview with Jack Fritscher"; *homomasculinity* appeared in *The Advocate*, the "gay journal of record" in the article "Daring to Be Bears," August 20, 2002; it also debuted in the benchmark *Village Voice* (June 22, 2004) describing the life's work of the legendary international artist Tom of Finland as the "artist whose drawings defined homomasculinity and S&M for the century"; Mary Louise Rasmussen and editor Eric Rofes—who was bearish, a professor, and part of San Francisco's historical leather community—introduced *homomasculinity* to a new generation in the anthology, *Youth and Sexuality*, 2004.

Homomasculinity is a coinage easily illustrated in the manner of dictionaries where "one picture is worth a thousand words." I have written about and published the homomasculine photographs of Robert Mapplethorpe whose first ever magazine cover, previously mentioned, I commissioned, designed, and cast for the triumphal homomasculine "Biker for Hire" cover, *Drummer* 24 (September 1978). I have also promoted photographers Arthur Tress in *Drummer* 30 (June 1979), Jim French (Colt Studio), Lou Thomas (Target Studio), Chuck Renslow (Kris Studio), Bob Mizer (AMG), and the man-defining films of the Gage Brothers, as well as the drawings of Tom of Finland, Rex, the Hun, and Domino. As a career photographer and videographer, I have shot and printed specific images of my interpretation of *homomasculinity* in magazine covers, centerfolds, and photo spreads as well as in my more than 160 feature-length homomasculine videos shot for Palm Drive Video since 1982 with box office at 250,000 units sold only in blue states. Doing the math: if four guys watched each unit sold.... Palm Drive Video's tag line is "Masculine Videos for Men Who Like Men Masculine."

Art critic Edward Lucie-Smith discussed the graphics of *homomasculinity* in his "Introduction" to the fifty-five photos he chose from my portfolio for the coffee-table book titled *Jack Fritscher's American Men* (Aubrey Walter, Gay Men's Press, London, 1994). Lucie-Smith wrote:

In these photographs, Fritscher focuses on what he calls "homomasculinity"—less the act of sex, itself, more a complete state of being. [These are] ritualized totems of the potent American Dream, taken from his own dream visions, as well as the dreams of the intense cult following whose tastes he has recorded and reflected for many years on page and screen.... He believes that, just as some women now legitimately investigate their own gender, so too, many men have become increasingly curious about their own gender identification. In his view, true homomasculinity, far from cancelling out the female principle, offers the valid gender balance of male animus that the female anima demands and deserves....his images may be...threatening to a certain type of gay Puritan....[8]

Frankly, *homomasculinity*, which was coined as a "Platonic blank of self-reliant male archetype," can be spun by biased misandry against the concept. *American Men*, which makes absolutely no reference to women was judged "misogynistic" by one very binary American gay reviewer. Sexist himself, his reactionary "key" did not fit the "lock" these iconoclastic images had on ur-masculinity. Because masculinity is as valid a unit of identity as femininity, it should not be vilified by anyone confusing the Platonic ideal of homomasculinity with the "sins of patriarchy" as defined by those who would be matriarchs: real or drag. This exact cultural fear of masculine-identified gay men led gays and straights alike into censorship of Robert Mapplethorpe's homomasculine photography; kept Patricia Nell Warren's homomasculine love story, *The Front Runner* (1974), from so far being filmed; and created "Don't Ask/Don't Tell" because gays may, in fact (shades of Adolf Brand), be more masculine than straights.

Homomasculinity, especially when made to sound political with an *ism* as in *homomasculinism* (a term I have never used), can incite male and female politicos as dramatized in *Some Dance to Remember* when the "Masculinist Manifesto," injected as a plot-pushing device to pinpoint the inflammatory sexual politics of the late 70s, causes curbside magazine racks selling the "Manifesto" to be set afire. One reviewer, who was not bilingual around "male stough" (*stuff* + *tough*), ranted under his headline, "The Rise and Fall of Butch," reviewing his own gender issues but not the book. The fictional "Masculinist Manifesto," with a facetious nod to Valerie Solanas' *SCUM Manifesto* (Society for Cutting Up Men), is a simple "declaration of masculine independence" that in the course of the narrative becomes politicized by reactionaries the way masculinity was politicized by the anti-patriarchist Arthur Evans, the self-proclaimed "Red Queen," whose broadside, pasted on Castro Street lampposts, I took up from the street and published as a very camp "editorial" in *Drummer* 25 (December 1978) with his title, "Afraid You're Not Butch Enough?" In truth, homomasculinity is no more patriarchal than the role playing of *daddies* and *boys*.

Building the homo-word-hoard was a clear necessity in the 1970s gay civil war over terminology as "gays" fought "queens" fought "clones" fought "men who happened to be gay." For historians who want to know how a keyword helps understand the past, there, recorded on the Rosetta Stone of *Some Dance to Remember* is, as written on the first page, the beginning of the 1970s "civil war between women and men and men"—a very uncivil civil war over keywords as *gay lib* morphed into *gay politics*. In a world of sliding gender, *homomasculinity* and *bear* actually have grown to include women: e.g., "Lesbears and Transbears: Dykes and FTMs as Bears."[9] And "Dykes on Bikes" has evolved from slur to trademark.

Psychologically, *homomasculinity*—and its attendant words from *leather* to *bear*—was needed as antidote to the self-hatred pushed at masculine-identified gay men whom other-identified gays considered part of straight masculine hegemony—particularly by queens ruling at the top of the hierarchy dominating early gay communities. (In 2005, *sissy* is now transforming as gay sites and publications use it—qualified—as in "'self-proclaimed sissy' Bill Porter's one-man Broadway show.") It is ironic when masculine gay men are blamed for the sins of straight men given that gay men get no "bump" from anyone for "being gay," and then are bashed by straight men "because they *are* gay" and then—double indemnity—cursed by politically correct abusers because they are "male." What's good for the goose is good for the gander: if a woman wants to transgender into the Platonic ideal of a man, why criticize a man who wants the same ideal?

My driving *Drummer*, and my cautionary tale *Some Dance to Remember*, with its fictitiously coded *Drummer* magazine, *Maneuvers*, was about finding the apt projection of that part of one's self that will control and discipline the self the way only self can. Therefore, only on the literal surface is homomasculinity about disciplinarian bikers and coaches; in truth, it is about identifying self discipline. Masculine-identified gay men have had to become positively self-reliant after the fashion of Ralph Waldo Emerson whose self-reliant person in mass media is the Marlboro cowboy who rides wordlessly across a subliminal *Brokeback Mountain*. That can-do erotic American cowboy image—reeking of homoerotic fraternity—I very specifically coopted off TV and billboards as the key subliminal behind every homomasculine face/body/attitude in every page, paragraph, and picture in *Drummer*. This iconic genesis out of the gay-friendly Emerson—by way of Walt Whitman's blue-collar lust for working men—is no stretch, really, because the very title of *Drummer* comes from Emerson's pal Henry David Thoreau who is quoted on the masthead of nearly every issue of *Drummer*: "If a man does not keep pace with his companions, perhaps it is because he hears a different drummer. Let him step to the music he hears, however measured or far away."

That non-aggressive Transcendentalist self-reliance is at the very heart of self-disciplined homomasculinity. Just as the Marlboro ads never reference women, *homomasculinity* is a Whitmanian he-festival, a moment out of time, place, and politics that allows men to consider their essence and identity as males in terms of themselves and other men, before they dare even consider themselves ready or worthy to approach females and family. Philosophically, *homomasculinity* is a meditational helix very like Thomas Aquinas' consideration of *ens qua ens, being as being, masculinity as masculinity, queer as queer*—a defensible intellectual exercise that is also legitimate emotionally, sexually, and politically on the human level. Masculinism and feminism both pale beside humanism which includes them both. That is why the first sentence of the masculine-identified *Some Dance to Remember* is very pointedly the tender homo-humanism of "In the end, he could not deny his human heart."

BIBLIOGRAPHY

Blake, Roger, *The American Dictionary of Adult Sexual Terms*, Century Publishing Company, 1964

Jung, C. G., *Aspects of the Masculine*, R. F. C. Hull, translator, Bollingen Series, Princeton University Press, 1989

Legman, Gershon, "The Language of Homosexuality: An American Glossary " in George W. Henry, editor, *Sex Variants: A Study of Homosexual Patterns*, New York: Hoeber, 1941

Leyland, Winston, editor, *Gay Roots: Twenty Years of Gay Sunshine—An Anthology of Gay History, Sex, Politics & Culture*, San Francisco: Gay Sunshine Press, 1991

Murray, Thomas E., and Murrell, Thomas R., *The Language of Sadomasochism: A Glossary and Linguistic Analysis*, Westport CT: Greenwood Press, 1989

Rodgers, Bruce, *The Queen's Vernacular: A Gay Lexicon*, San Francisco: Straight Arrow Books, 1972

Suresha, Ron, *Bears on Bears: Interviews and Discussions*, Los Angeles: Alyson Books, 2002

Thompson, Mark, editor, *Leatherfolk: Radical Sex, People, Politics, and Practice*, Boston: Alyson Publications, 1991

Townsend, Larry, *Leatherman's Handbook, Silver Jubilee Edition*, Los Angeles: L. T. Publications, 1997

Trimble, John, *5000 Adult Sex Words*, Brandon House, 1966

Van Leer, David, *The Queening of America: Gay Culture in Straight Society*, New York: Routledge, 1995

Williams, Raymond, *Keywords: A Vocabulary of Culture and Society*, Revised Edition, New York: Oxford University Press, 1983

Wright, Les, editor, *Bear Book II: Further Readings in the History and Evolution of a Gay Male Subculture*, Binghamton NY: The Haworth Press, 2001

Also:

Chapman, Robert L., *American Slang: The Abridged Dictionary*, New York: HarperCollins Publishers, Inc., 1998

Clampit, Mickey K., *The Religious Subculture of the YMCA Camp*, PhD Thesis, Harvard University, 1969

Dalzell, Tom and Terry Victor, *The New Partridge Dictionary of Slang and Unconventional English*, NY: Routledge, 2005

Fritscher, Jack, *Mapplethorpe: Assault with a Deadly Camera*, Mamaroneck NY: Hastings House, 1994

———, *Popular Witchcraft: Straight from the Witch's Mouth*, Madison WI: University of Wisconsin Press, April 2005

———, *Some Dance to Remember: A Memoir-Novel of San Francisco 1970-1982*, Binghamton NY: The Haworth Press, September 2005

———, *Jack Fritscher's American Men*, Photographs with an "Introduction" by Edward Lucie-Smith, London: Gay Men's Press, 1995.

———, *Gay San Francisco: Eyewitness Drummer - A Memoir of the Art, Sex, Salon, Culture War, and Gay History of Drummer Magazine from the Titanic 1970s to 1999*, San Francisco: Palm Drive Publishing, 2008; also at www.JackFritscher.com

Frum, David, *How We Got Here: The 70's, The Decade That Brought You Modern Life - For Better or Worse*, New York: Basic Books, 2000

Hemingway, Ernest, *The Sun Also Rises*, New York: Charles Scribner's Sons, 1926

Kimball, Roger, *The Rape of the Masters: How Political Correctness Sabotages Art*, San Francisco: Encounter Books, 2004

Lucie-Smith, Edward, *Race, Sex, and Gender*, New York: Harry N. Abrams, 1994

Mansfield, Harvey C., *Manliness*, New Haven and London: Yale University Press, 2006

Padurano, Dominque, The Horace Mann School, "'Dear Mr. Atlas': The Construction of the Masculine Self through the Bodybuilding Autobiography and Letter Writing, 1899-1945," The Chicago Seminar on Sport and Culture, Newberry Library, May 16, 2008

Paglia, Camille, *Sex, Art, and American Culture*, New York: Vintage Books, 1992

Pollack, William, *Real Boys: Rescuing Our Sons from the Myths of Boyhood*, New York: Henry Holt and Company, Inc., 1999

Smith, Paul, editor, *Boys: Masculinities in Contemporary Culture*, Boulder, Colorado: Westview Press, a Division of Harper, 1996

Sommers, Christina Hoff, *The War Against Boys: How Misguided Feminism Is Harming Our Young Men*, New York: Simon & Schuster, 2000

ENDNOTES

1. Breeding and taxes: "Two groups opposed to gay marriage rights...argued that the state has a legitimate interest in restricting marriage to opposite-sex couples as a way of encouraging procreation." —AP, FoxNews, 14 March 2005; "Connecticut could lose nearly $1 million a year because of decreased inheritance tax revenue if the state allows civil unions of same-sex couples." —AP, 13 March 2005, 365Gay.com
2. Jack Fritscher, *Some Dance to Remember: A Memoir-Novel of San Francisco 1970-1982*, Stamford CT: Knights Press, 1990; Binghamton NY: The Haworth Press, 2005.
3. Associated Press, 25 April 2005.
4. For thirty years, I have noted the failure of queer studies in regard to gay magazines' editorial and advertising contents, and applaud Paul Baker's latter-day efforts in "No Fats, Femmes or Flamers: Changing Constructions of Identity and the Object of Desire in Gay Men's Magazines," B. Benwell and T. Edwards (eds), *Masculinity and Men's Lifestyle Magazines*, 2004, which, nevertheless, overall, fails to bother to excavate the gay magazine roots of the 60s and 70s, particularly *Drummer*, which quickly grew hugely influential and became *International Drummer*.
5. Michael Bronski, "S&M: The New Romance," *Gay Community News* (Boston), Volume 2, Number 30, February 16, 1985.
6. Ron Suresha, editor, *Bears on Bears: Interviews and Discussions*, Los Angeles: Alyson Books, 2002, page 22.
7. Jack Fritscher, "Introduction: Leather *Dolce Vita*, Pop Culture, and the Prime of Mr. Larry Townsend," Larry Townsend, *Leatherman's*

260   Jack Fritscher

   Handbook Silver Anniversary Edition, Los Angeles: L. T. Publications, 1997, pages 9-22.
8. Edward Lucie-Smith, "Introduction," *Jack Fritscher's American Men*, London: Editions Aubrey Walter, Gay Men's Publishers Ltd., 1995, page 5.
9. Suresha, *op. cit.*, page 24.

III. Eyewitness Illustrations

New Words: *Homomasculinity* and *Bears*! "Virtual *Drummer*" was a concept bigger than *Drummer* which in the HIV 1980s shed its core 1970s sexuality and lost its underground edginess to Mr. *Drummer* contest coverage and video reviews. Continuing original-recipe *Drummer* "raw," *Man2Man Quarterly*, the first 'zine of the 1980s, edited by Jack Fritscher and Mark Hemry, was announced in *Drummer* 30 (June 1979). The "Virtual *Drummer*" of the *California Action Guide* (1981-1982), edited by Fritscher, and published by Michael Redman in San Francisco, was a people's tabloid that dared continue where *Drummer* left off. In the November 1982 *California Action Guide*, Fritscher was the first writer and editor to publish the word *Bear* on the cover of any publication. Filmmaker Wakefield Poole's model "Roger" on the cover signified how the salon Fritscher had created around *Drummer* traveled with him to other publications. The second *Drummer* publisher Anthony DeBlase also helmed the "Virtual *Drummer*" of *DungeonMaster* after the manner of the first *Drummer* publisher John Embry who started up the "Virtual *Drummer*" movement in *Mach* and *Manifest Reader*.

Men South of Market

> Written January 1977, this press-release essay was composed at the request of photographer Jim Stewart, and published in *Drummer* 14, April 1977.
> I. Author's Eyewitness Historical-Context Introduction written September 6, 2007
> II. The press-release essay as published in *Drummer* 14, April 1977
> III. Eyewitness Illustrations

I. Author's Eyewitness Historical-Context Introduction written September 6, 2007

We were all men South of Market.

Drummer was very DIY.

Just like the young Thoreau himself building his ten-by-fifteen-foot cabin with his own hands.

With my contributions to *Drummer* listed in the "Timeline Index," these four items show how, in my presence as editor in chief at *Drummer* from March 1977, I began to break the surface as a ghost-editor, ghost-producer, and ghost-writer before permitting my name to be signed in *Drummer* 19.

In *Drummer* 14 (April 1977), my first formal writing, producing, and ghost-writing was the small press release and photo spread, "Men South of Market."

My second writing, producing, and ghost-writing in *Drummer* was for the issue containing my three varietal pieces, "Stunning Omission," "Cock Casting," and "Durk Parker" aka Durk Dehner in *Drummer* 15 (May 1977).

My third writing, producing, and ghost-editing was for the issue with my two pieces, "Tom Hinde Portfolio," and the photo-feature for Jim Stewart's "Johnny Gets His Hair Cut" in *Drummer* 16 (June 1977).

My fourth entry as producer and ghost-editor was the photo-feature in *Drummer* 17 (July 1977), "Dungeons of San Francisco," for which I brought together three of my best friends: the leather priest Jim Kane and his lover, the former pro-football player Ike Barnes, and my traveling companion Gene Weber.

Having traveled on a Harley-Davidson road trip from Denver to Taos in June 1969 with Jim Kane, I traveled with Gene Weber to both Japan in 1975 and the Caribbean in 1976. I published Weber's underwater photographs of our scuba group fisting deep in the waters of the Cayman Islands in my "Gay Jock Sports" feature in *Drummer* 20 (January 1978).

In addition to my general editorial and re-write work on *Drummer* 18 which included my byline on "The Leatherneck Bar," these seven photo-and-art pieces in four issues are eyewitness of my first efforts to turn *Drummer* from a troubled Los Angeles magazine into a responsive San Francisco magazine featuring the esthetic voice and erotic eye of Folsom Street. To do so, I created for *Drummer* a San Francisco stable of talent from my circle of friends whose participation gave confidence to other talent still hiding in the closet. This was what publisher John Embry indicated he wanted me to do when he hired me in March 1977 to become editor in chief, a title that appeared first attached to my signed name on the masthead of *Drummer* 19 (December 1977).

There were only two people named editor in chief of *Drummer*: founding Los Angeles editor in chief Jeanne Barney (21 months: 4/1975-12/31/1976), and founding San Francisco editor in chief Jack Fritscher (3 years/34 months: 3/1977-12/31/79).

Harold Cox, publisher of *Checkmate Incorporating DungeonMaster*, wrote that "The tentative Los Angeles *Drummer*, reporting news about the uptight 1975-1976 LA leather scene, did not become an integrated *de facto* 'sex magazine' until Fritscher in San Francisco refashioned the *Drummer* writing, drawings, and photographs into frank erotica the readers could jerk off to."

What I did to virilize *Drummer* was add realism to the magical thinking of *Drummer* readers who wanted a magazine that made newly liberated sex seem possible and accessible. What they wanted they saw in the media image of themselves come alive in my *verite* pages reflecting what they really did at night. Sex sells. *Drummer* went from regional LA camp and drag (*Drummer* 9) to the international emerging soul of leather. It went from a two-handed magazine to a one-handed journal of erotic documentary of the way we leathermen were.

In the zero degrees of separation, director Gene Weber and I frequently worked together on his film projects, and I sometimes acted for him in front of his camera, appearing with Russell Van Leer in *Blood Crucifixion* (1977).

Gene Weber's multi-media film work has been archived since his death at the GLBT Historical Society in San Francisco.

As a kind of jokey internal signature, because *Drummer* 17, the second anniversary issue, had not yet been sophisticated to include a byline for "producer," I appeared — like Alfred Hitchcock signing his films by walking through a scene — in the Weber photograph at the top of page 11.

In the zero degrees of separation within our *Drummer* salon, my first "author's byline" in *Drummer* appeared in *Drummer* 18 (August 1977) at the top of my article, "The Leatherneck Bar," featuring photos, again, by my longtime friend and roommate Jim Stewart. (My first bylines as a writer were nineteen years earlier for my short story, "Timothy and the Shamrocks," in the bi-weekly national news magazine, *The Josephinum Review*, March 12, 1958, and for my poem in *America Sings: The Anthology of College Poetry 1958*.)

Our first-generation salon around *Drummer* was a crowd of cordial, and mostly Catholic, artists and writers, ex-pats from the Midwest and Manhattan. Jim Stewart was raised in the Church of Christ and, like the Catholic Mapplethorpe, tucked glimpses of Christianity into his photographs. In the Titanic 1970s, before gay lib turned into divisive gay politics, we weren't horn-locking male "arteests" aping Gauguin and Van Gogh who cut off his ear in a quarrel over which whore liked him best. Gay San Francisco, especially in the early art scene South of Market was more supportive than competitive.

As both *Drummer* editor in chief and as Robert Mapplethorpe's bi-coastal lover, I was eyewitness to a certain jealous evolution: competition among SoMa artists did not really ignite until after Mapplethorpe — who exhibited at Fey-Way Gallery — rose up out of gay ghetto art and began to become an international, and rich, artist celebrity. Dancing to remember, I detailed the minuet in our SoMa salon in "Take 10" and "Take 11" of the book, *Mapplethorpe: Assault with a Deadly Camera* (1994), pages 138-166.

In the 1970s, during the leather virilization of the pre-lib sissy stereotype, it was *de riguer* for gay male artists to have a female muse on their arms. Robert Mapplethorpe in New York had writer-singer Patti Smith as well as bodybuilder Lisa Lyon as his. (My 1977 intuition of Patti Smith's relationship to Robert is a fantasy of her singing a cover of the perfect short-story poem in *Hair*, "I Met a Boy Named Frank Mills.")

In San Francisco, the poet-singer, Camille O'Grady, an immigrant from Greenwich Village and CBGB and the Mineshaft, showed us what was the "state of being" when a gay man lives inside a woman's body which is somehow the opposite of the drag x-ray of a woman trapped inside a male body. Camille O'Grady wrote all her rock poetry and punk songs, like "Toilet Kiss," from a gay-male point of view. Robert Opel installed her as resident muse for Fey-Way. The extraordinarily beautiful Camille O'Grady became the central SoMa muse for the bunch of us leather photographers and homomasculine gender journalists playing South of Market and filling *Drummer*.

Jim Stewart (born November 11, 1942) photographed Camille O'Grady in an extraordinary series of black-and-white shots punning on Catholic iconography with crucifix and rosary. Even in the quick "Camille" portrait photos which I shot from the hip during my April 17, 1979, interview with her, Camille had "It." At that same interview, my lover David Sparrow as my backup photographer for *Drummer* added in several photos of Camille and me together, lounging about with Robert Opel, the founding owner of the South of Market Fey-Way Gallery. Performance artist Opel was always O'Grady's main man, and none of us had a clue that my April 17 shoot would be the last photographs of the power couple shot together. On Sunday evening, July 8, 1979, a gunman broke into the Fey-Way Gallery, demanding money, and threatening to kill Camille O'Grady in lieu of cash. When daredevil Robert Opel who had streaked the Oscars in 1974 foolishly dared to resist, the gunman shot him dead.

Jim Stewart shot the salon portrait of "Robert Opel Contemplating a Skull" that I published with Opel's eulogy on the last page of *Drummer* 31 (September 1979).

Within such an unfolding *mise en scene*, I drafted this bit of "Men South of Market" editorial-advertising copy to promote Jim Stewart and his Keyhole Studio in a runup to doing the same for the Leatherneck bar owned by my other roommate, Allan Lowery, in *Drummer* 18 (August 1977). In my freelance writing business in the 1970s, I wrote copy to create "brand names" for the "emerging new gay advertising" of "emerging new gay businesses" South of the Slot, such as "The Wizard's Emerald City" at 1645 Market Street which was owned by the darkly handsome Richard Trask, star of the fisting film classic *Erotic Hands* (1974). My text introduced the photographs of Jim Stewart at the moment he first presented them to *Drummer*.

This press release, similar to my gallery release on my playmate, the artist Tom Hinde, in *Drummer* 16, typifies the kind of thumbnail then given to artists at their first exhibitions. Upgrading *Drummer*, I wanted to present these talented people as artists first and as "hot" second.

Drummer 14: Men South of Market

A good example is my special "New York art" issue, *Son of Drummer* (September 1978), in which I presented Mapplethorpe in nine photographs, the pointillist artist Rex in five drawings, Lou Thomas of Target Studio in eleven photographs, and Bob Heffron in seven photographs. As an aside to the featured artists, I filled the issue with "Sparrow-Fritscher" as "Sparrow" in a proof sheet of thirty-five photographs, and "Fritscher" solo in two "film strips" of eight photographs.

This *Drummer* 14 Stewart photo-spread buoyed by the simultaneous "happening" of Jim Stewart's show, "Men South of Market," led to publication of three pages of six of his photographs, titled "Johnny Gets His Hair Cut!" in *Drummer* 17 (June 1977), the second anniversary issue. In *Drummer* 17, Jim Stewart's name as photographer was added to the *Drummer* contents page. On October 11, 2007, Jim Stewart wrote:

Dear Jack,

Here are my three contact sheets of the Shoot @ the Slot. There is one negative of me missing—I clipped it for a fan somewhere along the line. I took most of these photos but somebody took the ones of me, obviously, and it was you, Jack, as I remember you rolling around on your back on the floor in that green nylon flight-suit like you were shooting for an Antonioni film! Very David Hemmings in *Blow-Up*. Ah sweet bird of youth. We were all such exhibitionists and voyeurs.

—Jim [See Jim Stewart quote in the introduction to "Johnny Gets His Hair Cut" in this book.]

The addition of a name to the *Drummer* masthead meant that the freelance photographer, artist, or writer had contributed once and might do so again; but it did not necessarily mean that everyone listed was on the *Drummer* staff or was receiving any kind of salary or was part of the in-crowd. Some people like the first publisher John Embry and his virtual "indentured servant" John Rowberry were functionaries of *Drummer*, but were never part of the salon around *Drummer*. In the resulting drama, a civil war eventually broke out at *Drummer* after I exited *Drummer* December 31, 1979. In 1980, Embry and Rowberry forged an informal "Blacklist" to dictate who could and could not contribute to *Drummer*. (That Blacklist ended in *Drummer* itself when Embry sold the magazine and I returned to its pages in 1986. Fallout from that perceived Blacklist continued into the gaystream as Embry created new magazines and his apparatchiks moved to other gay publishing venues.)

The masthead is, nevertheless, kind of a permeable guide to the *Drummer* salon through December 31, 1979.

List of Jim Stewart's Photo Art Shows during the Golden Age of SoMa

- "Hot Stuff," 1977, Jim Stewart's first show; sponsored by the South of Market Artists Association
- "Men South of Market," 1977; Jim Stewart's first exhibition at the Ambush Bar
- "Double Exposure," 1978, Jim Stewart with Gregg Coates and Max Morales, Keyhole Studio, 766 Clementina Street; Stewart shot the urinals pictured on the invitation inside Allan Lowery's Leatherneck bar on Folsom
- "Jim Stewart - Photos," 1979; his second Ambush show
- "Town and Country," 1982; Jim Stewart's last show in San Francisco

---

Almost every deal at *Drummer* was done "in trade." *Drummer* wanted photos; Stewart wanted publicity. The deal was done; no money changed hands. Even though that blurred the strictly editorial separation from advertising, that's where I came in as copyrighting publicist and then as editor in chief to transmorph the deal into provocative editorial entertainment whose goal was to cause orgasm.

Because of "creative differences" and "lack of payment" from Embry, some freelance photographers, artists, and writers who were listed demanded that their names be removed from the masthead as I did upon my New Year's Eve exit. This seemed to happen much to Embry's chagrin because he wanted the masthead to give the impression he had a stable of talent rivaling *Playboy*. Demand for payment usually meant the writer or photographer moved from the masthead to the Blacklist.

Fleeing LA and a bust by the LAPD, Embry hired me, literally, an hour after we met in mid-March, 1977, at my home on 25th Street. We were introduced by my longtime intimate, Allen J. Shapiro aka A. Jay, whom Embry had hired two weeks earlier as art director. A. Jay presented us as a "can-do" team. I began ghost-editing *Drummer* in April, 1977.

Embry, new to San Francisco, wanted me—as much as he needed Al and me—to take over as founding San Francisco editor in chief, because he knew we knew the South of Market leather movers, shakers,

Drummer 14: Men South of Market

and fuckers who could help fill the pages of a hungry thirty-day beast. Anyone I didn't know, Al Shapiro did, and vice versa.

Embry hadn't a clue, nor did we at that moment, that we were about to re-conceptualize the potential that *Drummer* had frittered away in LA.

As an exorcist ordained by the Catholic Church, I took as my first mission the casting out of *Drummer* Embry's personal demons about the LAPD and about the *Drummer* "Slave Auction" arrests.

That molehill had become his mountain, and obsessive coverage of it was a boring waste of pages in *Drummer*.

On April 10, 1976, the bust of the "Slave Auction" was no Stonewall.

By agreement with Embry and Shapiro, I put *Drummer* on a four-month hiatus without a single issue: August 1977 to December 1977.

Embry needed a breather. From February 1977, through my hire in March 1977, until December 1977, he was virtually consumed with moving house and business from LA where he was still going to court over the *Drummer* arrests.

Leathermen and artists South of Market saw the arrival of *Drummer* as a new opportunity.

Drummer 17 (July 1977), the second anniversary issue, was one of several hybrid issues with both LA and San Francisco addresses on the masthead. It featured the lead article I produced, "Dungeons of San Francisco," showcasing Gene Weber's photographs of my two longtime pals Jim Kane and Ike Barnes in their dungeon on the first floor of their house at 11 Pink Alley, forty feet off Market Street near Pearl Street.

(It was in the Kane-Barnes playroom that Weber had lensed me for the photo on the top of page 11. David Sparrow and I, having lived with Kane-Barnes on 19th Street and Castro prior to their real estate purchase, helped them scrub, remodel, and paint 11 Pink Alley which was a second-floor garret over a street-level garage. In the way that men had to climb to the second floor of the Mineshaft to be able to go down the interior stairs to the "basement" on the street level, so did S&M tricks at Kane-Barnes have to climb the outside stairs to enter the living space, and then, lifting the secret trapdoor in the kitchen floor, climb back down to the street level of the Kane-Barnes playroom.)

Drummer 18, partially prepared in LA, was handed to me for massage and final edit (uncredited), and hit the bookstores in August 1977.

Drummer 18 was the last issue released during the hiatus of the next hundred days until I brought out *Drummer* 19 (December 1977) which was the first issue of *Drummer* listing "Jack Fritscher" as editor in chief on the masthead.

I had spent the summer and autumn of 1977 reading every word in every issue of *Drummer*, including the quintessential reader survey: the classified personals of the "Leather Fraternity."

Meeting formally at tables at the Castro Café (one door north of the Star Pharmacy at 18th and Castro) and informally at bars and baths on Folsom, I interrogated the South of Market demographic of leathermen whom I knew in order to refocus concepts, contents, and on-going editorial "philosophy." Besides lots of leather sex, I wanted to represent the then self-fashioning trend of virilizing gender that gay liberationists had not ever expected was in any closet. I wanted my *Drummer* to drum up the image of the under-served audience of masculine-identified gay males whom I personally witnessed marching in booted battalions through the streets and bike clubs of New York, San Francisco, Los Angeles, Chicago, London, Amsterdam, and Madrid.

We were a tribe. We were each and all *The Wild One* with *Scorpio Rising*. We were James Dean's *Rebel without a Cause*. I eyewitnessed the action and identity we ritualized after midnight when we all went prowling for masters and slaves. The new San Francisco *Drummer* was my chance to give that specific group of men at that specific time a specific magazine of specific desires.

As a writer requiring vocabulary to describe this emerging male identity, I probed my six years of high-school and college Latin (six class hours a week) and my four years of Greek (four class hours a week). At the tip of my pen, the keyword *homomasculinity* began to form in a drop of cum. Or was it blood? Or was it ink? The word evolved out of the way men self-fashioned themselves during witnessed acts of public sex and "Walt Whitman" comradeship.

Personal experience in face-to-face S&M sex led me to create a *Drummer* editorial policy reflecting on the pages the faces and psyches of its readers. Suddenly that summer, *Drummer* shifted to embrace masculine reality as well as leather fantasy. I became a gonzo journalist involved in the subject I was investigating: e.g., "Prison Blues" (*Drummer* 21), "Cowboys: Grand National Rodeo" (*Drummer* 26), and "The Academy Training Center" (*Drummer* 145). I wanted a men's adventure magazine whose pages didn't sound phony to reader-participants who cruised out at night looking for the real thing. That's why I preferred eyewitness photographers like Jim Stewart who was first of all an artist who also was a real-time player in leather culture.

Photographer Jim Stewart and I had been friends since 1973 when we both spent time in Kalamazoo, Michigan, where I commuted from San Francisco to teach for a number of years. He claims the underground world of leather opened for him in an epiphany one night when David Sparrow and I took him to his first bathhouse. At that time, in 1974, Jim Stewart lived with George Hale who — I thought, meaningfully — was a direct descendent of the brother of the handsome blue-eyed blond wrestler Nathan Hale, the young American martyr, who, hanged at age twenty-one by the British on September 22, 1776, pronounced his famous last words, "I regret I have only one life to lose for my country."

Before the dumbing of America, connections like that had meaning in the six degrees of separation that *Drummer* readers liked, especially after the example of Allen Ginsberg who connected himself sexually to Neal Cassady who slept with Gavin Arthur who slept with Edward Carpenter who slept with Walt Whitman. Joining in that gay heritage, David Sparrow and I in 1970 had a life-linking three-way with poet Thom Gunn (1923-2004) who slept with Neal Cassady (1926-1968) who slept with...

As a *Drummer* aside: Jack Kerouac fictionalized the wildly masculine Cassady, who was famously hung big, as Dean Moriarity in *On the Road*; Ginsberg mentioned him in *Howl*; novelist Robert Stone re-created Cassady in *The Dog Soldiers* which director Karel Reisz made into the brilliant film *Who'll Stop the Rain* (1978) starring Nick Nolte and Tuesday Weld. It played for weeks at the Alhambra Theater on Polk Street where some of our *Drummer* squad went repeatedly to see the surrealistic film on acid because it brought us to heroic, romantic tears about our identity.

My thought is that Herman Melville had in mind the aura of Nathan Hale when he wrote *Billy Budd*. Perhaps this connection homosexualizes *Billy Budd* even more, so that gay culture, always eager to "out" history, might accord gay canonization of the never-married Hale who was so hot his statue deserves fucking worship or fucking and worship.

(In *Drummer* 22 and *Drummer* 23, the trope underlying my drama, *Corporal in Charge of Taking Care of Captain O'Malley*, leaned on Billy Budd and Captain Vere; Billy appeared again at the opening of the *Drummer* novel, *Some Dance to Remember*, page 13, Reel 1, Sequence 6.)

Less abstractly, I lived domestically with my twenty-four-year-old lover, David Sparrow — the handsome, freckled, redheaded son of Ray and Nellie Sparrow — who said, "How would you like to be an insecure boy soprano, and answer the family phone when the caller's first question is, *Nellie?*"

In August 1969, I had moved my David Sparrow from working for Chuck Renslow at the Gold Coast bar in Chicago to Kalamazoo so he could attend college where I taught and where I funded his tuition and our commuter airplane tickets to San Francisco. In those days before gay liberation, when no one spoke of homosexuality, it was considered platonic and stylish in the open closet of academia to have one's lover also be one's student living under the same roof.

We were an arty little salon in Kalamazoo and we were about to become an arty salon in San Francisco. Jim Stewart was manager of the Campus Theater which was a commercial movie house not connected with Western Michigan University where I taught film and creative writing. In a freezing February 1973, I drove my tan Toyota Land Cruiser through huge snow drifts to meet Jim Stewart at his theater. On the telephone we had donned our professional disguises as the "film professor" and the "movie theater manager." Upon first meeting to arrange student screenings at student prices, gaydar instantly bonded us, and we exploded laughing at the big fat joke and the power it gave us to shape the taste of that open-hearted town with films by Andy Warhol, Kenneth Anger, the brothers George Kuchar and Mike Kuchar, and Jack Smith ("*Flaming Creatures*") tucked in among Bergman, Antonioni, Bunuel, and Fellini.

Had we known then that in four years we'd be creating together a magazine that did not yet exist, or that I'd be editor in chief of *Drummer* and he'd be managing the *Drummer* bar at 11th and Folsom—the heart of SoMa—for publisher Embry, we'd have said without any amazement, "Mais oui!"

The Longitude and Latitude of Tribal Identity in San Francisco

The intersection of 11th and Folsom was to leather culture what 18th and Castro was to gay culture. One was ground zero at midnight; the other was ground zero at noon.

So, in the way of small, prosperous, and liberal towns, two gay men set out to coordinate cultural bookings at our three film venues—mine at the university and at the Genevieve and Donald Gilmore Art Center (Kalamazoo Institute of Arts), and Jim Stewart's at the Campus Theater. The adventure made us fast friends, but never sex partners. We both liked the same type—which in this instance was the ever-ready David Sparrow who was everyone's type. (David Sparrow and I were domestic partners from July 4, 1969 to March 17, 1979; we were married by the Catholic priest Jim Kane on a rooftop in Greenwich Village on David's twenty-seventh birthday, May 7, 1972; George Chauncey Agustinella was our best man.)

Drummer 14: Men South of Market

After David Sparrow and I migrated full-time to San Francisco, vowing we would stay together and do everything "except shoot up with needles," the soft-spoken Jim Stewart, who was dark-haired with Mapplethorpean dark circles under his romantic eyes, telephoned long distance to announce he too was exiting Kalamazoo. Having never been to Mecca, he asked if he could move in with David and me. For his first six months in San Francisco, Jim Stewart lived with us at 4436 25th Street, and helped remodel my house and build my playroom dungeon. Made enthusiastic by the Castro-and-Folsom parade of handsome men, Jim Stewart picked up his Nikon with a brilliant purpose he had not had in Kalamazoo. He invented himself as Keyhole Studios and took his first photographs at our 25th Street house.

Rewinding the chronology exactly, Jim Stewart wrote to me on September 4, 2007:

> My first photos at your house were shot on Bastille Day 1975 when I flew out to visit you before I moved to San Francisco. To insure that I would return to San Francisco, you pierced my ear in your kitchen before a guy picked me up for the airport. You told me, Jack, that our lives are like films and we are all our own directors. I too am such a determinist. I quit my job at the Campus Theater and moved to San Francisco around October 4, 1975.

Even before the Bicentennial, July 4, 1976, we had a thriving neo-hippie commune of artists which was the seed for creating a salon at *Drummer*. Another commune at the time was the salon lounging about the Hula Palace at 19th and Castro Street where, among others living there, were the singer Sylvester, and the artist Robert Kirk, also known as Cirby, whose work often appeared in *Drummer*. In the 1970s, Cirby was the star bartender at the Midnight Sun on Castro.

(For intricate details, see *Some Dance to Remember: A Memoir-Novel of San Francisco 1970-1982*, Reel 2, Scene 4, to find more information on Robert Kirk, Sylvester, the Hula Palace, Harvey Milk, and how Castro Street grew. On May 7, 1989, I shot Robert Kirk for one of my Palm Drive Video features and clicked off more than a hundred photographs of him in fetish gear of his own choosing. Robert "Cirby" Kirk was born July 22, 1943, and died of AIDS on December 21, 1991.)

For "The Men South of Market" photo layout in *Drummer* 14, Jim Stewart lensed one of our sex pals, the very steamy Bill Essex. In the centerfold, Bill Essex is the hung model with beard and football helmet. After our rough sex that ended in a cum-gorgeous draw of "no surrender" in a third-floor toilet at the Slot, Bill Essex became my friend and training partner when the San Francisco Sheriff's Department first recruited gay men to become deputy sheriffs. Jim Stewart recalled:

> I remember a man, an off-duty San Francisco deputy sheriff, coming into the shop at the bar wanting to buy issue 14 of *Drummer*. It had my naked photos of his fellow deputy, Bill Essex, in it. Bill had told him to buy that issue as a preview of the treat he held in store for him.

There exists a previously unrevealed timeline of leather history in San Francisco. In 1976, the San Francisco Deputy Sheriff issued a Civil Service Commission call for gay recruits. Nearly a thousand straight and gay men and women took the physical, emotional, and IQ tests. I passed as Candidate #11, with a little help from a very handsome, straight, uniformed, moustached sheriff who during the physical testing (October 16, 1976) held my shins down with his big hands and his big biceps while I ground out a next to impossible hundred sit ups. (Rudi Cox became the first openly gay deputy sheriff in San Francisco and in the U. S.) During the following year, 1977, I turned down that deputy sheriff position on all three occasions that the very nice lesbian deputy sheriff offered it to me. During the same week, both she and Embry tried to recruit me. She sat in the same chair in my house that Embry sat in to hire me for *Drummer*. Upon my turning the sheriff's job down the third time (in order to take on *Drummer*), the position went to Candidate #12 on the list.

The hardcore temptation to be a deputy sheriff was as romantic as it was sociological, but I was more realistic. At the same workaholic instant, I also had a permanent and wonderful job writing engineering proposals and managing my own marketing staff of a dozen writers at a major corporation while at the same time I was editing and writing *Drummer*.

For me, declining the deputy position probably saved my life because when steroids were first released in the 1970s, oral and injectable steroids became the most used and abused drug among gay men who admitted using every drug in the world, but never steroids. Because Arnold Schwarzenegger, Pete Grymkowski, and the Venice Beach bodybuilding set bulked up, the first homosexuals to swallow and shoot steroids were, in my opinion of the gossip at the time, some of the gay men recruited to be San Francisco deputy sheriffs: a deputy had to be big enough to throw his weight around. As a result, many of the first to die of HIV were that first wave of gay deputy sheriffs—partly due to the steroids themselves, but mostly due to their ignorance in sharing needles to inject the steroids. Gay deputy sheriffs who only took oral steroids fairly much escaped alive.

Drummer 14: Men South of Market

When Jim Stewart moved from my 25th Street home, he rented a flat "South of the Slot." (The term "South of the Slot" defines the area south of the Market Street cable car slot—a literal slot in the middle of Market Street—which pulled cable cars east and west along Market Street, from the Ferry Building up to the Castro.) When David Sparrow and I loaded his stuff into his GMC pickup truck and my Toyota Land Cruiser, and drove him to 766 Clementina Street, Jim Stewart was one of the many guys to move South of Market, marking a psychological shift of personal investment more than simply slumming down to SoMa after midnight. Even though we all closed our eyes at how unhygienic was the Barracks or, especially, the Slot, my inner clean queen thought his old building (constructed after the 1906 quake) too ratty and roach infested, but it was centrally located for gay men not wanting to support a car, and for an artist seeking hot-and-cold running models. As 1970s leather identity grew, Jim Stewart and Robert Opel followed the earlier 1960s pioneers who had settled SoMa.

They mirrored the bohemian lead of Chuck Arnett, the dominant artist of Folsom Street who displayed his graffiti mural-art as majestically as a stone-age Druid on the stonewall of his gay bar, the Tool Box, because, he said, "Galleries are funeral parlors for artwork." Arnett's mural had been featured in *Life* magazine, June 26, 1964, five years before Stonewall, and his images drew, literally, millions of queer, faggot, gay, leather "sex tourists" from around the world to SoMa. Many of the early leather-sex pioneers were, as was I, university academics—the *luxe* class who had the most time to travel between semesters. Some of them were artists and writers and photographers and models and they were hungry for a magazine like *Drummer*. As early as *Drummer* 4 (January 1976), Robert Opel had pegged Arnett as "Lautrec in Leather." Life on Folsom was our leather *La Boheme*. In the 1960s and 1970s, we lived and fucked and loved in those falling-down workingmen's hotels reshaped into bars and baths and garrets where finally in the 1980s, coughing, selling earrings for medicine in Tijuana (like *Drummer* model and HIV-activist Richard Locke), we died in droves.

My press release for Jim Stewart references the already ongoing existence of the SoMa Open Studio movement (and the South of Market Artists Association) that had begun with Chuck Arnett and Bill Tellman who drew the ethereal "Valium-Blue Poster" for the Slot Hotel (1971), and Mike Caffee who created the sculpture of the *Leather David* (1966) for Fe-Be's bar. (For the magical conjure value of Caffee's "Leather David," see "Sex and Witchcraft" in *Popular Witchcraft: Straight from the Witch's Mouth* (1972, 2005), page 153.

The press release also references Jim Stewart's photographs of Christo's "Running Fence." This was a very huge work of conceptual art that thrilled the Bay Area, and the world, for two weeks in September 1976. Christo's enormous sculpture of fabric panels was eighteen-feet tall and stretched from inland Sonoma County, not far from my house in the country, and through Marin County twenty-five miles west into the ocean. It must have given Christo great satisfaction that every camera in the world focused on the photo op of his billowing ephemeral fence.

In the zero degrees of separation within gay heritage, panels from the Christo fence were chosen by *Boys in the Sand* director Wakefield Poole to decorate the interior of the famous "Night Flight" party he produced in San Francisco, New Year's Eve, as 1977 became 1978. (See *Drummer* 20, January 1978.)

I am not Lot's wife in Sodom, so I can turn back and look.

In my personal rear-view mirror, the white panels on Christo's "Running Fence" may have waved like flags on the ship of the Titanic 1970s; but ultimately, I see in time lapse how those white panels unnecessarily became a shroud, morphing into the panels of the AIDS Quilt which has also been displayed famously for the world to look at and wonder.

Finally, I will always be eternally grateful to my pal Jim Stewart for introducing me in May 1976 to one of the greatest talents I ever discovered for *Drummer*: my longtime dearest friend David Hurles aka Old Reliable Studio, a pioneer in the SoMa art scene. Hurles' introduction to this book, "A Thousand Light Years Ago," reveals the helix axis of the way we were at the moment *Drummer* was invented. In the zero degrees of separation, the genesis is this: deputy sheriff Bill Essex introduced Hurles to Jim Stewart who introduced Hurles to me who introduced Hurles' work into the gaystream of popular culture where his homomasculine photography and video beat down the resistant sissy domination of media and became legendary.

After six months' talking two hours every day on the telephone, David Hurles and I first met face to face at his SoMa apartment at 10th and Mission Street, kitty-corner from the Doggie Diner owned by my family's friend, Carl Mohn. (Our adopted "Uncle Carl" never realized how popular his chain of restaurants was with hustlers and johns.) Hurles' work was brilliant, sexy, and best of all as real as the high standard of masculine *verite* that I was setting for *Drummer*.

David Hurles was something altogether new.

It was my good fortune as editor and talent scout that every other gay magazine had refused to publish Old Reliable's dangerous photographs of ex-cons, rough-trade hustlers, and graduates of some of the best Youth Authorities in the American South. When I published Old Reliable in the pages of *Drummer* 21, he exploded into gay pop culture. Readers shouted for more. His hyper-masculine eye raised the bar of gay photography, made way for Mapplethorpe who collected Hurles' Old Reliable photographs, and changed the way virile gay men looked at themselves and the objects of their desire.

While Jim Stewart lived in San Francisco during the Golden Age from 1976 to 1982, he worked as a artist-photographer building a community salon South of Market with other artists such as David Hurles, Tom Hinde, Robert Opel, Camille O'Grady, Chuck Arnett, Gregg Coates, Max Morales, and Larry Hunt, the Mapplethorpe model who was murdered. Like "Old Reliable" Hurles, Rex, and Robert Opel at Fey-Way Gallery, Jim Stewart opened his own SoMa studio, Keyhole, at 766 Clementina Street with a literally underground mailing address in the basement at 768-A Clementina Street.

Having established his Folsom Street "cred" and reputation with his photos in *Drummer*, he was later employed by publisher Embry to manage the *Drummer* Key Club bar and swimming pool at 11th and Folsom Street (1981-1982) in the location that had been the Leatherneck bar.

Embry dubbed the venture the "*Drummer* Key Club" to ape Hugh Hefner's Playboy Club. See the pre-opening display ad in *Drummer* 40 (November 1980), page 48. Hefner had *Playboy* Bunnies, and Embry had Mr. *Drummer* contestants for centerfolds. "After the International Mister Leather contest in Chicago in 1981," Jim Stewart recalls, "Embry returned and announced he was changing the name of the bar to the 'Gold Coast' [spinning off the brand name of Chuck Renslow's venerable Gold Coast bar in Chicago]. See *Drummer* 46 (June 1981), inside front cover. By March 1982, the bar was closed."

Jim Stewart also wrote fiction for publisher Jim Moss who started up *Folsom* magazine in 1981; that glossy alternative that employed so many disaffected and often unpaid contributors to *Drummer* went belly up after several issues.

Knowledgeable in the way the real world does business, Jim Stewart remains rather shocked at the way *Drummer* did gay business, and how—as even word on the street knew—it often stiffed contributors and employees on pay day. He is an eyewitness whose *Rashomon* recall, which is his alleged opinion, he described to me in an email on September 21, 2007:

Dear Jack,

Working for John Embry [from LA] and Mario Simon [his lover from Spain] at their "*Drummer* Key Club" bar was a trip. Their heads didn't really seem to be into running a bar/swim club. Their ideas seemed to fit more into Southern California than San Francisco, South of Market. For instance, the leather shop in the bar had one mannequin to display leather harnesses, etc. It was a surfer boy. I convinced John to let me trade it in for two male mannequins that looked more like they belonged in an SF leather bar. John would sometimes call meetings of the bar staff for suggestions. However, he was very reluctant to follow through on any of them.

Either the two of them had no head for finance or they were working very close to the bone or both. I used to walk the previous night's cash receipts complete with tapes, paid bills, etc. over to *Drummer* offices on, was it Natoma?—in a bank bag. John would either say—just put it down over there—or—just give it to Mario. In either case, I never saw anybody ever count it to verify what was what. It sure was not like I had been taught by the scrupulous Butterfield Theater Chain when I managed the Campus Theater.

You must remember that when I worked for John and Mario in 1980-1982, these were the days before banks had widespread computer use and instant deposit.

When payday rolled around Mario would take the cash and deposit it in a branch bank way out in the Avenues [out toward the ocean and far from South of Market] just before John would write the paychecks. If you took your paycheck to the main branch downtown, the record of the deposit would not have been received and the account would be underfunded to cash the paychecks. If you waited a day or two and all paychecks were cashed, someone usually came up short. John would apologize and sometimes cash it himself, or tell you to go back to the bank again as Mario had just made another deposit. What a way to run a business. Well, Max Morales and I finally figured out what was happening. We'd try to predict Mario's moves and would get on Max's BMW motorcycle and go over to the branch bank in the Avenues to cash our checks. An added bonus of going to the bank in the Avenues—there was a great butcher shop just across the street from the bank—much better than anything I could get at the Dented Can grocery South of Market.

Let me know if I can help you with anything else with your book endeavor. Since I have seriously started writing, I realize how much work is really involved.

—Jim Stewart

Drummer 14: Men South of Market

After the burning of the Barracks Baths on Folsom Street in July 1981 which signaled the end of the Titanic 1970s in SoMa, Jim Stewart moved in 1982 to Chicago where he undertook doctoral studies at the University of Illinois and became Head of the History Department at the Chicago Public Library.

He has written: "The fusing of sex and art was what South of Market was all about in the 1970s."

Retired, he lives in Michigan and is author of the forthcoming fiction collection about the 1970s sex-and-art life South of Market, *Clementina Tales.*

II. The press-release essay as published in *Drummer* 14, April 1977

Introducing photographer Jim Stewart...

Men South of Market

Jim Stewart of Keyhole Studio in San Francisco has recently hung One-Man Shows at the Ambush bar, and currently is hanging on the walls of the Catacombs. His photographs of Christo's "Running Fence" will open in the fall at the Galeria Vandres in Madrid.

His work will be on public display at his studio at 768-A Clementina as part of the South of Market Open Studio.

Jim lives in the South of Market area and does much of his photography in that neighborhood, and at various locations ranging from Mount Tam to the Slot Hotel. On one side of our new centerfold are a few shots from his show "Men South of Market." Jim promises heavier examples for future spreads to follow this jock issue.

When not behind his Nikon, Jim does construction and carpentry work around San Francisco. His Keyhole Studios also makes prints of his exciting work available by mail.

III. Eyewitness Illustrations

"Gallery Invitation," Jim Stewart, Keyhole Studios, 1977. ©Jim Stewart. Used with permission.

"Bill Essex," June 1976, Mount Tamalpais. Photograph by Jim Stewart. ©Jim Stewart. Used with permission.

Bill Essex and his training partner Jack Fritscher were two of the first gay men to be recruited, tested (October 16, 1976: 9:48 AM), and accepted (March 4, 1977) as candidates for the Class 8304 Deputy Sheriff for the City and County of San Francisco. During that week of March 4, 1977, Jack Fritscher was hired as editor in chief of *Drummer*. Powerful man's man Bill Essex was also the doorman-bouncer at the Leatherneck.

KEYHOLE STUDIOS'
MEN SOUTH OF MARKET
PHOTOS BY JIM STEWART

"Arranging the Deck Chairs in the Titanic 1970s," Leatherneck Bar, August 1977, 11th Street and Folsom Street. Leatherneck bar publicity kit. Photograph by Jim Stewart. ©Jim Stewart. Used with permission.

"Camille O'Grady with Skull," 1979, *Drummer* salon portrait shot in Keyhole Studios, San Francisco. Fey-Way publicity kit. Photograph by Jim Stewart. ©Jim Stewart. Used with permission.

"Robert Opel with Skull," 1978, *Drummer* salon portrait shot in Keyhole Studios, San Francisco, published in Opel's obituary in *Drummer* 31 (September 1979). Fey-Way publicity kit. Photograph by Jim Stewart. ©Jim Stewart. Used with permission.

"Max Morales," 1977, photographed during lensing of the "Four Seasons of Ass Series" (after Alphonse Mucha) shot in Keyhole Studios as large-size advertising posters for the Leatherneck bar, one of which helped make *Drummer* 21 (March 1978) the most perfect issue of *Drummer*. Leatherneck bar publicity kit. Photograph by Jim Stewart. ©Jim Stewart. Used with permission.

DOUBLE EXPOSURE

PHOTOS & DRAWINGS BY JIM STEWART AND GREGG COATES
- OPENING RECEPTION: FRIDAY, 13 OCTOBER 1978: 8:00-MIDNIGHT
- AUDIO BY MAX MORALES / INVITATION ADMITS TWO
- 766 CLEMENTINA ALLEY, SAN FRANCISCO, CA (S.O.M.)
- PUBLIC VIEWING: NOON-5 P.M. SATS & SUNS, 14 OCT.-5 NOV.

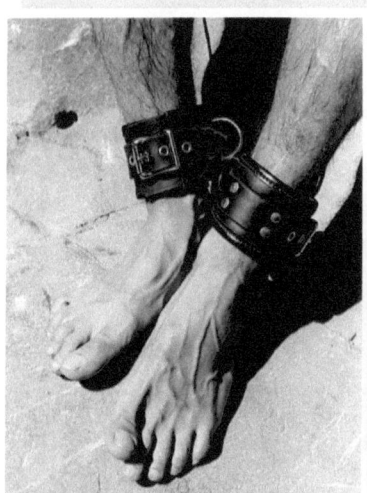

Top: "Three Toilets," Gallery Invitation, "Double Exposure Exhibit," Jim Stewart, Gregg Coates and Max Morales, 1978, when South of Market was "S. O. M." on the cusp of becoming the new word *SoMa*. Photograph by Jim Stewart. ©Jim Stewart. Used with permission. Bottom: "Bound Feet" and "Bound Hands," model Luc Alexandre, both shot at the Geysers, Sonoma County, California, 1978. Both photographs by Jim Stewart. ©Jim Stewart. Used with permission.

"Camille O'Grady Bead-azzled with Cat o' Nine Tails," *Drummer* salon portrait lensed in Keyhole Studios, 1979; poster for Jim Stewart exhibition at the Ambush bar, 1979. Ambush bar publicity kit. Photograph by Jim Stewart. ©Jim Stewart. Used with permission.

"Camille O'Grady, Bell, Book and Candle," 1979, shot in Keyhole Studios, San Francisco. Keyhole Studios publicity kit. Photograph by Jim Stewart. ©Jim Stewart. Used with permission.

Bottom: "Trash," and "High Heel Tango" 1979, featuring the hip of Max Morales and the high heel of "Pillow" who performed regularly together in their erotic dance act at a North Beach strip club. Both photographs shot on location at the Leatherneck bar, San Francisco. Keyhole Studios publicity kit. Photographs by Jim Stewart. ©Jim Stewart. Used with permission.

JIM STEWART—PHOTOS
"TOWN AND COUNTRY"
Reception—March 3, 9–11 p.m.
Public—March 4–28, 1982
544 NATOMA, San Francisco, 621-2683

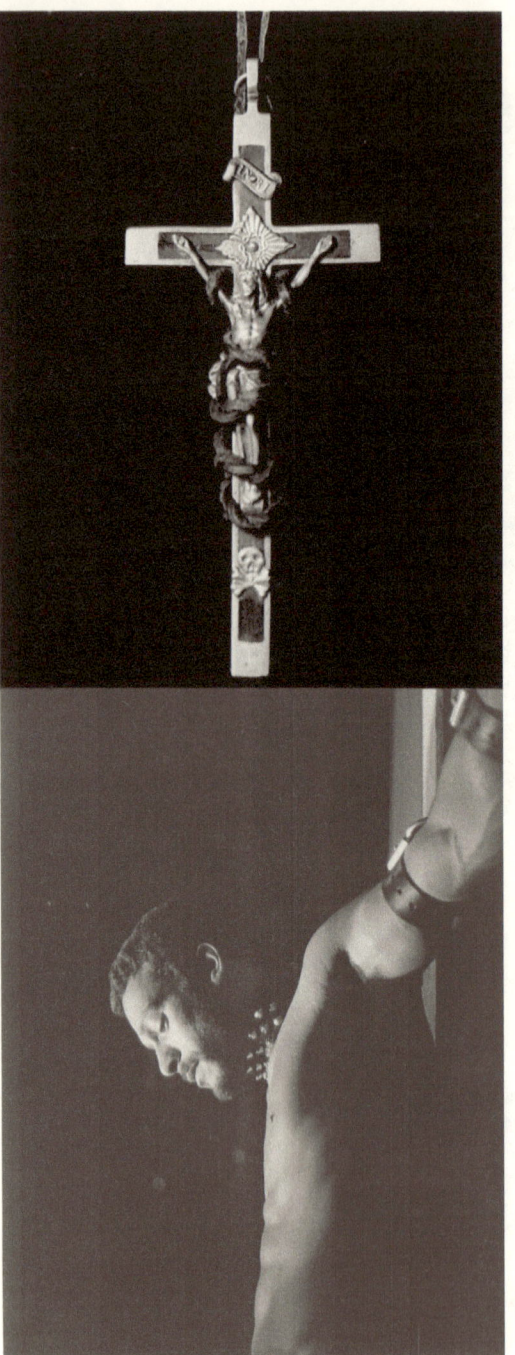

"Crucifixion Bondage," 1977. This photograph is the center frame of a triptych featuring reversed on the left and on the right, "Crucifixion: Rocky, the Bartender," 1977. Shot in the Leatherneck bar. Photographs and montage by Jim Stewart. ©Jim Stewart. Used with permission.

"Crucifixion: Rocky, the Bartender," *Drummer* salon portrait shot in the Leatherneck bar, 1977. Leatherneck bar publicity kit. Photograph by Jim Stewart. ©Jim Stewart. Used with permission.

Top: "Jack Fritscher and David Sparrow," Fritscher-Sparrow House, Kalamazoo, Michigan, 1969. Auto-photograph by Fritscher-Sparrow. ©Jack Fritscher. Bottom: "Ike Barnes and Jim Kane," Golden Gate Park, San Francisco, 1972. Photograph by Jack Fritscher. ©Jack Fritscher

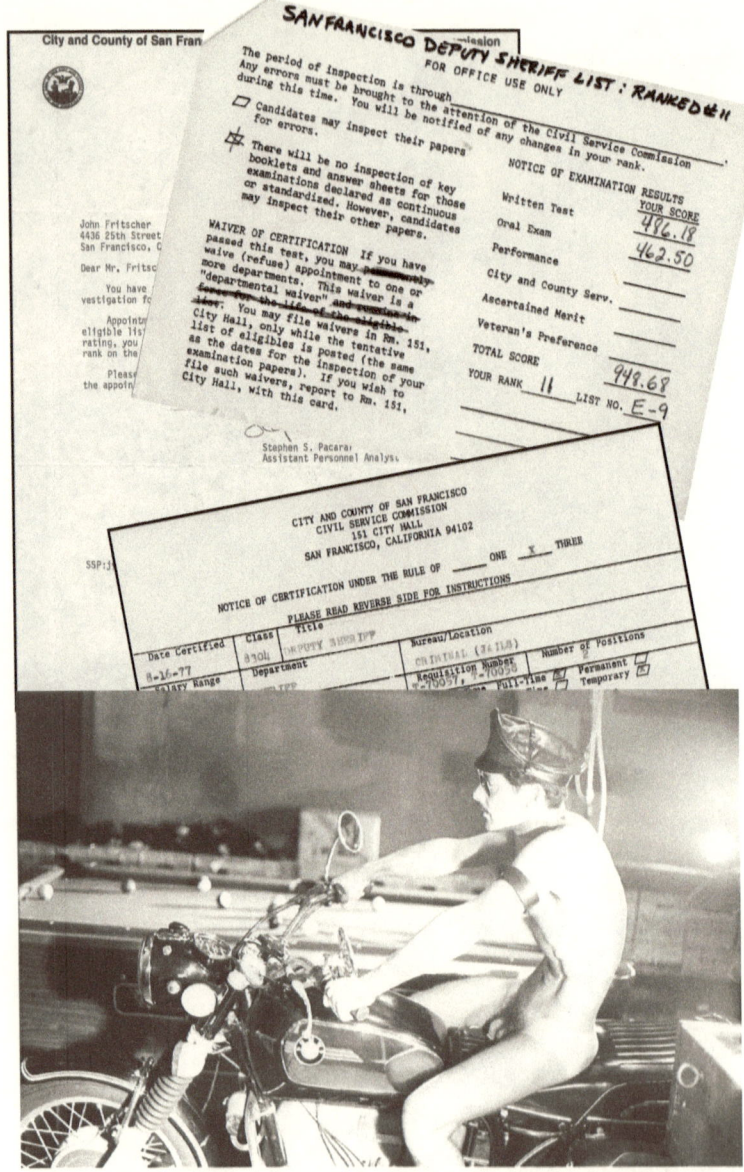

Top: Test Results, City and County of San Francisco, Civil Service Commission, certifying Jack Fritscher finishing as candidate #11 for Deputy Sheriff, March 4, 1977. This career in law enforcement was offered at the same time Fritscher was offered the position of editor in chief of *Drummer*. Bottom: "Max Morales: Nude Gunning Motorcycle through Leatherneck Bar," August 1977, interior 11th Street and Folsom Street, homage to Kenneth Anger and *Scorpio Rising*. Leatherneck bar publicity kit. Photograph by Jim Stewart. ©Jim Stewart. Used with permission.

"Psychedelic Leatherman 1960s," colorful Day-Glow blacklight-reactive painting; unsigned; possibly by Chuck Arnett who painted the legendary mural at his Tool Box bar (1963); from the Jack Fritscher and Mark Hemry Collection. Photograph by Mark Hemry. ©Mark Hemry

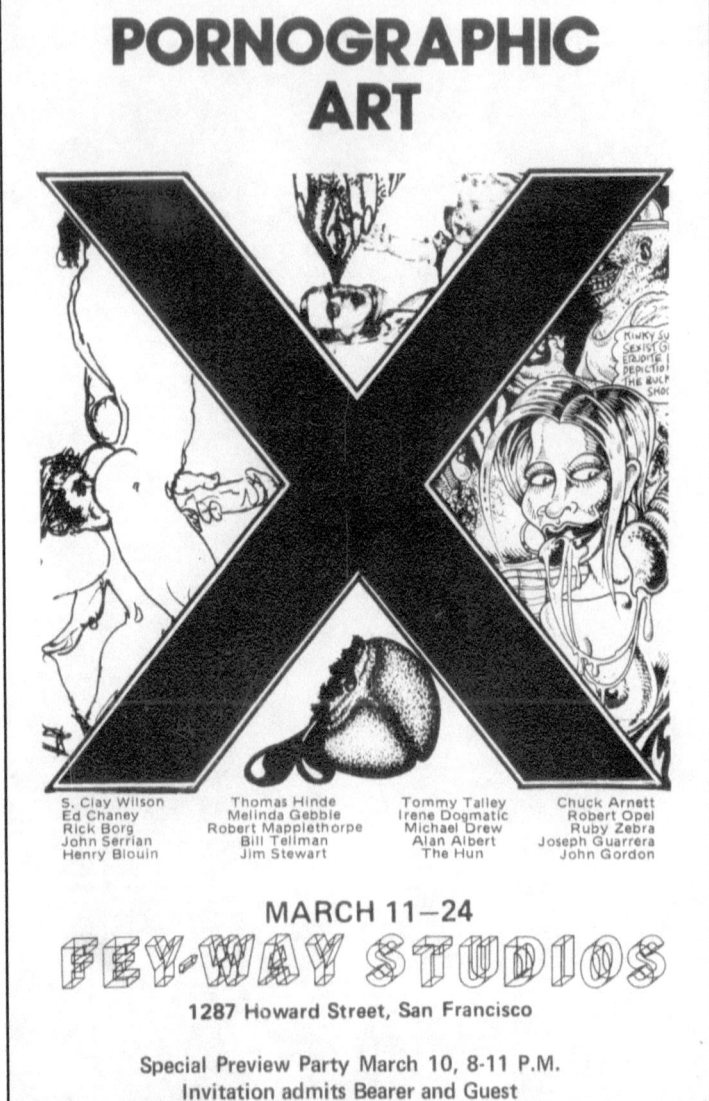

Invitation, Fey-Way Studios. This group show of twenty artists signifies the salon around Fey-Way that was part of the salon around *Drummer*: Tom Hinde, Robert Mapplethorpe, Bill Tellman and Chuck Arnett, Jim Stewart, and Robert Opel himself. Others included: S. Clay Wilson, Ed Chaney, Rick Borg. Not everyone who was published in *Drummer* or who worked for *Drummer*, or even owned *Drummer*, was part of the *Drummer* salon. Fritscher's eyewitness peek into a typical Fey-Way opening night was published in *Some Dance to Remember: A Memoir-Novel of San Francisco 1970-1982*, Reel 3, Sequence 1; the *Drummer* salon appeared in Reel 3, Sequence 3.

Drummer 14: Men South of Market

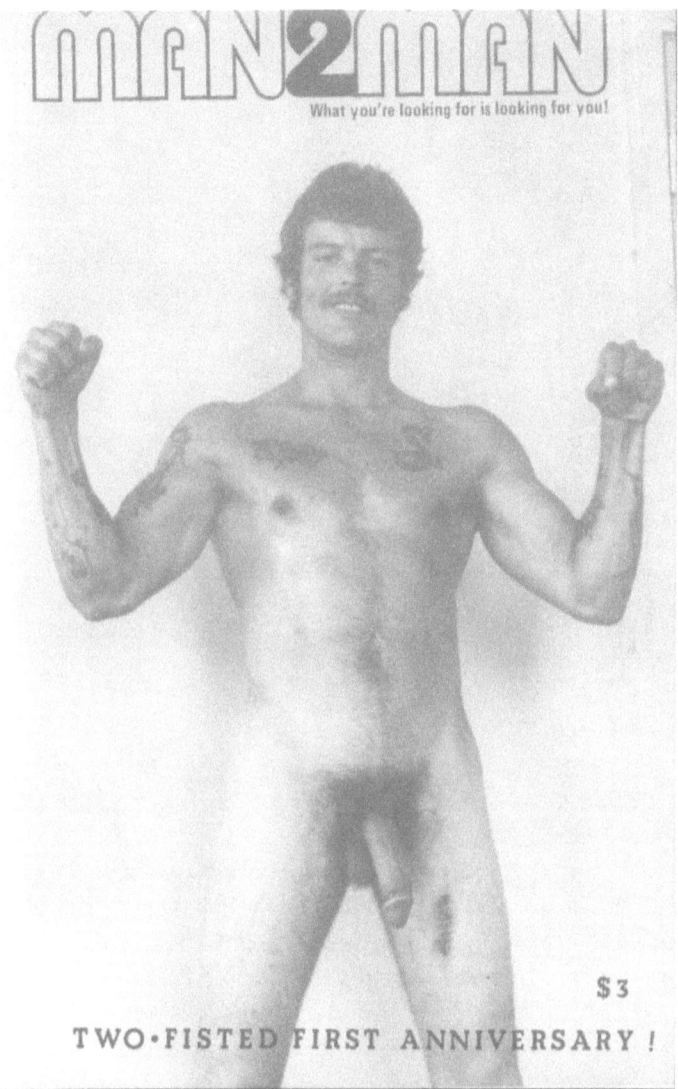

Cover. *Man2Man Quarterly* #6 (Spring 1981). Cover photograph by David Hurles (Old Reliable). ©David Hurles. Used with permission. *Man2Man Quarterly* was a "Virtual *Drummer*" publishing fiction, articles, photographs, and drawings that had become too edgy for *Drummer* beginning in 1980 when publisher John Embry allowed the Mr. *Drummer* contest to wag the magazine, and new "assignments editor" John Rowberry turned to corporate video companies for slick photographs to replace the grass-roots photographs of readers that *Drummer* had reveled in during the 1970s. David Hurles, the photographer known as Old Reliable, was first published by Fritscher in *Drummer*, and moved with Fritscher to *Man2Man*. Six Old Reliable photographs, including front and back cover, appeared in *Man2Man Quarterly* #6.

"Dore Street, Earthquake, 1906," site of the fabled Dore Alley Street Fair, between 9th and 10th streets, SoMa. Gay culture South of Market was built on quivering fill. In 1989, the Loma Prieta earthquake destroyed the *Drummer* office, and, in effect, the *Drummer* business whose *coup de grace* came from the Internet.

San Francisco, April 25, 1906

Dear Benny,

It's yer old (ha ha) pal Jimmy writin you from General Delivery in Frisco. Where you might of heard back in St Louie we had a little earthquake on my birthday Wednesday last. What a way to turn 19 (ha ha). No birthday cake for me like the one we had two years ago when we had that special birthday party at the St Louie World's Fair before I lit out for Frisco on the train. I ain't forgot what we did. Sorry I ain't writ you much but I bin thinkin about you, &, pal o mine, I wish you were here, but I'm glad yer not. What I seen in the last week could break a man's heart. This whole city it ain't gone, but sorely wounded. Ma Sloat's boardin house where I live is all gone down South of the Slot an so is all the buildins South of the Slot. It's all us workin men down here an pore families because nice San Franciscans never cross South of the Slot in Market Street. Remember I toll you last letter that the cable car slot ran down the center of Market Street from the Ferry

Buildin west toward Twin Peaks like a line between us an the rich folk we work for. It were terrible after the shakin woke us all up yellin in our longjohns runnin out into the streets at 5:12 in the AM. The Chronicle paper says 60,000 us souls live down South of the Slot, & we was all runnin for it, tryin to get away from the fire that started in a Chinee laundry near Ma Sloat's at Third & Brannan. It just spread & spread through all the broken wood & gas mains shootin flames into the air. I don't want to make you sick, dear Benny, but there was lots of men, some of um I knew, trapped in the wreckage & beggin at first to pull um out till they was beggin anybody to shoot um, & they was shot, because they was about to be burned to death. It was a vision of hell. Nothin none of us could do to keep somethin like 3000 souls alive in our disaster. Somethin like 500 looters was shot on site includin 2 fellas I knew who was just tryin to get their pants out of the wreckage. Gun fire & flames & smoke & explosions. I left Ma Sloat's with nothin. I don't know where I'm gonna live, despite rumors of Tetrazzini singing at Lotta Crabtree's fountain for us survivors at Geary & Market, as I am now campin next to a tent in Golden Gate Park which you may recall I once told you you'd like since I could see us walkin there, hand in hand through Paradise. So I was wondrin if you wanted to come out here to the ruins (ha ha, but I mean it) because you said you were needin work & there's lots of it. Just so's you know—I been takin my once-a-week salt-water at the Sutro Bath that's as fine as any building at the St Louie Fair. Maybe we could work for room & board for Ma Sloat. She says she's rebuildin over on Folsom Street upstairs over where her brother Hallam has a piece of property for a new saloon because he believes in the future of Frisco even South of the Slot. She says he believes in the future of thirst, & he be namin the little street next his after their father the older Hallam. If you have work there in St Louie then maybe you could send your old secret chum a couple bucks to help out, but, dear Benny, if I have to start over, & I do have prospects, I'd a damn sight rather start over with you by my side here in Frisco cause you never know what's gonna happen next, but this survivor can tell it's gonna happen here, & it would be good for us because our kind has to know how to take care of ourselves if you get what I mean. I can't meet you in St. Louie, Louie, but I can meet you at the Golden Gate. & you might want to see Tertrazzini as much as me (ha ha). Down on Folsom Street I found some French postcards like you never seen. I love this place, but not as much as you know who. Put that in your pipe, dear Benny, & smoke it. Two bucks would be fine. Your face an other assorted parts would be better cause I'd like to show you my South of the Slot.

Your devoted pal,
Jimmy

©Jack Fritscher

Stunning Omission

> Written March-April 1977, this letter to the editor was published in *Drummer* 15, May 1977.
> I. Author's Eyewitness Historical-Context Introduction written March 12, 1999
> II. The letter to the editor as published in *Drummer* 15, May 1977

I. **Author's Eyewitness Historical-Context Introduction written March 12, 1999**

Editor's Note: Jack Fritscher, the founding San Francisco editor in chief of *Drummer* magazine, met John Embry, the founding Los Angeles publisher, in March 1977, and worked with him, and observed him, during nearly thirty years, including twenty years after their *Drummer* partnership, writing for Embry's twenty-first-century magazines *Manifest Reader, Manhood Rituals*, and *Super MR*. Only two people were editor in chief of *Drummer*: Jeanne Barney and Jack Fritscher. I myself have been an eyewitness of Fritscher and *Drummer* since 1979. In fact, I met Fritscher at the precise moment in 1979 when he had edited half the *Drummer* issues in existence.

Fritscher was editor in chief of *Drummer* for three years, for thirty-two intense and seminal months: March 1977 to December 31, 1979. During this formative time as script-doctor, he was the sub-rosa editor in chief ghost-editing *Drummer* 14 to 18. He edited *Drummer* 19-30 as well as his hybrid issues, *Drummer* 31, 32, 33, plus his special extra issue, *Son of Drummer* (September 1978). He was a steady force of continuity through the *sturm und drang* of all three owner/publishers of *Drummer*. He was *Drummer*'s most frequent contributing writer and photographer for 65 of the 214 issues during three publishers over 25 years.

He is the historian of *Drummer*'s institutional memory.

—Mark Hemry, *The Drummer Salon* in the introduction to *Gay San Francisco: Eyewitness Drummer*

Before my friend Al Shapiro became art director whose first work appeared in *Drummer* 17 (July 1977), he had introduced me to publisher John Embry in March 1977. During that spring, *Drummer* was hysterical, and arriving in bits and pieces from LA, fleeing for sanctuary in San Francisco where porn-refugee Embry, driven out of town by the LAPD, set up his home and a temporary *Drummer* office at 311 California Street. Traveling between two cities, while trying to escape one and set up business in the other, Embry produced his "first hybrid LA-San Francisco issue" with *Drummer* 12 (February 1977). When I met him in March he had completely deleted *Drummer*'s founding Los Angeles editor in chief Jeanne Barney who had exited after editing *Drummer* 11. (Barney and I were the only two people who were titled editor in chief of *Drummer*; all the others were listed as associate editors, managing editors, and, sometimes, simply as editor.)

In that March 1977, Embry hired me immediately to help him anchor the refugee *Drummer* in San Francisco. Before my name appeared as editor in chief on the masthead of *Drummer* 19, I was a kind of ghost-writer, kind of a ghost-editor, kind of a script-doctor trying to fix the magazine (issues 14-18) broken by the April 1976 raid by the LAPD acting like the Keystone Cops.

At that time, I had a proper job, a real writing career as full-time manager of a writing staff of ten people at Kaiser Engineers (one of whom, John Trojanski, I recruited to freelance in *Drummer* with articles and photography). I had no intention of quitting a great job in the straight world to take on a fun job in the gay world. In fact, the whole time I was editor in chief of *Drummer* from March 1977 to December 31, 1979, I also kept my career at Kaiser Engineers, which, luckily, assigned me as the managing writer on a task force at the San Francisco Municipal Railway (MUNI). Our startup of the light-rail-vehicle (LRV) program, the new Muni subway and surface system, was run out of the main Muni office only seven minutes from the *Drummer* office.

In short, not depending on *Drummer* for income, I was free to experiment and to grow *Drummer*. That made me bolder than Embry who needed *Drummer* to pay his bills and buy his cheese. I never expected to live off my writing because I noticed a trend that most writers and photographers and artists who try to earn their living off their art very often compromise the honesty of that art in order to please a patron, or an editor, or the public. The only intimate friends I've known who became rich because of their talent were David Hurles aka Old Reliable, and my bicoastal lover Robert Mapplethorpe who never compromised his vision even while he waltzed pertinent patrons around the floor.

With a real job, I could afford to envision the risk of making *Drummer* be *avant garde* and dangerous and fun; Embry saw *Drummer* as a business, and as a glorified mail-order catalog selling cock rings and amyl nitrite. Like a salesman pitching with jokes, he preferred camp humor about leather. Much like Jeanne Barney considering *Drummer* a kind of leather *Evergreen Review*, I envisioned literary erotica and new photographs of the newly uncloseted masculine-identified gay men signified by the leather life emerging in a homosexual culture dominated by drag and petulant sissyhood.

I was first published in 1957, twenty years before Embry hired me. Writers, like actors, mostly always have experience in holding two jobs at once; it's the nature of the vocation. Embry rather liked that I had a job and an income independent of him. Maybe he thought I wouldn't pressure him to be paid as did the others—until I did demand he pay me back wages and we fell out in autumn 1979.

My straight job gave me also a kind of intellectual independence from him. I could dare stand up to him when other staff had to salute and say *yessir*.

Fresh from the front lines of civil-rights and anti-war activism in the 1960s, and as a founding member of the American Popular Culture Association in 1969, I wanted to buff up the potential of *Drummer* to capture realistically the first gay decade after Stonewall.

I set about studying page after page of each existing issue (*Drummer* 1 to *Drummer* 15), searching the internal evidence in the magazine to find if *Drummer* had a "voice" or not. By *Drummer* 21, which I think is the most perfect issue of *Drummer*, the new and distinctive *Drummer* voice was speaking to the decade.

I felt in my guts what a jumble *Drummer* had been in LA and I figured in my cock what a giant it could become in San Francisco.

My longtime friend Al Shapiro, the artist A. Jay, who did not have a day job, had gone ahead full-time on *Drummer* as art director while I reconnoitered as a ghost-editor producing this and doctoring that and recruiting friends as contributors. Al said: "I'm pasting up the last pages and I don't have enough for the 'Letters to the Editor' column." Al and I were flying by the seat of our pants; Embry was too often gone making round trips to LA to complete his move. As a clue to who did what in *Drummer*, it should be noted that whenever *Drummer* had no editor, the editor listed on the masthead defaulted to publisher John Embry's alter-ego "Robert Payne"—an S&M-pun a bit less corny than "Dick Payne." Embry, fresh from Hollywood, knew that whenever a writer's real name is deleted from the screen credits for whatever reason, the custom is always to substitute the code name of the anonymous "Alan Smithee."

"Robert Payne" was the "Alan Smithee" of *Drummer*.

With this "Robert Payne" persona, he covered the void between the time that Jeanne Barney had dumped him and the time that I was coming on board at a disintegrating magazine that had no San Francisco office.

Drummer 15 was a shameful issue assembled from file-drawer bits by Embry. The rotten core of *Drummer* 15 exhibited how desperate Embry was insofar as the issue consisted of three articles ghosted by "Robert Payne" who had seemingly cribbed them from straight men's magazines and books. Two pieces that seemed blatant plagiarism in *Drummer* 14 were "The Third Degree" and "The Foreign Legion," and in *Drummer* 15, "Devil's Island" and "The Greek Way."

In *Drummer* 15, I took the opportunity of the "Letters to the Editor," whom I imagined to be my new employer Embry, to address a little critique of what alternatives I thought worked or might work in *Drummer*.

In the letter, seconding the *Drummer* interest in pop-culture movies, particularly with S&M themes, I actively suggested some real-world standards for giving proper credit to gay artists, as well as for raising the level of presentation of art and criticism. This little letter recapped my March 1977 talks with John Embry about the direction I intended to drive *Drummer*.

Drummer 15 was one of the sad "transition issues" tossed together partly in LA, and finished off in its new home in San Francisco at 311 California Street.

Drummer 12 through *Drummer* 18 were "California Street *Drummer*."

This is the timeline of that period: Beginning in March-April 1977, I was sub-rosa editor in chief working out of my home at 4436 25th Street because Embry was still working out of his 311 California Street address. While he searched for a San Francisco office, I studied *Drummer* and initiated my editorial make-over on theoretical and practical fronts.

My first *writing* in *Drummer* appeared in *Drummer* 14 (April 1977) when I produced and wrote "Men South of Market," page 46.

- My first *byline* was in *Drummer* 18 (August 1977) when I produced Jim Stewart's photography for, and wrote, "The Leatherneck Bar," pages 82-85.
- My first *photograph* appeared in *Drummer* 20 (January 1978), page 10.
- I worked on the intermediate issues, *Drummer* 14 to *Drummer* 18, assuming with each issue more responsibilities such as producing, script-doctoring, and ghost-editing.
- Hiatus! Four months! Because *Drummer* was nearly dead in its emergency transplant from LA, Shapiro and Embry and I put the magazine on a four-month hiatus without any new issues from August to December 1977.

- That hiatus ended when I produced my first full solo issue, credited on the masthead as editor in chief, with *Drummer* 19 (December 1977).

Drummer 19 to *Drummer* 31 — "Divisadero Street *Drummer*" — were created by Al Shapiro and me at 1730 Divisadero Street. The second-floor office was a makeshift dump stacked up and spilling over in a walk-up flat in a dirty old Victorian. We were young; we laughed; we smoked dope; we fucked. We were part of the 1970s Gay Renaissance of writers, artists, and photographers who had converged on San Francisco.

Having known each other for several years before *Drummer* was invented in 1975, Al Shapiro and I were feeling our way toward a needed new identity for the dying *Drummer*. There had been so much trouble and infighting around the young *Drummer* in LA that after the "Slave Auction" arrest by the LAPD, *Drummer* very nearly did not survive the acrimonious divorce among all the LA personalities who had worked on LA *Drummer*. In fact, some of that acrimony exists into this century among the original LA principals who, like dinosaurs surviving the crunch, lunch — despite their differences and their advanced ages.

Because of the on-going legal problems after the arrest, Embry several times had to return to court hearings in LA. In addition, he was trying to crush Jeanne Barney in a struggle over who owned the classified personals section "The Leather Fraternity." Under the stress of fleeing LA, *Drummer* in 1977 was comatose when we San Franciscans took over and administered CPR. *Drummer* had landed on the yellow-brick road in Oz and we gave it a heart, courage, and a brain.

And a dick.

Having been preoccupied with his move which distracted him a bit from *Drummer* in 1977, Embry went virtually missing from *Drummer* for nearly half a year from late 1978 to mid 1979 because of a near-death experience with cancer, its onset and remedy. I visited him in hospital and brought him a goldfish in a bowl. Is kindness weakness? He rather expected Al Shapiro and me to continue the kind of creamed corn, 1950s gossipy, campy, and sometimes drag materials he famously favored.

Embry's drag cover of the "Cycle Sluts" on *Drummer* 9 created a huge controversy, and to this day remains a scandal and a blot on *Drummer* history as well as an absolute dipstick of why Embry, who advertised Naugahyde (!) vinyl sheets for sale in *Drummer*, was really quite unsuited to helm *Drummer* for eleven years of its twenty-four-year run, and for ninety-eight of its 214 issues which his regime made more "commercial" than "cutting edge."

Had Embry been left to his own devices, *Drummer* would have died after issue 11 when Jeanne Barney exited.

Al Shapiro and I had a new 1970s vision for "San Francisco *Drummer*." We wanted to make the pages reflect the heights to which gay sex culture was rising in San Francisco and New York where we both had been playing with leather, S&M, and art since the early 1960s.

During Embry's long absence, we set our sites on a high concept of *Drummer* as a magazine using leather as a hook and metaphor for presenting the breadth of homomasculine identity, culture, and sex play.

We both knew armies of masculine gays who were sophisticated and sexual, and we wanted to reflect them, so we could reflect the reader to himself, or to a new liberated "identity image" of himself.

No longer was *Drummer* to be an LA rag preoccupied by LA concerns. If San Francisco *Drummer* was to survive, a whole new national and, eventually, international, team had to be recruited to fill its pages, and that was quite fun for Al Shapiro and me to do: one at a time, bed after bed, bath after bath, club after club, friend after friend.

That's how we created the *Drummer* salon that created *Drummer*.

Recruitment was essential, because it wasn't every day that a fully functioning artist like photographer Robert Mapplethorpe walked into the *Drummer* offices (and fell into my bed for two years).

Unlike the end of the twentieth century and the beginning of the twenty-first, when everyone with a laptop is a "writer," and everyone with a digital web-camera is a "photographer," in the Titanic 70s, even actual writers and real photographers were so swept away by the glorious availability of sex that they were not producing on any dependable schedule.

I had to beg friends, acquaintances, and fuck buddies for material for *Drummer* the way A. Jay requested this letter to the editor from me.

Surprisingly, something as thin as this little letter was the Trojan horse I rode into *Drummer* where, at first, I had not known I was to change anything.

Finally, apropos this letter to the editor, the average *Drummer* reader in the 1970s knew popular culture and was hot for the much-talked-about military, uniform, and torture film, *The Battle of Algiers* (1966). Director Gillo Pontecorvo was nominated for an Academy Award as best director for this black-and-white epic shot in an extremely real documentary style (*cinema verite*) depicting the Algerian revolution against the French colonial army. Driven from Vietnam in the 1950s, the French had something to prove in Algeria, and they did it with amazing scenes of classic torture which inspired Algerian guerillas to place small terrorist bombs under tables in crowded cafes. *Time* magazine noted ominously in 1966 that *The Battle of Algiers* had the distinction of introducing bombing as a means of political protest. *The Battle of Algiers*, a truly great film, appeared early in the American Vietnam War, and helped galvanize anti-war protests as did Pontecorvo's later 1969 film titled *Z*. It's almost too easy to make the point that Americans driven from Vietnam in 1975 had something to prove in Iraq.

Since 1966, I have kept near my desk a paperback of the screenplay and photographs from *The Battle of Algiers* which so greatly influenced my kind of first-person documentary writing in *Drummer*.

Two films that come close to the intense torture scenes of *Algiers* are Charles Bronson's perfect B-movie *The Evil That Men Do* (1984), and director Luiz Sergio Person's Brazilian film *The Case of the Naves Brothers* (1967) which I saw at the Carnegie Hall Cinema in New York before every print of it mysteriously disappeared.

Note added June 30, 2001. The soap-opera history of what happened with creativity and cash at *Drummer* was rerun twenty years later in 2001 when legal and cash troubles destroyed *Bear* magazine. Publisher Bear-Dog Hoffman lost his entire Brush Creek Media empire of video and magazine production when the IRS, reporting a debt of $55,000, closed Hoffman's office doors at 367 Ninth Street, San Francisco, on June 20, 2001. Less than two years earlier, *Drummer* had closed Folsom Fair weekend, September 1999. This eyewitness participant knows that anyone who tries to live off gay art, writing, photography, or publishing has never heard Tennessee Williams' warning: "You can be young without money, but you can't be old without money."

For a detailed eyewitness narrative of how geography, ego, arrests, LA debris, money, greed, murder, hubris, and sex affected *Drummer* while I was its editor in chief, see the narrative history part of this *Gay San Francisco: Eyewitness Drummer* titled *The Drummer Salon*.

II. The letter to the editor as published in *Drummer* 15, May 1977

Letter to the Editor

Stunning Omission

Gentlemen:

My congratulations to you on your magnificent "Movie Mayhem" series. I really look forward each new issue of *Drummer* to see what other examples Allen Eagles [the *Drummer* reviewer in LA] has dug up. But there was one stunning omission in your Volume 2, Number 13, chapter of "Movie Mayhem."

The Battle of Algiers was not widely circulated. Perhaps it is still regarded as an art movie. But it vividly depicted the attempts that the French forces made to extract information from the Algerian captives. The captives were trussed up, beaten, and subjected to electrical shocks [on their genitals]. And all this was shown on screen. If Mr. Eagles has not yet seen *The Battle of Algiers*, I urge him to seek out the film.

My special congratulations to you for unearthing an artist as talented as the one who did the drawing which appeared on page 11 of Volume 2, Number 13. It is the most stunning physique art work I have seen in some time. The action taking place is imaginative; the drawing is superb; the contrast between the youthful "M" and the macho "S" is well-drawn and the little touches, like the phallic symbol sticking out of the ground all help to make the drawing a masterpiece.

Unfortunately, the artist is not identified on the page [and thus begins a long *Drummer* tradition of failure to credit the talent]. I would love to know who the artist is, whether he is offering work commercially, and whether or not he is accepting commissions. To facilitate a reply, I have enclosed a stamped, self-addressed envelope.

Thanks again for the high quality of the work you put out. Have Eagles continue to feed us more "Movie Mayhem." And let's show more of the work of the aforementioned artist. –Fred, Forest Park, Il [Coded with my father's middle name, Fred, and with Illinois, my home state, and Forest Park, near the campus where I attended graduate school.]

Cock Casting

> Produced in February-March 1977, this feature essay was published in *Drummer* 15, May 1977.
> I. Author's Eyewitness Historical-Context Introduction written August 25, 1998
> II. The feature article as published in *Drummer* 15, May 1977
> III. Eyewitness Illustrations

I. **Author's Eyewitness Historical-Context Introduction written August 25, 1998**

In 1976, word around San Francisco was that a newspaper centered on Folsom Street life was about to begin publication and be distributed free in the South of Market bars and restaurants. It was to be called *The Bridge*, but despite it being a great idea it never took off. At the same time, San Francisco leather men began to hear of *Drummer* in Los Angeles. A hundred days later when *Drummer* began arriving in February 1977, the idea of *The Bridge* collapsed.

From my 1960s eyewitness recall, the San Francisco leather community early on had a need for a dedicated newspaper or magazine when *Drummer* suddenly blew into town. I liked the idea because I sensed the support was there not only in potential readers but in a talent base eager to be tapped to fill the pages of a leather publication.

In 1971, my lover David Sparrow and I had appeared in forty or so S&M leather photographs in *Whipcrack* which was the first leather magazine published in San Francisco. *Whipcrack* was created as a one-time issue, but the response the magazine received encouraged me to keep the emerging idea of a leather publication on the burner.

Earlier, in 1969, I had already completed my first leather novel titled *I Am Curious (Leather)*. In its time, that little leather "classic" also known as *Leather Blues* sold 10,000 copies at $5.95 for Gay Sunshine Press. More than ten years before anyone ever saw the first copy of *Drummer*, I had a personal and professional feeling for the content and the demographic marketing of the leather culture I'd been playing in since the mid-1960s with partners in the scene since the 1950s.

With *Drummer* in mind, I produced and wrote this "Cock Casting" photo feature with several talented and fun-loving friends. The source for my process analysis was my pal, Joe Taylor, who ran his own leather-making workshop at 768 Clementina Street. His was the first-floor flat under photographer Jim Stewart's upstairs at 766. In the style of the times, Taylor billed his business identity as "Taylor of San Francisco" using a single name and a city name, as did so many others following the fashion set by "Tom of Finland." The photographer for "Cock Casting" was named Peter Munekee. His "headless model" was everyone's favorite model, Max Morales.

To follow up this *Drummer* 15 how-to article, I invited Taylor of San Francisco to return to *Drummer* to write and produce the "Body Casting" photo feature in *Drummer* 18 lensed by Gene Weber, a true documentary photographer of San Francisco S&M.

Within this circle of kinship, I had previously booked Gene Weber, who was my longtime traveling companion, to photograph two other intimates of my circle—the Catholic leather priest Jim Kane and his lover Ike Barnes (and me, top page 17)—for "Famous Dungeons of San Francisco" in *Drummer* 17 (July 1977), which was one of the first pieces I produced for *Drummer*.

Gene Weber also photographed several of us in the underwater fisting shots of my "Gay Sports" feature in *Drummer* 20 (January 1978). He also shot me with my longtime playmate and "co-star" bottom, the redheaded Russell Van Leer, in *Blood Crucifixion* lensed on location in the dungeon of S&M hustler John Pfleiderer. (Russell Van Leer, the sex-adventurer, is no relation to my other redheaded friend, David Van Leer, the gay studies professor at the University of California-Davis and author of the book *The Queening of America*.) *Blood Crucifixion* was one of Gene Weber's famous multi-media 35mm S&M extravaganzas which he frequently screened for invited audiences of gentlemen in his Upper Terrace home. He projected his images on his art-theater-sized 20-foot wide-screen using machines programmed so fluidly that his presentation looked like a movie when, in fact, it was a series of 35mm slides dissolving at different speeds into each other. When frequent *Drummer* photographer Gene Weber died, October 2, 1992, he bequeathed his vast 35mm-color transparency collection to the James C. Hormel Gay and Lesbian Collection at the San Francisco Public Library where his *Blood Crucifixion* and other photography may be viewed.

Besides having vacationed together in the Carribean (1977) to go on location for the *Drummer* 20 underwater scuba sex shots at Grand Cayman, Gene Weber and I had traveled together to Japan in October 1975, sleeping on floor mats in dormitories in Osaka with fifty snoring

Drummer 15: Cock Casting

working men, balling in Tokyo with a young Japanese Communist karate instructor, cottaging in the park with a friend of Van Cliburn's, and spending time in the outskirts of Tokyo at a Samurai house of bondage where the vibe was polite but a bit cool because the forty-year-old owners remembered World War II. Upon my return to the jaded sex scene of San Francisco, I introduced my fundoshi (and how to wrap it) as a new fetish and freshened a few scenes demonstrating Japanese rope bondage which I explained as a way of tying the body to itself rather than to something else.

The model in Gene Weber's photos for "Body Casting" in *Drummer* 18 (August 1977), pages 66-69, was, again, our friend Max Morales, who sometimes worked for *Drummer*, modeled for the Leatherneck bar, competed in the Mr. CMC Carnival, and was the handsome and energy-centered athlete who was great friends with Paul Gerrior aka Ledermeister, the archetypal Colt model on whose non-avoirdupois type the original "bear" movement was based. In our *Drummer* salon, it was a pleasure to produce "Body Casting" written by Taylor of San Francisco with fourteen photographs of Max Morales shot by Gene Weber.

I remember I was fascinated that in North Beach theater-clubs and cabarets featuring "Live Topless Girls," Max Morales appeared nightly, or at least, regularly, oozing male sex appeal. He was the exotic-erotic dance partner of several female dancers. Because I so appreciated the hot energy field around Max Morales, I invented a way to fictionalize his persona, for myself at least, in *The Holy Mountain* section of *Some Dance to Remember*, Reel 6, Scene 4.

Drummer salonista Max Morales was also famous for creating tapes of music for bars and baths and galleries. The Folsom Street flyer for "Double Exposure: Photos and Drawings by Jim Stewart and Gregg Coates" read

> "Opening Reception: Friday, 13 October 1978; 8:00 - Midnight. Audio by Max Morales. Invitation admits two. 766 Clementina Alley [Street], San Francisco, CA (S. O. M.) [The acronym SoMa was on the cusp of happening.] Public Viewing: Noon - 5 PM. Sats & Suns, 14 Oct - 5 Nov."

This is the kind of ambient salon of leather friends and talent that the lucky *Drummer* fell into when *arriviste* Embry found himself exiled out of LA and into San Francisco late in 1976 and early 1977.

It was my friend Sam Steward, the veteran of Gertrude and Alice's salon, who first used the word *salon* to describe what he saw as my interesting circle of friends around *Drummer*.

II. The feature article as published in *Drummer* 15, May 1977

Cock Casting

Here's a do-it-yourself section you won't find in any issue of *Popular Mechanics*! It's something for you more trophy-minded Masters—a step by step guide to casting your Slave's cock. The session pictured here is the handiwork of satyr/photographer Peter Munekee, who has a special relish for using the torturous *hot wax* casting technique.

To make your own casing of an erect cock, melt one pound of paraffin (or sealing wax). Place it over a fondue pot base or chafing dish candle unit to keep it at working temperature. Have your subject kneel on the floor or a table and spread his knees; then coat the pubic area liberally with grease. (Vaseline works best.) Paint a thick coat over his cock and balls (up to his asshole), inside his thighs, and across the belly up to his navel. Shave or Vaseline pubic hairs away from the casting area.

With a 1" brush, coat the front of the balls with the hot paraffin, building up several coats until the wax is 1/4" thick. Then move up the side of the sac and around to the base of the cock and coat it equally as thick.

Now work up the cock to an erection without touching it. Use some anal action, dirty talk, poppers, tit clamps, or whatever it takes to keep it stiff as you proceed up the cock with a 1/4" coat of wax. It must remain rock hard and totally immobile until you wax off the knob with the final coat.

As soon as the last coat is hard, the subject can relax. The best way to remove the finished mold is to have him piss it off—carefully. You don't want to drop it.

To cast a plaster replica of the mold, fill a box with sand or tightly stuffed newspapers and set the mold in it, the opening level with the top. Mix ½ pound of Plaster of Paris and pour it in slowly. The slave pictured took 3/4 pound.

As you pour, it is very important to bump, jiggle, and tap the mold to eliminate bubbling. Let the filled mold set for an hour. After it has cooled, lift it out of the box and lightly slice the wax coating with an Exacto knife, then peel it off. Let the plaster cast cure for at least eight hours before you sand it and patch any air holes. After that, it is ready to be painted, mounted, or whatever collectors do with their trophies.

Drummer 15: Cock Casting 307

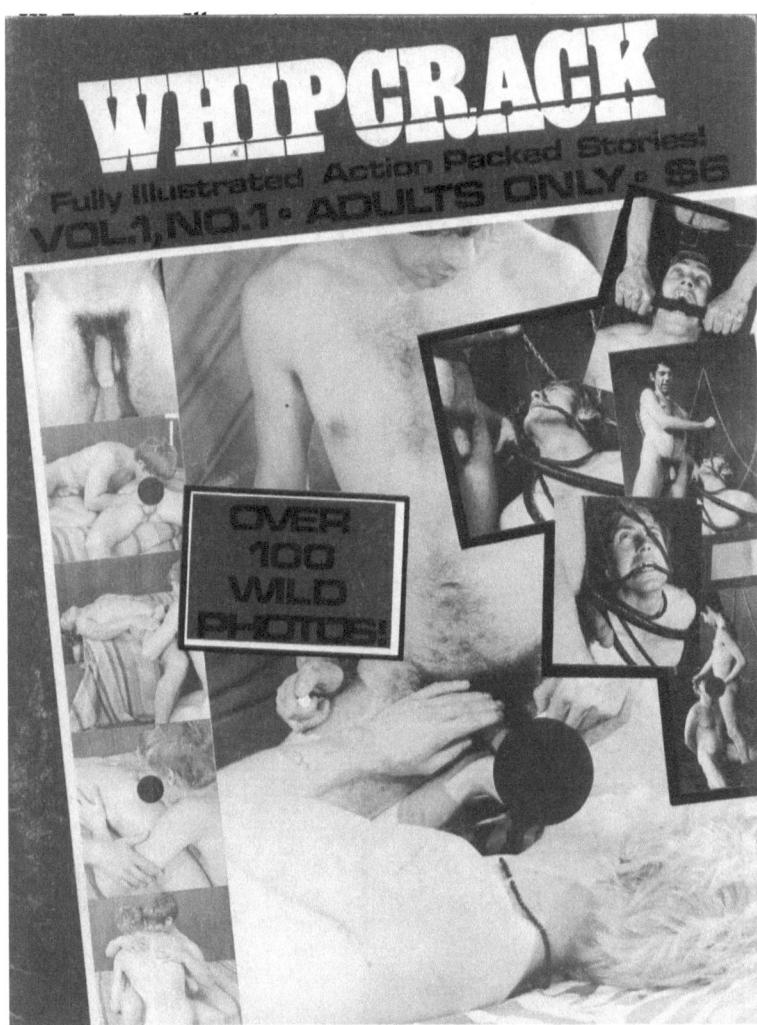

Cover. *Whipcrack* Magazine (1971). Before *Drummer* debuted in 1975, leather culture of the 1950s and 1960s formed its genome around magazines like the periodicals, *Mars, Triumph, Tomorrow's Man*, and *Physique Pictorial*, as well as one-issue magazines like *Leather!* (Guild Press, 1965), *The Rawhide Male*, (from the Chuck Renslow and Etienne Kris Studio, showcasing homomasculine archetypes such as Mike Bradburn), *Erotic Hands*, and the first leather magazine printed in San Francisco, *Whipcrack* (1971), which featured photographs of Jack Fritscher and David Sparrow shot by Walter Jebe above his camera shop at 19th and Castro, 1970. Walt "Jebby" Jebe was the first business in San Francisco willing to develop and print gay erotica shot by his customers. His store known as "Jebe's Camera" existed for nearly ten years before Harvey Milk came to "Manhattanize" San Francisco and opened his "Castro Camera" a few hundred feet from "Jebe's Camera." Used with permission.

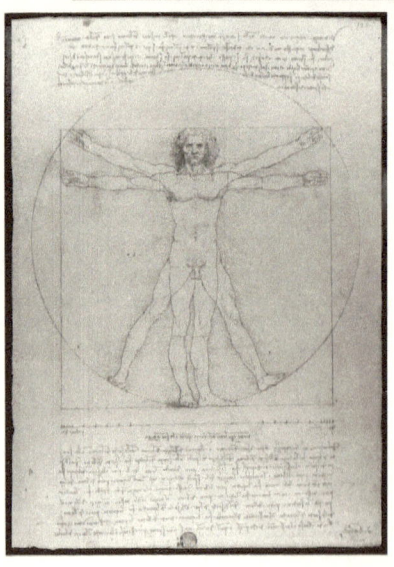

Da Vinci's *Vitruvian Man* is the specific symbol of homomasculine men in the way Michelangelo's *David* is the generic symbol of gay men. In the 1970s, Lou Thomas, Fritscher's longtime friend, adapted the image for his Target Studio which was the studio most published by *Drummer*.

Durk Parker

> Ghost-edited and produced with captions written April, 15, 1977, this centerfold photo spread was published in *Drummer* 15, May 1977.
> I. Author's Eyewitness Historical-Context Introduction written July 29, 2007
> II. The centerfold text and photograph as published in *Drummer* 15, May 1977
> III. Eyewitness Illustrations

I. Author's Eyewitness Historical-Context Introduction written July 29, 2007

In a kind of synergistic trifecta when I first began ghost-editing *Drummer*, I scooped up 1) my friend Lou Thomas' photographs of 2) model "Durk Parker" aka Durk Dehner whose leather style and sultry look channeled 3) pure Tom of Finland. Eight years before *Drummer* debuted, photographer Lou Thomas had started up Colt Studio (1967) with Jim French (aka Rip Colt) who bought him out and moved Colt from Manhattan to Los Angeles. It was a separation of geography, and a separation of erotic vision: Jim French photographed muscle gods who showed up on the sunny beaches of the West Coast; Lou Thomas shot leathermen who inhabited the dark leather bars in New York.

With the split in 1971, Lou Thomas invented his own Target Studio with Bob Lewis and operated Target for thirteen of the first fifteen years after Stonewall.

Like the neo-Californian Jim French and like the European Tom of Finland, the Lebanese-American Lou Thomas was formative in creating the 1970s Platonic Ideal of the emerging identity of the international homomasculine man whose archetypal symbol is DaVinci's strong *Vitruvian Man*. Michelangelo's louche *David* is the symbol of the effeminate gay male.

Carousing in Manhattan, Lou Thomas and I became longtime friends in 1968, and his seminal Target photography appeared on the covers of *Drummer* 13, *Drummer* 14, and *Drummer* 23.

As much as I liked my friend A. Jay's drawing on the cover of *Drummer* 15, I thought in 1977 that if Lou Thomas had not shot the covers of the two immediately preceding issues that his photograph of "Durk Parker" would have been chosen for issue 15 instead of simply as the centerfold. (Cover and centerfold traditionally are from the same shoot.) If that perfect trifecta of photographer, model, and magazine had happened, *Drummer* would have had an instantly iconic cover.

Never was it easy for a photographer or artist to get an image on the cover of *Drummer*. In the way I divided Lou Thomas' work, I also divided Robert Mapplethorpe's.

Gallia est omnis divisa in partes tres.

Near the beginning of expanding his career the young Mapplethorpe, age 31, was an American unknown, nationally, outside certain Manhattan galleries, European salons, and leather venues. On October 16, 1977, he flew TWA to California from JFK to my desk at *Drummer* where he hoped to get an "inside photo spread." When, instead, I said, "Wow!," I gave him the coveted front cover that officially introduced him to leatherfolk when I assigned him to shoot my pal Elliot Siegal for *Drummer* 24 (September 1978).

As editor in chief, I moved what would have been Mapplethorpe's photo centerfold to anchor *Son of Drummer* (September 1978), and within *Drummer* 24, I promoted the photography of David Hurles' Old Reliable Studio ("In Hot Blood: We Abuse Fags") and of my longtime domestic- and-photo partner David Sparrow and myself ("Castro Street Blues").

I gave the centerfold spread to Jocks Studio because it featured one of the hottest men on Castro, the blond model known as "Holst" who was part of our salon who ate breakfast everyday at the Norse Cove on Castro Street where he incarnated the image of the Marlboro Man over coffee and cigarettes. Holst was a pal whom I photographed a year later in Reno at the Gay Rodeo that Randy Shilts and I covered for the Associated Press and the San Francisco *Chronicle*, August 6, 1979. One of my Reno shots of Holst, produced by Mark Hemry, appeared on the front cover of my book of mostly *Drummer* fiction, *Rainbow County and Other Stories*.

This is how I parsed and sorted images at *Drummer* to keep a morphing flow page to page to accommodate the diversity of readers' tastes.

Looking back as a keeper of the *Drummer* institutional memory, am I the only person to note that Tom of Finland was never on the *Drummer* cover? The reason—which I have detected from archived documents—appears in volume four of this series: *The Drummer Salon*.

In disclosure of the zero degrees of our salon which preceded *Drummer*, Lou Thomas and I had been involved sexually and in publishing since 1968. We had been introduced by the Catholic leather priest, Jim Kane. In 1969 when I was thirty, Lou Thomas shot me with a tough 42nd Street hustler for a photo series he was producing before he started Target; and in 1972, he published a samizdat limited edition of my 1969 novel, *I Am Curious (Leather)* aka *Leather Blues*, later excerpted as "a *Drummer* novel" in *Son of Drummer* (1978) and in *Man2Man Quarterly*. We continued to work together into the 1980s when I wrote fiction such as "The Best Dirty Blond Carpenter in Texas" for his *Target Magazine*. Hugely successful, in 1983, he became editor of the mass-media gay magazines *FirstHand* and *Manscape*. After the death of Lou Thomas (March 10, 1933-January 7, 1990), the grave robbers at 1990s *Drummer* continued to publish his photographs uncredited, and, disrespecting Lou Thomas as the creative source, had the nerve to label them: "From the *Drummer* Archives."

In the reveal that is the uncloseting and documenting of true leather history, model "Durk Parker" was more than a model. Having internalized the leather ethos, he made the rounds of various leather ateliers and galleries as a patron and sometime model. He became the image and the champion of homomasculine art and artists. In the 1970s, the Target model "Durk Parker" came out as Durk Dehner, when he became friend, champion, and business partner of Tom of Finland. Dehner was mentored by *The Advocate* owner, David Goodstein, who understood startups for a business or for a nonprofit 501(c)(3)—(*Dispatch*, Tom of Finland Foundation Newsletter, Spring 2006). Dehner became the co-founder and longtime president of the Tom of Finland Foundation, and has dedicated his life to collecting, preserving, and protecting the art of Tom, as well as of emerging and established erotic artists and photographers.

Durk Dehner has given written permission for this *Gay San Francisco* reprinting of his photograph shot by Lou Thomas at Target Studio. On July 29, 2007, Durk Dehner confided in an almost mystical email that he, as did I, believed the most important contributors to *Drummer* were the men who poured their identities, hearts, and sexuality into the classified personals ads in *Drummer*. He wrote:

> *Drummer* magazine was a get-down-and-dirty experience where a real pureness existed. Artists like Tom of Finland, Etienne, A. Jay, Rex, and Domino, to mention just a few were delivered unto us amongst the prayers and salutations from the Hellion Priests of the times—known better as the classifieds where words and images were pure in cravings and desires; they were the new reality.

Durk Dehner understands the principle that popular culture is the distillation of what ordinary people like.

That's why I groomed *Drummer* to reflect the reader because I had studied the thousands of classified personals that revealed precisely what the demographic wanted.

Lou Thomas and I agreed on that theory of popular culture.

Colt Studio under master artist Jim French idealized men beyond one's reach; Target Studio photographed men one might touch; David Hurles lensed straight street toughs one could hire; for my Palm Drive Video, I shot masculine men one could meet at a bar, a street fair, or a building site.

Of that group of four studios all channeling the homomasculine mystique, Colt alone, except for a stray ad or two early on, was never published in *Drummer*.

In the interactive mix of editorial text (magazine leading the readers) and classified personals text (readers leading the magazine), fantasies could become realities. The ads offered reachable postal boxes and phone numbers.

As if anticipating reality TV shows, *Drummer* was the first gay reality magazine.

Durk Dehner is a perfect eyewitness of how the reciprocity in *Drummer* worked.

In 1979, Durk Dehner clipped a certain personal ad from *Drummer*, pasted it on his mirror, and memorized the text like a prayer. As a matter of history, that particular ad, which ran for years like a note in a bottle in *Drummer*, became famous as a classic among readers. After some time, and by chance, Durk Dehner was cruised by a man in LA. His nickname was "SS" and he turned out to be the author of the ad. They are still together at the Tom of Finland Foundation.

About SS's ad, Durk Dehner wrote to me: "The words were to my spirit. I first read them in 1979 and I keep them up to now, because I met the righteous one who spun them...."

Durk Dehner quoted the ad:

L.A. FILTH
Tough, hard, beer-drinking, cigar-smoking, foul-mouthed dirt dude with rank armpits, slimy asshole, and a cruddy uncut cock wears greasy, rotten, stinking boots, socks, jocks, T-shirts, Levi's and leather. Digs spitting, pissing, shitting, puking, sweating, and farting. Gets off with chains, tires, concrete, mud, tools, rubbers, and oil. Box 294V8.

Drummer 15 - Durk Parker

Because a picture is worth a thousand words, I kept my centerfold caption to a minimum when, with Lou Thomas and I trading favors, I produced this photo feature introducing Durk Dehner as a smouldering icon to the leather world of *Drummer*. He was what queer men were looking for in the *Drummer* classified personals where the most frequently used keyword was *masculine*.

In addition to their art foundation dealings, Durk Dehner was without question the favorite model of the homomasculine artist Tom of Finland; and, most importantly, they were legendary friends together.

II. The centerfold text and a photograph as published in *Drummer* 15, May 1977

Durk Parker is somewhat a *Drummer* discovery. In these heretofore unpublished photographs, he brings to the pages of this issue a strong, brooding sensuality unusual in photographs of real leathermen. Originally from the Rocky Mountain area of Canada, Durk has lived in New York, Honolulu, Los Angeles, and Seattle thus far.

III. Eyewitness Illustrations

Invitation, Tom of Finland opening and exhibition at the Ambush bar, Friday, February 9, 1979, South of Market. Long before gay galleries emerged in the late 1970s with Eons in LA, Stompers in New York, and Fey-Way in San Francisco, leather bars were the gay art galleries featuring their own original murals and the work of ever-changing artists and photographers. See *Life* magazine June 26, 1964. Tom of Finland's first shows in the United States were during his first trip to America in January 1978 when he met and dined with *Drummer* art director Al Shapiro and editor in chief Jack Fritscher who introduced him to Robert Mapplethorpe who shot Tom's most important portrait. Tom, in turn, drew an almost German Expressionist portrait of Mapplethorpe as a virtual Dr. Caligari. Eyewitness Fritscher is the first to ask, "Why was Tom of Finland never published on the cover of *Drummer*?" Invitation ©Tom of Finland Foundation. Used with Permission.

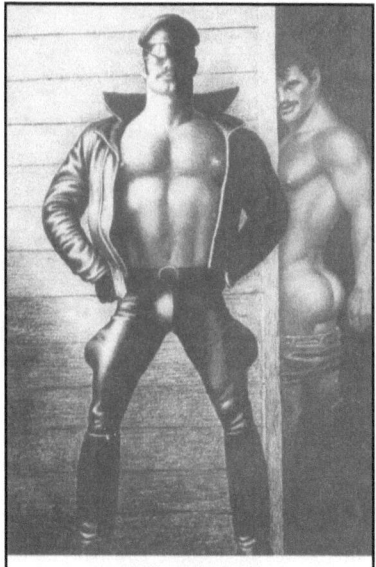

THE AMBUSH
is proud to present a showing of recent works
by Europe's foremost Erotic Artist

TOM OF FINLAND

February 9th through 24th
1351 Harrison, San Francisco

Opening Reception, February 9th, 6:30 PM

"Eyewitness Durk Dehner," billed as "Durk Parker," debuted in the quintessential 1970s sultry centerfold of *Drummer* 15 (May 1977), perhaps the hottest homomasculine centerfold ever in *Drummer*. Photograph by Lou Thomas, Target Studio. ©Lou Thomas. Leather pioneer Lou Thomas was co-founder with Jim French of Colt Studio. Dehner became a favorite model for Tom of Finland, and the two shared a legendary friendship that resulted in the creation of the Tom of Finland Foundation. Fritscher first wrote about Durk Dehner—and introduced the term *homomasculinity*—in *Drummer* 31 (September 1979) when Dehner was first runner-up in the first International Mr. Leather contest (1979). Used with permission of Durk Dehner.

Insert: In the salon around *Drummer*, the Chicago artist Etienne was one of the hosts of that first IML contest. Like Tom of Finland, Etienne idolized Durk Dehner whom he personally invited to compete live on stage. So taken was Etienne that, months before the contest, he painted a full-length color portrait of Dehner (face subliminal) that was published as the black-and-white logo for the international advertisements and posters for that IML, May 1979. Fritscher positioned Etienne's ad as the full page 69 in *Drummer* 28 (April 1979). Thirteen years later, Etienne's leather-heritage painting of Dehner was published as the full-color cover of *Drummer* 153 (March 1992). Used with permission of Chuck Renslow and the Leather Archives & Museum.

Tom Hinde Portfolio
The Artist Speaks
by Tom Hinde with Jack Fritscher

> Written and produced in March-April 1977, at the request of Tom Hinde as a press release to accompany his drawings and quotations for *Drummer* 16 (June 1977), Second Anniversary Issue.
> This same text was also published at Hinde's show at the Eons Gallery, 708 Heliotrope Drive, Los Angeles, August 2-31, 1977.
> I. Author's Eyewitness Historical-Context Introduction written December 22, 2001
> II. The feature essay as published in *Drummer* 16, June 1977, Second Anniversary Issue
> III. Eyewitness Illustrations

I. Author's Eyewitness Historical-Context Introduction written December 22, 2001

Gay art spontaneously combusted into the first designated "gay galleries." Lowell and Herb's Eons Gallery in Los Angeles, like Robert Opel's Fey-Way Gallery in San Francisco and Lou Weingarden's Stompers Gallery in New York, was one of the pioneer galleries for queer art in the 1970s. Eons opened in March 1976 showing the photographs of *Drummer* contributor, Robert Opel; the 1977 Eons show featured Tom Hinde, Tom of Finland, Go Mishima, and Zach of Los Angeles. Tom Hinde's first solo show at Fey-Way was January 20 to February 18, 1978. (See the telegram from Eons' "Lowell and Herb" congratulating Etienne and A. Jay on their dual opening at Fey-Way, May 1978, in the "Star Trick" entry in this book.)

Tom Hinde sold his S&M lithographs as 8x10 prints in limited editions of 125 signed-and-serially-numbered "suites" through his own mail-order company, Denim Publications, San Francisco. Through Denim, Tom Hinde published the 120-page paperback novel titled *Leather Boy, Leather Man*. Billed as "At last, a sensitive S&M Sex/Love Story," the novel was particularly well written by Robert Stewart (whom I always believed to be Tom Hinde toying with the heritage names of Jim Stewart and Sam Steward). The cover and the 10 interior illustrations—one for each chapter—were drawn by Tom Clave (aka Tom Hinde). Hinde's drawings in that book are original and distinctive, yet seem to share the nervous, speedy South-of-Market look similar to drawings by legendary drug-addict artist, Chuck Arnett. Tom gave me a copy of this limited edition novel in 1977, and I treasure it to this day.

Tom Hinde's personal story in a sense is the story of *Drummer*—out of many stories of *Drummer*. The 1970s were a Golden Age before HIV sucked out the gold and turned the light as fluorescent as an ICU.

Tom Hinde, born in San Francisco, was the kind of artist *Drummer* needed to invent itself. His story is typical of how personal sex encounters led into the pages of *Drummer* at a time when everybody was fucking everybody else. Tom Hinde, a brilliant erotic artist of submission, was both my friend and playmate. He starred as "the martyr" in my two-reel Super-8 color film, *The Imitation of Art* (1973), two years before *Drummer* was invented. The film trans-substantiated Tom's autobiographical S&M drawings onto his own flesh, which, of course, made him so much the more interesting as an artist whose lust included the performance art of his own erotic suffering. I filmed the movie at Allan Lowery's playroom on Castro near 15th Street. David Sparrow did the lighting. My films and videos usually focus on one man on screen from the photographer's point of view. If I walk into the frame, my camera is on my tripod.

Over time, Tom Hinde introduced me to several other artists and bodybuilders who also wished to appear as martyrs on screen as if, I think, to be able to see themselves lit and angled and shot in ways even more intimate than in a mirror. This "suffering artist" phenomenon in the 1970s in San Francisco was not new to me, even when "original-recipe martyr," Michel Foucault, showed up to play among the *Drummer* salon on Folsom Street, because in the 1960s in New York I had shot a number of rather severe films of several artists and critics and writers (the names of the dead, the famous, and the still living are deleted). In San Francisco, one in my series of S&M films, *Muscle Agonistes* (1972), was shot in the same location as was Tom Hinde. The little epic starred Tom Hinde's friend, the very handsome blond bodybuilder Robert Walker who was a painter famous as a muralist in Los Angeles interior design. He was also the personal chef for the very famous "name deleted," the doyenne of the San Francisco social scene whom Armistead Maupin fictionalized in *Tales of the City*.

(Many of my Super-8 films and 35mm transparencies—some shot with Tony Tavarossi at the Slot Hotel in the Stocks Room #226—premiered during a number of performance-art "happenings" staged with the poet Ron Johnson at the No Name bar on Folsom Street during

Drummer 16: Tom Hinde Portfolio

1972-1973. The No Name became the Bolt which became the Brig which became the Powerhouse.)

In 1972, the ever gracious Robert Walker asked my lover David Sparrow and me as a favor to him to pose for one of his very large paintings which was not meant to be a portrait of us. Because Robert Walker had appeared in my Super-8 film, turn-about seemed fair play. That experience of being made into the object of a painter's eye is recounted as an episode in my 1975 short story, "Rainbow County," in the female character named "Cleo Walker." Robert Walker after several sessions said, "I can't capture the two of you in one frame. There is too much tension." Neither David Sparrow nor I needed to ask exactly what that meant. The painting which was mythic in theme lies unfinished in some San Francisco attic. The short story that remains appears as the title story in *Rainbow County and Other Stories*, as well as in *Sweet Embraceable You: Coffee-House Stories* featuring my spin on Virginia Woolf, "Mrs. Dalloway Went That-A-Way."

David Sparrow and I were gorgeously tempestuous lovers, truly in love and loving each other, officially from July 4, 1969, through March 17, 1979. After that we became even more tempestuous friends who continued to fuck together, as well as tempestuously create together (mostly billed together, explicitly or covertly), shooting many photographs for *Drummer* under the names "Spitting Image" and "David Sparrow." Actually, from 1977-1979, the salon of friends and talent and fighting at *Drummer* drove David and me closer together in creative work, and drove us apart as a domestic couple. *Drummer* at that period of High Sex was the only game in town, and the very handsome David Sparrow—depressed by his genetically addictive and suicidal personality, confirmed by his sister—never felt he could compete with other players such as Robert Mapplethorpe, who, as I recall, bought several drawings by Tom Hinde, because, Robert said, he admired Tom Hinde's work at Tom's second Fey-Way Gallery show, January 21 to February 18, 1979. (David Sparrow, my first true love, is loosely fictionalized as the character Teddy in *Some Dance to Remember: A Memoir-Novel of San Francisco 1979-1982*.)

Everything about our lives in the Titanic 70s was in the fast lane, but at least we were celebrity passengers in a decade when everyone was a star. On March 3, 1979, Fey-Way, the first art gallery South of Market, celebrated its first anniversary hosted by founder Robert Opel and his muse, the poet and singer Camille O'Grady. On April 20, 1979, I recorded live my interview with Camille O'Grady and Robert Opel which was published in *Mapplethorpe: Assault with a Deadly Camera* (1994). On May 21, San Francisco gays, angered by the light sentence given to assassin Dan White, set police cars on fire outside City Hall during the

White Night Riot. A week later, Robert Opel appeared as Gay Justice in the Civic Center plaza and with a gun acted out "executing Dan White." Six weeks later, on July 8, 1979, a real gunman entered Fey-Way Gallery, cornered Robert Opel and Camille O'Grady and Anthony Rogers, and in an exchange of words shot Robert Opel to death. To handle the horror the leather-and-art salon immediately spun a joke about how cruel a critic could be.

Critics can be merciless. Rewind tape! Five months before the murder, on January 30, 1979, Camille O'Grady, distressed at a review of Tom Hinde's work in *The San Francisco Sentinel* newspaper, wrote me a letter introducing herself. She was that month literally "new in town" and she trusted that as *Drummer* editor I could help rebut the review. Her approach to me was typical of the power of not me but of the editorship of *Drummer*. Mapplethorpe approached me in the same way. (Camille and I discussed that her letter was both personal to me and an "open letter" meant for publication, and that her letter to the *Sentinel* was also an "open letter" which she gave me to publish at my discretion.)

> Camille O'Grady
> c/o Fey-Way Studios
> 1287 Howard Street
> San Francisco Calif 94103
> January 30, 1979
>
> Dear Jack:
> I have been in San Francisco for about a month—I read *Drummer*, & we have many friends in common both here and in N.Y.C.
> I thought that this article & my reply to it might be of interest to you & others at *Drummer*. Since I don't know whether my letter will be published in the *Sentinel*, I am sending you this copy of it. [Camille included a clipping from page 9 of the *Sentinel*, January 26, 1979]
> I am reachable through the gallery–626-1000. If you haven't seen Tom Hinde's show, come by and see it.
> —Camille O'Grady ©1979 Camille O'Grady

This letter opened a friendship. Camille and I bonded (over Tom Hinde) within our mutual circle of New York and San Francisco artists and writers who traveled back and forth between *Drummer* and Fey-Way. (We also bonded as quivering Catholics, and she gave me copies of dozens of her song lyrics and mystic poems. I gave her journal pages from *Some*

Dance to Remember.) Camille was to Robert Opel what Patti Smith was to Robert Mapplethorpe, except that Camille was hot. Forget comparisons to the intellectually engaging Patti Smith who is cool in her own right. Camille O'Grady seemed to me to be channeling Jim Morrison. In the early 70s, she was an artist who was a singer and a poet. She came up in the underground sex-art-punk milieu of Manhattan. At the Mineshaft, where no women were allowed, the crotchety Wally Wallace who founded and managed the Mineshaft (opening night, October 8, 1976, to the closing in 1985), told me in my videotaped interview with him (March 28, 1990) that he actually welcomed the full-leather Camille into his infamous sex club. (Wally Wallace died September 7, 1999.)

Camille O'Grady lived the liberated pop-and-art life Camille Paglia wrote about ten years later. To me, Camille O'Grady was the "Queen of the *Drummer* Women." She was second only to Jeanne Barney, the founding Los Angeles editor in chief of *Drummer.*

As an exorcist ordained by the Catholic Church, I know about witches: Camille was born a changeling. In the 1977 text-and-photo book *Hard Corps*: *Studies in Leather and Sadomasochism* by Michael Grumley and Ed Gallucci, she appears in two photographs: as a striking woman, and as a genderfuck leatherboy. (I wrote in 1979, "Camille O'Grady is a lady. And the lady is a tramp. That's hot.") In fact, Wally Wallace not only let Camille in to play, he invited her to sing at the Mineshaft's 1978 anniversary party where she belted out her piss song, "Toilet Kiss." She wrote all of her songs from a gay man's point of view. Camille had assembled her own band dubbed "Leather Secrets" who were a prototype of punk and new wave. Camille told me on audiotape that she played at Hilly Kristal's CBGB "before Patti." Her flyer announcing her appearance at Max's Kansas City, October 9, 1977, sported a drawing of her with a bullet-snifter of poppers (or coke?) up one nostril. Her temporary tattoos read "Wounded Not Broken" and "Stigmata Hari Bleeds for You."

She had messed around singing with Lou Reed who called her "Patti Smith without a social conscience." That whole Warhol Factory superstar scene, and *Interview* magazine crowd, welcomed Camille's creation of her own wild twin, "Stigmata Hari." Camille met Robert Opel about the time he streaked the whole wide world on live television at the 1974 Academy Awards. My former house mate Jim Stewart whose work I introduced to *Drummer* photographed Camille for his show at the Ambush bar. The show opened on March 3, 1979, with Camille appearing in a "Special Guest Performance." Jim Stewart had moved from Kalamazoo, Michigan, with David Sparrow and me when we all heard the call to head to San Francisco where Jim Stewart lived with us on 25th Street. Camille was, before the trauma of the murder of Robert Opel, a kind of earth mother, a leather lioness of the arts.

And Tom Hinde was one of her cubs.

Her significance emphasizes his.

Excuse me for thinking about these times, and these people, and that art the way some think about the lives and art of all charmed circles of their young adulthood.

At the time, I thought they were all of interest.

That's why I saved everything: letters, invitations, the last Quaalude....

And took notes.

And shot photos.

And made audiotapes and films, and then videos.

Camille's letter to the *Sentinel* is interesting and maybe important because she voices her own view of art and morality, which, while very liberated, reveals the reactionary Catholic underneath.

Her art-for-art's-sake letter is dated "January 27, 1979," and says:

> Dear *Sentinel*,
>
> In his review in the Jan. 26 *Sentinel*, Beau Riley has compared the art of Thomas Hinde as representing "evil," and the art of William McNeill as representing "good." This approach is unfair to both artists, and is irrelevant to the criticism of art itself.
>
> If Riley is to criticize art, he can not approach his subject as a moralist; he must leave his and others' lives and lifestyles behind, particularly regarding art of a sexual/sensual nature.
>
> Riley's major criticism of Hinde's work is a reaction to the subject matter, and his (Riley's) projections about it. He was obviously quite disturbed by the work. He was, on the other hand, quite delighted with McNeill's work.
>
> Riley then proceeds (very ambitiously) to declare that one man's work is "art" and that the other's is not—on a "good-evil" basis. What each artist is appealing to is an experience in a specifically sexual area—where one man's pain is another man's pleasure, where one man's "heaven" is another man's "hell."
>
> One of the main properties of successful "art" is its ability to place the viewer in the artist's spirit; in the case of these two artists, in his sexual persona and flesh. If one is to truly experience sexual art, he must approach it with an acceptance and willingness to have congress with the artist's own vision. If one is to criticize it and negate it as "art" outside of technique, the only

dismissal of sexual art is that the critic was totally *unmoved* [word is underscored by Camille's hand in ink] in any sensual way.

Art is the forum where men can transcend many limitations, one of them being the area of "good" and "evil": many physically uncommitted crimes have been transfigured by artists into great moments to be recognized and experienced by others. The critic's function is to determine whether that moment occurs—not whether he is physically repelled by it or not.

Sincerely,
Camille O'Grady [signed in black ink from a fountain pen]
©1979 Camille O'Grady

Tom Hinde's drawings were so controversial in the Titanic 70s that they made critic Beau Riley foam at the mouth like a right-wing Republican—in fact, like a 1979 prototype of the new wave of the politically correct. Riley reviewed two shows: William McNeill's "Seven Deadly Virtues," seven large mixed-media drawings at the Ambush bar, and Tom Hinde's "Thomas G. Hinde," forty-one small drawings at Fey-Way Gallery. The two South of Market venues were about two blocks apart.

Beau Riley was writing about not just Tom Hinde. He was also flaming on about sex, drugs, and rock-n-roll South of Market in the same fundamentalist way as had Richard Goldstein in his shock feature article "S&M: The Dark Side of Gay Liberation," *Village Voice*, July 7, 1975—two weeks after the first issue of *Drummer* was published, June 20, 1975.

In truth, in that time in that place in the politically correct *Sentinel,* Riley was really writing about *Drummer* and the culture of *Drummer.*

Odd, the way he perceived it, because at the same time he was writing his point of view for the *Sentinel,* I was writing my point of view about art, politics, gay leather culture, and the fashioning of homomasculine identity in *Drummer.*

I find it absolutely necessary to quote fundamentalist Beau Riley because he voices precisely the politically-correct bigotry that I was fighting against in the pages of *Drummer*. In the fair play of fair use, I quote the vanished Riley nearly in full because his militant article in smearing the leather culture South of Market as an "explicit hell" and "forum of depravity" is historical "Exhibit A" of swanning gay puritanism. He requires inserted line-item rebuttals and scholar-like comments. And, to be fair to him and readers who may want to judge if I have "bent the bent" of his primary text in then publisher Charles Morris' *The Sentinel*, I quote him for textual examination because his article seems otherwise irretrievable.

Beau Riley wrote in part:

> William McNeill's seven colossal-sized works are clearly idealizations. They all represent nude males, rendered in a mix of black, white and gray media, in a loose, quick, Zen-inspired style....The group has been given a satiric name, deadly virtues [*sic*], a warning to the wary not to take the works at face value, not to see them as only seven naked men.
>
> Thomas Hinde has been equally and oppositely direct. His forty-one small drawings are specimens of precise draftsmanship, mostly in pencil, a few with washes of ink or paint, one washed with the artist's own shit. The subjects are sado-masochistic sexual activity, including bondage, mutilation, and the (nowadays) inevitable fistfucking. No reference is made to abstractions, to ideals, or to anything which a camera might not have seen as well as Hinde. His men, trussed and slung for fisting, seem to insist that we not see a male nude, but merely the debased and dis-clothed [*sic*] human object.
>
> Clearly Hinde is an eroticist and McNeill is not, but this is where the ambiguity begins. Hinde's cold, even clinical approach seems to prevent an erotic response....
>
> Both artists are working from the milieu in which they are exhibited, the black-and-white, EXPLICIT HELL SOUTH OF MARKET, THAT FORUM OF DEPRAVITY [I added caps to emphasize Beau Riley's Jonathan Edwards-like preacher's approach to "Sinners in the Hands of an Angry God"; or is he more a campy version of Harold Hill singing "We Got Trouble" in *The Music Man*.] which has arisen in our troubled day, in part as a response to our confusion. We seem to be looking for something basic, durable and present which can be used as a referent [*sic*], and we seem to find this in ultimate forms of sexuality.
>
> But Hinde's appreciation of whatever is going on out there in the sex clubs and bars and deserted streets is typically American, short-sighted and mislead by appearances. He is content to locate and show the events, the symptoms of this social exploration, in this case the extreme sex acts themselves, together with their miasmic atmosphere of decay, ruin, and disgust, all of it neatly, nicely, medically framed under glass on white walls, and for a clientele in their dress-leathers.
>
> By contrast, McNeill's approach is typically Japanese, understated, lyric, ironic....

Two scenes: Hinde in a gallery, free wine, everybody seeing and being seen. McNeill in a scrufty [*sic*] bar, supply your own drugs and look out for reality....Hinde's work is a spectre, McNeill's a prospect....Hinde's work is ILLUSTRATIVE, his technique MAGAZINE-LIKE [I added caps to emphasize the prejudice that the "proper gay establishment" has always had against gay magazines as a genre], his ideas are those which are comfortable in their perverse way, and the works themselves [are] as easily dismissed or obsessionally retained as any pornographic image....

Clearly McNeill has bested our fractious times...to assert himself and to plea for goodness. Clearly Hinde has been bested by it all, been objectified and victimized like his subjects, has surrendered his own feelings to the crowd notion of what is real. Hinde has been specific, naked if you will; but McNeill has made art.

—©Beau Riley, "The Naked and the Nude," *The San Francisco Sentinel*, January 26, 1979, page 9.

Beau Riley makes me think of the German saying from the 1890s, "Just because you take it up the ass doesn't mean you're a critic." Like so many under-educated and agenda-driven gay critics in *The Sentinel* and in the *Bay Area Reporter*, instead of reviewing the art, he uses the art as an opportunity to stand on his moralistic, fundamentalist, bi-polar soapbox.

Of course, Tom Hinde was absolutely "illustrative" and "magazine-like." That's why *Drummer* published him. Of course, he had "perverse" ideas and had been "objectified and victimized." That's why we all had sex with him. And made movies of him. He suffered beautifully. He was like Christ in Gethsemane. He was a great bottom.

As of this date, Thomas G. Hinde, who gave me several of his drawings, is listed by his alma mater, St. Mary's College, San Francisco, among the "Lost Alumni" of 1964.

Camille O'Grady — God bless her — is rumored to be alive and well and living at an undisclosed location.

Tom Hinde was the kind of S&M player who, breathlessly over the poet, e e cummings, did not use upper-case capitalization he thought suitable only for masters and tops. He signed his drawings both as "T. Clave" and "Thomas G. Hinde" playing with S&M metaphor: that *clave* is a word for a hardwood stick used in a pair for percussion, and that *hind* can also mean *rear-end* and *deer*.

II. The feature essay as published in *Drummer* 16, June 1977, Second Anniversary Issue

Body Worship, Submerged in Sex...

Tom Hinde Portfolio
The Artist Speaks
by Tom Hinde with Jack Fritscher

Mr. Hinde was born in San Francisco and was raised in Mill Valley, California, and in the Napa Valley, north of the San Francisco Bay Area. He has studied art at the San Francisco Art Institute, College of Marin, St. Mary's College, and the University of California Extension Center, San Francisco. His training includes lithography, etching, silk screen, painting (oil), landscape, and portraiture with major emphasis upon life drawing and the human form. His current medium is graphite and pencil, turpentine washes, and pastel. His subject matter of sex, language, and worship can best be summed up in his own words.

I once saw an alley cat in heat, spread eagle on a concrete walkway between my house and the place next door. looking over the fence I saw her lying flat on her belly with her rear sticking up in the air, her tail whipping from one side to the other. her front claws dug into the concrete path pulling at it. gathering in the alley were several toms [Tom's own multiple personas] fighting with each other over who would mount her first. four of them fucked her savagely and with each thrust she backed farther against that captor mating as violently as she could; she didn't care who screwed her or how many times each one did. she simply lay there howling for more and wanting no pause between shifts.

man as animal, like that alley cat or a bull wild in his mating; man mounting man, the spirit all carnal. man feeling his body, not thinking, enjoying his instincts as he submits to his body, freeing that animal to act: to taste ass, cock, sweat, to slap, kiss, grunt, to fart, to fuck, to eat cock, to rim, to howl, to cry. the power enjoyed while controlling another body—whether fucking it, beating it, tying it down, or stringing it up. the joy of surrender. the celebration of the animal in man.

I draw people who are human, people completely submerged in their sex with bodies which are real, faces filled with feeling, playing with other bodies, bare expressions which are quite direct. in the intensity of this specific sexual language no thought is paid to any reality outside of the immediate. no value exists except the desirability of each body involved and the pride in which each person offers himself. "I am a man," his actions say, and as a man, he kneels or boastfully stands to take the pleasure he wants.

it is within this context, this personal climate that I draw my subject for it is here that a man lies exposed, his feelings expanded and open, his senses ignoring all caution or censure. the reverence demonstrated and acknowledged when one kneels before another "giving head or ass or body" is an act done in worship of the body. the cooperation between each person involved, seeking a common end produces that intensity experienced in their moments of climax; both work towards it, each one prodding the other on with a kiss or his hand. the reverence, the cooperation, the language, and each mood of this communication is what I acknowledge with my drawing. the dignity of those touches, and their intimacy, is worthy of respect.

—Thomas G. Hinde, May 24, 1977

III. Eyewitness Illustrations

Invitation, Tom Hinde Preview Party, Fey-Way Studios, 1978. Self-portrait by Tom Hinde.

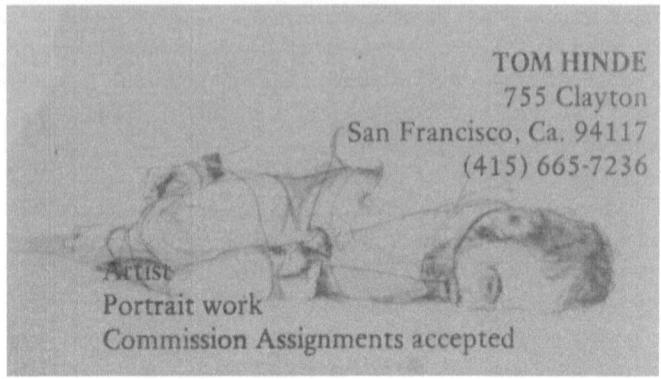

Top: Tom Hinde self-portrait business card 1970s. Bottom: Cover of paperback novel illustrated *and* published by Tom Hinde who was most likely also the author under the pseudonym of "Robert Stewart." In the 1970s, especially in gay publishing such as *Drummer*, authors and artists often had several alternative names. The desire was to make a few seem like many to gain business status for the publication by giving the impression that a large staff —and not just one or two dedicated people—had created the book or magazine. *Drummer* publisher John Embry frequently removed Jack Fritscher's byline because, Embry said, "It looks like you're writing the whole damn issue." As a result, Fritscher often assigned the credit for his own writing and photography solely to his domestic lover of ten years, David Sparrow, and to his longtime friend, David Hurles.

Invitation, Fey-Way Studios, group show, First Anniversary, March 3, 1979, drawing by Camille O'Grady. During the inclusivity of the Titanic 1970s, before the iceberg of the gay gender wars, women and men mixed together in the art and life of SoMa. Robert Opel paired with Camille O'Grady. Steve McEachern of the Catacombs paired with Cynthia Slater of the Society of Janus. Robert Mapplethorpe paired with Patti Smith, but did not bring her to San Francisco where she would have been *prima inter pares*. The artists listed were: "Camille O'Grady, Gill Mann, Tom, Jim Stewart, Jonni Marchant, Lionel Biron, Rick Borg, Lou Rudolph, Gordon Pollock, Christina McCabe, Michael Drew, Kent, Stryder, The Hun, Larry Hunt, Tom Hinde, Mark Kadota, Robert Opel."

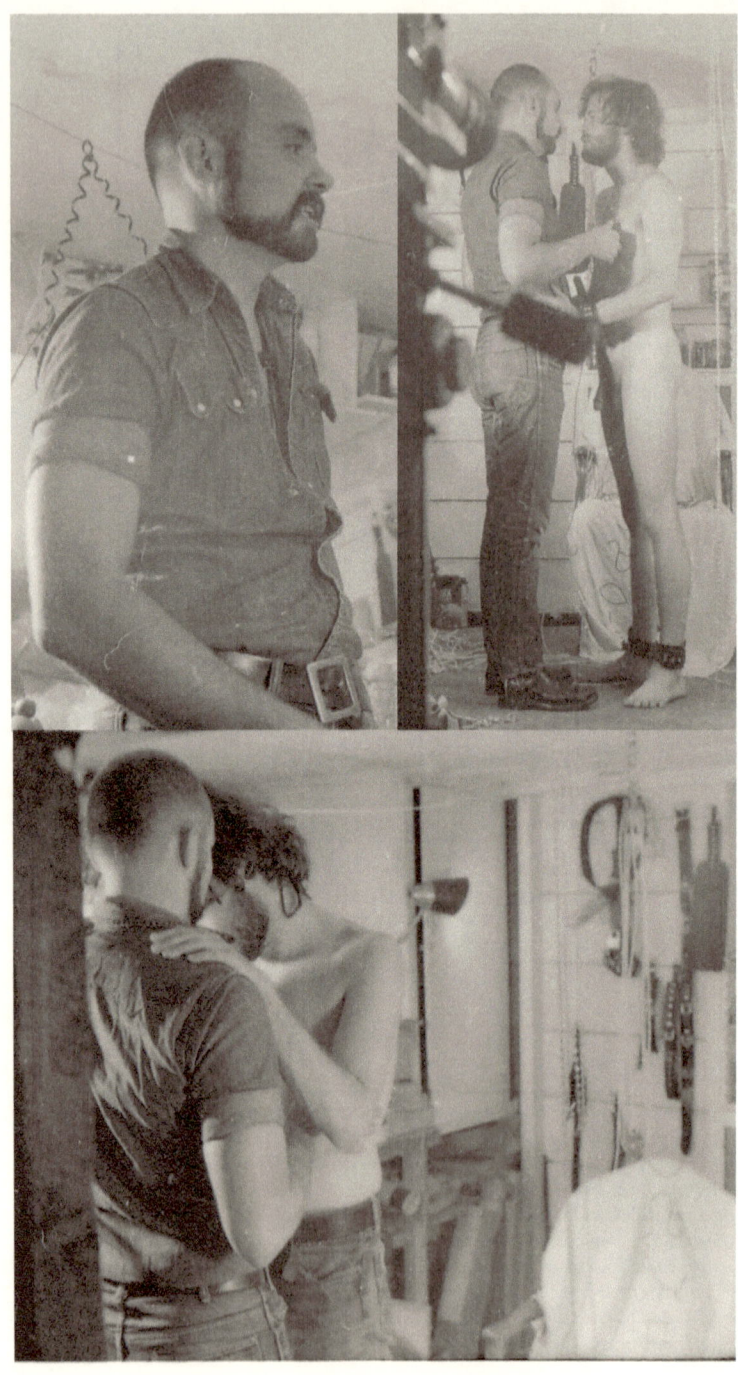

Opposite and this page. *Cinema Verite* Meets *Drummer Verite*. Four photographs of Tom Hinde and Jack Fritscher co-creating on the set of Jack Fritscher's *Imitation of Christ* film, *The Imitation of Art* (1973), on location at 15th and Castro Street. This documentary kind of reader-reflexive *verite* truth was what Fritscher's *Drummer* was all about. In this genre, *Drummer* picked as two of its video favorites Fritscher's *Buck's Bunkhouse Discipline* and *Hot Lunch*. Production photographs by Jack Fritscher assisted by David Sparrow. ©Jack Fritscher

Top: "Robert Opel and Singer-Poet Camille O'Grady with Interviewer Jack Fritscher of *Drummer*," Fey-Way Studios, April 17, 1979 (Tuesday, 7:30 P. M.). Fritscher's audiotape is Opel's last interview. These pictures are the last shots of Opel and O'Grady photographed together before Opel's murder, Sunday, July 8, 1979. Fritscher withheld his interview from *Drummer* and it was first published in the book *Mapplethorpe: Assault with a Deadly Camera* (1994). Photograph by David Sparrow. ©Jack Fritscher. Middle: Camille O'Grady and Jack Fritscher, same evening. Photograph by David Sparrow. ©Jack Fritscher. Bottom: Robert Opel, same evening. Photograph by Jack Fritscher. ©Jack Fritscher

"San Francisco's Muse Camille O'Grady," *Drummer* salon portrait, Fey-Way Studios, April 17, 1979. Photograph by Jack Fritscher. ©Jack Fritscher

Thieves Kill Gallery Owner, Get $5

By Maitland Zane

Robert Opel, who staged a mock execution of Dan White at the Gay Freedom Day parade and "streaked" at the 1974 Oscars ceremony, was shot and killed Sunday by bandits who invaded his gay art gallery South of Market.

All the robbers got was $5, a camera and a backpack, police said.

Witnesses told police they were at the Fey Way Productions, 1287 Howard Street, about 9 p.m. when two white men in their 30s came in demanding money and drugs.

One man had a sawed-off shotgun, the other — believed to be the killer — had an automatic and was wearing a brown leather jacket with a large diamond stickpin.

Opel, 39, begged the men to leave, saying, "I don't want to see that (the guns)."

Homicide Inspectors Jim Crowley and Mike Byrne said the gunmen threatened to kill witnesses Anthony Rogers, 32, and Camille O'Grady, 29, when Opel said he had no money.

"We are not violent people," Rogers reportedly told the robbers. "Please don't hurt us."

When the bandit with the shotgun pointed it at O'Grady's head and said, "Give us the money or I'll kill her," Opel replied, "You'll have to kill us all — there's no money."

O'Grady, Rogers and another witness, Ladon Palmer, 25, told police the bandit with the automatic took Opel into the apartment Opel shared with O'Grady behind the gallery.

A shot was fired, apparently to scare Opel, but he was heard to tell the bandit, "Get out of my space."

"I'm gonna blow your head off," the bandit threatened.

"You're going to have to," Opel retorted. "There's no money here."

The witnesses told police they heard another shot and the thump of Opel falling to the floor.

After taking $5, a camera, and a backpack, the gunman told the witnesses, "You haven't seen us before, but if you see us again, you're dead." The two men then fled the building.

Opel was pronounced dead at 10:40 p.m., soon after being rushed to San Francisco General Hospital.

Opel's mock execution of Dan White, the slayer of Mayor George Moscone and Supervisor Harvey Milk, took place at the UN Plaza, with Opel pretending to shoot a friend dressed all in white.

Five years ago, Opel, then an advertising man in Los Angeles, "streaked" at the Academy Awards ceremony, prancing across the stage just as David Niven was about to introduce Elizabeth Taylor.

A couple of months later Opel stripped at a Los Angeles City Council meeting to protest an ordinance banning nudity at municipal beaches. He was acquitted in October, 1975, of indecent exposure, but convicted of disrupting a public meeting.

Survivors include his mother and a sister in Pittsburgh, Pa., police said.

Robert Opel streaked the 1974 Academy Awards live telecast. Top: Opel streaking an LA courtroom protesting the closing of a nude beach; two-page photo spread from publisher Fred Halsted's magazine *Package* 6 (January 1977). *Package* was a "Virtual *Drummer*" which tried to dig deeper than publisher John Embry allowed *Drummer* to go. Photograph by Opel's associate, B. Moritz. Bottom: Opel's obituary as reported in the *San Francisco Chronicle*, July 10, 1979. ©*San Francisco Chronicle*

Drummer 16: Tom Hinde Portfolio

CAMILLE O'GRADY
Fey—Way Productions
1287 Howard Street
San Francisco, CA 94103
(415) 626-1000

Camille O'Grady photographed by serial-killer victim Larry Hunt, a member of the SoMa *Drummer* salon, who was himself a model (August 1978) for Jack Fritscher who introduced him to Robert Mapplethorpe who photographed Hunt in knee-high lace-up boots. Years after he went missing from a leather bar in Los Angeles, Hunt's jawbone was found in Griffith Park.

The "Christmas Fix Invitation" illustrated with Chuck Arnett's drug-drawing for the "Christmas Fix" salon party at "Fey-Way, Midnight, December 30, 1978," featured Santa injecting his forearm with a hypodermic whose old tracks spell out *NOEL*. Fritscher has suggested that the sharing of needles during the Titanic 70s, more than unsafe sex, was what killed many speed-driven leather players in the first wave of HIV. Besides Robert Opel premiering his film *Fuck You, Santa Claus*, "club" artists featured were "Camille O'Grady direct from the Mineshaft in her first West Coast appearance," Ruby Zebra's queer rock poetry, Spikey Dummer's live music, Tom of Finland, Rex, Chuck Arnett, Olaf, the Hun, A. Jay, and photographer Bill Moritz from the LA salon of Fred Halsted.

Drummer 16: Tom Hinde Portfolio

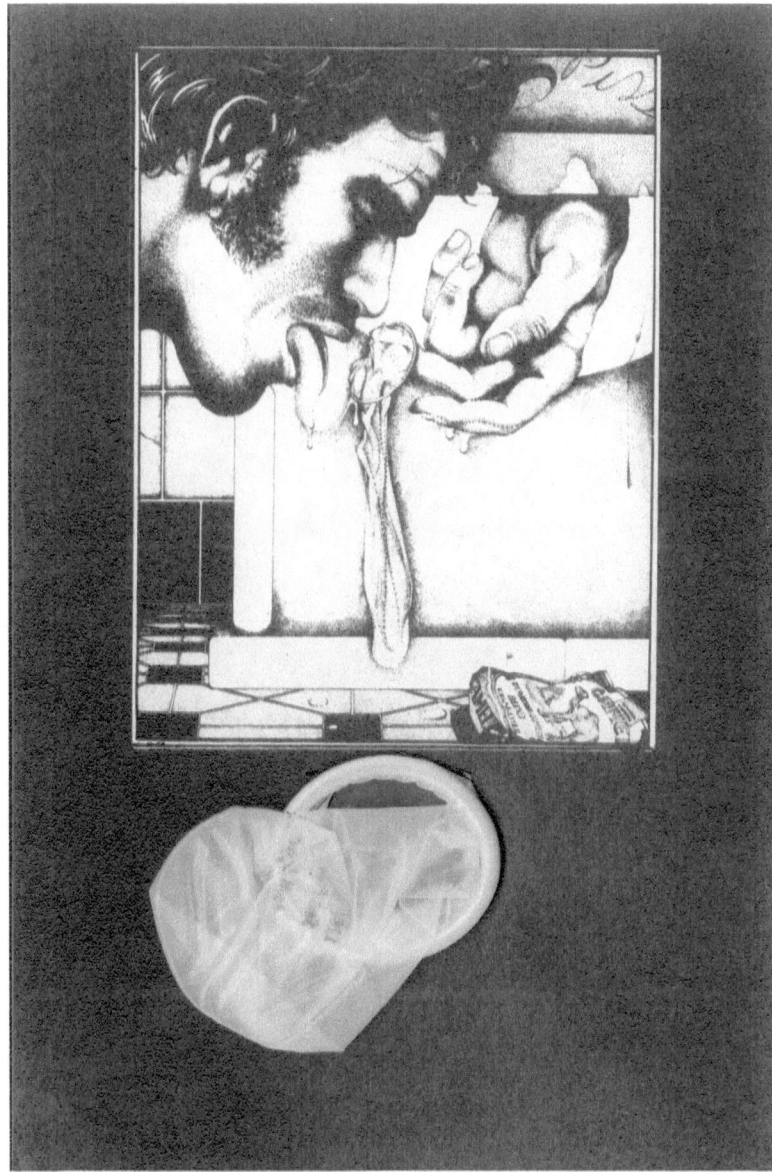

Invitation, Rex drawing—with actual condom attached by the artist's hand. On the condom the printing reads in tiny four-point black ink on yellow-white rubber: "Rex Originals, Fey-Way Studios, 1287 Howard St. San Francisco, April 8-19 [1978]. Reception for the Artist. April 7, 8-11 PM, Admits 2." Prime among the clever 1970s mixed-media pop-art objects, and second only to Aleister Crowley's ejaculation cover of *White Stains* (1898), this "Rex at Fey-Way" invitation is extremely fragile. Drawing ©Rex. Used with permission.

PIGS OUT OF CASTRO

WHAT IF A GAY ASSASIN HAD KILLED DAN WHITE?
They would have roasted that person alive, and that would have been the end of that.
Would straights have been excluded from the jury? The answer is obvious.

Last night, the gay community of this city rose up, in pain and in anger, and protested the outrageous verdict in the Dan White murder trial. The police rushed to assault us, beating on innocent people without hesitation, and we taught them a lesson they will never forget. Last night we learned that they are the enemy, that this is a war--a war between government and the gay community. While the liberal politicians and their gay flunkeys reassure us that there's nothing to worry about, that San Francisco is an "enlightened" city, and that Police Chief Gains is our "friend"--an all-heterosexual jury let Dan White off with a light rap on the knuckles, the police invaded the very heart of our community and people were clubbed on the street.

Police brutality is the living symbol of the evil inherent in the political control of lifestyles. Last night, the police assaulted innocent people and the people fought back--and WON. The pigs ran as the people kicked the brutal oppressors out of their community. The cheer that conquered the night was a cry of relief. In that moment, that dizzying, triumphant moment, we knew that we didn't need them. They needed our sanction, our cooperation, our consent.

Let that be our answer to them. When they call us outlaws, vandals, radicals, libertarians, our answer must be: we have withdrawn our sanction, our cooperation, our consent. We will tell them--and their gay allies-- that we refuse to apologize for acts of self-defense. If this makes us outlaws, then we will proclaim it to the skies--and let Feinstein's Gestapo make the most of it.

STUDENTS FOR A LIBERTARIAN SOCIETY
1620 Montgomery Street
San Francisco, CA 94111
(415)781-5817

LIBERTARIAN PARTY (RADICAL CAUCUS)
LIBERTARIANS OF SAN FRANCISCO

"Pigs Out Of Castro" samizdat flyer distributed on May 22, 1979, the morning after the White Night Riot when crowds of gays angry over the light sentence given to Harvey Milk's assassin attacked City Hall and set a dozen police cars ablaze. Immediately, the SFPD retaliated and stormed down Castro Street beating gays in their path. The Libertarian Party created this flyer protesting Mayor Dianne "Feinstein's Gestapo."

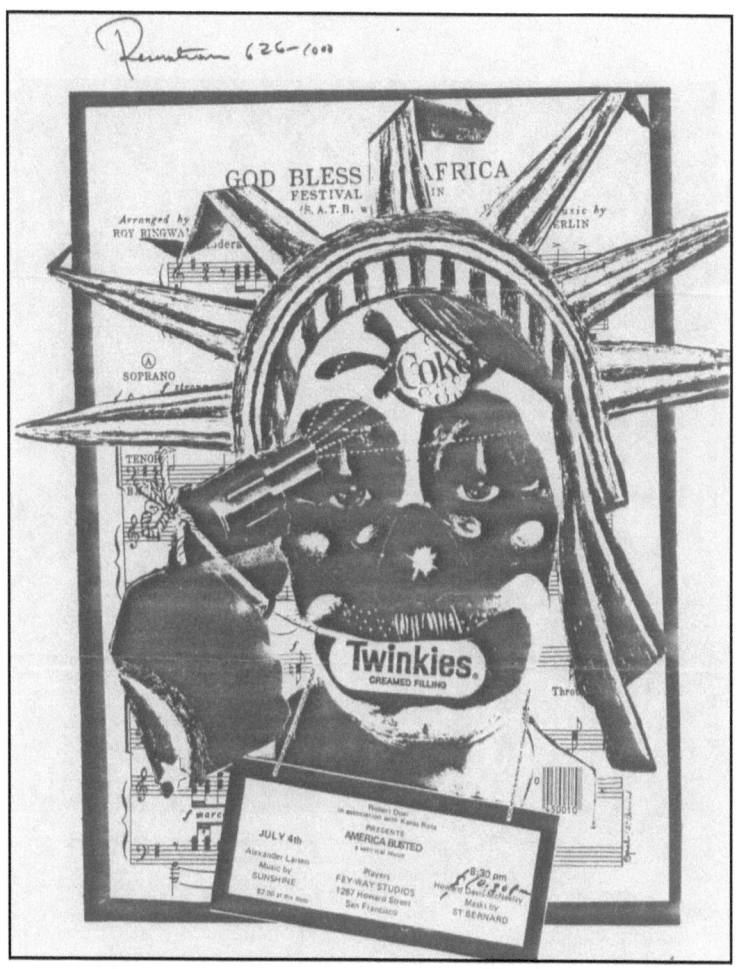

Poster. Robert Opel's samizdat advertising, *America Busted: A Satirical Revue*, was his response to the May 21, 1979, "Twinkie Defense" that let Dan White, the assassin of Mayor George Moscone and Supervisor Harvey Milk, off with a slap on the wrist. "Robert Opel in association with Katos Rota, presents *American Busted: A Satirical Revue*" with "players Alexander Larsen and Howard Davis-McNeeley; Music by Sunshine; Masks by St. Bernard. $2.00 at the door." In an earlier performance-art happening at San Francisco City Hall, Opel garbed himself as Gay Justice and with a prop gun "executed Dan White," the former fireman and cop; in his other satires, he had also appeared as "Uncle Sam" and as gay enemy Anita Bryant. *America Busted* played twice (8:30 and 10:30), one night only, July 4, 1979. Four nights later, on July 8, 1979, two men walked into Fey-Way Studios, forced Camille O'Grady to the floor, and shot Robert Opel to death. The turbulent week around July 4, 1979, and the murder of Opel at age 39, is dramatized in *Some Dance to Remember: A Memoir-Novel of San Francisco 1970-1982*, Reel 3, Sequence 9. Although someone was arrested and convicted, Fritscher's *Rashomon* inquiry poses: *Who Really Killed Robert Opel?*

In 1978, Robert Opel began promoting his own "Virtual *Drummer*" to be titled *National Pornographics*. A week after hiring Fritscher to write him a kickoff story, Opel arrived at Fritscher's home and sat at the kitchen table with Robert Mapplethorpe who laughed when Opel asked Fritscher to read the story aloud. When finally Fritscher agreed, performance artist Opel astonished both Mapplethorpe and Fritscher when he unzipped and stroked to the rhythms of the story. When the story and Opel ended, Opel wrote Fritscher a check as Mapplethorpe muttered, "I thought I had to work hard for the money." Opel retorted: "You should see my rejection slips."

Drummer 16: Tom Hinde Portfolio

"Olaf and the Hun," Invitation, 1979. Drawing by Olaf (1938-1997). Olaf and the Hun were two longtime contributors to *Drummer*. The two films, *The Hun Video Gallery: Rainy Night in Georgia*, and *The Hun Video Gallery: Chain Gang Gang Bang*, directed and photographed by Jack Fritscher and edited by Mark Hemry, were both Palm Drive Video feature releases (1992).

"Robert Opel Presents Rex," Invitation, 1979. Drawing by Rex. Drawing ©Rex. Used with permission. This announcement, the epitome of the zero degrees of separation in the *Drummer* salon, was also published as a quarter-page display ad in *Drummer* 30 (June 1979). Rex and his work were profiled in *Drummer* by Jack Fritscher in his special "New York Art" issue, *Son of Drummer* (September 1978). The bicoastal and reclusive Rex was the official artist of Wally Wallace's Mineshaft in New York. When a SoMa arsonist torched the Barracks bath on Folsom Street during the night of July 10, 1981, the neighboring studios of Rex and photographer Mark I. Chester were destroyed. The burning of the Barracks and the flaming disintegration of Rex's studio were fictionalized in *Some Dance to Remember: A Memoir-Novel of San Francisco 1970-1982*, Reel 4, Sequence 3. The film, *The Rex Video Gallery: Corrupt Beyond Innocence*, directed and photographed by Jack Fritscher and edited by Mark Hemry, was a Palm Drive Video feature release (1993).

Drummer 16: Tom Hinde Portfolio 341

"Domino and Rick Borg," Invitation, March 24, 1979. Drawing ©Estate of Don Merrick. Used with permission. Like Rex and the Hun, New York artist Domino (Don Merrick) functioned in the salon axis between Fey-Way Studios and *Drummer*. If Rex was a skid-row existentialist of "J. Alfred Prufrock" proportions, Domino was a romanticist of the same blue-collar sex in "one-night cheap hotels." *Drummer* art director Al Shapiro and editor in chief Jack Fritscher produced their interview "Drawings by Domino" in *Drummer* 29 (May 1979). *The Domino Video Gallery: Men Who Will Fuck You Up*, directed and photographed by Jack Fritscher and edited by Mark Hemry, was a Palm Drive Video feature release (1994).

"Haiku Headlines." As an eyewitness of San Francisco's nervous breakdown, Fritscher montaged some of the *San Francisco Chronicle* headlines that began with the Jonestown Massacre, November 18, 1978, escalated with the assassination of Moscone and Milk, November 27, 1978, and continued through the White Night Riot, May 21, 1979. During this exact same high-anxiety period, Fritscher was sole editor in chief of *Drummer* which was having its own nervous breakdown because its publisher John Embry withdrew temporarily with the onset of cancer, treatment, and cure. *Drummer* emerged with a new identity.

The "Gay Plea for Calm," May 22, 1979, was the fiery headline the romantic revolutionary evening that Jack Fritscher and Mark Hemry cruised and met for the first time under the marquee of the Castro Theater during the Castro street party celebrating the first post-assassination birthday of Harvey Milk that had morphed into a Peace Rally in the riot-torn City. Material for collage ©*San Francisco Chronicle*

Drummer 16: Tom Hinde Portfolio

Robert Opel's "Christmas Card, Fey-Way Studios, 1978." Sent to Jack Fritscher, this card, printed on one side only, was inscribed in Robert Opel's hand: "Love to you from Robert Opel."

As a post-mortem valedictory to the murdered Robert Opel in *Drummer* 32 (October 1979), Jack Fritscher published Opel's autobiographical religious poem, "The Men," written in praise of Sacred Eros in San Francisco. Opel concluded "Pray for us now and at the hour of our death" and ended with the promise of resurrection.

"Fey-Way Studios," storefront, 1287 Howard Street, the first gay gallery South of Market, founded by frequent *Drummer* writer and photographer, Robert Opel, who was murdered inside the premises on July 8, 1979. Photograph by Mark Hemry (2005). ©Mark Hemry

Captions: Eyewitness documentation of the existence of graphics providing internal evidence supporting Jack Fritscher's text are located in the Jack Fritscher and Mark Hemry GLBT History collection. Out of respect for issues of copyright, model releases, permissions, and privacy, some graphics are not available for publication at this time, but can be shown by appointment.

| Eyewitness Illustration | Two drawings by Tom Hinde, 1979. Jack Fritscher and Mark Hemry collection. |

| Eyewitness Illustration | "Camille O'Grady Proof Sheet," 1978. Photography by Fey-Way Productions (Robert Opel). |

| Eyewitness Illustration | Poster. "Camille O'Grady," Fey-Way Productions, 1978. |

| Eyewitness Illustration | Booklet cover. "Camille O'Grady, *Terminal Fascination: A Song Cycle*," cover for private printing of poetic O'Grady lyrics, 1978/1979. Photograph by Larry Hunt. |

| Eyewitness Illustration | Booklet covers. "Camille O'Grady, *Stigmata Hari Stories: The Continuing Visions of a Progressed Saint*," sent with a letter to Jack Fritscher, 1979. O'Grady wrote all her songs from a gay man's point of view. Drawing by Camille O'Grady. |

| Eyewitness Illustration | Invitation (featuring Mapplethorpe photograph of Cedric), reception for the artist, for the exhibition "Mapplethorpe Photographs," February 21, 1978, Simon Lowinsky Gallery, 228 Grant Avenue, San Francisco. |

Mapplethorpe, rising late, penned his handwritten note to Jack Fritscher after Fritscher had gone to work in the morning, and left it in the bed. "Jack—It was very hot—I hope to see you on Tuesday. Robert." The pair met during Halloween 1977 when a Mapplethorpe virtually unknown in the US flew from Manhattan to editor Fritscher's desk at *Drummer* to show his portfolio. They immediately clicked as bicoastal lovers. Fritscher assigned Mapplethorpe his first magazine cover: *Drummer* 24 (September 1978). The passion of the Mapplethorpe-Fritscher affair lasted from October 1977 to its amicable evaporation into friendship during spring 1980 after Fritscher had exited as editor of *Drummer*. It is chronicled in the erotic memoir *Mapplethorpe: Assault with a Deadly Camera* (1994). Fritscher published "Cedric" as the opening photograph of his feature essay, "The Robert Mapplethorpe Gallery," *Son of Drummer* (September 1978), page 14.

| Eyewitness Illustration | Album cover. Mapplethorpe's muse Patti Smith on the cover of her album *Horses* (1975). Photograph by Robert Mapplethorpe. |

Drummer 16: Tom Hinde Portfolio

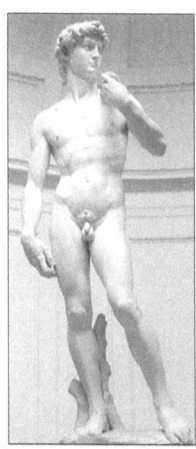

Eyewitness Illustration: Poster, "The Slot Hotel," Bill Tellman (1971). In the first-floor waiting room where no one ever waited because it was, after all, the Slot, there was a tiny table offering rolled-up Slot posters; over the years, thousands of men took this free advertising collectible home because it meant as much as a diploma.

Michelangelo hung out on Folsom Street.

SoMa artist Bill Tellman re-conceptualized the arms and one-legged posture of Michelangelo's *David* to draw his louche reverse spin for Jack Haines' Slot Hotel, displaying the new international signage of the signature "fisting tattoo."

Eyewitness Illustration: At the same time, artist Mike Caffee sculpted his slouching *Leather David* statue for Jack Haines' Fe-Be's bar, whose logo, designed by Caffee, was also spelled *Febes* and *Febe's*.

Eyewitness Caffee told Fritscher at the "Arnett Lautrec" Opening at the Gay and Lesbian Historical Society in San Francisco, January 28, 2008: "Sam Steward brought me a tourist-shop copy of Michelangelo's *David* in April 1966 to sculpt into a motorcycle cop. Three months later on July 10, Jack Haines brought me another copy which I made into the Fe-Be's statue. It took me two weeks to finish it in time for the bar's opening on July 26, 1966. I finished Sam Steward's statue early in 1967...I only recently discovered people were calling my statue *Leather David*. I have always called it the 'Fe-Be's statue.' I like *Leather David* better because it's a good description. Fe-Be's is long gone and mostly forgotten—only the statue lives on."

In 1972, Fritscher first wrote about Caffee's iconic *Leather David* and about leather occult rituals in the "Sex and Witchcraft" chapter of his book *Popular Witchcraft: Straight from the Witch's Mouth*; revised twenty-first-century edition, University of Wisconsin Press, 2005, page 152 and following.

Copyright images of the Slot poster and Fe-be's *Leather David* can be examined on the Internet.

Johnny Gets His Hair Cut

> Written and produced March-April 1977, this photo-feature paragraph was published in *Drummer* 16, June 1977.
> I. Author's Eyewitness Historical-Context Introduction written March 22, 2002
> II. The photo-feature paragraph as published in *Drummer* 16, June 1977
> III. Eyewitness Illustrations

I. Author's Eyewitness Historical-Context Introduction written March 22, 2002

Producing both this Jim Stewart photo-feature squib in *Drummer* 16 as well as the Jim Stewart photo feature in *Drummer* 14, I was connecting *Drummer*, after its arrival in San Francisco, with new local talent (such as photographer Jim Stewart) and into established local talent (such as author Sam Steward). Reducing the six degrees of separation among potential contributors was what publisher Embry had hired me to do to fill *Drummer*. Through naming me "founding San Francisco editor in chief," the newly arrived Embry meant that I was to be his San Francisco talent scout discovering a new group of contributors, ideas, and themes for *Drummer* orphaned in LA.

Jim Stewart and I had been friends since 1973. When he moved from Kalamazoo, Michigan, to San Francisco in October 1975, he lived with me and my lover David Sparrow at our home on 25th Street.

Out of the Folsom Street leather culture of the 1960s which focused on motorcycles and bars, in the early 1970s we began fashioning a kind of SoMa salon around art in which the motorcycle changed from transportation to icon, and our leather chaps and jackets morphed from safety clothes to fetish gear. In the early 1970s, beer was 15-cents, pot was $5 a lid, and a comfortable room for rent cost $20 per week. I was thirty, happy, and in love with David Sparrow who became my photography partner at *Drummer*. It was our leather *Boheme*. South of Market was glorious. Our new scene was the end of beatniks and hippies and the beginning of gay men. Peace, love, and granola gave way to sex, drugs, and rock-n-roll. By 1977, our decade-long sex-orgy fraternity of leather easily flowed into our *Drummer* salon.

In 1971, David Hurles was the first gay photographer to live South of Market; he managed a workingmen's set of flats on 10th Street at Mission Street across from the Doggie Diner. In May 1976, Jim Stewart introduced me to David Hurles aka Old Reliable Studio who was casting his photographs from the straight and bi-sexual hustlers working Polk Street and the Tenderloin from hangouts like the Zee Hotel at 141 Eddy—which was the hustler hotel of the Tenderloin—and from the Old Crow bar on Market Street, thirty feet from South of Market.

As editor in chief of *Drummer*, I had the opportunity to be the first to publish Hurles' photographs (*Drummer* 20, January 1978, pages 70-71). In early 1976, Jim Stewart moved South of Market and opened his homomasculine Keyhole Studio. In the fraternity of our intimacy, I produced his photographs for *Drummer* 14 (April 1977) and *Drummer* 16 (June 1977) because publisher Embry had already hired me in March 1977 as editor in chief of *Drummer* in charge of recruiting new talent. In that same *Drummer* 14, page 65, was a half-page display ad for Stewart's Keyhole Studio.

Jim Stewart was a fixture of our *Drummer* salon in March 1978 when *Drummer* writer and photographer Robert Opel, having moved north from LA, helped establish the South of Market identity of art and eros. Jim Stewart, who was also a carpenter, helped Robert Opel remodel a storefront at 1287 Howard Street into the first gay art gallery South of Market, Fey-Way. At the March 1978 opening, the underground of leather met the underground of art. Our *Drummer* salon came out in full force. It was like "old-home week" for all us friends. The baths and the bars had been the first gay art galleries, and suddenly we had, at this emerging stage of gay liberation, our own unqualified gay art gallery dedicated to leather, S&M, and transcendence.

A mega-hit from the moment Opel opened it, Fey-Way Gallery showcased Jim Stewart, Robert Mapplethorpe, Rex, the Hun, A. Jay, Lionel Biron, Lou Rudolph, Larry Hunt, Tom Hinde, Robert Opel, and Chuck Arnett, the first and founding artist of Folsom Street.

March 3, 1979, was the first and last anniversary of Fey-Way because Robert Opel was murdered in his gallery on July 8, 1979. To spare repetition of this eyewitness history of Opel, see *Mapplethorpe: Assault with a Deadly Camera* and *Some Dance to Remember: A Memoir-Novel of San Francisco 1970-1982*, Reel 3, Scene 1 and Scene 9. For details on Chuck Arnett, see my essay "Chuck Arnett" in *Drummer* 134 (October 1989) or in the anthology *Leatherfolk*, edited by Mark Thompson. For information on David Hurles, see *Man2Man Quarterly* #8 and any issue of the *California Action Guide* as well as the fictitious character, the video-porn mogul Solly Blue, in *Some Dance to Remember*.

Drummer 16: Johnny Gets His Hair Cut

The photographs for "Johnny Gets His Hair Cut" were shot during a real event at Jack Haines' Slot Hotel (979 Folsom Street) where cameras were usually not permitted. Permission was arranged with the Slot manager, my longtime friend, Tony Tavarossi. The 35mm camera and film belonged to Jim Stewart who shot all of the frames except for the few I shot of him during the scene. Jim Stewart told me on October 9, 2007:

> Dear Jack,
> The Slot Shoot—sometime in the spring of 1976—was I think April. The occasion? Sheldon Kovalski shaved both my head and John E.'s. It was planned in advance. I believe we let the management know what we were planning. The door was left open. Guys would come and go. Some stayed for the action. Major players, beside the three mentioned above: Jack Fritscher, and I remember that you called David Sparrow at home and he came over. Russell Van Leer is in the pictures too, as well as Steve Prokaski in the cap. I'll send you a few more pix to help set the scene. The room number is forgotten but it was the second room back from the stairway on the second floor. —Jim [See Jim Stewart quote in the introduction to "Men of SoMa" in this book.]

From 1975 when publisher Embry started *Drummer* to 1986 when he sold it, there was the constant low-grade friction of the "Credit War" and the "Reprint Controversy." Contributors were often miffed that their photographs were not properly credited, or that they were reprinted, or both. Subscribers complained about the frequent recycling of stories, photographs, and drawings. Jim Stewart was disconcerted when Embry republished some of his "Johnny" at-the-Slot photographs in one of the special magazine series Embry aka "Robert Payne" had written: *The Care and Training of the Male Slave II*. Stewart was not credited for the photographs, and Embry, reaching for Mapplethorpe's star, wrongly credited the Stewart photograph on page 26 to Mapplethorpe who by that time had refused to have anything to do with Embry's *Drummer*. Jim Stewart wrote on September 22, 2007:

> In *The Care and Training of the Male Slave II*, my photo at the top of page 26 was credited to Mapplethorpe. The other photo on that page, plus the photos on page 25, were not credited to anybody! The photo on the bottom of page 27 was correctly attributed to Mapplethorpe. All the photos of mine on pages 25-26 were previously published in "Johnny Get His Hair Cut,"

Drummer 16, pages 64-68. The whole photo spread in *Care and Training II*, except for a photo by Dave Sands, gives the impression that these were all Mapplethorpe photos."

II. The photo-feature paragraph as published in *Drummer* 16, June 1977

Johnny Gets His Hair Cut

We noticed an episode involving a hair cut (and shave) in San Francisco photographer Jim Stewart's "Men South of Market" series. We set these aside when we were running that series in *Drummer* 14 and asked Jim about it. He came up with three more shots to tell the complete story.

Jim lives in the South of Market area and does much of his photography in that neighborhood and at various locations ranging from Mount Tam to the Slot Hotel.

III. Eyewitness Illustrations

"The Slot Hotel" was the gay *Hotel California*. The Eagles sang "You can check in, but you can never leave" in the best-selling album of the 1970s. The Slot, which was cheekily covered by a hotel license rather than a bath license was created *ex nihilo* to be a fisting palace by CMC founder, Jack Haines, and was managed by longtime Fritscher pal and Folsom Street legend, Tony Tavarossi, who had created the Why Not? leather bar in 1960. When the gorgeous orgies and outrageous sex acts at the Barracks baths began to seem like bourgeois vaudeville, ever edgier erotic performances were always in constant invention at the Slot Hotel where Fritscher from his customary Room 326 (first door on the left at the top of the stairs) drove *Drummer*. The Barracks and the Slot were four blocks and light years apart on Folsom Street. Photograph by Mark Hemry. ©Mark Hemry

Drummer 16: Johnny Gets His Hair Cut

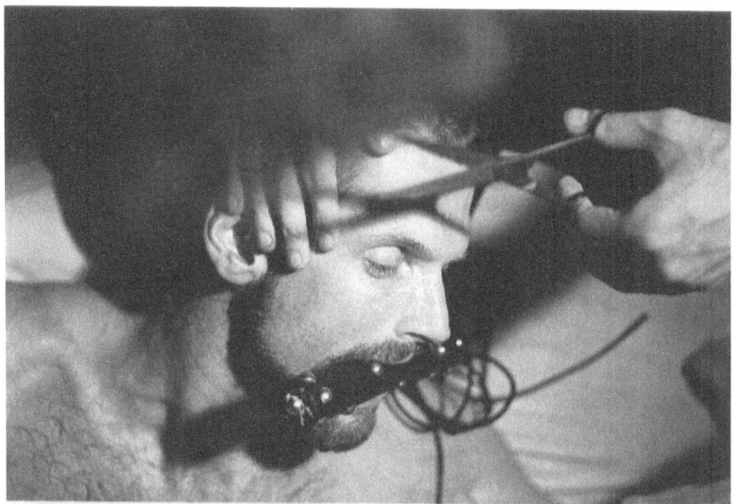

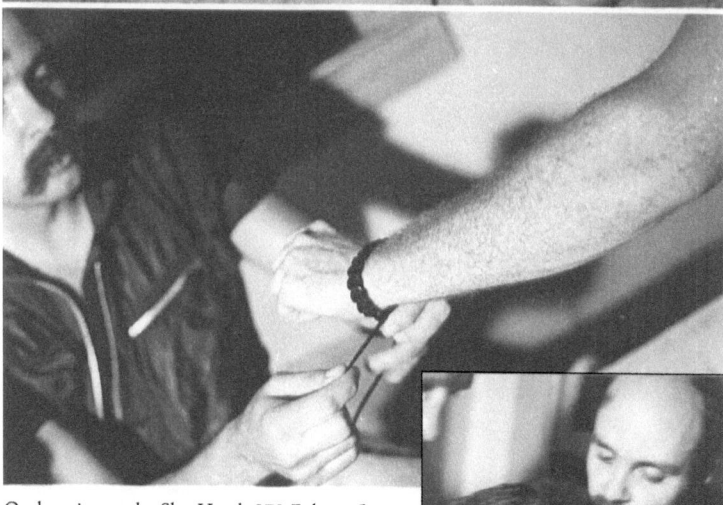

On location at the Slot Hotel, 979 Folsom Street, April 1976, photographer Jim Stewart and Jack Fritscher produced an erotic happening that became the *Drummer* feature "Johnny Gets His Hair Cut." Lensed with Stewart's Nikon which Stewart and Fritscher traded back and forth while participating in the *verite* action scene, the photographs were mostly shot by eyewitness Jim Stewart. Top: John E., "Johnny," gets his hair cut. Middle and right: Fritscher wraps the forearm of handballer Russell Van Leer, and then cradles a couple of "Johnny's" face to face. Keyhole Studio publicity shoot for *Drummer*. Photographs by Jim Stewart. ©Jim Stewart. Used with permission.

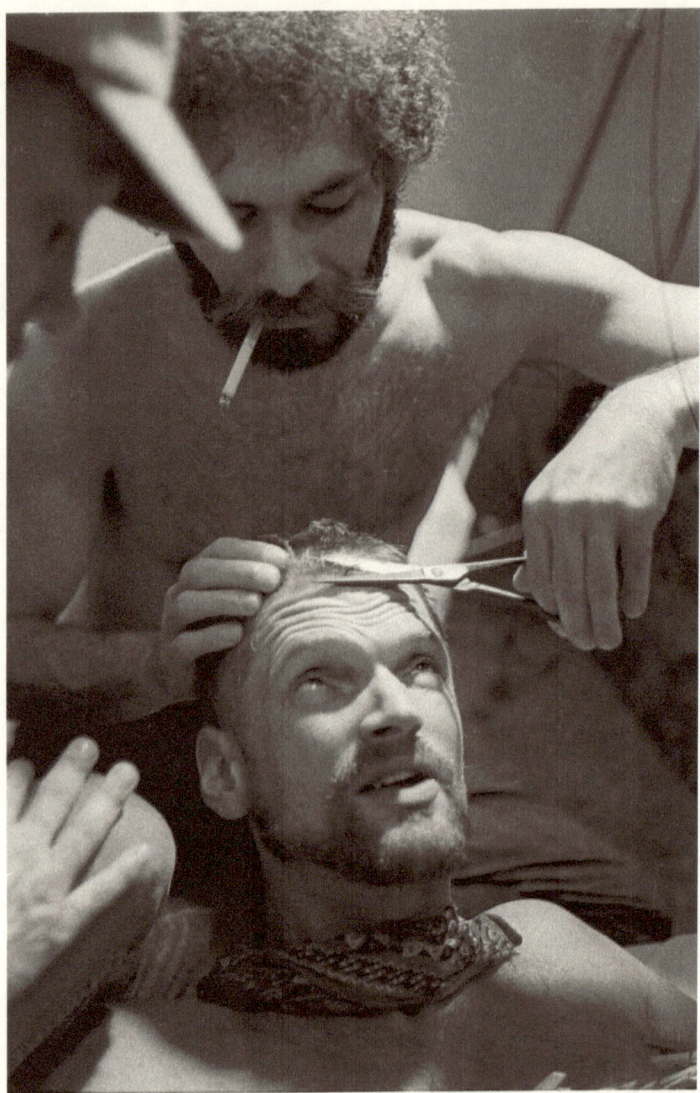

Before Stonewall, cameras were absolutely forbidden in gay venues because police and blackmailers exploited such eyewitness evidence. By 1976, cameras began to come out of the closet, thus breaking the kind of self-censorship that had made gay culture invisible. Fritscher wrote that "Mapplethorpe and Harvey Milk turned to cameras as power-tools of sexual liberation. Cameras gave us a face." Above: The Slot, April 1976. "Johnny Gets His Hair Cut." In a shot expressing how homomasculine men morphed their own self-fashioning identities during a disco era of Zapata and Zappa moustaches and permed hair and Afros, Sheldon Kovalski changes the received gay look of John E. Keyhole Studio publicity shoot for *Drummer*. Photograph by Jim Stewart. ©Jim Stewart. Used with permission.

Drummer 16: Johnny Gets His Hair Cut

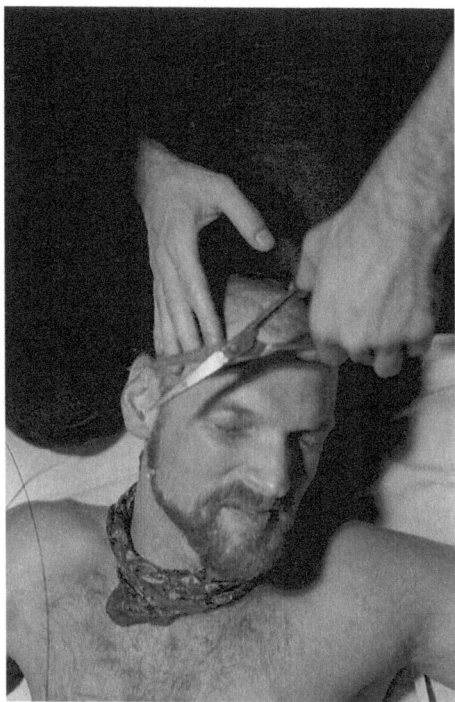

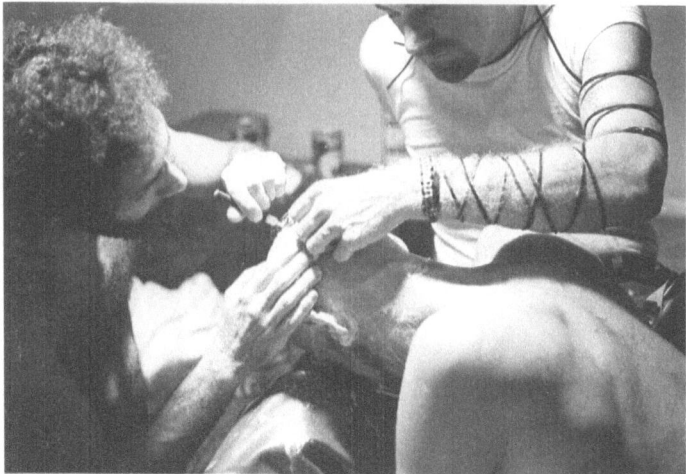

The Slot, April 1976. Top: "Scissors with Shadow." Catching the perfect moment and lighting, photographer Jim Stewart composed in action on location the same subjects and elements that intrigued Robert Mapplethorpe in the isolation of his studio. Bottom: "Hands." Sheldon Kovalski, John E., and redheaded Russell Van Leer. Keyhole Studio publicity shoot for *Drummer*. Photographs by Jim Stewart. ©Jim Stewart. Used with permission.

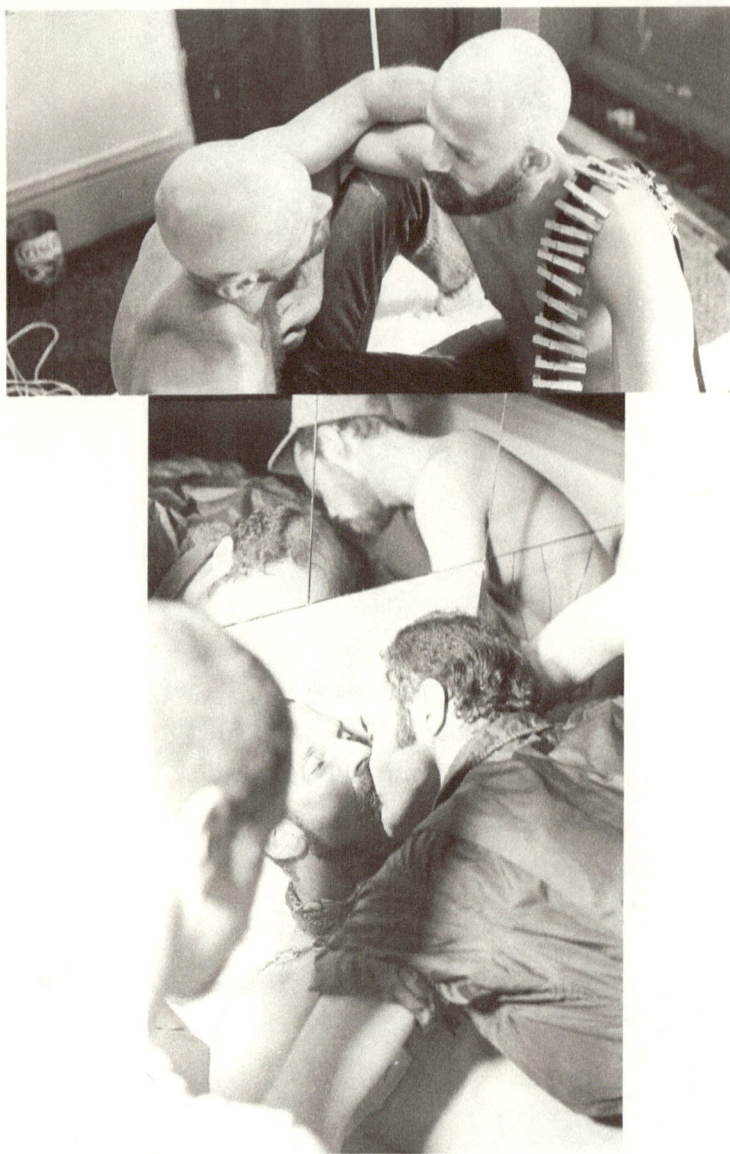

The Slot, April 1976. Top: "John E. and Photographer Jim Stewart with Crisco Can and Clothes-Pin Bandolier." Photograph by Jack Fritscher shot with Jim Stewart's camera. ©Jim Stewart. Bottom: "The Kiss." Doubling the information in his frame using mirrors, Jim Stewart documented Russell Van Leer (left) and Steve Prokaski (right) leaning in over John E. (bottom center) kissing Jack Fritscher. Keyhole Studio publicity shoot for *Drummer*. Photograph by Jim Stewart. ©Jim Stewart. Used with permission.

The Leatherneck:
The Ultimate Bar of the 70s
with Photos by Jim Stewart

> Written April, 15, 1977, this feature essay was published in *Drummer* 18, August 1977.
> I-A. Author's Eyewitness Historical-Context Introduction written October 2, 2001
> I-B. Author's Eyewitness Historical-Context Introduction, Part 2, written October 24, 2001
> II. The feature article as published in *Drummer* 18, August 1977
> III. Eyewitness Illustrations

I-A. Author's Eyewitness Historical-Context Introduction written October 2, 2001

Gay Bars Were the First Gay Art Galleries

As I was becoming the independently functional editor in chief with *Drummer* 19, this was my first actual byline in *Drummer*, written, coordinated, and produced for my friend and longtime roommate Allan Lowery who was opening his San Francisco dream venue, the new USMC-themed bar, the Leatherneck, June 1977. The article included documentary leather and S&M photographs by my other roommate Jim Stewart aka Keyhole Studio, featuring Leatherneck bartender Chris Meyrovich who became my Palm Drive Video model, Sweat MacCloud. Jim Stewart and I had been friends since the mid-1970s when I was teaching literature and film at Western Michigan University and he was the manager of the Campus Theater; together we coordinated several years of town-and-gown film festivals.

Allan Lowery owned a two-flat home on Castro Street at 15th where David Sparrow and I lived with him during parts of 1972, 1973, and 1974. (In the early 1970s at that address, we three hosted several then-famous leather S&M parties to a very pertinent A-list of leathermen.) Allan Lowery had asked if I had any interest in opening the Leatherneck together as a business, but I was coming off my sabbatical year as a tenured associate professor and was working as a writer at Kaiser Engineers in Oakland, and basically preferred my approach to gay business through writing and photography, although the glamorous lure of owning a piece of leather nightlife, and managing its hot bartenders (which was a lot like owning gladiators) was quite tempting.

We had a very sexy shoot staging these promotional Leatherneck photos in a very private performance before the bar's grand opening, because Allan Lowery designed his bar as a performance-art set, complete with props, so that customers could spontaneously act out S&M scenes. Chris Meyrovich appears in three photographs including one half-hoisted onto a cross (page 82). The sweet Allan Lowery is pictured profile, with beard, facing one of his famously beefcake bartenders over a beer bottle on the lower right of page 83.

In the grand and early tradition of having gay artists create murals for new bars, making them instant folk-art galleries, *Drummer* art director, A. Jay, made four huge mural panel-paintings for the Leatherneck. He continued the legacy of artists such as Tom of Finland painting the murals for Tom's Saloon in Hamburg, Etienne painting the murals for the Gold Coast bar in Chicago, Chuck Arnett painting the Lascaux murals for the Tool Box, and Skipper painting the four 4x8 panels for the Sanctuary bath in LA. One of the four panels painted for the Leatherneck by A. Jay aka Al Shapiro, is pictured in the photographs with this article.

Art in Bars: Of course, these core murals by key artists led bar owners and artists to hang other paintings, drawings, posters, and photographs displayed in revolving exhibits, often with special opening-night parties. In this way, before gay art galleries existed, huge crowds of men saw a vast amount of gay grass-roots art simply by going out to the bars.

Bars as Performance Space: The Leatherneck and the Ambush bar, both heavy S&M watering holes, were expansions on the 1960s and early 1970s ideas of bars as drinking establishments. The Ambush bar, with logo art work by Chuck Arnett (who had designed the Tool Box and the Red Star Saloon), was, besides being a bar, a practicing leather workshop where leather artists like Ambush owner David Delay created leather bondage gear and leather clothing which patrons, drinking a beer a few feet away, could watch him and his staff tool and dye. Among all the immortal bars of the 70s, the Ambush was, with its Folsom-defying location on Harrison Street, the lead pub in opening up the covenant of strict "leather" into the wider democracy of the homomasculinity of outdoorsmen and bears and mature men. When I took Robert Mapplethorpe to the Ambush in his full leather to meet poets Ron Johnson and Thom Gunn, he felt so out of place I had to drive him back to my home for a quick change into jeans and a flannel shirt.

Drummer 18: The Leatherneck

While the Leatherneck mixed the two intense genres of "leather" and "uniforms," the Ambush pitched its tent over a realistic crowd that embraced the fact that leaving one's twenties and thirties behind could be gladly celebrated.

The homomasculine Ambush was, in the "art form of a bar," precisely the demographic I was intending to address in *Drummer*.

Drummer publisher Tony DeBlase, much later, pointed out on page 5 in his *Drummer* 100 editorial, this delicate distinction—that I had stamped *Drummer* with masculinity first and leather second. "Issues 12 through 18," DeBlase wrote, "were edited by Robert Payne [publisher John Embry], then with *Drummer* 19, Jack Fritscher came upon the scene. Under Jack's direction, S&M per se became less prominent, and rough and raunchy male/male sexuality, often written by Jack himself, became the main theme."

I-B. Author's Eyewitness Historical-Context Introduction, Part 2, written October 24, 2001

Who Died and Left Vanilla Academics in Charge of S&M Culture?

Drummer, Leather Literature, and Magazines
Trashed by Gay Historians' Politics and Mistakes:
Claude Summers, Edmund Miller, and Robert Nashak in
The Gay and Lesbian Literary Heritage: A Reader's Companion to the Writers and Their Works, from Antiquity to the Present

This is as good a place as any to invoke "fair use" and to defend *Drummer* and my friends' and my own S&M literature.

History, especially the murky origin of gay history, should be as accurate as possible, and protected as an endangered species from the guns and poisons of revisionists. That is my goal in this collection about *Drummer* in which I take occasion to place a reader's *caveat* that, in 1997, editor Claude Summers published an encyclopedic book, *The Gay and Lesbian Literary Heritage: A Reader's Companion to the Writers and Their Works, from Antiquity to the Present*. At 786 pages, this ambitious book tries to codify gay and lesbian writers with a bit of their biographies and bibliographies incorporated with themes and genres, such as "American Literature: Colonial," "American Literature: Gay Male, 1900-1969," "Erotica and Pornography," "Sadomasochistic Literature," "Latino Literature," plus alphabetical entries of individual writers.

A work of this noble sweep, written by multiple authors, has much to recommend its lists of names and dates. However, my reading of the text causes me to take both historical and scholarly exception to its way-too-many mistakes and errors. Having written for encyclopedias myself—such as the "Mapplethorpe" entry in the prestigious British encyclopedia, *Censorship: A World Encyclopedia*, edited by Derek Jones for Fitzroy Dearborn, 2,950 pages (2002), and as the subject of an entry in the *Encyclopedia of Erotic Literature* edited by Gaetan Brulotte and John Phillips (2006), I am particularly sensitive to accuracy in this genre of books because what is published in them becomes, whether correct or not, set in stone as readers and researchers turn the pages unable to determine what is actually a fact, a mistake, or a political spin on the truth written by a particular author to pump his friends or stab his enemies. Sometimes pure insensitivity causes mistakes.

For instance, Claude Summers so disrespects *Drummer* that, although the magazine is mentioned many times in *The Gay and Lesbian Literary Heritage*, *Drummer* is not listed even once in the index. To me the index of any book gives instant evidence of its depth and integrity. For all the importance of *Drummer* in coaching and publishing beginning writers such as John Preston, Aaron Travis, John Rowberry, and championing many others, this 786-page book lacks a single page or paragraph explaining anything about *Drummer*. Actually, I was shocked by something personal in the book, which if the superficial take and misinformation is so factually wrong in the instance of the book mentioning my literary work and career history, then how off-key and wrong might it be in all its other pages.

Misinformation, and particularly the disinformation of gay politics, both appear on the page exactly like accurate information to the casual reader. I always taught my university classes in literary interpretation to be their own best critics, to trust no one telling them the "truth" about anything, and to look for the "vested interest" of the writer who is trying to maneuver facts and opinions in ways that may not be accurate or true. The ultimate goal of the intellectual life is the ability for one to become an analytical critic of all the misinformation, disinformation, and information printed and broadcast during the course of a lifetime.

It is curious that contributor Matthew Parfitt in his "War Literature" listings omits *Drummer* itself and all its war erotica, including my "Corporal in Charge." It is even more curious that in the section titled "Erotica and Pornography," contributor Edmund Miller, Professor of English and Chair of the English Department at the C. W. Post Campus of Long Island University, who himself is an author of erotic stories, poetry, and scholarly books about seventeenth-century British literature, writes with the rather air-kiss attitude that the East Coast gay literary crowd has regarding the depth and complexity of West Coast writing:

Drummer 18: The Leatherneck

Although he is also known for the experimental cinematic technique of his epic of San Francisco's Castro district, *Some Dance to Remember* (1990), Jack Fritscher (b. 1939) is known primarily as a writer [in *Drummer* which is not mentioned] of such short fiction as the stories of *Corporal in Charge of Taking Care of Captain O'Malley* (1984) [the first book collection ever of *Drummer* stories and articles, or, for that matter, the first book collection of erotic stories from any 1970s gay magazine] ....Fritscher began [*sic*] his career in pornography as editor of another true confessions magazine *Man 2 Man* [*sic*; besides his misnomer and mistiming of 1980s *Man2Man*, which was not a true-confessions magazine, Miller omits that my first erotic novel was *I Am Curious (Leather)* in 1968-69, and that I was editor in chief of *Drummer* beginning in March 1977, and was its most frequent contributor for twenty-two years]. (Pages 263 and 264).

On page 623, Robert Nashak, a doctoral candidate in English at UCLA, a recipient of a Mellon Fellowship in the Humanities and a Fulbright grant, writes in his essay "Sadomasochistic Literature":

Some of the best pornographic fiction to come out of the leatherman tradition is by Tim Barrus, whose *Mineshaft* (1984), like Leo Cardini's *Mineshaft Nights* (1990) before it, describes the sexual exploits of [*sic*; in] the infamous New York S/M palace of the same name. [My first writing about the Mineshaft appeared in *Drummer* 19, December 1977.] Phil Andros' *Different Strokes* (1986) and Jack Fritscher's *Leather Blues* (1984) and *Stand by Your Man* (1987) are three of the best erotic short story collections in this vein [even though *Leather Blues* is a novel, not a collection of short stories]. Larry Townsend is perhaps the most widely read writer of leatherman erotica. His landmark *The Leatherman's Handbook II* (1989) [*sic*] has received wide circulation and interest. [Townsend's landmark book was, in fact, published seventeen years earlier: *The Leatherman's Handbook* (1972); and, where — rather than the dismissive and vague Nashak toss-off "wide circulation and interest" — is the exact research mentioning the statistics regarding editions and copies sold of this seminal leather-heritage folk text written by Townsend from the "Tijuana Bible" questionnaires which grassroots leathermen sent to him?]

These disinformation quotes may be just the tip of the iceberg of inaccuracy in *The Gay and Lesbian Literary Heritage.*

Not to cavil, but to explain, some corrections need to be made on the sixty-seven words of Edmund Miller, and the ninety-five words of Robert Nashak. Their neglect of *Drummer* seems a shameless insult to the world of leatherfolk culture. In their rush to publish rather than perish, many queer academics live in an ivory tower twin to the tower of Babel; skimming material, some seem desperate to be promoted—not to be accurate.

I may be known for my signature novel of gay history, *Some Dance to Remember,* and for my short fiction collections, but, to amplify some of the shorthand inserts above, I did not begin my career in pornography as editor of a "true confessions magazine, *Man to Man* [sic]." I began my career with my novel, *I Am Curious (Leather),* written in 1968 and published in 1972. Over time, this novel entered the DNA of gay pop culture when excerpted in *Son of Drummer* (September 1978), then serialized with all of its chapters in *Man2Man Quarterly* 1980-1982, published fully again as a book titled *Leather Blues* by Winston Leyland's Gay Sunshine Press, 1984; and excerpted in *Stroke* magazine, volume 4, Number 4, 1985.

So how did the fact-checker for Summers, Miller, and Nashak miss it? In 1977, two years before I invented *Man2Man*, I entered high-profile gay publishing as the founding San Francisco editor-in-chief of *Drummer*. I developed *Man2Man Quarterly* in 1979 and ran it eight issues for two years, and its title was never *Man to Man*, as Edmund Miller mistakes it, and it was not a "true confessions" genre written by a lot of different and anonymous writers like Boyd MacDonald's *Straight to Hell*, because *Man2Man Quarterly* was all fiction and features that I myself wrote continuing the *Drummer* tradition from the 70s into the "Virtual *Drummer*" of the first 'zine of the 80s.

Also, Edmund Miller fails to note that my 1980s anthologies of short fiction are actually collections of my 1970s stories that first appeared in gay magazines, particularly in *Drummer,* where they were read every thirty days or so in each mass-market issue by thousands more readers than ever bought the books which have sold steadily through the years. Edmund Miller's failure to mention *Drummer* as the source of this pop culture magazine fiction is an intellectual mistake of the kind that is usually foisted by academic analysts who worship books but dismiss magazine culture.

A pop-culture fact that is worthy of note: *Drummer*'s press run in the 1970s, according to publisher John Embry, was 30,000 to 40,000 copies, which means that multiplied by the pass-along average to two other readers besides the original purchaser of the magazine, each *Drummer* issue was read by 60,000 to 80,000 gay men monthly multiplied by nearly twelve issues a year to an estimated one million readers then multiplied times twenty-four years. No gay book has ever enjoyed such statistics.

While I thank Robert Nashak for his assessment, because he is analyzing "Sadomasochistic Literature" as a genre, he might have deepened the information in his short sentences by mentioning that Tim Barrus was one of *Drummer*'s best editors in the 1980s during the time he wrote *Mineshaft*. Tim Barrus, always my friend, became my champion and hero, because after creating the "LeatherLit Writers Series" in San Francisco venues like A Different Light bookstore, when he left *Drummer* to work with LeatherLit publisher Elizabeth Gershman at Knights Press, he handed her my manuscript of *Some Dance to Remember*. Elizabeth Gershman wrote me an acceptance letter that said, "I'd fucking kill to publish your novel."

In the way that Matthew Parfitt in his essay "War Literature" omits all my erotic war stories including the very important Vietnam storyline of *Some Dance to Remember,* so Robert Nashak skips over the surface of sadomasochistic literature of "The Gay Renaissance of the 1970s" by misplacing the debut of another *Drummer* author, Phil Andros, with *Different Strokes* in 1986 (30 years late). By clock and calendar, my longtime friend Phil Andros aka Sam Steward, the grandfather of gay erotica, had famously been published internationally since the 1930s, and was revived in *Drummer* in 1975 and *Man2Man Quarterly* #2 (December 1980).

Robert Nashak also takes a wrong-genre belly flop when he lists my novel *Leather Blues* as a short story collection—which it is not. His nod to Larry Townsend is well taken except for Nashak's confusion: he writes, as previously noted, that "Larry Townsend's landmark book is *The Leatherman's Handbook II* (1989)" when actually Larry Townsend's landmark book was *The Leatherman's Handbook* published seventeen years before in 1972.

Timelines and facts are difficult when analysts skim the surface, but accuracy must be the job and goal of the historian and critic. That is why this *omnium-gatherum* book, *Gay San Francisco: Eyewitness Drummer*, exists with the original articles, boldly dated, with introductions that clarify the context and verify the back story of people, places, and events that surround these historical *Drummer* documents as a time-capsule eye into the history of our gay art and popular culture.

To some nasal-drip scholars, much of this magazine writing might be dismissed as light-weight because it was created as entertainment for a mass audience in gay popular culture. That purpose, design, and vernacular doesn't make it any less serious or any less literature. It makes it more interesting because it is reflexive of the audience.

II. The feature article as published in *Drummer* 18, August 1977

Allan Lowery's New Bar on 11th at Folsom...

The Leatherneck:
The Ultimate Bar of the 70s
with Photos by Jim Stewart

San Francisco's Leatherneck Bar ain't your ordinary meat-rack tavern. [Reference to Tim Buckley's then hugely popular album, *Welcome to L.A.*, which is a "texture and context" CD to listen to while reading this feature article in order to experience an audio-erotic and emotional evocation of that time.] Sure the 'Neck's a beer bar with wall-to-wall shitkickers, but upfront macho ain't no pose. Come night time, the right time, dudes head for the Leatherneck like an accident about to happen. Hot, man. Not a Lacoste alligator in the joint. A High Place.

About as high, in fact, as the elevated platform at the USMC Recruit Depot seems to 80 sock-footed jarheads sweating at attention, looking up as some 6-4, 245-pound DI's bootlace level.

GET THE PICTURE?

Hardass cruising. Like two-fisted combat at the USMC Depot where some little shaved-head boot is gonna be ordered for the first time in his life to take on another man with his bare hands. Palms and 'pits running sweat, man. Breathing hard. Crotch soaking his USMC jock.

Ain't that an OK fantasy walk into the Leatherneck!

Your eyes trip on the black leather. Your ears trip on the country-western wail. And your feet trip on the cleated boots standing toe to toe, crotch to crotch. Having a heatwave, man.

The Leatherneck's a "ball" room rotten to the Corps. Leather nights at 11th and Folsom are like the contact classes the USMC calls "Physical Instruction with Vigor." Outside, the big bikes and heavy pickup trucks are parked. *Waiting.* Inside, any little disciplinary problems with a dude and you can bet his buddies strap him down to the fastest bondage rack in town. Brig rats are a house specialty, stretched out in full leather, secured up on a cross six feet above the bar. That's how the Leatherneck does a social "security" number.

A NOTE TO PUSSYCATS

But don't worry if you're down there on your first visit. You're safe. *Heh. Heh.* The action is totally consenting. *S* and *M* at the Leatherneck means, above all, *Sensuality* and *Mutuality*. [This is the first time my keyword definition, which I first printed on one of my party invitations in 1974, is published in a commercial magazine.] The only thing that happens is what you want to happen.

MAN TO MAN

Shoulder to shoulder, dudes get bolder, hanging around the smoky back bars, shooting pinballs where guys with pinned balls score high. The front bar at the Leatherneck is long. The layout is laid-back into a maze of rooms with something for everyone. By midnight's wee bitching hour, pool balls are hitting hard in the side pockets. Guys in leather harnesses are eyeballing husky uniformed types whose handcuffs are gonna click-rasp down cold around the wrists of some very willing cowboy.

Drop your beer change on the floor and you go down to your knees to pick it up like a drowning man for the third time. A lifetime flashes by of piss-ripped denim, jockstraps, Crisco-ed leather, oiled chests rippling under pec-tailored vests, sweaty abdominals exposed through torn-off Leatherneck T-shirts, biceps banded with studs, cod-pieced "chaps" in chaps, thick belts, and boots of 1001 knights waiting for tongue-shine, and headed for the long porcelain trough in the back room.

When/if you come up for air/amyl, you know this ain't Alice's Restaurant. It's Allan Lowery's Basic Training Room. The Leatherneck has hot murals by A. Jay. It has oiled pecs and a yard of cock shared by four of the hottest barmen on the Coast. The Leatherneck ain't exactly fantasy. The Leatherneck trip is real.

Bar none, the Leatherneck is San Francisco's ultimate bar of the 70s.

The other night, at the christening of A. Jay's second of four murals, one of those green-fatigue type DI's was running a small conversation back in a dark corner on two muscled dudes of lesser leather rank.

"Choke 'im, fucker," the DI said to his recruit who was a bit too "gentle" with the man whose chest he was mauling on command. He rubbed the USMC tattoo on his forearm. (USMC tattoos get you discounts at the bar.) Like the Leatherneck itself, this leatherneck DI was the real thing. About thirty. Himself recent Marine meat. He still liked drilling. Especially after sundown. "Back at my playroom, I'll show you two what you do after you pin your man down."

A small part of the Leatherneck crowd circled tight in on this close encounter—to watch.

"First, you dropkick the fucker."

"Sir, yessir," the blond recruit whispered back.

"That's the real way. 'Course the way we're gonna play it," and the large man in the USMC fatigues put his sweat-ringed arms around his two boys, "is gonna be a little bit different." And he walked them out the Leatherneck door, past Bill [my San Francisco deputy sheriff pal, Bill Essex], the heavy-chested bouncer, who smiled after this good threeway match made in the heaven of the Leatherneck.

ANYPLACE IS WHAT YOU MAKE IT

So at the Leatherneck, you can love 'em tender, and you can love 'em nice and easy. But if [like Tina Turner] you "never do nothin' nice and easy," the Leatherneck's for sure your happy hunting ground. Because it ain't no statue bar, man. S&M don't mean *Stand* and *Model*. The Leatherneck means action.

At the Leatherneck, men celebrate being men.

Ain't nowhere else quite like Lowery's Leatherneck. It ain't a bad little nightspot for about 500 guys in a little 7-mile-by-7-mile fishing village called San Francisco.

For a celebration of male-hide and for close encounters of the leather kind, try it. Week nights 8-2. Weekends 2-2.

Man alive!

III. Eyewitness Illustrations

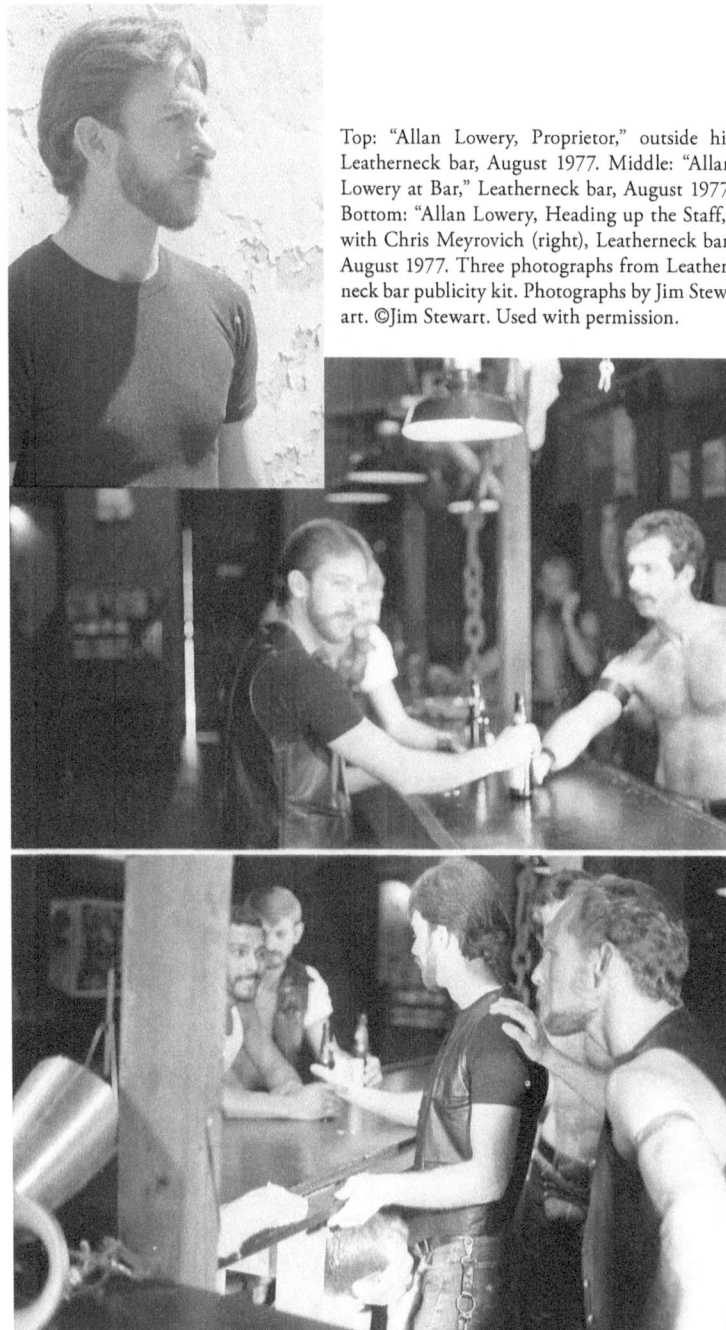

Top: "Allan Lowery, Proprietor," outside his Leatherneck bar, August 1977. Middle: "Allan Lowery at Bar," Leatherneck bar, August 1977. Bottom: "Allan Lowery, Heading up the Staff," with Chris Meyrovich (right), Leatherneck bar, August 1977. Three photographs from Leatherneck bar publicity kit. Photographs by Jim Stewart. ©Jim Stewart. Used with permission.

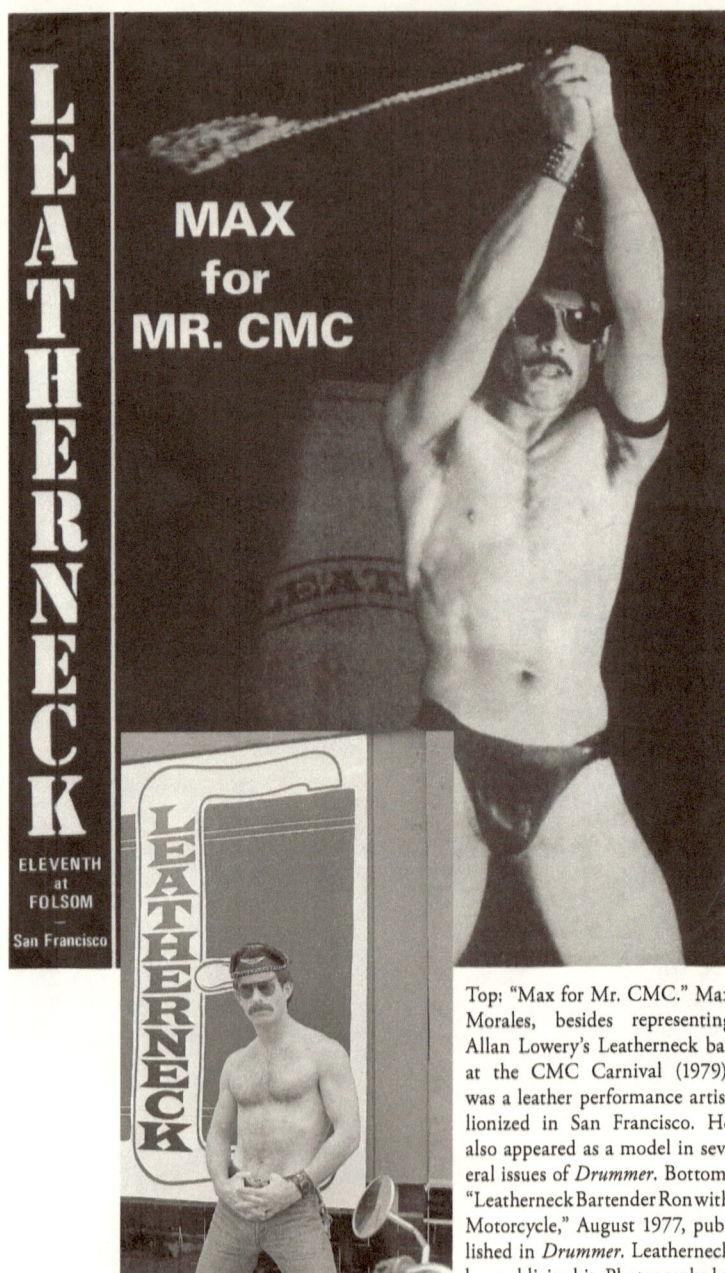

Top: "Max for Mr. CMC." Max Morales, besides representing Allan Lowery's Leatherneck bar at the CMC Carnival (1979), was a leather performance artist lionized in San Francisco. He also appeared as a model in several issues of *Drummer*. Bottom: "Leatherneck Bartender Ron with Motorcycle," August 1977, published in *Drummer*. Leatherneck bar publicity kit. Photographs by Jim Stewart. ©Jim Stewart. Used with permission

Drummer 18: The Leatherneck

Top: "A. Jay's Mural Installation," interior wall of the Leatherneck bar displaying the comic-erotic murals of A. Jay, Al Shapiro, art director of *Drummer*, August 1977. Eyewitness photographer and insider carpenter Stewart built the physical interiors of Fey-Way Studios, the Leatherneck, and other Folsom Street venues, and worked for years for *Drummer* publisher John Embry. Bottom: "Allan Lowery and Ron Opening the Leatherneck for the Evening," August 1977. Leatherneck bar publicity kit. Photographs by Jim Stewart. ©Jim Stewart. Used with permission.

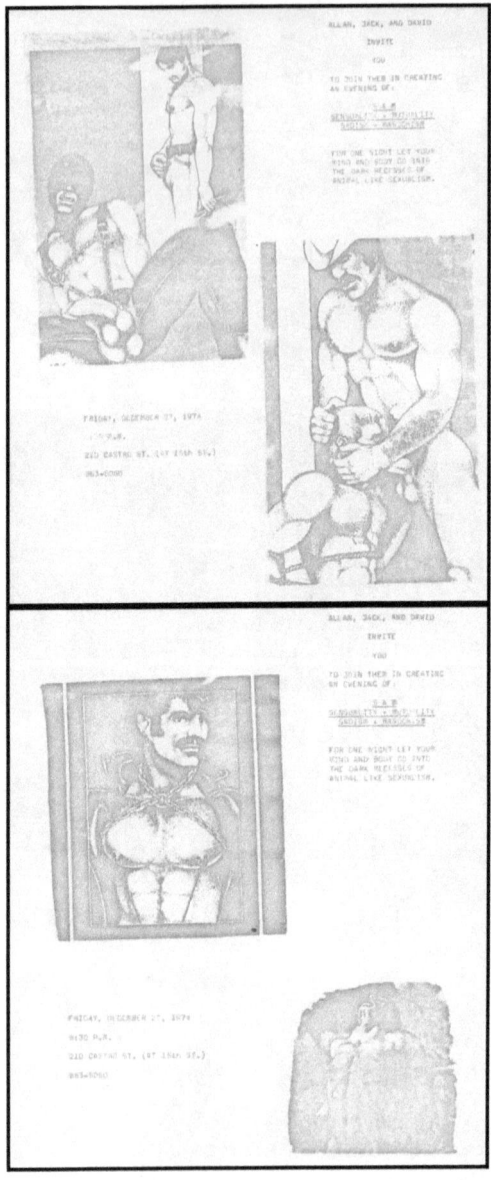

Two invitations to an S&M Party hosted by [roommates] Allan [Lowery], Jack [Fritscher], and David [Sparrow] who "invite you to join them in creating an evening of S&M, Sensuality + Mutuality, Sadism + Masochism," 210 Castro Street at 15th Street, Friday, December 27, 1974. Both flyers handmade by Jack Fritscher on non-electric portable Smith-Corona typewriter and early photocopy machine. ©Jack Fritscher. This is the earliest documented use in print of Fritscher's equation of *S&M* with *Sensuality* and *Mutuality*.

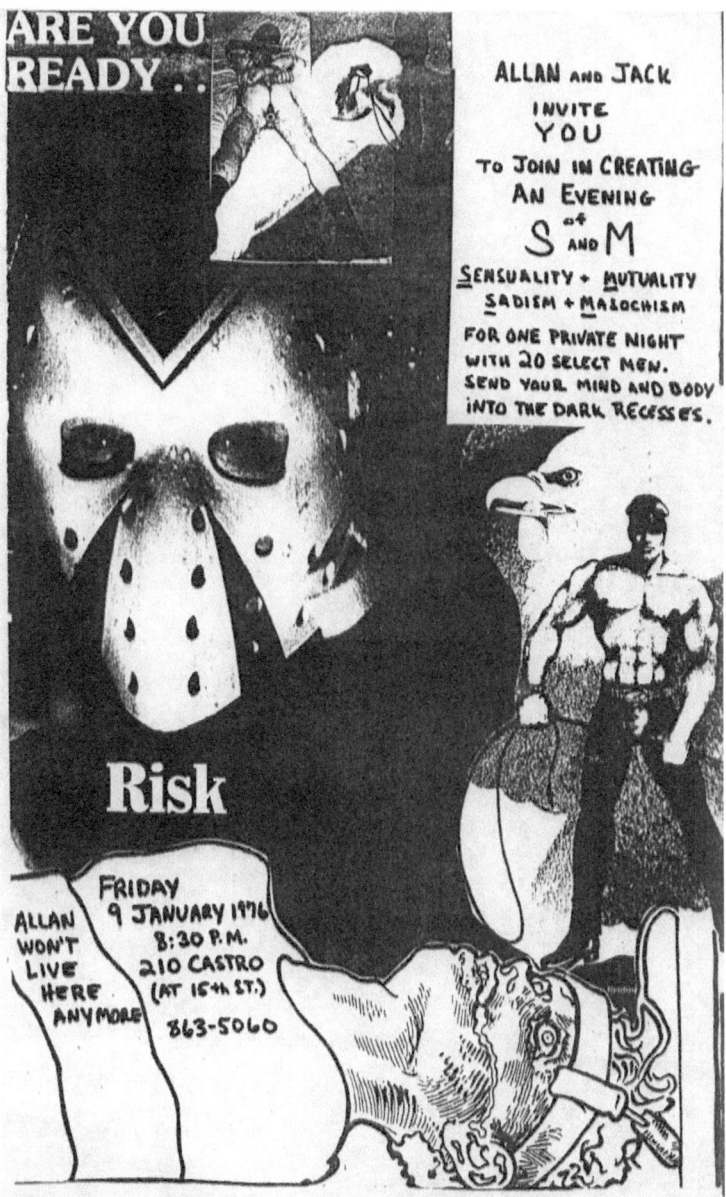

Invitation to party hosted by Allan [Lowery at his home] and Jack [Fritscher], extended to "20 select men," 210 Castro Street, Friday, January 9, 1976, marking the imminent move of Allan Lowery from his longtime address. Invitation created by Jack Fritscher. ©Jack Fritscher.

Christopher Meyrovich (1950-1992), star bartender at the Leatherneck (*Drummer* 18), also starred as the title character in the video *Sweat MacCloud*.

Top: "Chris Meyrovich with Cup and Billy Club," 1987, from *Sweat MacCloud* (1987), directed and shot by Fritscher for Palm Drive Video. Photograph by Jack Fritscher. ©Jack Fritscher. Bottom: "Chris Meyrovich Shirtless," August 1977, backgrounded by Leatherneck sound system playing tape mixes by *Drummer* salonistas Max Morales and Thom Morrison. Leatherneck bar publicity kit. Photograph by Jim Stewart. ©Jim Stewart. Used with permission.

Drummer 18: The Leatherneck

Captions: Eyewitness documentation of the existence of graphics providing internal evidence supporting Jack Fritscher's text are located in the Jack Fritscher and Mark Hemry GLBT History collection. Out of respect for issues of copyright, model releases, permissions, and privacy, some graphics are not available for publication at this time, but can be shown by appointment.

| Eyewitness Illustration | Photograph. "Allan Lowery," manager, Americania Hotel, South of Market, 1972. Photograph by Jack Fritscher. ©Jack Fritscher. |

| Eyewitness Illustration | Photograph. "Jack Fritscher with X, the lover of Herth Realty agent Terry Poe, and with Allan Lowery," 210 Castro Street, Fritscher's birthday, June 20, 1975, the same day as the publication of the first issue of *Drummer*. |

In 1977, Allan Lowery became the founding owner of the Folsom Street bar, the Leatherneck. Photograph by David Sparrow. ©Jack Fritscher

Leather Christmas 1977

> Written Christmas 1973, this feature essay was published in *Drummer* 19, December 1977.
> I. Author's Eyewitness Historical-Context Introduction written March 11, 2002
> II. The feature essay as published in *Drummer* 19, December 1977
> III. Eyewitness Illustrations

I. Author's Eyewitness Historical-Context Introduction written March 11, 2002

In this nonfiction article, "Leather Christmas," for the benefit of historians who tally up lists, I introduced several "firsts": the first use in *Drummer* of the high-concept homomasculine phrase "man to man"; the first use of my portmanteau word: *perversatile*; the first mention of women in S&M scenes; the first gonzo report on sex written in, and reported "live" from, a gay bath, specifically, the spectacular Folsom Street Barracks at 1147 Folsom with entrance on Hallam Street; the first of my many sexual-identity word plays on Descartes' "Cogito; Ergo Sum"; as well as first use of two of my early 1970s theoretical concepts of leather S&M defined as "Sensuality" and "Mutuality," and of leather S&M as "a second coming out." *Drummer* contributor, psychologist Guy Baldwin, later picked up on my "second coming out" and theorized further about my concept; for this I thank him because not all leatherfolk bother to credit the source of their information. In this article, I also began introduction of the popular culture of movies into reportage and analysis of queer sex, including the primitivism of the Sun Dance ritual and BDSM. As glossary, the terms "'lude" and "714" refer to the drug, Quaalude.

"Leather Christmas" with its irony, neologisms, and flaming Levi's is the first gay postmodern leather-sex article. Or perhaps it's a Duchamp parody. (What is more Cubist than a hand descending a cock—jerk-jerk-jerking off while reading?) Or perhaps it's a note found in a bottle, a journal entry of gay sex as it once was.

Oral History Transcription: When I was thirty-four, I wrote this true and erotic autobiographical feature article in 1973, two years before the advent of *Drummer* (June 1975), after spending many holiday nights at the Folsom Street Barracks, 1147 Folsom with entrance on Hallam Street, and at the Folsom Prison bar, on Folsom at 14th Street, which in the 1977 feature I updated to the Brig bar, 1347 Folsom Street.

The Folsom Prison bar opened 1973 and closed January 2, 1977 as the Brig opened. The closing was noted with a photo in *Drummer* 12, page 69:

> FOLSOM PRISON, at the beginning [the west end] of the Folsom Strip in San Francisco has been torn down..... Closing night festivities included the ripping down of the famous prison bars over the big horseshoe-shaped bar, and dismantling the beloved fireplace, brick by brick. A lot of people went home the night of January 2 with a lot of Folsom Prison souvenirs.

Drummer 19 (December 1977) was the first issue of *Drummer* to list "Jack Fritscher" signed in as editor in chief, even though I had also ghost-edited, uncredited, *Drummer* 14-18.

For a brief fulcrum of time in 1979, I had edited half the *Drummer* issues in existence.

I was editor in chief through *Drummer* 33, although publisher John Embry stripped my name from the masthead of issues 31, 32, and 33 while they were in production and at the printers.

Embry did this because in the time leading up to the day *Drummer* 30 was published, my lover David Sparrow and I dared request all the back salary owed me for my writing, and owed us (aka Fritscher-Sparrow) for our photographs. I was owed $4,000 and David around $2,000—which in 1979 was a lot for our two-person domestic household to absorb.

John Embry also switched out some of my writing after *Drummer* 30, but published some pieces without my byline.

He kept my photos going through *Drummer* 33 which was the last issue Fritscher and Sparrow, under the name of "David Sparrow" and "Sparrow Photography" contributed to *Drummer*—until Anthony DeBlase purchased *Drummer* and hired me back for *Drummer* 100.

David Sparrow never returned to the pages of *Drummer*; nor did others of my *Drummer* "salon" including my bicoastal lover, Robert Mapplethorpe.

However, in the rosy beginning, I arrived as editor in chief at *Drummer* with portfolios full of my writing including my S&M novel written in 1968 and first published in 1972 as *I Am Curious (Leather)* by Lou

Drummer 19: Leather Christmas   375

Thomas of Colt Studio and Target Studio in New York. Within this *Eyewitness Drummer* project, confer Lou Thomas' September 20, 1968, letter to me in my thumbnail introduction to *I Am Curious (Leather)* in *Son of Drummer*. I chose that *Curious* title as homage to the first truly ground-breaking and hugely popular commercial porno film *I Am Curious (Yellow)* shot in Sweden in 1967.

With the fading of the ubiquitous catch phrase "I Am Curious (fill in the blank)," I re-titled my leather identity novel into the list of Allen Ginsberg "blues" journalism I was creating for *Drummer*, and its title became *Leather Blues* to fit with my articles, "Prison Blues," "Rodeo Blues," "Jockstrap Blues," "Castro Street Blues," and on into fiction like "Wild Blue Yonder" which was published in several magazines and anthologies, including *The Burning Pen: Sex Writers on Sex Writing* (2001), a collective autobiography of authors compiled by M. Christian. *The Burning Pen* is as important to erotic literature as Mark Thompson's *Leatherfolk* (1991) is to leather culture.

In March 1977, when publisher Embry arrived at my San Francisco home on 25th Street home to interview me for the editor-in-chief job, I showed him, and Al Shapiro who was with him, the list of stories and articles I had already written which could be adapted to *Drummer*. (At the time we met, I was already deeply embedded in writing with a publishing career begun twenty years earlier as a magazine editor with several published books.) Embry's eyes lit up at my stack of stories and photographs — as well as my personal "sex" Rolodex of writers, artists, and photographers.

Always starving for material to fill a hungry monthly magazine, Embry saw me as a way to fill pages. Even so, I must clarify, he hired me as editor in chief only. My $200 per month was pay to edit the magazine; after a year or so, he promised me $400 per month for editing.

That's why I never gave up my day job while editing *Drummer*.

My writing for *Drummer* was totally independent of my editing and was sold freelance with one-time publication rights to Embry's Alternate Publishing. Embry propped up the lack of cash salary by promising that, as part of my hire, *I Am Curious (Leather)* would be serialized in *Drummer*, and then *I Am Curious (Leather)* would be published as one of the first of a new line of *Drummer* novels. From that, he said, I could earn royalties. This plan is mentioned at the end of the first serialized section of *I Am Curious (Leather)* in *Son of Drummer* (September 1978), page 47, where the excerpt — soon after renamed *Leather Blues* — was published with the original 1968 title, plus a subtitle for the opening chapter: "I Am Curious (Leather): The Adventures of Denny Sargent."

The irony was that soon after I started editing and filling the pages of *Drummer*, John Embry, who liked the "upside" of publishing my writing and photos, began disliking what he saw as a "downside" in crediting so much of my work: "It looks like you're writing the whole damn issue."

This was not, for me, an arm-wrestle over ego as much as it was an issue of law—specifically of the new 1977 copyright law and how it protected my intellectual property in *Drummer*. Always a notorious scofflaw (I thought), Embry balked at having both my byline and my copyright notice which the new law stipulated had to appear at the end of my articles in order to protect my copyright. I didn't want to surrender the one, and I couldn't surrender the other. He did not understand, or did not care, about the specifics of this change in the law requiring specific copyright notice to be published. Irritated by my insistence on following this inconvenient law, Embry, himself the seeming king of Byzantine intrigue, became suspicious that by doing the very thing I'd been hired for—fill each *Drummer* issue—I was hijacking his baby. After Jeanne Barney in Los Angeles had been the first editor in chief of *Drummer* and had fallen out with Embry, *Drummer* fled to San Francisco and Embry—made so initially suspicious of self-starting editors—had to deal with me who was no babe in the woods. Not counting the pro-tem editor "Robert Payne" aka Embry himself, I was the first male editor of *Drummer*, and a San Franciscan to boot. Embry who was very LA had a lot to learn in San Francisco where most of his business troubles around *Drummer* occurred because he acted, San Franciscans thought, "too LA."

It should be noted that when the names "John Embry" or his pseudonym "Robert Payne" appear listed on the *Drummer* masthead as "editor in chief," it means Embry was actually between editors and was himself stuffing the mag with all manner of writing that seemed—at least as some of us then gossiped— "stolen" from straight men's magazines (e.g.: *Saga* and *Argosy*). His *faux* editorial layouts were all too often masked advertisements for his mail-order sex toys. In my theory, Embry's 1970s concept of *Drummer* was that the magazine was little more than sheet-sugar to fold around his all-important mail-order brochure. In all my years of working with him, I was never of the opinion that he ever really much cared about the editorial content of *Drummer*. From start to finish, Embry was the tinker king of mail order. He has written that he never expected *Drummer* to take off and be anything much.

John Embry was not prepared for the *Being* and *Becoming* of *Drummer*.

How clueless was Embry about the essence of *Drummer*? In *Drummer* 1, Embry, acting as "Robert Payne," offered for sale through his Alternate mail-order "Leather Emporium" a set of bed sheets made from

Drummer 19: Leather Christmas

Naugahyde (!) which remains anathema, taboo, and camp joke to genuine leather fetishists. Among 1970s bar buddies, one line of code tossed off to dismiss a leather wannabe who was too new or too plastic to "dig the scene" was: "Lips that touch Naugahyde will never touch mine." (See *Naugahyde* as insult: *Drummer* 1, page 9.)

In 2003, Embry, the first publisher of *Drummer*, told Robert Davolt, who in late 1997 became the last editor and nominal publisher of *Drummer*, that he, Embry, "never foresaw the impact that *Drummer* would have. 'It was a big surprise to me....I'm amazed.'"

Embry's 1975 purpose for *Drummer* was to sell popper-like inhalants, cock rings, and butt plugs. He was, at age fifty-something, almost a generation older than the Youth Culture of the 1960s and 1970s. He seemed unmotivated to deal with the vision or the meaning or the content of the psychedelic convergence of drugs-sex-leather-and-gender that happened when *Drummer* met San Francisco. Sensing his disconnection, we drove *Drummer* as a vehicle of the newly liberated Titanic 70s.

In other places, I have mentioned that in the 1970s everyone spent so much time and energy having sex that not many guys wanted to take time out to contribute to a gay magazine which was then such a new phenomenon no one took the genre seriously. To build a network of reliable contributors took me a year, and during that year the only way I could keep up with our thirty-day production schedule was to work late into the night. Many a time I gave up going to the tubs or to the gay parade because I was churning out primary writing for *Drummer*. I wanted other authors on board; and I took time to develop them in various tutorials including my "Writer's Aid" program. Even so, I had always been, in my twenty years of freelance publication before *Drummer*, and have always remained, during and since, very strict about maintaining ownership of my intellectual property in writing, photographs, and videos.

That proprietary attitude was reinforced by the advice of my longtime pal, veteran gay writer Sam Steward. It was seconded by my eyewitness experience of seeing the work of Tom of Finland pirated left and right. Both Sam and Tom—when I met them—ranted and raved how their work had been famously and often ripped off. Durk Dehner gallantly rode to rescue Tom of Finland and his copyrighted work by founding the Tom of Finland Foundation. In the 1970s, I set out to champion a "New Generation of Gay Writers" resolved not to be exploited in terms of copyright and royalties as had authors like the young Larry Townsend. In 1968, I had not let Greenleaf Press rip me off for $300 for all rights to *I Am Curious (Leather)*; and in 1978, I wasn't about to let Embry rob me either. The 1972 limited edition printed by Lou Thomas nailed down my copyright just fine while I waited for gay book publishing to invent itself as a business. I had to be patient until 1984 when former Catholic priest Winston Leyland published the novel as *Leather Blues* at his Gay Sunshine Press, San Francisco; that 1984 edition sold 10,000 copies which made it a huge best-seller in the gay press where the standard press-run is 3,000 to 5,000 copies printed.

The following tale of one poetic little boy's "rise and calling" represents how a generation of boys grew up to converge as men in the leather culture that needed *Drummer*.

Was I prepared by my pop-culture and human nature to ride into *Drummer* in 1977? I'd been a leather cultist in Chicago even before I arrived for the first time in San Francisco in August, 1961. Recently I came across a bit of writing, some juvenilia—a poem—that I wrote in the 1950s when I was eighteen years old, May 14, 1957. I was well aware of the poetry scene in San Francisco and was in awe of Ferlinghetti, Corso, Spicer, and Ginsberg. That little beatnik poem, "Cry! The Young Hunters," written in those early years in my closet, when I was beginning to learn the extent to which homosexuality and leather existed, positively drips with my teenage desire for edgy, muscular, gay sex. The poem was one of two published in the teen poetry anthology, *America Sings 1958*, edited by Dennis Hartman for the National Poetry Association, 3210 Selby Avenue, Westside Village, Los Angeles 34, California. Was that then where WeHo is now?

I confess my poem's imagery was influenced by black-and-white beatnik and rock-n-roll movies. At that time, I played bongo drums, grew my first chin-strap beard, and was a great fan of *The Wild One*, *Blackboard Jungle*, and *Rebel without a Cause*. In fact, I was perhaps the first mid-century teen author to write a serious published article about the legend of James Dean whose death to me, when I was sixteen, was like the end of the my teenage world. My 1,500-word feature—which was my first pop-culture article—was titled "James Dean: Magnificent Failure" and was published in *The Catholic Preview of Entertainment: The Family Entertainment Guide*, June 1962.

The 1950s did not end until the world changed on November 22, 1963. So when I analyze my "1950s" James Dean piece now I am amazed at how intuitively queer I was as a teenager at writing code to mask the homosexual longing that simmers under the text. I was at the time a closeted "altar boy" who thought I could save the "bad boys" who attracted me. At least, that was my plan. It was the usual queer transposition of all the then-new teen movies and songs in which a good girl falls for the wild heart-throb of a bad boy. I bought tons of 45rpm records themed like Jerry Leiber and Mike Stoller's 1955 hit "He Wore Black Denim Trousers (and Motorcycle Boots and a Black Leather Jacket with an Eagle on the

Back)." By the time Kenneth Anger released *Scorpio Rising* (1963), I was so overheated I nearly fainted when in 1966, with a crowd from the Gold Coast bar, I saw his film mixing Jesus and leathersex!

My teen-poetry may be raw, overwrought, and embarrassing, but it is real. The writing and psychology show how my peer-group leather pioneer personalities—John Embry, Larry Townsend, and Fred Halsted, and all the rest: Terry LeGrand, Roger Earl, and others—came from adolescence in the repressed 1950s to working on *Drummer* in the 1970s.

The poem, "Cry! The Young Hunters," is reprinted below, after this "Leather Christmas" feature, as a peephole into us "leather boy" teenagers who grew up to invent *Drummer* and to read *Drummer* after spending our boyhoods anticipating the precise world of leather that would emerge from our psyches in *Drummer*.

Drummer was not created from nothing. *Drummer* was created from individual personalities who spoke for themselves and mirrored the times. We *Drummer* creators, born in the Art Deco 1930s, were children during World War II, teenagers during the repressed 1950s, and college age during the Swinging 60s when JFK's assassination changed everything and all we head-feeding hippies dropped acid with Timothy Leary, Ken Kesey, Allen Ginsberg, and Thom Gunn at the "Human Be-In" in Golden Gate Park, January 14, 1967, the winter before the Summer of Love.

Before I actually came out with another person, I had come out solo-handed with several 1950s magazines including my favorite, *Tomorrow's Man*; in the 1960s, I was seduced by *Rawhide Male*, and the one that eventually influenced me in *Drummer* the most, *Leather!* That was a small-format 'zine featuring a short text with photographs compiled under the direction of Avery Willard, Guild Press LTD, Washington, DC, 1965, 72 pages. *Leather!* was an archetypal collection of photographs from the 1950s and 1960s from six studios: Chuck Renslow's Kris Studio of Chicago, Avery Willard of New York, Bob Anthony of New York, Scott of London, David of Cleveland, and R. A. Enterprises.

Another studio that in the 1960s formed my taste—that led to me homomasculinizing *Drummer* into being about male identity as much as leather—was the inimitable Royale Photography, 110 Denbeigh Street, Victoria, London, England, with glorious photographs of muscular young military men disciplining one another in a fetish display of military kit with no frontal nudity.

The Guild Press' *Leather!* photographs featured leather, whips, chains, rope, and motorcycles, again, with no frontal nudity—yet how they steamed in 1965! The Willard model, Gary Adams, featured on four pages, including the first photograph, I was certain then and now, was also, under the name of Gary Lockwood, the star of *2001: A Space Odyssey* (1968).

Leather History Alert: The opening essay of the Guild Press *Leather!* was, I think, the first "leather manifesto."

Upon its homomasculinity I found the solidarity to build the attitude and plot of *Leather Blues*, which is, despite its publishing odyssey, very much a quintessential *Drummer* novel. The Guild Leather "manifesto" was the masculine-leather ethos I injected into *Drummer*, and then dramatized politically in the very *Drummer* novel, *Some Dance to Remember*, with its plot about a leather magazine with its own controversial "Masculinist Manifesto."

I chose to write "Leather Christmas 1977" in a mix of present and past tenses to intensify its immediacy. This essay is not fiction. All of it, including the "Bible-sex scene" at the Folsom Baths, is true. The man who called himself, "Thumper," was the San Francisco actor, David Baker, and should not be confused with my other pal, the famous San Francisco barber Jim "Thumper" McPherson, pictured in *Drummer* 115, page 32. The leather S&M priest was the Reverend Jim Kane.

II. The feature essay as published in *Drummer* 19, December 1977

S&M's New Definition...

Leather Christmas 1977

Christmas gives me fucked-out eyes. Lots of looks at lots of parties. Terrific tumbles at the tubs. Men visiting San Francisco for the Holidays. Remembrance of the whole year's close encounters of the male kind. Man-ghosts of Christmas Past. Eyeing wise men in threesomes. Enduring inevitable S&M Christmas cards that say: "ChriStMaS: Two "S's" and one "M." Have a well-hung Holiday." Omigod.

Christmas celebrates toys, toy soldiers, and men of good and consenting will. Estranged lovers decide to speak. Love is found with the proper stranger. Childless men celebrate the birth of the Basic Male of Western Civilization.

CHRISTMAS *DRUMMER* BOY

Already this holiday season, at the new Folsom bar called the Brig, which was the No Name before it was the Bolt, a guy named Thumper, says "Hi" to me. We talk. I buy him a Lite. He rubs my chest. I spotted him a moment before as across the bar a hot man in full leather toyed with Thumper's ass through his jeans. The man reached around, loosened Thumper's belt, dropped his denim to his knees, and kissed his butt in the shadows of the bar. Flattered by the compliment, Thumper prolonged the moment of his tonguing, then re-dressed himself, tucking the tail of his Rudolph-the-Red-Nosed-Reindeer T-shirt into his jeans, moving slowly my way.

He rubs my chest again. I stroke his bicep through his leather jacket. He is bearded. His red hair is clipped short, cut by the other Thumper [whose real name was Jim McPherson] who barbers up on Castro. A gap between his two front teeth makes me a sucker for his kisser. There's mistletoe in his green eyes.

A Top Man, we agree, should be believable.

He claims to play Top.

Later in his van we eat fresh strawberries. Again he touches my chest. He lights a Marlboro. In the glow, his tan deepens. His van smells of freshcut pine branches.

I wonder the same old wonder we all wonder: Is this guy believable? Maybe. He's offbeat enough. Looks like a genuine *BST*: Bent, Sick, and Twisted. We cruise specific types and read iconic fantasies in their faces: ranchers, truckers, bikers, linebackers, cons, mechanics, mercenaries, Mafiosi, and Marines. Symbolic men with a husky taste for celebrating male sex: whiskey in a glass, a baseball chaw of Red Man chew, a two-day beard, a cigar butt — bizarre, but exciting!

As the song goes, "All I want for Christmas is..."

At my house Thumper rolls a couple jays. We pass the sweet blue back and forth, lust rising with the high. "You got good arms," he says. "Want a 'lude? It's fun. We can sleep when we want."

Down with the 714s. Down with the wine. Down to my cellar.

He eyes the rack, stocks, cage, hooks, eye-bolted bed, and footlocker filled with toys. "I like imagination," he says. He grabs my chest twisting my tits too heavily, too painfully, too little sensual build-up.

We're hardly beyond the foretalk.

But I let him grind my pecs because of the delight in his eyes. My cock is hard. My head analyzes his moves. Judging. Taking — in this raw situation, in this pared-down human relationship where everything is upfront — the measure of us two men.

JINGLE BALLS

Recently on a night around Thanksgiving, at Allan Lowery's Leatherneck Bar on Folsom, with only twenty guys or so, I approached a man in a leather jacket, cap, jeans, no shirt. We nodded. He grabbed my crotch. Hard. Rough.

Men do to others what they really want done to themselves.

I grabbed him back. Never do nothin' nice and easy. He moaned. "Take care of my balls," he said.

I pushed him up against the empty back bar. He spread his feet. I laid forty, maybe fifty, kicks with my boot into his groin. *Thunk* of scuffed black leather against warm denim crotch. Balls bouncing hot in his big sac. He moaned out a smile. We minded our business. The crowd minded theirs. One last kick and I pulled his bruiser body into mine, jerking my knee up into his piss-soaked crotch.

Once. Twice. Three times. He made a low pleased sound and pressed hard into me. A direct hit. He shot hot and slick through his torn denim into my hand. "Thanks," he said.

Don't know his name. Don't need to. Wouldn't recognize him again. But for what it was, an honest engaging moment, we worked some meaning into the meaninglessness of what passes between people over holiday tea and ices. Something hot, maybe blessed, passed honest between us. Man to man.

I do remember he was a tourist, because he surprised me. He did what a tourist would do: he hugged me, shook my hand, and wished me a Merry Christmas.

WE FUCK. THEREFORE, WE ARE

Being men who prefer men has never been our problem. Society's problem, maybe. We never set ourselves apart. Society did. We are who we are.

We are worthy, worth something.

We can touch men or be touched by men in ways most people go their whole lives-long untouched by anyone. We are worth much. And we don't live our lifestyle out of show, sham, or shame. We live for ourselves. Honestly. At least most of the time. So here's to some kind of special merry little Christmas to us!

WON'T YOU GUIDE MY SLEIGH TONIGHT?

Thumper held on to my chest. I to his. But then began that hypnotized look in his eyes, falling back, down, and away from the Top position he projected in his macho bar pose. Grab a dude's tits and down he goes. That old black magic: I saw it happening. The way it usually does. Fuck. In sex or out of it, almost always stuck playing Top. Not that I am only a

Top. Who is? Just that in sex, business, or relationships, I usually end up dominant, not by my choice, but by others' deference.

Keys worn on the right always mean *Bottom*. Keys on the left mean no more than *Negotiable*. Get the picture?

To balance our scene's energy I turned on the negotiable Thumper. He glided gladly out of his Top space. A real down-hill racer. I tied his arms with rope behind his back.

"I've never been tied up before," he said.

"I'm not tying you," I explained "I'm making you secure." I attached his bound wrists to a pulley in the ceiling and hoisted his hands up toward his shoulders. His feet, booted on the cool cellar cement, ferreted for a footing.

"Be good to me," he said.

"I'll be very good to you. Very good."

S&M: A NEW DEFINITION

S&M does not stand for *sadism* and *masochism*. *S* and *M* stand for *Sensuality* and *Mutuality*. *Sensuality:* the action must feel good to both men. *Mutuality:* both men consent to a definite energy exchange.

Sensuality and Mutuality, as practiced in San Francisco, LA, New York, and all the farmburgs in between, is not only healthy sexual encounter, it is very often extraordinarily good therapy. One man, for example, gets very nervous when he hasn't recently played a bottom scene. He works as a radio dispatcher for a police department, and every six weeks or so, when his hunger and his tension peak, he submits himself to a Catholic priest [Jim Kane] who is one of the heaviest leather disciplinarians in the USA and gets his body well worked over, his head nicely shrunk out, and his "sins" conveniently forgiven.

THUMPER BOTTOMS OUT

"Come on, Thumper," I said. "Give it to me." I looked directly into his beautiful eyes. He focused on mine. His mouth fell slack. Receptive. I came in to him through his eyes. Talking, in through his ears. Close enough in the candlelit heat of the cellar for him to smell my body hot in my leather. Massaging his tits, to come into him through his sense of touch. "You are," I said, "Where you want to be. Say *yes*. Say *yes*."

And he focused through the "Vitamin Q" [Quaalude] on the reality flooding forward from his pituitary, from his adrenaline, from his *cojones*, from his subconscious. He said *Yes*.

"Yes. Yes. Yes. Anything."

Because the reality was he hung helpless, tied and hoisted, not by Superman, but by another quite ordinary man who had the will, inclination, and hardon to string him up.

Torture. He repeated the word five or six times. Rolling it in his mouth. "Please torture me."

What a man-with-a-hardon says, especially in night-games, needs subtitles. "Torture me" means "Give me heavy sensation on my body." There is no real torture and no real pain and no real humiliation in ritual. It is suggestion more than reality. But the truth is you can play plenty hard without physical damage. Without a mark. *Heavy* is measured by sensual and mutual respect for limits.

When a man contracts with a consenting man for a heavy trip, the possibilities begin as basic as clamps on his tits, balls, and cock. All the obvious places. Then a few not so obvious: in a circle around his asshole as foreplay to fisting, on both his lips and his tongue, across his eyebrows, and in his nose. If a guy lives in his head, use his head. The clamps and clothes pins get his attention. His hardon holds his interest.

In this way Thumper hung, treated with the great respect due a man, but worked over. Heavy. In a delicate balance.

STRAIGHT RITES OF PASSAGE

Working over straight guys is a whole other trip. I've topped several because movies like *Rollerball, The Holy Mountain,* and *Marathon Man* raise the ritual fantasy-consciousness in their hetero heads. Richard Harris, hanging by his pecs in *A Man Called Horse,* all for the love of a girl, awoke an "endurance hunger" in quite a few completely straight guys. They wanted their own personal rite of passage, their own initiation into adult masculinity, in our society that has never definitely signaled when a boy is definitely a man.

Mostly these dudes were macho athletic types. To the ones I agreed to conduct through ritual passage, I indicated they had to mutualize the energy by putting out sexually. So hungry were they for a safe experience they knew no other way to satisfy, they each in their own turn agreed.

For their head's sake I kept their sexual involvement fairly passive by simply fucking the shit out of them near the end of the scene. Jocks, used to hard coaching, seem the most susceptible to this kind of man-to-man ritual sexuality. Trained to accept the orders of another man, they follow those orders at even the greatest hardship and pain to themselves in order to make the team. They are ripe and ready to deal with a masculine Top who will modify his gayness to accommodate their needs while still satisfying his own. And these men are truly sexually straight. It's just that for once, in our too-soft society, they feel they must endure with all manly fortitude the primal therapy of the ritual vigils, pains, and humiliations endured by every ancient warrior worth his manhood.

THUMPER HANGS ON

Thumper began to moan. I turned on even more. The sight of his tanned muscular body hanging taut led to a truism: every body looks better in the strain of bondage. The sculpture of bondage. Definition of muscular bulk becomes clearer. Sweat rolls from under the arms, glistens down the trim sides. The cock, a length of rawhide tied tight around its base, distends, hard-veined. A clear string drools from its anxious mouth.

Electrical clips clamp his tits. Chains from each clip run up through eye hooks and dangle down to the lead weights swinging opposite his erect cock. This magnificent man whom girls turn to cruise in the streets hangs strung up in back by his wrists between his shoulder blades, strung up in front by his tits stretched up toward the ceiling.

WORKING ON WOMEN: 'ROUND YON VIRGIN

Working on women or married couples can be fun. For a fee. Because my hard really isn't totally perversatile. Women tend to be more dramatically masochistic in a psychodrama situation. On one extreme, a woman will play the innocent virgin captured and abused. On the other, she will play the outraged bitch who when she gets loose, you motherfucker, will barbecue your cock *en brochette.*

With husband-and-wife scenes, after she has called Palo Alto to double-check with the babysitter, the couple can be strung up opposite each other for who-loves-who-more games: "Who gets the next ten lashes? Who gets the dildo? Where?" Or spouses can be worked on one at a time. The most frequent scene is to tie, say, the wife into a chair and make her witness the abuse of her husband. Many women get hot and enraged at their old man's getting tied, degraded, and fucked. They yell and scream and attack his manhood as cock goes up his ass or down his throat.

She cums. He cums. I cum.

Later, all shrunk out, they kiss and hug and carry on like they've spent a week at Esalen. [The Esalen Institute founded south of San Francisco, 1962, is a human potential "sensitivity" movement based on Aldous Huxley whose gonzo-journalism book of mescaline-enlightenment, *The Doors of Perception* (1963), inspired Jim Morrison to name his group "The Doors" and gay men by the millions to drop acid. In 1970s San Francisco, gay men, particularly leathermen, considered Esalen a joke for its perceived excess of touchy-feeliness, especially as merchandised by CEO David Goodstein at *The Advocate* in "*The Advocate* Experience." As HIV and AIDS terror struck, it was this kind of corporate "sensitivity training" merging with the Marxist "politically correct" that in a perfect storm, a perfect hurricane, ruined the gay liberation movement and the gay press.]

THUMPER'S SECOND ROUND

I took Thumper down from the hooks and led him obediently across the cellar to the rack and tied him down again. For a good hard bellydown fuck. Leather restraints tighten around his ankles, his thighs, his waist, his neck, his biceps, and his wrists. His butt shines like Christmas ornaments in the candle light.

"I'm secure," he says.

I smile and plunge on in. Like quicksand, the more you wiggle, the deeper you go.

NEAPOLITAN SEX: 3 FLAVORS

Sex is Neapolitan ice cream. *Vanilla* is for plain old kissy face. *Strawberry* is for *S* and *M* exotica, because a "strawberry" is jocker talk for the bruise you get on the playing field. *Chocolate* covers the currently trendy, but understandably closeted, interest in scatology. (See *Salo,* Pasolini's last film before a Roman hustler caved in the side of his head with a two-by-four.)

Lovers of vanilla sex often have as much fear of strawberry sex as straights have of gay sex. Vanilla fans fear, or fantasize, that if they hit a leather bar or bath, they will be attacked like Sebastian Venable in *Suddenly Last Summer.* Hardly.

While men sometimes get pantsed, spread on pool tables, beaten with belts, and maybe fisted, you can believe they gave their consent one way or the other. As long as you don't wear cologne or deodorize your pits, you're safer in a leather bar than in twink bar where All-American boys might toss you and your leathers into a Lacoste alligator pit.

As Joel Grey said in *Cabaret:* "Live and let live."

NEW YEAR'S NOSTALGIA: FOLSOM STREET BARRACKS

Sometimes places like the classic Folsom Street Barracks conjure so much energy, they go up in flames. When the Barracks was golden [from 1972-1977], not only were you safe, you were transported. For guys liking the best bodies mixed with the farthest fantasy, the Barracks was Christmas every night of the year. You entered expectant that something lurid, raunchy, wild, even slightly dangerous might happen. And it did. But, generally, except for the reborn Jesus-freak who tied a guy up in his room and browbeat him for two hours with a Bible until his screams brought rescue, Barracks behavior was all within the realm of sensual mutuality.

Barracks guys suffered no failure of imagination. Fistfuckers inched their knuckles into rings Ripley would not believe. Men created trips of leather and sweat. Hides spread on the bed. Three layers of Crisco-ed leather wrapping a man's hot body. Bodybuilders poised to be touched, worshiped, fucked. S&M types with guys hanging upside down in the doorways to rooms. Spontaneous gangfucks. Wrestling in one room. Boxing next door. Big pecs. Big dicks. Smooth buns. Long hair. Crewcuts. Shaved heads. Oink of Crisco and chocolate. Piss and denim. Jockstraps. Uniforms. Armpits. Tongues. Asshole. Dim red light. Loud acid rock. Bodies laid back on asphalt-tile stairs. Uncut cock flipped up on a tight belly inviting a sucking. Easy access man to man. Dance: 10. Looks: 10. And the vibes, good.

But now, this holiday season, I flash: "Think tonight I'll hit the Barracks." Then comes the pang I can't. No one can. Except the local filmmaker who wants to shoot a porno, rumor has it, in the Barracks' charred halls. Love, I guess, among the ruins.

The Barracks' burning broke up that bunch of boys. No more hot new Year's Eve's like 1973 with the muscleman standing on a sink, stroking his meat, rubbing his oiled chest, while thirty men knelt on the tile floor, worshiping him, jerking off, reaching toward his golden calves straight out of some C. B. DeBiblical movie [Cecil B. DeMille: *The Ten Commandments*]. Gone are the days. San Francisco this Christmas has no pansexual High Place. [The Barracks was remodeled and reopened and burned down one last time in the great Folsom Street fire in July 1981.]

The best bodies currently check into the Technicolor Club Baths at 8th and Howard. [I used the word "Technicolor" because gay men enjoyed the fact that the previous tenant of the building had been the Technicolor Processing Lab, South of Market.] The best bent, sick, and twisted trips slide into the Slot on Folsom. The fistfuckers descend to the Catacombs, a private handballing palace, so elbow-decadent that if you want to leave your heart in San Francisco, you can probably store it there in a footlocker. The jerkoff/oral fans now hang ten, or less, or if you're lucky, more, through the gloryholes in the maze at the South of Market Club on 6th Street and Mission where Wino Country raunch reigns supreme. ["Wino Country" acknowledged that getting to the gloryholes required stepping over the skid-row drunks on the sidewalk.]

SWINGING NIGHTLY ON THE CHANDELIERS

My sweat drips down on Thumper. Two space heaters run to warm the perpetual San Francisco chill off the cellar. Nothing worse in a scene than a discomfort not intended. A Top has to be sensitive. I figure to move the one space heater away from the rack. Over it I notice—fuck!—my best faded Levi's hang on the heater's edge, scorching. Without pulling out of him I yank my jeans free of the heat. I don't care. All that counts is this man and me. Higher and higher.

We may never see each other again. But for what it is, for now: bliss-out! Too much of a good thing is great. Less isn't more. Only more is more. Ask any Medici.

DAYS MERRY AND BRIGHT

But, cuming, butt-cuming, with too much great sensuality, I think on this night before Christmas of the daytime street of that straight world so many gay men insist on functioning in so well, because we are—Thank God—not just creatures of the night. I hope people will be able to see in our eyes, in our fucked-happy eyes how we love the men we've laid and the men we've yet to lay; that they will see in our fuck-filled eyes what we have experienced, what we look and live for; that they will see in our eyes the dimension of human sex and sensuality and mutuality that we recognize in our gay brothers' eyes when we pass them on straight streets; that our fuck-full eyes will be forever the badge of our identification to those who should know, and our badge of fulfillment to those who barely imagine where our heads are, but yet love us enough to hope we're having a good time, the time even of our lives.

The only fucking immortality any man can expect, after we play it as it lays, is to be a story told in beds around the world on nights before Christmas. And even nights after.

Ain't that right, Thump, old buddy?

Editor's Note

The following poem, written August 14, 1957, offers a profile into the adolescent feeling and writing style of one teenager who grew up to be a formative editor in chief of *Drummer*. Jack Fritscher was an eighteen-year-old Catholic seminarian out in the world on summer vacation in Greenwich Village when he wrote this poem of shock and admiration. Many lines of the 1957 poem forecast a description of gay life in 1970s bars and baths, as well as give a nod to the author's

Drummer 19: Leather Christmas

1950s teenage awareness of leather, hustling, drag, transgenders, and drugs. —Mark Hemry, editor

CRY! THE YOUNG HUNTERS

I did not think they searched for God
When on weekends they razed the neon world
Or in the nights poured out in screaming emergency
Wards carbolic and tiled echoing
The surprised stares of the suddenly mangled.
Him they carted in—then brought his legs
Still the bloodied wheels railroad along impersonal tracks
Morphine and plasma for a dirty drunk?
He can sell pencils (RR's compliments)
Outside amber bars till some young tough
Kicks in his head for condom quarters.
All the king's horses foul the city streets
And dogs drink in the gutter
Petticoats Petticoats see the petty pretty coats, inviting.
The bruised once-woman tumbled from the stained bed
Fainted in her own vomit
Desecrating, they seek empty gods
In the arched chapel of a crotch
Eternal syncope of ends open to the pubic public.
Dead seed of dead seed.
Mechanical march through a vast
Urinal flushed of hope.
Adrenalin in full flow
Panting down a running alley they flee
Thinking that they chase. Stop.
Breathe in dark doorways.
Young muscle flexed hard against limp city dryads
Bistrodeep in beer, worship the golden hubcap.
Scream of jazz and rag of rock.
Anguish of breath strangled saxophonically.
Dancing shadows of aborted fullness.
The beat and black and blare
Drug with false strength the zombie faces and secret
The driving atomic fear. Unknowing,
Adonis dies fearing
Only that someday he shall die. Missing
The point. Dying like seconds in

Dark theophany ecstatic with a fix a fifth a fuck.
Searching
Fetid darkness, fleeing fear, thinking
He must be here somewhere but
Too tangled in frightened running searching
To find him.
©1957 Jack Fritscher

III. Eyewitness Illustrations

Detail of page from *Son of Drummer* (September 1978) showing first serial publication in *Drummer* of Jack Fritscher's 1969 novel, *I Am Curious (Leather)* aka *Leather Blues*, which was first published in a limited private edition by Lou Thomas of Target Studio, New York (1972).

Opposite page. Right and left: "Jack FritscherX8, First Beard," photo-booth strips, San Francisco, August 15, 1961. ©Jack Fritscher. Center top: "Jack Fritscher," Los Angeles, 1970. Photograph by David Sparrow. ©Jack Fritscher. Center bottom: "Jack Fritscher, Editor in Chief of *Drummer*," Castro Street, January 1978. Photograph by David Sparrow. ©Jack Fritscher.

Drummer 19: Leather Christmas

"Jack Fritscher, University Professor," May 1968, photographed during the writing of *I Am Curious (Leather)* aka *Leather Blues*. Auto-photograph by Jack Fritscher. ©Jack Fritscher

Like a vocation inside a vocation, coming out to oneself in specific homomasculinity is the same epiphany as coming out to oneself in generic homosexuality.

When Jack Fritscher's character Ryan O'Hara wrote his controversial *Masculinist Manifesto* which was so pivotal to considerations of "body fascism in GLBT culture" in *Some Dance to Remember: A Memoir Novel of San Francisco 1970-1982*, he was a fictive dramatization of the leather identity movement of the twentieth-century in which men self-fashioned masculinity as legitimately as feminists self-fashioned their identities.

Homosexuality is a primordial Old Religion more ancient and wise than Druidism, Judaism, Christianity, and Islam. Among its sects, homomasculinity is perhaps the most unexpected "click" on the Kinsey Six scale. Always present and almost invisible, it existed for millennia before its recent outings in Adolph Brand's 1896 magazine *Der Eigene*, William Carney's 1968 epistolary novel *The Real Thing*, Jack Fritscher's 1969 novel *I Am Curious (Leather)*, Larry Townsend's 1972 *Leatherman's Handbook*, and the 1975 debut of the leather-identity magazine *Drummer*.

In the 1960s, Fritscher was a practicing eyewitness in porno bookstores on the legendary 42nd Street in New York. When he was twenty-six in 1965, three years before he wrote *I Am Curious (Leather)*, he found the one-issue booklet, *Leather!*, compiled by Avery Willard for the pioneering homomasculine Guild Press, Washington, D.C. Willard was also the 8mm filmmaker who created the classic 1960s film, *Leather Narcissus*, starring New York leather icon Fernando.

Avery Willard's editorial essay, "Men of Leather," was the first American "Masculine Manifesto" of Leather Identity, and was an essential influence on Fritscher exploring the frontier of his own homomasculinity personally and in *Drummer*. In 1965, Avery Willard's "Men of Leather" was as important to the leather subculture as Susan Sontag's 1964 essay "Notes on 'Camp'" was important to gay culture.

Avery's leather-defining essay was precisely the kind of enthusiastic identity-fiction and nonfiction Fritscher went on to write for *Drummer* (1977-1999).

Drummer 19: Leather Christmas

Excerpt from Avery Willard's "Men of Leather" essay in the 1965 Guild Press booklet *Leather!*

"The part that Marlon Brando created in *The Wild One* has had an incalculable influence on the Leather world. His contempt for the square world, his scorn..., his love for the thrills of the moment, for life at its highest pitch—these became holy virtues in the eyes of boys and men who found in this way of life more excitement and meaning than in their own humdrum, monotonous, repetitive existence. All of his gestures, originally meant to be cruel and loutish, became, in the eyes of a million restless boys, the actions of a hero. In Leather and its rites, the Leather men find an escape from the marshmallow-soft, cloyingly sweet, TV, synthetic, deodorized, almost dehumanized everyday way of life promoted by this age. In Leather, with its sensuous touch and smell, they have found a symbol which helps them escape from the over-feminized present into a past where men of strength and muscle, power and determination....were admired and emulated. Through Leather, a small but intensely dedicated band of men are trying to capture and preserve the value of innate virility, and by doing so they could very well be performing an important service for us all." ©Guild Press

The Rawhide Male, Issue 2 of Four Issues (1966-1969). There was a mid-twentieth-century thirst for gay magazines years before small gay book publishers were founded in the late 1980s. In 1945, Bob Mizer of AMG in LA began publishing *Physique Pictorial*. In the 1950s-60s, Chuck Renslow and Etienne of Kris Studio in Chicago showcased their aggressively homomasculine photographs in the pre-*Drummer* magazines they published: *Mars, Triumph*, and *The Rawhide Male* featuring men such as Mike Bradburn, and the redheaded and bearded Irish lumberjack Don Dunne. It is a gay popular culture truth: millions more people read the 214 issues of *Drummer* during twenty four years (1975-1999) than have read all that period's best-selling gay novels combined. Used with permission of Chuck Renslow and the Leather Archives & Museum.

Captions: Eyewitness documentation of the existence of graphics providing internal evidence supporting Jack Fritscher's text are located in the Jack Fritscher and Mark Hemry GLBT History collection. Out of respect for issues of copyright, model releases, permissions, and privacy, some graphics are not available for publication at this time, but can be shown by appointment.

Eyewitness Illustration | Photograph. "Thumper Stradling Motorcycle, South of Market." Blue-eyed biker and wrestler Jim McPherson aka Thumper was the most popular barber in the Castro in the Titanic 1970s. He was upbeat and dripped virile sex appeal. Men wanted his strong hands on their heads. He was exemplar and participant in "Gay Jock Sports," *Drummer* 20 (January 1978), and was the star of Jack Fritscher's Super-8 film *Thumper* (1974). He appeared in *Drummer* 115 (April 1988). Photographer unknown.

Astrologic *Capricorn*

> Written October 1977, this feature essay was published in *Drummer* 19, December 1977.
> I. Author's Eyewitness Historical-Context Introduction written April 23, 2007
> II. The feature column as published in *Drummer* 19, December 1977
> III. Eyewitness Illustrations

I. **Author's Eyewitness Historical-Context Introduction written April 23, 2007**

Astrology, Comedy, Scofflaws, *The Advocate*,
and the *Drummer* Bloomsbury

Written October 1977, this feature column was published in *Drummer* 19 (December 1977). The LA author Aristide had invented "Astrologic," but warfare and attrition inside *Drummer* caused me as editor in chief to step up and take over the writing of "Astrologic" for seven issues (plus one): *Drummer* 19 (December 1977), *Drummer* 20 (January 1978), *Drummer* 21 (March 1978), *Drummer* 22 (May 1978), *Drummer* 23 (July 1978), *Drummer* 25 (December 1978), *Drummer* 26 (January 1979), including a reprint of my work pirated by John Embry and John Rowberry in *Drummer* 41 (December 1980).

To write this *Drummer* history I searched out eyewitness Aristide who revealed for the first time his role as a charter member of the original LA *Drummer* salon.

During "The Dawning of the Age of Aquarius" in the 1960s and 1970s, the most common pick-up line in bars was "What's your sign?" Spinning that joke, Aristide Joseph Laurent, a French Creole-Irish-Cajun whose birth sign is September 15, 1941, created "Astrologic" for the original-recipe of *The Advocate*.

Marking the fortieth anniversary of the founding of *The Advocate*, Aristide wrote in an email on September 19, 2007:

> After Dick Mitch was arrested in a bar raid and charged with lewd conduct in the late 1960s, he became a fired-up activist;

and, with his lover, Bill Rau, and friend Sam Allen, they bought the *Pride Newsletter* and changed the name to *The Advocate*. Since it was dangerous to be a "pervert" prior to the liberation movement, you didn't use your real name for fear of reprisals, not only from harassment by the LAPD but the ever-present possibility of losing your day job, family and friends. Dick Mitch became "Dick Michaels," the editor; Bill Rau became "Bill Rand"; and I became "P. Nutz," jack of many trades....I provided the so-called "humor" of the early *Advocate* in a monthly column titled "*Mariposa de la Noche*" (Butterfly of the Night). When I look at those columns in my mature years, I shudder. What a flamer I was! (No rebuttals, please). The defining purpose of the early *Advocate* was to unite and inform the gay community of what was happening in their closed society. When David Goodstein purchased it and took over, it evolved into a glossy fashion/celebrity magazine.

Aristide chose "P. Nutz" because in the United States Air Force his nickname had been "Peanuts." He also wrote for *The Advocate* as the Anglicized "Joseph Laurence" because the publisher wanted to list more names to make the staff seem larger.

Moving "Astrologic" to *Drummer* at the invitation of editor in chief Jeanne Barney because the humorless investment banker David Goodstein had bought *The Advocate*, Aristide wrote without benefit of byline when he penned his first eleven "*Drummer* Astrologic" columns ending in *Drummer* 18 what he had begun in *Drummer* 8. By *Drummer* 18, the magazine had moved to San Francisco, leaving behind in LA many original contributors including Jeanne Barney who had credited Aristide not specifically for "Astrologic" but more generally on the masthead list of "Contributors" under his third nom de plume "Aristide Laurent."

Having filled in for Aristide for seven issues, and having over-ruled the objections of LA office-boy John Rowberry, I negotiated his open return for forthcoming issues beginning with *Drummer* 27 in which I gave him his first byline in *Drummer* as "Aristide."

I was personally grateful because I needed him back. At that time, I was editing and producing *Drummer* as well as writing much of each issue and hadn't time to write "Astrologic." Deadlines had caused me to omit it from *Drummer* 24. In fact, in *Drummer* 23, I had "cheated" by writing no more than a simple astrological limerick.

Why Aristide had never been bylined on the *Drummer* contents page or at the top of "Astrologic" before I listed him remains a mystery to both Aristide and his longtime pal, Jeanne Barney.

- At the beginning of *Drummer* before Aristide's debut in *Drummer* 8, each astrology page in *Drummer* issues 2 through 3 consisted of a text-free illustration by the artist Bud who had drawn the cover of *Drummer* 1 in which there was no astrology page.
- In *Drummer* 4 and 5, the drawing by Bud was accompanied by quoted text from *The Gay Book of Astrology* by Jay Perry.
- With *Drummer* 6, the astrology page was renamed "It's All in the Stars" with a byline by "Ken" and with an illustration by the artist "KT."
- In *Drummer* 7, Bud returned to illustrate the second and last appearance of "It's All in the Stars."
- In *Drummer* 8, the column "Astrologic" first appeared minus a byline for Aristide.

Keeping with the humor of Aristide who was wrongfully fired after my December 31, 1979, exit from *Drummer*, I mixed satire for my seven "Astrologic" columns out of my experience with leather and with the occult. By chance, I had both academic and street credentials. In 1968, I had begun researching gay magic, astrology, leather wicca, and S&M rituals on Folsom Street for my book *Popular Witchcraft: Straight from the Witch's Mouth* (1972, 2005). Investigating the psyche of pre-Stonewall leather, I had also worked up the texts of leather author William Carney who pioneered his "S&M Way" as spiritual ritual in his epistolary novel *The Real Thing* (1968).

Popular Witchcraft featured the first American interview with the gay witch Frederick de Arechaga, and, according to *Fate Magazine*, a pitch-perfect interview with the straight Satanist Anton LaVey. The pagan de Arechaga was the founding Pontifex Maximus of the Sabaean Religion in Chicago. LaVey was the legendary founder of the Church of Satan in San Francisco.

While LaVey and I bonded as subject and journalist in his gorgeous diabolically decorated Black House at 6114 California Street, Frederick de Arechaga's El Sabarum sanctuary was a wondrous and campy Babylonian temple as imagined by the art department at MGM. Aristide would have loved it. Of course, de Arechaga and I smoked grass. Of course, we had sex. Of course, the doves in his cages cooed. It was the 60s.

Aristide played his part in the *Drummer* salon and on the *Drummer* Blacklist.

As editor in chief, I tried to maintain the "Astrologic" column which Aristide had written intermittently for *Drummer* from 1976 until he was fired in 1980 through the machinations of sometime *Drummer* freelance writer and fulltime queen John Rowberry who finally erupted in a character-revealing jealous rage because one of his lovers had a fling with Aristide.

That firing by Rowberry was typical of the spite and revenge inside the *Drummer* office where in the 1980s Rowberry and Embry created their Blacklist. The petulant Rowberry had "control issues" against everyone in the *Drummer* salon and the *Drummer* office who in the 1970s had dissed and dismissed him. For thirty-one months as editor in chief (1977- 12/31/79), I had to hold Rowberry in check as he oiled his way across the floor. It was like pinning a snake with a forked stick. He had arrived on the door step of San Francisco *Drummer*, hat in hand, looking for work. He had quit, or been fired, from his oleaginous career as the night porter at the tacky Ramada Inn on Santa Monica Boulevard in West Hollywood.

Considering the famous 1974 cult film *The Night Porter* (starring Dirk Bogarde trampling Charlotte Rampling), I think life was imitating art insofar as night-porter Rowberry's lover—who hit the sheets with Aristide—had a Nazi fetish.

Rowberry, who had Embry's ear, had written a couple of non-erotic murder-obsessed pieces for *Drummer* that had been heavily retooled by editor in chief Jeanne Barney. (I knew that Rowberry never really understood that *Drummer* was a sex magazine for one-handed reading; he always wanted it to be something more like *The Advocate*.) That gave Rowberry "motive" to hate Barney the way that Rowberry's puppet master Embry impugned Barney in *Drummer* 30, page 38, for knowing the secrets of Embry aka "Robert Payne." Allegedly because of Embry's problematical mail-order practices, Barney reported that the artist Sean dubbed Embry and his alias "Robert Payne" as "Robert Rip-off." See *Drummer* 1 (June 1975) for the "Robert Payne Leather Emporium."

The staff at San Francisco *Drummer* giggled and dismissed "Highway Rowberry" as the "office boy." We ignored him because in the 1970s tops rarely spoke to bottoms even out of scene. He was also one of that caste of men who likes young men of legal age who can pass for fourteen. When he took up critiquing videos for *Studflix* magazine, I told him if sperm could act, he'd give it a good review. For the thirteen months after I exited *Drummer* on December 31, 1979, Rowberry acted as "assignments editor." It was only with *Drummer* 40 (January 1981) that "assignments editor" Rowberry metastasized into "editor."

(Please re-set all the leather timelines regarding *Drummer* including the "DeBlase Timeline" of record at the Leather Archives and Museum.)

John Rowberry was never "editor in chief" of *Drummer*.

That was his leather "glass ceiling."

It burned him. In 1982, in the crowded lobby of the Castro Theater at the premiere screening of Rainer Werner Fassbinder's *Querelle*, Mark Hemry and I nodded hello to John Rowberry who fizzled like he might explode. He spit out: *"You* like Fassbinder?" I said, "Ich mag ihn auf Deutsche—aber er ist sehr ausgezeichnet auf Englisch—okay?—mit Brad Davis und Franco Nero. Hahaha." It was enough high-school cuntinental German to end that conversation!

[I said, "Actually, I prefer Fassbinder in German, but he's brilliant in English—okay?—with Brad Davis and Franco Nero. Hahaha." See a similar theater scene in *Some Dance to Remember: A Memoir-Novel of San Francisco 1970-1982*, Reel 6, Scene 3.]

During 1980-1984, Rowberry and Embry drove *Drummer* into a tailspin—by dumping talent such as Aristide and others—that caused Embry to sell the magazine to Chicagoan Anthony DeBlase who, during very early negotiations in the viral-death summer of 1985 made certain that Rowberry was "gone" from *Drummer* as a condition of the oncoming sale in 1986. By autumn 1985, Embry had eased Rowberry out the door.

Earlier, in 1973, two years before Jeanne Barney started up LA *Drummer*, she had worked with Aristide at the original *The Advocate* founded and owned by publishers Dick Michaels and Bill Rand who sold ownership of their *LA Advocate: The Newsletter of Personal Rights in Defense and Education (P.R.I.D.E.)* to New York investment banker David Goodstein.

At *The Advocate*, Aristide, as mentioned, had begun writing his "Astrologic" column. When Goodstein fired most of *The Advocate* staff, Jeanne Barney invited Aristide and his "Astrologic" to *Drummer*. In 2007, I queried Jeanne Barney about her eyewitness of that early history of *Drummer* in Los Angeles in 1975-1976. In the zero degrees of separation, she contacted Aristide for his eyewitness. On February 4, 2007, Aristide wrote:

> ....First off let's get this completely clear: John Rowberry did NOT like me [Aristide] and I did not like John Rowberry. Rowberry had a fleeting mini-affair with a good friend of mine at ABC-TV, Bob McWilliams. Bob was as much "in love" with Rowberry as Bob was capable of caring about anyone other than Bob. Bob had a Nazi fetish (Nazi flags in his bedroom; photos of Adolf, etc.) and would only fellate uncircumcised penises....Since Rowberry was see-through white and uncut [he had a translucent Aryan foreskin]...not to mention "easy"

(OK—so that was strictly *opinion*), Bob thought he had died and gone to München.

Since I am presently suffering the debilitating effects of what is commonly known as "chemo brain," my memory for details is a bit sketchy, but, it seems like when the 3 of us [Aristide, Bob McWilliams, Rowberry] were together there was noticeable tension. I don't know if it was the fact that Bob had one of the civilized world's largest uncircumcised cocks (pix available upon request) and Rowberry wanted sole possession of it, or the fact that John [Rowberry] & I just disliked each other because, given our clash of personalities—I had one; he didn't, it was doomed from the start. Finally, Rowberry & his lover (I forget his name [Charles Musgrave]—I wish I could forget Rowberry's) moved to SF and I had Herr gross und unbeschniten [Mr. Big and Uncircumcised] Bob [McWilliams] all to myself....

Naturally, when personality-challenged Rowberry wound up at *Drummer* [as assignments editor, following Fritscher, in 1980], it was his great opportunity to exert his final act of dominance over me by canceling my ["Astrologic"] column (regardless of the excuse in his letter to me). Well, this was actually a total relief to me because I had long since burned out on having to be creative when I was long burned out on doing it. After all, I AM a fickle kween. For some reason, Embry was always on my ass to do it every month and, like with everything else in my life, I would eventually say "ohhhh, alllllright" and send one in. If you look at the last dozen or so you can easily see that my heart was not in them. ©2007 Aristide Laurent

In 1980, Rowberry's unprofessional response to this sex triangle at *Drummer* proved he had no clue regarding the gentlemanly code in our 1970s *Drummer* salon where everyone was sleeping with everyone but him.

Rowberry's co-dependent in destroying the salon around *Drummer* was publisher Embry who in the 1970s failed to make timely payments to such talent as Aristide, Fred Halsted, and other LA contributors including book and movie reviewer Ed Franklin aka Ed Menerth aka Scott Masters. When the talent ran screaming for the exits, the sucking vacuum necessitated that I not only had to write material such as "Astrologic" to fill *Drummer*, but I also had to find new contributors.

Historians might note that from "day one" *Drummer* suffered even as its founders fought over control which defaulted to Embry. In "Astrologic" in *Drummer* 17, Aristide took a shot at the 1975 fight that destroyed the other *Drummer* founders' magazine *NewsWest* much to Embry's glee. In addition, when the LAPD busted the *Drummer* "Slave Auction" in 1976, Embry fled LA and *Drummer* lost what LA talent base it had left. To build a San Francisco salon around *Drummer* I hit the "re-set button" and changed *Drummer* from an LA bar rag into a San Francisco magazine with international appeal.

I regretted that LA personality Fred Halsted, whose best friend in life was Jeanne Barney, had stopped contributing his columns and photographs to *Drummer* and had begun his rival magazine, *Package*.

Unlike Halsted, LA writer-photographer Robert Opel—famous for streaking the 1974 Academy Awards—followed *Drummer* to San Francisco where he was murdered.

Details of this wonderful "Titanic 70s" Bloomsbury salon of writers, artists, and photographers who gathered around my *Drummer* can be found throughout this series: *Gay San Francisco: Eyewitness Drummer*. During the first post-Stonewall decade which let all kinds of sexuality—including masculine-identified homosexuality—out of the closet, I was fortunate to be in the right place with the right friends at the right time.

During that wild golden age of gay liberation, my "Astrologic" column honored the style that Aristide had invented: tongue-in-cheek humor satirizing leather foibles.

Before my editorship, and during and after me, codependents Embry and Rowberry stopped at nothing. The monkey business they had done in LA, they repeated in San Francisco. They created that Blacklist of contributors "who had done them wrong." Through sins of commission and omission, they became scofflaws of copyright, and their unlicensed reprinting of intellectual property disrespected individual authors, artists, and photographers.

For instance, after he fired Aristide, Rowberry and Embry pirated my "Astrologic" column from *Drummer* 21 (March 1978), page 30 and reprinted it in *Drummer* 41 (December 1980), page 63.

Trying to cover up the loss of Aristide, Rowberry and Embry colluded in this direct violation of my copyright for which I was neither contacted for permission nor paid. They also falsely assigned my byline to "Aristide" and, most deceitfully to consumers, set out to dupe the *Drummer* readership by rearranging the line items within my "Astrologic" for my original "Aries 1978" so that they could recycle and resell what would appear as if written for "Sagittarius 1980."

Playing with language in "Astrologic" (*Drummer* 19), I introduced one of the several words I had coined around *Drummer*. It was *perversatile*. In the decade after Stonewall, to write about newly uncloseted sex for the first time in the 1970s required a new vocabulary, including the word for masculine-identified homosexuality: *homomasculinity*.

See *Gay San Francisco: Eyewitness Drummer* for "Homomasculinity: Framing Keywords of Queer Popular Culture in *Drummer* Magazine" from the Queer Keyword Conference, University College Dublin, Ireland, April 2005.

II. The feature column as published in *Drummer* 19 (December 1977)

Astrologic *Capricorn*
(New Year's 1977 Becomes 1978)

CAPRICORN S: (Dec. 22 - Jan. 20): You're a cold fucker whose sun sign, bridging one calendar year to the other, indicates slaves by the pair for the New Year. Your executive-executioner ability will keep them sufficiently servile, so your domestic scene should keep quite scrubbed up unless you prefer to live like the raunchy goat you are. On the first day of Christmas, budget some cold cash for the tattooing of at least six M's this coming year with your capricious birth sign.

CAPRICORN M: In the New Year, expect competition. Be everything your S desires. Be the genuine reflection of your Top's affection. If by February you fall lax from his top style, get yourself together. Maintain. After all, your supportive imitation of him is not only the sincerest form of flattery, it's also the fastest free lunch in the West. Beg him to tattoo you for Valentine's Day.

AQUARIUS S: (Jan. 21 - Feb. 19): On the second day of Christmas, tie your M to a tall pine in a cut-it-yourself lot. Pull out whatever ax you have to grind. Yell "Timber!" Take bets on which way he will fall.

AQUARIUS M: Read Kilmer's "Trees." Tell your Top you're pining for a good needling. Try to land on your face.

PISCES S: (Feb. 20 - Mar. 20): On the third day of Christmas, prepare your New Year's party. Buy imported champagne. Avoid using the cliche of a rented bubbly fountain.

PISCES M: Douche thoroughly.

ARIES S: (Mar. 21 - Apr. 19): On the fourth day of Christmas, fill glass ornaments with piss. Hang them through the tits of an especially green M.

ARIES M: Buy your S a pellet gun. Prepare to be decorated. Stand very still.

TAURUS S: (Apr. 20 - May 20): On the fifth day of Christmas, buy a roll of barbed wire and a "how-to" book on macrame.

TAURUS M: Begin to empathize with hanging ferns. Remember: a plant never speaks unless spoken to first.

GEMINI S: (May 21 - Jun. 21): On the sixth day of Christmas, become a toker and a taker. Buy a year's supply of macho cigars.

GEMINI M: Learn the niceties of storing cigars in dark places where the air is properly humidified.

CANCER S: (Jun. 22 - Jul. 21): On the seventh day of Christmas, clip your nails, practice your ambi-dexterity, and insert both fists at once.

CANCER M: Fall on your knees and hear the angel voices.

LEO S: (Jul. 22 - Aug. 21): On the eighth day of Christmas, invite a surgeon specializing in circumcisions over for a threeway.

LEO M: Cross your legs, hit your amyl, and kiss your smegma goodbye.

VIRGO S: (Aug. 22 - Sep. 22): On the ninth day of Christmas, bike out to the local lovers' lane. Make your M collect the scumbags. Take them home to the microwave he insisted on for Christmas.

VIRGO M: Pretend you're Barbara Hale. Punch your Amana and learn how to hum "Green Sleeves" with your mouth full. [Reference to actress Hale who made a last stand in her career as a TV pitch-woman for Amana kitchen appliances.]

LIBRA S: (Sep. 23 - Oct. 22): On the tenth day of Christmas, reserve the bathtub at the Mineshaft in New York City. Buy beers for the house.

LIBRA M: Since you hardly ever have any fun, beg Santa for scuba gear and a straw. Even recycled, boycott Coors.

SCORPIO S: (Oct. 23 - Nov. 21): On the eleventh day of Christmas, resolve to live your 1978 life in the fast lane. [This is a reference to the Eagles' *Hotel California* and their song "Life in the Fast Lane" with its line "Everything all the time." At this time, I was writing *Some Dance to Remember* whose title is a line quoted from *Hotel California*.]

SCORPIO M: You are insatiably perversatile. Your answer to any S is "Everything all the time." (Also stop trying to turn Virgo S's into M's.)

SAGITTARIUS S: (Nov. 22 - Dec. 21): On the twelfth day of Christmas, pump up an even heavier sweat at the gym. Save water. Don't shower. Go directly home.

SAGITTARIUS M: Ditch your color-coded handkerchiefs. Stick a yellow washcloth in your right rear pocket. Wait at home. Then tongue and groove.

III. Eyewitness Illustrations

Top: John Rowberry displaying his notorious attitude in his office on Folsom Street, 1986. Photograph by Jack Fritscher. ©Jack Fritscher. Bottom: "John Rowberry, Night Porter, LA, Clawing His Way to the Top." Rowberry typically acted like he was starring in a student production of *Sunset Boulevard*. Publicity kit photograph given by Rowberry to *Drummer* art director, and longtime intimate of Fritscher, Al Shapiro. Photographer unknown. Used with permission of the Estate of Al Shapiro administered by Dick Kriegmont.

John W. Rowberry, the night porter from the Ramada Inn on Santa Monica Boulevard in West Hollywood, looking for a job in San Francisco, became editor—never "editor in chief"—of *Drummer* with *Drummer* 40. Almost single-handedly in the 1980s, he dismantled the reader-reflexive grassroots erotic photography in *Drummer* so much in favor of corporate video companies' photographs that there were whispers of "Payola" kickbacks of cash. Eased out under first publisher John Embry at the insistence of new *Drummer* publisher Anthony DeBlase, Rowberry moved on to work successfully in tandem with Fritscher throughout the 1980s on half a dozen other gay magazines.

In the interest of free speech, *Drummer* publisher John Embry decided to accept advertising money from the National Socialist League. Fritscher objected, and insisted on the deletion of the Nazi ad that played seductively with a song title from the popular 1972 Kander and Ebb musical *Cabaret*.

El Paso Wrecking Corp.

> Written October 1977, this feature essay was published in *Drummer* 19, December 1977.
> I. Author's Eyewitness Historical-Context Introduction written April 18, 1998
> II. The feature essay as published in *Drummer* 19, December 1977
> III. Eyewitness Illustrations

I. **Author's Eyewitness Historical-Context Introduction written April 18, 1998**

How Movies Shaped *Drummer*

Written October 1977, this tiny feature essay was published in *Drummer* 19 (December 1977) because *Drummer* readers loved movies and *Drummer* created itself publishing photographs from movies, as well as printing movie reviews and erotic scripts for plays and films. (For film list, see below. For plays, see entry for *Crimes Against Nature, Drummer* 20, January 1978.) When *Drummer* was new, Ed Franklin was the monthly movie reviewer (1976-1978), and Allen Eagles' on-going column "Movie Mayhem," detailing the history of S&M in Hollywood movies, debuted in *Drummer* 8 (August 1976).

I was eager to showcase in *Drummer* the filmmaking Gage Brothers who were a perfect fit with their homomasculine trilogy: *Kansas City Trucking Co.* (1976), *El Paso Wrecking Corp.* (1978), and *L.A. Tool and Die* (1979). The Gages were narrative story tellers of episodic sex featuring the picaresque escapades of actors like Jack Wrangler and the mature Richard Locke who was *Drummer*'s first "Daddy" — at age 37! In content and style, the Gage *mise en scene* embraced technique, material, eros, and casting that were a revelation embraced by fans of the new genre of homomasculine action movies.

There is a back story of how the Gage Brothers arrived on the film scene, and there is a back story of how cinema built an audience for *Drummer*.

Parallel to the emergence of gay bars as the first gay art galleries, gay movie theaters were film galleries screening the moving image of newly liberated homosexuality. In the Titanic 1970s, gay movie theaters were erotic performance-art spaces. Movie-palace sex (on film and live in the audience) was a gay community social phenomenon that went extinct with the 1982 arrival of VCRs and HIV that emptied the theaters, sent everyone home alone, and destroyed the high concept of group sexuality celebrated on screen and in the seats, aisles, and toilets. A man hasn't lived until he's had orgy sex on the stage behind the giant screen in a gay porn theater with the dots of Technicolor light flickering through making him and his partners shimmer as if they themselves were glimmering on celluloid. That's a "gay film festival"!

Live sex also occurred on stage. Continuing a sexed up version of the G-rated vaudeville tradition that was very much alive in first-run family movie theaters in the 1930s and 1940s, gay film theaters often included erotic stage shows between features. It was a kind of performance art of male burlesque. See my article, "Pumping Roger: A Night at the Nob Hill Theater," in *Drummer* 21 (March 1978) and my review of the live show starring Colt model Clint Lockner and Dan Pace, the star of the Gage Brothers' *L. A. Tool and Die*. (Because I was exiting *Drummer*, my article, "In These Last Days of the American Empire: Dan Pace & Clint Lockner Together," was published as part of my "Virtual *Drummer*" collection in the premiere issue of *Skinflicks*, Volume 1, Number 1, January 1980.)

Anthropologically, gay films of the 1970s are lightning caught in a jar. They were *Mondo Cane* "documentaries" anticipating "reality TV" showing the way we were. When anthropologist Margaret Mead died in Manhattan in 1978, was she headed to the Adonis Theater to add one more culture to her *Sex and Temperament in Three Primitive Societies*? The gay film genre of the 1960s and 1970s was a kind of educational *cinema verite* that taught newly uncloseted primitive audiences the new ways to self-fashion gay identity and have more exotic sex. The Gage Brothers shot primers of masculine-identified eros.

Most gay movies of the 1970s were scripted silent films with music added. Not until the advent of the video camera did silent gay cinema find it could talk; but by then it had nothing to say except the unscripted "Yeah. Uh-huh. Give it to me. I'm gonna cum!"

That decade's cinema silence is one reason the 1970s is often misinterpreted by latter-day revisionists who don't "get" the Titanic 70s and the original-recipe sexual revolution before it was turned into gay politics. They wonder about us survivors whose memory of the 1970s is akin to William Wordsworth who wrote of the joys of the French Revolution: "Bliss was it that dawn to be alive, but to be young was very heaven."

Unfortunately, 1980s video moved 1970s film away from art and into business. Instead of gay movies with forward momentum of plot, eros, and character, the video "grind formula" devolved to eight guys in four scenes with eight cumshots in eighty minutes. Gay video of the 1980s and 1990s (with no art roots) was a travesty of the gay art-and-eros films of the 1970s with their pedigree in the wonderful world of 1960s experimental and underground cinema in which Kenneth Anger, Andy Warhol, the Kuchar Brothers, and Jack Smith created the gay film esthetic.

In a direct line of homomasculine descent, film DNA shaped *Drummer*. In the Swinging 60s, American culture had been swept up into the "experimental cinema" of underground films, and many foreign films, and some Hollywood movies which, in fact, created a ready-made audience for experimental *Drummer*.

Drummer shaped gay culture.

For thirty years, among the millions of leatherfolk, there was hardly a person alive who had not heard of or had not read *Drummer*. With its 1970s press run of 42,000 copies per issue, more people have read one issue of *Drummer* than have read any one book by any deeply established GLBT author on the top hundred list of literary best-sellers in the so-called "gay canon." That's why I added the line to the masthead of my *Drummer* 23 (July 1978): "The American Review of Gay Popular Culture." This makes *Drummer* worth study and research in GLBT culture.

The Gage Brothers' DNA comes from this lineage: Kenneth Anger's leathery *Scorpio Rising* (1963) and butch-fetish *Kustom Kar Kommandos* (1965); Andy Warhol's long-take *Blowjob* (1963), *My Hustler* (1965), and chatty *Lonesome Cowboys* (1969) which was connected through Joe Dallesandro to the 8mm films of Bob Mizer at Athletic Model Guild; Wakefield Poole's actioner *Boys in the Sand* (1971) and muscular *Bijou* (1972); Fred Halsted's MOMA features *L. A. Plays Itself* (1972) and *Sextool* (1975); Roger Earl and Terry LeGrand's leather-cherry popper *Born to Raise Hell* (1972); Peter Berlin's auto-portrait *Nights in Black Leather* (1973); the uncredited fisting classic *Erotic Hands* (c. 1975); and Michael Zen's leather-occult *Falconhead* (1976) usually double-billed with C. Michael McCullough's gorgeously sleazy, smokey, and primitivist *Tattoo* (1975).

Beginning with the first issue, *Drummer* was always illustrated with movie stills: *Sextool* photos appeared inside *Drummer* 1 (June 1975), and on the front and back covers of *Drummer* 2 (October 1975); *Born to Raise Hell* on the front cover of *Drummer* 3 (October 1975); and full-page ads for *Falconhead* inside the front cover of *Drummer* 7 (June 1976), and for *Kansas City Trucking Co.* inside the front cover of *Drummer* 11 (December 1976). Publicity stills from mainstream features such as *Mandingo*,

Deliverance, and *Salo* appeared repeatedly. In the 1980s and 1990s, photographs of men I lensed for Palm Drive Video, such as Keith Ardent, Larry Perry, and Donnie Russo, appeared on the covers of *Drummer* 118 (July 1988), *Drummer* 140 (June 1990), *Drummer* 159 (December 1992), and *Drummer* 170 (December 1993). A further supply of film stills to *Drummer* happened in 1989 when Mark Hemry and I shot six films in Europe for Roger Earl and Terry LeGrand, the helmers of *Born to Raise Hell*. *Drummer*'s love affair with film embraced also the Super-8 films and video features of David Hurles and his Old Reliable studio. For details of film and video photos in *Drummer*, search the "Timeline Bibliography" of *Gay San Francisco: Eyewitness Drummer*.

From its first issue wherein "Sidney Charles" reviewed *Sextool*, *Drummer* included film reviews written regularly by Ed Franklin aka Ed Menerth aka Scott Masters. *Sextool*, forbidden by the LAPD, premiered simultaneously in San Francisco at the fratricidal Mitchell Brothers' O'Farrell Theater and in New York at the Lincoln Art Theater on June 4, 1975, three weeks before the first issue of *Drummer*. Eschewing straight theaters, the Gage Brothers booked their films into San Francisco at the Nob Hill Theater where their friend Wakefield Poole directed the legendary stage show for the Colt model Roger in 1977.

Because readers responded to film coverage, I added op-ed cinema features such as "Pasolini's *Salo*" in *Drummer* 20 (January 1978), and my interview with *Boys in the Sand* film director Wakefield Poole, "Dirty Poole," in *Drummer* 27 (February 1979), and made humor with movie stills in "Steve Reeves' Screen Test" in *Drummer* 19 (December 1977) and "Nobody Fucks Lex Barker Anymore" in *Drummer* 26 (June 1979).

When Ed Franklin wrote me that he was quitting reviewing movies because publisher Embry fell in arrears paying him, I turned to reviewing significant films such as Derek Jarman's *Sebastiane* in *Drummer* 22 (May 1978) and the homomasculine *The Deer Hunter* in *Drummer* 28 (April 1979). Covering films was natural to me because I had been reviewing movies since 1953, and my love of film led into my 1960s career as director of a museum film program and as a university professor in the 1960s and 1970s teaching courses such as "History and Esthetics of Cinema" and "Women in Film." I assigned other movie reviews to my protégé, John Trojanski, a former Catholic seminarian whose photographs appeared in *Drummer* 25 (December 1978) and other issues. Had I still been teaching when the Gage Brothers debuted, I would have invited them to speak in my classes and at my museum film program where during the 1960s and 70s I screened gay underground films and hosted filmmakers from the National Film Board of Canada.

Drummer 19: El Paso Wrecking Corp.

(*When Sex Meets Art*: In a taxi leaving the New York Eagle or, maybe, the Spike at 3 AM in 1973, my new best friend who was taking me back to ball at his apartment introduced himself as "John Boundy, the U. S. manager of bookings for the National Film Board of Canada," and I introduced myself as the professor-director who needed to fill my museum and campus film programs.)

In the zero degrees of separation in gay culture, Fred Halsted starred in *El Paso Wrecking Corp.*, and he was also a regular *Drummer* columnist published in this same *Drummer* 19, page 24. This was my first credited issue as editor in chief, and I believed everything was possible. I wanted to mix all these great guys and these great talents together in the salon around *Drummer*. In my brief paragraph accompanying the nine *El Paso Wrecking Corp.* photographs, I promised to interview the Gage Brothers for an upcoming *Drummer*. In the zero degrees, that opportunity never rose so that we could converge.

Nevertheless, Wakefield Poole made certain that Mark Hemry and I connected with Georgina Spelvin who was the star of Poole's *The Bible* (1974), of the Gages' *El Paso Wrecking Corp.*, and of the blockbuster porn hit by Gerard Damiano, *The Devil in Miss Jones* (1973). (I featured one of Wakefield Poole's Fellini-like color production stills from *The Bible* on the cover of *Drummer* 27, February 1979.) Fresh from exiting *Drummer* as editor in chief, in 1980, and with Mark Hemry carrying the cameras and the single red rose that warmed her heart, I interviewed the very bright and funny Georgina Spelvin on a bed in a pretty Sausalito motel for my feature article "The Devil in Ms. Spelvin" published in *Hooker* magazine (May 1981).

Having withdrawn from the warfare inside *Drummer*, and bruised by publisher Embry's cancerous Blacklist of disgruntled contributors, I kept my writing moving forward—not in *Drummer*, but in the "Virtual *Drummer*" of other 1980s magazines *Honcho, Man2Man, California Action Guide, In Touch, Uncut, Just Men, The Target Album, Dan Lurie's Muscle Training Illustrated, Skin*, and *Bear*, as well as in the straight *Hooker, Expose*, and *California Pleasure Guide* which published my fiction and features that could have been in the *Drummer*stream.

Editor's Final Note and Film List

Scripts such as the following were frequently published in *Drummer*: George Birimisa's *Pogey Bait* serialized in *Drummer* 12 (January 1977) and *Drummer* 13 (March 1977); Jack Fritscher's *Corporal in Charge of Taking Care of Captain O'Malley* serialized in *Drummer* 22 (May 1978) and *Drummer* 23 (July 1978); Jack Fritscher and Old Reliable David Hurles' one-man show *Ex-Cons: We Abuse Fags*, serialized in *Drummer* 24 (September 1978) and *Drummer* 25 (December 1978).

Fritscher recalled, "In 1980, I co-wrote the script with filmmaker J. Brian for his vanilla porn film *J. Brian's Flashbacks*. Having fallen out with *Drummer* publisher Embry who had started his *Mach* magazine to steal thunder from his competitor *Honcho* magazine, I couldn't resist selling my novelization of the J. Brian film to *Honcho* where the six chapters were serialized as twin bills in three issues." Perhaps one future day a new young Kenneth Anger will come along and shoot several reels of film based on scripts published in *Drummer*.

II. The feature essay as published in *Drummer* 19, December 1977

Drummer Previews the Flicks
Richard Locke packs meat for Gage Brothers...

El Paso Wrecking Corp.

Drummer presents an exclusive peek into what promises to be another hot, new film from director Joe Gage and producer Sam Gage, the brothers who excited us all last year with their *Kansas City Trucking Co. KCTC* was made with a professionalism generally lacking in gay male porn. We don't know yet the story line. But we do know the stars include: Fred Halsted; Richard Locke; and our *Drummer* 19 cover man Steve King [*sic*], with Jeanne Marie Marchand, Stan Braddock, Mike Morris, Jared Benson, and a hot new discovery Guillermo Riccardo. *Drummer* will feature an interview with the Gage Brothers and their dedication to the upgrading of male films in an upcoming issue.

III. Eyewitness Illustrations

New York artist Domino, profiled in *Drummer* 29 by Fritscher and Shapiro, idealized San Francisco erotic celebrity Richard Locke, star of *El Paso Wrecking Corp.* The cover of *Drummer* 19 was a still of actor Mike Morris from the same Gage Brothers film. Drawing by Domino. ©Domino. Used with permission. In 1988, Jack Fritscher directed and photographed the feature film, *The Domino Video Gallery*, produced and edited for Palm Drive Video by Mark Hemry.

Steve Reeves' Screen Test

> Written September 22-24, 1977, by Jack Fritscher with additional line-item material by Al Shapiro (A. Jay) and John Embry (Robert Payne), this feature essay was published in *Drummer* 19, December 1977.
> I. Author's Eyewitness Historical-Context Introduction written December 11, 2000
> II. The feature essay as published in *Drummer* 19, December 1977
> III. Eyewitness Illustrations

I. Author's Eyewitness Historical-Context Introduction written December 11, 2000

Gladiator Muscles and Beard:
Constructing the Subtext "Look" of Drummer

Steve Reeves (1926-2000)
Drummer Publisher John Embry (b. 1926)

In the "School of Camp," publisher John Embry seemed a graduate student who had studied and taken his orals in the best cocktail bars in LA during the 1950s.

He knew how to cut to the chaise longue.

He never saw a photo layout that did not need cartoon balloons. In fact, because he was such a fan of the camp cartoon strips, such as *Harry Chess*, in the 1960s *Queen's Quarterly* (*QQ*), he hired the author of that strip, A. Jay (Al Shapiro) to be the founding San Francisco art director of *Drummer*. In the Great Gay Migration, we were all three sex-immigrants to San Francisco: Shapiro (in 1974) whom I knew from Manhattan; Embry (in 1975) whom I had just met from Los Angeles; and myself, visiting as often as possible since August 1961, and arriving officially in May 1970.

We were the three-way that transformed LA *Drummer* into San Francisco *Drummer*.

For details of our salad days together, see my A. Jay obituary, "The Passing of One of *Drummer*'s First Daddies," in *Drummer* 107 (August 1987).

In this last issue of the "Teen-Age *Drummer*," *Drummer* 19, Steve Reeves caused Embry and me to debate whether *camp* and *eros* can exist together; actually, we were in truth arm-wrestling about the identity of *Drummer*. Was the mag merely a *QQ* clone in leather drag as Embry portrayed it with his Cycle Sluts gender-bender drag cover of *Drummer* 9, or was it to be serious male erotic entertainment readers could jerk off to while still getting the "*Drummer* Philosophy" modeled on Hugh Hefner's *Playboy*. (Notice the Hefner-style of three photos of the interviewee at the bottom of the first page in interviews with Richard Locke, *Drummer* 24, and Wakefield Poole, *Drummer* 27.) The little tempest over camp was one of many of our creative differences.

At that beginning, none of us gents wanted to be a spoilsport; so we three had a fun time tossing around captions satirizing Hollywood, because the pop culture of movies was always a huge part of *Drummer*.

Citing that most of the publicity photos were from my personal collection, I made one request: that the jokes be printed as text under the photographs, where true fans and mastubators could ignore them, and not, as Embry's dreaded cartoon balloons, be pasted on the pictures or over Steve Reeves's body. I felt a responsibility toward Steve Reeves. In 1959, I came out on his *Hercules*; I went in "straight" and came out "homomasculine." I found out about "gayism" only later.

It was in this pictorial feature that I first printed one of my many satirical names for Arnold Schwarzenegger whom I have always scorned, not for being 260 pounds of ham in a two-ounce nylon posing brief, but for being unforgivably not hot. Arnold was 180-degrees of separation from Steve Reeves who was the bearded muscle god of my nocturnal emissions. He was to me what heroic Catholic martyr-saints and Catholic priests should look like. In the secret subtext of Joe Weider's muscle magazines of my perfervid 1950s, Steve Reeves defined the homomasculine Platonic Ideal.

Steve Reeves was thirteen years old when I was born and I don't really remember his first movie appearance in Ed Woods' rock-n-roll teen-movie *Jailbait* (1954) which I most likely saw in some double-feature; but that same summer when I was fifteen, he rocked my world on the big screen when I went to see the MGM musical *Athena* (1954) and watched the unsinkable Debbie Reynolds upstaged by the luminous screen heat of Steve Reeves.

Five years later, I was twenty years old and hot to trot when producer Joseph E. Levine released the widescreen Italian movie *Hercules* (1959).

Steve Reeves shot to international stardom, and I shot all over the balcony seats. That summer, the overgrown boy, Schwarzenegger, posing in a mirror in Austria, was nearly thirteen years old with visions of what dancing in his head?

Hercules imprinted me forever with the erotic metaphor of muscle. That day I began my search for the perfect body. I was a Platonist raised by two Platonist parents; and that day my mind and my dick knew instantly that the noble ideal of an uncompromised man was possible. I didn't really know what homosexuality was. So in memory I wonder if I looked like a silly young fairy, standing on my tongue in the lobby of the Madison Theater in Peoria, bargaining with the manager to sell me one or two publicity photos of Steve Reeves. "It's illegal to sell them," he said, "but if you never say where you got them, I'll give them to you for ten cents each." I countered with an offer he couldn't refuse, and afterwards he who was an old man of twenty-eight gave me the photos in gratitude.

Steve Reeves grew up in Oakland and in San Francisco where he built his legs bicycling up the hills. He was a natural beauty with a sweet personality. Schwarzenetc, whom I met in 1971 at the Muscle Beach iron pit in Venice, was not, never was, never will be. "Vy are you taking my picture?" Arnold scowled. "I'm not taking your picture," I said, "I'm shooting him. [Ken Waller]." Waller was a strawberry blond hunk, freckled, affable, and my type.

"You must ask," Arnold said, "to take my picture."

"I didn't take your picture. In fact, you got in the way of the picture I was taking."

"Fag," he muttered.

"Kraut," I muttered.

(We are both of Austrian extraction.)

As he turned his back to me, I snapped my camera again just to piss him off.

I walked away with four color transparencies of the incident. My camera is my eyewitness.

Arnold was, to my eye, Exhibit A of why steroids as a concern entered my 1970s journals of Folsom and Castro which turned into the steroid-rage-driven plot of *Some Dance to Remember*. All these crystal-meth generations later, many queer historians do not realize that steroids—not coke or speed—were the most abused drug in 1970s gay culture. Ironically, steroids became for some a therapy to treat symptoms of AIDS, and the hard, basketball belly became an emblem of AIDS culture in the bear community.

Anyway, the harmonious three-way of Embry-Shapiro-Fritscher was interrupted when John Embry grew suddenly and then increasingly ill.

While the declining John Embry pasted his dialog balloons on every photo in sight, and while I wanted the graphics to speak for themselves, the extremely patient and diplomatic Al Shapiro spent much of his time pasting down balloons John Embry told him to put back after I had told Al to peel them off.

Actually, in these early San Francisco issues (18, 19, and 20) before John Embry became so seriously ill that he had to be absent from *Drummer* for several months, we three had strained but rather good times.

I was no stranger to long-term illness; I had become editor less than a year after my own father died from a terrible twelve-year ordeal during which he had twenty-two surgeries and was frequently in ICU — one time for over six months. So my empathy, sympathy, and my life experience was there for John Embry when he was struck with what we all were told at that time was colon cancer.

Al and I, left to our own devices, went to bat to make the new kid in town, *Drummer*, into a success.

After a regimen of many months, including surgery, treatment, and recovery, by the time John Embry had returned to relative health and to *Drummer*, the magazine in his absence had become a new kind of hit (no one had seen anything like it before), and his mood toward Al Shapiro and me in the *Drummer* office changed dramatically. Was he depressed? Was he jealous? He seemed disgruntled. We had not hijacked *Drummer*; we had simply plugged it into the times.

Who can read anyone else's mind, but, in my opinion, Al and I — plus catastrophic illness — inadvertently made Embry feel his age smack dab in the middle of the revolutionary 1960s-1970s American Youth Culture intensified by gay culture's fetish of youth. Born in 1926 — the same year as Steve Reeves, Embry was a generation older than all of us. He had certainly been formed during a different gay time in a different pre-gay age. His persona seemed more of the "Johnny Ray 1950s" than the "acid-rock 1960s" and he seemed not attuned to the emerging post-Stonewall macho of 1970s leather culture that turned *Drummer* into a hyper-masculine world full of bizarre new sex trips. The most leather I ever saw John Embry wear was a black leather vest — oh, and one of those de rigueur Muir leather caps from Canada. We all wore that hat in homage to Brando in *The Wild One*. I especially prized as fetish wear my 1950s, pre-Muir, biker cap made of black cloth with a shiny white plastique brim given to me in 1969 by the Catholic leather priest, Jim Kane, who also gave me an authentic swastika pin, large as a brooch or medal, but I could never justify wearing it, even as a fetish item, on the front of the cap where he pinned it.

Drummer 19: Steve Reeves' Screen Test 417

Summary: In LA, *Drummer* had been strangely conceived by eros out of politics. *Drummer* 9 camped up a virtually "suicidal" drag cover that had readers threatening to cancel subscriptions. And 1) when *Drummer* was ten months old, the publisher and editor in chief got busted by the LAPD for hosting a "Slave Auction." At that point, the infant *Drummer* imploded, and nearly died. Then 2), the publisher became at least a bit distracted from editorial production by the lawyering and by his court appearances stemming from his LA arrest as well as from his culture-altering move of *Drummer* from LA to San Francisco that changed the *Drummer* staff, the talent pool, and the demographic. Finally, 3), the publisher seemed rather withdrawn because of what turned out to be the worrying onset of cancer in 1978, and unavailable during his Spring 1979 cancer surgery and recuperation when he turned over production of the magazine to art director Al Shapiro and editor in chief Jack Fritscher.

My mission was to keep "camp" out of *Drummer*—which didn't work in these "Steve Reeves" captions referencing the pop culture of the cruising novel *Looking for Mr. Goodbar*, the musical *A Chorus Line*, and television commercials for Charmin Toilet Tissue: "Please, don't squeeze the Charmin!" I added the sexual slam against comedian Richard Pryor (who was from my hometown) because Pryor had in 1977 ranted against queers and fags during his performance with Lily Tomlin at the Hollywood Bowl: "You Hollywood faggots can kiss my happy, rich black ass." The slap against John Briggs was included because he was the California legislator who began the anti-gay "Briggs Initiative" (Proposition 6, 1978) that cost the gay community so much in time and money to defeat so that gays could continue to teach in public schools. Briggs was the West Coast pal of cuntry-western singer Anita Bryant in Dade County, Florida.

In San Francisco, *Drummer* had to change its essence in order to reflect the readers. (Note my inclusion of the East Coast code for wearing chains on the "left" or "right" versus the West Coast code.)

Here was the theorem I concocted: *Drummer* got its identity from the identity of the readers and then reflected their identity back to them.

I had grown up in a family of priests and sales people. My father was a champion salesman; my mother worked in marketing. As a teenager, I sold Hoover vacuum cleaners door to door, learning empathy for shut-ins and how to deal with the human condition in the privacy of lonely people's homes. I was a teenage seminarian from age fourteen to twenty-four. I was like a visiting priest, but, more, I was a visiting writer. I learned how to turn those depressing death-of-a-teenage-salesman encounters into writing for Catholic magazines. I learned how to make the stories and features reflect the reality I saw behind closed doors as well as the beliefs and identities of the readers.

With Embry missing in action, and with Al so cooperative, I took my whip and began driving *Drummer* with all the talented contributors I could find. The "Letters to the Editor" changed, and circulation rose to 42,000—its highest point then or since.

This "Steve Reeves" feature is, queer historians may note, listed at the "Unofficial Steve Reeves' Page" at geocities.com which lists "Fritscher, Jack, 'Steve Reeves' Screentest," *Drummer* 19 (December 1977) and reviews it as "a parody of a typical Steve Reeves movie with captioned stills. Kind of mean, but really funny!"

So, maybe John Embry was right!

Humor and *eros* can co-exist.

Not.

Nobody ever jerked off to a joke.

Nobody ever came to camp.

On my book shelf is a privately produced book, *Worlds to Conquer: An Authorized Biography of Steve Reeves* (1999) by Chris LeClaire, 190 photos, many previously unpublished; 256 pages, Chris LeClaire Publishing, PO Box 116, South Chatham MA 02659, $29.95.

I wrote the single paragraph introducing the photo feature and co-wrote, and then edited, the one-liner photo captions from the three of us.

Finally, in the zero degrees of separation, I connected the dots from Steve Reeves to the world heavy-weight champion boxer, Primo Carnera, who co-starred in *Hercules Unchained* (1959). In 1989, when it was time to pick the cover of the first edition of *Some Dance to Remember: A Memoir-Novel of San Francisco 1970-1982*, I insisted that publisher Knights Press print a George Mott photograph of the Art Deco statue of Primo Carnera commissioned by Mussolini in the 1930s for the 1944 Olympic Games planned for his Foro Italico in Rome. When Knights Press suddenly declared bankruptcy, I so respected Mott as a fellow artist that I personally paid him the fee Knights Press owed him for the use of his intellectual property. Because people judge a book by its cover, Mott's photo helped make *Some Dance to Remember* both popular and controversial. In 2003, thirteen years after Mott's photograph appeared on *Some Dance to Remember* (1990), his book, *Foro Italico: Photographs by George Mott*, was published by Powerhouse Books, New York, with introductory essays by Giorgio Armani, Michelangelo Sabatino, and Luigi Ballerini.

Editor's Note: This feature is early documentation of Fritscher's long-standing satirizing of Schwarzenegger. Visit a search engine such as Google for "Schwarzenegger + Mapplethorpe + Fritscher" to read about the political eBay censorship scandal as reported by the Associated Press, October 5, 2003. —Mark Hemry

II. The feature essay as published in *Drummer* 19, December 1977

A Photo-Spread of the Movies' Most Handsome Muscle Man...

Steve Reeves' Screen Test

It is no secret that the dialogue for most Italian-produced muscle epics is put in later and the voices belong to actors other than those on the screen. Many have wondered what the voice of mighty Steve Reeves really sounds like. That, we can't bring you. But we can fill you in on what was *really* being said in some of these Reeves' *pas de deux* from the muscle-musical *Barbell Romance*, an Arnold Schwarzeneanderthal film in Steroidoscope. Photos courtesy of Alan Tuck. Dialogue by Jack Fritscher, Robert Payne, and the hangers-on around the art room [A. Jay], who would be most happy to give Mr. Reeves equal time, should he care to come around.

"Okay, Steve. You can breathe out now. Steve...Steve?"

"Let's see. For an S, it's chains on the right. Or is it left? Or is it left for Top on the West Coast and right for the Top in New York? Or is it in the middle for the Midwest?"

"I swear I'll never again squeeze the Charmin."

"Tits and ass won't get you jobs—unless they're yours."

"Get down, sweathog, and lick my pits."

"Alright, who threw that pie?"

"What do you guys mean the scene isn't over? I distinctly heard the director yell, 'Cut.'"

"What the fuck you mean you gave my name at the clinic?"

"Are you positive this is how Nureyev auditioned for *Valentino*?"

"Steve stretches between two horses' asses. Co-starring as the gelding on the left is Richard Pryor. The mare on the right is Rep. John Briggs."

"I told you to fuck off. I'm looking for Mr. Goodbar."

"When something's over, whatever happened to shaking hands and saying goodbye?"

"Steve [swinging a huge chain above his head] warms up for one of singer Anita Bryant's greatest hits...."

III. Eyewitness Illustrations

Steve Reeves, Mr. Pacific Coast (1946), Mr. Western America (1947), Mr. America AAU (1947), Mr. World (1948), Mr. Universe (1950). Steve Reeves, raised in San Francisco, set the 1940s-1950s standard for heroic American manhood. Tim Curry as Dr. Frank-N-Furter opens *The Rocky Horror Picture Show* singing, "We could take in an old Steve Reeves movie." He was born in 1926, the same year as *Drummer* founding publisher John Embry. Publicity photo.

Steve Reeves's gladiator movies inspired Steven Saylor (Aaron Travis), author of *Slaves of the Empire* and his ongoing series *Roma Sub Rosa*. Having been an early AIDS-Era 1980s fiction editor at *Drummer* under publisher John Embry, Saylor wrote a line consonant with editor in chief Jack Fritscher's Titanic 1970s experience. Working at *Drummer* was "mind-boggling and mind-numbing—we were underpaid, disrespected and overstimulated on a daily basis...."—*Steam*, Vol. 2 #1 (1994).

Reeves represented the epitome of virile nobility and homomasculinity to teenage boys in the 1950s who grew up to be subscribers to *Drummer* magazine in the 1970s where they wanted to see variations on the kind of masculinity that was their spring awakening. Reeves' beard, quoted on various faces of 1960s Colt models such as Ledermeister, greatly influenced the beards, moustaches, and sideburns that graced gay faces in the 1970s, and led to the glorification of male secondary sex characteristics (facial and body hair, musculature, deep voice) within the bear movement organized by Richard Bulger in the 1980s.

"Why should you be on the cover of *Some Dance to Remember*?"

Top: Publicity photo. In *Hercules Unchained* (1960), Steve Reeves wrestled with longtime international sensation, world-heavyweight boxing champion Primo Carnera, the Italian athlete sculpted in the 1930s into an heroic statue for Mussolini's Foro Italico stadium in Rome. As thematic warning against the tyranny of "body fascism" in gay culture, Fritscher insured that a photograph of the Fascist statue of Carnera by New York photographer George Mott appeared on the cover of the first edition of *Some Dance to Remember: A Memoir-Novel of San Francisco 1970-1982*. On page 195 of the 2005 edition, the oracular Solly Blue says: "Gays and Fascists. Both consider themselves the ultimate elite. Don't forget that." Bottom: Publicity photo of Steve Reeves published as the cover of *Physique Pictorial*, Summer 1959.

Star Trick
Artist Dom Orejudos Is Etienne!

> Written September-October 1977, this editorial promotion essay was published in *Drummer* 19, December 1977.
> I. Author's Eyewitness Historical-Context Introduction written February 16, 2002
> II. The editorial promotion essay as published in *Drummer* 19, December 1977
> III. Eyewitness Illustrations

I. Author's Eyewitness Historical-Context Introduction written February 16, 2002

Dom Orejudos, Sam Steward, and Chicago DNA in *Drummer*

Written and produced October 1977 for my pal, Chicago artist Domingo Stephen Orejudos, and for my longtime friend and sexmate, Lou Thomas of Target Studio, who was announcing his publication of *Star Trick*, the new Target book of drawings by Dom-Etienne-Stephen Orejudos.

This editorial essay amounted to "advertising" in *Drummer* 19 (December 1977). Synergistically, I also planted it to promote the upcoming "Etienne and A. Jay - Joint Exhibition" at Robert Opel's Fey-Way Gallery, May 27 - June 9, 1978, San Francisco.

For that show, Opel commissioned two single drawings to be created for the Fey-Way invitation. It was a genius union. Chicago's Etienne drew one side of the pictures and San Francisco's A. Jay drew the other.

Within our growing salon of in-laws and outlaws, Lou Thomas also published my writing including my 1969 novel *I Am Curious (Leather)* in a limited private edition (1972).

This eyewitness-participant introduction to *Star Trick* is an example of the inclusive ways I worked to connect *Drummer* in San Francisco to leather culture in Chicago. Jeanne Barney had featured "The Etienne Portfolio" sold by Target Studio in the centerfold of *Drummer* 10 (November 1976).

As a favor within our *Drummer* fraternity, I wrote this little essay to accompany four pages of the cartoon narrative, *Star Trick*, by Dom

Orejudos with a photograph (page 74) of artist Orejudos lying in front of one of the large murals he painted for the Gold Coast Bar which he and Chuck Renslow, his partner from 1950-1991, had founded in 1958. By means of having their traveling "personal leather salon" spontaneously congregate at various Chicago bars, Renslow and Orejudos invented the first distinctly leather bar *during the first five years* after Marlon Brando brought leather biker culture out of the closet in *The Wild One* (1953).

Born in 1933, Dom Orejudos was seventeen in 1950 when the twenty-one-year-old Chuck Renslow spotted the muscular teenager on the sand crescent that is the Oak Street Beach, a block north of the Drake Hotel and the Miracle Mile. The man who would be their significant mentor, Samuel Steward, was forty-one, and living in Chicago since 1936.

All this Chicago leather action occurred during the 1950s-1960s beat-hippie-gay-leather revival on the Near North Side of Rush Street and Old Town. Doing research at the Newberry Library in the early 1960s, I often stared out the windows down into the trees and bushes and pathways of Bughouse Square to watch the hustlers signaling the johns cruising around the block in cars. It was while he was hustling there that the teenage David Sparrow — three years before he became my lover — was hired by Renslow and Orejudos as a back-bar bottle boy for the Gold Coast.

Dom was twenty when he gayed up his middle name to the French "Etienne" for the publication of his first art work in *Tomorrow's Man* #8 (1953) published by Irv Johnson who ran the gym that Renslow and Orejudos would buy in 1958.

As a matter of fact, I grew up on Renslow-Orejudos' homomasculine tastes. When I was a closeted teenager, *Tomorrow's Man* was my favorite guilty-pleasure magazine. I was so imprinted and impressed that in 1965 I mentioned *Tomorrow's Man* specifically in my first novel *What They Did to the Kid* (1965 and 2001), page 112. (Much of *Kid* takes place in Chicago; *Kid* is the prequel to my memoir-novel *Some Dance to Remember* which is the story of the main character in *Kid* moving from Chicago to San Francisco where he becomes editor of a magazine very like *Drummer*.) Beginning at age fourteen, my personal erotic maturation in homomasculinity was zero degrees of separation from Renslow's models and Orejudos' art direction. I understood that *Tomorrow's Man* was an occasion of mortal sins against purity — as I confessed to priests — because it tempted me to masturbation, but I could not stop looking. I did not know then that Dom (1933-1991) was only six years older than I and Renslow (born 1929) only ten years older. People ten years senior to or younger than a person are that person's generation.

Latin Leather Pioneers

The quintessential presence of the Latin artist Domingo Orejudos as one of the central action figures creating leather culture, and as a universally beloved person as well, indicates the ethnic diversity at the formative core of our inclusive leather culture. In San Francisco, Mario Simon, the longtime partner of founding *Drummer* publisher John Embry, was an immigrant from Spain who became associate publisher of *Drummer*. In October 1979 when *Drummer* art director Al Shapiro (a very close friend of Etienne) and Embry and I picked the first Mr. *Drummer*, we chose the Brazilian immigrant Val Martin (Vallot Martinelli) who appeared dozens of times on the cover and in the pages of *Drummer* as well as in films by Fred Halsted. In face, physique, and sweet temperament, if Dom Orejudos had been separated at birth, his twin would have been my longtime intimate, Tony Tavarossi, who was legendary in San Francisco leather the way Dom was in Chicago leather.

For more on race and ethnicity in *Drummer* and leather culture, see *The Drummer Salon* in this *Gay San Francisco: Eyewitness* series, and my erotic biography *Mapplethorpe: Assault with a Deadly Camera* (1994).

Having come out in Chicago in the early 1960s, I became personally familiar with the Renslow-Orejudos leather family. Everyone drooled over their Triumph Gym, was imprinted by their photography at Kris Studio (1950-1979), and cruised through their bar businesses like the Gold Coast and the Man's Country Baths. I played in the heady and "outlaw" leather culture spun out of the Black Castle where they lived. When I moved to San Francisco, I took many Chicago leather values and ideas, and years later folded them into my version of *Drummer*. I also "married into the Renslow clan" when on July 6, 1969, I met the Gold Coast bartender David Sparrow who quit to become my domestic lover for ten years (1969-1979). With our Chicago values, we moved permanently to San Francisco and photographed many covers and centerfolds as a duo shooting for *Drummer* during the issues I edited from March 1977 to December 31, 1979 (*Drummer* 18 - *Drummer* 33).

This thin slip of an article on *Star Trick* occasions this introduction of its surrounding history that emphasizes that gay life exists at six—maybe three, maybe zero—degrees of separation.

It also demonstrates the roots of *Drummer,* and how everything that rose within leather culture converged to make *Drummer* possible. *Drummer* did not spring full-blown from the head of John Embry, Jeanne Barney, or me. Without Chicago's on-going leather heritage, *Drummer* would not have been invented in LA and perfected in San Francisco.

Blaine Cunningham, my travel partner in Europe in the wild spring of 1969, introduced me to Dom Orejudos during a concert at the Lincoln Park band shell, July 4, 1969. The bunch of us were picnicking in a leather group together, and Dom and I laid in the grass sharing a joint, surrounded by John Philip Souza and fireworks and shirtless men in leather vests, beginning an acquaintance that lasted until his death; we were both judges for Mr. *Drummer,* and before his final illness we were in correspondence about my directing and shooting an *Etienne Video Gallery* in the style of the other video galleries I had created for Dom's peers: Rex, the Hun, A. Jay, Domino, and Skipper.

In a zero-degrees letter from Boulder, Colorado, October 12, 1988, Dom "Etienne" Orejudos expressed his interest in my translating his drawings from page to screen:

> Hi Jack:...Yes, let's follow through on discussing the possibility of an Etienne video gallery by you at Palm Drive. I've had some ideas in that area (video) for some time now, and I'm sure we could come up with something interesting. I enjoyed visiting with you during the Mr. *Drummer* Contest weekend [We were both judges]...I'll look forward to seeing you again....
> Sincerely, Dom
> Used with permission of Chuck Renslow and the Leather Archives &Museum.

His last thirty-six months of illness kept Dom from going forward with our project. Without his own video gallery, and before the public had access to the Internet, he died September 24, 1991, with our video feature unfinished. During the sad time of his oncoming death, Renslow, his partner of forty years, was inspired to create—with *Drummer* publisher Anthony DeBlase—the Leather Archives and Museum of Chicago which was founded in 1991 to preserve the artwork of Etienne and then by extension other artists and artifacts of leather heritage. Seven years earlier in Los Angeles, the nonprofit Tom of Finland Foundation had been created in 1984 with its own mission to preserve the homomasculine artwork of Tom of Finland and other gay artists.

In the way that Renslow-Orejudos ran a salon of artists and bohemian leathermen out of the Gold Coast in the 1950s, and in homage to their style (in which Dom would later introduce Durk Dehner to Tom of Finland in 1979), I figured it made sense for me in 1977 to follow their model and create a salon around *Drummer* because a magazine requires many talented people — and an erotic magazine requires a salon of even more specifically talented people, all having tons of sex (often with each other). It was, in fact, former Renslow-Orejudos family member Sam Steward who first used the word *salon* to describe the team of friends and pals I pulled together around *Drummer* in the 1970s.

I made sure there was less than one degree of separation between Chicago leather and San Francisco leather in *Drummer*. Dom appreciated my fidelity to my Chicago leather roots. He was an enterprising businessman who saw publication of his drawings in *Drummer* as free international advertising for the Renslow-Orejudos Chicago enterprises that had worldwide consumer appeal. Wally Wallace, the founder of the Mineshaft in New York, wrote in the *Mineshaft Newsletter* that he felt the same way about my coverage hymning the Mineshaft to leather tourists from around the globe in *Drummer* 18 (December 1977).

When I took over the reins of *Drummer*, I did not know that my allegiance to Chicago leather, which was so formative to my personal coming out, would be questioned by publisher John Embry. He wanted to compete with Renslow and Orejudos who had invented their International Mr. Leather contest from their experience running sanctioned AAU physique contests in venues like the Lawson YMCA.

Chicago: The Lawson YMCA

I feel compelled to make this eyewitness *tableau vivant* aside: The Lawson YMCA was a block from where I lived at 60 East Chicago Street at the foot of Rush Street and not far from the cruise-y Oak Street Beach. I had rooms above a socialist bookstore that was bombed one afternoon in 1964 while I was writing *What They Did to the Kid*. (Luckily, it was a small bomb.) In the 1960s, when I was in my twenties, the Lawson YMCA was a sperm-o-rama orgy party from the roof sundeck down through the rooms and toilets, down through the stairwells where I had to step over writhing bodies, down to the showers and the pool. This was the Chicago scene in which Renslow and Orejudos flourished — years before Stonewall.

Meanwhile, back at *Drummer*, I watched Embry grow green with envy (in my opinion) over the new idea of IML. He immediately ordered me to begin a Mr. *Drummer* contest. (I refused.) That arm-wrestle is detailed in *Gay San Francisco: The Drummer Salon*.

It was in my *Drummer* 31 (September 1979) that I wrote the first national and international coverage of the first IML in order to salute and support Renslow, Orejudos, Chicago, and IML.

My review was reprinted by leather scholar Joseph W. Bean in his history of IML, *International Mr. Leather: 25 Years of Champions* (2004) published by the Chicago Leather Archives and Museum.

In fraternity in *Drummer*, I promoted Dom-Etienne, who was already a legend as a bodybuilder and dancer and artist from the 1950s, because I wanted the DNA I was injecting into *Drummer* to show off its gay leather roots out of the heartland in Chicago.

Some people—who don't know we suspect they're playing "Where's Waldo?"—say they got stoned at Woodstock in 1969, and thousands claim they were in the Stonewall Bar which must have been as crowded as the Black Hole of Calcutta. In the 1960s, I was carried out of Mayor Daley's office during a civil rights demonstration while working with The Woodlawn Organization (TWO) in August 1962. I was laid by my first leathermen in Chicago in 1964, and I was beaten up by the Chicago police during the Democratic Convention in August 1968. Wonderfully turned on by the eroticism of it all, I always ran off to the nearby Gold Coast bar for comfort and safety and sex.

Chicago-San Francisco connections were everywhere in my extracurricular *Drummer* life in the 1960s and 1970s. Cliff Raven aka Cliff Ingram, another member of the extended Renslow family, was the artist who tattooed David Sparrow and me in 1969. Raven had taken his name from advice given him by Chicago personality Samuel Steward who had pulled off the double-identity act of being both a university professor at DePaul and a tattoo artist in the Loop—until the university stopped his moonlighting. Sam in his tattoo parlor lusted, as did homomasculinist photographer Renslow and artist Orejudos in their Triumph Gym on Van Buren Street, for the hot young sailors coming into the Loop on leave from the Great Lakes Naval Training Station where the glittering North Shore of Chicago sucked them down from industrial Waukegan.

With his credentials from Gertrude Stein, Sam Steward was the avatar of intellect and esthetics within the Renslow and Orejudos salon. Sam was a kind of Super-Ego to their Ego and Id. He taught Renslow how to tattoo and tutored the tastes of the twenty-year-old Orejudos whom he casually schooled in the homoerotic ballet photography of George Platt-Lynes who was a friend of Stein and Toklas. To them Sam sent a black-

and-white snapshot of himself appearing as an "extra" with the New York City Ballet. (This impressed Orejudos.) Sam was a teacher and a reporter; he was a constant analyst collecting information and statistics about the emerging Chicago gay sex scene, leather culture, and tattooing folkways that he personally reported to Dr. Alfred Kinsey at the nearby Kinsey Institute. In the Titanic 70s, he pumped me to keep him up with every detail of the latest sex fads in San Francisco.

If history wants an illustration of what was the main *idee fixe* stored and replayed on a loop inside Sam Steward's head, I would point to Paul Cadmus' *The Fleet's In*. That infamous painting, as a national American art scandal, pre-dated Mapplethorpe in 1934 when Sam, an impressionable young man of twenty-five, was soaking up the world and had already corresponded for two years with Stein. Sam, tippling on the edge in France with Gertrude's "Lost Generation," had only just met his Stein and Alice B. Toklas in 1937 at Bilignin, a year after he was fired from his college teaching job at State College in Washington for writing the novel *Angels on the Bough* (1936) which echoes E. M. Forster's *Where Angels Fear to Tread* (1905). Sam admired Forster who was thirty years older than Sam and was the author of *A Passage to India* (1924) and of *Maurice* published posthumously in 1971 to the delight of "Samuel Morris Steward" fresh out of his tattoo parlor in Oakland and sitting pretty in his arts-and-crafts cottage at 2016-x Ninth Street in Berkeley.

Sam Steward was an esthete who wrote, sketched, and painted referencing cool classical museum culture warmed with hot-blooded sensuality from the streets. Upper crust and lusting after "les miserables," Sam was magnificently carnal in his hands-on tattooing of the young flesh of muscular rebels without a cause (including the original *Rebel without a Cause*, James Dean whose forearm Sam tattooed with a black panther before that image became racially political). Sam who was the artful dodger "Phil Andros" and "Phil Sparrow" liked his homomasculine tough guys "down and dirty" in real occupations like sailors and cops. Dom who was "Etienne" and "Stephen" liked his homomasculine "chaps in chaps" idealized as irresistible leather tops and cherry-ripe leather bottoms with no more real occupations than Betty Page. Sam *pere* brought every innuendo he had to his tutorial of Dom *fils*. The art historian Justin Spring, author of *Paul Cadmus: The Male Nude* (2002), is writing the forthcoming biography of Sam Steward. He informed me on April 19, 2007, that Sam and Dom occasionally worked together on drawings, and that Dom turned his hand to illustrating Sam's story "The Motorcyclist."

Cadmus' pop-style satire *The Fleet's In* influenced the queer zeitgeist — and ballet dancer Orejudos — when legendary gay choreographer Jerome Robbins and bisexual composer Leonard Bernstein based their ballet *Fancy Free* (1944) on the Cadmus painting. Gay men of that era, including Steward and Renslow and Orejudos, watched the queer evolution of "sequels" as that famous painting became that famous ballet which became the Broadway musical *Fancy Free* (1944) which became the musical-comedy dance film *On the Town* (1949) starring Frank Sinatra, Gene Kelly, and Ann Miller.

With show business in his blood, Dom Orejudos was a classic ballet choreographer and principal dancer with the Illinois Ballet Company. At the same time he was art director for Kris Studio. Lightly guided by Sam, he chose Kris' dramatic, classic, often stage-y themes, designed the Platt-Lynes' Balanchine-meets-Hollywood glamour lighting, and posed the heteromasculine models that the more technical photographer Chuck Renslow artfully lensed.

In the indie-movie narrative of their relationship, whose screenplay I'd like to write in the fashion of Christopher Hampton's *Total Eclipse*, Dom intermittently grew his own identity and absented himself from Renslow and Kris Studio to dance in touring companies of *Song of Norway*, *The King and I*, and *West Side Story*. Leather artist Chuck Arnett was also a chorus boy. He arrived in San Francisco with the touring company of *Bye Bye Birdie* (1960) and never left. He settled into the waterfront gay scene of San Francisco at the foot of Folsom Street, created the Tool Box bar in 1961, three years after the founding of the Gold Coast which he had enjoyed while *Birdie* played Chicago. As the "Leather Lautrec of Folsom Street," Arnett, unlike Orejudos, was listed under "Contributors" on the masthead of *Drummer*. As a muralist, Arnett inspired Orejudos.

In *Gay San Francisco: Eyewitness Drummer*, see my leather-history feature "Artist Chuck Arnett," *Drummer* 134 (October 1989); Arnett was one of the original charter members of the *Drummer* salon.

Because of cross-pollination inside Renslow's Chicago leather salon, I think it reveals something about Orejudos to examine a bit about his senior mentor Sam Steward.

The aristocratic Sam Steward was a different class than Renslow and Orejudos, but they both had more testosterone. Sam, the sage and teacher, had this lyric whimsy that tattooists, at least tattoo artists under his tutelage, should be named after birds. Cliff Raven followed his advice, but Sam's protégé Ed Hardy and others did not convert.

(Sam was immensely amused that *Sparrow* was truly David Sparrow's family name. He found it very "Edna St. Vincent Millay, very 'Passer Mortuus Est.'" *Spero* in Latin means "I hope." Sam wrote a monthly column, 1942-1949, for the *Illinois Dental Journal* using the pen name "Philip Sparrow.")

I think Sam's romantic idea of the role of the tattoo artist inflicting beauty and pain at the same time was reinforced by Tennessee Williams' very popular bird imagery of the 1950s. Savage birds of beauty fly through Tennessee Williams' stories and dramas such as *Sweet Bird of Youth* and *Suddenly Last Summer*. Williams' first play has a title that sounds in fact like a description of a tattoo: *I Rise in Flame Cried the Phoenix*. After Williams penned *The Rose Tattoo* (1951), Sam, who began tattooing in 1952, had a rose tattooed on his own chest. As Gertrude might have claimed, the link of ink may have signified nothing more than "a rose is a rose is a rose." The S&M theme of beauty inflicting pain was the subtext of Kris Studio's photographs and of Etienne's artwork of heroized sadists.

Sam was especially fond of Williams' short story about a stunning young sailor, "One Arm," which he told me that he wished he himself had written. Sam appreciated my writing of the first doctoral dissertation on Tennessee Williams in 1967. He also appreciated that my doctorate was from Chicago's Loyola University where he himself had taught for ten years (1936-1946) before transferring to DePaul University, also in Chicago. In 1964, before we knew each other, we had both met Tennessee Williams, separately, when Williams was in Chicago for the premiere of *Eccentricities of a Nightingale* at the Goodman Theater. On Sam's book shelf, he had an autographed copy of the New Directions anthology called *One Arm* with its final story "The Yellow Bird."

In the helix of art and imagery, Sam made Dom aware that his first short-fiction anthology was *Pan and the Firebird* (1930). Dom himself famously choreographed both *The Firebird* and *Metamorphosis of the Owls*. As the resident literary guru in the Renslow-Orejudos clan, before he fell out with Renslow and Orejudos (they later reconciled) and took off for greener pastures in California (tattooing Sonny Barger and the Hells Angels), Sam Steward also suggested the name for the Renslow drag-show bar "Sparrows." The Renslow-Orejudos Chicago Eagle, like Eagle bars everywhere, is part of this almost universal gay-bird bar imagery whose roots lie somewhere in the mythic rising of the phoenix firebird.

A veteran of the Renslow-Orejudos family and the Stein-Toklas charmed circle, Sam Steward required "salons." When he moved to Berkeley, six years before *Drummer* began, he moved into the 1970s San Francisco leather salon of Jim Kane and Ike Barnes and David Sparrow and me which he remained part of until his death in 1993—even after I exited that group because Kane wanted my Sparrow, and I wasn't a bottom. Individually, Sam and I had much in common in personality and synchronicity. In 1966, again, three years before we met, we had both attended the wild Chicago premiere of Kenneth Anger's *Scorpio Rising* at the Illinois Institute of Technology in the company of Chuck

Renslow, Dom Orejudos, Cliff Raven, Bob Maddox, and a gang from the Gold Coast. In 1969, Sam was introduced to me by my longtime leather partner, the S&M Catholic priest Jim Kane, with whom I toured the American West by Harley-Davidson in June 1969. Kane and I cycled from Denver to Santa Fe and Taos where one night of a thousand stars, tripping, I floated barefoot, in jeans, shirtless in a swimming pool wearing Ken Kesey's brown leather jacket and dreaming of Neal Cassady after whom I lusted.

In 1961, so much had drawn me to San Francisco. That summer of 1969 so much kept drawing me back to Chicago. It gives me a palpable chill to write this, but that "Summer of 69," that summer of Dom Orejudos and David Sparrow, that summer before Stonewall even happened, this erotic leather-salon "incest" signified a brotherhood of homomasculinity. That summer of 1969 focused a very high-energy on sexual liberation in the gay male world. Everything went wild. In Chicago, and other large cities, very "out" elaborate and scheduled orgies happened on the erotic numerology date 6/9/69.

As told, Sam Steward, who had been mild-mannered enough to be an intimate of Gertrude Stein, Alice B. Toklas, James Purdy, Chuck Renslow, and Dom Orejudos, was a university professor teaching English in Chicago when he took up tattooing in 1952 in a parlor under the El tracks around the Loop in order to get his hands on the tough straight guys that for him, and for many gay men, are the *sine qua non* of desire. He told me he learned how to tattoo by practicing on potatoes. Sam Steward was Chicago's Jean Genet. DePaul University, hearing of his "inappropriate activities" at first refused to give him tenure and a raise. In fact, his biographer Justin Spring wrote to me on July 3, 2007, that DePaul decided not renew his contract and told him to resign. Like his friend James Purdy (and I) who quit teaching university because he was underpaid and wanted to write full time, Sam traded the ivory tower of academic sheepskin for the tattoo parlor of death-before-dishonor cheap skin.

Having had a "quarrel" with Renslow, Sam exited Chicago for California in 1967 at the age of fifty-eight. Playing the "old gent" card as if he were seventy-eight, he was the male version on the West Coast of Quentin Crisp playing the female spinster on the East Coast. Drawn to the university ambience of Berkeley, he wisely bought a property with two houses, one of which, he rented to generate income.

In 1974, the first post-Stonewall decade, before the liberated gay world had heard of its forbear Sam Steward, I received a National Endowment for the Humanities (NEH) Grant at UC Berkeley, and a Western Michigan University Research Grant to finish several hours of interview of Sam Steward and his fabulous life that I had begun audio-taping in 1972. He modestly said he was interesting because of his friends like Gertrude and Alice and Kenneth Anger and Etienne, but I thought he was interesting in himself. Sam and Etienne were similarly modest and self-effacing, but they brooked no shit. Frankly, I loved Sam as a friend. In many ways, we were doppelgangers who did not fawn over each other. We were living the same life thirty years apart—him thirty years ahead, with me following in new improved, more liberal times. He thought so too. We both had in common: higher education in Columbus, Ohio; sex and university teaching in Chicago; gay and non-gay writing, S&M, cops, Catholicism, bad boys, *Drummer*, and on and on.

Sam and I appreciated critic Michael Bronski who linked our erotic writing together in his seminal article "S/M: The New Romance" in *Gay Community News* (Boston), Volume 2, Number 30, February 16, 1985. It was too narcissistic for us to have sex. "Take off just your shirt," he'd tease, because neither of us was the other's type. I gave him police patches for his fetish collection to feed his addiction to cops. After I went undercover as a gonzo reporter for *Drummer* in 1989 to role-play with real cops at the famous Academy Training Center, Sam invited me to lunch, and at the steam-table cafeteria he preferred near his home, he milked me for details beyond what I published in *Drummer* 145 (December 1990). His only real-world request to me had been that I not use the information on my tapes until after he was dead, because he said, "I have to live off these stories in my writing and lectures."

On April 23, 1990, Sam, who was a superb memoirist, wrote me a letter about my novel *Some Dance to Remember*:

> My god, what a book!...a real page-turner...beautifully handled crises of the golden age, all gone and lost....I wouldn't be surprised if you have written what will come to be looked on as that period's Great American Gay Novel....you really got me with the ten pages of Ryan's memories [the operative word behind all my writing of gay history] beginning on page 35. What lovely stuff! Thanks...especially for page 19...
>
> ©Estate of Sam Steward administered by Michael Williams. Used with permission.

...on which I mentioned him because I owed him for pioneering the path.

In early 1970, reading Sam Steward's fiction, published in Europe but unknown in the United States, I decided, with this precise verb, to *resurrect* him. (He had no American identity and I thought he should be a gay "brand name" like Etienne, like John Rechy, like Kenneth Anger.

In 1990, smirking, he thanked me for priming the post-1978 stream of "gay groupies," and literary fans like John Preston, who sought to pay him court after his publication in *Drummer*.) I edited him by lightly updating several of his stories which I told him to send to Jeanne Barney who was the editor of *Drummer* in LA in 1975. Because of Sam, his friend James Purdy also sent a story to *Drummer*, but, as Purdy himself told me in 2007, his agent blinked and withdrew the story.

Sam's fiction appeared several times in *Drummer*:

- "Babysitter," illustrated by Chuck Arnett, *Drummer* 5 (March 1976), and
- "Many Happy Returns," illustrated by Arnett, cover created by Sam's Chicago protégé Cliff Raven, *Drummer* 8 (September 1976).
- When I was editor in chief, I published Sam's "In a Pig's Ass," illustrated with photos by Falcon Studio, *Drummer* 21 (March 1978). Attached to Sam's typed manuscript for "A Pig's Ass" was a letter to me dated January 9, 1978. Sam wrote: "Dear Jack...The enclosed Xerox is by Dom Orejudos." He thought Dom's drawing perfect for his story, but that issue needed photos.
- Again, as editor in chief, I published his Catholic short story "Priest: This Is My Body - Hustling in Chicago" in the "Virtual *Drummer*" of *Man2Man Quarterly* #2, December 1980.

In "Priest," the disciplined hedonist Sam Steward wrote the wonderful principle he lived by: "Man should be called to account for all the permitted pleasures he failed during life to enjoy."

For my introduction to the 25th Anniversary Edition of Larry Townsend's *The Leatherman's Handbook* (1997), I wrote an homage:

Chicago leather society, inspired by the Kris standard of masculinity, led the charge of the Leather Liberation Brigade. Renslow's zeitgeist, with photo images and drawings and paintings by Dom Orejudos, was as pivotal to the creation of the American leather archetype as was the fine-art "cartooning" of Tom of Finland who was introduced to the United States by Bob Mizer via his LA-based *Physique Pictorial* magazine in 1957.

Mizer began Athletic Model Guild (AMG) in LA in 1945 and *Physique Pictorial* in LA in 1950. Renslow and Orejudos, having debuted

Kris Studio in Chicago in 1950, published the small-format magazines *Triumph* (one issue in 1960) and *Mars* (1963). *Tomorrow's Man* had rolled out in 1952. Together and separately, Mizer, and Renslow—supported by Orejudos, fought the 1960s laws against posting frontal nudity through the United States mail. They won, and thereby opened the gates for the creation of gay liberation, gay publishing, gay magazines, subscriptions, and gay mail order. Etienne was part of that social action, and he was published widely. Those men were humanists who were essentialists who knew that nudity is one specific element required by homosexual art.

The Leather Mural Movement: Gay Bars as Gay Art Galleries

Dom Orejudos aka Etienne aka Stephen helped invent the "Leather Mural Movement" (1962-1979) that re-conceived "gay bars as the first gay art galleries." That titanic concept inspired the founding of the first gay gallery businesses such as Fey-Way in San Francisco, Eons in LA, and Stompers in Greenwich Village.

If there is a gay Mount Rushmore of four great pioneer pop artists, the faces would be Chuck Arnett, Etienne, A. Jay, and Tom of Finland. If there could be a fifth face, I would nominate Skipper aka Glenn Davis. When I was editor in chief, all of them were associates in the salon around *Drummer*.

- In 1962, Chuck Arnett painted the cement wall inside his San Francisco bar, the Tool Box, with the legendary Lascaux mural that shocked the world in the pages of *Life* magazine, June 26, 1964, five years, almost to the day, before Stonewall, June 27, 1969.
- In 1972, Etienne painted his mural-posters for the Gold Coast. (Uncredited murals adorned the Mineshaft.)
- In 1974, Tom of Finland painted the murals for the wall of Tom's Saloon in Hamburg.
- In June 1977, A. Jay aka Al Shapiro, the founding San Francisco art director of *Drummer*, painted the murals for the new Leatherneck bar in San Francisco.
- In 1979, Skipper whose work first appeared in *Drummer* 15 painted the Sanctuary bath panels later installed at Dick Saunders' Probe disco in LA, and those installations can be

seen in the background of the scenes in the Richard Gere film *American Gigolo* (1980) shot on location at Probe.

Dick Saunders, *Frontier Bulletin Gazette*, and Probe Disco

Dick Saunders was the founding publisher and pioneering editor of the *Frontier Bulletin Gazette* which he started up in Los Angeles in January 1965 as a homomasculine newsletter for his cowboy-western themed Frontier Club. Very pre-Stonewall, and pre-dating *The Advocate* by two years and *Drummer* by ten years, *Frontier Bulletin Gazette* made the well-built model, Dick Saunders, a household word in LA fifteen years before he began writing and publishing the *Probe* newsletter from December 1980 through the arson fire in September 1983. In the zero degrees of separation, Saunders sold Probe disco to the man who founded *Frontiers* magazine after asking Saunders for permission to approximate his *Frontier* title. For years, Saunders and I shared—without then knowing we were sharing—a significant lover who was a great beauty in his day, and about whom we still compare (sniggering) notes while time marches on across the two-timer's face.

Search elsewhere in this *Gay San Francisco Eyewitness* series for "gay bars as art galleries" and for "Tom of Finland" in *Gay San Francisco: The Drummer Salon*. See also the related articles I wrote on Etienne's peer group of artists: "Tom Hinde," *Drummer* 16 (June 1977); "The Leatherneck," inclusion of A. Jay, *Drummer* 18 (August 1977), "Rex Revisited" (*Son of Drummer*, September 1978), "Domino," *Drummer* 29 (August 1979), "Martin of Holland," *Drummer* 31 (September 1979), "A. Jay," *Drummer* 107 (August 1987), and "Chuck Arnett: His Life, Our Times," *Drummer* 134 (October 1989).

Like the homomasculine Tom of Finland, Etienne had a natural erotic eye untrained by any academy. His style, open to eros and comedy, was like the best sex graffiti lifted off the walls of the toilets from Lascaux to Montmartre to the present. In the way one can tell a Pissarro from a

Picasso, and a Monet from a Manet, one can immediately identify an Etienne drawing or painting in a line up of his equally distinct peers, Tom of Finland, Rex, A. Jay, Skipper, Domino, and the Hun—all of whom followed Etienne into leather publishing and owe him respect as an activist pioneer who helped remake the laws that made their graphic careers legal in the United States. Many fans compare Etienne to Tom of Finland, but Etienne compares perhaps more closely to A. Jay with his comic-strip style of images, dialog, and humor which he debuted as his *Harry Chess* in *Queen's Quarterly* magazine in 1969. Etienne and A. Jay linked themselves together forever with their joint show at Fey-Way (1978). In their particular artists' salon, Tom of Finland and Etienne and A. Jay were personally the best of friends.

Etienne's style was suitably hyperbolic for a commercial leather culture that in the psychedelic 1960s and 1970s saw gay sex through a gorgeous haze of pot and poppers. Arnett, who was a primal artist, saw masculine sex through a rainbow quiver of acid and crystal meth.

Etienne's view of the homomasculine ideal is of an iconic Olympus populated with men as leather gods as imagined in a mix of Brando's *The Wild One* (1953), Steve Reeves' *Hercules* (1959), and Kenneth Anger's *Scorpio Rising* (1964). His talent for dramatic movement and story arcs, developed on stage in his choreography, informed his cartoon-strip narratives. Nevertheless—and this is the elephant in the X-rated room—Etienne's work, quite important historically, is, like A. Jay's, revered for its heart and humor and qualities other than generating a universal masturbatory response. Unlike cum-minded artists Rex, Skipper, Domino, Martin of Holland, and the Hun, Etienne had other goals than causing guys to jerk off.

Much of Etienne's work—and this is nothing against its inherently beautiful esthetic—was zoned "commercial" in that it was produced as posters and advertising for venues and events within the leather world invented, owned, managed, and promoted by Renslow and Orejudos. Etienne was exceptional in that he is one of the few gay artists who actually made a living from his art.

He succeeds historically because his images relish the fun of leather sexuality, and because he maybe even dares to satirize the golden *gravitas* of the 1960s and 1970s leather scene that was ruined in the 1980s when leather culture went all balls-up, kumbaya, and commercial in the gaystream.

One thing is certain, and this is no idle eulogy, because it was true when he was alive: the person Dom Orejudos was a sweet, gentle, and beloved man. In that regard, he was exactly like the very sweet and gentle

A. Jay and the sweet and beloved Tom of Finland, and very like his mentor, the universally beloved Sam Steward.

- A. Jay (Al Shapiro): February 7, 1932 - May 30, 1987
- Tom of Finland: May 8, 1920 - November 7, 1991
- Etienne (Dom Orejudos): July 1, 1933 - September 24, 1991
- Sam Steward: July 23, 1909 - December 31, 1993
- Skipper (Glenn Davis): November 14, 1944 - Living

For anyone wishing to consider the link between the private art of Sam Steward and the popular art of Etienne, Sam's heretofore mostly unseen drawings, engravings, and paintings can be surveyed in the book *The Visual Art of Sam Steward* by Justin Spring, forthcoming from Elysium Press.

II. The editorial promotion essay as published in *Drummer* 19, December 1977

Reviewing the Best Gay Artists...

Star Trick
Artist Dom Orejudos Is Etienne!

Darth Vader has nothing on Dom's "Captain Kirk." In fact, *Star Trick*'s Captain Kirk has nothing on at all. At last, *Star Trek*'s best special effects hang revealed. No longer is the enterprising spacemeat basketed in those bouncy JC Penney pajamas.

Strip a Trekie. Get a Trickie.

Drummer gladly sneak previews *Star Trick*. This strip is the latest by starwalker Dom Orejudos who signs his murals and paintings as "Etienne" and "Stephen." Dom aims to please. *Drummer* aims to tease. After all, no preview ought to expose the great lengths to which Dom's drawings go. Suffice it to say that a long time ago in a galaxy far, far away, Captains Outrageous dived head first into the ultimate space probe.

Star Trick is a marvel of a comic. For men who appreciate uncut cockamamy plots and tongue-in-cheeks humor, *Star Trick* is a collectible available in this galaxy from New York's Target Studio.

May the farce be with you.

Opposite page. Top: Invitations, Eons Gallery, Los Angeles, Sunday, May 7, 1978, and Fey-Way Studios, San Francisco, Friday May 26, 1978. Etienne and A. Jay each drew half of each invitation. Used with permission of Chuck Renslow and the Leather Archives & Museum and the Estate of A. Jay, administered by Dick Kriegmont.

III. Eyewitness Illustrations

Bottom: "*Drummer* Salonistas A. Jay (Al Shapiro) and Etienne (Dom Orejudos)," at the opening of the Etienne and A. Jay Joint Exhibit, Fey-Way Studios, Friday, May 26, 1978. Editor in chief Jeanne Barney had first published Etienne in *Drummer* 10 (November 1976). Publicity kit photograph by Efren Ramirez. ©Efren Ramirez.

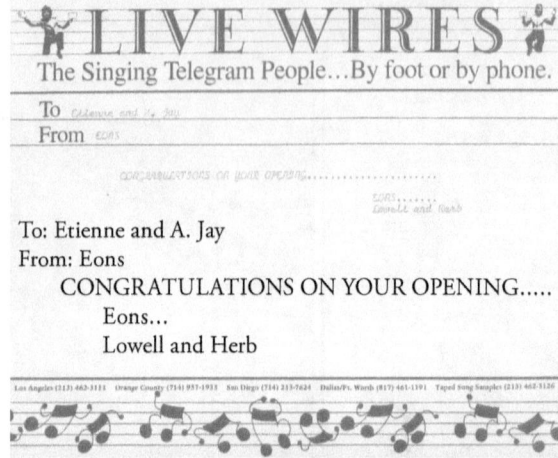

Telegram from owners "Lowell and Herb" of the Eons Gallery to Etienne and A. Jay on their joint opening at Fey-Way Studio, May 26, 1978. The last closet in the world is exited by revealing one's true surname. Used with permission of Chuck Renslow and the Leather Archives & Museum and the Estate of A. Jay, administered by Dick Kriegmont.

Left to right: Tom of Finland, Chuck Renslow, and Dom Orejudos, 1983 International Mr. Leather Contest, Chicago. Publicity kit photograph by Jack Sitar for IML Inc. Used with permission of Chuck Renslow and the Leather Archives & Museum.

Drummer 19: *Star Trick* 441

Two posters by Etienne for the Gold Coast bar, Chicago. Top right: The inscription is to Tony Tavarossi from Etienne, and in Etienne's hand reads: "For Tony—Fondness & Hickeys [*sic*]. —Etienne (Dom)." The poster itself was a gift from Tavarossi to Fritscher. Used with permission of Chuck Renslow and the Leather Archives & Museum.

Longtime Fritscher intimate, Lou Thomas, co-founder of Colt Studio, founded Target Studio and was quintessential in creating the *Drummer* look. He and Fritscher worked together on several projects: photography, writing for the *Target Album*, and the private publication of Fritscher's 1969 novel, *I Am Curious (Leather)* aka *Leather Blues*. Lou Thomas shot the covers of *Drummer* 13 and *Drummer* 14, and his work continued to appear inside *Drummer* long after his death January 7, 1990.

Out of the salon around *Drummer*, Lou Thomas presented the triumvirate of Etienne, A. Jay, and Fritscher.

PRIEST

THIS IS MY BODY

BY PHIL ANDROS

Just where it was in Chicago that Clint and I first met, I don't remember. Probably prowling the dark alleys of the Loop or walking along the Lake front at night, but it sure as hell wasn't in a bar because at eighteen he couldn't go in one. He mentioned the name of someone — maybe a score, maybe another hustler, so I knew he was safe. He was a tall lanky undeveloped kid, not yet filled out, with blond necklength hair, and he was about as green as they come. He wore shoes size twelve, had a long nose and a long middle finger which meant — if old wives' tales were right — that he was gratifyingly sized in the most important place.

I do remember that he looked at me that first night, with those eyes so pale blue the iris seemed almost white, and said, "Hey man — I wanta be a hustler. Will you teach me how?"

Since it was a dull evening and he was younger than I by about ten years, and my ashes hadn't been hauled for about twelve hours, I grinned and said, "Well, there's always room for one more, I reckon. Wanta come home with me?"

On the way, I found out a little more about him. There was almost no sexual experience behind him, except for a few fumbling unsatisfactory attempts with cunts and some jack-off sessions with boys his own age up near the St. Ignatius playground under the El. Having no background, he really wasn't very smart; but he was full of the big talk, the impossible dreams of the untalented young. For him the world had begun at the moment of his birth at Michael Reese Hospital and he knew little and cared less about what had gone on during all the centuries before. About all that he had to offer was his long-legged charm, his strong slender hands, and his good face. He was an unholy temptation for me, I must admit, for here was something to be molded, to be helped over the rough spots. But when he came out with his answer about why he wanted to be a hustler, he floored me.

PHIL ANDROS is the great grand man of homoerotic writing. As a World Class Hustler, Phil has written more than thirty novels and hundreds of short stories that have appeared in the best and worst of men's magazines. Dell recently included several of his classic stories in its Anthology of Gay Writers. Under the name Sam Steward, Phil has been publishing the memoirs of his adventures with James Dean, Hell's Angel Sonny Baroer, Kenneth ("Scorpio Rising") Anger, Thornton Wilder, and Gertrude and Alice. Dear Sammy, Phil/Sam's edited collection of letters from Stein and Toklas is his newest release.

"Le Sport des Matelots," metal circle plate, etching, by Samuel Steward, signed and dated December 12, 1954. Gift from Samuel Steward to Jack Fritscher, 1970. More than just an intimate of Gertrude Stein and Alice B. Toklas, Sam Steward was an author of novels and short fiction as well as a fine artist who, in the 1950s and 1960s, wittily combined his love for art with his love for men and set up his own tattoo studio in Chicago and in Oakland. Editor in chief Jeanne Barney published two of his stories in *Drummer* 5 and *Drummer* 6. Used with permission and copyright by the Estate of Samuel Steward, administered by Michael Williams.

Opposite page: The *Drummer* salon segued absolutely to the "Virtual *Drummer*" of *Man2Man Quarterly* in 1980 with the publication of the Phil Andros (Sam Steward) story, "This Is My Body." Ever-true Samuel Steward and Jack Fritscher met in 1969 through the Catholic leather priest Jim Kane. Longtime pals Kane and Fritscher took a formative and fabled 1969 road trip by Harley-Davidson from Denver to Taos and Santa Fe. Riding together and writing together for editor Kane's diocesan newspaper in the early 1970s, they developed roots for the gay press that emerged with Fritscher editing *Drummer*. In the first decade after Stonewall, Fritscher, with permission, edited the elderly Steward only enough to keep his nostalgic stories from seeming dated.

Samuel Steward in his 20s in the 1930s

The 1966 *$tud* book jacket was drawn by Etienne referencing Chuck Arnett's Tool Box Mural.

What happened in Bilignin did not stay in Bilignin. In 1969, the diligent leather priest Jim Kane introduced Jack Fritscher and the elegant Sam Steward (1909-1993) into a mutual-admiration friendship. In 1974, forestalling the demise of the frail sixty-five-year-old Steward who fanned himself gallantly feigning eighty, historian Fritscher received a grant to record the oral history of the author, tattooist, and longtime confidant of Gertrude Stein and Alice B. Toklas for the documentary, *My Shy Bashful Sammy: A Literary Biography—65 Years in the 20th Century*. Steward, whom Fritscher lightly edited and published in *Drummer* and *Man2Man*, autographed many of his books to Fritscher whose *Some Dance to Remember* (1990) he called "possibly the great gay American novel." On June 6, 1978, a playful Steward wrote on the first page of the first edition of his priceless 1966 hardcover *$tud*: "Pour Jack Fritscher—co-travailleur dons le vignoble, en souvenir d'une nuit memorable a Cap d'Antibes. —Tou amant fidele, Phil Andros. [For Jack Fritscher—co-worker in the vineyard, a souvenir of a memorable night at Cap d'Antibes—Your faithful lover, Phil Andros]." In 1984, Steward penned on the cover page of his *Different Strokes*: "For Jack Fritscher—He knows more different strokes than I ever did. —Phil Andros aka Sam Steward." In the zero degrees of separation, Tom of Finland's drawing of Fritscher's lover Jim Enger with Clint Lockner was published on the cover of Sam's *Bullenhochzeit*, the German translation of his novel *The Boys in Blue* (1984). It was Sam Steward, intimate of the Alfred Kinsey "salon" and the Stein-Toklas salon, who coined what he called "the moniker" for Fritscher's *"Drummer* salon." Photograph and dedications used with permission and copyright by the Estate of Samuel Steward, administered by Michael Williams. Cover used with permission of Chuck Renslow and the Leather Archives & Museum.

Top: Two 1950s photographs of Dom Orejudos document the evolution of the Kris Studio image. Photographs by Chuck Renslow. Bottom: Artist Etienne (Orejudos) and photographer Renslow at Kris Studio turned the style of Chicago-American leather international in their publication *Mars* which joined the homomasculine movement in *Tomorrow's Man* and Bob Mizer's *Physique Pictorial* which Jack Fritscher injected directly into *Drummer* for 1970s readers raised on virile Old School 'zines predating 1980s political correctness. Photographs and covers used with permission of Chuck Renslow and the Leather Archives & Museum.

"The Football Huddle: Go, Fisters, Go!" Felt-tip ink on paper, color drawing by Skipper, 1979. ©Jack Fritscher. First published in *Gay San Francisco* from the Jack Fritscher and Mark Hemry collection. Skipper Davis' first work in *Drummer* appeared in *Drummer* 15, and he created a specific drawing to illustrate Jack Fritscher's story, "Foreskin Prison Blues," in *Drummer* 186 (July 1995). Along with Chuck Arnett at the Tool Box, Etienne at the Gold Coast, Tom of Finland at Tom's Bar in Hamburg, and A. Jay at the Leatherneck, Skipper was part of the "Gay Muralist Movement" of the 1960s-1970s: he painted the large panels at the Sanctuary bath which were later installed at Dick Saunders' Probe Disco in LA. The film *The Skipper Video Gallery*, directed and photographed by Jack Fritscher and edited by Mark Hemry, was a Palm Drive Video feature release (1994). Because the quintessence of gay art is eros, it often must censor itself in public venues in order to reassure the GLBT community of its remarkable survival in underground collections. (As shown, the original is obscured.)

The Mineshaft

> Written June 1977, this feature essay was published in *Drummer* 19, December 1977.
> I. Author's Eyewitness Historical-Context Introduction written March 8, 2002
> II. The feature article as published in *Drummer* 19, December 1977
> III. Eyewitness Illustrations

I. **Author's Eyewitness Historical-Context Introduction written March 8, 2002**

Over the holidays, the Mineshaft played host to the FFA, UYA, and countless single guys from all over the world. Many of the latter came to us during their New York visit after reading a fine article about the Mineshaft in *Drummer* magazine. Although we did not seek this publicity, it was a positive statement for the Mineshaft and we thank....writer, Jack Fritscher, for his fine words.

—Wally Wallace, Founding and Only Mineshaft Manager, *The Mineshaft Newsletter*, February 1978. All Mineshaft Newsletters and announcements as well as letters from Wally Wallace are copyright Wally Wallace and are printed with permission.

As editor in chief of *Drummer*, I took the opportunity to write the first (as well as the second) national and international article about the "Number One 1970s sex club," the immediately legendary Mineshaft which orbited Earth at 835 Washington Street, New York, from its opening October 8, 1976, to November 7, 1985, when shut down, shuttered, and slammed closed by the health department of the imperial City of New York. The second article "Pissing in the Wind: A Night in the Mineshaft Bathtub" appeared in *Drummer* 20 (January 1978).

"We lasted nine years and nine days," Mineshaft manager, Wally Wallace, told me.

(Note: Except as specifically noted otherwise, all Wally Wallace quotations are from the video *Jack Fritscher Interviews Mineshaft Manager, Wally Wallace, March 28, 1990*, recorded at 206 Texas Street,

San Francisco. A copyrighted excerpt of this article and interview was published with permission of the author in *Leather Times* 1 (2007), the newsletter of the Leather Archives and Museum, Chicago, published by Chuck Renslow and produced by Rick Storer.)

Fourteen years earlier, that second week in October 1976 was a busy one in Manhattan: the S&M Eulenspiegel Society was incorporated on October 14, 1976, six days after the Mineshaft opened. *Drummer*, founded June 1975, was sixteen months old and on sale at gay New York shops.

In leather-heritage synchronicity, Wally Wallace and I knew each other for twenty-three years. Few in the salon around the Mineshaft knew his name was "James Wallace" who to intimates was known as "Jim," or that he had transferred his theatrical experience — mid-1960s through early 1970s — as actor and stage manager with La Mama to the theatrical set and dress-code costumes at the Mineshaft.

In the zero degrees of separation, it was at La Mama that Wally Wallace first met Robert Mapplethorpe and Patti Smith; and it was at the Mineshaft in 1976 that Jacques Morali saw Wally Wallace's blue-collar dress-code archetypes that became the pop stereotypes of his disco group, the Village People. Glenn Hughes, the original leather biker in the Village People, was a frequent sex-player at the Mineshaft as well as part of the S&M leather salon around *Drummer* in San Francisco.

My "Mineshaft" *Drummer* article, delivered up in the limited format of our monthly "Men's Bar Scene" column, is brief because the Mineshaft had been open only seven months when I wrote about it in June 1977, and the legend of the Mineshaft sex circus was just beginning to launch. Mythologizing the Mineshaft was not my point because I was writing frank PR to promote the Mineshaft — as Wally Wallace acknowledged in 1978 — with readers who lived outside Manhattan.

Perhaps someday I will write a lengthy, humorous, and scandalous article for *Vanity Fair*, or, better, a screenplay that will reveal the players, the mystery, the comedy, and the sexuality of the legendary Mineshaft. Chaucer would love such a framing of the newer, sexier, raunchier *Canterbury Tales*. Host Wally Wallace fills in as the Harry Bailey of leather and the Mineshaft is Bailey's Tabard Inn where the pilgrims as sex-tourists meet up. The Wife of Bath becomes the Husband in the Bathtub; and the ass-kissing and red-hot poker up-the-bum in "The Miller's Tale" recreates itself nightly.

Attending the opening night of the Mineshaft, I recalled Kenneth Anger's film title *The Inauguration of the Pleasure Dome* (1954). As a journalist and a sex commuter to New York, I was staying with my longtime pal Jack McNenny who was, in the zero degrees of our salon around

Drummer, also a friend of Wally Wallace and a founding member of the Mineshaft. Jack McNenny owned the scatalogically named flower shop "The Gifts of Nature" on the northeast corner of Sixth and Houston where he provided Robert Mapplethorpe with flowers for his photo shoots at his 24 Bond Street loft. (See "Take 2: Pentimento for Robert Mapplethorpe " and "Take 3: Adventures with Robert Mapplethorpe" in the 1994 erotic memoir *Mapplethorpe: Assault with a Deadly Camera*; thanks to the request of Tony Deblase, "Take 2" was first published as the lead cover article in *Drummer* 133 (September 1989). Jack McNenny was also the New York distributor for my Mineshaft-like *Man2Man Quarterly* 'zine which I began as a "Virtual *Drummer*" in 1979.

Through hundreds of visits, I experienced the Mineshaft as the 1970s quintessential frame of homomasculine sexuality. Years later in San Francisco, on March 28, 1990, Wally Wallace recalled again that this first *Drummer* article gave the Mineshaft some welcome initial traction because it was like an alert, an invitation, sent out worldwide to *Drummer*'s passionate subscription base which Wally Wallace always considered the house magazine of the Mineshaft where "a regular Saturday night drew five hundred or six hundred guys and I'd have fifteen guys on duty at the door, the coat check, and the bars. The night of the annual Barnum and Bailey Circus, I'd have a crowd of a thousand guys."

Actually, this *Drummer* 19 "Mineshaft" article is a prequel to a second Mineshaft feature that I wrote for the next issue, *Drummer* 20 (January 1978) titled: "Pissing in the Wind: Wet Dreams, Golden Showers (Or, A Night in the Mineshaft Bathtub)." Writing as a gonzo participatory journalist a month after the publication of the first Mineshaft article, I went into erotic detail about the fabled extreme sexuality of the Mineshaft. These two articles might be read together.

I like to put gay history into objective correlative context that is as sensual and descriptive as possible. I also like to back up my pioneer eyewitness testimony with internal evidence from letters, interviews, and printed articles.

Without initial irony, the Mineshaft was situated in the Meatpacking District of West Greenwich Village. In the pre-dawn hours on the shared loading dock, Mineshaft members, arriving and leaving, crossed steps within inches of butchers in bloodied white aprons shouldering huge, stiff carcasses from waiting trucks into their meat-cutting shops. It was very *Twilight Zone*: two worlds existing in the same dimension, each invisible to the other, one leathery and dark, the other bloody and lit with extraterrestrial fluorescence.

Time Capsule Sidebar: A daytime and deserted view of the street and the warehouse loading docks was used as a location in the Robert

Mulligan film *Love with the Proper Stranger* (1963), which featured Natalie Wood and the leathery biker Steve McQueen in a very long scene shot virtually on the doorstep of what would later become the Mineshaft.

Wally Wallace's Letter of Invitation to the Opening of the Mineshaft (Presented as Written, without Editing, from the Jack Fritscher and Mark Hemry Personal Archive Collection)

October 2, 1976

Howdy,

  On Friday October 7th [hand-corrected by Wally to 8th] at 9 pm I will begin managing a new club in THE MINE SHAFT [two words at this point quickly changes to *Mineshaft*] at 836 Washington Street by Little West 12th Street. You may have visited it under its present name or as the old Zodiac years ago. In any event you will find it different in terms of decor and concept.
  We have taken away the lovely wall-to-ceiling silver foil Reynolds Wrap decor and made the main bar area [up the stairs from the street and built on the second floor] into a comfortable Western style club complete with new murals and a pool table.
  From this room you go through a set of swinging doors into a tunnel leading into a cave style bar area with smaller caves for exploring off to the sides. A perfect setting for underground graphic viewing. In the middle of the room is the Mine Shaft [a door in the floor of the second floor that pulls up to reveal rugged lumber stairs] leading down to a lower level [the first floor or ground floor or street floor] for shafting sports. It is indeed different!
  Conceptually the club activities will be different as they revolve around special interest groups during the early hours starting at 9 pm. On Tuesdays we have the Wrestling guys and on Sundays the P.G.T. Club. [The meaning of "P.G.T. Club" seems lost to history, but it was probably was a code for piss or grunge activities.] For them we have installed a new shower.
  There will also be a SCHOOL FOR LOWER EDUCATION [run by GMSMA, Gay Men's S&M Association, with an occasional show-and-tell by Chicagoan, Tony DeBlase] beginning in early October with limited size classes in subjects

relating to improving one's sexual techniques. I can not for obvious reasons describe this further in print.

We will also have special events such as a BLACK AND BLUE PARTY for our members. Setting the tone for this and the place itself there is a dress code of levi, leather, uniforms, and similar casual attire required at all times. No fluff allowed!

So, come on down and see what we have going on. The sooner the better as the number of memberships will be limited. During the month of October we will be open to you and your friends between the hours of 10 pm and 6 am Weds through Sunday. But for a sneak preview come Friday October 7th [sic] at 9 pm.

Try it! I know you'll like THE MINE SHAFT!

Wally

On that opening night, October 8, 1976, Wally Wallace, a protector of male space in Manhattan as was Steve McEachern at the Catacombs in San Francisco, was intent on keeping intact a sanctuary for masculine men. Wally Wallace wrote in his homomasculine *Mineshaft Manifesto* about sex, identity, performance art, politics, and civil war over gender:

THE MINESHAFT IS NOW, AND FOREVER WILL BE,
A UNIQUE MEMBERSHIP

The MINESHAFT is basically a unique playground conceived by and dedicated to the fun-loving raunchy gay male minority who exist in the underworld of gay society. It is truly a place where many a gay man would never come because it is surely not a place for everyone.

The facilities include three bars, a roof, several playrooms, a [bath] tub room, and various pieces of equipment [slings, bondage equipment] located in a half block long building at 835 Washington Street in the middle of the New York Meat Market. It is all to be used and shared to enhance your wildest sexual fantasy and more!

As a social club, the MINESHAFT provides the opportunity for guys to meet and to play with men of a like persuasion, or with men so rare and so different that they inspire new ways to play, or might even change their entire life. This is mentioned as many couples have first met and found new type lives through the club. Yes, we are ever changing and the changes are due to the various men from all over the world who meet and play here in international play.

Within minutes of opening the Mineshaft, the liberation zeitgeist of the 1970s changed Wally when as a business man he observed a truth of the way white gay males kept company with women at that time. This is an excerpt from the video *Jack Fritscher Interviews Mineshaft Manager Wally Wallace, March 28, 1990*:

> Wally Wallace: The night of the opening, the word had got out through my letter and that word of mouth got to people who were looking for something different. The Eagle and the Spike, which were the leather bars at the time...had become rather inundated with people who were not into the leather scene. People were looking for a new place to go. I promised a dress code, although at the time I didn't know what it would be.
>
> Jack Fritscher: Your dress code was like the dress code Chuck Arnett enforced at the Tool Box in San Francisco in the 1960s. The one difference was that Arnett nailed a pair of sneakers to the ceiling with a sign saying "No sneakers." And you...."
>
> Wally Wallace: ...allowed sneakers in as a fetish. [Laughs]...To have the dress code, I had to make the Mineshaft a membership club. Well, the first night we opened—we were on the second floor, and I was standing at the entrance greeting friends at the top of the stairs. Then I noticed an attractive female standing halfway up the stairs.
>
> Jack Fritscher: I know this story. I love this story. It's canonical. She herself told me.
>
> Wally Wallace: So I said to her, I'm sorry but you can't come in here. This is a men's club, a gay men's club. It might be embarrassing for a woman. She said, Well, I go to the Spike and the Eagle. She was dressed in leather and a very attractive girl. I said, I'm sorry but we determined that this was to be a private club for leather men. I was worried about getting into trouble with women's rights groups. We had some trouble at the Ramp...
>
> Jack Fritscher: Nureyev's favorite sex bar...
>
> Wally Wallace: ...with women trying to get into the backroom, but that was a public bar. So this great looking girl in leather turned and walked down the stairs and left, and when she left all these hot men standing on the stairs also left. The hot

guys were with her! So I said to myself, I've got to find out who this woman is....

Jack Fritscher: When legends collide.

Wally Wallace: That's how I met Camille O'Grady who became our sort of token female member of the Mineshaft, but she could only go to the bar area and she couldn't bring any of her women friends, which she didn't. She pretty well stuck to those rules. I know that sometimes when I wasn't there, she would end up in the back rooms, but I wasn't supposed to know. I'm sure she got involved in some pretty hot scenes....

Jack Fritscher: Camille was very involved with your entertainment events.

Wally Wallace: We had S&M demonstrations like bondage and body painting. I remember she was involved in one contest. She was a talented artist.

Jack Fritscher: She exhibited her drawings at Fey-Way Gallery in San Francisco.

Wally Wallace: Where she was almost shot to death.

Camille O'Grady was rivals at CBGB with punk diva Patti Smith who was coupled with photographer Robert Mapplethorpe the way Camille O'Grady was coupled with *Drummer* writer and photographer Robert Opel who streaked the 1974 Academy Awards, and was murdered in his San Francisco gallery, Fey-Way, on July 8, 1979. The gunman mercifully did not shoot Camille O'Grady who was forced to lie on the gallery floor during the robbery and murder. (For dramatized details, see *Some Dance to Remember: A Memoir-Novel of San Francisco 1970-1982*, Reel 3, Scene 1 and Scene 8; for documentary details, confer *Mapplethorpe: Assault with a Deadly Camera*, "Take 11: Robert Opelthorpe: Streaking the Academy Awards.") The first Mineshaft flyer for Christmas 1976 advertised: "Upcoming special events include the opening of our new tunnel playroom, a 'Criscomas Party,' and a repeat performance by Camille O'Grady." Wally Wallace also invited Camille to sing her piss song "Toilet Kiss" at the Mineshaft 1978 anniversary party. Patti Smith's own first single was "Piss Factory"—but it was not literal as was Camille's.

Jack Fritscher: When did you notice that the Mineshaft was getting to be a lot kinkier than you first planned?

Wally Wallace: In the beginning, I thought it would be just a basic fuck and suck in the back room. Well, it was fairly early on that we put up slings.

Jack Fritscher: That signaled something new.

Wally Wallace: I remembered seeing a place in San Francisco, a place called the Barracks.

Jack Fritscher: The kinkiest place in San Francisco next to the Slot.

Wally Wallace: It had a bathtub, where somebody was in the bathtub, fully clothed, getting soaked with piss, surrounded by a big crowd pushing in to piss on him, which I thought was kind of hot.

Jack Fritscher: So you put a bathtub on the ground-level floor of the Mineshaft.

Wally Wallace: That bathtub became famous. I didn't realize how many people were into bathtubs.

Jack Fritscher: Into piss.

Wally Wallace: I'm sorry I didn't keep a nightly diary. We had a group, the FFA [Fist Fuckers of America]. In the bar business, except maybe in Las Vegas, there are so many dead times during the week. When the Mineshaft opened there were maybe thirteen leather clubs in the city. Several of them fisting clubs. So we tried to attract them in on the slow nights....The FFA was a very heavy drug scene as I realized when their orgies went on for days....

Jack Fritscher: You knew Leather Rick who shot outrageous, extreme S&M videos at the Mineshaft featuring the club guys from the "Skulls of Akron." The action is astounding as in *Fisting Ballet*, but the videos also show a lot of the interior set of the Mineshaft rooms.

Wally Wallace: I became good friends with Leather Rick....and it was on a New Year's Eve, I think, he nailed somebody's cock down on the back bar. The guy climbed up and sat on the bar....In the Mineshaft for the first four years, I would not allow photos. Although I let George Dudley shoot a poster for our tub room and one of our American flag display that had Christmas lights behind the flag.

Jack Fritscher: It is really unfortunate that so much of the 1970s went unphotographed because it took nearly the whole decade for everyone to catch on after Stonewall that it was okay to be in a gay snapshot. Even in the early 1970s, a camera could empty a gay bar. By 1977, everyone was ready for his close-up. I'm glad that you let Robert Mapplethorpe in to shoot.

Wally Wallace: Yes...he shot one of the Mineshaft Man contests. It was David O'Brien that year, about 1979–1980. Somebody

> thought Bob could take pictures of the event. But that wasn't his thing.
> Jack Fritscher: He couldn't shoot from the hip in spontaneous conditions. He needed the formality of a studio.
> Wally Wallace: ...I liked Bob, although we weren't close friends...
> Jack Fritscher: We were.

Mapplethorpe and I were bicoastal lovers from October 1977 until our lovely affair evaporated into simple friendship in the Spring of 1980.

Robert Mapplethorpe shot many photographs in the Mineshaft, including the print he gave me of David O'Brien, "Mr. Mineshaft 1979." Over the years, Wally Wallace grew quite conscious of the documentary value of photography within the Mineshaft where history was made nightly. In his flyer, "MINESHAFT FIFTH ANNIVERSARY, OCT 25 1982," his archetypal sense of Mineshaft identity was evident: "The Men! The Music! The Mystery! The Magic! The Myth!" He wrote that! Most of the Mineshaft photos shot by Mapplethorpe have disappeared, presumably into the vaults of the Mapplethorpe Foundation, because, perhaps, they are not as formal and "perfect" as Robert's exquisite studio photography. (See the outlaw memoir of what happens to outlaw art, *Mapplethorpe: Assault with a Deadly Camera*.) For all his bad-boy reputation as an artist as well as his involvement with Wally Wallace socially at the Mineshaft, Mapplethorpe really preferred private sex to public sex, and told me so frequently. With regard to unclosetting gay photography, the Mineshaft truly did break the historical taboo against cameras in gay bars and baths. Thousands of photographs, shot by dozens of photographers in the Mineshaft, actually exist, as do videos such as *Fisting Ballet* shot by the Skulls of Akron and long-since proscribed by government censorship.

> Wally Wallace: Bob liked Black men and he had heard of a Black bar in Midtown in the 40s [between 40th and 49th Street] called "Blues"...and Bob was afraid to go there....So I went up there with him one time. He was like a kid so eager to go, but afraid to go alone.
> Jack Fritscher: His insecurities were endearing. I squired him around town on his first trip to San Francisco to introduce him to everyone in the leather scene.
> Wally Wallace: You might have thought we were headed to the depths of Harlem. The night we were there, there weren't many hot men, but only a couple of drag queens with their white boyfriends. It was not what he imagined.

Jack Fritscher: "Blues" was not the Mineshaft. [When Mapplethorpe broke through the calla-lily-white ceiling of his racial fear—he had no racist fear—he created brilliant studies of black men. For a consideration of racism in Mapplethorpe, see *Mapplethorpe: Assault with a Deadly Camera*, Take 16, "White Art, Black Men." In his will, Mapplethorpe left the sum of $100,000 to one of his Black models, Jack Walls.] ...Camille told me she was in a video shot early in the Mineshaft.

Wally Wallace: Before Leather Rick made a video, the first video was shot by a director from France who was a friend of one of the guys who worked for me at the Mineshaft. Supposedly this would only be seen in Europe and not in America. We got a little money, but it was a strange film.

Jack Fritscher: Even in an age of Warhol and John Waters and underground films?

Wally Wallace: It was a French version of the Mineshaft. What the French thought we were about. They tied one guy up and put Christmas lights around him.

Jack Fritscher: Very teenage Kenneth Anger.

Wally Wallace: I remember Camille O'Grady was in it, singing. She was a good singer. But the soundtrack on the video had a terrible echo...

Jack Fritscher: Maybe it was the punk rock sound that had just become so popular from CBGB.

Wally Wallace: The movie did nothing for Camille's career. She thought it would. I remember her. She did sing at the Mineshaft a couple times for benefits. We did a lot of benefits like after the fire at the Everard Baths in 1978 when so many died. We also did a Casino Night to raise money for Rex...I just love Rex. Our heads are complementary. Very private. But he's nowhere near as quiet as he seems. He's a wonderful human being. Rex drew three posters for the Mineshaft. I feel fortunate in having known so many great people in male porn. Rex is our Michelangelo and so is Tom of Finland and A. Jay [Al Shapiro, art director of *Drummer*].

In the zero degrees around *Drummer*, Rex was the official Mineshaft artist who illustrated my "Mineshaft" article in *Drummer* 19. He had drawn the cover of *Drummer* 10 (November 1976) which was on the stands when the Mineshaft debuted. I also wrote a major feature article about his work in my special issue, *Son of Drummer* (September 1978), pages 48-51. In 1980, I formally interviewed Rex who had moved in the migration of Manhattanites to San Francisco. For the excerpted interview, see *Mapplethorpe: Assault with a Deadly Camera*, "Take 14: Merchandising the Magical, Mystical Mapplethorpe Tour." Rex moved South of Market and opened up a gallery called "Rexwerk" in his home on Hallam Mews, fifty feet across the lane from the Barracks baths on Folsom. Rex who has rarely had good luck had some very bad luck. An arsonist set the Barracks on fire during the night of July 10, 1981. Rex, along with more than a hundred others, including *Drummer* photographer, Mark I. Chester, escaped with their lives; everything they owned, all their artwork, was lost in the disaster. (For a fictive "documentary" description of what may have happened in Mark I. Chester's studio and Rex's studio as the fire raged, see *Some Dance to Remember*, Reel 4, Scene 3.)

In the *Mineshaft Newsletter*, Wally Wallace wrote:

> A "CASINO NIGHT TO HELP A BUDDY OUT"
> (Rex Benefit) TUES. OCT 20 [1981] 9-12
>
> In July the largest fire since its Earthquake swept the Folsom Street area in San Francisco leaving 120 totally homeless. One of the victims was Rex, the artist of the Mineshaft logo, who lost all his earthly belongings in one night. The MINESHAFT gave a benefit for him in San Francisco and now we are having one in New York from 9 until Midnight on Tuesday October 20th. It's a Casino Night with lots of prizes for the winners...with some recent Rex work on display.... Please note that another Casino Night will be held in early November for the Gay Men's Chorus and their Bux for Tux Fund.

May I, as an eyewitness participant, alert latter-day researchers, historians, and cynics: anything and everything anyone has ever said or written about the hedonistic Mineshaft is true, including George C. Scott shouting in the 1978 musical camp film, *Movie Movie*: "More sequins! More sequins in the 'Mineshaft' number!" See my review of *Movie Movie* in *Drummer* 27 (February 1979). That kind of camp was not welcome in the sex rooms around the Mineshaft bar. Wally Wallace sent out a flyer that said:

> Keep Your Damn Mouth Shut When Playing in the Playground!
> The MINESHAFT playrooms are for one purpose and it surely is not the place to gossip, discuss your European trip, or how well Joan Sutherland sang "Carmen" at the Met. This you

do in the Main Bar which is a social area. Please remember this simple rule when visiting the Shaft.

He also posted warnings about violence: "This summer has been one of the worst in terms of street crimes in the Village/Chelsea area."

He told the following anecdote, characteristic of Mineshaft culture, in *Jack Fritscher Interviews Mineshaft Manager, Wally Wallace, March 28, 1990*:

> At one of our Mr. Mineshaft contests, one of the judges thinks he recognizes one of the contestants [Michael Garrison] as a man who seven years before had murdered the lover [Tom Strogen] of a mutual friend [Rob Kilgallen] to both the judge and me. So the judge tells me this during an intermission. The two of us go to our mutual friend out in the crowd and he confirms this. [The contestant] had murdered the lover, had gone to trial, and three years later he was out of jail, and now, a few years later, was in the Mr. Mineshaft contest.

On another existing videotape in Wally Wallace's collection—authenticated by reporter Bob Bailey in *New York's Gay Newspaper Connection* (June 11, 1985), the unsinkable Wally Wallace can be seen calling winner-killer Garrison back to the stage, disqualifying him, and humiliating him even as Garrison stands stripped to his contest costume of chains, jockstrap, and Muir leather cap. "This is a man," Wally Wallace said, intoning the shunning to the crowd, "I never want to see again in the Mineshaft because he took home a man who is no longer alive."

Even so, males of every class, caste, and nationality felt safe and secure under the omnipresent Wally Wallace's watchful eye, his clothing-check system, and his fire-safety regards.

> Wally Wallace: Our building was safe, but the sex definitely wasn't. AIDS was still in the unforeseeable future.
> Jack Fritscher: What was the dominant sexual activity at the Mineshaft? It seemed, "Anything goes."
> Wally Wallace: The most basic thing was cocksucking, then fucking, then fisting, then other things. Oh, rimming. And a lot of tit play. S&M. You know, you start at the top and go to the bottom.
> Jack Fritscher: That's gay sex to a T.

Reminding me of an after-hours joint that closed in 1978, Wally Wallace differentiated his integrity from his competition: "The Toilet [an after-hours club] hired pickpockets who worked for the house." He handed me an undated sheet from a *Mineshaft Newsletter* in which he wrote:

> Reporting a pickpocketing incident is important, but when you report it, give facts! Where were you when you first noticed something was gone....Who was around? Were there one or more? Were your pants up or down? Who do you suspect? Remember that all pickpockets are not Black or Hispanic! [The Mineshaft was famously international and inter-racial.] ....Our batting average has been good lately, but we remember a time in the early days when we had a real problem it took a long time to cure. Finally it was discovered that it was a team of three. One was really hot and always nude. His partners were the pass off men. He'd pick the pocket and pass it off to one of the who would relay it to another! Naturally the nude was never the suspect nor was the runner—a naked runner.

The Mineshaft could easily have disintegrated into a den of thieves. In the demimonde of leather, sex, drugs, and *haute culture*, a diversity of outlaws sometimes took advantage of its consensual and permissive milieu. In 1985, sex and art and death collided coincidentally in the S&M ritual-murder of model, Eigil Vesti, detailed by David France in *Bag of Toys: Sex Scandal, and the Death Mask Murder* (1992). As if playing the stabbing "*E-E-E*" violin notes from the shower scene in *Psycho*, France wrote on page 312, "When the phone rang outside the Mineshaft, on the morning of September 20, 1984...."

Almost from its opening night, the urban legend of the Mineshaft became part of American popular culture. Most urban legends are larger than life, but no urban legend can begin to capture nightlife inside the Mineshaft. According to Wally Wallace's report in the *Mineshaft Newsletter* (January 1977), a member named Howard went "beyond the call of duty [sucking off] 74 loads in one night."

Former *Drummer* editor Tim Barrus tried to capture the private club in his novel *Mineshaft*, and Leo Cardini tried in his picaresque book *Mineshaft Nights* which opened with a good description of the Mineshaft as a theater stage set up for erotic performance. It's what I tried to do for the Mineshaft with my article in *Drummer* which I dubbed on its masthead: "The American Review of Gay Popular Culture."

The very word *Mineshaft* grew to connote a certain de Sade-like shock value of sex beyond the pale.

Wally Wallace kept the Mineshaft ship on course. He wrote in his *Mineshaft Newsletter* (January 1977): "...we want to acknowledge the guys who have done so much to make THE MINESHAFT a pleasurable experience; especially the young ones we see growing up into new experiences they only fantasized about before."

Timing is everything if everything that rises is to converge. The mystique, action, and sexual power of the Mineshaft could have happened only in the Titanic 70s, an innocent, but not naive, time which those who were there remember, and those who weren't there often trash out of envy and bitterness because they missed the decade-long party.

> Whoever did not live in the years
> neighboring the revolution
> does not know what
> the pleasure of living means.
> —Charles Maurice de Talleyrand

The Mineshaft existed in that wonderful window between penicillin and HIV where sex galloped out of the closet completely unleashed in the heady first decade of sexual liberation. A real camaraderie existed. A few months after the Mineshaft opened, Wally Wallace became ill with the kind of heart problems that eventually killed him in 1999. In the first *Mineshaft Newsletter* for 1977, he wrote on page 5:

> A note of thanks to all you guys who thought of me during my hospital stay with your prayers, letters, and love. I am doing better every day; but like all affairs of the heart, it will take a while to really recover. May I return your love many fold. —Wally

In gay iconography, Wally Wallace, guarding the rope and the door at the Mineshaft, early in his life became a beloved star to gay and straight New York City where James Wallace was known by a single name. There was only one "Wally."

Jack Fritscher: Describe a cross section of the Mineshaft crowd.
Wally Wallace: We had every profession and business. Journalists. Critics. The cream of the crop. Bob Mapplethorpe, of course. Clergymen. It was a change for men dispensing holy water to receive holy water in the bathtub. Theater people.

Directors, writers. Not just performers. Performers of note stayed away, although some arrived in disguises. Nureyev showed up at the door in his huge fur coat, took it off and was in full leather, but the son of a bitch I had as doorman was a French-Canadian who thought he had to enforce the dress code to the nth degree. He wouldn't let him that night because he wouldn't leave his fur at our coat check. Rudy never came back. I fired the French-Canadian kid. I know that Rock Hudson came in. Pacino came in. I let him in one night just so he could research his role in *Cruising*. The music was low. So you could hear the person next to you.

Jack Fritscher: Who did your music tapes?

Wally Wallace: Jerry Rice...

Jack Fritscher: *Mon amour*, and house guest for years [since 1967].

Wally Wallace: ...and Michael Fesco who ran the Flamingo disco...

Jack Fritscher: Michael and I spent the Jonestown weekend together. [November 17-19, 1978] Luckily, we were in San Francisco, not Jonestown, drinking beer, not Kool-Aid.

Wally Wallace: ...and a guy named Ashland, and myself. I asked all kinds of people to make new tapes to fit our scene. We played anything in the world, from western to classics. A lot of classics actually. Electronic variations on classic themes. Ella Fitzgerald, jazz. Tomita, new wave.

Jack Fritscher: I remember hearing Kitaro, and Kraftwerk's *Trans-Europe Express*, and Tim Buckley. His "Sweet Surrender" was more seductive than poppers for fisting.

Wally Wallace: We tried to avoid basic disco, references to females, references to "let's dance," things like that. Our music became famous because we didn't follow the mainstream. We were about kink. Mineshaft members knew what kink was. They weren't out to blind date, nor to emulate the straight world in terms of sexuality, lovers, dogs, and family. Single guys.

Jack Fritscher: Every detail. Your main bar had sawdust on the floor. Inside the Mineshaft you created an alternative universe.

Wally Wallace: Most people don't know. Art, business, politics were conducted. Sex at the Mineshaft was like going to the gym to work out. An exercise. But also spiritual, like going to church. The Mineshaft was a form of recreation for people in high-pressure jobs whose stress came out as sexual intensity. It was not just a business; it was a labor of love. Other businesses tried to copy the Mineshaft but didn't succeed because they did it for money.

Jack Fritscher: The Mineshaft helped shape the way we were in the 1970s and 1980s.

Wally Wallace: I think we allowed everything. We gave guys a sense of freedom, to sort of sow their oats.

Jack Fritscher: Sow their oats and spill their seed.

Wally Wallace: Right. Sex is many things, never a cut and dried subject.

Jack Fritscher: Including sex, the Mineshaft provided much support to the community.

Wally Wallace: Stonewall didn't happen over night. The Stonewall Rebellion was one night. It didn't just grow spontaneously. It took a long time and a lot of people to develop what some people think exploded all at once in 1969.

Jack Fritscher: You ran a gentlemen's club for some wild gents who were building that first decade of gay liberation.

Wally Wallace: The staff and I gave a lot back to the community. We were there when people needed things, especially when they needed a space for a fund raiser. All these special-interest organizations came out: gay bankers, and the gay chorus needing tuxedos for their concert at Carnegie Hall. We raised a lot of money for charities and politics, and gay churches, and then AIDS. Just read the Mineshaft newsletters. The Mineshaft was so good at raising money that we caused people for the first time to realize the importance and the power of gay money.

Harold Cox was partners with Wally Wallace in the bar, The Lure, in the 1990s. Cox is the legendary editor of the magazine, *Checkmate Incorporating DungeonMaster*. He told me:

> When it came to money, Wally was no crook. He was personally very honest, but he had worked for some shady types. So when we started The Lure, kind of to give him a job after the Mineshaft closed, we had to tell him he did not need to drive to New Jersey to buy liquor, and he did not have to pay people under the table. We were not a Mafia bar.

I wouldn't say the Mafia was slow on the pick up, but in 1984 profits dropped so sharply at the Mineshaft that the good fellas called in Wally

Wallace and his staff, one by one, and accused them of skimming the cash register. It took nearly six months for the godfather to believe what Wally Wallace said: AIDS was killing their paying customers.

A notorious Hollywood "fictionalization" of the Mineshaft, featuring real Mineshaft "regulars" as atmosphere extras, was the William Friedkin film *Cruising*, finally released censored and cut in 1980. The *Cruising* script was loosely based on a fact-based novel of the same name by *New York Times* reporter Gerald Walker. During the film's 1979 location shooting in the streets of the Village, crowds of gays picketed the filming because they feared that Friedkin's dark image of gay leather men as murderers would cause a backlash against gay liberation.

Talk about the double standard in queerdom! These same anti-leather gays nonetheless defended drag queens and guys in butterfly costumes on roller skates as normative in the broad daylight of Pride Parades. Perhaps their attitude was bitchy payback against Friedkin whom they hated for his outing—ten years earlier—of the self-hating archetypal bitch-queens in his acerbic film of Mart Crowley's lacerating play *The Boys in the Band* (1970).

The fearless Friedkin also trolled the nihilistic dark side of drugs, satanism, and gangsters in classics like *The French Connection* (1971), *The Exorcist* (1973), and *To Live and Die in LA* (1985). Friedkins' sharp nihilistic formalism on screen was, I think, very like the formal, perfect-moment dark side of Robert Mapplethorpe, a Mineshaft charter member, who was honored by leatherfolk and disdained by the majority of the eponymous "gay community."

Some scholar needs to investigate how this disconnect within queer culture is similar to the culture war waged by straight fundamentalists against homosexuals. I addressed this dramatically in the "gay-politics civil war" story arc in *Some Dance to Remember: A Memoir-Novel of San Francisco 1970-1982* (1990).

Wally Wallace gave his eyewitness testimony about *Cruising*, Friedkin, and the allegedly corrupt *French Connection* cops in the video *Jack Fritscher Interviews Mineshaft Manager, Wally Wallace, March 28, 1990*:

> Wally Wallace: *Cruising* was not filmed at the Mineshaft but it gave us notoriety. We had a lot of sex tourists from all over Europe. One time I had [in a kind of shocking statistic worthy of both Kinsey and the Center for Disease Control] our doorman keep tabs for one week—we called it "Seven Days in May," but it was really ten—on where everybody was from who came through our doors, and I think it was something like thirty-three states and over forty countries....About the

only countries not represented were from behind the Iron Curtain.

Jack Fritscher: The CDC might like to profile that statistic.

Wally Wallace: The film representative came into the Mineshaft maybe six months before filming. He wanted to do still photographs, but he said the ceilings were not high enough for a movie. I refused because we had a rule at the beginning about no photographs. We only let friends like Mapplethorpe take some...And then a couple of my staff got involved with the movie. Others on the staff didn't want anything to do with it because it portrayed gays as murderers....

Jack Fritscher: So, to end the rumor: it was not filmed at the Mineshaft.

Wally Wallace: *Cruising* was not filmed at the Mineshaft—although to this day people think it was. The bar scenes were done at a place now known as the Cell Block, but at that time it was—before it was Hellfire—another after-hours place in the basement of the Triangle Building at 14th Street and Ninth Avenue. It is a unique space that is under the street and not under the building.

Jack Fritscher: It was always a more hetero mix there. My friend Frank Vickers, the Colt model who was also a model for Mapplethorpe, liked to play there. [Having photographed Frank Vickers on video in 1981, I asked him to appear on the cover of the first edition of my erotic fiction anthology, *Stand by Your Man* (1987).]

Wally Wallace: They continued to want to shoot stills in the Mineshaft, but I refused. [In a much longer and complicated dialog, Wally Wallace alleged to me, the film company purposely "set up" the first police bust of the Mineshaft by bribing the cops who had helped Friedkin direct *The French Connection* in Manhattan a few years earlier. During the raid, while Wally Wallace and his staff were arrested and]...taken downtown in a paddy wagon....a crew from the movie company came into the Mineshaft and photographed everything [ostensibly to build a similar set on a sound stage]...Friedkin had this obsession to re-create the Mineshaft interior and exterior.

Jack Fritscher: It certainly looks real on film.

Wally Wallace: In order to create the exterior, he hired the meat company which is right next door to the Mineshaft, where he filmed all his entrances and exits to the bar in the bar scenes.

In the movie, people go downstairs after entering, whereas in the Mineshaft, you had to go upstairs. Otherwise, it looks the same.

Jack Fritscher: Is it ironic that when you began to have a movie night, the first 16mm film you projected on the screen in the Mineshaft main bar was *Cruising*?

Film critic, Gary Morris, wrote in *Bright Lights Film Journal* #16 (April 1996):

> Friedkin's sweaty tableaux of leather-clad, popper-snorting, fist-fucking, sadomasochistic hedonists was bound to trigger a reaction from gays who feared society would assume all homosexuals were busily engaged in these activities....This sounds dangerously similar to the middle-class queens who complain about the presence of leather, drag, or nudity in gay marches....What they failed to note is how *Cruising* points the finger for a violent decadent society far past the gyrating leather queens, who come off more as fun-loving party-boys than sinister psychopaths...it's the leather boys [from the Mineshaft] who are the targeted innocents...while the cops (read: society) are shaking down, brutalizing, raping, and probably murdering gays....

Here's my two-cents' worth of contribution to original scholarship: *Cruising* is the unspoken dark "back story" of the kind of Mafia-and-cop-subculture that tyrannized the Stonewall Inn and all the other gay bars in New York in the 1960s. It explains why that gay rebellion was so self-defensively energized and important. That homophobic, authoritarian, and Fascist subculture of cops did not evaporate in the vapor trail of the Stonewall Rebellion, June 27-28, 1969. It was pervasive nationally. In Chicago, when Chuck Renslow opened the world's first leather bar, the Gold Coast, in 1957, he had to pay off both the cops and the mob well into the 1970s. On April 11, 1976, the LAPD raided the Mark IV Bath and arrested forty-two people at the fund-raiser, the *Drummer* "Slave Auction." Harassment continued in New York even as the Mineshaft opened its doors in 1976 under legal and civic threats exactly like the fire-code and health-code dodges used to close the Mineshaft doors in November 1985 ending the sacred shrine's fabled nine-year and nine-day sleaze party.

What further original analysis I can add from my own experience is that the 1970s vanilla culture of Manhattan gays was terribly upset, set up, and misguided by a seminal anti-S&M screed written by the infamous Richard Goldstein at the *Village Voice*.

There was a political as well as erotic reason behind the dress code at the Mineshaft. In the *Mineshaft Newsletter* (April 1977), Wally Wallace wrote:

> The Queen, England's Elizabeth, is celebrating her first 25 years on the throne. Without her pomp or her circumstances, the MINESHAFT will celebrate its first six months on the weekend of April 15th. Fortunately we don't expect a queen in sight. Thrones [toilets], yes, but "queens" no!

Exercising "crowd control" against invasive cologne and Lacoste queens, Wally Wallace wrote in the *Mineshaft Membership Application*:

> Approved items in the MINESHAFT DRESS CODE as originally adopted are leather cycle styles, western gear, Levi's, T-shirts, tanktops, official uniforms, plaid and plain shirts, some rugged work pants, cut offs, gymwear, jockstraps, and just plain sweat.
>
> The items *not* approved are those which do not fit in a man's club where visions of leather, cowboys, uniforms, and jocks are a reality and not just sugar plums at Christmas. In other words: NO COLOGNE, PERFUME, or STRONG AFTERSHAVE, NO SUITS, TIES, JACKETS, DRESS PANTS, or FANCY SHIRTS, NO DISCO DRAG, NO MAKE-UP OR FEMININE HAIR STYLES, NO FANCY DESIGNER SWEATERS, NO RUGBY OR OTHER STRIPED SHIRTS, NO HEAVY OUTERWEAR OR PARKAS, and, last but not least, LACOSTE STYLE SHIRTS. This is a NO, NO even if manufactured by those who ignore the original alligator and replace it with foxes, sailboats, pigs, or monograms. The administration of the DRESS CODE is the responsibility of the MINESHAFT Doorman, and should he err, someone on the very capable staff will probably catch it. So buy it, don't defy it!
>
> ....When you go to the Baths, you are requested to wear a towel.
>
> ...Problems arise in the dress code when a guy dressed properly tries to bring in a friend who is not so attired. It is equally hard to turn away an out-of-towner, especially a foreign visitor, who may be of the right head, but of the wrong dress. Exceptions

have been made, but in the future they will not be without a loan of the shirt off our back to the right guy.

....We feel that suits, ties, sport jackets, sweaters, fur coats, sparkles, spangles, and dresses have a place in gay society, but it ain't here.

Richard Goldstein was a lickety-lickety crusader of the correct. He seemed to have a special hatred for the Mineshaft and for Rex. He got his buzz poking his stick into the gay beehive. He specialized in anti-leather, anti-S&M, anti-fisting articles, such as "Flirting with Terminal Sex" which continued his cautionary rant begun in "S&M: The Dark Side of Gay Liberation," in the *Village Voice*, July 7, 1975.

Goldstein hit a diva's high note that shattered glass.

Timing is everything.

Seventeen days before the *Village Voice* published Goldstein's article, *Drummer* had published its first issue June 20, 1975.

Objective corollary: seven weeks before *Drummer* was first published—that is, while the first issue was being written and edited, the Vietnam war, which drove draft-age gay men to excess to stay alive, ended on April 30, 1975, as helicopters lifted the last Marines off the rooftop of the American embassy in Saigon.

Never underestimate the pervasive violence of the Vietnam war, and the resistance to it, on the psyche of gay men in the Titanic 70s. Queer scholarship needs to address this unspoken nexus between war and hedonism.

If, as an eyewitness participant, I made *Drummer* homo-aggro (aggressive), particularly in my editorials (eg.: *Drummer* 24, September 1978) and in my hard-hitting "resistance" themes of *masculinity* and *homomasculinity*, it was part of my stance against anti-leather queens like Goldstein who in 1975 was the first voice I heard of the politically correct who later abducted gay culture when it was brought to its knees by HIV, and thus made so very vulnerable to hostile take over.

About Hollywood, Katharine Hepburn famously said, "Most people in this profession are pigs." About the politically correct in publishing and academia, I'd say the same thing. I have withstood the PC pigs for thirty years and I will rejoice when their politically correct fad fully fades like the Marxism whose bastard it is.

I suspect that at this moment most leatherfolk are yet as unaware of Goldstein's pioneering anti-leather, anti-edge rants as they were unaware of the *Life* (June 26, 1964) article which I was the first to "out" to the attention of leather history in *Drummer* 134 (October 1989). That was the issue on the stands during the huge Loma Prieta earthquake, 5:04

PM, October 17, 1989, that wiped out the *Drummer* office, demoralized its owners, and caused the magazine to be put up for sale, and turned over to the last owner's mostly greenhorn-tinhorn editors.

The politically correct quake was worse.

Why is the West Coast always ahead of East Coast leather? Like Rex, even NY-centric Mapplethorpe left Manhattan and came to San Francisco, to my *Drummer* desk, to begin his West-Coast-driven "leather period" which to this day his East Coast heirs probably wish would disappear so they can sell calla lily photographs printed on dinner plates and shower curtains.

Much that I have written in *Drummer* in defense of leather, edge play, fisting, and S&M, as well as much that I have written in defense of, in fact, Robert Mapplethorpe, was caused, as scoped out here, by crap such as Richard Goldstein's hysterical take on masculine-identified leather. Goldstein's anti-male prejudice was the East Coast twin of self-described sissy publisher, David Goodstein, whose fear and loathing of men permeated his magazine, *The Advocate*.

Are some gay men so "'whipped" by feminist Marxism that they fight the fact that homomasculinity is a legitimate measure on the Kinsey scale?

What makes these urban oracles, who have a right to be surrounded by coteries of sissies, forget this fact: the true gay-male demographic within all races is more than ninety percent masculine identified. For incontrovertible proof, I offer as internal evidence of self-fashioned gay identity the millions of personal sex classifieds of magazines and papers ranging from *Drummer* to *The Advocate* which pivot on the word *masculine*.

Contemporaneous with Anita Bryant and the religious right, Goldstein and Goodstein set up the judgmental and fearful attitude that grew to excite the United States federal government when Republican Senator Jesse Helms denounced S&M, leather, and Mapplethorpe on the floor of the United States Senate, and destroyed the National Endowment to the Arts as well as federal funding to uncensored voices and visions. No one can convince me that these anti-sex Cassandras weren't all vindicated by the advent of AIDS.

Drummer's voice and vision is totem of leather culture within gay culture within straight culture.

Drummer, from first issue to last (*Drummer* 214), stood like a lighthouse against the dark censorious shadow cast by attitudes such as Goldstein's, Goodstein's, and Helms' who represent legions of repression from the Marxist left and the religious right.

The positive energy pole of West Coast *Drummer*, appearing at the same time as the negative energy of East Coast Goldstein, charged up the electrical field that shaped and censored *Drummer* throughout the

Drummer 19: The Mineshaft

1970s, 1980s, and 1990s: in problems *Drummer* had with Puritan printers and fundamentalist distributors, with customs agents seizing *Drummer* between the US and Canada, as well as the specific video censorship of *Drummer* publisher Anthony DeBlase's and Zeus Studio's *Drummer* S&M series, *USSM* —which I've always thought was the most brilliant title ever for a video series.

Nevertheless, "*Drummer* served, and still serves," wrote PlanetSoma. com, "as the guidebook to the national leather/SM community." So I was happy when PlanetOut.com wrote that "Fritscher was the groundbreaking editor of *Drummer* magazine."

I was equally happy when an anti-Semite website listing the takeover of "Jews in Homosexual Vocations in America" named me specifically in terms of *Drummer*: "Fritscher became editor in chief of gay *Drummer* magazine in 1977." Others listed were: Tony Kushner, Larry Kramer, Leslie Feinberg, Dan Savage, Sarah Schulman, Martin Duberman, Rex Wockner, Gayle Rubin, and even black-leather's nemesis, Richard Goldstein, himself. Even though I am an Irish-Austrian American Catholic, I realize that *fag* and *Jew* are one and the same epithet to bigots, and in that I relish solidarity.

Always in the eye of a Category 5 storm, *Drummer* was the leather magazine of record which dared proclaim masculine-identified homosexuality as alternative to the queenstream. Such issues of sexual identity interested Friedkin. Had he submitted his screenplay for *Cruising* to *Drummer* I would have gladly serialized it—Vito Russo not withstanding, because Friedkin's depiction of leathermen holds up as a psychological inquiry, as well as a *film-noir* murder mystery in which the "virilization issues" of male sexual identity are the main theme.

Also, for leathermen of a certain age, it is nostalgic fun to freeze-frame *Cruising* to see a veritable gallery of otherwise lost-to-history familiar faces—including the 1960s Latin porn star, Fernando—"acting" all around the sexy and brooding star Al Pacino who could have been that year's Mr. *Drummer*. I wrote in *Mapplethorpe: Assault with a Deadly Camera*, pages 189-190:

> Between 1979 and 1980, Robert Mapplethorpe was the "official" Mineshaft photographer. Wally Wallace asked Robert to shoot a party at the club....In October, 1979, he shot David O'Brien, that year's "Mr. Mineshaft," at the bootblack's stand....

As Bogart said in *Casablanca* (1942): "Sooner or later, everyone comes to Rick's."

The Mineshaft was instantly the hottest spot in New York during the Titanic 70s even after Studio 54 debuted five months later on April 26, 1977. Everyone who was anyone traveled from wherever they were in the world, from over the rainbow, from Max's Kansas City and the Saint and CBGB to the north end of the West Village, twelve to fourteen blocks away from Christopher Street, to try to be admitted into the after-hours Mineshaft.

"It is an odd thing," quipped Oscar Wilde, "but everyone who disappears is said to be seen in San Francisco. It must be a delightful city, and possess all the attractions of the next world."

Substitute the word *Mineshaft* for *San Francisco* to understand the Bali Hai call of the Mineshaft and the litany of the rich and famous, talented and beautiful and legendary who were, so urban legend gossiped, seen down on their knees at the Mineshaft—from Nureyev and Minnelli to Fassbinder and Foucault. Mick Jagger was turned away for showing up with a couple of women, who, like business suits and Lacoste shirts, were not on the list. Once in awhile, some women disguised as men did make it into the Mineshaft. As with the Woodstock wannabes ("I was at Woodstock!) and the Stonewall revisionists ("I was at Stonewall!"), Wally Wallace assured me, lots of people—men as well as women—who bragged they made it into the Mineshaft were lying.

During my 1990 interview, Wally Wallace—who was the founding (and only) manager of the Mineshaft, as well as its total creative force and code enforcer—offered me more than one hundred photographs shot inside the Mineshaft for inclusion in the video documentary as well as for historical publication in *Eyewitness Drummer*. Wally Wallace had a couple of original Mapplethorpe prints tossed unprotected into his suitcase with all the other photographs, his underwear, and socks. I lifted the Mapplethorpe photos up with two fingers by the corner, as if they were sacred objects, and told Wally what iconic images they were and how much they were worth.

He shrugged.

He was totally unassuming, but he was also in interview so very monumentally disgusted with gay culture at large that he damned the whole of it. What happened next at *Drummer* didn't sweeten his tongue. Wally Wallace knew I intended to excerpt his interview in *Drummer*.

I wrote a letter to him dated April 10, 1990:

Wally Wallace
183 Christopher Street 2nd Floor
New York NY 10014

Dear Wally,

Thanks for a very pleasant afternoon. You made the interview much more fun than interviews often are. Actually, it was nice just to be able to sit and talk with you. Next time you're out [to San Francisco], we must visit again, without both of us having to work at the same time.

Enclosed is a copy of *Palm Drive Video's Greatest Hits* which you might find amusing. Sort of short clips from a wide variety of our offbeat videos.

Especially enclosed is a copy of *Some Dance to Remember*, my new novel, which we spoke about. Hope you enjoy it. Reader response has been excellent as have the reviews that have come in so far [in the two months since the book's publication].

Your photos which you left with me are safe, and I'll be giving them to *Drummer* as soon as I finish [transcribing] the interview, which should be sometime in May.

Again, thanks for your time. I'll be sending you a draft of the interview before it's published in *Drummer* so you can check it to make sure I haven't misrepresented you in any way. It's very important to me to keep things clear among people, particularly in the gay business of publishing.

Best regards,
Jack Fritscher

cc. Anthony DeBlase, *Drummer* publisher
Joseph Bean, *Drummer* editor

On the same April 10, 1990, I wrote to *Drummer* editor, Joseph Bean:

Dear Joseph,

...The Mineshaft interview took 12 hours, 2 meals, but it was worth it. Interview should be to you mid-to-late May. Also took pix of Wally, so that bottom of 1st page might have 3 horizontal pix ala *Playboy*. However, you use them, they're the only current pix of WW around....
Yours,
Jack Fritscher

cc. A. DeBlase

When the October 17, 1989, earthquake destroyed the *Drummer* office, the magazine never recovered despite the efforts of editor Joseph Bean and the publisher Anthony DeBlase who felt compelled to sell *Drummer* to the Dutch businessman Martijn Bakker in September 1992.

In the turmoil, my interview with Wally Wallace lay in turnaround, unpublished.

Seeing the handwriting on the wall, and feeling abandoned and ignored, Wally Wallace knew he was being double-fucked. It hurt my feelings that *Drummer* hurt him. I thoroughly liked him. He was not even a year older than I, but he had a hundred years of wear and tear from his long nights at the Mineshaft. He was always a difficult personality, but he was no curmudgeon. And his heart condition was worsening. He knew the primacy of *Drummer* in leather history, and he felt his legacy slipping away through DeBlase's negligence.

Wally Wallace sent me a copy of a bitter letter he sent to Anthony DeBlase because, failing a response from DeBlase, he wanted me publish the letter; it was postmarked April 7, 1992. Two years had passed since I had given Wally's photographs to *Drummer*, and still DeBlase refused to cooperate with Wally Wallace with whom he had once been so close, famously even hosting S&M workshops at the Mineshaft. The irony was that it was DeBlase who roped both Wally Wallace and me into doing the interview in the first place.

Of course, there was a back story.

Because I was involved with former Chicagoan DeBlase in the startup and the writing of the *Drummer* feature on leather history titled "Rear-View Mirror," I was aware as early as 1988 that DeBlase's interest and loyalty was shifting from repairing *Drummer* in San Francisco to inventing the Leather Archives and Museum in Chicago in partnership with Chuck Renslow. DeBlase was founding director and president of the LA&M board of directors. I know, from my eyewitness participation, that he asked me—and others—to write about leather history and to interview personalities such as Wally Wallace so that, as *Drummer* publisher, he could funnel our raw data and essays into the new Leather Archives and Museum which was a brainchild born out of a partnership with Chuck Renslow who was casting about for a place to archive the artwork of his terminally ill partner Dom Orejudos aka Etienne. The Leather Archives and Museum was incorporated in August 1991 and Etienne died on September 24, 1991.

Even so, DeBlase, dejected over *Drummer*, was no longer motivated to publish the Wally Wallace interview in *Drummer*. Even before the 1989 earthquake, DeBlase devalued *Drummer* because on his watch plague and politics had turned the former erotic giant into a self-help and gender-esteem magazine, and he was trying to unload it on anyone (including me) who would buy it.

Primarily, he wanted my personal historical research about Chicago leather culture and Folsom Street life, as well as my Wallace-Mineshaft videotape to build up his LA&M history archives where he was worthily engaged in building a *Leather History Timeline*. (He once thanked me and admitted he mined my archeological information in my *Drummer* writing, particularly my "Rear-View Mirror" columns, in order to build parts of that vast timeline. I also helped him construct his later issues of *DungeonMaster*.)

No one has yet noted the important role that *Drummer* once perforce played in adding its DNA to the GLBT genome at the LA&M.

In the zero degrees of separation, the morbidly ailing DeBlase chose former *Drummer* editor Joseph Bean, who moved his expertise from San Francisco to Chicago, to become executive director of the LA&M in July 1997. Anthony DeBlase died in Oregon on July 21, 2000.

Wally Wallace's letter is presented with his punctuation, spelling, and feeling intact:

April 6, 1992

Dear Mr DeBlase,

Two and a half years ago I was asked by you if I would be willing to be interviewed for a feature article in DRUMMER on my experiences as manager of The Mineshaft. I believe that it was part of a series of articles on Seventies Sleaze spots. It was shortly after the earthquake and I believe that the intent was to revitalize your membership [subscription lists]. Although I agreed to what appeared to be an urgent request it was another four or five months later before I was directly contacted by Jack Fritscher who was assigned to write the article. [I contacted Wally Wallace quickly after DeBlase had waited months to give me the assignment.]

Jack suggested we set a time for him to call me and we would do it over the telephone. I felt that if it was to be the important feature that a person-to-person phone conversation would be inappropriate as I have had a couple of bad experiences in being misquoted and generally am uncomfortable in extended telephone conversations.

After making one personal schedule change, arranging for a Friend to stay with and an inexpensive flight, I went out to San

Francisco to meet with Jack. I had cash flow problems, which I still do, but thought the story well worth making the trip. I NEITHER ASKED FOR NOR REALLY EXPECTED COMPENSATION FROM DRUMMER. [Nor did I who received none for this project.] That is, other than a fair shake, or should I say a rather timely publication of the article resulting from my face-to-face interview with someone whom I both knew and still respect. Naturally, as you are the one who initially approached I thought that you would also be involved with the end product.

In any event I thought I was doing someone whom I respected a favor. I also looked forward with sharing my experience in a leisurely manner in an unpressured atmosphere away from New York. With Jack this worked very well as we talked for hours on the balcony of a friend overlooking San Francisco. The early spring March day was perfect and as we talked he videotaped every word. I think that I was candid and we covered many, many subjects. I was excited because I finally opened up a lot of thoughts that I had had to contain within me to that day. And most important, I was certain that the resulting feature by Jack would be both a pleasure for your readers, who had either visited the Mineshaft or had heard tales about it.

So, where is it? Where is a copy of the video of that experience that I thought I would show my other half? [He presumed I would release a copy of that original video footage. I never promised that. What I promised was to send him a transcript of the interview. As a journalist, I would never release into the wild my private notations on paper or on tape. I also think he presumed that my video was some kind of production by my company, Palm Drive Video. In truth, I set up my camera on a tripod in a full-on medium close-up of Wally Wallace, in the same way that I interviewed Robb of Amsterdam and others. It was electronic note-taking. As I wrote his words on my yellow legal pad, I let my camera—with its wonderful microphone—run untouched as a way to record his words more precisely than a small audiotape recorder. He knew that the video was for archival use.] Where are my personal pictures that I left in your or Jack's care. [I had handed them to DeBlase so that he could begin photostating them for the page-layout design of the interview. Ultimately, I went to DeBlase and asked for the photos which he held for another six months. Immediately, on October 20, 1992, I mailed them to Wally Wallace, and the letter that accompanied them follows this letter.]

Drummer 19: The Mineshaft

Jack was kind enough to send me a short and wonderful note shortly after, but that is the last semi-official written notice that I have ever had regarding my efforts to give you the DRUMMER story that you wanted.

....I also want immediate return of all my photographs and other materials that I supplied for this thankless endeavor....In truth I am glad that I did participate in that experience for like many of life experiences it served as a lesson in the art of wasting time which seems to be just what most of my endeavors on the behalf of the DRUMMER image have been.

[Wally Wallace then shifts to *Drummer* and his discontent with DeBlase's lack of help in staging the Mister Northeast *Drummer* Contests.] ...Behind the scenes, cooperation on the part of DRUMMER this year was to say the least, minimal. Each year our expenses are raised through the program ad inserts with the ticket proceeds going to the cause [AIDS].... Shortly after we mailed our letter solicitating ads we received a call from someone in your organization wanting a quotation on the subscription prices in last year's ad as they couldn't locate the copy we had sent with our letter. It turned out that the prices were still in effect, but the post office box number was wrong. So, the caller said he would send another tearsheet or mechanical which he did. To it our layout man added the expression "Keep on Drummin'" in the space between the cover photos and the order form. Then in a blank space on another page we devoted a 3/4 page to a free promo for the San Francisco main event [the annual international Mr. *Drummer* contest].

Then later a few days...I called John Ferrari [at *Drummer*] about the payment for the ad. He said he'd look into it, but as you were having cash flow problems he doubted that you wanted an ad. After two days I called again only to find that he was in Atlanta and you were away. I left messages at two Atlanta locations for Ferrari, but he never called. But, we went to press with the belief that you would come through. I sure made a mistake.

The army taught me never to assume anything. I guess that I forgot that when I mistakenly thought that DRUMMER magazine would repeat their support, in a DRUMMER Contest program, for an AIDS...fund raiser.

...The shock of your "cash flow" decision was not only difficult to explain to our beneficiary organization, but lost us two vital committee members on the eve of the contest who basically indicated upon exiting that...they have had it up to here with the piety of the Almighty DRUMMER....In truth you use, but certainly don't know how to appreciate the people in the various regions who work damn hard to keep the name and publication of DRUMMER alive.

This has not been an easy letter to write. In fact on a personal level it has been most difficult to write as I seem to remember a cocktail party in my former home congratulating you on your acquisition of DRUMMER Magazine. Enough said.

Enough indeed. Wally Wallace apologized for speaking truth. Wallace had feted DeBlase in New York after the wealthy doctor Andrew Charles purchased *Drummer* for his lover DeBlase on August 22, 1986. In San Francisco, our long-standing salon around *Drummer* also welcomed Charles and DeBlase to *Drummer*. There was an especially wonderful and intimate supper for ten held in their honor on the Thursday before the Folsom Leather Weekend, September 25, 1986. We writers, photographers, and artists—including Rex—hoped for a restoration at *Drummer* after the botched ownership by first publisher John Embry.

It wasn't long before new publisher DeBlase was believing his own press. The toy his lover had bought him brought him power, and power corrupts—at least, relatively. (The *Drummer* mystique—and here's the elephant in the room—was also a way for both Charles and DeBlase to get laid by leathermen who otherwise would not touch them for love or money.) Embry had used *Drummer* to fund real estate. DeBlase, even though married to the Charles fortune, used the energy and cash of *Drummer* the way Evita, even though married to Peron, funded her foundation and her Rainbow Tour. His interest was not in *Drummer* itself; he was using *Drummer* as a means to an end.

Owning *Drummer* was like waving a gun: the sense of power made everyone look, and get out of the way.

Whatever insecurities or jealousy that DeBlase had felt in the 1970s trying to break into the Chicago leather empire created by the legendary Chuck Renslow, he was out to prove something. He had issues. He had been the archetypal fat john standing in the Gold Coast leather bar knowing that every thirty pounds he was overweight took a half inch off his penis. By 1990, he was determined to return to Chicago as a player and a winner and a cult personality no one there could dismiss or exclude.

As eyewitness in his April 2, 1992, letter, Wally Wallace insinuates the storyline of how DeBlase came to San Francisco, climbed his way to power, forgot who he was, fell from grace, and had to flee the City. I had been friends with Andy Charles since 1969. I knew him "when": before he met DeBlase. My first lover David Sparrow and I, and then Mark Hemry and I, were their friends. It saddens me to remember that as an eyewitness on the inside track at *Drummer* and at their home, I watched as their personal modesty turned to the same kind of prehensile hubris that infected John Embry.

In closing I ran into Rex last night who was about to return to San Francisco. I told him of my intended letter on the article that never happened. He said, "what did I expect from the laxidasical [*sic*] world of the porn publishing world." Somehow, from you, Tony, or rather Master DeBlase, I did expect something more.
(Signed) Wally

Acting as apologist for *Drummer* and DeBlase, I wrote to Wally Wallace on October 20, 1992:

Dear Wally,

You've heard of all the changes at *Drummer*, I'm sure, since it's been sold. Tony stays on [so I was told], which is good, because he's a calming influence; Joseph Bean remains editor, which is also good. Now with a new publisher perhaps a solid new direction will pump some life into the magazine — life that was lacking mostly due to censorship. *Drummer* always gets picked on for things that aren't *Drummer*'s fault. Once this presidential election is over — and decides things somewhat about what the gay media can expect [to print] — the pace of publishing will pick up.

As I mentioned to you [on the telephone], I have worked on your interview...and so it will happen, but not, of course, without your reading it and updating or changing whatever you like. That's not just a courtesy to you for all the courtesy you showed me the day I drove from the country to the City to see you; it's a courtesy and more. I want the interview to be accurate and to reflect how you want to see yourself presented in print.

So again, thank you, for meeting with me and for being so open and fresh in the stories you told and how you told them. History will be all the more exact for your testimony to the Golden Age of the Mineshaft.

Enclosed are the photographs you left with me. I hate sending them through the mail [as he requested], but I'm packing them safely and sending them CERTIFIED etc to enhance the chance that the Post Office can actually deliver.

I hope you got that original Mapplethorpe framed — the one I pulled from your stack of photographs. It's quite valuable.

As things take shape with the latest new *Drummer*, I'll let you know the schedule and will send you the manuscript for your reading prior to publication.

All the best,
Jack Fritscher

When DeBlase bought *Drummer* from its first publisher John Embry in 1986, hostilities broke into a blood feud almost instantly. When DeBlase sold *Drummer* to its third publisher Martijn Bakker in 1992, a nasty business quarrel erupted within hours.

Egos and cash done 'em all in.

Martijn Bakker, the new owner of *Drummer*, lived in Holland and quickly parted ways with DeBlase who, besides being a morbidly obese gourmet cook and cigar smoker, suddenly "suffered some kind of emotional collapse." Escaping Bakker and *Drummer* and San Francisco, DeBlase fled to Oregon where, growing more eccentric, he edited his magazine *DungeonMaster*, which he sold to my longtime friend Harold Cox, publisher of *Checkmate* magazine. Guiding the Chicago LA&M from Oregon, DeBlase died of complications involving liver failure on July 21, 2000.

Bakker's amateur American editors Robert Davolt and Wickie Stamps, twisting *Drummer* to their own agenda, shunned the very idea of an interview about a long-gone sex club by "Wally who?"

Even though I offered Davolt-Stamps some of the Mineshaft photos, I was told the interview was "too much text" for their taste! Their readers wanted pictures.

Rex said, "What do you expect?"

This snub by neo-gay culture pissed Wally Wallace off even more. He felt further justified in his bitterness toward the ignorant, young, history-free queers who took over in the 1990s after the generation who should have been running gay media had all suddenly died.

An historian wanting to know how *Drummer* fizzled to its demise in 1999 need look only at the magazine's failure of originality and vision during the entire 1990s. For instance, *Drummer* staff, Davolt and Stamps, missed the perfect journalistic "hook" to publish my Wally Wallace interview when there was a hot news flash about a "new" Mineshaft resurrected by the French in Marseille in 1995. As it turned out, *Drummer* was scooped by rival magazine, *International Leatherman* (September 1996), whose editor (in the zero degrees) was former *Drummer* editor Joseph Bean. Even so, in the *IL* "Euro-Leather" column, Bean's history-free reporter Thomas Schwartz wrote about the French Mineshaft without mentioning the original Mineshaft or Wally Wallace or Rex whose artwork was badly imitated in the advertising for the Mineshaft, F.S.M.C., rue Mazagran, F-13001, Marseille, France.

Wally Wallace was insulted by both the French imitation and the leather-heritage omission in both *Drummer* and *International Leatherman*.

Even as we remained friends, Wally Wallace often phoned to chat, bitching and wondering why *Drummer* wasn't interested in his story of the Mineshaft. My hands were tied.

He said, "Gays are always embarrassed by the leather community the way straights are embarrassed by fags."

We both believed that *Drummer* in the 1990s had been captured in a coup by vanilla queers. He and I both remained at a loss why *Drummer* did not want to hear his vivid oral history, because *Drummer* had eagerly published my histories of other leather luminaries such as Chuck Arnett, Robert Mapplethorpe, and Tony Tavarossi in my "Rear-View Mirror" leather-history columns.

Ten months before DeBlase died, Wally Wallace, betrayed by gay culture and embittered by the century, died September 7, 1999.

His heart clutched.

He died in a panic to remember.

Everything ends in panic.

Like Magnus Bishop, my narrator in *Some Dance to Remember*, I was left holding baskets full of notes, diaries, letters, recordings, photographs, and videotapes.

In "THE MINESHAFT FIFTH ANNIVERSARY NEWSLETTER," Wally Wallace wrote about remembrance:

> In one hundred years will anyone remember? In one hundred years will anybody care? Lyrics from a long ago Broadway show

[Kander and Ebb's *Chicago* (1975)] echo through my head as I put together this *Newsletter* celebrating the MINESHAFT's fifth anniversary. Well, I can't comment on one hundred years to come, but as far as today goes it can be said that the club is in the thoughts of guys the world over who have either been in the MINESHAFT or fantasized about it from printed word or the word of mouths. So for you and them I hope that the mystery, the myth, the magic, the music, and the men remain hot for at least five years if not for one hundred. —Wally

My own experiences at the Mineshaft, which I attended religiously for years, are glossed, of course, in my 1977 feature article in which I was tub-thumping for the Mineshaft as a place of necessary pilgrimage for any grown-up masculine-identified gay man. As editor in chief, I presupposed my *Drummer* readers believed Auntie Mame's first commandment that life is a banquet and most poor suckers are starving to death.

Back in that day, I lived bi-coastally between New York and San Francisco all during the 1960s and 70s. When I was in Manhattan, I'd see the latest films during the afternoon, the latest plays in the evenings, and after a tour of the leather bars, I'd alternate the late nights between the not-so-vanilla Everard Baths, a filthy, glorious, matchbox maze which burned often (one of many times in 1977, and finally in 1985), and the Mineshaft (which was so wet it burned partially only once) with its more extreme action of nipples, slings, fisting, piss, bondage, whipping, and scatology.

At the Mineshaft, the group dynamic was such high energy that a man had to be in control of himself so as not to get swept away in action that was too extreme for himself. That meant grass and poppers—and staying away from acid, MDA, and angel dust.

Sometimes the very personal is the way to, if not universality, at least to historical feel.

Eyewitness Scenario 1: Interior Mineshaft. 2:30 AM. A very handsome leatherman and I, both stripped to the waist, pec to pec, nipple to nipple, began bumping belt buckles, and playing with our leather belts, which turned into a mutual belting session, chest and back and shoulders, which "turned on" a third man who joined us, increasing the round of beltings, as the energy shifted and two ganged up on the third, and the trio of us migrated slowly away from the crowded room to a more private corner, and the belting increased to the intensity of, say, two guards in a Georgia prison beating an inmate, escalating in consensual intensity until the ferocity rose to a level of awareness of what "being beaten by belts" was about, to the moment where the quintessential intellectual curiosity is satisfied, is transcended, and the scene having reached its apogee begins to descend into nothing but physical subjection to brutality, and I said, *stop*, and they continued, and I said, *No, stop*, and they continued, and I crawled out from under them and said, *Really, no, stop*, and they stopped in the wonderful bonding, knowing finally that I meant *stop*. I got the point—the experiential definition of what belting and beating is—and reached my limit in a spontaneous scene I had not expected to be part of, and we smiled, and I rose up, and as quickly as I rose to my feet from under their belts, a fourth man, who had been watching from the doorway, fell to his knees at the booted feet of the three of us, and the belting began all over again, on him.

The very architecture of the Mineshaft as well as the shifting crowd allowed scenes to flow from one intensity to the next, and the players to change within a scene, so that a man could enter any scene, upstairs, or leave any scene downstairs, exactly when and how he chose, free, always careful not to break the erotic trance of the participants in the scene.

In fact, *erotic trance* was goal and mantra at the Mineshaft.

"Fantasy imagined" was exchanged at the door in favor of "fantasy actualized into new reality."

In the Mineshaft, a man knew there were men who would gladly do to him the things he never thought anyone would do to him.

Eyewitness Scenario 2: Interior Mineshaft. 3:30 AM. Another night. In a corner, on the first floor of the Mineshaft, an incredibly handsome man, well built, started out giving a certain vibe in the middle of the room. He was soon backed into a corner by a dozen men worshiping his wonderful body. For almost a half hour, the small gang stroked, petted, and licked at his god-flesh naked but for a dirty piss-soaked jockstrap and boots. On their knees and standing, they shuffled in towards him, and reshuffled themselves among themselves, sucking on each other's cocks, working nipples, writhing in orgy between his big, hairy thighs. On a close look at him, he was well worthy of desire.

So I reached my right hand over and through the scrum of men thrashing around his legs and torso and I touched his nipple. Surprisingly, he looked up, smiled, and reached out toward me, leaning into him, both arching above the worshipers, judging what this erotic negotiation might mean. He had that light in his eyes that made me feel he read us both. He was so hot I figured to do anything he wanted. He wasn't shy. He grabbed onto my nipples and pulled himself out of the worshiping suction toward me, and kept flowing by me, towing me by the pecs into the next room where a sling hung vacant and waiting. We danced a primordial, ancient, prehistoric, genetic, and sacramental choreography. Neither asked the other our motivation. And what happened, happened very fast.

He walked me up to the sling hung from huge 8x8 posts, unbuckled my belt, peeled my jeans down around my ankles, knocked me back into the sling, and I was thinking *Am I ready?* for this specific trip within all the general erotic possibilities of the Mineshaft, when my ankles went up into the stirrups, and loose change fell to the floor from my jean pockets, and he leaned into my biggest arch, and drove his hand skillfully, and most importantly, realistically, into me, with no foreplay but an intense smile, and no drug other than grass and desire, because we both had clicked into the "whatever" of the perfect moment, and I was glad I had hosed out a couple of hours before, receiving his big fist on his powerful arm driven by his tectonic torso and his intense face. He wanted me to cum. Maybe his game was harvesting cumshots from as many guys as possible. Sometimes a hardon is hard to come by during a butt trip, but his drive summoned up all my cooperation, and I came to please him, and myself with him, the two of us connected fist to ass.

Tennessee Williams' Blanche says, "Sometimes there's God so quickly."

And as fast as I came, he leaned over and kissed me, turned and walked off into the crowd. Two other men, witnesses to the collision, unhooked my ankles, and I had to make the only crucial decision one had to make at the Mineshaft: whether to go upstairs to the bar to reload for a second round, or to head to the street hoping that, among the butchers in white shouldering bloody carcasses of meat, I could shout, "Taxi."

> It was always beautifully symbolic to me
> that gorgeous sides of fresh red meat
> were hanging from bright hooks
> outside the warehouses around the Mineshaft.
> And, oh, what a gift it was
> in those years to be able to be meat
> every once and awhile
> in a lifetime surrounded by people
> so moral and ignorant they think
> it is a bad thing: this enfleshment,
> this incarnation of self,
> this becoming flesh that is,
> well, the actual very heart of Christian theology.
> I always hear of neo-religious people
> talking about how physical sex
> led them to spirituality.
> I'm talking about how physical sex
> leads to animality.

> After all, I am equal parts
> meat and spirit
> and I have never minded celebrating either.
> In the sanctuary of the Mineshaft,
> the word was made flesh.
> And for a writer, what could be better.

II. The feature essay as published in *Drummer* 19, December 1977

**Men's Bar Scene
Manhattan's Divine Decadence...**

The Mineshaft

Hot spots get too hot not to cool down. So hit them while you can. Like The Mineshaft in New York, New York. Two floors and a roof of whatever flips your switch. In San Francisco, a friendly stranger asks your sign. In LA he asks what part of town you live in. New Yorkers just do a two-handed fine-tuning on your tits and lift an armpit, either yours or theirs, for openers. That's the "Manhattan Hello."

UP A STEEP AND VERY NARROW STAIRWAY

Cab it to The Mineshaft. It's tucked in among the meat-packing houses at the Little West 12th Street. Head on up the stairs. At the entrance, a man checks your membership or issues you a card renewable every three months. For members the door charge is minimal and the stub is money at the bar.

Best of all you can check any or all of your clothes. You aren't going to need them anyway unless they are fetish items. For instance, a new group called The Jock Strap League tends the bar Monday nights. Those quiet dudes you see roaming around in their Bikes are actually in their club uniform. (You can join the JSL by calling (212) 580-9582, but don't wash your jock first.)

The jock fans are typical clientele. Tuesdays, for instance, during this first year of Mineshaft festivities, have been reserved for live bouts by the New York Wrestling Club. Wednesdays the FFA takes over both slings and the pool table: left ball in the side pocket. A can of Crisco sits behind the bar. Ask for some with an outstretched hand and you get an ice cream scoopful to lube up to your elbow. Thursday the A.E.A. (Ass Eaters

Association.) takes over the downstairs, although they're there every night everywhere. Other nights, uniforms are as varied as a surplus fantasy can get. Obviously, The Mineshaft has a Dress Code, basically macho and fetish, and strictly enforced.

OTHER VOICES, OTHER ROOMS

The Shaft is an amazing two-story maze of rooms, stairways, toilets, closets, hallways, bathtubs, gloryholes, and sex equipment. Light varies from shadows to darkness. Men sit, stand, kneel, hang, crawl, drink, and eat. After midnight: something for everyone. The music is truly weird, but played low enough not to cover the slurps, moans, whippings, and piss scenes.

Anything you can fantasize is available somewhere in The Mineshaft which is not for those with low Fantasy Quotients. The Shaft now offers a "School for Lower Education" to aid men in their descent. Currently, an M.D., a psychiatrist, and a psychologist are needed to conduct the timid through courses geared to release their inhibitions. Dial 924-4978.

The Mineshaft is the pits. In the best sense. The Shaft is no place to take your daytime identity. The Shaft is the place of the night-time ID. Abandon inhibition all ye who enter here. Any joint up front enough to advertise SUNDAYS ARE FOR SLUMMING, you can figure goes all the way down on Friday and Saturday nights. The Shaft is true raunch.

Besides the variety of body types, the New York attitude, the films, the genuinely far-out trips, and all the gimmicks any good bar exploits to jazz up a cooking atmosphere, the best thing at The Mineshaft is the men who make it go: Wally Wallace, Bruce, and Bob. They really care about your safety inside the oasis they have created. Clothes checking is totally safe; members have special valuables envelopes which are placed in a newly fire-proofed safe. The current newsletter, in fact, is full of sensible advice on how to keep Mr. Goodbar out of The Mineshaft and out of your life. So if you don't live in The Big Apple, but still want a hot trip, rest assured inside The Mineshaft everything is cool. (Outside, remember to take a taxi.)

THE SHAFT IS A FANTASY BY REX

The essence of The Mineshaft is found in page after page of Rex's drawings in *Icons* and *Mannespielen*. If you get off on Rex, you'll like The Mineshaft and you'll understand why The Shaft chose him to design its 1978 poster and T-shirt. Rex epitomizes in his work the concept of The Mineshaft man.

Drummer 19: The Mineshaft

THE CURRENT SHAFT HOURS

Monday, Tuesday, & Wednesday 10 pm-6 am
Thursday Happy-Hour Prices 5 pm-9 pm
Thursday Evening Hours 9 pm-6 am
Friday (Everything Goes) 10 pm-9 am
Saturday (Around the Clock) 10pm-?am
Sunday (Happy Hours) 4 pm -8 pm
Sunday Evening Hours 8 pm-6 am

The Mineshaft is located at 835 Washington Street, New York 10014.

III. Eyewitness Illustrations

EYEWITNESS PHOTOGRAPHS. In the following pages of Mineshaft publicity kit photographs, all were shot for promotional purposes in the Mineshaft and were given to Jack Fritscher by the manager of the Mineshaft, Wally Wallace, from his personal collection, with the express purpose of illustrating Fritscher's eyewitness history of the Mineshaft in conjunction with advertising materials, Mineshaft Newsletters, personal letters, and transcripts of the videotape *Jack Fritscher Interviews Mineshaft Manager, Wally Wallace, March 28, 1990*. Out of an age of joyous anonymity in the 1970s and through an age of AIDS in the 1980s, where identification was simply not uncloseted and then became impossible, names of subjects and photographers are strictly noted as known. All photographs ©Wally Wallace. One hundred Mineshaft photographs in the Jack Fritscher and Mark Hemry collection may be seen by appointment.

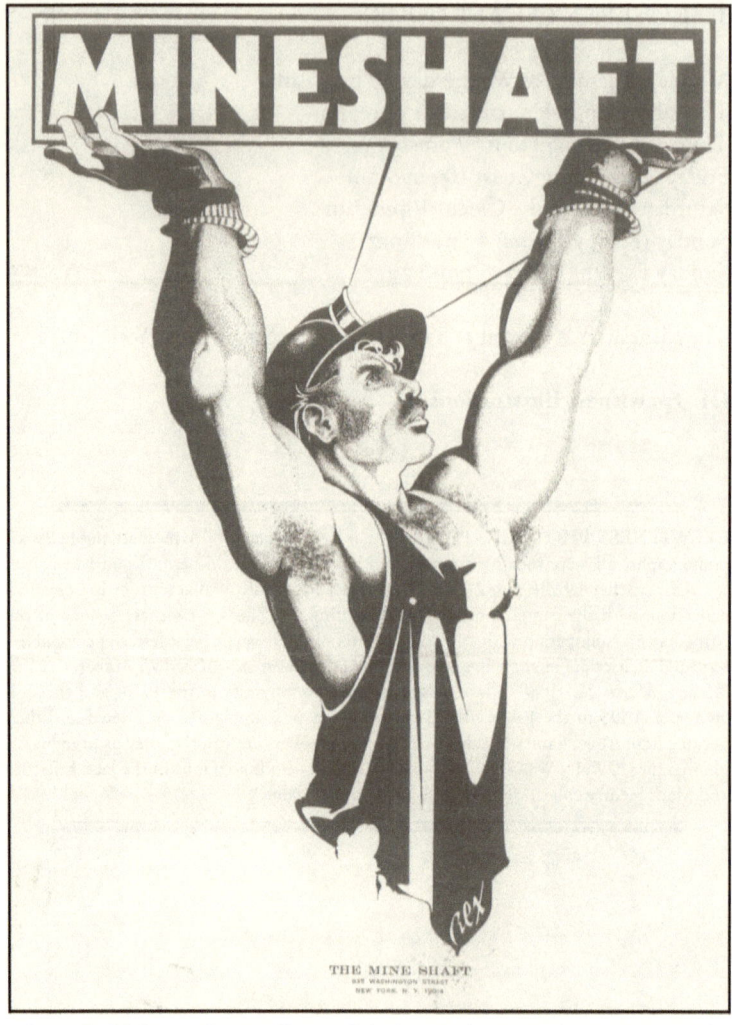

"Mineshaft," drawing by Rex, illustrated the first article written about the Mineshaft which was authored by Jack Fritscher in *Drummer* 19 (December 1977). Drawing ©Rex. Used with permission.

Drummer 19: The Mineshaft 487

"Wally Wallace, Mineshaft Manager," San Francisco, March 28, 1990. Photograph by Jack Fritscher. ©Jack Fritscher. Following the muralist tradition, Wallace commissioned the large panels installed on the walls of the bar in the Mineshaft.

"Mineshaft 1983 Calendar," drawing by Rex. Drawing ©Rex. Used with permission.

This page and opposite. Top: "Protest Poster V. *Cruising*," William Friedkin, the director of the acid-tongued *The Boys in the Band*, shot the controversial film *Cruising* in streets and locations round the Mineshaft in 1979. "Correct" multi-grain vanilla gays, not particularly fond of meat-wearing leather gays, and not understanding the subculture of leather gays' secret society, protested that *Cruising* would be bad publicity for the emerging gay identity because straights would think that all gays acted like the characters in *Cruising*, as opposed to straights thinking that all gays acted like *The Boys in the Band* or Quentin Crisp in *The Naked Civil Servant*. Worth the price of admission in *Cruising* is Friedkin's brilliantly shocking scene in which a muscular booted black cop, naked but for a white jockstrap and a cowboy hat, barges suddenly into an NYPD interrogation room and slaps leather cop Al Pacino across the face. Every diverse behavior in the Mineshaft, and every promise of lustful aggression, and every subliminal desire crying out in the Mineshaft, was summed up in the erotic interracial code of that slap.

Back: Protest Poster V. *Cruising*

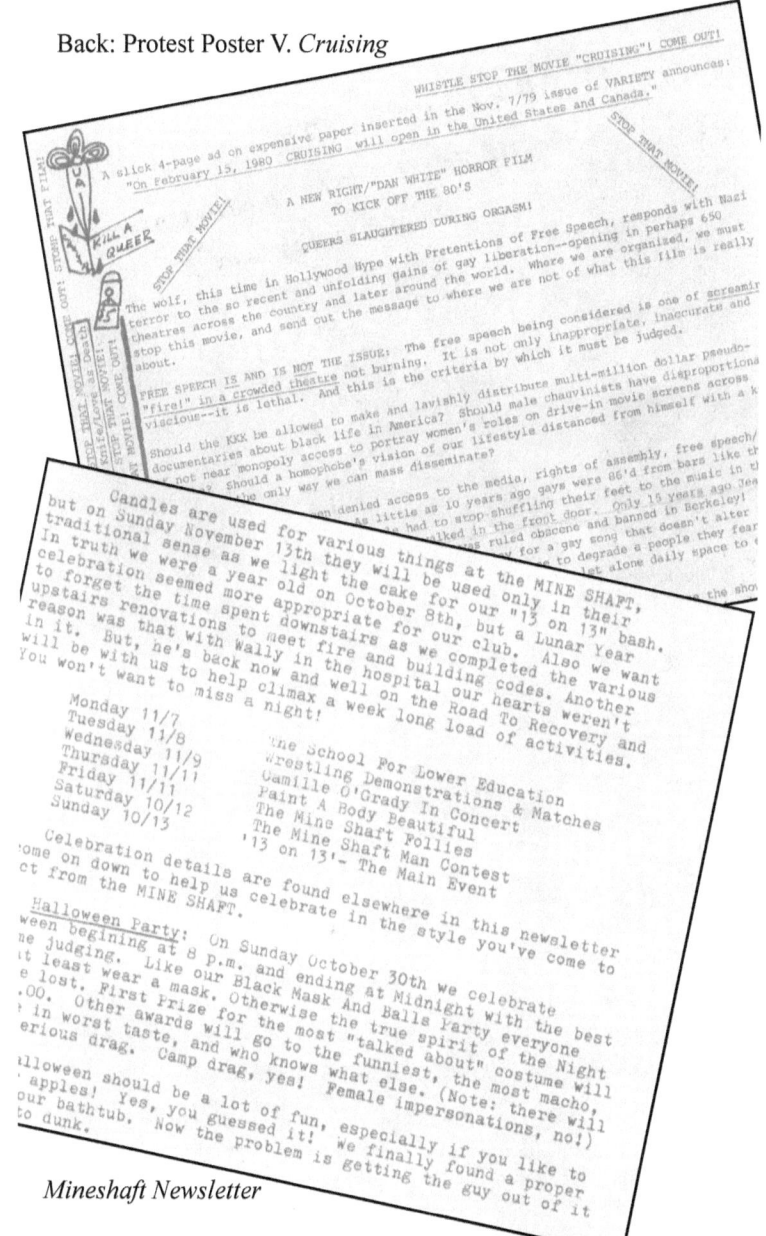

Mineshaft Newsletter

Bottom: *Mineshaft Monthly Newsletter*, October 1977, written, edited, and produced by Wally Wallace. Sample page: The School for Lower Education, Camille O'Grady concert, fire code compliance, Halloween fete, drug use, politics.

Crisco was the lube of choice at every gay bath in the world. Free cans of Crisco hung on chains next to the slings at the Mineshaft in New York, and Crisco was sold for 25 cents in three-ounce white paper cups at the Slot Hotel in San Francisco. At the Safeway on Market Street near Castro in San Francisco, late on a Saturday night there was always some optimistic leatherman pushing a grocery cart empty but for a can of Crisco and a six-pack. Having written that gays exist to inject irony into the lives of straight people, Jack Fritscher, as if by providence, found this camp treasure of a book, *The Story of Crisco* (1913), in 1974.

Drummer 19: The Mineshaft 491

Captions: Eyewitness documentation of the existence of graphics providing internal evidence supporting Jack Fritscher's text are located in the Jack Fritscher and Mark Hemry GLBT History collection. Out of respect for issues of copyright, model releases, permissions, and privacy, some graphics are not available for publication at this time, but can be shown by appointment.

| Eyewitness Illustration | Photograph. "Wally Wallace and Rex," standing at the bar in the Mineshaft, New Year's Eve 1982, exhibit the cover of the 1983 Mineshaft calendar drawn by Rex. In the way that Rex was the official artist of the Mineshaft, "Bob" Mapplethorpe, as Wally Wallace called him, was a |

favorite photographer who once set up his camera in the Mineshaft itself to shoot on location the winner of the Mr. Mineshaft contest. (Although Mapplethorpe gave Fritscher a copy of that photograph, no Mapplethorpe photographs are included in this book.) In 1981, after Rex's San Francisco home and studio and drawings were destroyed during the July 10, 1981, Barracks fire on Folsom Street, Wally Wallace hosted a "Casino Night" on October 20, 1981, to help Rex, who was not personally injured, get back on his feet. This gesture was typical of the kind of fund-raiser and community charities the Mineshaft community supported.

| Eyewitness Illustration | Four photographs. Clockwise beginning at top right: In the style of Studio 54 uptown, a "Caped Customer" poses downtown on the stairway leading from the Meatpacking District street to the Mineshaft entrance |

on the second floor. "Disco Ball Bondage" against the rough wooden frames purpose-built into the Mineshaft interior. Two contestants strut on the bar for one of the many Mr. Mineshaft contests. In the anti-war climate of the 1970s, many gay bars displayed the American flag.

| Eyewitness Illustration | Three photographs. Top: This group photograph is a peephole into the "look" and diversity of men in the homomasculine culture of the Mineshaft. Bottom left: Fritscher pal "Lyle Heeter" whom Mapplethorpe shot |

for the famous salon portrait "Lyle Heeter and Brian Ridley." Bottom right: The reel-to-reel music tapes played at the Mineshaft were created by Jerry Rice and Michael Fesco and Ashland and Wally Wallace, and were absolute key in a perfect mix of classical themes, jazz, energetic beat, and S&M themed lyrics, with a special fisting favorite, Tim Buckley's "Sweet Surrender." The Mineshaft dress code inspired Jacques Morali's creation of the four archetypes of the Village People.

| Eyewitness Illustration | Photograph. "Leather Rick [left] with the Skulls of Akron" who were the only group allowed to shoot sex videos inside the Mineshaft. Farther out than Cirque du Soleil, the Skulls shot aerial trapeze videos like *Fisting Ballet* and extravaganzas which remain *video verite* documentaries of a |

lost civilization. In the 1980s, the Skulls of Akron videos went beyond censorship when the master tapes were confiscated by government authorities.

| Eyewitness Illustration | Photograph, "Candle Fire." Nightly at the Mineshaft, men played erotically with elements of "earth" sex, "water" sports, "fire" edge play, and the "air" exchange of breath control, pot, poppers, and ether. When |

Hollywood director William Friedkin, mimicking Mineshaft culture, was filming *Cruising* with Al Pacino in 1979, he cast his "atmosphere" extras from Mineshaft regulars whose faces appear like ghosts if one freeze-frames the film.

Eyewitness Illustration Three photographs. Three unencumbered views of Mineshaft bartenders and the bar near the entry where Wally Wallace, the Autocrat of the Mineshaft, ruled who could enter his club. Having once mistakenly turned away Camille O'Grady, Wally made her the official singer of the Mineshaft. When the Beautiful People spilled very late out of Studio 54 and tried to crash the Mineshaft, they had to have a certain *je ne sais quoi* to get past Wally who said he turned away Mick Jagger, but admitted, he said, Nureyev, Minnelli, Fassbinder, and Foucault.

Eyewitness Illustration Three photographs. "Butt Parade on the Mineshaft Bar as a Runway." Top to bottom: Compared to the exclusive fisting palace of the invitation-only Catacombs in San Francisco, the Mineshaft in Manhattan was an open and inclusive parade of real "fundament"-alism. Butts that shimmered in contest pageants on the main bar enticed logical conclusion in the dark maze of Mineshaft rooms where men hung, waiting in slings, like the raw carcasses hung on hooks outside the door of the Mineshaft at 835 Washington Street where bloody young butchers, aproned in white, worked nights shouldering huge sides of beef lit by the blinding fluorescence of the loading dock.

Eyewitness Illustration Three photographs. At the Mineshaft, slings, hoists, and trapezes removed gravity from sex and added to the circus of sexual acrobats. Bottom: In a Skulls of Akron performance art piece, Wally Wallace received the "New Year's Baby" doll birthed from inside the butt of the man lying on the covered pool table. The man handing Wally the doll was one of the most able of masochistic leading men in the Skulls of Akron videos.

Eyewitness Illustration Photograph. Every night was Halloween, Santeria, or homo-religious leather ritual in some corner of the Mineshaft lit with black light that showed off Day-Glo body-painting that was popular in the 1960s and 1970s.

Eyewitness Illustration Photograph. Mummified and hung on a rough-hewn cross in the Mineshaft, a gent discovers the rare human satisfaction that he has finally found the place where men will do to him the kinds of things he always dreamed men would do. In the 1970s, New York sculptor Nancy Grossman fashioned life-size wooden heads sinisterly hooded with tight black leather and industrial zippers that sold in galleries for thousands of dollars. The Mineshaft admission for the real thing in a hood (including one's own head) was no more than the three-buck cost of a Mineshaft membership card.

Eyewitness Illustration Two photographs. "Blacksmith 1" and "Blacksmith 2" were lensed outside at night on the roof of the Mineshaft. What at first glance seems like a festive barbecue morphs into serious S&M because of the anvil in the lower left corner as two blacksmiths heat and shape branding irons for red-hot action.

Gifting

> Written September-October 1977, this feature essay was published in *Drummer* 19, December 1977.
> I. Author's Eyewitness Historical-Context Introduction written December 14, 2003
> II. The feature essay as published in *Drummer* 19, December 1977
> III. Eyewitness Illustrations

I. Author's Eyewitness Historical-Context Introduction written December 14, 2003

As a writer who is a stylist, I tried to make even *Drummer*'s editorial advertising amusing through wordplay. Historically this "Gifting" piece is as much clock as calendar. It marks the first mention in *Drummer* of some leather heritage artists, such as Bob Mizer offering Harry Bush at Athletic Model Guild, David Hurles offering audio tapes years before he began to create video tapes at Old Reliable Studio (1981), and the Wizard's Emerald City, one of the first gay businesses to widen its way out of the Castro to an Upper Market Street location near Van Ness.

The uncredited model for the Accu-Jac device is the porn star Jack Wrangler. He finally took his pump, and exited gay culture to marry the legendary 1940s Big Band singer, Margaret Whiting, who, when Wrangler protested (as did we all) that he was gay, told him, "But only around the edges, dear."

The model "Tom" was a popular hot man in San Francisco whose name, as written in my sex Rolodex of friends, was "Leonard Sylvestri." He also appeared as "Tom" in the David Warner photo layout, "Construction Workers," which included "Richard Moore" who wrote the photo captions in *Drummer* 18 (August 1977), page 21.

In the 1970s, I knew "Richard Moore" as "John Adams," but he was also known as "Ivan" and "Olaf." He was a man-about-town who shaved his balding head and nearly always wore a curly wig. Sometimes he costumed himself as a silvery, glittering, and nearly nude "Mercury on Roller Skates" for the gay parade and for street fairs.

(The two David Warner "lumberjack" photographs of "Richard Moore" appeared in *Drummer* 18, page 20; "Richard Moore's" text for the photo spread is a good example of the weak, coy, and silly prose that I labored to delete from *Drummer* beginning with the first full issue that I signed as editor in chief, *Drummer* 19.)

Before "bears" came into existence in the 1980s as an acceptable body style possible for men like him, "Richard-John-Ivan-Olaf" struggled with his own bald, beefy look that he buffed with weightlifting. Like "Tom," he was a bearded muscle guy living on Polk Street in a gay youth culture fixated on chicken. I saw that he and men like him might appreciate *Drummer* coming to their rescue through articles and illustrations celebrating the secondary male sex characteristics of men in their thirties. "Richard Moore" was an entrepreneur who hustled himself and his stable of gladiator musclemen out of his second-floor apartment on "Polkstrasse" where we often spent languorous afternoons on madras cushions, lying under his Casablanca ceiling fans, chatting among his potted palms.

(The afternoons I spent with another San Francisco entrepreneur, David Hurles/Old Reliable, in his apartment of hustlers were a different kind of languor; Old Reliable's rugged models, mentioned in this "Gifting" feature, were essential to my virilizing *Drummer*.)

As a writer and editor, I was never one of "Richard Moore's" clients, but we did work together on several projects. On July 30, 1987, he introduced me to one of his latest ingenues, Larry King, who was a twenty-five-year-old African-American freshly discharged from the US Navy for being gay. The deeply complexioned Larry King was built like a football linebacker at five-foot-eight and 235 pounds. He could afford to be the strong silent type because he also sported nine inches uncut. John Adams sat intent on set as I directed and lensed Larry King for my Palm Drive Video feature, *Big Black Dick Black* (1987).

The last time I saw "Richard Moore," I was spending a week videotaping the 1988 Police Olympics in Bakersfield, California. In a sad *Sunset Boulevard* scene, he pulled up in front of the arena in a drop-dead vintage yellow Rolls Royce stretch convertible driven by a uniformed bodybuilder-chauffeur who helped him walk from the car. He was so gaunt, I did not think he would survive sitting in the audience of the Cop Olympics bodybuilding.

Standing on the stage, and shooting the physique contest close-up, I confess that in the midst of all that healthy male flesh, death mesmerized me, overcame me, dissolved me with sadness; I could not turn away; I discreetly panned my video camera into the audience to film a half-minute cameo of him sitting alone with his bodybuilder-caregiver in the twentieth row. I panned back to the rowdy physique action, stifling small gasps of tears and panic I had to hide by pressing my face into my viewfinder because my tripod stood on stage in the midst of bright lights, sweating muscle, and hearty rounds of applause and cheers. That moment defined an existential archetype that Michelangelo could have painted, opposite his "Last Judgment," at the other end of the Sistine Chapel: gay sexual outcasts, threatened by plague, surrounded by nearly nude straight law-enforcement heroes exuberant with health.

In 1989 during the Great Dying when I could no longer reach "Richard Moore"—John Adams—by telephone, I wrote in my Rolodex: "Dead, I think. He just disappeared."

The model "Tom"/Leonard Sylvestri, if memory serves, had himself gone missing during the late 1970s after he seemed to become ill, grew gaunt, and probably went back to wherever he had immigrated from, because in the 1970s it was unfashionable to become sick in San Francisco. Of course, by the mid-80s, remembering Leonard, I figured he may have been one of those extremely early cases of AIDS that occurred in the 1970s before anyone connected the dots of the emerging pattern of deaths. How horrible it must have been for this sweet hot man, leaving the Titanic 70s party, not knowing what was afflicting him, while the band played on.

Hanging Tree Ranch, an early S&M leather mail-order business was famous for employing Richard Locke as a bondage model (*Drummer* 10, page 4) before Locke himself became legendary as the leading man in the Gage Brothers' films, and as a face in the pages of *Drummer*. Although Locke was never on the cover, as editor in chief I produced an interview with him in *Drummer* 24 (September 1978), and introduced him and his manuscript for his autobiography then titled *I Didn't Do It for the Money* to my own publisher Winston Leyland at Gay Sunshine Press. Eventually, the synergistic-genius film producer Jerry Douglas published *Locke Out: The Collected Writings of Richard Locke,* Firsthand Books (1993).

Tuffy's Sport Shop at 597 Castro was the first commercial and community-minded articulation—and "alert"!—that gays could dare play the sports we weren't allowed to play in high school. See more about Tuffy's in my feature article "Gay Jock Sports" in *Drummer* 20 (January 1978). My gay sports article appeared two years before Tom Waddell first began talking publically in 1980 about creating the first Gay Olympics (Gay Games 1982) whose first physique contest Mark Hemry and I videotaped as a documentary at the Castro Theater for our Palm Drive Video company.

II. The feature essay as published in *Drummer* 19, December 1977

Gifting

OWN A PIECE OF THE ROCK. Give that special artist or photographer (who has everything but inspiration) a shot at Tom. Versatile modeling.

TUFFY'S SPORT SHOP can get your rear in gear for sports you once thought you'd never play. Athletic uniforms, shoes, equipment, and university insignia clothes are Tuffy's specialty. In addition, Tuffy sponsors the USA Athletic Club whose 500 professional, collegiate, and just-plain-fun jocks get into flag football, basketball, boxing, wrestling, tennis, skiing, and racquetball. Suit up your jock with something from Tuffy's and then gift him with a USA Athletic Club membership. Check it out with Tuffy. 597 Castro, San Francisco. (415) 621-2128.

CUZ NOBODY DOES IT BETTER. Accu-Jac is the perfect fit for the man who "vants to be alone" with his Target movies, his Old Reliable audio tapes, his titclamps, his dildo, and his Rush [a brand of poppers]. Accu-Jac won't supplant human relationships; but on a rainy night in Rio it comes in handy. Recommended for men who want to make really hot love to themselves. Bionically yours from JAC MASTERS, INC. $3 gets you a Catalog of Adult Toys: 757 North La Cienega Blvd., Los Angeles 90069.

BOX IT ALL UP in brown leather from Hanging Tree Ranch in San Diego. Send $3 for color brochure for hides to highlight your hide.

AMG Athletic Model Guild offers a set of six 8x10 drawings by Harry Bush for $9 and their latest issue of their magazine *Physique Pictorial* for $1.25.

VELCRO MAD-MONEY BANDS. Your asshole may have more deposits, withdrawals, and interest than the Bank of America. So stash your cash inside the secret compartment of this watchband in brown or black leather. $7. Wristband and cockring stashes also available for the truly paranoid. Take in the whole trip at The Trading Post, 960 Folsom, San Francisco.

SCULPTURE by Michael Drew. Sand color, glazed terra cotta, 11x7½. One-of-a-kind commissions for $40. Exclusively through THE

WIZARD'S EMERALD CITY, 1645 Market Street, San Francisco. (415) 863-1901.

HOT STUFF from Old Reliable is hot, reliable, and *authentic*. Cons, bikers, and punks are only a few of the tramps and trade who will burn your ears. Stick something nasty in your [audio] cassette [player] on a cold night alone. If you state you're over 21, a buck gets you a jerkable brochure that comes all year long. OLD RELIABLE, PO 5927, San Francisco 94101.

III. Eyewitness Illustrations

In the 1970s, the "very out" advent of gay-owned small businesses was the first sign of the dawn of the gay economy that was to grow into the fabled GLBT billion-dollar disposable income. While editor in chief of the small business known as *Drummer*, Jack Fritscher often wrote promotional copy for gay startups such as the Wizard's Emerald City owned by Dick Trask, one of the stars of the handballing independent-film classic *Erotic Hands*. In the business-mind of publisher John Embry, *Drummer* seemed to exist primarily as a vehicle to sell merchandise by mail order.

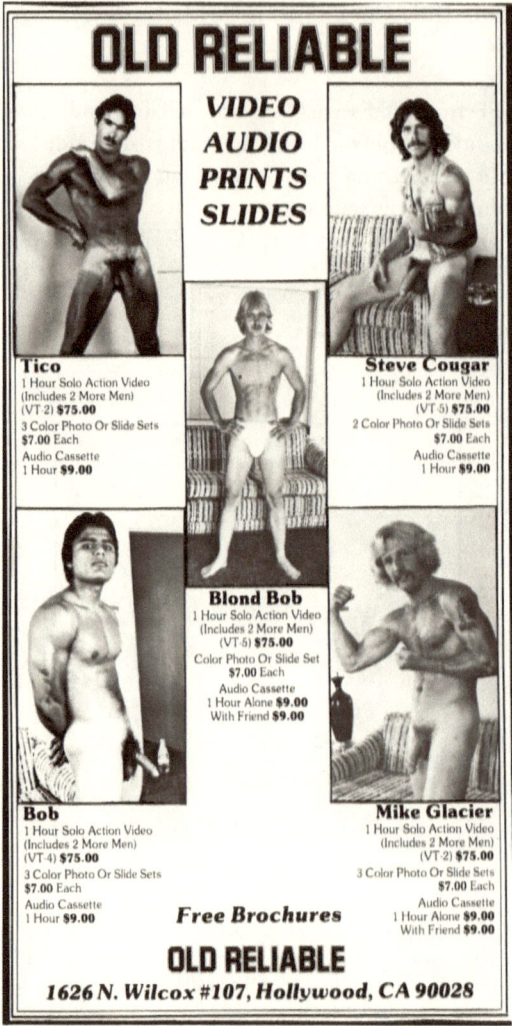

Display ad in *Drummer*. Old Reliable was the wildly successful photographer who was most responsible for expanding the *Drummer* concept of homomasculinity and S&M as rough sex. When other gay magazines ran in terror of Old Reliable's scary ex-cons and drop-dead sexy rough trade, editor in chief Fritscher coaxed Old Reliable into *Drummer* 20 (January 1978) and brought him out aggressively as a "personality" in *Drummer* 21 (March 1978). Because of Old Reliable alongside all the other fresh *Drummer*-forming essentials of that issue, *Drummer* 21 is the best issue of *Drummer*. *Drummer* 21 is the perfect *Drummer* issue. *Drummer* 21 is the Platonic Ideal of what *Drummer* could be. In 1986, *Drummer* publisher Tony DeBlase wrote about 1970s *Drummer*: "Fritscher's discovery David Hurles' Old Reliable photos and A. Jay's drawings characterized this era....and A. Jay's illustrations for stories and ads had exactly the right look for Jack Fritscher's version of *Drummer*." Photographs by David Hurles. ©David Hurles. Used with permission.

Drummer 19: Gifting

Back Cover, *Man2Man Quarterly* #6 (Spring 1981), "Mongoose." In 1978 when Sam Wagstaff and Robert Mapplethorpe began to collect David Hurles' Old Reliable photographs, Mapplethorpe's first purchase was "Mongoose." Photograph by David Hurles. ©David Hurles. Used with permission.

| Eyewitness Illustration | Front Cover, *Speeding: The Old Reliable Photos of David Hurles* (2005) illustrates the "Zero Degrees of Separation in the *Drummer* Salon." When longtime *Drummer* and Mineshaft artist Rex wrote and designed the coffee-table book *Speeding*, he chose for his front cover the exact same Old Reliable photograph of the model Mongoose that Jack Fritscher had published on the back cover of *Man2Man Quarterly* #6 (1981) which also included a full-page drawing by Rex. Twenty-five years on, it was perhaps exigencies of the culture war that caused Rex to crop the image that Fritscher in freer times had published full-frontal. |

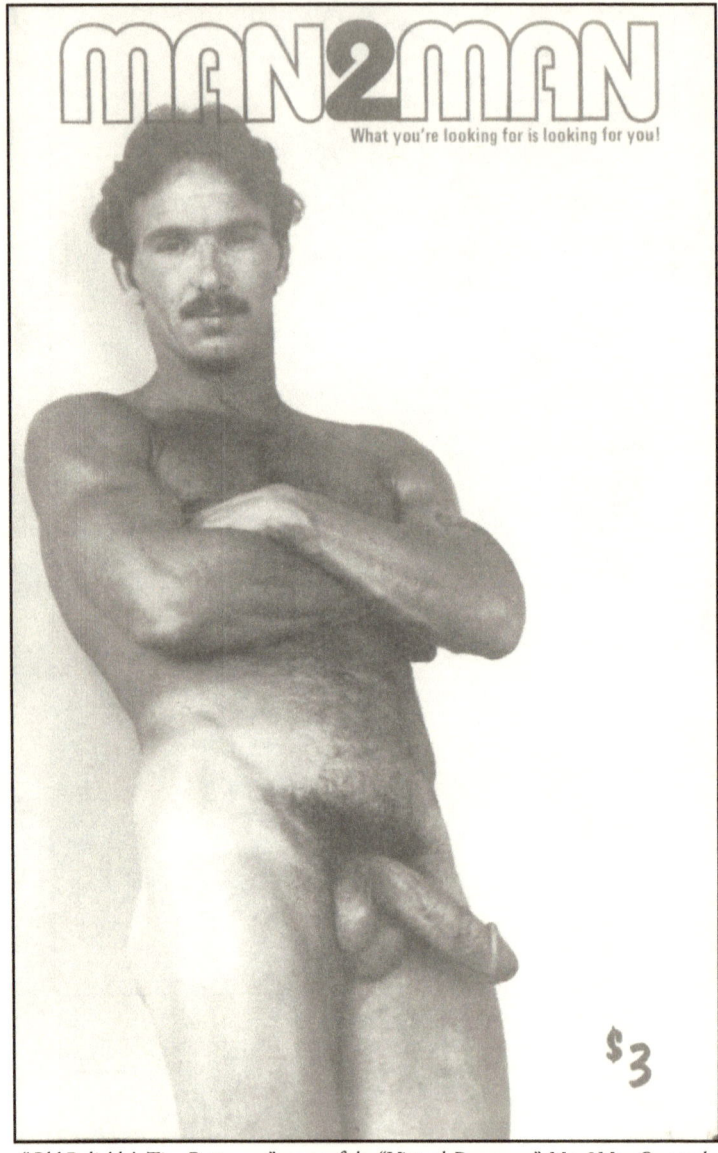

"Old Reliable's Tico Patterson," cover of the "Virtual *Drummer*," *Man2Man Quarterly* #4 (Spring 1981). As he did in the pages of *Drummer*, and on Santa Monica Boulevard where he worked hard for the money, Tico Patterson typified the kind of rough and handsome Latin flavor that had so much appeal in the 1970s with *Drummer* coverman, Val Martin, who was the first Mr. *Drummer*. Tico folded out like stapled origami in his classic centerfold in *Man2Man Quarterly* #4, and in his solo action video from Old Reliable Studio. Cover design by Mark Hemry. Photograph by David Hurles. ©David Hurles. Used with permission. See *Drummer* 19, page 20.

Drummer 19: Gifting 501

 Captions: Eyewitness documentation of the existence of graphics providing internal evidence supporting Jack Fritscher's text are located in the Jack Fritscher and Mark Hemry GLBT History collection. Out of respect for issues of copyright, model releases, permissions, and privacy, some graphics are not available for publication at this time, but can be shown by appointment.

| Eyewitness Illustration | Photograph. The model "Tom," Leonard Sylvestri, was an intimate in the *Drummer* salon *via* the popular Castro barber, Jim McPherson aka Thumper. See *Drummer* 19, page 21. |

| Eyewitness Illustration | Photograph. "Richard Locke with Bridle Bit." With his universal sex appeal, Locke was a model for Hanging Tree Ranch mail order at the same time he appeared in *Playgirl* and in the Gage Brothers films. When editor |

in chief Fritscher looked around and saw that the 1970s *Drummer* demographic was approaching forty years old, he set in motion the further glamorization of Richard Locke to prove that a gay man could be more than twenty-one with a twenty-eight-inch waist. Fritscher's concept in *Drummer* 24 (September 1978), "In Praise of Older Men," sparked the already simmering "daddy" concept and led to the several special issues of *Drummer* titled *Drummer Daddies*. "Richard Locke with Bridle Bit" appeared on the cover of Fritscher's special issue, *Drummer Rides Again*, 1979, which, after Fritscher had prepared it, publisher Embry re-edited subtracting most of Fritscher's writing and photography because Fritscher had exited *Drummer* over money issues.

Crimes Against Nature 1977

> Written October 17, 1977, this feature essay was published in *Drummer* 20, January 1978.
> I. Author's Eyewitness Historical-Context Introduction written April 15, 2002
> II. The feature essay as published in *Drummer* 20, January 1978
> III. Eyewitness Illustrations

I. Author's Eyewitness Historical-Context written April 15, 2002

Drummer and Theater
Drummer and Performance Art

"To survive, I'm butch."
—David Baker, author, *Crimes Against Nature*
Now THAT'S acting!

As eyewitness editor in chief and as author of a couple plays in *Drummer*, I find this a chance to remind GLBT history that *Drummer* as a lifestyle-generating magazine was essentially theatrical in its mission and presentation of gender identity and sexuality. I mean something more essential than the total obsession *Drummer* had with S&M-themed Hollywood films, or with the erotic art films of early *Drummer* contributor, Fred Halsted, the MOMA-enshrined Los Angeles director who so perfectly formed the dominant theatrical film images in the first issues of *Drummer*. It is also something more ritualistic than the bumptious burlesque theater of the extremely popular Mr. *Drummer* contests that provided great bonhomie and free leather-fashion runway photos for covers and centerfolds.

At its substantial best, *Drummer* frequently published the scripts of plays and performance pieces including in *Drummer* 5, *Isomer* (1975), a one-act play by Richard A. Steel with author photo by J & R Studios; in *Drummer* 12 and *Drummer* 13, *Pogey Bait* (1977), a two-act play by George Birimisa; in *Drummer* 22 and *Drummer* 23, *Corporal in Charge of*

Taking Care of Captain O'Malley (1978), an erotic drama by Jack Fritscher from a draft concept by David Hurles who has been the performance-art and photography studio "Old Reliable" since 1971; in *Drummer* 22 (May 1978), "Cigar Sarge" by Jack Fritscher, collected and republished by Richard Labonté (with Fritscher's "USMC Slap Captain") as "Sexual Harassment in the Military: 2 Performance Pieces for 4 Actors in 3 Lovely Costumes" in *Best Gay Erotica* 1998; in *Drummer* 24 and *Drummer* 25, *Ex-Cons: We Abuse Fags* (1978), a one-man show by David Hurles (Old Reliable) and Jack Fritscher; in *Drummer* 25, "Horse Master," an erotic performance piece by Jack Fritscher, plus an excerpt from *Equus* which upset playwright Peter Shaffer because publisher Embry did not responsibly follow through my advisement for him to secure written permission; and in *Drummer* 57, *Delivery* (1982), a play by C. D. Arnold.

In addition to my friend and frequent collaborator, the screen director David Hurles, the *Drummer* salon had many theatrical links including my longtime intimate, Richard LeBlond (1924-2000), president of the San Francisco Ballet (1975-1987), who was so practically supportive of my "script" for *Drummer* that he provided the rope-and-harness photographs of the San Francisco Ballet that I requested and published with my "Bondage" feature in *Drummer* 24 (September 1978). (Richard LeBlond is not Richard Labonté, my literary critic pal who was the guiding light among the founders of A Different Light bookstore which was the first 1970s venue to invite gay authors in to perform their works.)

Complementing the Hollywood Halsted and the local LeBlond, New York stage-and-screen director Wakefield Poole, who had moved west—like Harvey Milk during the 1970s Manhattanization of San Francisco—was one of the most glamorous talents circling the *Drummer* salon from his swank studio and home on the Panhandle of Golden Gate Park where he and I co-produced at least one invitation-only salon centered on the physique performance of my lover Jim Enger, the championship bodybuilder whom Wakefield had gorgeously lit, after the manner of Caravaggio's stark tenebrism, with his dramatic chiaroscuro film-studio lighting.

Responding once to my concerns about publishing his photographs to his liking, Wakefield generously defined my role as editor in chief of the *Drummer* "script" saying, "You're the director." He and his partner Paul Hatlestad provided noble support because their tastes, films, theatrical photographs, and stage shows were so essentially homomasculine that they were a perfect fit for my conception of *Drummer*. I published a 35mm color-still from Wakefield's feature, *The Bible* (1974), on the cover of *Drummer* 27 (February 1979), and featured an inside spread of ten Poole photographs from the films *Bijou* (1972), *Moving* (1974), and *Take One*

Drummer 20: *Crimes Against Nature*

(1977). This was the same *Drummer* 27 that published my *Playboy*-style interview with Wakefield who had also produced the participant-cabaret party extravaganza, "Night Flight." (See *Drummer* 20, January 1978.) On August 24, 1978, Wakefield told me:

> Technically, we're moving into the Videotape 80s....My fantasy for the 1980s is to produce a live Broadway show. Multi-media. Using all the pornstars I could employ. Just like *A Chorus Line*. Have it all take place in a discotheque.

Having filmed *Roger* (1977), Wakefield proceeded in early 1978 at San Francisco's Nob Hill Theater to incorporate that film into the mixed-media SRO stage show he produced and directed for the Target and Colt model, "Roger" (Daryll Hanson), whose orgiastic Nob Hill performance as an erotic "Eugene Sandow" I profiled in "Pumping Roger," *Drummer* 21 (March 1978), and whose nude pose, shot by Wakefield, I featured on the "Homomasculinity" cover of the "Virtual *Drummer*," *The California Action Guide* (November 1982). In 1980, Wakefield introduced me to his friend, Georgina Spelvin, the star of his film, *The Bible*, and, most famously, the star of *The Devil in Miss Jones* (1973). In the zero degrees of separation, my literally embedded interview with the *grande dame* porn star, "The Devil in Miss Spelvin," was published in *Hooker* magazine (1981).

In a letter dated September 7, 1978, Wakefield wrote:

> Dear Jack, Enclosed is a copy of *A la Recherche du Temps Perdu, The Proust Screenplay* [written by Harold Pinter]. I hope you enjoy it as much as yours truly. I'm on my third reading and it gets better each time. — Love, Wake.

The book itself is inscribed,

> To Jack, I found a copy for you today. Now you need only read and enjoy. — Wakefield

He sent the Pinter film script because we had talked earnestly of our "Proustian" responsibility as artists in the 70s to write and create the 70s from the inside out—he in the recorded visions of his films, and I in the recorded journal entries which he knew I was shaping into the 70s drafts of *Some Dance to Remember* which I shared with him and with Robert Mapplethorpe who was also capturing esthetic documentary "takes" on the 1970s. I had titled my 1978 *Drummer* interview of Wakefield Poole with the inevitable pun, "Dirty Poole." Twenty-three years later, Alyson Publications printed Wakefield Poole's memoir with the same title: *Dirty Poole: Autobiography of a Gay Porn Pioneer* (2001).

With the Manhattan luster of Wakefield Poole and Robert Mapplethorpe shining in the pages of *Drummer*, I cultivated the "decadent" international S&M-leather esthetic of the Berlin photographer and film director, Gerhard Pohl, who was so sensational in his evocative Weimar ways that Christopher Isherwood might have blushed long before Pohl's retrospective at the Schwules Museum. (Pohl is not Poole.) When Pohl spied the huge stack of journal pages I was editing into *Some Dance to Remember*, he said, "Alfred Doblin, *Alexanderplatz*?" That was at least a year before Americans had heard of Fassbinder's film, *Alexanderplatz*. So I asked my German immigrant friend, Hank Diethelm, about what was then simply the novel, *Alexanderplatz*. Diethelm at age fourteen had been conscripted into the Nazi Youth, escaped the Russian front in 1945, starred in my underground film *Castration* (Super-8, 1972), helped me remodel my Victorian in 1975, and became the founding owner of the legendary Folsom Street bar, the Brig, from where his murderer took him home. (Hank Diethelm: March 18, 1928 - April 10, 1983.) Diethelm explained Pohl's allusion joking that Doblin's Berlin was like Joyce's Dublin in *Ulysses*. Both wrote novels of a specific group of people in a specific time in a specific city that itself became a "character" which was my goal in my memoir-novel. In his stunning spins through San Francisco, Gerhard Pohl was a popular house guest who was dedicated to "'feeding' the downtrodden." He contributed much "off-the-page" *frisson* to the *mise en scene* in our *Drummer* salon where, in our homes of an evening, he frequently unspooled his exotic and daring and very beautiful underground Euro-leather films of totemic dominance and taboo submission that expanded our San Francisco consciousness and encouraged us locals to make *Drummer* even more global in appeal. The secret of success in *Drummer* was that the editor had to be a top because the readers were ninety-nine percent bottoms seeking someone who would top them on page, stage, screen, and real life.

(My collaborative relationship with Old Reliable David Hurles, my personal relationship with Richard LeBlond, and my intimate relationship with Robert Mapplethorpe, as well as my professional relationship with Wakefield Poole were all four between me and each one of them, and none was ever between them and *Drummer* and its publisher, John Embry. When I exited the daily drama around *Drummer* on December 31, 1979, their relationships to *Drummer* evaporated. It was their choice; no gauntlet was thrown down. By 1986 when I returned to *Drummer*,

Drummer 20: Crimes Against Nature

Hurles and LeBlond and Mapplethorpe and Poole each had other interests as did the new AIDS-era *Drummer* publisher, Anthony DeBlase.)

In the 1970s, through plays such as my *Coming Attractions*, and through actors such as my pal, the leathery S&M hunk David Baker, *Drummer* was attached to the invention of gay theater in San Francisco. I had met David Baker at the Folsom Prison bar during Christmas 1972, and I wrote the story of our erotic tumble that set my faded Levi's on fire in the feature essay, "Leather Christmas," *Drummer* 19 (December 1977). Actors and performance artists were drawn to the *Drummer* salon because of our sincere and welcoming coverage of happenings and performances in leather bars, galleries, and staged parties, as well as *Drummer*'s eager photographic search for erotically dramatic leather models posed in tableaux of S&M. David Baker also acted at the 544 Natoma Gallery founded by Peter Hartman in 1977 at the same moment *Drummer* moved to San Francisco, and everything converged.

Besides Andy Warhol's Factory films and traveling musical S&M show, *The Exploding Plastic Inevitable* (1966), performed live by the Velvet Underground, and because of Broadway successes like the rugby-masculine *The Changing Room* (1972) and the masculine inquiries of *A Chorus Line*, experimental plays became important to *Drummer*'s text and mindset. (*A Chorus Line* opened one month before the publication of the first issue of *Drummer* on June 20, 1975.) The experimental plays were often naked, sexual, and violent "60s Revolution" plays (and their film versions) that *Drummer* readers—having been educated in the 1940s, 1950s, 1960s, and 1970s—attended, or learned about over brunch. They were familiar with the form and content, and intellectually and erotically, they liked what they saw on stage and they wanted it on the page. Gay Liberation of the 1970s was a pop-culture gay lib whose consciousness grew out of the theater of protest of the 1960s when civil rights for Blacks and for the anti-war and anti-government movements both expressed themselves first in the open air as street theater and then in actual theaters as writers reflected on what was going on, what was worth fighting for, and what was worth rebelling against in influential plays from Jean-Paul Sartre, Albert Camus, and Jean Genet to Kenneth Brown's exercise in brutal S&M, *The Brig* (1963); director Peter Brook's *Marat/Sade* (1966); Andy Warhol's *Pork* (1971); and stage work by the Cockettes in San Francisco, and by Charles Ludlam's Ridiculous Theatrical Company in New York. Art and politics in the 1960s made sex worth something. *Worthiness* was the key word. "Male worth" was the main value behind my concept when I was driving *Drummer*.

Art usually tidies up the ragged edges of life with Aristotelian unities of time, place, and action so life can be both felt and analyzed. Art is an invaluable walk-through rehearsal of life's problems and joys so when people begin to experience their own inescapable life, they have at least been exposed to options as to how artists have their characters live, love, suffer, problem-solve, or resign themselves. Before "theater of gay lib" itself existed, gay-themed plays represented lesbigay life in various daring and tortured ways. It is symptomatic of the anti-gay times of the mid-twentieth century that many original gay-themed works found their contents, and even their titles, censored as they crossed from novels to plays to films.

Three plays that became part of the canon of gay consciousness, particularly in the last two decades before Stonewall, were:

- the discreetly coded Broadway hit about "outing" lesbian love by Lillian Hellman, *The Children's Hour* (1934), which homophobia twisted into a straight film re-titled *These Three* (1936). After twenty-five years of social evolution, the director of *These Three*, William Wyler, remade Hellman's drama into a psychological thriller with the restored title, *The Children's Hour* (1961), starring gay divas Shirley MacLaine and Audrey Hepburn suffering the kind of shocking pain that happens when people are dragged out of the closet. In a great life-affirming departure from the worst gay dramatic cliche that the gay character must die on page, stage, or screen, in *Drummer* fiction, no character ever committed suicide.

- novelist Calder Willingham's gay-themed-S&M military-school drama, *End as a Man*, which as a 1953 Off-Broadway play at the Theatre de Lys was publicized as a 1954 Broadway vehicle starring the young prince, James Dean, who instead went west to star in *East of Eden* (1955). Besides my 1950s gaydar lust for the edible James Dean, the provocative title, *End as a Man*, resounded in my throbbing teenage DNA as a mantra about "secret rituals that make a boy a man"—which, of course, is the main theme of most *Drummer* stories, and of most *Drummer* "Leather Fraternity" personal ads articulating a real effemiphobia that counter-balances sissies' real fear of homomasculinity. In 1957, two years after James Dean was killed and went iconic on September 30, 1955, homophobia caused Hollywood to retitle the film version as *The Strange One* which was a marketing pun on the Ur-gay leather-biker film, *The Wild One* (1953), starring Marlon Brando who was James Dean's doppelganger. And

- the very coded Tennessee Williams' *A Streetcar Named Desire* (play, 1947; film 1951). My doctoral dissertation was *Love and Death in Tennessee Williams* (1967), and only the most flat-faced heterosexuals would ever not get that Sebastian Venable was cannibalized for being a bacchanalian gay in *Suddenly Last Summer* (1958); only the most flat-earth straights would not be able to decipher that Blanche DuBois was a drag version of an effeminate man who liked rough sex servicing young soldiers, and who had a lech for his/her hyper-masculine blue-collar brother-in-law—himself recently mustered out of the army, played on stage and screen by the twenty-something Marlon Brando who merged his sweaty hard-man image from *Streetcar* into his combustion-engine rebel image in *The Wild One* to become a huge biker icon behind the leather culture of early *Drummer*.

In 1967, Mart Crowley wrote a powerfully pentecostal play that spoke with tongues of fire. *The Boys in the Band* became a Broadway hit, a Hollywood movie, and a cultural benchmark. The self-eviscerating comedy, no more bi-polar than the ever-lovely (perhaps drag drama), *Who's Afraid of Virginia Woolf?* (1962), became popular with regional and community theaters. As a matter of fact, my domestic lover and photography partner at *Drummer*, David Sparrow—when he was a student at Western Michigan University where I was tenured on the English Department faculty—starred in the 1972 WMU production of *The Boys in the Band* directed by David Karsten. Much to our amusement, he was cast as "Alan," the only straight character in the play, while straight "college-boy" actors—who kept their balance on such thin ice—played swishy gays. David Sparrow was accurately typecast on stage, because he was a homomasculine man playing an evolving heteromasculine character, and masculinity carried his performance as much as his presence. Some latter-day gay critics don't approve of Mart Crowley's snarly dialog, which, whatever they imagine, is an exact time capsule of the way many homosexuals of a certain age bantered with a kind of "gay gallows humor" in the oppression before Stonewall. Up through the 1960s, suicide—beginning with social suicide through alcohol and tobacco, and then physical suicide—was the only way out of the existential horror show of being outcast with other outcasts. If the brilliant Mart Crowley were figure-skating an "Olympic version" of *The Boys in the Band*, he would win a perfect 10, crowned with another perfect 10 for overcoming the degree of difficulty in nailing his quadruple-lutz routine with an accuracy that some found disconcerting.

Gay theater in the 1970s raised its profile in New York with Al Carmine's musical, *The Faggot* (1973); A. J. Kronengold's *Tubstrip* (1974) starring Casey Donovan aka Cal Culver, the star of Wakefield Poole's film, *The Boys in the Sand* (1971); Christopher Hampton's *Total Eclipse* (1974) which in Hampton's 1995 film version starred Leonardo DiCaprio and David Thewlis; Lanford Wilson's *Hot L Baltimore* (1973) featuring Richard A. Steel whose play *Isomer* was published in *Drummer 5* (March 1976); Terrence McNally's satire of the Continental Baths, *The Ritz* (1975); James Kirkwood's *A Chorus Line* (1976); David Rabe's *Streamers* (1976), and Harvey Fierstein's *International Stud* (1978). Besides *Isomer*, the most directly related to *Drummer* were Kenneth Brown's *The Brig* and Doric Wilson's *West Street Gang* (1977) which was staged in the leather bar, the Spike, near the Anvil bar, not far from the Mineshaft. My *TV-Guide*-like Thumbnail for *West Street Gang*: a hot young gay basher is caught and put on trial by the leather-bar patrons. (My longtime sexmate from 1969-1974, Don Morrison, was one of the owner/managers of the Spike, and one of the producers behind *West Street Gang*. Another owner/manager/producer was Morrison's partner, Frank Olson, who was also the lighting director for the CBS-TV soap, *The Secret Storm*. Because of our incestuous sex synergy in 1970, Olson gave me an old-leather-boys-club entree to *The Secret Storm* director, cast, and set in CBS Studio 43 when I was writing my book on "electronic" theater, *Television Today*, published in 1971).

Outside New York, gay theater in San Francisco in the early 1970s was mostly drag versions of warhorses like *Hello Dolly*, staged by my friend, the actor-director Michael Lewis, at the Yonkers Production Company which also produced my one-act *Coming Attractions* (1976). There were notable exceptions mirroring the tremendous art behind gay liberation. In 1977, the Gay Men's Theater Collective created, after the style of *A Chorus Line*, the theatrical event titled *Crimes Against Nature*. It caused a sensation and gay culture-vultures may note that *Crimes* was the first gay play in San Francisco to be videotaped. Directed by Edward Dundas, a three-camera video copy of this original production saved an extraordinary documentary of the Titanic 1970s. As I have mentioned elsewhere, because of corporations warring over VHS and Beta formats, the new consumer video cameras and VCRs did not reach ordinary people until 1981 and 1982. As a result, the first decade of gay lib in the 1970s is virtually invisible because what moving images exist were mostly shot on film and were mostly silent—and as a result were mostly porn. The 1970s corporate war over VHS and Beta was a gay tragedy. Had video existed, the 1970s would be critiqued quite differently by those who missed the era, and only attended the 1980s after-party.

Drummer 20: *Crimes Against Nature*

I speak from experience as a filmmaker once limited by technology and budget to shooting on Super-8 while lusting for video. (Pioneer Andy Warhol had a video camera as early as 1966.)

In the 1960s, San Francisco actor Paul Gerrior was the first Colt Studio icon: on silent film and in print. In my eyewitness observation, Colt Studio gained its first reputation from presenting the universally handsome Paul Gerrior as "Ledermeister." If Gerrior had been separated at birth, his twin would have been the actor Clint Walker, the muscular, noble, and hairy-chested star of the TV show *Cheyenne*. (I printed a shirtless waist-to-face torso photo of Clint Walker on the last page of *Drummer* 27 as precise nostalgia because so many *Drummer* readers had come out as teenagers ogling Walker who performed his signature scenes—stripped to the waist—week after week.) Colt founder Jim French featured Gerrior in many homomasculine erotic films, including *The Meterman*, which was appropriate because Paul Gerrior worked as a lineman for a utility company in San Francisco.

Paul Gerrior was also the legendary model in the slick-paper *Catalog* for Leather 'n' Things, which was the leather clothing store at 4079 18th Street, on the south side of 18th east of the Hibernia Bank on the corner of 18th and Castro. In the early 1970s, every man in the City, and every tourist, picked up multiple copies of the handsomely produced catalog which was first published in 1969 and was kept in print until around 1974. That *Leather 'n' Things Catalog* was like a pre-*Drummer* mockup of *Drummer* and should be included in every really complete collection of *Drummer*. There are twenty-seven iconic photographs of the hairy and muscular Paul Gerrior stripped to the waist in leather, in sheepskin, with gun in holster, with cigarette, and ultimately sized up with a cloth tape measure in two photos in which his awesome body, wearing briefs, is divided into a grid to guide mail-order customers how to measure themselves. (Measuring oneself in the 1970s was the original gay Olympic event.)

In the zero degrees of separation, Paul Gerrior was the 1960s traveling companion of my longtime friend Al Shapiro, the artist A. Jay, who was the art director of *Drummer* when I was editor in chief. (I have inherited Al Shapiro's vacation snapshots and Polaroids which often feature the private Gerrior.) In the 1960s, Al Shapiro and Colt founder Jim French lived in the same apartment building in Brooklyn Heights off Joralemon Street in a building so gay it was called "KY Flats." When French decided to shoot an on-location brochure to advertise his precisely registered "COL-TOURS" to the Carribean, Al Shapiro designed French's shoot of model Paul Gerrior. Even though we had friends in common, Paul Gerrior was too beautiful for anything but my worship from afar.

For six weeks, from July 13 to August 19, 1978, during the nearly three years I was editor of *Drummer*, Paul Gerrior, who remains a very popular actor in San Francisco theater with the Actors' Collective, starred in *The Firebirds*, a play written by Max Frisch, and presented by the San Francisco Actors Ensemble, 2940 16th Street. My protege Tony Plewik, whose work I often mentored in *Drummer*, was photographer for the show which featured a fetishized fireman with fireman boots in a fireman uniform. Paul Gerrior, who was the perfect Jungian archetype of a very hairy muscleman with a Marlboro face and chin, played the part of "Sepp Schmitz, a wrestler." He was also one of the men influencing my creating the positive aspects of the muscular character of Kick in *Some Dance to Remember*.

In the intersecting worlds of leather, film, and theater during the 1970s, Paul Gerrior appeared regularly with the San Francisco Actors Ensemble, beginning in 1972 with his starring role in *Lucifer and the Good Lord*. "Sepp Schmitz" was his ninth role in SFAE plays including *Ghosts*, *Detective Story*, Tennessee Williams' *Summer and Smoke*, and as Judge Brack in Ibsen's *Hedda Gabler*. When my background in Tennessee Williams converged with Colt's iconic actor, Ledermeister, my esthetic and erotic fate was sealed. Most gay men then alive lusted after him. Naturally, every play he appeared in sold out with standing room only. I couldn't keep my eyes off him on screen, on stage, or in bars like the No Name and Ramrod, or in Riley's Gym (which became the Golden Gate Gym) which was one of the gyms where our salon worked out. In fact, once in the mid-70s when he wrecked his Harley-Davidson motorcycle and broke his leg, I marveled that the next weekend he was back in the Folsom bars, stoic, smiling, and very handsome with his leg in a plaster cast—and on crutches. I remember thinking: Omigod, I can finally catch him! Knowing that cruising can become stalking, I behaved.

In 1972, I was artist enough to recognize Ledermeister in a piece of street theater that reflects exactly how roleplaying mirrors reality. I was walking east of 15th Street and Divisadero where David Sparrow and I were living with Allan Lowery, owner of the Leatherneck bar, when the spontaneous apparition every documentary filmmaker desires appeared. There, sitting with his legs down in a manhole, with his butt sitting on the pavement of the little side street, wearing all his Pacific Gas & Electric lineman gear, and one of the white-cotton wife-beater tank tops he famously filled out, was Paul Gerrior, Ledermeister, peeling the ends off wires with a knife in his big hands between his knees. Instead of cuming right there, I sprinted uphill back to my bedroom at Allan Lowery's thinking the apparition would be gone before I could get my silent Super-8 camera. I ran downhill and knelt in the street, twenty or so feet away from Paul Gerrior doing brilliantly in real life in real time what everyone thought was acting on screen. He knew exactly what I was doing and he knew exactly what he was doing, and without so much as either of us acknowledging the other and breaking the fourth wall, I shot him, peeling wires, his biceps naturally flexing, his big hairy pecs working, for over twenty minutes to fix his real image on two four-minute reels of silent, color film. I did not interrupt him and he did not interrupt me. We both seemed, locked into that street scene, bonded, two artists knowing exactly what the other one was creating. Had the perfect voyeur found the perfect exhibitionist?

It was not until Sunday, June 24, 1979—the zenith summer of my three years of editing *Drummer*—that we converged in the same bed.

When a famous porn star and a famous bodybuilder cruise each other on the public promenade of 18th and Castro, hook up, and leave together *entourage* with a known magazine editor, that's newsworthy on the Richter Scale! Heads turn; paparazzi shoot; phones ring; gossip ripples with aftershocks.

On a hyper-cruisy Sunday afternoon, standing outside the Elephant Walk bar at 18th and Castro, my lover-bodybuilder Jim Enger and I saw Paul Gerrior and his friend Craig Caswell walking up the crowded sidewalk toward us. (Caswell—whose name I think is correct—and I were lucky enough each to be half of a very public couple.) It was a fireball of energy when Gerrior and Enger saw each other. Fifteen minutes later, the four of us were mixed into an only-in-the-70s performance on my bed at my house on 25th Street. Let me backtrack for a moment. This is the way it is with worship: before the four of us went to the bedroom, I had Jim Enger stall our guests while I excused myself in a stealth move to take Paul Gerrior's photograph off the wall over the bed where I had kept it from 1972 and keep it even today, so perfectly the Platonic Ideal of the archetypal man was he to me. My Paul Gerrior film still exists. (The color photograph of Ledermeister called "Stoner" was by Jim French, Colt Studio, and was published in the centerfold of *Queen's Quarterly*, January-February 1972.)

Here I discreetly draw the curtain across our private theatrical (which was an archetypal 180-degree antithesis from the stereotypical *The Boys in the Band*), but my beige designer sheets with the one bold red stripe next to the one bold green stripe, like a *madeleine* from Proust, have been saved as holy relics which to this day have never been used again, or washed. Can one brew tea from DNA? Those sheets, and their shelf-life, are among my souvenirs with a lock of David Sparrow's strawberry-roan hair, a small chunk of cement from the Berlin Wall, a fragment of bone from the leg of Saint Isidore, the posing briefs of Jim Enger, a tiny Titian, the key to Mapplethorpe's Bond Street loft, and my personal ticket and program from August 7, 1961, when Merman opened in *Gypsy* at the Curran Theater in San Francisco. I dance to remember and to think.

Exuding masculine gay appeal, another theatrical production that rocked San Francisco's pre-*Drummer* community was staged with a very new kind of uncloseted gay heart that moved self-defining gender one click farther in the evolution of identity. In the early 1970s, the drama department of Lone Mountain College premiered a nearly all-male production of *Tommy: The Who's Rock Opera*. The muscular young actor-dancers, stripped to the waist, and wearing sailors' white bell bottoms—referencing the seafood fetish of Herman Melville in *Billy Budd*, Tennessee Williams in "One Arm," Jean Genet in *Querelle*, and Kenneth Anger in *Fireworks*—set the hippie-Castro and leather-Folsom crowds on their ear. These benefit-of-the-doubt "straight" young men were the first sign of "something new" in the post-Stonewall sea change. Their debut revealed the arrival of an emerging and twenty-something homomasculinity that was a 1970s "way of being" beyond the early 1950s trope of thirty-something "leather, motorcycles, and S&M." Printed on the *Tommy* program, the twenty-two athletic actors were listed with hippie names: Charming Fred, Tommy John, Golden Gai, Starlight Alan, Psychedelic Ron, and so on.

Less musical and sexy, in 1976, the Yonkers Production Company produced a one-act play I had written about gay life emerging in San Francisco on 24th Street and Castro. It was titled *Coming Attractions* (aka *Kweenasheba*) and played on a double-bill with Lanford Wilson's one-act homage to—and "out-take" from—Tennessee Williams: *The Madness of Lady Bright*. The plays were headlined on the front-page of the *Bay Area Reporter* (BAR), Volume 6, Number 5, March 4, 1976, and were noticed in the San Francisco *Chronicle* Pink Section (March 21, 1976), because *Coming Attractions* was the first little gay play written in San Francisco *at that time* about gay identity in San Francisco *at that time* and produced *at that time*.

In August 1977, spurred on by the local Theatre Workers production of Brecht's translation of Christopher Marlowe's *Edward II* (whose poster I later printed with my purposely claustrophobic two-person dialog playlet, "Bondage," in *Drummer* 24), I wrote a kind of quintessential dominance-submission play, *Corporal in Charge of Taking Care of Captain O'Malley*: *Drummer* 22 (May 1978) and *Drummer* 23 (July 1978). (In the

Drummer 20: *Crimes Against Nature*

six-hundred degrees of separation, Christopher Marlowe was murdered in 1593 in self-defense by Ingram Frizer—a British collateral cousin from the Northern European Fritscher line: Fritscher/Fritcher/Fritzer/Frizer. Some people become dyslexic trying to spell or pronounce my surname that sports an internal "s" and rhymes with *richer*.)

It is an historical note that my friend David Hurles, with whom I have never traded stabs, collaborated on the background authenticity of my version of *Corporal in Charge*, and he recorded his own wonderful "audio book" performance version that is still available from his Old Reliable studio. In 1991, literary historian and critic Winston Leyland included my *Corporal in Charge* text as the only drama in his Lammy-Award winning canon, *Gay Roots: 20 Years of Gay Sunshine: An Anthology of Gay History, Sex, Politics, and Culture* (1991). *Corporal* has become a classic *Drummer* chestnut. It also appeared in three anthology editions of my writing titled *Corporal in Charge and Other Stories*, published in 1984 by Gay Sunshine Press, San Francisco; in 1998 by Prowler Press, London; and in a text-definitive edition in 2000, Palm Drive Publishing, San Francisco.

The power of some of the writing in *Drummer* has endured and has entered the canon of the literary gaystream.

Crimes Against Nature which premiered in 1977 about the same time as I became *Drummer* editor in chief grew out of this early climate when theater of gay lib was finding its voice which was to nurture some of the strength of gay culture. *Crimes Against Nature* seemed to me to be of great interest to the men who I figured were the demographic of *Drummer*. In fact, the homomasculine David Baker, who co-authored and starred in the psycho-dramatic *Crimes*, was key to the drama collective that staged the play to reveal their own personal stories after the fashion of *A Chorus Line*, but using drumming and tub-thumping and movement that was years ahead of *Stomp* and *Tap Dogs*. David Baker appeared in a photograph by Robert Pruzan, *Drummer* 57 (October 1982), page 22; he was performing in another play, also printed, as mentioned, in full in *Drummer*, titled *Delivery* by C. D. Arnold, which opened March 5, 1982, at Studio Rhino (Theater Rhinoceros) and again on June 16, 1982, at the 544 Natoma Gallery.

When David Baker was performing *Crimes* in the round in 1977, after we had not seen each other for a couple of years, I had the anonymous advantage of being a blurred face in the audience while he was brightly lit solo on stage. The cast had invented a kind of dance movement that was very stylized and sensual, and when the play ended, several of the cast, including David Baker, sat casually about on the floor of the stage-in-the-round as the audience slowly mixed and exited. Through the milling people, David Baker and I made eye contact that, because he seemed to recognize me, impelled me to rise from my chair to begin the exact stylized movement, traveling mainly on the knees—with much leg jack-knifing—toward him. It was the 70s. Nobody cared how outrageous anyone acted. The dance thrilled us both—that night, again, and for a couple of weeks, as it had when we first had met in December 1972.

David Baker was sometimes called "Thumper." He should not be confused historically, however, with my other pal, the legendary "Thumper," the uber-popular and handsome San Francisco barber and wrestler Jim McPherson mentioned in my "Gay Sports" feature; in 1974, I shot Super-8 footage of McPherson's wide smile, and his photo appeared in *Drummer* 115, page 32. It was David "Thumper" Baker who was the man I wrote about in 1972, and published, as noted, in "Leather Christmas," *Drummer* 19 (December 1977).

Years later, in the 1990s, David Baker sent me an invitation to a revival of *Crimes Against Nature*. He had moved to Eugene, Oregon, where in the diaspora of the zero-degrees salon around *Drummer* he was living with the long-haired redhead Michael "Misha" Workman whom I had photographed on March 22 and 29, 1988, as the model, "Outlaw Red," for my Palm Drive Video feature, *Bellybucker*. David and I hadn't seen each other in years; so the reunion involved much hugging in the lobby of the New Conservatory Theater building at 25 Van Ness in San Francisco where the producers of the revival were seeking backing. (The evolution from "fucker" to "backer" takes about twenty years.)

In fact, David Baker and I hadn't seen each other since February 1983 when Mark Hemry and I walked up to the apartment (kind of a rehearsal space, I think, perhaps for Studio Rhino) at 2926 16th Street, San Francisco, for the preview opening night reading of *The Ubu Cycle* by Alfred Jarry, the father of theater of the absurd, who had started riots in Paris in 1896 when the opening word of his *Ubu* play was a word that had never been said on a stage: *merde, shit*. This was as culture-changing as Lytton Strachey suddenly announcing the word *semen* in 1905 when he looked at a spot on the dress of Vanessa Bell who was Virginia Woolf's sister. He said simply, "Semen?" His daring unlocked the Bloomsbury stuffiness the way that semen on the dress of Monica Lewinsky changed the national discussion in America in 1995.

My friend, the often scatological artist Claude Duvall, who had produced Beat poet Ruth Weiss' *The Thirteenth Witch* (1980), was producing Jarry's three plays:

- *Ubu Roi* (or *Ubu Rex*) 8 PM, Mondays, 14 and 21 February, 1983, retitled and re-phrased by Duvall as *King Turd*;

- *Ubu Cocu* (or *Ubu Cuckolded*) , 8 PM Tuesdays, 15 and 22 February, 1983, retitled *Turd Cuckolded*; and
- *Ubu Enchaine* (*Ubu Enchained*), 8 PM, 16 and 23 February, 1983, retitled *Turd Bound*.

The evenings were whimsically billed as

a staged reading by the Noh Oratorio Satiety commandeered by Claude Duvall, with the phamous Noh Orchestre de Salon du Vay Say, playing pata-physical phavorites for hornstrumpot, importuned by Nick Shryock and Roger Anderson, David Baker, et al.

With his shaved head, big hooped gold earring, and wise-owl glasses, Claude Duvall, always in a green nylon jumpsuit, always smelling of scatological play, charged $5 for one or more performances, and when patrons called for reservations, he gave "frank advice" about the literal scatological nature of the evening's performance for which the audience sat on the hardwood floor of the apartment, trying to live up to the implicit dare—which came from Mapplethorpe—that "if you don't like this, you're not as *avant garde* as you think."

The Ubu Cycle was one of those tiny gay triumphs, a success of art, particularly as, in February 1983, AIDS was still a big mystery and the 1970s' fascination with scatology included theatrical nights not only dramatically at Studio Rhino but literally at the baths. Duvall thought his fetish was ready-made for *Drummer*, but *Drummer* failed to respond, and the scatological-fisting-crystal crowd elbowed its way into the classifieds of underground experimental 'zines like *Man2Man*, which, also, eventually, fled from the devotees of scatology, handballing, and drugs. When Sam Steward asked me in 1974 what was new in San Francisco's sex scene, and I answered, "Scat," he said, "That's the end of everything." The way that steroids were the most popular secret drug in the 1970s, scat was the most popular secret sex game that grew out of the douching for handballing as well as the abandon that came from handballers tweaking on speed. Anyone walking with their eyes wide open through the Titanic 70s observed a scatological awareness in places as public as the baths, the clubs like the Mineshaft, and the Catacombs, and on "Brown Hanky Wednesdays" sponsored by the Scatalogical Society of America at Dan's Compound at 11th and Folsom—the site of the former Leatherneck bar and of the *Drummer* Key Club. The readership demand for scatology in *Man2Man* became a request publisher Mark Hemry and I ultimately could not deal with. That—combined with the fact that there were no home computers or consumer-size word processors in 1980 and 1982, and the fact we both had careers in the real world—made the matter and form of producing that anthropological 'zine something we could no longer do. We did, however, send each subscriber a check for the amount of his remaining subscription. Leather-artist Jim Stewart of Fetters in London and David Stein of GMSMA in New York both wrote that the demise of *Man2Man* was the first and only time that a subscription refund ever happened in gay or straight publishing.

My first play, *Continental Caper* (1957), an undergraduate all-male musical written in high school, had been produced in 1958. Like walking a poodle named "Bruce," writing an all-male musical should have signified I was gay long before I thought about tying guys to a rack and dialing their nipples like a radio. Like most gay men, with telescopes up, assessing the sea change of the late 1960s and early 1970s, I jumped at the opportunity of enjoying community theater as a gay mixer and played in the four-character comedy, *Generation*, and the musical, *The Canterbury Tales*, singing "What Is It That Women Want" (which I didn't get) and "I Have a Noble Cock" (which I did). So by the mid-1970s, with an arts-writing-and-leather life lived in New York, Chicago, London, Los Angeles, and San Francisco, theater seemed to me an apt metaphor for the kind of dramatic S&M games that shaped *Drummer*, because plays—like sexual psycho-drama—activate the players and keep them from becoming passive which is the worst thing that can happen to a gay man, particularly gay S&M bottoms who tend to become energy vampires. As a genre, *Drummer* was not afraid to publish male-driven plays, favoring particularly those by George Birimisa, who later became a contestant in the Bodybuilding Seniors Division of the Gay Games.

At theatrical venues that were like Weimar cabarets gone mad, I often showcased in *Drummer* huge parties like *Night Flight* and *CMC Carnival* as well as many exotic theme bars, like the No Name, that all seemed to me to be gay theater which queer keywords turned into the term "performance art." For the same reason, in my writing I championed actors like Richard Locke in *Drummer* 24 (September 1978) and his directors, the Gage Brothers, in *Drummer* 19 (December 1977), as well as Roger in *Drummer* 21 (March 1978), and his director, Wakefield Poole, in *Drummer* 27 (February 1979).

The No Name bar nightly encouraged outrageous performance behavior among its pot-smoking customers sniffing poppers and cruising and moshing together in the theater-in-the-round rear-section of the bar where cardboard beer boxes were stacked like a banquette along the walls surrounding the pool table. In the midst of the sex-crush, late one midnight in 1973, I stood back in the crowded shadows watching, ten-feet away, a muscular man, aloof and costumed for role play, in full leather resting his butt against the lighted pool table. All around me in the dark corral of boxes, men were stroking themselves under the dim red light, sharing joints, and nipping at one another, but I had eyes only for the leatherman who stared from under his leather Muir cap like some dude from Ipanema into mid-distance. After twenty minutes of teasing myself up to eruption, I felt someone (watching me watching the leatherman) slip a bottle of popper up to my nose. I sniffed and strode hard-on-first directly up to the leatherman whose long legs and boots were kicked out and crossed at the ankles. I straddled his leather chaps and looking directly into his mirrored shades, I shot hot white clots all over his thigh. He screamed, "You can't do that!" I said, "Why not?" He said, "I'm from LA!" The surrounding audience roared with laughter and applause. Like *The Reluctant Debutante*, he rushed out of the bar, pulling at his costume, running from his reviews, shouting "That's not my *scene*!" Did he know he had caused me to suspend my disbelief? (I thought he was a man.) Did he realize he had been paid the ultimate compliment of orgasm? Did he appreciate the improvisational stand-up comedy of gay bars in the 1970s when *in situ* radical sex upended tradition through the unexpected juxtaposition of opposites? Did he comprehend that a man shooting San Francisco cum on his regal LA leathers was a comedy of manners virtually born among the groundling humor at Shakespeare's Globe Theater?

It does not harm the deep-dish metaphor of leather as a fetish to point out the quite literal theatrics of leather culture. Before irony deconstructed the roleplay "scene" in the 1980s, performance sex had to be honored if I were to create a reciprocal editorial policy for a magazine that voiced—and echoed—the identity of the readers. They were all suddenly actors, activated by the times, relieved from the passivity of the closet as they cast about to find their new playmates, partners, and friends. The behavioral keywords of early leather culture—as it got "the show on the road" from the 1950s through the 1970s—were, pointedly, theatrical terms.

Drummer was always a theatrical magazine filled with a colorful cast of actors, scenarios, erotic sets, exotic costumes, bizarre props and fetishes, stage-y sex in "play" rooms, and casting calls for role-playing characters. S&M sex is at essence theatrical ritual. In leather bars, we were "Method actors" kitted up to signal the part we would play in the "costume drama" of ritual acting: leather + denim + tit clamps + yellow hankie on the left." Under dim red lights, we cruised for "leading men" with the standard 1960s-1970s opening line: "What's your *scene*?" Eyewitness evidence exists in the fourth word of the title of the handmade magazine, *The Way Out Scene*, whose publisher, D&W Enterprises, described in Volume 1, Issue 8 (September 1975) that the little samizdat folio was a thousand copies per issue "printed on a silk-screen mimeo made by Gestetner of Yonkers, NY."

The mimeographed ads of *The Way Out Scene* and the personals ads of the "Leather Fraternity" in the glossy *Drummer* were filled with intimate *cri de couer* pleas that—today making me weep with nostalgia—were, I state, "Casting Calls" written by horny men directing their own "sex scenes" and seeking "character actors" as tops, bottoms, studs, bearded men, muscle guys, sadists, slaves, hippies, huskies, and even "inexperienced" ingenues. (John Dagion, the creator of *The Way Out Scene*, quickly evolved that periodical into his long-running small-format 'zine, *TRASH: True Relations and Strange Happenings*. Dagion, my long-time acquaintance in the zero degrees of gay publishing, has continued publishing his stylishly under-produced *TRASH* for the twenty-first-century underground. *TRASH* is to *Drummer* what the skid-row Tenderloin is to bike-row Folsom Street.)

Editing *Drummer* with such theatrical reality in mind, I massaged its thirty-day format to address the readers' genuine ever-morphing stage-iness. I aimed to give them a magazine that in editorial content and masculine attitude was a positive environment in which to re-write their "scenes," re-cast their "actors," and re-invent the narrative arcs of their Id-fetish "scripts " in *Drummer* every month.

It is amusing that this introductory essay is longer than the original notice in *Drummer*, but when the editorial "manifesto" was originally published most readers were, as it states, "dudes" steeped in the culture, innuendo, and personalities that it seemed necessary to reconstitute here—these many years later—for context.

A *madeleine*, after all, is just a tiny cookie.

II. The editorial essay as published in *Drummer* 20, January 1978

Getting Off

Crimes Against Nature 1977
Gay Guerrilla Theater

Crimes Against Nature, written and performed by the Gay Men's Theater Collective, has been the held-over hit of the 1977 San Francisco Season: Like *A Chorus Line* and *Hair*, *Crimes Against Nature* is a high-energy semi-musical in which the characters/actors expose the most private truths of their lives. *Crimes*, headed for Los Angeles and New York, deals specifically

Drummer 20: *Crimes Against Nature*

with athletics, jockstraps, and All-American dads' attempts to program their All-American boys into sports against their nature. *Crimes* is subtitled "A Play about Survival." As with *Hair,* one of the characters is shot, but in *Crimes* the fun and games turn serious. This play, like *Drummer*'s sports issue, is about fun that becomes self-defense. Like *Network*'s Peter Finch, gay men today are mad as hell and won't take it anymore. If a gay man wants to jock it up, it's not only okay, it's a celebration. Why should straight guys wear all the juicy equipment? When you grow up, you can play the way your nature calls.

CONTENTS: *DRUMMER*'S NEW BROOM SWEEPS

Taste is as taste does and *Drummer* tastes a bit of everything. *Drummer* has pinned its nuts on. Reality and fantasy both are in this issue. Jerk to what you like: drawings, comics, hot fiction, articles about the actualizing of fantasies, new photos by new photographers, the CMC Carnival, the I-Beam macho disco, and parties like *Night Flight. You* name it.

This masturbatory self-congratulation is to warn you that a new *Drummer*, good as the old, and even better to come, is in your hand right now.

DRUMMER GETS MORE AUTHENTIC

If you don't have *Drummer,* buy it. If you can't find *Drummer* to buy, subscribe, because in our next issue you're gonna get put in "PRISON" so authentically you wouldn't believe, and on top of that, the biggest upfront pumped-up exclusive of 1978 will be heading your way: ROGER'S BACK AND *DRUMMER*'S GOT HIM! (And Roger's ten inches is no crime against nature!)

NATURAL *VS* NORMAL

As Capote's Holly Golightly said in *Breakfast at Tiffany's,* "I'd rather be natural than normal." The "norm" is what most people do: Dull. The "natural" is what men do according to their nature: Fanfuckingtastic! As David Baker, author/actor of the *Crimes*' collective says: "To survive I'm butch." He survives, as does the play, in the best *Drummer* tradition. If it's okay to be straight macho, it's just as okay to be gay macho. If it's okay to be straight kink, it's okay to be gay kink. After all on a desert island which would you rather have? *Drummer*'s gay machismo or *Reader's Digest*'s "I Am Joe's Pancreas."

You read *Drummer*, dude, because you're macho, mad as hell, hot, horny, jocked, leathered, and getting in shape for THE SURVIVAL OF THE FITTEST!

III. Eyewitness Illustrations

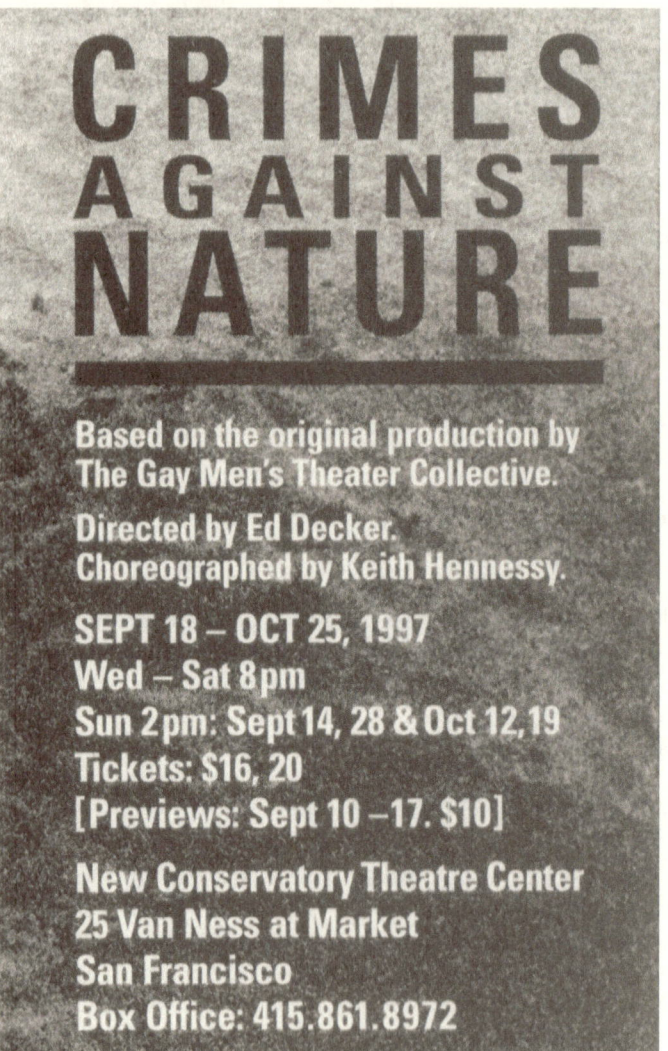

Advertising flyer from the 1997 revival of the 1977 original production of *Crimes Against Nature*. *Drummer* succeeded because its issues so often featured erotic plays that seemed to catch the essence of sexual action in an age when *Drummer* readers followed edgy gay theater of the S&M kind on stage and in playrooms at home and at the baths.

"Thank you for supporting my theater work."

Eyewitness Document
"Letter from David Baker to Jack Fritscher"
Keeping the Voice of David Baker Speaking

David Baker
xxx-A States Street
San Francisco 94114
December 27, 1997

Dear Jack,

Greetings from your old friend, David. What a wild adventure this last year has been. My father died on April 15....Fortunately, I had a chance to spend some quality time with him in Portland...in the hospital for his final week....I miss my dad tremendously [his biological father was gay]. During the next month, I got sick with a cough and was in bed for several weeks, isolating myself and grieving. I had this very weird condition where I would pass out if I started coughing vigorously. Several times, I would be standing, start coughing, and the next minute find myself face down on the floor and bruised. It was scary. I learned to get on my knees with my head on the floor whenever I started coughing (a position that I grew to call the "crash position.")....Fortunately, it wasn't TB or pneumonia either. My dad left all he owned to me....I let his life partner [man's name] stay in the house....

So, it happened this year, the 20-year-revival of *Crimes Against Nature*, the show that 11 of us wrote, directed, produced, and were in (even Off-Broadway), in the 70s. It was astutely directed, as you know, because you were there, by Ed Decker at the New Conservatory Theater. There was a cast of 8, and we told 8 of the original stories with very tight choreographed movement done by Keith Hennessy. It was a thorough joy to see the old girl back up on her feet again. Only this time it was much tighter and fuller. The biggest delight was having the 5 living of the original 11 cast members spend time together. We even shot some film footage of us discussing the show and how we'd changed since the original production in 1976. Just think how much you've changed since 1976. I am so thankful to be conscious and free....

The production also connected me with my grief over the loss of 6 of the original cast. I found myself crying during the show just to hear the voice and lives of my old compadres coming alive again. This was the first show I've done in 10 years and I was pleased to see what a professional job I did acting. I was interesting and real which felt rewarding to be so creative. Actually, I've changed over the years so that the story I told was much closer to who I am now than was my original story....They say the show took 10 years off my look which I think it did....Nevertheless, my T-cells are down to the 300's and my viral load is edging up. My interior infant feels helpless with this looming disaster. I am doing what I can to stay healthy at the same time I feel helpless....

Jack, I hope your holidays were bright and filled with cheer. Great to see you again after all these years. Thanks for supporting my theater work too. The years have treated you well....May comfort and joy surround you this holiday season! Hope to see more of you this coming happy new year. Love, David [Baker].

Text below was written on the back of the photo of David Baker and Michael Workman on the opposite page.

Christmas Solstice 1989

Jack,
May Peace fill your hole heart.
Happy Solstice.
I hope you have a great New Year. All is well here and I hope all is well with you. I think of you often. Be well and big bear hugs.
Misha and Dave

PS This picture was taken the last day I shaved. I ran out of shaving cream so the beard is coming back.

San Francisco actor, David Baker, star and producer of *Crimes Against Nature*, set up camp in the lap of the redheaded bear Michael "Misha" Workman for this Solstice card sent to Jack Fritscher (1989). Fritscher had photographed Workman in stills and video for the Palm Drive Video feature, *Bellybucker*, March 22 and 29, 1988 and for a full page in *American Men*. Three of his photographs of Workman appeared in *Drummer* 119 (July 1988).

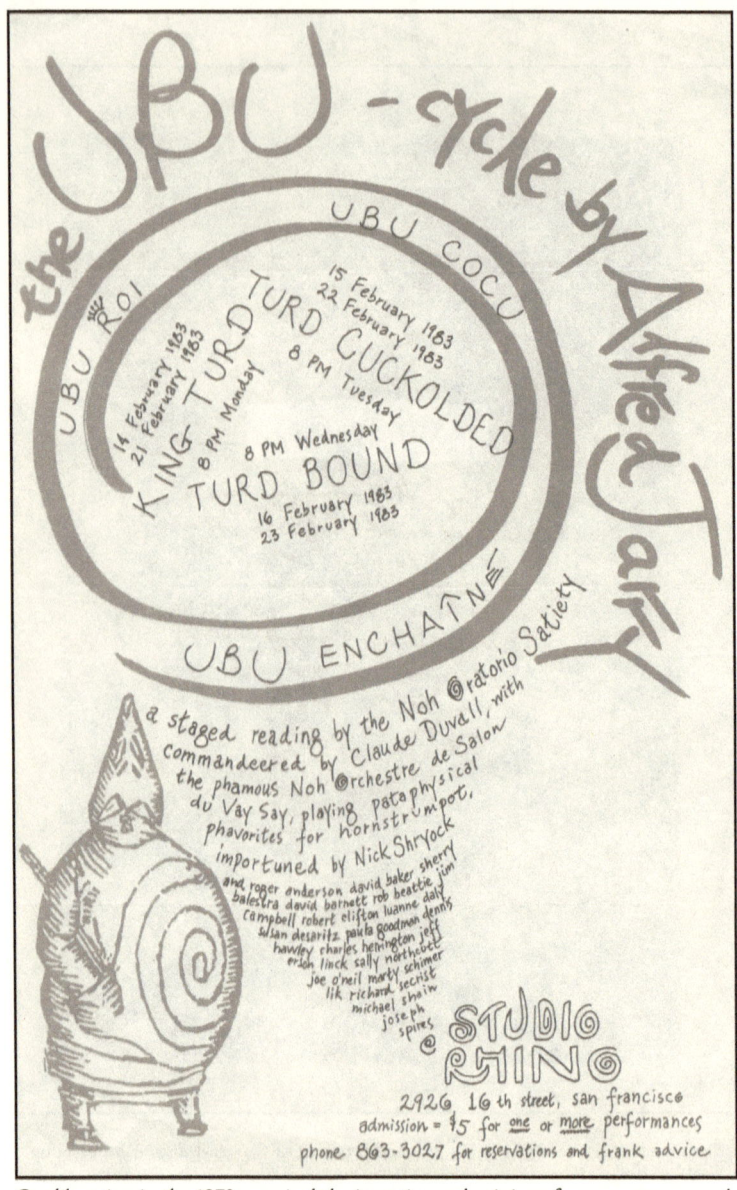

Gay liberation in the 1970s required the invention and coining of many new gay words such as *homomasculinity* to deal with the uncloseted concepts of the love that formerly dared not speak. In order to fill *Drummer*, Fritscher and other authors had to pioneer a new gay linguistics beyond Polari. *Drummer* was akin to the way that Lytton Strachey said the word *semen*, and Alfred Jarry said the word *merde*. *Drummer* salonista Claude Duvall's Noh Oratorio Society shocked San Francisco with Jarry's scatological *Ubu Cycle* at Studio Rhino, February 1983. Studio Rhino publicity kit. (continued bottom next page)

Delivery, advertising poster for the San Francisco production of the play by C. D. Arnold which was published originally in *Drummer* 57 (1982). Poster publicity photograph (not shown) by *Drummer* salonista Mark I. Chester.

Tommy, the early 1970s rock opera that was the mega-hit at San Francisco's Lone Mountain College, taught Castro Street and Folsom Street the new style of being a masculine-identified homosexual whose quintessential core identity was as valid as that of the then dominant and dominating identity of drag queens, androphobic sissies, and the politically correct controlling almost all of the gay press except for *Drummer*. *Tommy* publicity kit.

(continued from previous page)

In the gorgeously incestuous DNA of the *Drummer* Salon, Claude Duvall through his Noh Oratorio Society commissioned *Inquiries of Hope: Ten Poems of Kirby Congdon*, the first musical piece mourning AIDS (1984), by composer Louis Weingarden who also founded Stompers Gallery on 4th Street in New York which featured the first exhibits of Mapplethorpe and Tom of Finland. Louis Weingarden, an intimate part of the Fritscher-*Drummer* salon, was peer to Lewis Friedman, the legendary founding impresario of the Manhattan cabaret, Reno Sweeney, where Mapplethorpe and Fritscher went on dates, as they did to Stompers, to see and be seen. Lou Weingarden died of AIDS in Manhattan in 1989. Fringe *Drummer* salonista Lew Friedman, HIV positive, exited New York and opened his Sweet Life Café north of San Francisco in Santa Rosa, and died nearby in the Russian River village of Cazadero in 1992 close to his neighbors *Drummer* editor Jack Fritscher and *Drummer* publisher John Embry.

Are there sexists who hate masculinity and sexists who practice sissyphobia across the range of the Kinsey Six? The minute after gay liberation broke out, the gay gender wars began. In the 1970s, graffiti began to appear on toilet walls across San Francisco, and high on the outside wall of the abandoned Falstaff Brewery South of Market: "Queers Against Gays." From before the 1849 Gold Rush miners, San Francisco, countering a kind of "Viva Las Divas" metastasis, has long been the prime mover of gay masculinity. The gay civil war over gender was a central and controversial theme in what *The Advocate* called the "Gay *Gone with the Wind*," Jack Fritscher's story of Ryan "Miss Scarlett" O'Hara and the burning of the Barracks baths: *Some Dance to Remember: A Memoir-Novel of San Francisco 1970-1982*, Reel 2, Sequence 6 and Sequence 8. Plutonium Players publicity kit.

B.A.R.

free

IN THE BAY AREA
25 ELSEWHERE

VOLUME 6   NUMBER 5   March 4th   NEXT ISSUE OUT MARCH 18   NEXT DEADLINE: MARCH 12

THE LARGEST CIRCULATION AND READERSHIP IN THE BAY AREA

GAY HATE CAMPAIGN GROWS
... SEE PAGE 4

"Lanford Wilson writes with understanding and sensitivity"

THE NEW YORK TIMES

Yonkers Presents

"COMING ATTRACTIONS"
by Jack Fritscher

"THE MADNESS OF LADY BRIGHT"
by Lanford Wilson

March 13, 14 - 20, 21 - 27, 28 8:30pm SIR Theatre
TICKETS: 673-4258

Cover, *Bay Area Reporter* (March 4, 1976), headlined Jack Fritscher's play, *Coming Attractions*, double-billed with Lanford Wilson's *The Madness of Lady Bright*." *Coming Attractions* (1973) was the first gay play written and produced in San Francisco about life on Castro Street. Actor Michael Lewis who starred in both plays was the founding owner of the gay small business, the Nelly Deli, inside Dave's Baths where one lazy afternoon, serving Jack Fritscher a cup of coffee, he mentioned that his Yonkers Production Company was looking for new one-act plays. Fritscher wrote the short story for *Coming Attractions* in 1972. The story and play were published together in the anthology *Sweet Embraceable You: Coffee-House Stories*. B.A.R. cover used with permission.

DAVE'S

San Francisco
Palm Springs
San Diego
Seattle
Reno

Captions: Eyewitness documentation of the existence of graphics providing internal evidence supporting Jack Fritscher's text are located in the Jack Fritscher and Mark Hemry GLBT History collection. Out of respect for issues of copyright, model releases, permissions, and privacy, some graphics are not available for publication at this time, but can be shown by appointment.

Eyewitness Illustration — Magazine cover. The "Superman" cover of *American Theater* magazine, (November 1985, Vol. 2 No. 8) begins to reveal what Jack Fritscher contends is an essentially Shakespearean drama in search of an author who can do poetic justice to the motives and hubris of the quartet of "Dan White, Harvey Milk, George Moscone, and Dianne Feinstein" tangled in the helix of San Francisco politics and sexuality.

Eyewitness Illustration — Video box cover and three advertisements. San Francisco Colt Model Ledermeister in the 1960s and 1970s was the Platonic Ideal of the homomasculine leatherman who loomed like desire above Folsom Street and *Drummer* magazine. Appearing on page, screen, and stage, he was the star model in the Colt magazine *Manpower #6: The Leather File*, and in the catalog for the Leather 'n' Things store at 18th and Castro. In the early 1970s, every man in the City, and every sex tourist, picked up multiple copies of the handsomely produced catalog which was first published in 1969 and was kept in print until around 1974. That *Leather 'n' Things Catalog* (top right) was like a pre-*Drummer* bespoke mockup of *Drummer* and should be included in every really complete collection of *Drummer*.

531

Gay Jock Sports

Written September 17, 1977, this feature essay was published in *Drummer* 20, January 1978.
I. Author's Eyewitness Historical-Context Introduction written April 2, 2006
II. The feature article as published in *Drummer* 20, January 1978
III. Eyewitness Illustrations

I. Author's Eyewitness Historical-Context Introduction written April 2, 2006

Bullies, Gods, and Gay Bodies:
Without Pecs You're Dead!

Years before Tom Waddell, the Gay Olympics, and the Gay Games,
This 1977 "Jockstrap Declaration of Independence"
Framed and Reclaimed Sports, Gyms, and Balls
for Gay Men Self-Fashioning Their Masculine Gender Identity

This is the first magazine article written on gay sports, and the politicizing of gay sports. Written two years before Tom Waddell announced his idea for the Gay Olympics, this "Gay Sports" feature reclaimed for gay men the playing fields and locker rooms denied them in high school and college. Waddell, traveling the same path, found the article an encouraging assessment of the temper of the times. Many readers liked the article's focus on black men (O. J. Simpson, Ken Norton), on the idea of sports as a metaphor of rethinking gay masculinity, and on the analysis of the politicizing of gay men.

As editor in chief of *Drummer* and as a theorist of queer culture, I have always tried to stay "on message" regarding the self-fashioning esteem of homomasculine men emerging from the deepest closets of the pre-Stonewall world.

Historically, clock, calendar, and circumstance have put me in a pro-active position to reflect homomasculine men's lives in an immediate way in monthly magazines. Unlike books that take years to produce, magazines must be responsive monthly to new currents in culture; and magazine writing goes deeper than weekly gay papers.

In *Drummer* 99, page 5, and in *Drummer* 100, publisher Anthony DeBlase wrote that I was driving *Drummer* with a purpose: to celebrate and empower the most deeply closeted gay men, the masculine ones no one had ever considered might be lovers of other men. Patrick Califia, in one of his books, mentioned that "Fritscher is a prophet of homomasculinity." Like the zealous Patrick, I am sometimes apostolic about forging new identities and making them available.

I meant this cover lead feature to stir up even more the awakening jock consciousness among gay men who in American pop culture had been historically denied the "jockstrap role" and instead assigned the "victim-magnet role of the sissy."

Without any mention of campy cheerleaders, I interviewed, wrote, and produced this reflection of the "Gay Sports" movement as a key metaphor of emerging male-gender identity in *Drummer* where internal evidence shows that the keyword printed most frequently, particularly in the self-describing personals, is *masculine* (including *masculinity*).

In March of 1977, I coined the new word *homomasculinity* to clarify a newly visible "way of being" for men.

[Edited in October 5, 2007: For more on the use of language in *Drummer*, see the "Eyewitness *Drummer*" article: "Homomasculinity: Framing Keywords of Queer Popular Culture in *Drummer* Magazine" from the Queer Keywords Conference, "The(e)ories: Advanced Seminars for Queer Research," University College Dublin, Ireland, April 15, 2005.]

I may have invented the empowering word, but I did not invent the empowerment of homomasculinity itself which has long burned in the hearts of many homosexual men.

Like Adam in the Garden of Eden with his task of naming everything, queer pioneers immediately after Stonewall had much to name within the sex culture that till then dared not speak its name. Through the years, some men in the leather culture and in the bear culture, have taken my queer-theory word to heart. Long used in the alternative sex world, the word *homomasculine* went fully into the gaystream in *The Advocate*, August 20, 2002, on page 55, in the article "Daring to Be Bears" by Larry Flick, senior talent editor of *Billboard* magazine. On August 1, 2003, the conservative talking head Andrew Sullivan came out on Salon.com as a bear, one of the largest identity movements in homomasculinity. This linguistic evolution is a response to real life in which time and hormones change men's bodies through the maturation of the male secondary sex characteristics that identify men as a gender.

Drummer 20: Gay Jock Sports

> Years before the Gay Olympics existed and before all the rainbow leagues of gay sports suited up, the term "Gay Sports" in *Drummer* served as code and metaphor for homomasculinity. With a light touch, this "Gay Sports" essay, written in 1977, analyzes the genesis of the archetypal homomasculine "Castro Street" look in grooming, clothing, and physique. Its antithetical stereotype, the "Castronaut" look of the "Castro Clone" sent up by the Village People, was humorously satirized in my "Gay Deteriorata," *Drummer* 21 (March 1978) and in "Castro Street Blues: 1978 Style," *Drummer* 24 (September 1978).

Homomasculinity has liberated masculine-identified gay men.

Homomasculinity is a way of being, as valid as being a traditional sissy, even though the politically correct misjudge that homomasculinity means macho or sexist, which it doesn't.

Homomasculinity also recognizes homofemininity.

This aspect of the male paradigm does not tread on the female paradigm, nor on any paradigm in between.

Homomasculinity is often a personal choice within gender style as much as it is genetic destiny.

Many gay men do "their mother's act."

Other gay men act out the best of their fathers. See *Some Dance to Remember*, Reel Two, Chapter Six.

Neither "identity act" is better than the other, but one is less likely to make a man a target-victim.

Consider this theory: as long as homophobes feast on the idea that gay men are, or want to be women, they will abuse us the way they feel free to abuse women.

Homomasculinity threatens heteromasculinity way differently than does sissyhood.

Because of this horn-locking assertion of virility, men in straight sports and the military fear the queer who might outshine them man-to-man.

I shaped *Drummer* as an on-going "masculinist manifesto" to uncloset a repulsion-attraction demiurge in masculine-identified gay culture.

In what turned into a serious and sideways review of *Drummer*, Michael Bronski wrote of my *Drummer* writing collected into my 1984 book *Corporal in Charge and Other Canonical Stories*: This anthology of *Drummer* features and fiction written by Fritscher is

> graphic, explicit...and unabashedly romantic in a truer sense than are most books [magazines] aimed at gay audiences....[This is a] collection of [Fritscher's *Drummer*] pieces which deal with individual consciousness. Like Genet's work, these [*Drummer* writings] are essentially masturbatory fantasies...about the actual fantasy of romance...and gay men love to read about romance. —Michael Bronski, "S/M Fiction: Isn't It Romantic," *Gay Community News*, Boston, February 16, 1985, Volume 12, Number 30, pages 8-11

Some gay men—sissy, mid-range, and butch—have been, or have fantasized, they were somehow misunderstood or abused by their rugged blue-collar or white-collar fathers. They fairly or unfairly demonize their straight dads who, despite the anti-patriarchal poison of gay culture, were the *very essence of the masculine erotic authority gay men advertised for* specifically in *Drummer* personal ads.

I wanted to "out" that desire for the Platonic Ideal of masculinity so that gay men did not have to go against their personal gender identity as masculine men who prefer men masculine. The readers responded positively as *Drummer* tub-thumped for masculine-identified liberation of grown-up men who preferred each other rather than twinks, sissies, drags, or clones.

As editor in chief I made *Drummer* the first magazine to iconize mature men in each issue. In this article, besides O. J. Simpson and Ken Norton, erotic assessment was made of Ted Turner, Gordon Liddy, and Ken Stabler. What I did was different from Colt Studio romanticizing grown-up and hyper-groomed bodybuilder gods no one could touch; I lionized men edgy with reality who reflected the ages and looks of men seen as available on the street and in bars and baths.

I began with the concept "In Search of Older Men" and initiated it fully in *Drummer* 24 (October 1978) with my Mapplethorpe cover, my editorial, and the cover feature "An Interview with Porn Star Richard Locke: 37 & Hot." This "mature man" angle on homomasculinity—which I spun out of my longtime analysis of the Marlboro Man advertising campaign—played so big in every issue that *Drummer* published three extra "special issues" titled *Drummer Daddies*.

The reason publisher Embry went for this thematic issue of "Gay Sports" was that in late 1975 he had commissioned some pictures from the popular photographer Joe Tiffenbach who, like other photographers at that moment, had not yet heard of Robert Mapplethorpe. Embry had a few left-over Tiffenbach images that he insisted I use.

Joe Tiffenbach had lensed his shoot in the desert outside Palm Springs, and several were published, for instance, in *Drummer* 6 (May 1976) to illustrate the serialized story, "Five in the Trainer's Room," by Scott Masters who was a frequent *Drummer* author also known as Ed Menerth aka Ed Franklin. Squeezing the nickels out of those photos was almost okay (See "Dune Body"), because I'd told John Embry when he hired me that I had lots of existing writing I could stick in *Drummer* and also that I did not mind backfilling with material to match photographs and writing already in the *Drummer* files.

In the mid-70s before "Gay Lib" became "Gay Politics," gay men knew a freedom unparalleled before or since in the window between penicillin and HIV.

Bodies turned very muscular in gyms. Without pecs, you were dead.

Steroids were, in fact, the most used drug in the 1970s.

Masculinizing steroids were the secret designer drug of choice.

During the French Revolution (1789-1799), the ideal was "Liberty, Equality, Brotherhood." During the Enlightenment of the Gay Revolution (1970-1982), "Masculinity" was added as inalienable goal and Platonic Ideal; and it endures in the bear movement celebrating male secondary sex characteristics, in the quintessential images of gay porn, and in the heart's desire personal classifieds of the gay press. The words *masculine* or *masculinity* are used six times in my purposely assertive 8,000-word article written for gay popular culture way back in 1977.

The minute steroids pumped up the testosterone, competition sports broke out. The gay male body changed and morphed into something new. Speed cut gay body fat to micro-percentages less than a long-distance runner. Gay T-shirts shrank three sizes too small. Body hair and moustaches bloomed with beards after the fashion of the nineteenth-century frontier of cowboys and gents. A fresh archetype of masculinity became instantly sexy even as its stereotype, the clone, became a joke. Homomasculine men left off dancing in discos and headed out to have fun in gyms and on the playing fields. Gay fitness was the rage that dragged aerobics out of the disco and led in 1981 to the gay-smart Jane Fonda's fitness empire.

In the San Francisco sports scene, the San Francisco Police Department challenged the gay softball team which gave the SFPD team a run for its money. I shot some Super-8 color film at the 1978 game—not of the action, but of the players, particularly every gay man's favorite hunk, the young and handsome Officer Walter Scott who was the son of former Police Chief Donald Scott. He had the same universal appeal and mystique as Mike Dayton, the bodybuilder and karate champion, whose father was a cop. Dayton from the East Bay appeared frequently around San Francisco with his strongman show, bending bars, escaping shirtless from handcuffs and restraints, and being hanged by the neck until parents complained. (See my feature "Mike Dayton: The Last Gladiator" in *California Action Guide*, November 1982, pages 9-14, San Francisco.)

Because of the Scottish novelist Sir Walter Scott who wrote *Ivanhoe* and popularized kilts as review-proof menswear, the straight Walter Scott's name was instantly memorable and stays so years later because of his cop look, his mustache, his arms, and his buoyant personality. In that same June 1978, he and his straight partner obliged me and Bob Cato by driving around in their police car in a way I directed so I could shoot some additional footage of them chasing Cato.

Little did any of us know then that the SFPD would be arresting Cato for real on Sunday, September 5, 1982, for driving his Dodge van into a cab carrying Broadway star Mary Martin, 68, and Oscar-winner Janet Gaynor, 75, and killing Martin's press agent Ben Washer, 76, for which, at the insistence of Mothers Against Drunk Driving, Cato went to prison.

Cops *versus* Gays:
"He Loves Me. He Loves Me Not"
How Softball Games Turned into the White Night Riot

In the background of my 1978 cops-gays softball film, of course, are the inevitable drag cheerleaders and their pom poms trying to get to "second base," but the real back story was this. On that 1978 playing field, the SFPD cops and gay men met in detente as community equals who did not divide until the White Night Riots, May 21, 1979, when gays set twelve police cars on fire outside City Hall and the cops marched down Castro Street beating everyone in their path.

The White Night Riot occurred almost exactly ten years after the Stonewall Riot, June 28, 1969, and is described in *Some Dance to Remember*, Reel Three, Scene One.

(In my drag-driven story, alternative to *Drummer*, comic eyewitness details of the Stonewall Riot appear fictively in "Stonewall, June 27, 1969, 11PM," *Harrington Gay Men's Fiction Quarterly*, 2006, Volume 8, Issue 1.)

During the time I was editor in chief of *Drummer*, I was recruited by the San Francisco Sheriff's Department which led to my doing outreach with the SFPD. "Sensitivity training" meant my taking a dozen young recruits on an introductory evening tour of gay spots on Castro Street and on Folsom Street. I cut a deal with manager Tony Tavarossi and owner Jack Haines at the Slot to let me lead my troop through the hallways. That night Tony told every sex maniac checking in about the visit of young SFPD cops which, of course, escalated everyone's exhibitionism.

The Slot hallways were like a night in the red-light district of Amsterdam. The door to nearly every room was left open on some intensely posed and in-progress S&M athletics. When my troop of young troopers reached the third floor, one of the recruits freaked out and hyperventilated all the way down the stairs as we helped him to the front door and set him down on the pavement. (I always wondered what became of him. Had he some pentecostal revelation of his own desire? Did he return the next night as a paying customer?)

Sports have always been a gay metaphor from ancient times to the present-day gym culture. The Greek word *gymnos* actually means *naked*. What could be more ideally gay than bodies moving naked? Read *The Naked Olympics: The True Story of the Ancient Games* by Tony Perrottet. In *Drummer*, the sports metaphor expressed itself in terms like "S&M *games* with *players* in a *playroom*" which was more rollerball and dangerous than the 1980s therapeutized "safe spaces" for urban aboriginals spanking their outraged inner child for politically correct Marxist gender issues.

The 1980s was a whole 180-degree spin away from the 1970s. Blame viruses, Marxists, and faux fags and imitation lesbos who weren't really gay, and only acted gay, because they were actually straight men and straight women afraid of the opposite gender. Where else but in the inclusive gay press could kinky straight people run their ads in search of each other? Our GLBT crew are all empathetic travelers on Noah's Arc where we have seen two of everything, but when a self-described "lesbian" seeks a "gay man" to fist her, that seems more like refracted heterosexuality than homosexuality. For all the power of *Playboy* and *Penthouse*, I've never seen either corporation's magazines run "Classified Sex Personals" that were always the backbone of *Drummer* and of *The Advocate* whose "Pink Section" kept it alive during the 1970s.

"GLBT" is destined to become the alphabet soup of "GLBTETC" because anyone and everyone can hitch a ride on our momentum, and we never throw them under the bus.

Nevertheless, that's the great element of "blank" in homosexuality and lesbianism: both are such open existential positions that they let any and all come into the tent whether they essentially belong there or not.

This existential irony has helped deconstruct pure homosexuality and pure lesbianism.

Unlike much of the gay press, I am not heterophobic nor anti-Catholic nor a gender separatist. However, I have the queer *idee fixe* that in all the years in which "Sandinistas in wheelchairs" are invited to lead the gay pride parade, "diversity politics" removes focus from the "same-sex principle of like seeks like" which is the only defining absolute for homosexuality. Does this change the focus, and rather much mandate and presume that all gays are leftists bound to accept any behavior and any character who attaches to the gay movement?

For this reason, when I set out to define the Titanic 70s culture in the *Drummer* novel, *Some Dance to Remember*, I mixed the sports metaphor into the sex games and brought in bodybuilding as the gayest sport of all because of its esthetic, philosophical, and theological implications. Body sculpting is about physical beauty as the base for spiritual beauty in the way Saint Thomas Aquinas wrote that "grace builds on nature." There is not a tribe on earth that does not believe that the more perfect one's body, the greater the capacity for grace, for love, for happiness, and for reproducing one's DNA. Plato himself believed in the perfect statue as the perfect form of the perfect man or the perfect woman. Has anyone in Western Culture recently looked at its "main art image" of a handsome, muscular, thirtysomething blue-collar carpenter Christ hung sculpted on the cross like a Calvin Klein gymnast on Olympic rings? The absolutely essential "Gay Sports" plot line of *Some Dance* is about a bodybuilder and an average-body gay man whose esthetic, theological, and political quest pursues the perfect body the way the Hispanic Man of La Mancha pursues "The Impossible Dream" in his Ideal Woman. This is lust, but could this be Fascism? Well, yeah, it could be. Maybe. Maybe not. Is Schwarzenegger's ideal body a Fascist expression learned from his Nazi father? Is the ideal Colt model Fascistic? Is the whole existence and popularity of Colt Studios, featured in early *Drummer*, Fascistic or the Platonic Ideal? Was the soon-to-be Colt model I shot for the cover of *Drummer* 25 Fascistic? Colt renamed him "Ed Dinakos" which I always thought was the clumsiest porn name in history, but when I shot him, his ethnic name was Michael Glassman. I further enjoined "the Fascist question" by putting a photograph of a statue of the boxer Primo Carnera—lensed by photographer George Mott at Mussolini's Foro Italico—on the cover of the first edition of *Some Dance to Remember*.

In that novel-memoir, I made dramatically certain that the protagonist gets what's coming to him, and that the antagonist gets what he deserves. That's the point of art for art's sake. I am not a moralist such as the politically correct would have artists be. In this case, as an artist who is a writer—which is different than simply being a writer, I wanted to do more than moralize and entertain. I wanted to outrage the self-satisfied status quo of the sissy-establishment with its gay agenda to program young gay hearts and minds through the endlessly effeminate gay press such as *The Advocate* or *The Bay Area Reporter* or a dozen other publications.

I want to alarm the reader and frighten the horses and stick needles into modern and post-modern homosexuality till it bleeds.

I want to whip the politically correct. I want to pinch the nipples of straight people who hang lasciviously around the edges of our homosexual shrines.

I want to drive the pretenders from the temple so that men can be with men again, and women can be with women again, without the politics of separatism or the religion of matriarchy using the playrooms of homosexuality to try to kill off patriarchy which is a heresy as bad as matriarchy.

I am not a masculinist.

I am not a feminist.

I am not a separatist.

I am a humanist, because I think that the quintessence of homosexuality is to make one more human.

Politics usually makes people less human.

These are dangerous words, maybe, but if writing isn't a thrill, then it's just jerking off.

History buffs may note that my *Drummer* of the 1970s was very "West Coast" going "international." After I exited *Drummer* on December 31, 1979, *Drummer*, like S&M itself in the 1980s experienced the pressure of East Coast sexual politics which changed face and direction.

Gay Liberation, for instance, became Gay Politics.

And those are two different ways of being.

Sports ain't just about jock straps, locker rooms, and sucking off the coach.

This kind of civil war, between the Left Coast and the Right Coast, was as bad as the civil war between *Drummer* and *The Advocate*, and between the gay Marxist left and the gay Log Cabin right. All these gay-civil-war battles of liberation hurt many artists and writers as much as the McCarthy Communist witch hunts in the 1950s hurt Hollywood writers. This is one of the reasons that the gay-civil-wars are one of the main themes in *Some Dance to Remember*, Reel 2, Scene Fifteen.

In 1990, Brian Pronger, aware of how for years I continued creating *Drummer* images for my erotic-athletic Palm Drive Video company, contacted me for some of my sports photographs. He had liked the pioneering "Gay Sports" idea of *Drummer* 20. His nonfiction book then in progress was *The Arena of Masculinity: Sports, Homosexuality, and the Meaning of*

Sex. He published one of my quintessential *Drummer* photographs featuring the two "Gay Sports" boxers, Dan Dufort and Gino Deddino, from my video *Gut Punchers* which, shot July 26, 1987, was the first gut-punching video. It was reviewed in *Drummer* 115 (April 1988). I kept the gut-punching theme going in the videos *Rough Night at the Jockstrap Gym*; *Larry Perry Raw: Naked Came the Stranger* starring Mr. *Drummer* contestant Larry Perry; and *My Nephew, My Lover* starring Mike Jacob who touted himself as the German International Mr. Leather (IML) contestant.

To illustrate my "Gay Sports" essay I used the Joe Tiffenbach photographs; a wrestling drawing by Matt; a Mr. California physique contest photo cut to make the headless competitors anonymous; one still photo each from *Rocky* and *The Longest Yard*; one photograph of baseball player Ron Cey with fist rampant which I used again on the cover of my *Man2Man Quarterly* #2 (December 1980); two photographs by Bob Heffron of a water skier who looked as if he might be the Colt model Ledermeister aka Paul Gerrior; a cartoon of a track-and-field athlete in a kilt—the first kilt to appear in *Drummer* (See also my Highland Games' photographs in "Men in Kilts," *Drummer* 25, pages 92-93); two photographs of the newly "out" football player Dave Kopay; two photographs shot by my traveling companion Gene Weber of us doing some underwater fisting in the Caribbean; one wrestling photograph by Bob Mizer at AMG; two "boxing bag" and "boxing chair" photos with three wrestling photos by David Hurles featuring John Handley of the Manhattan Boxing and Wrestling Club shot at the private ring owned by Golden Gloves coach Greg Varney (with the byline wrongly attributed to Handley on page 84); and one photograph of the staff inside Tuffy's gay sporting goods store at 597 Castro. The photograph on page 10 of the jockstrap-view of football quarterback Ken Stabler in *Sports Illustrated* is bylined as "David Hurles" whose name I sometimes used with Hurles' permission when publisher Embry balked at my bylining all my input into *Drummer*. I designed and shot this jockstrap photograph in my own bed using the popular San Francisco muscleman, my pal, Paul Merar as my model.

Before *Drummer*, *Sports Illustrated* was one of the main sources of erotica for homosexuals in the way that *National Geographic* was used as porno by heterosexuals. In fact, I made *Sports Illustrated*, like the Marlboro Man campaign, one of the informing images that drove the ethos of *Drummer*. *Sports Illustrated* was often mentioned in *Drummer*.

My "Gay Jock Sports" article is a manifesto about how we gay men reacted to being politicized by the fundamentalist culture war started by Protestant Republicans. To quote the 1978 article: "Everyone is rethinking masculinity today."

II. The feature essay as published in *Drummer* 20, January 1978

The Gay Sports Revival:
Should Only Straight Guys Have All This Fun?

Gay Jock Sports
Wrestling, Boxing, Rollerballing, Soaring, Scuba, Bodybuilding, Dune Bodies, Films

He chews Redman tobacco, wears a railroad engineer's cap at the helm, and often pisses over the side of *Courageous,* the 12-meter yacht he skippered to the America's Cup crown. Before the America's Cup races, he pep-talked his crewmen as if they were a football team, playing the theme song from *Rocky* to fire them up. His name is Reginald Edward Turner III, although he's more often known as "Captain Outrageous."

Ted Turner is a perfect 38 years old, a Georgia peach of a jock who stretched his RET initials to name his own WRET-TV station [which became his global super-station CNN]. He sees himself as Scarlett's Rhett modernized. International yachtsman Turner owns Atlanta's baseball and basketball franchises. He buys and sells pro-ball players like Big Macs. In a former existence, the dashingly handsome Turner no doubt owned a stable of gladiators. In this existence, he's a macho, married, handsome, straight, millionaire jock.

SPORTS MASTURBATED

Of all the current gladiator dreamjocks, Oakland Raiders' quarterback Kenny Stabler is a man of a southern class more redneck than the aristocratic Turner. "My lifestyle," Stabler confessed to *Sports Illustrated,* "is too rough—too much booze and babes and cigarettes to be a high-school coach." Stabler is big, bearded, and so butch that after winning the Super Bowl, he described the Raiders' locker room victory party as a great release: "Coach Madden was all red and grinning and the guys were hugging each other like a bunch of fruits."

Twice-divorced Stabler now keeps Wickedly Wonderful Wanda so close that she emerges "like a bauble from the shadow of his armpit." (Jock reporters, like Robert Jones, have a way with words to make your mouth water.) Always an athlete, Stabler, nicknamed "Snake," was 6-3 and 185 before pro-ball weight training boosted his bulk to 215. "The stronger you are, the more muscle you got around those joints, the less likely you are to get hurt."

Check out *Sports Illustrated* (9/19/77) to see Snake's Wicked Wonderful Wanda, to see the shining Stabler shot in loving-color "beefcake" full-page and cover photos. "Ken Stabler is a man in motion," *SI*'s Jones writes. "Furious, violent motion. Exultant motion."

Motion just like a lubed hand.

No reflection on Stabler as a private person, but when a private person goes public and is openly touted as a sexual beast, the tempted reader who buys the magazine can stroke up whatever fantasy he wants. Stabler can take the energy as the compliment it is: his manly *mana* only encourages lust in the grandstand. What jock-groupie wouldn't stir at Jones' story that Stabler is so tough, that when he was at Alabama he topped his girlfriend by putting her in her place in the corner and fed her with a slingshot.

SHOULD ONLY STRAIGHT GUYS HAVE ALL THIS FUN?

Even the tall, dark, and handsome Gordon Liddy, the only man who took Watergate like a man, while in prison buffed himself up to a tight-lipped 190 pounds and was bench-pressing over 300 by the time he went home to his wife *sans* slingshot. Liddy's dominant face suggests the look of the Castro Street type matured. Having achieved the character a man's face takes on passing through his thirties, Liddy's got the macho. He's got the magic. He's got the dark S&M look. He is so heavy, he offered himself for execution if his symbolic death would help clean up the Watergate mess. Instead, like most cons, he worked out what he had to work out through the channeled aggression of sports and the stoicism of cold showers.

JOCULARLY STRAPPED AND LATENT

Jock is British slang for *penis*. *Jock* with *strap* means *athletic supporter*. *Jock* in American slang means *athlete*, especially a *college athlete*. Edward Albee's *American Dream* boy is a jock "who works out a little bit." Tennessee Williams' Brick in *Cat on a Hot Tin Roof* is an over-the-hill jock, terrified, remembering that with his football teammate Skipper, "Sometimes late at night on the road in our hotel room we'd reach across the space between the beds…" The American dream is the golden boy who blooms early in high school, makes all the teams, and graduates to date the college homecoming queen. The American nightmare is the beefy jock type who, ten years later, divorced from the homecoming queen, cruises singles bars, presses his beer can up against his dropping double knit chest, and admits to having "played a little ball in college."

FUCKING: THE PRIMAL PUSH-UP

Charles Atlas made millions merchandising muscles to keep sand-kicking bullies from stealing away the heart of beach blanket Annettes. Atlas' successor, Joe Weider, publisher of *Muscle Builder*, one of the world's truly great catalogs of beefcake, peddles classic sex in ads with Arnold Schwarzetcetera [Schwarzenegger] touting protein powder while a bikini-girl hangs over his bionic shoulder with a *National Lampoon*-tang look on her face. Weider's catalogs are wonderfully illustrated for one-handed reading late at night for anyone who gets off on a hyperbole of bodies.

Athletes have long endorsed products promising first of all a terrific body (Bruce Jenner for Wheaties), then a body with sex appeal (Joe Namath for you-name-it), then clothes with success appeal (Bob Griese for leisure suits from Sears), and finally the unstoppable Joe Willie [Namath] — in his classic pantyhose [ad]. Woody Allen summed the Jock Sell up in *Everything You Always Wanted to Know about Sex* in the sequence with the two jocks, stripped down to white towels and tan torsos at the locker-room mirror, endorsing the irresistible qualities of some sexy product on an athletic body. Naturally, they fall into each other's hot embrace, as naturally as ballplayers pat ass, snap towels in the shower and talk chauvinist talk about broads and fags.

Athletics is attitude. Players spend as much time psyching as practicing. A jock is only as good as his body and his psyche. So when chased by jock-groupies of both sexes, players can get cynical or jaded. One baseball player recently claimed San Francisco was the worst place for a jock to try and get laid, because everybody in the Bay Area was either a hooker or a fag. Somehow, that should make it easier.

When the sport is as good as sex, as in *Pumping Iron* when Arnold rather truthfully states that a good muscle pump is as good as cuming, then the sport includes its own sexual end. Uniforms often exaggerate body parts with protective padding or expose the body for freedom of movement. I have Super-8 movie evidence I'll be glad to show any man who himself is around 6', 190, with 18" arms, that at more than one physique contest, my zoom lens has, by sheerest of accident, caught certain bodybuilders during their posing routines growing erect in their sheerest of posing briefs. That's not only okay. That's the point. Among other things that it is, sports is exhibitionism. And what's the Ultimate Exhibit? The Body.

Schwarzenegger wasn't booked in as an "exhibit" at the Brooklyn Academy of Music for nothing [during the 1969 and 1970s Mr. Olympia Physique Contests]. He was booked to exploit his body. His acting career, going back to the Italian spear-and-sandal epics when he was billed as Arnold Strong, always was and always will be based on his delts and not his diction. He and other sports-to-movies jocks are like the tone-deaf dancer in *A Chorus Line*. She doesn't need to sing. Her body itself has "men cuming in their pants." Her pigtailed counterpart affirms the body as exhibit: tits and ass. The body is the one singular sensation, sensed in the athlete's body and sensed in the sports fan's head.

Every man wants an athletic body. Lots of men want athletes' bodies. Back in the 1950s when Elroy "Crazy Legs" Hirsch was America's football idol, after one particularly rousing game, the fans streamed onto the field and literally tore Hirsch's uniform off for souvenirs: jersey, cleats, socks, everything, pad by pad, strap by sweaty strap. Hirsch escaped in a shred of jock. He is also remembered for one of his three movie roles. The film, a 1955 classic, was *Unchained*. Its main title theme was "Unchained Melody."

Norman Lear's short-lived sit-com *All That Glitters* featured a professional baseball player turned actor exercising his naked chest while explaining to the camera, "Without pecs, you're dead."

WITHOUT PECS, YOU'RE DEAD?

Naked to the Greeks, who had a word for everything but poppers, is *gymnos*. Gymnastics, like all events in the original uncut Olympics, was movement performed naked. In the 1950s, Bonnie Prudden in *Sports Illustrated* went so far as to recommend that high-school boys attend gym class shirtless to spur competitive pride in their bodies. Nothing was said about quick-glance comparisons made later in the overheated and underventilated shower. Gays have no corner on that kind of looking. At that age, every boy looks to see how he compares. The only difference is that gay guys never stop looking. Comparison shoppers to the end, they remember. For instance, a former student manager [David Sparrow, my lover 1969-1979, and my partner in photography at *Drummer* 1977-1979] at Evansville, Indiana's Rex Mundi High School fondly recalls watching their all-star straight jock head into the shower. To this day he can describe to the inch the sudsy vision of a cut Bob Griese, long before he became the Miami Dolphins' star quarterback whose blondness contrasted so perfectly with the macho darkness of those two other drop-dead Dolphins, Jim Kiick and Larry Czonka, whom the sportswriters called "Butch and Sundance."

[See the cover of *Sports Illustrated* (August 7, 1972). Jim Kiick inspired the name of the character, Kick Sorensen, in *Some Dance to Remember*.]

OH MY, O. J. SIMPSON

Equally well remembered is O. J. Simpson working out at the gym at City College of San Francisco [1965-1966; corrected from UC Berkeley in the original]. O. J. Simpson long before he hurtled suitcases in TV ads for Hertz [Rent-a-Car], pleased more than one pair of adoring eyes while he minded his own business at USC [University of Southern California]. As only [Boyd McDonald's] *Straight to Hell* # 32 magazine could juicily put it:

> Before going to Stanford, I was working in Hollywood and going to USC part time. This was during O. J. Simpson's last year at USC (1969-1970). Because I used to run, lift weights, swim and generally hang out at the gym, I met the straight O. J. a number of times.
> One afternoon I was in the weight room working on an exercise machine called a Universal Gym. The leg-press part is lowest to the floor and faces the south wall which is covered with mirrors. I was on this part of the machine when O. J. and a couple of his Black buddies came in to work out. They were bareassed except for bulging jockstraps. We exchanged nods and greetings and O. J. came over to work on the bench press section which was raised and to my left. Since I'd seen O. J. stripped to gym shorts several times before, I already knew he had a great bod: thick neck and arms, gigantic thighs, and beautiful dark reddish-brown skin. So this time I concentrated on the private parts. His jock pouch was filled out quite well, and because the bench press user has to spread his legs wide to the sides of the bench, he unknowingly gave me a fantastic panoramic view of his beautiful tight buns bulging out of the jock: dark, moist, curly-haired crack; fuzzy crotch; plus just a hint of asshole and a peek of one large thick nut sac. What a juicy mouth-watering straight stud. I wonder if the sports writers realize how appropriate his pro-nickname, "The Juice," really is.

In this media-mad world, anybody can fantasize almost anything about anybody, and Simpson even way back then, minding his own business, was already larger than life.

WIDE-SCREEN JOCKS

Boxer Ken Norton infuriated Muhammed Ali by appearing in a tabloid wearing only a jockstrap. That strap covered a lot considering the package the classically built Norton displayed in *Mandingo*. In that Dino DeDemented [DeLaurentis] movie, plantation mistress Susannah York summons slave Norton to her bedroom. Norton wears only white cotton trousers held up by a drawstring. The camera shoots Norton's broad-shouldered, sweaty, and lickable back. York, standing in front of Norton, faces the camera, but looks straight at Norton's face. Her hand reaches up and pulls slowly, sensually, and long on the symbolic drawstring holding his light trousers against his beautiful dark skin.

Not one to be undone without being done, Norton stands stock still as his trousers slide slow down his naked buttocks. The camera tracks equally slow down his noble backside as the fair-skinned York sinks to her adoring knees down his frontside.

This is acting? She gets paid for this?

One Black moviegoer shouted out in the hypnotized theater silence: 'HOLLEEE-WOOOOOOD!" And this perfect review was right on. Yet through it all Norton's innate nobility and incredible body carried the scene with a dignity Ali long ago lost. Norton's athletically disciplined body on exhibition, preserved for all time on film, is worth twice the admission price. Norton seems both to understand and be willing to share the vision of his naked body perfected by sports.

Hollywood has always trafficked in athletic bodies: Brando, Newman, Douglas, Voight, and Stallone boxed in *On the Waterfront, Somebody Up There Likes Me, The Champion, The All-American Hero,* and *Rocky* long after the humpy young John Garfield broke jaws and hearts in movies of the 1940s. Currently, Ryan O'Neal boxes for real, owns a piece of a boxer, and wants a boxing script for himself.

Wrestling was never better before or since it peaked in Ken Russell's *Women in Love*, produced by Larry Kramer, when Alan Bates, who shows ass in nearly every movie he's ever made, grapples sweaty and naked before a roaring fireplace with the very macho Oliver Reed.

Robert Redford's body, looking good as Natalie Wood's gay husband in *Inside Daisy Clover,* has been through a litany of athletics: leathered and shirtless dirt-biking in *Little Fauss and Big Halsey*; skiing in *Downhill Racer*; hiking and rafting in *Jeremiah Johnson*; running in *Three Days of the Condor*; and sailing in *The Way We Were,* in which he also out-wrestled Streisand frame-by-frame for face space.

Richard Harris, sailing in *Mutiny on the Bounty*, was stripped, tied to an iron grate, and flogged. That took care of his backside. The Native

American athletics of tribal life in *A Man Called Horse* took care of his front side. The power warriors strung Harris up with wooden pegs through his pecs, hoisting him up for a test of his endurance. In the Sun Dance ritual, he becomes a "man" through his initiation in pain.

Appropriately, *pain* is the one word all athletes use in common. Training, like sex, can become an obsession. It feels so good it sometimes becomes compulsive-addictive. The body aches for a workout. The more miles a long-distance runner logs each day, the better his threshold of pain. No man races against any clock. All men race against themselves. The mind takes control of the body and the miles pile up. This running analogy fits all sports as well as it explains much gay sex, which is the Greatest Sport, and why so many gay men ground their sexuality in endurance of SM, fistfucking, and marathon fuck sessions.

This Sporting Life [1963], made at the same time as *The Loneliness of the Long Distance Runner* [1962], was the jock movie that took care of Richard Harris' face. *Sporting Life* featured nude bathing and brawling similar to David Storey's Broadway rugby drama *The Changing Room* [1972] where twenty men enter the set, strip, stretch, massage, horse around, head out to get bloodied up on the field, re-enter the locker room, doggedly strip off their muddy uniforms, shower, towel dry, and exit.

Rugby has its own rituals of communal baths and bawdy ballads. The rugby player is more than just a member of the team. He's part of a more latent than blatant global fraternity that emphasizes bonhomie and plenty of beer-guzzling off the field. Rival teams usually share the same locker rooms and dip in the same team bath tub, communally, after their afternoon tussle in the mud. Every match ends with the "Third Half," a booze-up contest of bawdy ballads, where usually one or more players break into the traditional Zulu Dance, a tipsy male striptease. Admits Michael Smith who boosts US rugby out of Chicago, "I work in stockbroking because I have to live. But if I could, I'd spend all my life in rugby."

No wonder show biz types like to buy jock types. O'Neal has his fighter. Elton John has his football team. Mick Jagger, Paul Simon, Peter Frampton, and Bill Graham recently bought up the Philadelphia franchise in the North American Soccer League.

Burt Reynolds, sprung from a *Cosmo* centerfold, played football in college and starred in two movies since: *The Longest Yard* and *Semi-Tough* with the really tough Kris Kristofferson. Paul Newman's passion for real-life race-car driving was featured in *Winning*. Peter Firth in *Equus* played a boy who loves horses so much he hates them, and tortures them and himself (with a bloody bit tied tight into his own teeth) until "cured" by an incredible shrinking shrink.

They Shoot Horses, Don't They? And with puritan good reason. Horses in films are always symbols of passion. Equestrians always gallop toward passionate disaster: Christopher Jones' stallion forbode sexual danger every time he fucked *Ryan's Daughter*, Sarah Miles [1970]; Brando's Captain Penderton in *Reflections in a Golden Eye* [1967] gets carried away by his gay passion on his wife Elizabeth Taylor's horse. Throughout that film, in which Julie Harris cuts off her nipples with the garden shears, fetishist Robert Forster, the young Army private after whose privates Brando lusts, rides naked, wild, and free. The horse's eye, the eye of passion, reflects life, love, lust, and Liz.

Gay horseback riding has long been established in a very low-profile Los Angeles riding club whose members project a very heavy Marlboro Man image. Farther north, riding with a posse of gay men through redwoods and down a Mendocino creek bed conjures a galloping sensuality of horse-sweat, creaking leather saddles, Levi's-asses posting in a canter of foreplay, crotches pushed up against the horn, looks cast one man to another back at the corral, leather reins in gloved hands, uncinching the horse, carrying the saddle over the shoulder to the barn, currying down the horse, turning him out to graze, and heading toward the hayloft with the rider of choice. Such weekends are often arranged out of San Francisco. [The reference here is to a famous November 5-7, 1976 run to a dude ranch outside the village of Philo in Mendocino County, three hours north of San Francisco. It was organized by a certain Earl (surname deleted), M. D. who in the 1970s was, out of his Marina home office, the main healthcare provider to gay men frequenting Folsom Street baths and bars, and the Catacombs. His waiting room was always interesting because the other half of his clientele consisted of young Latinas. He was a wonderful medical realist and a leading "master of revels." Another doctor, Richard Hamilton, M. D. who assisted me in writing my "Dr. Dick" for *Drummer* also appeared in the mid-1970s.]

Horseback riding, of course, is not all overt sexuality. Gay men, like other men, can get into a sport for itself. The triumphant [first] Gay Rodeo held in Reno in the fall of 1977 received national press coverage and helped establish a positive sports image of gay men as men competitively capable of traditional American manliness in its best sense. This is affirmative gay action. Many gay athletes coming out into sports in their twenties or thirties admit to fears of athletics when they were very young—fears of "pitching like a sissy." A new liberated attitude now allows them to tackle whatever sport they like. People are learning that *gay is* not a synonym for *effeminate*. No more in sports than in bed is the ordinary gay man interested in "playing the passive female role." In both arenas, gay men celebrate their masculinity.

Masculinity is what really lies behind the gay sports revival.

Previously, the obvious way to be gay, maybe the only way, say men who remember the unhappy days of the 1950s, was skirt-and-sweater camp-scream-outrage. Liberation has let real, traditional manliness out of the locker and onto the field. Suddenly, the alternative to *nelly* stands on its own two Adidas.

It's okay to be *macho*.

MOVIES AND GAY SPORTS

Movies stylized the gay subculture (and *vice versa* if you've ever been blown in Hollywood): from the mad-queen stereotype of a Bette Davis, who is her own best cliche, to the grooming of movie males on an increasingly macho scale—from the effete Valentino to the insipid Leslie Howard to the tough gangster-cowboy actors to the Ivy-League grooming of Troy/Tab/Rock to the womanless romantic coupling of Newman and Redford, Voight and Hoffman, and Reynolds and Kristofferson. Movies have long taught gay men their attitudes. Movies came out of the hetero-marital closet at the closing line of *Women in Love* when wrestler Bates' wife asks, "Aren't I enough for you?" His answer prepared the way for Butch and Sundance. "No," he answers. And the movie ends.

Semi-Tough's Kristofferson says, "I figure the first year and a half of marriage is lust. After that, you just settle into a basic friendship." The boys, like Brando in *Streetcar*, go back to bowling with the boys. Movies of the 1970s have taught America a new attitude toward male relationships, just like Hollywood musicals, dead as *New York, New York,* taught a whole generation of males how to be queens. Currently, thanks to Stallone, Hollywood's second biggest trip is the Jock Movie. (The first is the horror-science-fiction movie.) And it is the Jock Movie that is teaching gay men the unqueenly other end of the masculinity spectrum: semi-tough macho.

Women might not like macho men. But men like macho men. Women often dislike very muscular men. So these hetero women make choices different from the gay preference. For instance, go to a straight gym. You'll see straight men, married and single, who are out-and-out Straight Queens: mincing, prancing, camping in nelly voices; but, aha! Their sexual preference is women with whom they watch football, go four-wheeling, and skiing.

Then hit a gay gym. Sure, you'll see some Muscle Queens pumping pecs they deep down wish were tits; but you'll also see the heavy Muscle-Buddy trip. These guys look like stereotype straights: strong, silent, practiced movements, "spotting" each other on their heavy sets, into rag sweatshirts they work to get really soaked, eyes only for each other's correct athletic form. Yet their sexual preference is each other.

How will Anita Bryant who reads people by stereotypes, ever figure out who's doing what with whom? With the uncloseting of sports has come a new viable gay lifestyle, visible and suitable: the athletic, genuinely masculine gay male.

Movies and TV have opened to gay men the possibility of participating in sports they long thought closed to them, because they were, from grade school on, a little "shy" as Lily Tomlin would say, or "marching to a different *Drummer*" as Thoreau would say. Somewhere, with the debunking of all the Great American Myths, sports has finally lost its straight cherry, its false modesty, its phony purity, its stupid prudishness. No one anywhere any more believes an athlete tackles better, runs faster, serves more accurately because he is straight. Since Dave Kopay came out and Johnny Carson asked Joe Namath directly about the number of gay quarterbacks, American attitudes have necessarily changed.

The famous *Washington Star* article on rumors of gays in professional sports [December 10, 1975; the article by reporter Lynn Rosellini was an extrapolation that did not name names until Dave Kopay contacted the paper for a follow-up article], Kopay's own dignified disclosure of his sexuality, and Anita's Big Squeeze Play were the three best things to happen to the gay movement. Before this trinity converged, if a gay man came out, he came out. Point and period. What was he to discuss with good old mom and dad? Details of our midnight gymnastics? They needn't hear all *that* about their best little boy in the whole world. Now, a man can discuss something after disclosure. Kopay and the *Post* gave us a topic: *athletics*. Bryant gave us *politics*, since she politicized us to the point where a man can say, "I'm gay and the implications of this constitutionally include you who are straight." These people, for better or worse, have given us the material we need: being gay is more than sexual calisthenics energized by poppers.

HIGH ANXIETY: COLLEGE GYMS

At the university in the Midwest where I taught for years, I had various close encounters with a baseball star, an assistant freshman football coach, one gymnast, and innumerable ordinary jocks mutually cruised in the shower where students recruited the more tactful faculty. Wrestling late Saturday afternoons on the mats in the second-floor gym of the field house led more often than not back to my house.

At UC Berkeley, right now, not only is the library lav [toilet] a study in tangled Adidas, the maze of showers in the gym is highly active.

Sunbathing is nude around the outdoor pool, and in the johns outside the Olympic gymnastics room and the weight room, the sex is subtle, free, and easy. At UC Berkeley, every man is issued regulation blue shorts and a jock. I've cruised there for years. In fact, my first workout, I hit the john and within three minutes, tanned bare feet padded in, turned, and curled all ten toes in the age-old signal for "lewd conduct" in a toilet stall. I pivoted my own foot slightly. Immediately, blue shorts and white jock dropped down over the tanned feet. His knees knelt to the floor and he slipped his thighs, knees first, tanned with mats of golden hair, under the partition. His cock followed, standing erect from a blond bush, hard, wet, and ready, with the foreskin stripped half-back. I stared in disbelief like some fucking tourist fisherman who catches a marlin in the first three minutes of his charter. Jocks, I knew, did IT but didn't talk about it. Was this the Berkeley custom? When in Rome, do. I did. After all, Zorba the Greek said: "There is one mortal sin in life: when a woman calls a man to her bed and he will not come." This athlete called me to the vaulting pole of his cock and I'm no mortal sinner. He was the first of many good sports that summer.

If gay men are anything, they are often insecure. Los Angeles psychologist Ralph Greerson believes that men generally deal with anxiety by compulsively facing it. "If they are afraid of violence, they may become addicted to football, play it, see it again and again." When a man fears something, he counters the phobia by doing exactly what scares him. So years ago you got a "D" in Phys Ed, or got beaten up on the playground. So what! Fuck explanations of behavior.

On any playing field or any white-water raft, the reasons for being present are as many as the men involved. Fear. Fun. Fucking. Walk into a gym and shout, "*What insecurity brings you here?*" (You can also shout it in offices, busses, and churches.) Do jocks buff up with tremendous muscle motivated by the cliche of a four-inch cock? Then let's hear it for four-inch cocks. As a coach told an embarrassed bareassed boy at Chicago's Lawson Y: "Big cock, small cock. Yours gets hard, doesn't it?" The kid nodded yes. "Then that settles that."

Gays once were afraid to be anything but closeted or queenly. The hot David Sparrow, *Drummer*'s favorite freelance photographer, says about coming out: "When I was sixteen, I thought I was the only one like me in my home town. When I was nineteen, I discovered others. They were hard not to discover because they were so nelly and outrageous. I thought to be queer I had to affect a limp lifestyle. Then I moved to New York, found out I wasn't queer but that I was gay, and that the Limp Style was only one of many ways to be gay. I turned in my ruby slippers for something I'd wanted all my life: boots, cleats, and Adidas."

Now that gays are a political issue we are forced into community relations and we gladly play softball tournaments with the local San Francisco cops. Just as Blacks have gained greater acceptance through fronting Black athletes who were first of all heroes to their sport, so ordinary gays gain acceptance as sportsmen through upfront softball with teams fielded by the San Francisco police. When a sports team that "happens to be gay" beats a sports team that "happens to be straight," the straights figure they were outclassed by some better jocks and they realign their opinion about the opponent "cocksuckers," and they all go off to a gay bar for a victory beer ordering neither Coors nor screwdrivers. The game and its aftermath are a celebration of two varieties of ways to be masculine in America: straight macho and gay macho.

Everyone is rethinking masculinity today. Read *Semi-Tough, Ball Four, The Boys of Summer, Cat on a Hot Tin Roof, The Front Runner,* plus Mary Renault's cock-and-bull-jumping novel *The King Must Die* where nude athletes do tricks in the arena. Best of all is Gary Shaw's *Meat on the Hoof,* a straight non-fiction expose of college football and the battle of a player to get into the big leagues. (Dell publishes it.) Shaw wrote:

> Probably the varsity's most popular game was "Record Races." Here they would strip several of us (football players) naked and divide us into two groups. Then, they would bring out our "toy"—an old 45-rpm record. They placed the toy between the cracks of our asses. We had to carry it from one end of the hall to the other without using our hands. We would then have to—again without using our hands—place it in our teammate's ass. If he happened to drop it, his partner had to pick it up with his mouth, and put it back in place. These races were considered the highlight of the evening.

Not to imply anything about Shaw's straight sexuality, but he adds:

> It seems rather ludicrous now, but my best moments as a freshman Longhorn were spent at the same time every day, in the same toilet stall, and on the same john. Being able to lock that stall, and then sit and read a magazine in total privacy for thirty minutes each day, enabled me to survive that first year.

HOT SPORTS

All sports until recently were heavy team sports: major equipment for ten to thirty guys, either seven feet tall or 250 pounds. Anything less than basketball, football, or baseball was sissy. Schools today emphasize individual sports a man can play his whole life. Tennis, once strictly for women and Latin males, has a whole new machismo. TV has internationalized sports, junking All-American Babe Ruth baseball, and going beyond seasonal football and basketball to include hockey, soccer, handball, racquetball, soaring, sky and scuba diving. To find the full variety read the bumper stickers. DIVERS DO IT DEEPER is one sticker that the accompanying photos taken off Grand Cayman Island by Gene Weber at an 80-foot depth gives a raised fist salute to.

Admittedly, the jockstrap boxer in *Waiting for Mr. Goodbar* was about as hot as DeNiro steeling himself to endure in *Taxi Driver* through hard workouts. But the ultimate jockstrap movie is Paul Newman's *Slapshot*. Actor Michael Ontkean plays a hockey goalie who skates around the ice arena crowded with spectators cheering on an illegal ice-brawl. Ontkean breaks it up by stripping his hockey uniform piece by piece to the strains of "The Stripper," getting down bare-assed to nothing but his skates, socks, and his chock-full-of-nuts jock. All in slow motion. It is a High Moment of cinema fetishism. Ontkean's slow strip stops the disbelieving brawl, proving, if nothing else, that sex, especially in Ontkean's overflowing cup, can stop violence.

GAY SPORTS: TUFFY

Peeled down the same way, Tuffy's Sportswear on Castro in San Francisco caters to outfitting the gay jock from the jockstrap on out, layer by layer, *out* to whatever sports uniform is needed. Tuffy himself is behind the competition between San Francisco and Los Angeles for the First Annual California Cup in gay all-star football, basketball, and volleyball. Through Tuffy's USA Club, whitewater rafting trips are currently coordinated by Larry Kratzer, a veteran tour guide of whitewater trips through northwestern Colorado and northeastern Utah.

Tennis, racquetball, and squash are coached by Jim Stacy, athletic director for gay racquet sports. Stacy has instituted a challenge system for advanced, intermediate, and beginning players. Stacy is one of northern California's top squash players. The caliber of coaching and play for tennis, racquetball, squash, and badminton is geared to provide the good gay athlete with quality competition while insuring adequate instruction for the beginning player.

Bodybuilding, sponsored by Tuffy's USA, likewise looks to the interests of the beginner. Since most gay men belong to either a traditional weight gym or a Nautilus Fitness Center, this bodybuilding association addresses itself to the needs of gay pumpers wherever they work out.

Utilizing the buddy system, advanced bodybuilders share their training tricks with men on the threshold of a properly bulked and defined physique. An openly gay physique contest is planned for the near future.

Tuffy's interesting shop is located at 597 Castro in San Francisco. The USA Club phone is (415)621-2128.

BAY AREA BOXING CLUB: GREG VARNEY

Greg Varney is a man who knows what he wants and how to organize what he gets. Native to the Bay Area, Greg has wrestled and boxed in a variety of cities, but chose San Francisco as the founding city for his Boxing and Fighting Club. The disarming Varney, who has the face of a Botticelli boxer, has plenty to say about sports and the gay men who play them.

"I started boxing when I was eight years old," Greg tells me, "and I won a Golden Gloves title when I was seventeen. I've always loved boxing for itself. Those locker-room romances are porn-film fantasies. Not that boxers aren't gay. Just that most male athletes at the mere mention of homosexuality really tighten up. I mean when I watch a bout I don't go to see the bodies per se. I go to watch the technique. Secondarily, the bodies from light to heavyweight interest me.

"What turned me on sexually to boxing was once when I was thirteen I boxed naked with another kid for about thirty seconds. I tried not to think about that during my amateur career; but when I was twenty-four, I came out. Ever since then, my main purpose has been to open up boxing to gay men who never were aware that this sport could be available to them. For instance, my roommate, Mike Mooney, started boxing in May, 1976. When I started teaching him to box, I found he was really good and highly motivated. So I took him to my local gym and we started his amateur career. So far, he's had two amateur bouts and is scheduled for his third. Something Mike always dreamed about doing, but thought he couldn't, has happened—so far successfully.

"Meeting men such as Mike who like boxing and fighting doesn't happen easily on the streets or in the bars. So I put ads in various gay publications and got a real flood of letters and calls. Right away I knew I had to weed out the phonies, and there were plenty—about 75 percent. A phony, I judged, was a guy more interested in jerking off looking at himself or me in our Everlast gear than he was in actual training or sparring. Sex is for-sure involved, but secondarily. With this premise, I started the Bay Area Boxing and Fight Club in 1976.

"Mike and I looked for the right place, both to live and to box. We finally found a super-big apartment with an attic space large enough to set up our regulation-size boxing ring. Our facilities now include different weight boxing gloves, headgear, and other protective boxing gear, heavy bags, speed bags, and a general workout area near the boxing ring itself. [Many photographs which David Hurles and I shot especially for this feature were staged in Varney-Mooney's attic boxing ring which was a very private inner sanctum within the *Drummer* salon.]

"We offer private bouts, instruction and workouts, and a lot of times, we function as an outlet for guys who just like to roughhouse on the canvas with other guys. More formally, our instruction and sparring is aimed at the growing number of men who come regularly for workouts to learn boxing techniques. We also like wrestling, but tend to exclude it so as not to duplicate the trip of the various wrestling clubs.

"We also have a majority of members heavy into the leather-sweat-contest aspect of boxing. Some of the bouts have some special rules determined by the participants. Some guys like to box in full leather. Others spar nude. Some like body-punching fights, with no hitting of the head. Some dig wearing headgear and mouthpieces to box with full-body contact above the waist. The 'contest' boxers like to fight to submission for a prize. That kind of prize, claimed in the ring on the canvas, I leave to your imagination.

"Any man interested primarily in boxing and other contact fighting sports with other gay men can contact the Bay Area Boxing and Fight Club by writing 681 Ellis Street #111, San Francisco 94102. The club and gym phone is (415) 861-1006. Novices, intermediates, pros: we respect them all at their level."

OLIVE-OIL WRESTLING: TERRIFIC TURKS

Each August in Gallipoli, Turkey, 500 male wrestlers pair off, slap their leather thighs, and clasp each other to rub the olive oil onto their naked torsos and into their leather breeches. The breeches are fit like American football pants from waist to mid-calf. They are made from 45 pieces of leather and 200 yards of cotton, cost $30, and last two years. They are soaked in water, sweat, and oil to soften the leather. Each wrestler, stripped to the waist, usually sporting a heavy dark moustache and a crewcut, lavishly coats his leather breeches and his torso, arms, head, and feet with olive oil. He knots tight his breeches' waist cord, and the ritual, dating back to ancient Greek vases, begins.

Over the centuries, Turkish olive-oil wrestling has become more than a sport. It is a macho ritual woven from the stuff of young men's wet dreams. Immensely popular as a tourist attraction today, Turkish wrestling peaked 100 years ago when Sultan Abdul Aziz, a massive athlete and himself a wrestler, under his own imperial blessing (and fetish), added the refinement of coating the marble floors of his palaces as well as the bodies of his wrestlers, with oil—a baroque, murderous, hardon touch.

Olive-oil wrestling has few rules. Anything goes in the free-for-all of 500 men, oiled, sweating in the sun, identified only by silver studs spelling out their names on the back waist of their leathers. There is much man-to-man macho chivalry and little shame in losing a match that goes on for hours and sometimes days. The only real shame is when a handsome young wrestler loses his leather breeches and is left standing oiled and naked in the sunswept field of brawling men. To him it's shame. To a tourist it's a prime Turkish Delight.

GAY WRESTLING: JOHN HANDLEY

Equally delightful is American gay wrestling. The Wrestling Club network now spans from California to Chicago to New York with the New York Wrestling Club somehow the most colorful because of its founding president and chief promoter, the dark-mustachioed John Handley, who, during an interview, will answer questions and lay out the NYWC future plans most fluidly, as he pretends to reach for his cup of coffee only to feint the disarmed interviewer into a half-nelson. No exaggeration. Handley is such a wrestling aficionado that an interviewer gets his best answers being drop-kicked across Handley's NYWC wrestling mats. Meeting John is a bruise forever, and a joy, once you realize that for Liza life is a cabaret, and for John life is a basic body slam to the canvas.

Handley describes his wrestling style as *mean*. His favorite holds are the body scissors, head scissors, and hammerlock. His Dewar's Profile quote: "I wrestle because I like beating the shit out of guys."

No wonder the world is beating a path to this man's door.

CRUISIN' FOR A BRUISIN'

The New York Wrestling Club was created to afford civilized men a chance to get down and grapple. Its newsletter, membership roster, and social events foster the network of matches between athletes, gay and even straight, for whom wrestling is a prime interest. "Whatever else happens between the two men," Handley says, "is their business."

Handley twists my arm. "In urban life men need to rebuild primal physical encounters. Man to man," he says. "Wrestling is one path. The most personal of all sports." He pushes his knee into my groin. "We expect wrestlers to be sensitive human beings who will make an effort to perceive in a match all the levels of encounter a one-on-one grapple involves. Some guys wrestle okay in private, but are afraid to wrestle in a gym or bar." He twists my arm tighter, for real. "Failure in a success-oriented society is hard to take."

"And it hurts," I say, dropping my notepad and pushing the butt of my palm into his chin.

"We all like to win matches but not everyone can be a winner." He speaks through clenched teeth, holding my arm immobile. "Some guys think of wrestling only as a contest."

"No shit," I say. Do I look to him like George Plimpton? [Plimpton was an American intellectual and author turned gonzo participatory journalist who dared play quarterback for the Detroit Lions and write about the reality in *Paper Lion*. In June 1968, he was walking in front of Bobby Kennedy, escorting the presidential candidate through the kitchen of the Ambassador Hotel, when Kennedy was shot; Plimpton grabbed the assassin by the throat.]

"It's more than a contest."

"It's murder," I say. I'm not ready for this encounter.

"I like spontaneity," he says. "Do you?"

"The Japanese liked spontaneity," I say. "Pearl Harbor didn't."

"Gay wrestling is a process of mutual discovery, interaction, exploration of the self as well as the other man who is of mutual interest."

"You're breaking my arm," I say.

"The other man is a person. Not just an object to toss around in a ring."

"Uncle," I say. "I'm a person."

"Again." (This guy's got style.)

"Uncle." I repeat it. "How the fuck can I write notes with you breaking my fucking arm?"

"You got to admit wrestling's fun."

"I love it," I say. "I'll remember every minute of this." I punched him in the stomach. The free-for-all was on.

Handley ain't no cupcake. He's a wrestler's cup of tea. Bouts with him can be arranged along with information about the NYWC by writing: Handley, 59 West 10th Street, New York 10011. The Chicago Wrestling Club, directed by Jim Tomnitz, can plug you into Midwestern grappling if you write to Box 4491, Chicago 60680. Larry Lane is the contact for California wrestlers. Write: The Gym, 5919 Franklin Avenue, Hollywood 90028.

John Handley wisely urges all wrestlers that the reality of the sport advises accident and disability insurance as much as a protective jock. He ain't just whistling "Dixie." [In this sentence, I was referencing that during the wrestling matches in Varney-Mooney's attic ring, while Hurles and I shot photos, Handley accidently injured the handsome and popular barber, Thumper McPherson, whom I had invited and whom I visited in the hospital after his shoulder surgery. A photo of Jim "Thumper" McPherson appeared as "Thumper" in *Drummer* 115, page 32.]

HAND-JOB ATHLETES: SUPER-8 MOVIES

For armchair and hand-job athletes who get off on the male body in the triumph of victory and the agony of defeat, the following three firms—endorsed perhaps against their will—give excellent service on fine quality Super-8 films which you can show through your projector at normal speed or at slower speeds as low as three frames per second in order to see each ripple of muscle, each drip of sweat, and each celebration of manflesh.

AMG (ATHLETIC MODEL GUILD)
1836 W. 11th Street
Los Angeles 90069

AMG understands gay interests. Its catalog is, in fact, a very hot magazine. As usual, state you are over 21 and enclose $1.25. AMG magazines have long been collectibles. Nearly everyone in the Midwest came out looking at good old *Physique Pictorial*. The wrestling films featured vary on a scale of 1 to 10 according to your tastes in hustlers, ex-cons, and make-believe cops going at each other. Good fantasy stuff.

FILM ASSOCIATES
P.O. Box 545
Venice, California 90291

If you like bodybuilders, you'll never find better posing, oiling, and contest physique footage in the world. Reels feature the incredible Mike Mentzer, Scott Wilson, Roger Callard, Joe Means, and hundreds of other top bodies in Super-8 films. Film Associates' product is expensive, but its quality of visual fidelity and satisfyingly quick service, in addition to bodybuilders you will never any other way get close to, make judicious purchase a continuing nightly joy. Especially recommended for athletes looking for a jolt of motivation. Film Associates features little, if any, nudity. They are forthrightly straight, but certainly worthy of use as a gay resource by men who appreciate the male body as the ultimate sculpture. Send $1 for the latest brochure.

SPORTSFILM INTERNATIONAL
415 Belleview Avenue
Normal, Illinois 61761

If you think pro-wrestlers are fat comics of the mat, Sports Film International will quickly disabuse you with its array of Super-8 color professional wrestling matches featuring men for every hot taste in real rough-and-tumble choreography. Football being a seasonal sport, many hunky players like Dick Blood and New England Patriots' Russ Francis who could fold out of *Playgirl* for days exhibit their talents on the pro-wrestling circuit. Lovingly photographed by Sports Film International, the slamming is for real. The quality of color film is exceptional. The mail-order service, trustworthy. It is also straight and clothed in wrestling trunks and lace-up boots. Send $1 for the current catalog. The product is a turn-on for men into man-to-man confrontation.

TOUGH IS AS TOUGH DOES

Sports is a way to practice competition, a way to learn physical/political/moral self-defense, even if only expressed through busloads of men heading Tuesday nights to South San Francisco to roller skate. More than pirouetting, the Folsom Street men turn the rink into a poppered roughhouse of rollerball. [Every Tuesday night, the big motor-coach bus, parked on Castro Street across from the Castro Theater, sat with its motor running as it filled up with men carrying skates and bottles of poppers for sniffing while skating around the roller rink.] The politicizing of gay men has caused an increase in aggression as expressed on the fields, the courts, the rinks, and the baths. Since Anita Bryant, more gay men are into combative sports and sex than ever before. This phenomenon seems a definite sign that gays are in training to counter the attacks so unreasonably launched against us. Trained physically, we build the endurance to resist morally and politically those who would have us not live a lifestyle different from theirs.

Sports literally gives gays another arena in which to speak out and communicate to a nation that prides itself on understanding sports.

Recently in New York, an organization of gay athletes announced a $100,000 national advertising campaign against Florida citrus products the day after the Florida Citrus Commission's decision to renew Anita Bryant's contract. Craig Liebermann, a spokesperson for the International Union of Gay Athletes, said the bulk of the money for the campaign was donated by professional athletes whom he would not identify.

So far, Anita and company has only been hit with a fruit pie and a gaycott. Her jock husband better warn her what fury can be conjured at halftime in a locker room.

Her next hit could be a well-placed gay upper-cut to the chin.

Now that we're all in training...

III. Eyewitness Illustrations

Top and bottom: In the 1977 *Drummer* salon, San Francisco Golden Gloves boxing promoter Greg Varney, photographer David Hurles (Old Reliable), and editor in chief Jack Fritscher produced an evening of man-to-man wrestling and boxing with a group of athletes including Jim "Thumper" McPherson and John Handley of the New York Wrestling Club (NYWC). (Handley broke Thumper's shoulder.) In addition to the *bonhomie*, the goal was to shoot photographs for Fritscher's upcoming "Gay Jock Sports" article for *Drummer* 20 (January 1978). Photographs by David Hurles (Old Reliable) ©David Hurles. Used with permission.

Opposite page. Top: "Dan Dufort," bodybuilding champion, Gay Games 1986, and "Gino Deddino," in the first gut-punching video, *Gut Punchers, Drummer* 115 (April 1988). Photograph by Jack Fritscher. ©Jack Fritscher. Dan Dufort appeared fictively under his own name in the memoir-novel *Some Dance to Remember*, Reel 1, Sequences 9 and 10. Brian Pronger (alert like Tom Waddell) to the "Gay Sports" aspects of *Drummer*, published this photo for his groundbreaking book *The Arena of Masculinity: Sports, Homosexuality,*

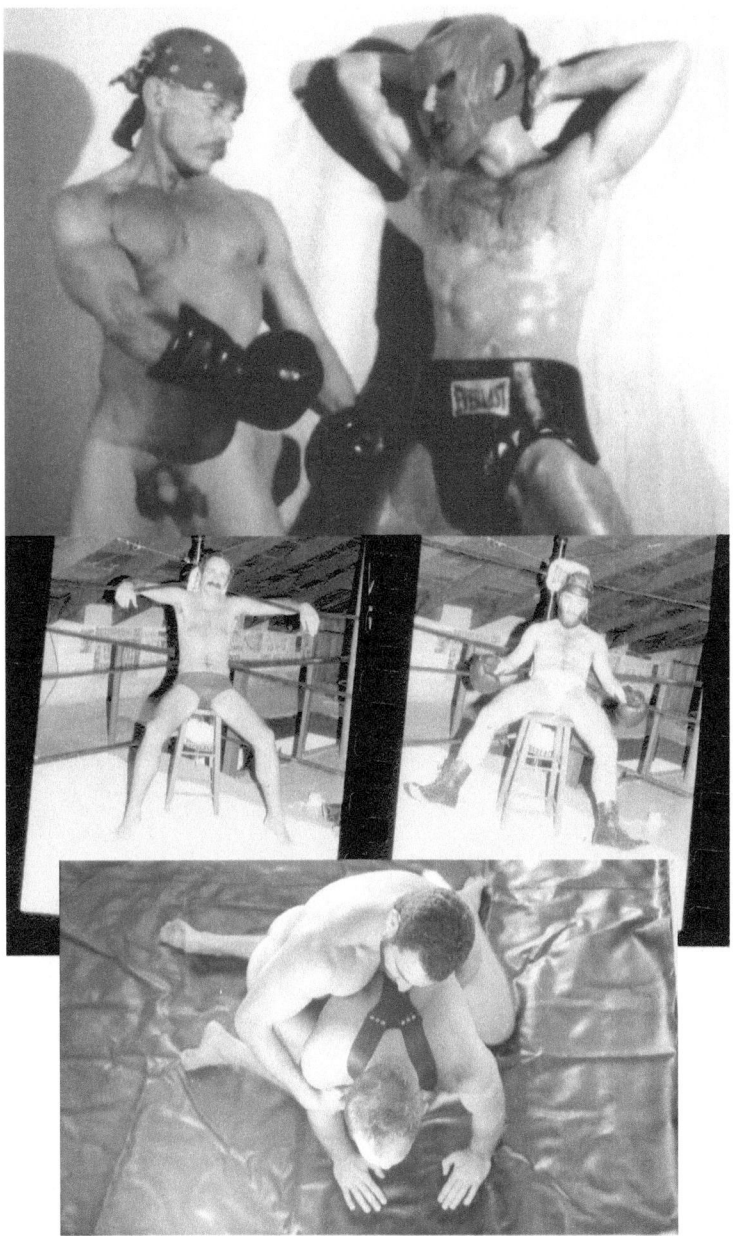

and the Meaning of Sex. Middle: NYWC founder John Handley (left) and opponent. Both photographs by David Hurles (Old Reliable). ©David Hurles. Used with permission. Bottom: Frequent *Drummer* model Mike Glassman (aka Colt model Ed Dinakos) on top of wrestling partner. Photograph by Jack Fritscher-David Sparrow. ©Jack Fritscher

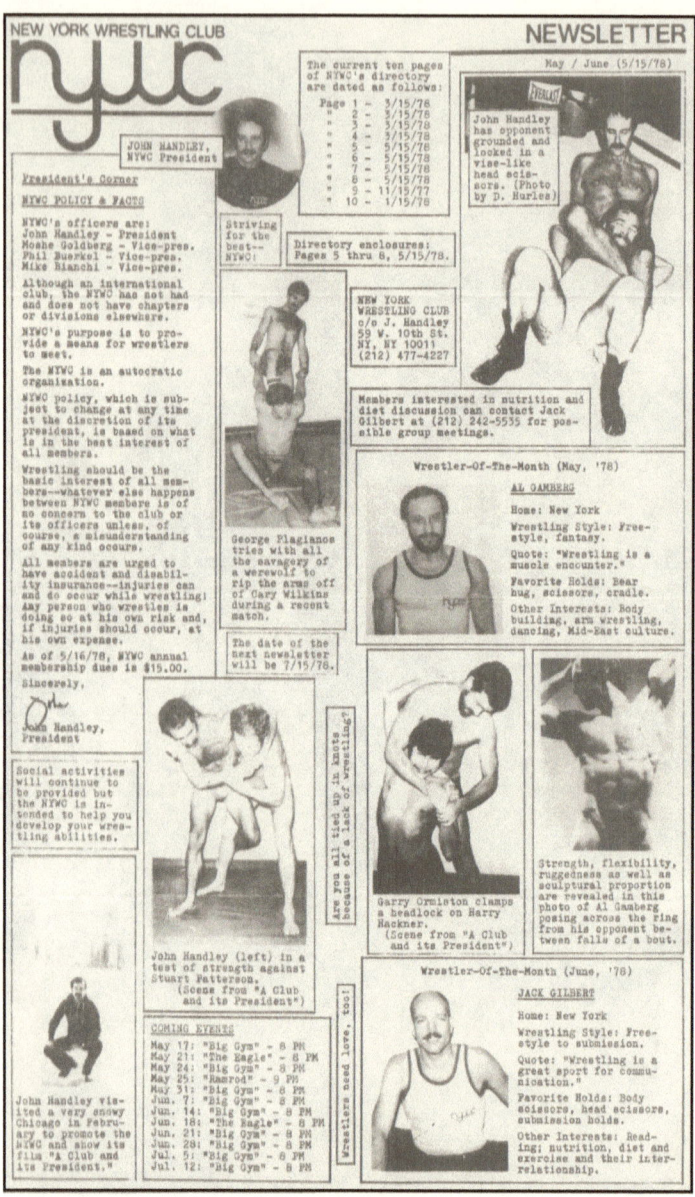

NYWC. *New York Wrestling Club Newsletter* (May-June 1978) written and edited by NYWC president John Handley, May-June 1978 issue. ©John Handley. This kind of grass-roots documentary *verite* was precisely the kind of reader-centered "New Journalism" content that Fritscher developed and injected into the writing and images in *Drummer*. In the 1970s, *Drummer* reported the very lifestyle it created. From 1977-1980, every month, Fritscher had to up the ante.

Drummer 20: Gay Jock Sports 563

"Moustached Bodybuilder," straight Mr. California Contestant, San Francisco, 1980. Photograph by Jack Fritscher. ©Jack Fritscher. This photograph appeared on the cover of *Drummer* 157 (August 1992) ten years after its debut as the cover of the "Virtual *Drummer*," *California Action Guide* (August 1982), founded and edited by Jack Fritscher with Mark Hemry creating magazines without borders of *gay* and *straight*. Beginning in 1970s *Drummer*, as chronicled in the bodybuilding novel *Some Dance to Remember*, the Male Body itself emerged—with all its "secondary male sex characteristics" in bloom—as both source and fetish of the homomasculine way of being and becoming.

Cover, *Man2Man Quarterly* #1, Premier Issue (October 1980). If there is one ruling Rohrshach of the "Perfect 1970s Gay Look," it is this quiet masculine image emerging from the inky dark at the foot of the bed. This archetype was where *Drummer* itself was heading when the Titanic 1970s party, cruising on, struck the iceberg of HIV.

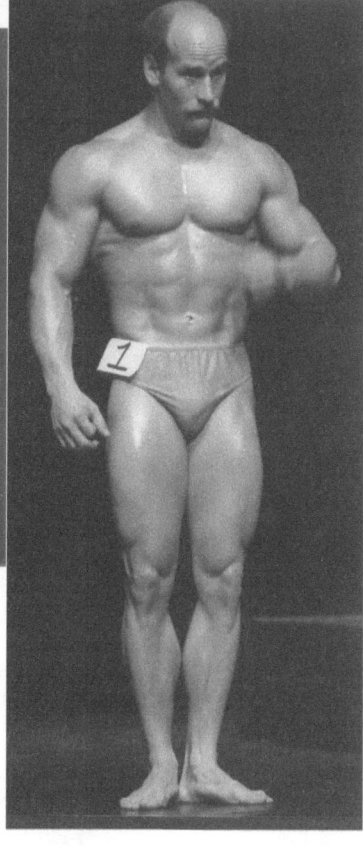

Top: "Pairs Posing, Gay Olympics 1982," Castro Theater stage, Gay Games 1982. Photograph by Jack Fritscher. ©Jack Fritscher. Bottom left and right: "Bodybuilder Contestant #3" and "Bodybuilder Contestant #1," San Francisco, 1978. Both photographs published in *Drummer* 124 (December 1988). Both photographs by Jack Fritscher. ©Jack Fritscher

First Gays V. SFPD Softball Game (1976). Three photographs by Jack Fritscher. ©Jack Fritscher. After police harassment in the 1960s calmed down, there was a brief shining window in gay liberation when gays and cops played ball, until the night of the White Night Riot, May 21, 1979. That night angry gays, attacking San Francisco City Hall, set police cars on fire, and the SFPD retaliated by marching down Castro Street using their billy-clubs. Top: Third from left, profile, glasses (circled): Jack Green, director of Fritscher's play *Coming Attractions* (1976). Middle: Profile (circled) Mark Hemry three years before meeting Fritscher in the zero degrees of separation.

First Gays V. SFPD Softball Game (1976). "San Francisco Police Officer #8." Photograph by Jack Fritscher. ©Jack Fritscher. In 1973, Jack "Irene" McGowan founded organized gay softball in San Francisco

Gay Rodeo, Reno, August 5, 1979. "Blond Cowboy Dave Wilson," "Shirtless Cowboy #1," and "Shirtless Cowboy #2." Three photographs by Jack Fritscher. ©Jack Fritscher

    Randy Shilts as reporter and Jack Fritscher as photographer together covered the Gay Rodeo for the Associated Press and for the *San Francisco Chronicle*. Shilts' article and Fritscher's photograph of "Dave Wilson" were published nationally by the AP and in the *Chronicle*, August 6, 1979. *Drummer* editor Tim Barrus wrote: "In the 1970s, there were two gay jobs in San Francisco. Randy Shilts had one [reporter at the *Chronicle*]; Jack Fritscher had the other [editor in chief of *Drummer*]."

Gay Rodeo, Reno, August 5, 1979. Top: "Partners," Twenty years before *Brokeback Mountain*. Bottom: "Steve Hawks," rumored source for the fictitious Logan Doyle in *Some Dance to Remember*. Both photographs by Jack Fritscher. ©Jack Fritscher. Shooting the gay rodeo, Fritscher intended some of his photographs for *Drummer* and others for the *San Francisco Chronicle* until he withdrew them from *Drummer* when he resigned as editor in chief on December 31, 1979, and wrote for a dozen other magazines.

Gay Rodeo, Reno, August 5, 1979, "Horst," on the cover of the *Drummer*-themed fiction anthology *Rainbow County and Other Stories* first published by Larry Townsend at LT Publications in 1997, and in a second edition by Palm Drive Publishing in 1999. At the National Book Expo America in Los Angeles, *Rainbow County* won the "Small Press Award 1998" for "Best Book, Erotica" from a level playing field of straight, lesbian, and gay authors. Photograph also published in *Jack Fritscher's American Men*. Photograph by Jack Fritscher. ©Jack Fritscher.

Gay Rodeo, Reno, August 5, 1979, "Three Cowboys." Photograph by Jack Fritscher.
©Jack Fritscher

Captions: Eyewitness documentation of the existence of graphics providing internal evidence supporting Jack Fritscher's text are located in the Jack Fritscher and Mark Hemry GLBT History collection. Out of respect for issues of copyright, model releases, permissions, and privacy, some graphics are not available for publication at this time, but can be shown by appointment.

| Eyewitness Illustration | Two photographs. "Scuba Fisting 1" and "Scuba Fisting 2," *Drummer* 20, page 17, top and middle. Taking "water sports" to a new depth (times 2). Two anthropological photographs documenting legitimate homomasculine behavior below the waterline of the Titanic 1970s. San Francisco |

photographer Gene Weber and Jack Fritscher were frequent traveling companions to Japan (bamboo house of bondage, 1976) and the Grand Cayman Islands (private dive charter, underwater handballing, 1977). Prior to travel, the intimate *Drummer* scuba group trained for certification in the pool at the Leatherneck bar at 11th and Folsom. At Grand Cayman, guarded by a safety instructor (right), gonzo journalist Jack Fritscher, daring anything for a *Drummer* photo shoot, twice directs and enacts a penetrating maneuver into the synchronized swimming. Photographs by Gene Weber. ©Gene Weber

| Eyewitness Illustration | Photograph. "Boxer Ken Norton" angered recent Muslim-convert, the boxer Muhammad Ali, by appearing in this jockstrap photograph that circled the world in every kind of underground gay 'zine there was in those days of cut-and-paste-and-photocopy. Norton starred in the Hollywood |

hit *Mandingo* which was frequently featured in *Drummer*. In the liberated 1970s, this famous photograph inspired the muscular black cop in a jockstrap in the film *Cruising*. Soon after, Black Muslim puritanism dictated long and baggy trunks for boxing and basketball.

| Eyewitness Illustration | Brochure. "Physique Movies in Super-8mm," Film Associates Brochure, Venice, California. Bob Mizer, Athletic Model Guild, published *Physique Pictorial* as a magazine-brochure to sell his 8mm and Super-8 films of muscular young men. Fans of AMG were often also fans of Film Associ- |

ates who featured very sexy, but sex-free, competition bodybuilders posing in classic routines. Secret Soundtrack: From the end of World War II to the advent of the VCR in 1981, the noise most heard in a gay man's bedroom was the clacking sound of his Super-8 movie projector. Film Associates publicity kit. ©Film Associates.

| Eyewitness Illustration | Magazine article by Jack Fritscher. "Mike Dayton: The Last Gladiator," feature article and centerfold spread, written for *Drummer*, appeared in the "Virtual *Drummer*," *California Action Guide* (November 1982). Local |

hero, former Mr. America Mike Dayton, the straight and charming and heroic Bay Area bodybuilder and karate champion, whose father was a cop, appeared frequently around San Francisco with his professional strongman show, bending bars, and (in a guileless metadrama of *Drummer* fetishes) escaping shirtless from multiple handcuffs and steel restraints, being shot at through a phone book, and being hanged by the neck until parents complained. He starred in the film *Mike Dayton Strength Show* (1984). Personalized publicity kit photograph ©Mike Dayton, given by Mike Dayton to Jack Fritscher (1979).

| Eyewitness Illustration | Photograph. Gay pro-footballer "Dave Kopay" in *Drummer,* publicity kit photograph |

Dune Body

> Written Thanksgiving 1977 and published in *Drummer* 20, January 1978.
> I. Author's Eyewitness Historical-Context Introduction written July 25, 1998
> II. The poem as published in *Drummer* 20, January 1978

I. Author's Eyewitness Historical-Context Introduction written July 25, 1998

Gay magazine writing was the GLBT reality show of the 1970s. In 1974, I wrote a magazine book analyzing TV titled *Television Today*. The twin media of magazines and small screen intermeshed. Television was finding its true signature and fundamental style in the immediacy of "reality TV" which began with the Loud Family in the hit series *An American Family* on PBS in 1973. In 1975, gay magazine writing in *Drummer* had to invent its "reality vision and voice" on the spot, ad-libbing reflexively, to keep up with the speeding styles of emerging gay life spontaneously combusting in the bars, baths, and on the street: Castro Street, Polk Street, Christopher Street, and Santa Monica Boulevard.

A magazine is a hungry beast that must be fed every thirty days, and it's a finicky eater.

As editor in chief, sometimes I had a full page of rambunctious journalism in *Drummer* that needed to have three empty "column inches" filled, and I needed something tasty: a photo, a drawing, a joke.

Sometimes a photographer from Nowhere, Indiana, or Hubbub, Texas, would send in a snapshot that worked as an image, but needed suggestive caption words to point up its grass-roots *verite*, or to pump up its literal look into erotic fantasy.

Other times, byzantine business conducted in trade under the table, and pillow talk shared in a tiny room at the tubs, shaped the pages and sometimes the covers of *Drummer*. In summer 1977, LA photographer Joe Tiffenbach sent us some photographs that publisher John Embry said he had commissioned in West Hollywood in 1976 before Embry was "ridden out of town on a rail"—which is the way most gays leave their hometowns.

Embry insisted he had paid good hard cash for the photos which I did not like because they seemed like Palm Springs "camp" starring a blond twinkie who did not drip "essence du *Drummer*." The willowy model was perfectly fine if an audience got off on young vanilla twinks; but my judgement was based on the criterion of how he would be received or rejected in the leather bars or leather bathhouses frequented by *Drummer* readers. Embry and I had a heated discussion over what was "the *Drummer* Look." (Our first tiff was over Tiffenbach.) A publisher trumps an editor, but mostly I surrendered because I respected some of Tiffenbach's other credentials. Historically, Joe Tiffenbach (aka Lou Alton) was the founder with Bud Berkeley of the crusading anti-circumcision group, the Uncut Society of America (USA), and he had directed sometime *Drummer* columnist and full-time LA leather personality Fred Halsted in the film *Truck It* (1973). After his photos appeared in *Drummer*, Tiffenbach went on to direct videos in the 1980s, and with Bud Berkeley penned the book, *Foreskin: Its Past, Present, and Future* (1984); he died, age 67, January 27, 1992.

Even though Tiffenbach's twink, who had no tread on his nipples, was too much the tyro to be leather, the desert images were—if I screwed up my eyes and squinted to erase the "camp"—at least vaguely fetishistic in a "sports sex" sort of way. The sunny photos themselves lacked the shadows and drama essential to S&M art, and were not ominous the way, for instance, that Mapplethorpe made his outdoor photography fetishistic and threatening.

At a glance, the subject was a neutrally naked male solo in the sand dunes. Like a human "4-wheeler all-terrain vehicle," he was spreadeagle horizontally holding onto (not tied to) one axle with two hands while his feet stretched out to a second axle. Both axles were fitted out with two bicycle tires. The male body was taut between the axles, his butt was high off the ground, and he seemingly was rolling face down through the sand on the four wheels. Because I was well advanced in prepping my "Gay Jock Sports" feature article, I figured I could shoehorn the twink in if I tried to re-conceptualize him as a kind of "Arthur Tress man" as "sports machine." (See "Meditations on Arthur Tress, *Drummer* 30, June 1979, pages 22-25.)

Muddying the aggressive butch theme of *Drummer* 20, Embry at first gave no indication that he was planning to put the deadpan twink on what was to have been the lively cover of the homomasculine gay sports issue which was based on an original theme that I had built conceptually from the ground up almost two years before anyone even heard of Tom Waddell's scheme for his Gay Olympics. I wanted *Drummer* and leather to be sexually *avant garde*. Embry's *retro garde* 1950s camp twink—lacking

Drummer 20: Dune Body

even basic 1970s *de rigueur* facial hair—was almost as wrongheaded a *faux pas* as was his widely scorned "Cycle Sluts" drag cover on *Drummer* 9.

In this *mise en scene*, I tugged on Tiffenbach's photo-image—as if it were one of those new 1976 "Stretch Armstrong" dolls—to reference the hit TV series *The Six Million Dollar Man* (1973-1978). (Its bionic hero, pop icon Lee Majors, *Drummer* 25, page 70, led to the complete bio-machinery of the perfectly cast action puppet, the never-erotic Arnold Schwarzenegger, in *The Terminator,* 1984.) As it turned out, these desert photos, and this poem, anticipated by more than a year the gasoline-and-leather epic of the sandy desert outback, *Mad Max* (1979), featuring the debut of the gay leather favorite, Mel Gibson, before he outed himself as a seeming homophobe and drunken anti-Semite.

To twist the Tiffenbach pictures into a specifically *Drummer* theme, I made his literal concept symbolic (or at least fetishistic) by turning the wheels into a rolling sex machine and the hairless twinkie body into a kind of android car.

Under Embry's retro taste and penny-pinching, I held my nose and dropped the pics into a poem sidebar to—what turned out to be—the first magazine article ever written on gay sports, the cover lead feature article: "Gay Jock Sports: Wrestling, Boxing, Rollerballing, Soaring, Scuba, Bodybuilding, Dune Bodies, and Films," *Drummer* 20 (January 1978).

But was that enough? Of course, not. This was *Drummer*!

John Embry was the prince of reprints. The general observation was that his re-run reputation eventually hurt *Drummer* subscriptions and sales because of the way he repeated stories and recycled photos and drawings. His practice also dismayed some writers and artists, and photographers like Mapplethorpe, who often felt they had not been paid royalties for such reprint rights.

Some battles are not worth fighting when faggots work together in a creative environment trying to turn out a magazine that is so interactive with the reader that it causes orgasm.

Nevertheless, I was chagrined, but not surprised, when nine months later, Embry squeezed one more dime out of Tiffenbach's twinkie's ass. Perhaps thinking that "sand is sand," he had art director Al Shapiro paste three spreadeagle-bondage photographs from the sands of Palm Springs into the copy of my desert-sands article, "Arab Death," in my special edition, *Son of Drummer* (September 1978).

Embry might not have dared cross swords had he decoded my byline on "Arab Death" which I signed as "by Denny Sargent." I suspect he had no idea who "by Denny Sargent" was on page 9, but all he had to do was turn to page 41 where I published an excerpt from my 1969 novel,

I Am Curious (Leather), which I subtitled in *Son of Drummer* as "The Adventures of Denny Sargent" — "by Jack Fritscher." The first line of the novel and the excerpt included the name of my protagonist in ALL CAPS: "DENNY SARGENT, eighteen, kicked his sheets to the floor."

I always thought Embry seemed rather curiously vague about the actual contents of *Drummer*. Did he ever really read it? Did he ever jerk off to it? Was he like a movie-studio mogul who never watches his pictures, and only discusses box-office tallies?

Embry, always keen on mail-order sales, wanted to reprint *I Am Curious (Leather)* because gay book stores had yet to be invented, and closeted gays in Speed Trap, Florida, needed mail-order goods. If they were going to order *Drummer* poppers, they might as well order *Drummer* books. Embry announced on page 47 that "*I Am Curious (Leather)* is to be a forthcoming *Drummer* novel." Earlier, the 1969 novel had been published in a limited private edition by Lou Thomas at Target Studio (1972), and after *Son of Drummer*, after Embry defaulted, it was serialized in *Man2Man Quarterly* 1980-1982, excerpted in several magazines, and then sold 10,000 copies for Winston Leyland's Gay Sunshine Press under the title *Leather Blues* (1984).

In "Dune Body," the line "Oasis of erect palms" is the first intimation of my "Palm Drive Video" play on words. "Palm Drive" is not the name of a street. "Palm Drive" is what a man does with his hand while reading or watching porno.

From the day I first edited *Drummer*, and as a former university professor teaching cinema, I calculated that the magazine could grow its brand name into a very successful Super-8 film business. In the 1970s we all knew about the coming joys of video, but the corporate wars between the Beta and VHS systems kept consumer cameras and VCRs out of our driving palms until 1981 when it was too late to tape the sights and sounds of the Titanic 1970s which history would regard quite differently had video offered up eyewitness documentation of the way we were before VHS and HIV. At a Boston book reading in the 1990s, I was asked by a young woman working on a college paper if she could see the videotape I shot of the Stonewall Rebellion!

In "Dune Body," echoing Allen Ginsberg chanting, I intoned my DJ mix of mythology, Joycean portmanteau words, erotic parallax metaphor, and world-weary sexiness. I wrote a free-association rap-and-slam poem to amuse *Drummer* readers who, in that literate day and age before the Great Dumbing of America, could rather "dig" this kind of beatnik stuff.

Marching to something different in *Drummer*, Thoreau might have smiled at the beatnik bongo drums punctuating the rhythm of the lines.

II. The poem as published in *Drummer* 20, January 1978

Dune Body

Dune body babyman,
stretched on spreadeagle wheels,
the CHP oughta getta shotta you:
hot mirage of *haute* stuff.

High noon of dust and lust,
Icarus rolling,
sunsweat of your solar-power body,
a quart of Quaker State to oil you up
with my calloused hand.

Oasis of erect palms.

I wanna fill your tank,
blow your carbs,
drive you all the way home
(9 inches: highway; 10 inches: city),
take flying leaps
at your silver spokes.

Christ. Your shock-absorbing back;
shooting over hot desert humps,
rolling down dunes at me, dick in hand,
ready for your pit-stop lube job, baby.

Ain't mirages when you rub 'em
s'pose to disappear? Thought you'd vanish
like some golden-tan dust devil,
leaving in the sand the trail
of your steel-radial cock and balls.
Swing lower, sweet chariot!

So come on, Sport,
show me what you do
for your next trick.

Pissing in the Wind

> Written September-October 1977, this feature essay was published in *Drummer* 20, January 1978. This feature essay was written as sequel to the "Mineshaft" feature in *Drummer* 19, December 1977.
> I. Author's Eyewitness Historical-Context Introduction written April 16, 2002
> II. The feature article as published in *Drummer* 20, January 1978
> III. Eyewitness Illustrations

I. Author's Eyewitness Historical-Context Introduction written April 16, 2002

Editor's Note: The first collection of *Drummer* fiction and features into a book was Jack Fritscher's solo anthology of twenty-one stories, *Corporal in Charge of Taking Care of Captain O'Malley and Other Stories* (1984).

That *Drummer* collection was published by Winston Leyland, Gay Sunshine Press, San Francisco. "Pissing in the Wind" was one of the selections. The British edition of the anthology *Corporal in Charge and Other Stories* was published in 1998 by Prowler Press, London. A text-definitive edition of *Corporal in Charge of Taking Care of Captain O'Malley and Other Canonical Stories* was published in 2000 by Palm Drive Publishing, San Francisco.

Censorship and the Culture War
(The Greeks Had a Word for Everything except Poppers)

I used *Drummer* as a recruiting manual to corrupt my readers with my apologia for sexual abandon. [And I was spot on foreshadowing the exact torture at Guantanamo Bay thirty years later.]

In my metasexual writing, I meant *Drummer* always to seduce the reader into doing at least in his fantasy what he had not yet done in reality. My duty was to pervert the pervertible.

This was the second article I wrote for *Drummer* about the Mineshaft where men turned fantasy into life. The first was in *Drummer* 19. To break down any residual "gay shame" or reticence left over from the closet,

I equated what was a "happening" in the Mineshaft as being no different than what straight guys like the Marines or SERE recruits do when their survival training gets them into some really twisted stuff: bondage, interrogation, torture, sexual abuse, piss, and scatology. I've always thought that everybody always does what they want and calls it by the best name possible. The message of the Golden Age of the Titanic 70s was that a man could liberate himself to do whatever he wanted.

The tactics and behavior of self-fashioned identity that were good enough for the Black civil rights movement, for the peace movement, and for the women's movement were good enough for us gays liberating ourselves, but we had to tell ourselves that this equation was valid. That was always the humanist political message coded behind my erotic writing in *Drummer*.

Unlike latter-day puritan kveens who strangle gay literature and castrate gay studies, I have always believed gay writing should be about sex, even though such dead-on honesty runs the risk that such writing, no matter how journalistic or literary may be dismissed as pornography. I chose early on, in 1968 in my first gay novel, *I Am Curious (Leather)* aka *Leather Blues*, to skip fantasy and to write about the actual sex lives and real sex practices of contemporary gay men.

I was lucky. In the first decade of gay liberation the gay press was not its own worst censor—as it became with the politically-correct puritans who in 1982 were swept to power in gay culture on a disaster-wind of AIDS rather like the dubiously elected George W. Bush was swept from mere presidential to imperial power by airliners crashing into the World Trade Center. Talk about two acts in the Theater of the Absurd! No one told me not to write about the real lives of actual gay men. Well, once or twice, publisher John Embry censored a piece or two that I wrote. He always blamed the fundamentalist printer who had religious and moral reservations about going too far.

Embry, having been arrested by the LAPD for the *Drummer* "Slave Auction," was correct in his fear of the religious right. In the 1970s, the Christianazi Anita Bryant was running her anti-gay crusade in Florida where she taught the Republican Neocons who came after her to hijack government to support traditional values. So I forgave Embry for not publishing my very psychedelic poem, "Jesus Depressed; Or, Kenneth Anger, Make a Movie." I also forgave him for pulling the feature article in *Son of Drummer* titled "Scum That I Am," because that special "New

Drummer 20: Pissing in the Wind

York art" issue featuring the leather debut of Robert Mapplethorpe was three-times gutted by the iron-fist of the fundamentalist printer. Who knew then, or knows now historically, about the uphill battle in the 1970s against all the straight religious tradespeople who, before the rise of gay businesses, called the shots on what *Drummer* could publish? "Not that cover! Not that photo! Not that article!" Talk about the censor's fist up the sock-puppet of gay publishing! In the 1970s, the censors were hypocritical printers who would print porno for cheap after midnight and go back to printing Bibles by day.

It was because they were cheap that Embry hired them. And it was a miracle that I got away with illustrating my "Pissing in the Wind" with four photographs from the Gage Brothers' film, *El Paso Wrecking Corp*.

Those 1970s straight fundamentalist printers on the right were the model for the 1980s politically-correct censors on the GLBT left.

Because of the pioneering times, nearly every topic I could get past all the censors—even the daring subject of "piss"—was a "first" in gay culture, not because of any particular brilliance, but because I was in the right place at the right time, and I dared move real gay behavior and gay linguistics forward into print. *Drummer* wasn't *Queen's Quarterly* with its queen's vernacular. We needed new words to describe the new way we were.

For more on the "outing of language" in *Drummer*, see "Homomasculinity: Framing Keywords of Queer Popular Culture in *Drummer* Magazine" from the Queer Keyword Conference, University College Dublin, Ireland, April 2005. It may be worth noting that I purposely headlined a feature on the cover of my *Drummer* 24 (September 1978) with the forbidden word *fag* as in "We Abuse Fags!" *Vis-a-vis* the S&M keywords words *slave* and *boy*, which are also racist words, confer *Drummer* 174, page 5, for the editorial, "The Slavery of Words," by Graylin Thornton who happens to be both Mr. *Drummer* 1993 and African-American.

The first post-Stonewall decade was as wild as an uncloseted preacher's kid. The nights of the 1970s, everywhere for adventurers, were wilder than the Roaring 20s—or so I was told by Sam Steward who came out in the 1920s, and who in the 1930s made the obligatory pilgrimage of artists and homos sexing their way through Gertrude Stein's pre-war Paris, Isherwood's Berlin, and Mussolini's Rome, pressing on into the international zone of Tangier where he and Cecil Beaton danced on barracks tables with young Moroccan soldiers.

Time is relative. The past is the past, and I don't live there. I tasted a *madeleine* and found it to be a cookie. Long ago on a May afternoon in 1995, while I was sitting on the stones next to Proust's tomb in Pere Lachaise, Mark Hemry shot a candid photograph of what looks like me laughing in the face of omnipotent death. A sweeter shot would have been the two of us at the shared tomb of Joseph Croce-Spinelli and Theodore Sivel, two young balloonists who ascended so breathlessly high in 1875 that they—dying in thin air, lying side-by-side, holding hands—floated back down to earth where, in the tender tangled repose of two lovers sleeping, their intimacy was sculpted into marble.

Memory is fragile as ice breath on a window pane.

But it is not futile comfort.

Yesterday was as interesting as today and certainly deserves some dance to remember.

II. The feature essay as published in *Drummer* 20, January 1978

RUN! Or Men Will Do Things to (Lucky) You....

Pissing in the Wind
Wet Dreams, Golden Showers
A Night in the Mineshaft Bathtub

"Drink up. Drink up. Let me fill your cup with the promise of a man."
— Neil Young, *Harvest*

Gay reality often reads like fiction. Mainly because the gay sense of adventure, that sense of openness to experience, causes fantasy to turn into fact and, once turned, that fact is often so outrageous in its reality, it sounds like fiction to people too chickenshit to pursue their fantasies. "What," they ask, "would happen if you actualized your fantasies? There would be nothing left to fantasize about."

Wrong. There would be new fantasies, one-step-further fantasies, push-the-limit fantasies. There would be new lost horizons to celebrate.

A man without fantasies is a man of the First Kind.

A man afraid to actualize his fantasies is a man of the Second Kind.

A man who acts out his fantasies is a man of the Third Kind.

[The pop-culture reference was to Steven Spielberg's *Close Encounters of the Third Kind* (1977).]

BACKROOM BARS: STAND-UP SEX, MINESHAFT

The backroom bars, watering holes for night bloomers, are phenomena of the Third Kind: *Contact.* They are native to San Francisco and New

York. They began as literal backrooms, spontaneous, in bars like the Tool Box, Folsom Prison, and the Ambush. They came out on their own at the Covered Wagon, the Anvil, and with increasing intensity, the Zodiac, the Toilet, and the latest "infleshtation," the Mineshaft.

After midnight, after the lights go down low, a man of the Third Kind can see what the boys in the backroom will have: fantasy actualized a la carte. New York's Mineshaft is the current frontrunner. Down a steep stairway, the Mineshaft offers "The Lourdes Room," featuring a full-length white porcelain bathtub suitable for baptizing and initiating any man who dares.

Any given night, a man can climb into the tub for nonstop Golden Showers. Fairer faucets, major and minor (less than seven inches), than he ever dreamed of, turn on–literally–to him and all over him. Saturday nights, especially, on three sides of the tub, men press in, six or seven deep. Men nearest the tub unbutton their Levi's, unsnap their leather codpieces, or go for their meat by peeling down their jocks. They are the front line of the Third Kind, pressed from behind by dozens of others chugging their beers as they press forward toward the tub. [The topical pun referred to the biggest blonde female icon of the 1970s, Farrah Fawcett-Majors.]

BATH-TUB PISS ORGIES

A single red light illuminates the dark faces, the blond moustaches, the bared chests wet with the humid cellar sweat. Often, a man of no patience drops to his knees to drink the piss of a man three rows back from the tub. The pissers move around the private scene toward their target: the man, laid back in the white tub, sometimes naked, more often wearing only construction boots, athletic socks, a piss-soaked jock, maybe a USMC fatigue hat.

One night, a perfectly groomed dude climbed into the tub wearing wingtips, a Brooks Brothers dark wool suit, Ivy League tie, a white oxford cloth dress shirt which, when he pulled open the suit coat, exposed holes cut out over his large nipples on his hairy chest. His hands found his crotch and fished his own cock hard from his white jockey shorts. On all sides, he looked up at the fifty or so piss-filled men looking down on him. A guy in full leather hawked up some deep spit and flumed it down on the dark suit. His baptism had begun.

The ritual runs nightly the same. The dozen men closest to the tub rim are in various erect stages of pissing. Some unbuttoning, some whipping it out fast. Others teasing it out slowly. One peels back his lip of heavy foreskin through his full hardon. One stands, muscular arms folded across his thick pecs, eyes closed, waiting for his piss to work its way down from inside his tight belly to his dick hanging out of his jeans: untouched, untouchable, but willing to piss down hard and heavy on the right motherfucker laid back in the tub. One by one, then in pairs, building to four and five at a time, they join together in a waterfall of piss.

Each chooses his own target. A man in the tub can study how some guys choose to piss on his boots. Others on his jock. Many on his chest. Most on his face and shoulders. The streams come thick. Some with firehose force. The hard ones piss straight down on his body. The thicker soft cocks rain down in a curved arc of beer-rich piss.

Ordinary to great bodies climb into the tub. Every body looks better hosed down with gallons of shiny piss. The look of the wet skin. The sound of hot piss splashing on warm flesh. The feeling, from celebration to humiliation, of aiming cock to piss on another man's cock and balls. The feel, to the man in the tub, of twenty streams of piss hitting him at once. The hot energy trade-off, man to man, in a communion of piss.

SIGHTS TRULY SEEN: PISS JOCKS

One dark-headed guy stands at the head of the tub with a dozen orange-and-blue Bike supporter boxes. He opens them slow and deliberate. One by one. Pulling out of each a clean new jockstrap. He opens the first box and throws the jock on the belly of the body soaked in the tub. Three dudes turn their dicks directly on to the new jock. It soaks up their piss fast. The second Bike box opens and the second jock lands in the tub. Again and again. The bearded guy tosses each box to the floor as he tosses each jock on top the man in the tub.

Another guy, one of those blonds with a thick red Marlboro moustache, sticks a finger through a small hole near the neck of his own white T-shirt. Slowly he tears the white cotton, shredding it to strips of rag, revealing his good pecs and smooth belly. He holds the rag of T-shirt balled up in his hand. His other hand pulls out his cock. He pisses long and heavy into his torn T-shirt. His cock hardens as he pisses.

The other men, except for one with a piss-load that won't quit, stop leaking to look at the big blond. When his T-shirt is soaked, he balls it up, wrings it out over the face of the man in the tub. Then he pisses in the shirt some more. Two other guys piss toward his cock pissing into the shirt. One hits the shirt. The other hits the blond's jeans.

Nothing bothers him. Pissed out, he lobs the dripping T-shirt like a wet softball into the face of the man in the tub. He catches it in his mouth and sucks it. Loud. His eager sucking causes six or seven more cocks to piss in his face.

The dude with the dozen jockstraps stuffs one of them into the tub drain. The tub fills up fast. Piss waves slosh side to side as the man in the tub twists and bobs for all the piss he can handle. As row after row of men moves in, the piss level covers most of his body. Once he slips. In the dripping, shuffling silence his hand makes the squeak of flesh sliding in a wet tub. For a moment, his whole head disappears under the piss and floating jockstraps.

A big fucker in full leather reaches down into the piss and dredges him up by the hair. The man in the tub gasps. Swallows. Wallows. Kneels up. Jerking off. Mouth open. Piss hitting his face. With him kneeling, the tub has room for two. Another guy climbs in for the same treatment. Both of them make gurgling sounds, mouths open, hunched back waist deep in the piss.

The guy with the jocks starts dredging them out. Fully soaked. No reason to wring them out. One at a time he steps into and pulls on the dripping jocks until his cock and balls are completely padded beneath a dozen straps soaked with the piss of nearly a hundred guys. He moves off into the darkly lit cellar and is lost in the crush.

The second guy into the tub dives for the T-shirt in the drain. He comes up with it in his teeth. The men piss harder in his face. He's working for it, begging for it, drinking it, as the tub level goes down. Slowly. The last piss swirls, gurgles, and leaves the tub slick. The first man climbs out, helped by the men standing nearest the tub. He's satisfied. He's had his turn. His scene is over.

Now the tub is ready for the new guy. He's busy already sucking the piss off the thigh-high rubber boots of a man who has thrown his fireman-booted leg across the tub. A fresh dozen dicks stream into the changing scene.

Off in another Mineshaft corner, in more private spaces, other men have waded off to bridge waters of their own. Near the bar, a short muscular man pisses into his empty beer can. He hands it to his buddy. They nod. They smile. The buddy drinks.

WET REALITIES: USMC

Camp Pendleton survival training teaches the young Marine recruits that to survive they can drink their own piss twice and eat their own shit once. Navy survival training is even better. For years, in fact, naval officers and cadets have whispered about the Navy Torture Camps: beatings by guards, "tiger cages," the starvation, and especially the exotic water tortures.

The source of all this cruel, unusual, and hardon punishment of young American males is not a foreign prison camp. It is the U.S. Navy's own hard-assed school for Survival, Evasion, Resistance, and Escape (SERE). Designed to train servicemen to survive the rigors of POW life, the Navy's two SERE programs, one at Warner Springs near San Diego and another in northwestern Maine, lost their secrecy recently when an embittered SERE graduate filed suit against Navy personnel, exposing the SERE training as an S&M reality.

NAVY PISS: SEX ABUSE OR PATRIOTISM?

Navy Lt. Wendell Richard Young, rejected the secrecy forced on every SERE graduate, telling tales of fetid tiger cages, beatings and jarring judo flips by Navy instructors he called "gorillas," and a torture device called the "water board." Young also charged, though not in his suit, that SERE students have been tortured into spitting, pissing, and shitting on the American flag, masturbating on order before Navy guards and, on one occasion at least, engaging in sex with an instructor.

The Navy denied the unsubstantiated charges of sexual abuse, but it did acknowledge the use of water torture and physical punishment in its training camps. A Navy spokesman, Comdr. William Collins, insisted that these activities were mostly "illusions of reality" that were not as dangerous as they seemed.

These "illusions of reality" done in the name of "patriotic military training" sound very close to the "illusions of reality" done nightly in the name of "sleazy sexual ritual." In America, it's not what you do, it's what you call it in order to excuse it.

NAVY HAZING TURNS SAILOR GAY

An ex-Navy officer, who was not gay at the time of his SERE training, explained that only after he was out of the Navy and had come out sexually that he realized the full implications of the weeklong SERE training which he was forced to take on threat of disciplinary action.

He was stripped to his skivvies and boots and made to stand at attention in a line with the other young officers forced to take the San Diego training. They were hooded one by one, "sacked" the guards called it, with a heavy canvas bag tied around the neck. After that he saw no one except for contact with the guards. His hands were tied behind his back and he was locked in a kneeling position inside a small wooden box where he was left hooded, tied, and cramped for twenty-four hours. He figured the large tin can between his thighs was for his piss. Hooded he couldn't see it. Tied he couldn't get his cock out of his skivvies anyway. He held back as long as he could, hearing the muffled sounds of the other men isolated in other wooden boxes. Finally he had to let go of his piss which wet his shorts, ran down his thigh, and pooled around his knees.

He found out that his piss was to be the excuse.

When the guards opened his box, still hooded, he could not rise from his cramped position. His boots and socks were wet with his piss. The guards, pretending outrage, lifted him bodily and dragged him across the compound, shouting at him about how even a dog won't piss in its own box. His legs were pins and needles, useless beneath him. They carried him into a room, unhooded him, and with a guard for each foot and hand, laid him out on a plywood torture board, tying him in place spreadeagled. A hose was brought near his mouth. He was thirsty from the desert heat and the twenty-four hour isolation. He drank. They pushed the nozzle closer to his face. He drank some more. They pushed the nozzle into his mouth. A strong, pair of hands held his jaws closed. The water flooded his mouth, forced out his cheeks, ran out his nose, into his ears, down his throat. He was drowning, choking, drinking to stay alive. They knew what they were doing. Right before unconsciousness, they pulled the hose from his mouth. He thought they were finished.

He was wrong. The waterboard torture lasted over an hour.

A tube was forced through his left nostril and fed the three-foot length to his belly. The water hose was attached to the tube. His belly filled to full distention. He admits to begging them to stop. Instead, they shoved a water-soaked T-shirt into his mouth, leaving only one nostril free for breathing. Then a guard posing as a foreign interrogator, climbed up on the waterboard, astraddle his bound waist, and kneaded his bloated belly until he was screaming into the T-shirt. He felt he could take no more. They knew he could. He knew he had to. They continued. The guard, kneading his belly rising and sitting, rising and pushing on his belly, then sitting back across his piss-soaked skivvies, worked him over with obvious pleasure.

MORE GRATUITOUS PISS AND VIOLENCE

Such isolation and forced feedings continued for the week. And with good reason. In his book *P.O.W.: A Definitive History of the American Prisoner-of-War Experience,* research-writer John Hubbell writes of how the enemy always tries to attack the macho American prisoner by belittling his manhood. He exposes how prisoners were forced to crawl through enemy latrines on their hands and knees, left for weeks tied in their own waste and sexually tortured. To paraphrase Hubbell: The interrogation the next day took place in an ancient pagoda. A crowd of civilians was present, apparently invited to witness the humiliation of the American "air pirate." As the interrogator asked questions, guards slipped the rope loops around the prisoner's shoulders turn-buckling them tighter. He was made to climb onto the seat of a chair. An end of the long rope that held his shoulders in torture was tossed over a rafter and pulled taut. The interrogator turned to the audience, smiled, waved an arm, and the chair was yanked from beneath the prisoner, who hung in the air by his agonized shoulders. The torture continued, and the interrogator began to masturbate....

Such realities both cause the Navy to prepare its men for sexual abuse and cause civilian belief in the secret details coming to light: the spitting, pissing, shitting, masturbating, all juicily excused as preparation for patriotism.

THAT'S STRAIGHT PISS FOR YOU

For relief, comic and cockwise, Burt Reynolds wins the Wet Oscar for Best On-Screen Piss in *Semi-Tough* when he inserts his dick into a rubber hose, straps it down his leg, and pisses into a metal flask strapped inside his boot. The loud soundtrack outdoes rain on a hot tin roof. Pasolini, in his version of *Something for Everyone*, called *Teorema*, films the humpy teenaged son pissing off the family balcony. In Kenneth Anger's *Scorpio Rising*, a classic gay version of *The Wild One*, the lead biker stands on an altar in a church and pisses into the chalice of his helmet, and finally pisses down on all the worshipers gathered around him.

In prison plays and films like Miguel Pinero's *Short Eyes* or Kenneth Brown's *The Brig*, the piss scene is obligatory. Experienced cons usually take to shoving a new dude's head into the cellblock toilet in an initiation as time-honored as the Hell's Angels' initiation of pissing on a new member's colors. And his leather jacket. And his jeans. From then on an Angel pulls off the road strictly for a good shit. Piss just goes off like a rocket in his pocket.

SOME LIKE IT HOT

Ancient warriors bathed in piss. Victorian athletes rubbed themselves down with piss before a good cricket match. Health addicts for years have claimed piss perfect for brushing the teeth. India's Prime Minister Norarji Desai announced recently: "For the past five or six years, I have drunk a glass of my own urine–about six to eight ounces– every morning. It is very good for you, and it is even free. Even in the Bible it says drink from your own cistern. What's your own cistern? It is your urine. Urine is the water of life."

Some men, always working toward versatility, often take a liking for piss: from beer-clear to early morning thick. The range of preference is an acquired taste—the reasons for taking another man's piss range from the sacred to the profane.

Some guys start off early in life pissing, as little boys, into the family john with their brother having races to see who will finish first. Others start later, at college bars, pissing into the same trough. Refinements set in: going off to bars across from police stations to give the porcelain a good lick when the cops come in after duty for a quick beer quickly pissed out; pissing up a guy's ass before, during, and/or after a good hard fuck; and preparing the basic water sports emblem, a piss-soaked jock, tucked into the back pocket.

RECYCLE

Variations on any theme, even Handel's "Water Music," are as endless as the inventive mind of man. Run an ad in *Drummer*'s personals, The Leather Fraternity, for Mason Jars of dirty bathwater and takers will beat a path to your P.O. Box. You just can't out-fetish and out-fantasize and out-actualize all of the people all of the time. But that is The Joy of Piss, like the joy of almost everything else: finding out that you as a man of the Third Kind are not alone, and in piss, more than almost anything else, together men sink to swim.

III. Eyewitness Illustrations

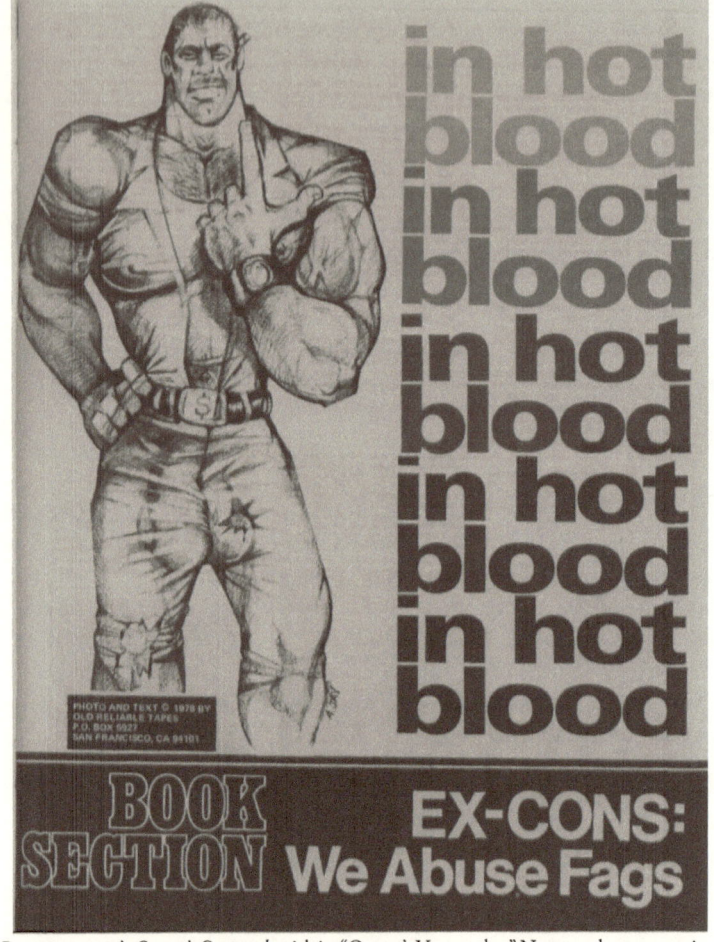

Drummer wasn't *Queen's Quarterly* with its "Queen's Vernacular." New words were required to describe the new way gays were. For specifics on the "outing of language" in *Drummer*, see in this book "Homomasculinity: Framing Keywords of Queer Popular Culture in *Drummer* Magazine" from the 2005 Queer Keyword Conference, Dublin, Ireland. To shock and defuse "touchy" language, Fritscher provocatively headlined a feature on the cover of *Drummer* 24 with the forbidden word *fag*: "We Abuse Fags!" *Vis-a-vis* the S&M keywords words *slave* and *boy*, which also happen to be racist words, see *Drummer* 174, "The Slavery of Words," by Graylin Thornton who wrote as Mr. *Drummer* 1993 and an African-American. For thirty years, Fritscher's coinages and chronicling of gay words have funneled gay lingua franca into mainstream linguistics collections. More than twenty examples of gay language are quoted directly from his *Some Dance to Remember*, the companion book to his *Gay San Francisco: Eyewitness Drummer*, in the encyclopedic *The New Partridge Dictionary of Slang and Unconventional English*, authors Tom Dalzell and Terry Victor, New York: Routledge, 2005.

Drummer 20: Pissing in the Wind

The first collection of *Drummer* stories and articles outside of *Drummer* was *Corporal in Charge of Taking Care of Captain O'Malley and Other Stories*. Clockwise from top left: First edition, Gay Sunshine Press (1984); British edition, Prowler Press (1998); textually correct edition, Palm Drive Publishing (2000), with cover featuring Jack Fritscher's photograph of Chris Duffy aka Bull Stanton. ©Jack Fritscher. The *Drummer* Salon threw a catered buffet and book-signing party for Fritscher at the Ambush bar, South of Market, celebrating publication of the first edition of *Corporal in Charge*, Friday, November 16, 1984.

Captions: Eyewitness documentation of the existence of graphics providing internal evidence supporting Jack Fritscher's text are located in the Jack Fritscher and Mark Hemry GLBT History collection. Out of respect for issues of copyright, model releases, permissions, and privacy, some graphics are not available for publication at this time, but can be shown by appointment.

| Eyewitness Illustration | Photograph. "Mineshaft Bath Tub," 1977. If this cropped documentary photograph were printed in full in *National Geographic*, it would be regarded with respect. However, because GLBT anthropology is an erotic culture, "culture war" censors rant against the legitimacy of its absolutely necessary core images. Margaret Mead should have had such luck in *Coming of Age in Somoa* as to find this evidence of the tribal baptism and bath rituals in the Mineshaft. Publicity kit photograph from the collection of Wally Wallace. Used with permission. Photographer as yet unknown. |

Astrologic *Aquarius*
The Dawning of the Age, 1978

> Written October 1977, this feature column was published in *Drummer* 20, January 1978.
> I. Author's Eyewitness Historical-Context Introduction written December 21, 1998
> II. The feature article as published in *Drummer* 20, January 1978
> III. Eyewitness Illustrations

I. Author's Eyewitness Historical-Context Introduction written December 21, 1998

For introductory history to the "Astrologic" columns, confer "Astrologic: Capricorn" in *Drummer* 19.

I often coded playful and personal messages into each "Astrologic" to entertain the mob of us doing *Drummer*—some of us living together and others of us fucking together. In the way that venerable author Sam Steward saluted our friends, the leather priest Jim Kane and his partner, the pro-football player Ike Barnes, in "Babysitter" in *Drummer* 5 (March 1976), I often wrote "internal signatures" into the text and subtext of my *Drummer* articles and stories to acknowledge my pals.

"Bent, sick, and twisted" was a catch phrase on Castro Street in the 1970s. "Jaded Degenerate Man" referred to New Yorker Don Levine who was one of the first truly original Titanic 70s "characters" to emerge in the Castro and South of Market. He was a nightclub singer and friend of the cabaret pianist John Trowbridge whom David Sparrow and I photographed for the cover of *Drummer* 21 (March 1978). Levine was like *Godot*. Always in rehearsal for his show that never happened, the dramatic Don Levine, who never saw a Broadway musical he didn't like, sold pot, and designed T-shirts emblazoned with his characterization of each and all of us: "Jaded Degenerate Man." Although he was swept away with the 1980s and seemingly lost from history, Don Levine was the wag who first dubbed Harvey Milk "The Mayor of Castro Street."

In the early 1970s, the Castro Café was the tidal pool of a group of us bohemian leather artists and writers on whom Don Levine pinned the donkey tail of the "gay Algonquin Club." It was this group that evolved into the first salon around *Drummer*.

The legendary Castro Café was on the west side of Castro Street, two doors north of the corner of 18th and Castro, and next to the Star Pharmacy. The Castro Café was the 24-hour place to see and be seen between afternoons in the backroom of Ron Ernst's Jaguar Bookstore and nights down on Folsom Street. Not until the Castro Café shuttered around 1975 did the Norse Cove across from the Castro Theater rise as the diner of choice. For a detailed narrative of how the 1970s Castro neighborhood grew from the Castro Café to the brunch culture inside Mena's Norse Cove, see *Some Dance to Remember: A Memoir-Novel of San Francisco 1970-1982*, Reel 2, Scene 4.

Don Levine and I (a Gemini) shared a mutual concern: we looked so much like each other—virtual twins—that when we were not together, people could rarely tell us apart. It became such a cliche that we both answered to the other's name just to add to the confusion. His Jewish name was "Don Levine," but we joked that his Irish-Catholic name was "Lon Devine." In the Ambush bar, a trick once warned us both to be great sex or we'd ruin each other's reputation.

My "Astrologic" quip about "Any Pisces named David" referred to David Wycoff who was roommate and lover in a "two-year three-way affair" with David Sparrow and me during our ten-year marriage. David Sparrow and I photographed David Wycoff for this same *Drummer* 20, page 39. My reference to "a taxi driver - especially if he is strawberry-blond, mustachioed, and muscular" described David Wycoff who was all that. He was also hung a full nine uncut inches, and a San Francisco taxi driver who gave blow jobs with the meter running, and a sweet-tempered young man except for one occasion referenced in this column when he and David Sparrow had a two-way spat and David Sparrow kept finding nails in his motorcycle tires. (There was no proof it was David Wycoff and the incidents were quickly forgotten.)

In 1980, David Wycoff found his own true love, Brian Dalgleish.

Then, without any warning from the astrological stars, the Titanic 70s party hit the iceberg of HIV.

After five years together as the best of lovers, Brian Dalgleish died on April 29, 1985, and David Wycoff lived only thirty more days, dying under care for dementia in the San Francisco Veteran's Hospital on May 29, 1985.

David Sparrow and I chartered a boat and on a way-too-brilliant spring afternoon spread David Wycoff's ashes on the waters of Paradise Cove near Angel Island in San Francisco Bay.

David Sparrow died seven years later on February 20, 1992.

He was born a Taurus on May 7, 1945, and my 1978 Taurus quips in "Astrologic" were meant for him.

My Capricorn swipe that "...there has never been a Capricorn of any importance" was meant as a barb of irony shot into gay culture's Marxist dismissal of Christianity.

II. The feature article as published in *Drummer* 20, January 1978

Astologic *Aquarius*
The Dawning of the Age, 1978

AQUARIUS S: *(Jan. 21 - Feb. 18)*: Admit it, asshole. You are *BST*: Bent, Sick, and Twisted. You have an inventive mind, inclined to be into PROGRESSIVE S&M. You fear you've already gone too far sexually when in reality you're only half as *BST* as 1978 will make you. By the end of the 70s, you will be a fully jaded, degenerate man. Sit on your own hand.

AQUARIUS M: *(Jan. 21 - Feb. 18)*: Inclined to be careless in your choice of masters, you will make the same stupid mistakes repeatedly until finally you learn how to project mastery of yourself. THEN the Right S will pick up on you. Currently you say NO too much too often. Relax. You need to be severely whipped and permanently pierced. You're old enough now to take possession of your body and give it away piece by piece.

PISCES S: *(Feb. 19 - Mar. 20)*: Careful this winter of M's who want to turn the tables on you. Secretly you desire to bottom out to a Satanic Warrior who will pin you to the mat. If you're not seriously working out, get your physique act together. An event is about to occur requiring from you a very muscular response.

PISCES M: *(Feb. 19 - Mar. 20)*: Any Pisces named DAVID had best be careful as the combination sign and name will this month earn you a very bad reputation among your immediate friends who find you quite possibly attack former lovers' motorcycles with nails and do terrible things to small animals when alone in your apartment. You rarely ever get what you want, but you are about to get what you deserve.

ARIES S: *(Mar. 21 - Apr. 19)*: Consider an affair with a taxi driver. Especially if he is strawberry blond, mustachioed, and muscular. Keep his meter running. You need another top man to play with, as your current bottom tricks are not fully satisfying you. Seek out mutual scenes.

ARIES M: *(Mar. 21 - Apr. 19)*: You are the asshole type and might as well celebrate the fact that most guys hold you in contempt. You are quick-tempered, impatient after midnight, and always scornful of advice. You are not very nice. Men should piss on you.

TAURUS S: *(Apr. 20 - May 20)*: You are bullish on yourself and, by god, you deserve it.[The gorgeous David Sparrow was a Taurus referenced here in the "S" and "M" entries for Taurus.] You are practical and persistent. Your bull-headed determination makes you cruise with specific purpose. M's know you've got ATTITUDE.

TAURUS M: *(Apr. 20 - May 20)*: Secretly, you're a scat freak. And you think your friends don't know that you eat your own bullshit.

GEMINI S: *(May 21 - Jun. 20)*: You are a quick and intelligent thinker. Both of your heads are better than one. Men like you because you are bisexual (some of the time) and on the head of your cock they can taste p-u-s-s-y j-u-i-c-e. Before the winter is out, you may need H-E-L-P.

GEMINI M: *(May 21 - Jun. 20)*: Uh-oh. You are too narcissistic these days. Stop jerking off alone in front of your mirror. It is a necessity for you to go to a bath for a heavy degradation trip. Find the ugliest dude you can and go down on him. If he rejects you, all the better. That could be your ultimate trip: to be rejected by a real scumbag.

CANCER S: *(Jun. 21 - Jul. 22)*: Wrestling has sometimes been a spontaneous part of your sex scene. Add in more sports touches. Drop some of your heavy leather, and jock up your wardrobe. You will come on and get off differently if you advertise the true sexual athlete hidden in your real self.

CANCER M: *(Jun. 21 - Jul. 22)*: You whine too much. Lower your voice a tone. Currently, other men think you're a sucker. You procrastinate. That's why you never make anything of yourself except a mess. No wonder most welfare recipients are Cancer people.

LEO S: *(Jul. 23 - Aug. 22)*: You are the sunshine of several men's lives. They'd like you to be even more of a bully. Add to your innate arrogance. M's will adore you, and in any sports contest you'll immediately establish psychological dominance.

LEO M: *(Jul. 23 - Aug. 22)*: No trick should let you stay over night, unless you are in total bondage. After dark, you turn into a thief. Keep your hands off the downers you find in your host's medicine cabinet. If he's going to trick with a creep like you, he'll need all the Valium he can get.

VIRGO S: *(Aug. 23 - Sep. 22)*: This month make your clean act even cleaner. Shower twice a day at the Y. Avoid sex with others. Tempt them instead by standing under the shower spray with a hardon. If uncut, spread a long, lingering time pulling back your delicious foreskin and sudsing your cockhead. This month your game is Turn-On-And-Turn-Down.

VIRGO M: *(Aug. 23 - Sep. 22)*: Your logic and hatred of disorder make you sickening to your friends. You are cold, unemotional, and often fall asleep while making love with your socks on. Virgo M's make good bus drivers. You ought to try it.

LIBRA S: *(Sep. 23 - Oct. 22)*: Practice your artistry by learning how to do prison-style tattooing with pins and India ink. Find a pierce-able M and decorate the space between his balls and his asshole. Who cares if he objects? He IS an object.

LIBRA M: *(Sep. 23 - Oct. 22)*: If you haven't, you should try hustling. You will be good at it. You should also be quick, as most Libras die of VD.

SCORPIO S: *(Oct. 23 - Nov. 21)*: You are shrewd in business and in bed and cannot be trusted any farther than Bruce Jenner can toss a cow-pie discus. You have achieved the pinnacle of your late-night reputation because of your total lack of sexual ethics. Remember that most Scorpios are murdered and their passing is only back-page news.

SCORPIO M: *(Oct. 23 - Nov. 21)*: Consider joining the Trappists. They keep their mouths shut. You kiss and tell. So it's either the monastery or pursuit of an S who will sew your loose lips together.

SAGITTARIUS S: *(Nov. 22 - Dec. 21)*: You are optimistic and enthusiastic. You need a reckless tendency to rely on luck since you lack the talent a true Top man needs to hit his mark. Most Sagittarians are dope fiends. You are no exception. When you are on Quaaludes, people laugh at you a great deal.

SAGITTARIUS M: *(Nov. 22 - Dec. 21)*: Buy a stature of Saint Sebastian stuck full of arrows/eros. He is your patron this month as you will be besieged on all sides by the slings (good) and arrows (better) of outrageous (best) fortune-hunters. Be ready to suffer.

CAPRICORN S: *(Dec. 22 - Jan. 19)*: Post-holiday let-down should not affect you, as you have Lent to look forward to. Improve your performance as a Top by denying yourself half the sex you're used to having and spending your new-found time building up your latent athletic skill. M's will worship your pumped-up forearms.

CAPRICORN M: *(Dec. 22 - Jan. 19)*: You are afraid to take risks. You don't do enough of anything. All you ever want is to lie back with a fist up your thankless butt. No wonder there has never been a Capricorn of any importance. Don't stand still too long as you tend to take root and become a tree, unless—that is—you're into dog piss.

III. Eyewitness Illustrations

Love Is a Three-Way. Top: "David Sparrow and Jack Fritscher," San Francisco, 1972. Bottom left and right: "David Wycoff (left) and Jack Fritscher," American Bicentennial Celebration, July 4, 1976, Marina, San Francisco. Photographs by David Sparrow. ©Jack Fritscher

Drummer 20: Astrologic Aquarius

"John Trowbridge," 1977, bunker, Marin Headlands, test shot for cover of *Drummer* 21 (March 1978). Photograph by Jack Fritscher-David Sparrow. ©Jack Fritscher

Ron Ernst, 1960s-1970s gay business activist and founder of the legendary Jaguar Bookstore with its 25-cent turnstyle entry to its lascivious back room at 18th and Castro, during interview on September 12, 1988, by Jack Fritscher for *Drummer*. Photograph by Jack Fritscher. ©Jack Fritscher

Toward an Understanding of *Salo*

Written October 14, 1977, this feature essay was published in *Drummer* 20, January 1978.
I. Author's Eyewitness Historical-Context Introduction written February 15, 2007
II. The feature essay as published in *Drummer* 20, January 1978
III. Eyewitness Illustrations

I. **Author's Eyewitness Historical-Context Introduction written February 15, 2004**

Fighting American Fascism: The American Civil War (1860-1865) Continues as the 21st-Century American Culture War

On October 14, 1977, I wrote this review-essay which was published in *Drummer* 20 (January 1978), pages 66-67, with six photographs from the Italian film *Salo* (1975). Based on the book, *The 120 Days of Sodom*, by Marquis de Sade, *Salo* was directed by international filmmaker Pier Paolo Pasolini who, shortly after the release of *Salo*, was murdered, age fifty-three, on the beach at Ostia, near Rome, by the rough-trade hustler Pino Pelosi. In this world, there are the dreamers and the predators who follow them. Then come the legends and the acolytes.

On a brilliant spring day, March 22, 2006, Mark Hemry and I, having taken rooms at the Hotel Quirinale in Rome, set out from Pyramide Station on the Roma-Lido railway for a day trip to Ostia, making pilgrimage to lay roses near the beach where Pasolini was killed thirty years before on November 2, 1975. In our camera bag we carried from home in San Francisco a copy of Pasolini's *Roman Poems* translated by Lawrence Ferlinghetti at City Lights Books. Outside the train window, huge quadrangles of apartments gave way to tenement slums, and at EUR Magliana Station to the large white cube of Mussolini's Pallazzo della Civita del Lavoro, and then to the suburbs of trackside country villages Pasolini had satirized with Terence Stamp in *Teorema* (1968). We exited the graffiti-covered train at the seaside village of Ostia Antica. Pasolini himself had made this exact trip many times by train, by car, and by slow boat down the Tiber.

Outside the tiny deserted station, we climbed the pedestrian overpass, and through the pine trees saw Ostia Antica spread out before us: a once busy city abandoned in ruins. In its maze of empty streets, grass and ivy covered the brick outcroppings of Roman baths, merchant warehouses, Agrippa's theater, and ancient restaurants with inlaid floors of intricate black-and-white mosaics. It is a wild place where young men easily prowl at night, vandalizing this wall, stealing that statue's hands. The Romans have so much antiquity that they select what to secure.

Ostia, the first harbor for Rome, is no "perfect moment in time" like Pompeii because Ostia's people drifted away as the mouth of the Tiber silted over and closed the port. We were alone; it was only the second day of spring and the summer tourist buses had not yet arrived. As if left behind centuries ago, gentle but wary dogs, the unpetted kind, the cruising kind who had gone back to nature, watched us making our way through the ruins. Had their eyes seen Pasolini? And Pelosi? Had they seen Mafiosi? Had they barked at the violence? Had they run in fear when Pasolini was run over repeatedly by his own car? Over our heads, huge jetliners roared in low over tall Corinthian columns to land one after the other at the new port, Leonardo da Vinci Fiumicino Airport.

The perfect morning folded down under a March storm sweeping in from the Tyrrhenian Sea. Dark clouds, lightning, and chilly winds, but no rain, alternated with intense humid sunshine while the sky fifteen miles to the north hung unmoving and black with cold drizzle over Rome. Any gay man instinctively knows that the labyrinth ruins of Ostia have been a hot spot for cruising since its founding as a naval base in the third century BC to its demise as Rome's commercial port in the third century AD. In the way that the abandoned West Side maritime piers along the Hudson River in New York became an equally abandoned orgy of industrial-strength outdoor sex in the 1970s, Ostia smacks of its own pagan roots as a port town filled with laborers, sailors, slaves, and prostitutes. On the very night that Pasolini was killed, the dilapidated piers, and the jeopardy of trucks parked near Keller's leather bar in the West Village, were jammed with a thousand men, including *Drummer* readers and pickpockets and assassins, doing the same thing he was. The choreography of Pasolini's night out cruising ended not in wonderfully anonymous sex but in the kind of murder that moralists figure is the luxury tax on the evolved state of being born gay.

The barbaric attack against Pasolini remains mysterious because the suspicion is that Pino Pelosi was hired by the very kind of conservative

Fascist politicians and Mafiosi whom Pasolini dismantled in films such as *Salo*.

The film caused an international sensation that only increased with Pasolini's murder two years before this feature essay, "Pasolini's Last Picture Show," was published in *Drummer*. His murder rocked the gay world. Pasolini and anti-gay Fascism were extremely hot topics in the politics and pop culture of the 1970s. I wrote this essay to pique reader interest and to make *Drummer* respond realistically to homophobic attacks by American Fascists such as Anita Bryant and John Briggs who began the culture war that continues to this day.

Pasolini was born March 5, 1922, the year Fascist dictator Benito Mussolini came to power over Italy. He took esthetic cue for his irony from Dante who also punctured politicians. Lest anyone be confused about precisely why the S&M images in *Salo* are so extreme and so tailored to history, note that Pasolini lifted his title from the Repubblica di Salo. This Salo Republic during World War II was a sham government much like the Vichy government in France. At Hitler's orders, it was established in the North of Italy by Mussolini after Mussolini had been driven out of Rome. The Salo government was Hitler's hand puppet in rounding up hundreds of Italian Jews, gays, and gypsies. However, before Salo officials—living aristocratically in art deco palazzos—sent them to concentration camps, they played terminal sex games with them. Such is the *mise en scene* of the film, *Salo*.

Pasolini, always bucking authority, was very much part of the 1960s and 1970s gay lib *zeitgeist*. Fascism specifically is an authoritarian political movement that flourished in Italy under Mussolini and in Spain under Franco. World linguistics often applies the Fascist label to any oppressive government limiting civil liberties. I use the term, always capitalized, both ways.

That said, now, so many years past the Titanic 70s, the films named in this essay may guide S&M enthusiasts and queer studies professors seeking "must-see viewing" within BDSM culture. These 1970s films have been resurrected on DVD as leather-heritage art objects.

American Fascism 1

If there is an Absolute Timeline on an Absolute LGBT Calendar, one date requiring annual observance is February 19, 1942: President Franklin D. Roosevelt signs Executive Order 9066, the internment order requiring Americans who happened to be of Japanese descent to be held in concentration camps for the duration of World War II.

I believe that the "Leather Decade of the Titanic 1970s" began on November 25, 1970, with the world-shocking suicide of Yukio Mishima at age forty-five. The homomasculine author had directed and starred in his own internationally acclaimed sadomasochistic film *Rite of Love and Death* (1965) in which he acted out his own future muscular *harakiri*. Moralists rarely condemn Mishima's film, although both the right-wing and the left condemn his politics. Leatherfolk romanticize him for his dreamy S&M self-portraits that—while very similar in pose to the Kris Studio leather-muscle esthetic—so shaped the work of many gay photographers in *Drummer* including Mapplethorpe.

It is not fair, and it may be quite sexist on their part, that politically correct fundamentalists single out the gay, male-identified *auteur* Pasolini for condemnation when other filmmakers of his era, particularly the wonderful women directors (Liliana Cavani, Lina Wertmueller), dealt with similar sadomasochistic material for similar political reasons. In addition, the French male director Barbet Schroeder made his shocking S&M film *Maitresse* (1976) without being, as Pasolini was, undeniably political. In Spain, Fernando Arrabal, founder of the surreal Panic Movement, directed his political and violent S&M film *Viva La Muerte* (1970) which was every bit as brutal as *Salo* and ran many weekends as the "midnight movie" at the St. Mark's Theater in the East Village. Undisturbed by politics, *Maitresse* with its graphic scenes of pain and mutilation was cast with masochists who paid to be in the film and it was, in those pre-reality-TV times, a huge hit among S&M afficionados. As mainstream as was *Maitresse*, Nagisa Oshima's *In the Realm of the Senses* (1976), often referred to as *In the Realm of the Censors*, was another explicit S&M hit wherein sexual transgression through edge-play relieved Fascistic repression. When this feature essay was written in 1977, I mentioned some of these films as akin to *Salo*.

My eyewitness presumption was that *Drummer* readers had seen most of these mainstream movies as part of how we lived—and how we used gaydar to discover S&M where we could in heterosexual films in those days when there was hardly any gay publishing or gay film industry.

Having taught the history and esthetics of cinema at university for ten years before becoming editor of *Drummer*, I introduced a bit of European and Japanese film culture which expressed my intent of growing *Drummer* into *International Drummer*. (I had been traveling east to gay culture in Europe since May 1969, and west to Japan since October 1975.) On September 14, 1972, I had been immensely impressed when the startling Brazilian film, *The Case of the Naves Brothers* (1967), had its quiet little American premiere at the Carnegie Hall Cinema. Director Luiz Sergio Person's black-and-white palette and *verite* camera made the explicit torture of this brutal film a landmark in anti-government cinema.

In the hardon helix between art and sex, I can attest, *The Naves Brothers* greatly enhanced the subtext and the actuality of S&M games played by gay men in 1972. If somewhere a film print of *The Naves Brothers* exists, it should be digitally preserved like a note in a bottle from a lost civilization.

Might I note that in the 1970s, gay men in their thirties had come to first consciousness during the violence of World War II that was projected on screen in newsreels shown between double-feature musical comedies. Has anyone ever bothered to study the causative impact of that war on the sexual abandon of the 1960s and 1970s? Connecting the dots of the leather, uniform, and S&M interests of the Nazi-obsessed 1970s, I find comparative films shot at the same time as *Salo*. "S&M literacy" requires some knowledge of Antonin Artaud's Theater of Cruelty theories as well as the viewing of both high-art films and pop-culture movies. Pasolini, similar to the rest of us, had feasted on the anti-Fascist film *Viva la Muerte* by Fernando Arrabal (1970) and the not-to-be-missed fetish feature *The Holy Mountain* (1973) by Alejandro Jodorowski, which leathermen made so popular at the Ghirardelli Square Cinema that I included the erotic experience of watching that very film in a significant scene in *Some Dance to Remember: A Memoir-Novel of San Francisco 1970-1982*, Reel Six, Scene Four.

The hit list continued.

Pervy British filmmaker Derek Jarman directed *Sebastiane* (1976), the first "gay" S&M film to gain international notoriety with its spear-and-sandal story of gay icon and long-suffering martyr Saint Sebastian tortured and killed by rough young Roman soldiers on the hot, burning desert sands of Sardinia—northwest of Ostia.

The deliciously decadent *The Night Porter* (1974) by Italian director Liliana Cavani, starred the incomparable Dirk Bogarde trampling the peerless Charlotte Rampling. *The Night Porter* reveled in the same highbrow sadomasochism as *Seven Beauties* (1976) by Lina Wertmueller. Both were popular and highly respected during the same season as the lowbrow gore-genre sexploitation blockbuster *Ilsa She-Wolf of the SS* (1975) directed by Don Edmonds and starring Dyanne Thorne. *Ilsa*, gorgeously advertised as "One of the Most Notorious and Reviled Films of Our Time," showed its hotsy-totsy Nazi fantasies continuously—grinding through projectors 24/7 to the end of the 1970s—at the Apollo Theater on 42nd Street and at the Strand Theater on Market Street where leathermen bought tickets time and again for *Ilsa*'s extreme torture of bound males, as well as for the anonymous "balcony blow jobs" ready to finish the viewers off as they sat in full leather masturbating to the S&M Nazi high camp on screen.

This feature essay appeared soon after the first American release of *Salo*, less than two years after Pasolini's shocking death, and, since then, films *about* Pasolini have become numerous if not definitive: Paesi Bassi's *Whoever Says the Truth Shall Die* (1981); Aurelio Grimaldi's *Un Mondo d' Amore* (2002); Marco Tullio Giordana's *Who Killed Pasolini?* which Mark Hemry and I viewed at its premiere screening in Paris at a small Left Bank movie house in May 1995. Abel Ferrara, the director of the mortally sinful *Bad Lieutenant* (1992), has announced plans for a feature film about the life and death of the Italian icon whose mystique so captivated the fancy of intellectuals and straights. Besides Pasolini's own novels, poetry, and film scripts, the book to read is *Pasolini Requiem*, the definitive biography by Barth David Schwartz (1992).

In the Dumbing of America, which has taken its toll even among homosexuals, there is no artist of recent memory, and certainly no gay artist, who like Pasolini, transcends his politics, his art, and his own faulty self to become an icon of art, intellect, and politics. Italians mention Pasolini's name with reverence; and, while the "S&M philosopher," Michel Foucault is worshiped by the French, his world-class intellectual body of work does not have the populist diversity of Pasolini's films, fiction, poetry, and political theory.

Pasolini's "death by rough trade" is perfect archetype of gay bashing from Saint Sebastian to Saint Matthew Shepard.

Apropos *Drummer*: Pasolini's taste helped shape *Drummer* because his hustlers whom he cast on screen prompted me to be the first editor to dare publish the street hustler photographs of the American photographer most like Pasolini, Old Reliable (David Hurles). That was in *Drummer* 21 (March 1978) when every other gay mag had rejected Old Reliable's gritty erotic aggro photos that were too scary for the vanillarinas, but not for the leatherstream. In the late 1970s, David Hurles and I thought the death of the bashed Pasolini — as most likely engineered by politicians — was a warning shot to gay culture at the time when ever-onward-marching Christian soldier-homophobes like pop-singer Anita Bryant, California politician John Briggs, and comedian Richard Pryor were waging war against gay liberation. (Pryor's nasty gay jibes were particularly offensive to me because we had both grown up in Peoria which wasn't too fond of either one of us. So we should have stuck together.)

In Florida, former Miss America Bryant who was the TV advertising "spokeswoman" for the Florida Orange Juice Commission campaigned with her "Save Our Children" group to get the then just-passed 1977 Dade County Human Rights Ordinance repealed. As a result, even to this 21st-century day in Florida, GLBT people may not adopt. However, as certainly as a tornado dropped Dorothy's house on the Wicked Witch of the West, there was a 1970s "spin." The GLBT reaction to the attacks by Bryant and Briggs galvanized gay liberation and drove us to change its character from fun "gay liberation" into serious "gay politics."

In California late in 1977, conservative Orange County state senator John Briggs, emboldened by Ronald Reagan's two terms as governor of California, began tub-thumping "Proposition 6: The Briggs Initiative" that intended by law to ban gays from teaching in any public school.

Also mentioned in this review-essay is "avowed heterosexual Ed Davis" who was the chief of police in Los Angeles. In the Swinging 60s and the Titanic 70s, the Fascist Davis famously deployed his LAPD cops as some kind of New Wave Brown Shirts to terrorize and raid innumerable gay bars, baths, and to destroy the LA publishing base of *Drummer* magazine.

April 10, 1976, was a defining moment for *Drummer* and homomasculine culture when Davis busted *Drummer* for hosting a "Slave Auction" for charity. This social event was about as sinister as a church auction, but Davis, planning his attack long before the event occurred, characterized the glamorous evening as some kind of medieval sex orgy of queers.

In my opinion, 1) the LAPD police attack and raid on the *Drummer* Slave Auction (April 1976) is a West Coast version—in fact, a Keystone Cops version—of 2) the NYPD attack on the Stonewall Bar seven years earlier (June 1969), and both prefigure 3) the SFPD attack on gays on Castro Street the night of the White Night Riot in San Francisco (May 21, 1979).

These three police attacks connect the dots of major physical battles in the new American civil war between homophobe citizens and homosexual citizens. Some call it a culture war. I think this war is the same as the unresolved issues of the Civil War (1860-1865) which was about states' rights, the Constitution, and human rights vis a vis slavery wherein, by extension to our day, the state of *being Black* stands in for the state of *being homosexual* by nature.

Being born Black is no more a choice than being born gay. You know homosexuality is not a choice when your dreams, over which in sleep you have no control or choice, are gay.

(Tell me what you dream and I'll tell you your sexual preference.)

Being redneck, however, is different because redneckery is a choice.

The theocracy of the American South, toting its Bible as a weapon and waving its Confederate flag, literally believes—in the way fundamentalists believe everything literally—that "the South will rise again." Red State voters are in angry denial that the South lost the Civil War and they seek a restoration of their confederacy of dunces.

In the *sturm* and *drang* of the operatic 1970s, the cast of characters was huge and the plot lurched forward on events that were epic. (That's why, as critic Michael Bronski, pointed out, *Some Dance to Remember*, like *Gone with the Wind*, sweeps through fifteen characters and a dozen plot points.)

It is an intellectual mistake, especially for GLBT people, to dismiss the 1970s because of cliched and jokey attitudes about disco, grooming, clothing, political incorrectness, and pre-AIDS behavior.

In the 1970s, we took the virtual world that had been the gay world before Stonewall and worked to turn the virtual dream into actual life.

The night of that LA "Slave Auction," April 10, 1976, Davis arrested approximately forty gay personalities and stars including *Drummer*'s first editor in chief Jeanne Barney, *Drummer*'s first publisher John Embry, porn legend Val Martin, and director of *Born to Raise Hell*, Terry LeGrand.

They were charged—and here's a pattern!—with breaking the 14th Amendment to the US Constitution forbidding slavery. Invoking an antique law twenty-eight years later (2004) was the same way that then Massachusetts governor Mitt Romney denied gay marriage in his state to people who did not reside in Massachusetts.

The LAPD asked Jeanne Barney if she was a real woman and she answered, "Honey, if I were a drag queen, I'd have bigger tits."

The way John Embry, ever ambiguous, handled the advertising, charged for the event, and changed his story about the nature of this event (was it for charity or was he charging admission for profit?) had played into Davis' hands. Whatever happened, this raid drove *Drummer* to San Francisco to escape Davis's clutches the way that Jews fled Hitler.

One cannot help but remember that the inspiring text for gays in the 1970s was the iconic, political, and sexually liberating film *Cabaret* (1972) which as a 1960s Broadway musical initiated an equation between Nazi Germany and Fascist America beyond, I think, even what Christopher Isherwood intended in what he called his *Berlin Stories* which were Herr Issyvoo's combination of his two short novels, *Mr. Norris Changes Trains* (1935) and *Goodbye to Berlin* (1939).

His autobiography, *Christopher and His Kind* (1977), was a gay best seller at the same time I became editor in chief of *Drummer* and *Christopher and His Kind* colored the way many participants felt about the *Drummer* salon and its kind.

Sprung from Isherwood via Kander and Ebb, the Weimar musical *Cabaret* dramatized how 1970s San Francisco mirrored 1930s Berlin: decadent, dazzling, diverse, doomed.

Following the exodus of *Drummer* out of LA by only a few months, Robert Opel (the performance artist and *Drummer* contributor who had streaked the 1974 Academy Awards) fled to San Francisco after he was arrested by Davis for indecent exposure when Opel protested nude inside a courtroom against the censorious legislating away of Los Angeles' nude beaches.

Opel was murdered in San Francisco on July 8, 1979, 1) only eight months after Harvey Milk was assassinated, 2) six weeks after the White Night Riot, and 3) only five weeks after Opel appeared in his own performance art in the wide-open UN Plaza in front of City Hall where he had protested the jury's soft "Twinkie Defense" verdict that had pillowed rather than pilloried assassin Dan White.

At high noon, in the Gay Parade crowds, Opel had costumed himself as "Gay Justice," and, brandishing a gun, he "executed" a fellow actor costumed in white as the former policeman-fireman-and-conservative-politician "Dan White" who in his own private Fascism had shot both Milk and the liberal Mayor George Moscone. I created an entire section around Opel's life and murder in *Some Dance to Remember*, Reel Three.

I think Opel's death less than four years after Pasolini's fits a pattern, especially factoring in the bass-boom archetypal 1936 death of Federico Garcia Lorca shot, literally up the ass, by Fascists. The leftist poet Lorca was, like Pasolini and Opel, masculine-identified, and evinced the roots of his homomasculinity in his "Ode to Walt Whitman."

The rumor that Pasolini's murderer was an operative of darker political forces is exactly what I was once told about Opel's murderer. On March 4, 1990 at a San Francisco cocktail party for a hundred men in uniform, a man pulled Mark Hemry and me from the gay chatter to a dark stairwell, and, because, he said, I had been the editor in chief of *Drummer* he had a story to tell us....

Let me ask you to sit on the ground in a circle as I tell the sad deaths of queens.

I wrote this *Salo* review because immediately post-Watergate and post-Vietnam all of us gays could feel the hate explode in the American air; gains we had made after Stonewall were beginning to be attacked by the fundamentalist religious right.

I thought *Salo* was a convenient pop hook on which I could hang some of our gay angst while at the same time I mobilized *Drummer* readers by showing them that what they could take from *Salo* was not just S&M but also political rage against what all we leather hippies accused much of the establishment: Fascism.

Besides, "Gowns and Uniforms" were in the air. ("Gowns and Uniforms" is my code phrase for the modern anti-Nazi genre of movies nostalgic for World War II.) A year after this Pasolini essay was published, the Museum of Modern Art in 1979 hosted a "Fascism and Gays" symposium in which gay historian Martin Duberman participated.

American Fascism 2

Fascism is totalitarianism marked by a fundamentalist right-wing dictatorship supporting war-driven patriotism and nationalism. What we feared in the 1960s and the 1970s came true on 9/11 with members of the Senate and the Congress singing a fundamentalist arrangement of "God Bless America" on the Capitol Steps while some of them made threatening gestures to suspend the Constitution and declare the sitting president dictator-for-life. When George W. Bush reaches the end of his second term, he may decide not to leave the White House.

Down Castro Street, a few blocks from the *Drummer* office, Supervisor Harvey Milk was warning gays not to let their civil rights be taken away as they had, Milk said, in Nazi Germany.

On November 7, 1978, the Briggs Initiative was defeated.

Twenty days later, on November 27, 1978, Supervisor Harvey Milk and Mayor George Moscone were gunned down in San Francisco City Hall by Dan White, the only supervisor to have supported the Briggs Initiative.

The alarm I tried to sound in this review went off.

My career thumbnail: Internal evidence in my *Drummer* writing shows that while I always wrote sex-text about living life in the fast lane, I also wrote a sub-text about being careful medically and astute politically.

As Pasolini had been murdered, as Milk had been murdered, as Opel had been murdered, so were we all at risk—faced with the murderous Fascism of our anti-gay enemies.

It did not please me that I had to write my column on Harvey Milk's death, on the very day he died, while his body was still warm, for *Drummer* 26 (January 1979).

American Fascism 3

What happened in the 1970s was archetypally repeated in 1989 when the government, driven by the tobacco-funded Republican Senator Jesse Helms, prosecuted and censored the S&M gay photography of my bicoastal lover Robert Mapplethorpe. In the first years of the 21st century, the same crap has been reeling out again in the fundamentalist opposition to gay marriage.

There may be a point here: gay art, such as *Salo*, is a cautionary tale that prompts us to look at the principles we stand for even as we are attacked by Fascists of whatever stripe simply because they have to point at somebody they say is bad so that nobody will notice that they themselves are evil. They need us the way Hitler needed Jews to get his way.

Pasolini is template of many gays, particularly Catholic gays, who are anti-clerical yet profoundly religious. To me, trained as a social-worker priest, his film of the life and death of Jesus, *The Gospel according to Saint Matthew* (1964), is a Catholic-Marxist "take" on the gospel, by way of Saint Francis. It is equal to Martin Scorsese's erotic *The Last Temptation of Christ* (1988) and far superior to the fundamentalist S&M Jesus created by the right-wing director Mel Gibson in his blood-dripping whip-fest *The Passion of the Christ* (2004).

On November 3, 1992, *The Advocate* (Issue 615) published a huge black swastika on its red cover headlining its lead article, "The Rise of Fascism in America."

My *Salo* essay, because its subject matter and argument were relevant to Robert Mapplethorpe, was re-printed (albeit censored) in my erotic-bio memoir *Mapplethorpe: Assault with a Deadly Camera*, Hastings House, New York (1994). Robert Mapplethorpe and I were bicoastal lovers. I cast the models in some of his San Francisco and New York photographs, including the cover of *Drummer* 24 (September 1978). I gave Mapplethorpe his first magazine cover (the same *Drummer* 24) and was the first gay magazine editor to print his photographs in America in my special "New York art" issue *Son of Drummer* (September 1978).

In his book *Outlaw Representation: Censorship and Homosexuality in Twentieth-Century Art*, the critic Richard Meyer cited the pioneering importance of my feature essay and my photo captions, "Robert Mapplethorpe Gallery (Censored)," the first article on Mapplethorpe in the gay press, in my special *Drummer* edition *Son of Drummer*; see also my "Pentimento for Robert Mapplethorpe: Fetishes, Faces, and Flowers of Evil," *Drummer* 133 (September 1989).

Finally, I should make an eyewitness note that Mario Simon, the lover and business partner of publisher John Embry, was a singer born and raised in Franco's Fascist Spain. He immigrated to America as an adult, met Embry in LA, and was arrested with Embry by the LAPD which made him two-times a Fascist victim when he fled LA for the open city of San Francisco in 1977. In the 1980s he was type-cast in local stagings of *Evita* as Magaldi, the over-the-top tango singer who gives Evita her first leg up singing "On This Night of a Thousand Stars." Long after I exited *Drummer*, Embry listed "Mario Simone" on the masthead of *Drummer* 57 (October 1982) as "General Manager" which was flattering—and, one opines, tax-deductible, which made legitimate sense for benefits because he was not unknown as "Mrs. *Drummer*," the owner's "wife." The tempestuous "Mario Simone" was more often "Mario Simon" as spelled in his obituary; he lived from March 5, 1942 to December 12, 1993.

II. The feature essay as published in *Drummer* 20, January 1978

***DRUMMER* Views the Flicks...**
The last and best review of
the controversial *Salo* you'll ever need.
What's an S&M man to think of leather and Fascism?

Toward an Understanding of *Salo*
(*Drummer*'s Farewell to Pasolini's Last Picture Show)

Let's cut through all the queenly bullshit about *Salo*, the last and most controversial vision of Italian filmmaker Pier Paolo Pasolini. If you're alive and gay, you waited two years for the U.S. release of this film. Now that you've seen *Salo*, how do you handle its scenes in your own head and explain them to unkinky gays? Especially since *Salo*'s explicit scenes, at first viewing, seem so directly tied to the S&M lifestyle. You can't laugh *Salo* off like *Pink Flamingo*'s outrageous Divine eating shit. *Salo* is no joke.

TWO KINDS OF CINEMA

Make a distinction: movies and films. You go to a *movie* to escape life's tension. You go to a *film* to intensify life. You go to a movie for entertainment. You go to a film for intensified input. Some guys short-circuit when they pay admission for a movie only to find out what's on screen is more than they bargained for: a film.

Before you approach the box office, read reviews and listen to word-of-mouth to determine if the feature showing is a *movie* or a *film*. Then figure out if you're in a movie-mood for entertainment, or in a film-mood for intensity. Since most reviewers are confused assholes trying to judge movies by film criteria, and films by GP-movie standards, you basically pay your money, take your chances, and wind up as your own best movie/film critic.

With an entertainment-movie, you get pretty much the sound of music that you bargained for. With the intensity of a film, you can bet you'll be yanked into some artful spaces you never expected to go. When you leave a movie, you exit much the same as when you entered. When you leave a film, you exit changed by an experience that really opened your eyes and your mind.

SALO IS A FILM

Poor Pasolini: more misunderstood dead than alive. He filmed clues to his murderer's identity. His murder is our attempted murder. His clue is *Salo* itself: a film about the Bryants and Briggs and Pryors (whose grandmother's name is Bryant). Pasolini's *Salo* is a cautionary film, a warning flag. He is frankly blunt in his message about political Fascism that kills the individuality of sex. For Pasolini there is no pentimento in *Salo*. No regret. No change of heart or mind. Certain murder, he cautions gays, lies in wait.

Salo is a dark film shot in a narrow space.

SALO IS ABOUT AMERICAN GAYS TODAY: 1978

There are two kinds of S&M: ritual and real. Ritual S&M men go to see *Salo* hoping that Pasolini has made a gay porno-fantasy movie as innocuously entertaining and ritualistic as the gay porn film *Born to Raise Hell* (1974) shot by Roger Earl [Warnix] and Terry LeGrand. Instead, Pasolini, although a fan of ritual-macho S&M, in *Salo* presents a scary film of real S&M. (And rather disappointingly straight at that!) Gay ritual S&M is Black Leather Therapy acted out for mental health with mutual consent.

Straight real S&M is the evil stuff of a Hitler born again in a Bryant, Briggs, or in the LAPD Police Chief Ed Davis. Real S&M is Fascism. Chances are that American Gays in the coming 1980s are in for a fantastically Fascistic bad time. Goodbye, glitter, and, hello, Anne Frank!

CABARET TO JULIA

Films find Fascism fashionable. *Cabaret* insightfully showed the easy seduction by Fascism when the handsome blond Nordic boy sang "Tomorrow Belongs to Me." This sequence detailed Fascism's bandwagon seduction as, on screen, face after face joined his rousing song. Director Bob Fosse's own filmic power seduced the American audience right into the spirit of the sunny beer-garden song, so that in movie houses everywhere audiences were shocked to find themselves so suddenly, so easily sucked into the thrill of what began as a gloriously innocent song and built to an impassioned Fascist anthem of the Master Race.

Julia, directed by Fred Zinnemann, more gently shows American dramatist Lillian Hellman (Jane Fonda) rescuing liberal Europeans from pre-World War II Fascism which eventually murders Julia herself (Vanessa Redgrave). Less delicately than *Cabaret* and *Julia*, the films of Lina Wertmueller such as *Seven Beauties* (1976) and the films of young Spanish director Fernando Arrabal— *Viva la Muerte* (1974) and *Guernica* 1976)—portray the grotesquely real S&M of Franco's Fascism under which Arrabal and the current generation of young Spaniards have grown up knowing the fact that gay men, like the gay poet/dramatist Federico Garcia Lorca, are shot up the ass with pistols because they are gay; the fact that Arrabal's own father is buried to the neck in sand so his head can be used by four horsemen as a polo ball; the fact that a woman shits on a male prisoner's face. In Wertmueller's *Beauties*, a Nazi She-Wolf performs shockingly cruel and scatological S&M inside a concentration camp. These are strong images meant to stir up strong audience reaction by these filmmakers. A moviemaker like Ken Russell, on the other hand, rolls singer Ann-Margret around in chocolate syrup in *Tommy* (1975), and this movie-brand of "pretend-shit" the audience of faint-hearts think is "just a wonderful camp."

SOME GUYS WON'T FACE TRUTH

So what has Fascism to do with Gay Americans in 1978? John Dos Passos, author of *USA Trilogy*, warned, "We will have Fascism in America, but we will call it Americanism." Bigots from Bryant to Briggs who wrap themselves in the flag and scream "family" are Americanists. Americanists do what Fascists did. Hitler burned books and censored radio. Germans were not allowed to see what they wanted to see nor say what they wanted to say. Americanist/Fascists always want other people, their victims, in tied-up situations.

Pasolini dared demonstrate this by literally tying up *Salo*'s victims, by literally gouging the eye (to symbolize you may not see what you wish), by cutting out the tongue (to symbolize you are not free to speak your opinion), by scalping the head (to symbolize you may not use your head according to the fashion of your own thoughts), by forcing one couple to make love on command (to symbolize you may not fuck except as ordered), by shooting an interracial pair of lovers (to symbolize you must not only procreate with your own kind, but you must also have passion for nothing but the Movement). And always, Fascism makes you eat its shit.

Americanist/Fascist "morality" will not allow gay people to see with the perspective of gay vision, nor stand up to speak out with opinion for gay human rights. Anita wants your eyes, your tongue, and like *Cuckoo's Nest* Nurse Ratched, she wants your balls. Dade County, remember, has "tied-up" gay housing. Add insult to injury: TV gouges your eyes, your ears, and your wallet with Anita's plastic face shilling the Orange Shit Juice Americanists/Fascists automatically swallow.

THE WIZARD OF OZ MEETS MUSSOLINI

Salo offers strong images to strengthen the viewer in his sequences "Circle of Obsessions" and "Circle of Shit." Pasolini was so aware of the horrors of his third section titled "Circle of Blood" that he softened the images by distancing the audience from the bloody action with a telephoto lens that gauzed out the edges. Sometimes assault is the only way to raise consciousness.

Throughout *Salo*, which is not salacious, Pasolini artfully staged his cautionary political warning at a gut-level. *Salo*'s images are contrived to get your attention. *Salo*'s message is to hold your interest. *Salo* is a political film in the anti-Fascist tradition of Gillo Pontecorvo's *Battle of Algiers* (1965) and Costa-Gavras' *Z* (1969) and *State of Siege* (1973).

Despite his serious message, Pasolini has the sense of humor to add the comic relief of a bunch of silly women dragged up in his film like Glinda the Good Witch, coming down the Hello-Dolly staircases telling their naughty, campy tales. But, he vehemently warns, behind their fashion lurks Fascism.

WHATEVER HAPPENED TO MGM MUSICALS?

Lots of gay men don't like real things. They hide in fantasy and ritual. They prefer life in a gay ghetto. They need nobody to cover their eyes and ears. On their own, they ostrich-like refuse to look or listen farther than their cocks can shoot. They miss Pasolini's value of using parallax gay vision in a twisted straight world.

Pier Paolo's images are strong. His message is clear: FASCISM IS COMING OUT OF ITS CLOSET, TOO. His film won't let us ignore it. He shakes us so bodily we want to turn away our faces from the screen. We may not emotionally like what we see; but, understanding his visionary point of view, we can intelligently distinguish and explain how what he films is not about our Ritual S&M, but about a real political-moral reality that, like something dreadful, this way comes.

GET THE PICTURE?

In defense of her own bizarre short stories' strong images, Flannery O'Connor wrote about people who have eyes and see not and ears and hear not: "To the almost deaf you have to shout; and to the almost blind, you have to write in very large letters."

Pasolini's death-cry, *Salo*, shouts very large.

III. Eyewitness Illustrations

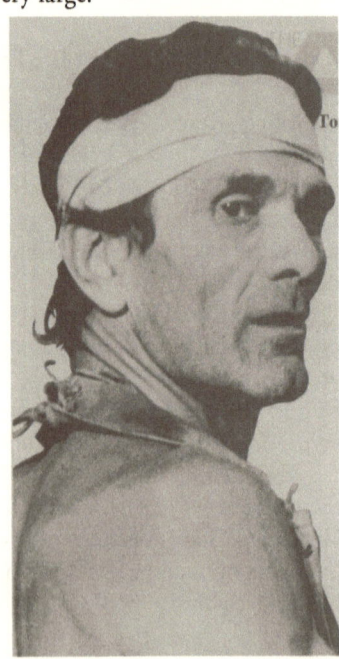

"Pier Paolo Pasolini," 1974, publicity photograph.

Drummer 20: Salo

Two publicity kit photographs from Pasolini's film *Salo* (1975). Six of them appeared in *Drummer* 20 (January 1978). Based on the book *The 120 Days of Sodom* by Marquis de Sade, *Salo* was directed by international filmmaker Pier Paolo Pasolini who, shortly after the release of *Salo*, was murdered, age fifty-three, on the beach at Ostia, near Rome, by the rough-trade hustler Pino Pelosi.

Movie ad, *New York Times*. On September 14, 1972, the startling Brazilian film *The Case of the Naves Brothers* (1967) had its quiet little American premiere at the Carnegie Hall Cinema. Director Luiz Sergio Person's grainy black-and-white *cinema verite* made the explicit torture of this brutal film a landmark in anti-government cinema. In the hardon helix between art and sex, *The Naves Brothers* enhanced the subtext and the actuality of real torture and S&M games played by some *Drummer* men. The *Naves* film, like its victims, has mysteriously disappeared.

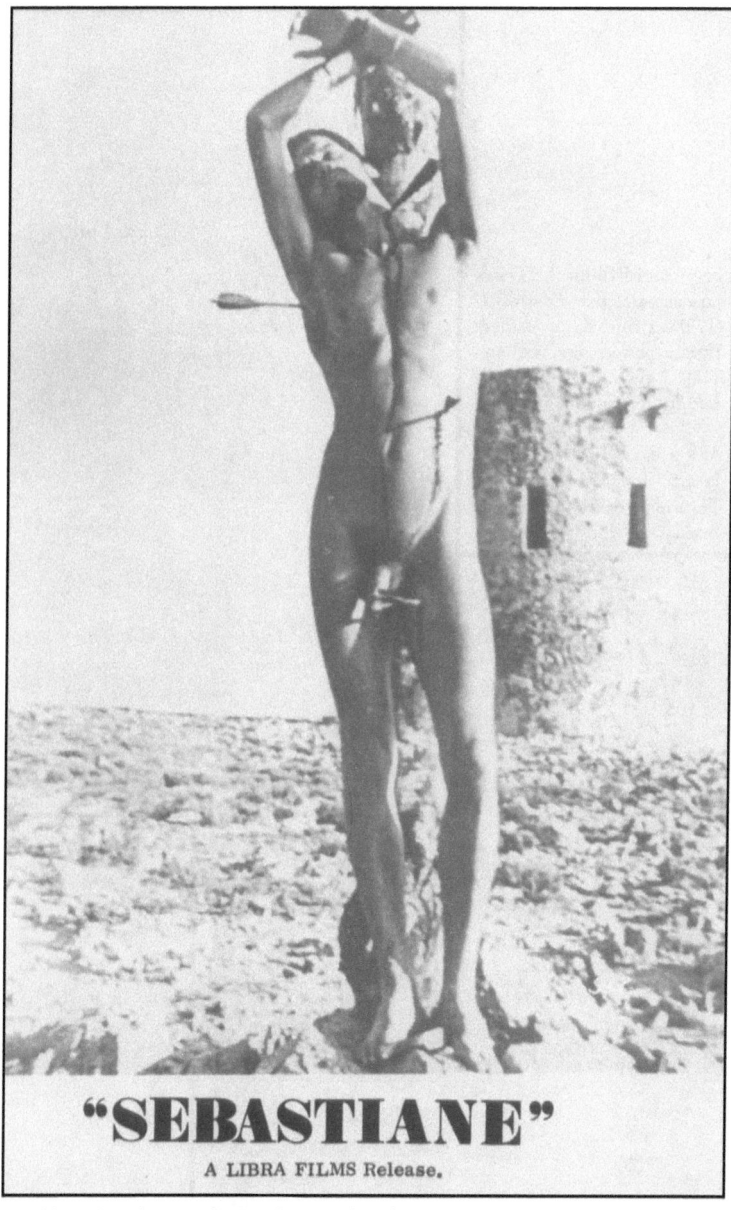

Publicity kit photograph. Derek Jarman's *Sebastiane* (1976) was the first gay S&M film to gain international notoriety with its Steve-Reeves-like spear-and-sandal story of gay icon Saint Sebastian tortured and killed by rough young Roman soldiers on the hot, burning desert sands of Sardinia—northwest of Ostia. The dialog of *Sebastiane* was in Latin with subtitles.

Pervy British filmmaker Derek Jarman directed *Edward II* (1991), a film about leathery Fascist power, gay sex, and Tilda Swinton. Premiere *Edward II* program.

At the same time, the dying Jarman designed the Queen's Theatre production of Samuel Beckett's *Waiting for Godot.*

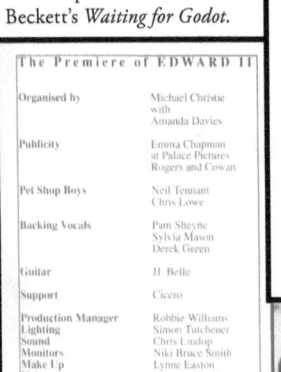

Drummer 20: Salo 621

At Fascist dictator Benito Mussolini's Foro Italico, Rome, each statue is twelve feet tall on a six-foot pedestal. "Statue of Boxer Primo Carnera #1," and "Statue of Primo Carnera #2." Photographs by Mark Hemry (2006) ©Mark Hemry. Inset: Statue of Primo Carnera on the cover of the first edition of *Some Dance to Remember: A Memoir-Novel of San Francisco 1970-1982*. Photograph by George Mott. ©George Mott

"Jack Fritscher," March 2006, Ostia Antica, the ancient cruising ground where Pasolini was murdered, and, top, "Ostia Antica." Photographs by Mark Hemry. ©Mark Hemry

Top: "Jumbo Jets Stream in Low over Ostia," the abandoned ancient "sea port" of Rome, to land nearby at the modern "air port" of Rome, March 2006. Photograph by Mark Hemry ©Mark Hemry. Bottom: "Mark Hemry," March 2006, Ostia Antica. Photograph by Jack Fritscher. ©Jack Fritscher

Captions: Eyewitness documentation of the existence of graphics providing internal evidence supporting Jack Fritscher's text are located in the Jack Fritscher and Mark Hemry GLBT History collection. Out of respect for issues of copyright, model releases, permissions, and privacy, some graphics are not available for publication at this time, but can be shown by appointment.

Eyewitness Illustration: DVD and book cover. In the 1970s, both the films and writing of right-wing Yukio Mishima and left-wing Pier Paolo Pasolini became required viewing and reading in the canon wars over establishing gay art and literature.

Eyewitness Illustration: Four DVD covers. After the Prague Spring of 1968, Fascists and Nazis invaded the popular culture of the 1970s. Franco reigned in Spain; Nixon ruled over Watergate; and the Vietnam war did not end until one month before the first issue of *Drummer*. Top: Fernando Arrabal's *Viva La Muerte*; Christopher Isherwood's *Berlin Stories* morphed into *I Am a Camera* and *Cabaret*; the underground grind-house "guilty pleasure" of *Drummer* readers was *Ilsa: She-Wolf of the SS*.

Gay Source: A Catalog for Men

> Written September-October 1977, this book review was published in *Drummer* 20, January 1978.
> I. Author's Eyewitness Historical-Context Introduction written July 25, 1996
> II. The book review as published in *Drummer* 20, January 1978
> III. Eyewitness Illustrations

I. Author's Eyewitness Historical-Context Introduction written July 25, 1996

This book review was written in tandem with my friend Bob Zygarlicki, a moustached blond with a wide-open and smiling face. As a very young part of the stable and salon around *Drummer*, he supported my editorial work with his writing and his photography. At first I had mentored him and his writing through my personal tutorial advertised in *Drummer* as "Writer's Aid" helping young authors get started in the emerging 1970s style of erotic magazine journalism. Other *Drummer* graduates of my "Writer's Aid" included—among some notables whose names I cannot reveal—Skip Navarette, John Trojanski, and Anthony DeBlase who became owner and publisher of *Drummer* in 1986. As Zygarlicki matured into the *Drummer* style, we worked together to produce several articles including a review of the bar, the I-Beam.

Like all publishers, including *The Advocate* founders, Dick Michaels and Bill Rand, who had six people writing under twenty-six pseudonyms, John Embry wanted to give the impression that *Drummer* was written by a boatload of talent. To satisfy Embry, I assigned this tandem review a solo byline crediting Bob Zygarlicki only.

As editor in chief, I performed as a constant and "serial ghostwriter" in *Drummer*.

Zygarlicki really existed, although few believed it.

On Folsom Street, my pals, including especially my longtime friend, Hank Diethelm, the founding owner of the Brig bar on Folsom Street, often made references to "Mr. Cigar Licky" and made jokes that my funny fetish pen name didn't fool anybody.

However, at the CMC Carnival 1978, I photographed a shirtless Bob Zygarlicki, wearing a black leather collar and chain, followed by his dark bearded partner Jack Wilburn; both sport dark glasses. I published the photograph in *Drummer* 26 (January 1979), on the bottom half of page 85. Zygarlicki also shot Wilburn for the cover of the "Virtual *Drummer*" magazine titled *Folsom*, issue #4 (1981).

II. The feature essay as published in *Drummer* 20, January 1978

Drummer Reads The Books

Gay Source: A Catalog for Men

Dennis Sanders
Berkeley Publishing Corporation New York, 1977

Conventional gay cruising areas like bars, parks, and public restrooms are currently declining in popularity as gay awareness opens alternate avenues of meeting. These days, everything from sports to church socials provide gay activities through which we can meet, cruise, and encounter legally and with dignity. An awareness of this trend appears to be the basic motivation of *Gay Source: A Catalog for Men,* compiled, written, and edited by Dennis Sanders who states in his Preface: "There is a broad, somewhat informal, but nevertheless highly functional network of businesses, communications, and services which have arisen in response to the needs of our great gay community."

Gay Source is a 290-page compilation of what is happening where within a sweeping variety of gay-oriented activities around the country. Topics covered range from the serious to the whimsical: arts to health to drugs to body awareness to fashions to legalities to religion to vacation paradises. Sanders prefaces each topic with an informative, and often entertaining, article detailing what the area is all about, followed by listings, descriptions, and up-to-date correspondence information for organizations, books, periodicals, and resources.

Sanders is upfront with giving *Gayellow Pages* [founded 1973] its due credit while explaining how the *Gay Source Catalog* has angled its useful perspective without duplicating *Gayellow Pages*' work. His preface explains his *Catalog*: it is for men; bars and retail businesses are excluded as are poetry and fiction listings while gay musical composers and theater are included. Where other directories provide information Sanders has chosen not to include, he lists them and recommends cross-reference. He has chosen a selection of fresh topics which "...will give a cross section of information, viewpoints, and areas of interest."

Twenty-eight writers, each credible in his own field, have been chosen to author the thirty-five succinct prefacing articles, many of which are reprints from a variety of national publications. Each article describes the history and the current state of each particular topic. Some articles offer insightful direction for the future. Others emphasize where more work is needed.

Sanders has chosen not to dwell on the oppression that gays face in the non-gay world, but rather to point out the amicable relationships that exist in many areas between the gay and non-gay worlds. *The Gay Source Catalog* emphasizes our human sameness rather than our sexual differences.

Sanders' energy shows in his detailed listings of the organizations, books, periodicals, and resources he has chosen for his catalog. In these lists, he presents thoroughly all appropriate information concerning the listing and then very objectively evaluates it from several different perspectives. He states why the one book chosen is the best available, supporting his evaluation with objective evidence. He never negates absolutely any listing. Whatever is included is obviously relevant and worthwhile.

As with any book of lists, none can ever be completely up-to-date. *Gay Source* works well even with this handicap; very few out-dated listings caught my eye. Sanders states that he was often disappointed by the lack of response from many businesses and organizations who neither provided or updated information. Within the listings, he offers alternative directories and publications to bridge this gap in up-to-date information.

Often *The Gay Source Catalog* contains interesting surprises: a history of "gay pirate buccaneer homosexuality" is detailed; a state-by-state summary of sodomy, indecent exposure, lewdness, solicitation, and disorderly conduct laws; a positive approach toward government assistance for gays. Many articles offer a "how-to-do" approach: how to publish your own book, how to pump-up in ten minutes without a gym, how to go about making the decision of "coming out" professionally, how to handle an arrest situation, how to choose a therapist, etc. Sanders' book takes a most positive descriptive approach of how things are, rather than a negative proscriptive attitude on how things should be.

Gay Source: A Catalog for Men is a sound investment for any gay man, no matter where he is geographically located. For those not having the freedom of gay interaction offered in larger U.S. cities, *Gay Source* is a practical and even necessary reference book for finding alternative means to meet and communicate with other gay men. For those of us surrounded by the freedom of The Big Time, *Gay Source* is still very good news.

III. Eyewitness Illustrations

Top: "CMC Carnival 1978," San Francisco. A shirtless Bob Zygarlicki, wearing a black leather collar and chain, is followed by his dark bearded partner Jack Wilburn; both sport dark glasses in *Drummer* 26 (January 1979). Photograph by Jack Fritscher. ©Jack Fritscher. Bottom: "Jack Wilburn" on the cover of the "Virtual *Drummer*" magazine titled *Folsom* (#4, 1981). Photograph by Bob Zygarlicki. ©Bob Zygarlicki

WRITER'S AID
P.O. BOX 31730
DIAMOND HEIGHTS STATION
SAN FRANCISCO, CALIFORNIA 94131

Dear Author:

WRITER'S AID works with authors professionally and personally. We frankly assess the pluses and problems of your writing. We suggest changes gently. We encourage your strengths realistically. Because we truly care about your sensitivity and talent, we respectfully pull no punches in suggesting the ways you want your writing to improve. Writer's Aid promotes good writing by good writers.

FICTION OR FEATURE ARTICLES

No matter the length, your short stories or feature articles receive:

- o a basic critique of both your content and your style
- o a light editing for a more polished readability
- o suggestions on manuscript presentation: how to please an editor's eye
- o recommendations for placing your manuscript with the proper editor at an appropriate publication.

Fiction or feature rates: up to 1,500 words/6 pages $15
up to 3,000 words/12 pages $20
up to 6,000 words/24 pages $25

A double-spaced typed manuscript averages 250 words per page.

Longer fiction or non-fiction manuscripts are individually and reasonably negotiated upon query with sample chapters or sections.

POETRY

Your poetry receives the same thorough and frank critique, light editing, placement recommendations, and manuscript presentation suggestions as the fiction and feature articles.

Poetry rates: 7 poems (up to 30 lines each) $15.
Add $1 for each poem after 7.

Longer poetry manuscripts negotiated upon query and sample.

OTHER LITERARY SERVICES

Through heavy editing, rewriting, or complete ghosting, WRITER'S AID will work your research, notes, or rough draft into a marketable manuscript. WRITER'S AID has helped authors with manuscript sales ranging from religious to erotic publications, from small literary magazines to professional journals. Query with particulars: any subject, any medium.

Always keep a copy of your manuscripts. Photocopy submission to WRITER'S AID, as well as to editors, is acceptable practice. Although we handle your manuscripts precisely and professionally, we cannot be responsible for their loss or damage. Always enclose a self-addressed stamped envelope-- with sufficient postage--for the speedy return of your edited manuscript.

Sincerely,

Flyer for "Writer's Aid." Working to grow new writers for *Drummer*, editor in chief Fritscher offered an ongoing tutorial through *Drummer* (see *Drummer 26*) to coach authors during the immense learning curve of the first decade after Stonewall when few knew how to write, edit, or sell an erotic story or article. The fees were $15, $20, and $25 per story.

ceiling. Other gear I have adapted for sexplorations includes horse thigh warmers which make great padded bondage belts; a rubber bite which makes a comfortable gag; reins which make wonderful whips (flexible like ropes and just like an extension of your hand); saddle strings good for bondage as they are wider and thicker than the thongs on sale in most bars and S/M stores; horse brushes I love to brush down men with lots of body hair as I would a prize pet. Also good for getting things out of hair, such as wax and other nasties.

Some common equipment that you are likely to find at flea markets include lineman's belts, boots, harnesses, tree-climbing gear, rubber suits; parachute harness, hand and hand-held vibrators; weights, pulleys, belts, and wood/metal boxes for toy storage. Occasionally you find someone who has to sell their leather and toy collection. When the rich get bored or married, you can get beautiful whips and leather accessories at minimal cost.

And if you keep your eyes open you can find special items that are one-of-a-kind. I found some spears that are made with bamboo shafts and wood or metal tips. With someone else to play a hand drum that I keep in my playroom, I use the spears in a sensual/sexual exploration trip with my bottom. The point is to create a different reality where all the normal rules, regulations and behavior patterns do not apply. With the right person, it leads to a jungle/aborigine/canabalism fantasy.

Good hunting and remember— WE ARE EACH OTHER'S RESOURCES. Hope to hear from you. Until the next time— from the EDGE OF MADNESS.

Sample page of typed manuscript submitted to *Drummer* (1978). Handwritten marks and comments are edits made by Jack Fritscher who as a professional editor since 1957 polished nearly every page in late 1970s *Drummer*, including the draft manuscript of John Preston's *Mr. Benson*.

CMC Carnival
The World's Best Annual Gay Party

> Written November 27, 1977, the first feature article was published in *Drummer* 20, January 1978.
> I. Author's Eyewitness Historical-Context Introduction written December 29, 2002
> II-A. The first feature essay as published in *Drummer* 20, January 1978
> II-B. Written November 26, 1978, the second feature essay as published in *Drummer* 26, January 1979
> III. Eyewitness Illustrations

I. Author's Eyewitness Historical-Context Introduction written December 29, 2002

How the CMC Carnival Became the Folsom Street Fair
The Role of Photography in the Psychology of Leather and
the Image of Homomasculine-Identified Gay Men

My first feature article about the CMC Carnival (1977) was written November 27, 1977, and was published in *Drummer* 20 (January 1978) with seventeen photographs shot by "David Sparrow and Jack Fritscher."

My second feature about the CMC Carnival (1978) was written November 26, 1978, the Sunday before the Monday Harvey Milk and Mayor Moscone were assassinated; it was published in *Drummer* 26 (January 1979) with thirteen photographs shot by "David Sparrow and Jack Fritscher." The second article appears again in proper serial order with the contents of *Drummer* 26 in *Gay San Francisco: Eyewitness Drummer.*

In *Drummer* 20, my second issue edited fully under my byline, I wrote my first of two essays about the annual bacchanalian saturnalia, the CMC Carnival, hosted by the California Motor Club. (Not "California Motorcycle Club.") In the first report, I celebrated that long-running San Francisco party *cum* orgy as if it would never end.

Things fall apart. Things fell apart.

A year and six issues after that first article in 1977, and mere days after the CMC Carnival in 1978, Harvey Milk and George Moscone were assassinated on November 27, 1978.

That was the day the Titanic 70s first scraped the first cube of the iceberg.

Months before the November 1978 CMC Carnival, we all knew the party was about to be uprooted. Fielding our sense of loss because the host site, Seaman's Hall, was for sale, I wrote my lamentation "CMC 1978" for *Drummer* 26 one day before the Moscone-Milk assassinations. "Everything must change," I quoted Judy Collins. "Nothing stays the same."

I did not know that the next day I would be writing another kaddish essay for the very same *Drummer* 26 titled "Harvey Milk and Gay Courage." In my opening I keened:

> Less than two hours ago, San Francisco supervisor Harvey Milk was shot to death, reportedly by an ex-cop. Two years ago, I watched that ex-cop, Dan White, stripped to the waist and out to prove himself one more time, in his last Golden Gloves bout." (For a dramatized description of Dan White boxing at the Golden Gloves, see *Some Dance to Remember*, Reel 1, Scene 16.)

My recitation of how tragedy looked like a curse on minorities continued:

> Two months ago, Milk returned home from his supervisorial duties to find that his lover, Jack Lira, a Latino in his twenties, had hanged himself after taping the paperback of the TV miniseries, *Holocaust*, to the door. The Jew cut the Latino down and held the dead boy while the WASP media watched for a crack in Milk's composure. Lira's suicide served rather to firm up Milk's personal resolve to campaign heavily against California's anti-gay Prop 6, which Dan White, a recognized homophobe, apparently supported. Milk's Prop 6 victory three weeks ago [in the November election] was his last.

Several paragraphs later, I added in the even more personal:

> *Drummer*'s David Sparrow [my lover] was in City Hall at the time of the shooting. Within minutes, Harvey's body, shot twice in the head and three times in the chest, was wheeled past Sparrow and out to the coroner's office.

My last paragraph was an explanation of my intent as editor in chief:

> *Drummer* is dedicated to fun, fantasy, and fetish. But between the lines lies some social conscience, or, at least, we like to think, some recording of our gay social history.

That recording of gay history was what—the day before the killings—I had been writing about: the onrushing end of the CMC Carnival which was being ousted from the San Francisco Seaman's Hall.

Like the seventeen photographs of CMC for *Drummer* 20, the thirteen documentary photographs in *Drummer* 26, pages 82-85, were shot by my domestic lover of ten years, David Sparrow, and me dba "Photos by David Sparrow." We featured our *Drummer* cover man Mike Glassman aka "Big Mack Macker" who became the Colt model Ed Dinakos. In my ongoing credit and byline war with publisher Embry, both of my CMC articles (text and photos) were credited on the contents page solely to David Sparrow. The signature style of writing clearly identifies authorship even without byline.

THE CMC & THE SLOT

The first bike club to be officially incorporated in California was the CMC on April 15, 1963. The California Motor Club (not "Motorcycle") was organized at 111 Gilbert Street, San Francisco, in a warehouse used by Jack Haines' father to clean used refrigerators and stoves. Its industrial atmosphere made for a perfect clubhouse. The idea of the club was Jack Haines' and another man, currently unnameable, as he is allegedly still in Mexico waiting for the statute of limitations to run out on whatever he has been accused of doing.

The CMC had nothing to do with Jack Haines' two other ventures. Jack Haines was also one of the first celebrants of fisting in San Francisco in 1960; he brought the ritual from Los Angeles to his acolyte in San Francisco, Tony Tavarossi. He was also the founding owner of Fe-Be's and the legendary Slot Hotel, the crystal palace, which seemed sprung from the mind of T. S. Eliot whose J. Alfred Prufrock was describing the Slot when he whispered on about "certain half-deserted streets," about "restless nights in one-night cheap hotels," and about being "etherized upon a table."

"Oh, Baby, never ask, 'What is it?' on your visit! You may not be able to handle it." —Jack Fritscher, "Leather's Founding Daddies," "Rear-View Mirror," *Drummer* 129 (June 1989)

Beginning in 1966, the annual CMC Carnival was the main leather event of the autumn. The reason the Seaman's Hall stopped renting to the CMC Carnival was because the once-small event had grown to a mob scene, always orderly, but huge, and sexual, with the first-floor parking area turned into a pissoir of wild sex on drugs celebrated by thousands of men in leather.

I think the CMC chose Seaman's Hall, 350 Fremont Street, South of Market as a gayification of Ken Kesey's throwing his successful "Acid Test" parties in San Francisco venues such as the Longshoremen's Hall in North Beach in 1966. So many of us from South of Market attended Merry Prankster Kesey's "Acid Test" happenings at the Fillmore that it seemed a natural progression when acid—versions of LSD—became the basic drug for mind-expanding gay sex. At the Barracks bath, for instance, an "office" water-cooler burbling with free Kool-Aid mixed with Owsley acid often stood in the lobby—especially on holidays like July 4, Halloween, Christmas eve, and New Year's eve—with tiny white-paper cups for anyone who wanted a hit.

At the CMC Carnival, the mix of men and drugs and open-mindedness was so rich that a man's life could be changed, revolutionized, and transmorphed in a moment. At the CMC Carnival in November 1977, an LA bodybuilder named Dan Dufort tripped me so we could fall into each other's leather arms, and, although he and I after an initial affair turned out to be a lifelong friends rather than sexmates, he months later introduced me to the championship bodybuilder Jim Enger who became my lover for twenty-eight months while I was editor in chief of *Drummer*. In turn I introduced Enger, who ennobled my writing in *Drummer*, to my bicoastal lover Mapplethorpe who found it absolutely necessary to photograph the drop-dead blond physique champion. Life happened and art happened, and *Drummer* happened, because of the CMC melee which was the tip of the Titanic 1970s.

For details on how I directed and staged our on-location CMC photographs for *Drummer*, see the volume titled *The Drummer Salon* in this series *Gay San Francisco: Eyewitness Drummer*.

The CMC Carnival was such a representative and "high leather ritual event" that *Drummer* 3 (November 1975) bragged on page 46 that cover man Val Martin, star of the films, *Boys in the Sand* (1971), *Sextool* (1975), and *Born to Raise Hell* (1975), was voted "Mr. Leather" at the Hawks' annual Leather Sabbath in Hollywood, and would be representing *Drummer* and "the Southern California Leather community at the even larger CMC Carnival in San Francisco in November." Surfing a wave of homomasculine popularity, Val Martin also appeared as "Renso" on all thirty-six pages of *Impact 1* (1974), a Ramon Publication, and in the one-

Drummer 20: CMC Carnival

issue magazine, *Born to Raise Hell* (1975), a *Drummer* Publication of stills from the film directed by Roger Earl and produced by Terry LeGrand.

In the zero degrees of separation, Mark Hemry and I, traveling on location in Europe with Roger Earl and Terry LeGrand, spent the summer of 1989, the last summer of West Berlin, shooting—up against the Berlin Wall in leather bars like the Knast—six video features for their *Bound for Europe* series which was the sequel to their *Dungeons of Europe Trilogy*. In LA, Val Martin was a business partner with my pal, Dick Saunders, owner of the throbbing Probe disco chronicled in the Richard Gere film, *American Gigolo* (1980). Val Martin died April 13, 1985.

In 1978 when Al Shapiro, John Embry, and I handpicked Val Martin, he became, by our appointment and not by contest, our first Mr. *Drummer*. For details of Val Martin featured on four *Drummer* covers and in many centerfolds, including my forty photographs of Val Martin with Bob Hyslop in *Drummer* 31 (September 1979), see in this *Gay San Francisco* series, the volume titled *The Drummer Salon*.

In my 1977 and 1978 articles on the CMC, I did not detail the Fellini-Jarman-Pasolini sexual *mise en scene* of the "Louis XIV" Carnival, because back in the 1970s everyone took the wild accessibility of surreal sex in public places for granted. The news story was not the "wet, escalating group-sex-on-drugs," but the hard-knock realism that the straight corporate world was getting its fingers into the underground gay world that up till then had been so outlaw that corporations had no way of making money off it. (Except for the Mafia.) Having dismissed and ignored the CMC Carnival as a silly gay event, suddenly the Seaman's Hall management, and the City of San Francisco, both woke up and began to increase the rental rate for the building and demand insurance coverage for the sex event. Insurance coverage was one of the reasons that our Pacific Drill Patrol, San Francisco's first uniform club (founded 1972), stopped throwing our annual uniform orgy parties as early as 1975. The concern about the orgy being fun turned into worry about assumption of risk: "What if somebody falls down the elevator shaft?"

I am connecting historical dots of real conversations.

The demise of the CMC Carnival evolved into the Folsom Street Fair. However, it was not until five years after the annual CMC Carnival went out of business in 1979 that the Folsom Street Fair began in 1984. That first Folsom Fair was organized by native San Franciscan, leatherman Michael S. Valerio, who was also the Folsom Fair's first executive director. Valerio died of AIDS at age forty; his memorial was January 15, 1995; and his obituary was in *Drummer* 182.

Entering into gay pop culture where the CMC left off, the Folsom Street Fair, meant to be a leather alternative to the ten-year-old vanilla

Castro Street Fair founded by Harvey Milk in August 1974, did not become a wildly popular international draw until the dying time of the late 1980s brought 100,000 men out into the streets. In the way that David Sparrow and I had historicized the CMC Carnival in the 1970s with hundreds of photographs and with my reporting in *Drummer*, Mark Hemry and I began shooting our Palm Drive Video documentaries of the Folsom Fair in 1984 when the crowds in the street—mostly local leather-bar types—were quite small.

What is interesting to see in our chronicles of these street documentaries is how, as the years go by, the Folsom Street Fair crowd evolves in numbers, attitude, and intensity. Every three years, or so, the videos show a generational change in the tenor of the homomasculine leather look, even though, over-all, the iconic look of a defined muscular man in chaps and stripped to the waist wearing a chest harness, his skin tanned like a saddle, remains virtually unchanged. The strangest Folsom Street Fair we shot was two weeks after 9-11 when restricted air travel shrank the somber crowd to only the bravest souls. By 2002, the gay leather crowd was being morphed by straights pushing baby strollers while ogling men and women being whipped for AIDS charities by Peter Fiske and the 15 Association.

I mention this to show the documentary value of what an eyewitness *Drummer* was in its photographic images: reflexive of real readers in the 1970s before video changed *Drummer* photography into an album of video porn stars in the 1980s.

The sociological value of our video street documentaries, shot not helter-skelter, but with a big-game hunter's disciplined and controlled point of view, is that they collect outside in the sunlight the actual faces and bodies of men who are usually only seen under the dim red lights of leather bars. The value of daylight events like the CMC Carnival and street fairs such as Folsom Street Fair and Castro Street Fair is the ability to check out, document, and analyze that part of the gay population that only comes out at night, exhibitionistically wearing gear and get-ups usually only worn at night. The Folsom Street Fair is the libidinous gay homomasculine Id parading itself proudly. Mark Hemry and I pro-actively capture diverse images ranging from trophy gods to sexy trolls, because beauty is in the eye, as well as in the "fast-forward" and "freeze frame" of the ultimate beholder cruising the Folsom Fair from his couch.

Shooting the CMC Carnival and shooting the Folsom Street Fair, or any large group of gay men, is a real test of an analytic photographer's steel—and theory. As one photographer among the hundred who filled *Drummer,* may I explain my work regarding what as editor in chief I thought *Drummer* needed. I even asked Mapplethorpe to do the same when I cast his *Drummer* 24 cover. In all my photography, my camera style reflects my psychology. My angle anchors my point of view for the viewer. I cannot be detached and aloof from the subject because I must heat up the viewer to connect to the subject. That's my job. This is not just documentary; it's erotic documentary. I must become the viewer. I must turn his ignition to engage his willing suspension of disbelief that occurs when the viewer becomes his voyeurism—and his head and his heart and his cock leap up and become one with the screen.

My photography is the same as my erotic writing: intentionally interactive. In my erotic art theory, on page and on screen, my aim—using standard literary devices—is to connect with the readers or viewers in a way that causes them to experience orgasm.

I like my art on page and screen to start in men's heads and work its way down.

That connectivity is what I hope distinguishes me as an artist who is a writer and a photographer from the other artists—the gay-genre writers—who are my unthawable peers, but don't, won't, can't compose orgasmic erotica. I mean writers, for instance (and this critique is not meant as a pot shot), like the Violet Quill book club of Edmund White, Andrew Holleran, Felice Picano, and all the usual suspects who are the pale darlings of the increasingly bourgeois and totally corporate mega-business of the gay establishment made up of professional homosexuals. Who of them was writing, and publishing erotica, popular or literary, back in the Titanic 70s when wide-open gay liberation would have allowed them to experiment any way they were clever enough to pioneer? I would have welcomed any of them into *Drummer*, but none of them was far enough along in his writing skills to pen erotica—or ballsy enough, perhaps, to come out of the closet as authors of eros. As an objective correlative of this sniffy 1970s attitude, I offer that it took until the twenty-first century for the *Lambda Book Report* to dare grant a Lammy Award to—eek!—an erotic book.

Writing is a solitary act and art. Photography is a cooperative act and art. One has to be sensitive to the men being photographed out in public, who because they are being outrageous in public, become newsworthy, and the more outrageous they dress or act, the more newsworthy they become. Sometimes they do not know this legal distinction. Public behavior determines whether or not a person can be photographed in public. The only two restrictions for such photographs is that in the photograph or caption the subject is not ridiculed, and that the subject shot in public is not used for advertising. A street documentary photographer must be ready to handle any response—including a punch in the face.

I have a relentless camera. As an artist, I have to have. To get meaningful footage that is not the kind of "tourist footage" that most video cameras shoot at Folsom Fair, one must be, well, actually, truly relentless and fearless of rejection—just like "cruising for sex." I try to reinvent the public image of gay men with each shoot. How can I best present what is best about what they have done to themselves? I have to think my way into camera moments that tourist photographers coast through on autopilot.

The posed "snapshot" photo of three or four shirtless gay guys lined up, arms around shoulders, may be Whitmanesque, but it is an unfortunate tourist-camera "take" on street-fair and pride-parade photography precisely because it is posed. Maybe I'm too Weegee or too paparazzo, but a good photographer does not interrupt a man being natural and ask him to pose and grin for a picture.

Not only must the sensitivity of the subjects about the camera be considered, but their sex-appeal for the viewers must be instantly judged: are they hot, and how can I suck that heat into the camera so it warms the viewer alone in an apartment on a winter night. All the while the "clock" is also ticking on the shoot. The Folsom Street Fair rises like Brigadoon for five hours one Sunday once a year. Actually, fewer than four men in all these years have said, "No. Stop!" when I was shooting.

The ideal shot is to take candid footage of men simply "being." The next most ideal is to shoot cooperative footage of performance art, such as men being walked on all fours as dogs, set-scenes of intricate Japanese bondage, whippings, wrestling, boot-polishing, and displays of huge silicone-enlarged penises. When appropriate, I communicate with the subject I'm shooting by smiling, or while I'm shooting, with hand gestures that indicate "A-OK" or "thumbs up" or a hand gesture that obviously means "keep giving me more of the same." Also, I either say or mouth the words "Thank you."

The placement of the camera is as important on the street as it is in a studio video. Most videos are shot from a camera held on the cliche of a shoulder. I spend a lot of time at the Folsom Fair actually creating shots instantaneously so the angle will erotically interpret what I see to shoot, by both moving the camera itself intimately in on body parts, as well as falling to my knees, shooting up at the men who are enlarged and heroized and empowered by that angle. Guys "get" it that it's empowering when I kneel before them in a position of seeming subservience, reverence, and worship, but...it's not personal. After all, I'm winning. I've got the camera and the footage forever.

My camera goes where the viewer would like to put his eyes and nose.

I'm also kneeling for a diversity of home viewers cruising the Folsom Fair from their lounging recliner chairs. In actuality, I am totally anonymous on the street, because I wear a hat as protection from the blazing sun, and the video camera covers two-thirds of my face, and I am just one of thousands of cameras shooting every which way. All this combines to give me the leeway, like a hunter in a duck blind, to imprint the documentary with my own point of view, which, after thirty years of feedback from readers and viewers fairly understands the market of gay erotic taste.

While my camera seeks out archetypal leathermen, musclemen, fetish men, bears, and cigar smokers, the context around them reveals the Sisters of Perpetual Indulgence and other GLBT types also in attendance. This collection of homomasculine archetypes is for me the erotic documentary point: to capture the essence of "Folsom" at the Folsom Street Fair the way, for twenty-two years I captured quintessential males for *Drummer*. I confess I love these intensely interesting men who dare to put their sexuality out so publicly. My relentless camera is my post-HIV attempt to save them all for posterity, to have them all on digital video to admire forever.

Years from now when there is a gay satellite network streaming 24/7 programming to the Space Shuttle and Mars and beyond, my promise as a cameraman to these men I've shot will come true: "Want to become immortal?"

Sometimes, after editing the footage, and sitting back and watching an hour of all these men montaged together, I can only admire the Fellini-thon of men that gay culture offers to western civilization as an alternative to traditional ways of being a quiescently frozen male.

The journalism of this *Drummer* article on the CMC Carnival? And the video documentaries of Folsom Fair?

This work is all about storing documentary words and images in a time capsule.

After all, the final thirty years of the twentieth century were host to the first generation after Stonewall. That era was populated by men who grew up in closets and secrecy. Back then, all of us continued on in amazement that cameras finally were allowed in to chronicle the public image of a culture that once had dare not record more than one or two Polaroids of itself.

In 1969, a camera in a gay bar started a stampede to escape out the exits. At the end of 1999, a camera at a gay event makes men ready for their close-up.

Actually, I think one street South of Market should be renamed "*Drummer* Way" or "Leather Lane." (What a photo opportunity for tourists!) It must intersect Folsom Street between 6th Street and 12th Street. It need be no longer than one short block like Dore Alley or Hallam Close where the Barracks Baths once lit up the SoMa night and then burned down. Because gay culture traditionally has been so much a street culture, this is a significant way to rename an existing street or, while remodeling the grid of SoMa, to create a new mews to acknowledge all the style and character that *Drummer* culture and leather culture have introduced to San Francisco. From *Drummer* to Foucault (who tested his "power" philosophy on hot fists late night South of Market), such a dedicated street name is as legitimate as renaming other San Francisco streets representing the contributions of Martin Luther King, Jr., Cesar Chavez, and Harvey Milk and his main competitor, Jose Sarria.

My "Berserker" description in the last paragraph is one of the first public definitions of the homomasculine look of the yet-to-emerge bear community.

II-A. The feature essay as published in *Drummer* 20, January 1978

Always Remember November...

The CMC Carnival 1977
The World's Best Annual Gay Party

New York, New York, hardly knows what it misses every November when San Francisco hosts the CMC Carnival. The annual autumn bash for Viking-like Berserkers at the Seaman's Hall began modestly a decade ago as a charity bazaar and has immodestly grown bizarre enough to be A Major Event of the West Coast Season. Multiple charter busses ferry LA-landers to the party, and San Franciscans prefer the November CMC at Seaman's to October's Halloween in the streets.

IS IT RICH? IS IT RARE?

Some guys think the CMC Carnival is overcrowded: two floors of booths, beer, and 10,000 bodies. CMC addicts, on the other hand, get off on the press of flesh, the long lines to the outdoor Port-a-Sans, the straight security cops staring into midspace as if they see stand-up orgies for thousands every Sunday afternoon.

SOME ON THE GROUND

The first floor of booths peddles food, drink, leather codpieces, T-shirts, amyl, and games of chance. Wandering among the predominately

Drummer 20: CMC Carnival

leather crowd are the year's *muy macho* contenders for Mr. CMC whose nomination may be determined by his looks, but whose winning is decided by the cash he raises for charity. They glad-hand with genuine friendliness, climb good naturedly up on stage to rousing cheers at their lengthy charms, pumped chests, and cleft chins. The crowd by 4 PM is shoulder to shoulder, peeling off layers of leather, unable to move more than five feet in ten minutes.

SOME IN MID-AIR

Some guys meet, marry, consummate, and divorce all in one glorious CMC Sunday afternoon. For men more adventurous, the lower-level disco orgy teaches the Funk and Wagnalls truth that *carnival* means "a celebration of meat." Performing on your knees on top of a cement floor, piled three-feet-deep with beer cans, makes walking on water an easy trick. Dancers dance and a sucker is always a sucker. The only hitch in the crush is getting back up from your knees to your feet. If ever a man fantasized about his face surrounded by a dozen loaded groins, and a lot of chest-to-chest action, then there is no mall to maul him nearly so good as the CMC carnival.

SEND IN THE CLOWNS

So, New York! Book all of Manhattan onto your charter flight for next November. CMC Carnival is a date not to be missed. Mark it firmly on your *Drummer* Calendar of Autumn Events.

Proper Berserkers are mighty of stature, hairy of face and body, generously thewed and sinewed. Their interest is not war but battle. In time of peace, they sharpen their wits and mend their scanty battle harness. They are inclined to drink. Experienced Berserkers are able to transform themselves entirely into animals. Wise Berserkers provide themselves with wooden shields covered in leather, for it is their custom to chew upon the rims as they wait for battle. Metal shields do great damage to teeth and gums. Berserkers' spit is thought to be more corrosive than most. If not paid attention to, Berserkers show interest in little, except becoming werewolves.

II-B. The feature essay as published in *Drummer* 26, January 1979

Lost Our Lease.
Everyone Must Go...

Seaman's Semen's End
CMC Carnival 1978

Everything must change. Nothing, not even the California Motor Club (CMC) Carnival stays the same. So give us an *OI*! Give us a *VAY*! Gone are the CMC's of yesterday!

This season's bash at San Francisco's Seaman's Hall was the last ever in that sanctified location. And the change of place will inevitably change everything. Remember how London Bridge changed when moved to the U.S. southwest? Un-believable! Remember how you changed when you moved your ass out of your cedar-lined closet in whatever Cedar Rapids or Cedar Falls? Even more un-believable.

NO MORE MR. CMC?

The CMC Carnival, like every good show, must go on. After all, some events become institutions that resonate with an importance beyond themselves. Think of the Super Bowl. Think of the Academy Awards. Some events start out ordinary and end up as annual tribal rituals. The CMC Carnival, with proceeds donated to charity, plays in this league. The show must go, but shouldn't the show go on?

So where? Seaman's two floors of wall-to-wall wet, leathered bodies was the perfect ritual ground. The Cow Palace next? Too big–unless we either start to propagate or start to recruit. Somewhere there's a place for us.

Meanwhile, just keep clapping your hands and believing so Mr. CMC will continue to live.

FISTING FOR DOLLARS

In one wild aberration even in wild San Francisco, several carnivals ago, one inventive booth offered a willing ass propped up and ready to go (for charity, remember!) at 50¢ per fist. Now, THAT'S entertainment!

Some CMC veterans may blush to remember, but any group up front enough to sponsor a bash that turned from a simple beer bust into one of the world's wildest standup encounter groups, not only can't be bad at all, but must make sure their charity show goes on and on and on. CMC forever! No matter where!

III. Eyewitness Illustrations

Top: "CMC Bike Run, Saturday Night Drag Show," mimicking the "Willkommen" Tiller Girls from *Cabaret*, Rainier Creek, California, July 4, 1972. Photograph by Jack Fritscher. ©Jack Fritscher. Bottom: "Jack Fritscher with David Delay," owner of the Ambush bar, CMC Bike Run, Rainier Creek, California, July 4, 1972. Photograph shot by poet Ronald Johnson, manager of the No Name bar, with Jack Fritscher's camera. ©Jack Fritscher. Years later, Fritscher shot stills and video of David Delay in the high-concept title, *Daddy's Beerbelly in Bondage*, for Palm Drive Video from which a photograph of Delay was published full-page in *Drummer* 119 (July 1988).

"Dan Dufort," 1977. Photograph by Jack Fritscher. ©Jack Fritscher. At the CMC Carnival 1977, Dan Dufort introduced himself to Fritscher, and then in August 1978 introduced Fritscher to his friend, bodybuilder Jim Enger. As a model, Dufort appeared several times in *Drummer*, including *Drummer* 22 (May 1978).

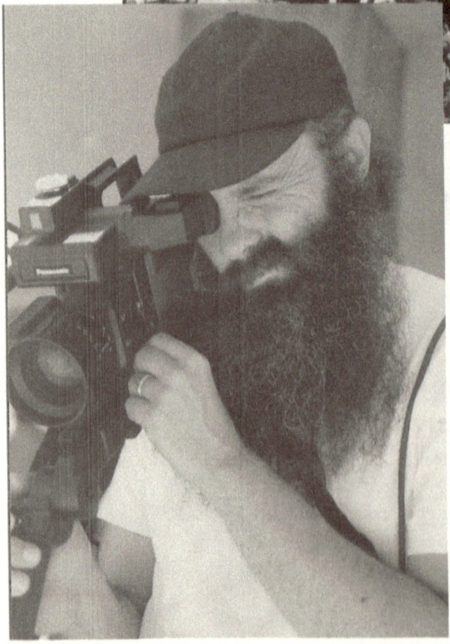

Middle: "Jack Fritscher and Mark Hemry, West Berlin, 1989." In the zero degrees of separation in the *Drummer* salon, Fritscher and Hemry, traveling on location in Holland and Germany with Roger Earl and Terry LeGrand, spent summer 1989, the last summer of West Berlin, shooting—up against the Berlin Wall in leather bars like the Knast—six video features for the Earl-LeGrand *Bound for Europe* series which was the sequel to their *Dungeons of Europe Trilogy*. Left: "Jack Fritscher, Bearded with Camera," filming documentary of the Folsom Street Fair, 1994. Photograph by Mark Hemry. ©Mark Hemry

Manhattanization destroyed gay South of Market leather culture that gay men dubbed *SoMa* in 1977. On January 24, 2008, Seaman's Hall, 350 Fremont Street, the hallowed site of the annual CMC Carnival and orgy, stood waiting for the wrecking ball in the shadow of the first new skyscrapers being built exactly where in the 1970s the A-Z List of leathermen made drop-dead entrances and exits on its terrazzo stairs. It was at the 1978 CMC Carnival that the threesome of art director Al Shapiro, publisher John Embry, and editor in chief Jack Fritscher personally handpicked Val Martin as the first Mr. *Drummer*. Referred to as "Seaman's Hall" by the joking leather crowd, 350 Fremont was a Marine Labor Union building that in 1980 was bought by the Brotherhood of the Sea, Seafarers International Union, SIU AFL-CIO. At that time, the CMC Carnival had to leave 350 Fremont. Photographs by Mark Hemry. ©Mark Hemry

Captions: Eyewitness documentation of the existence of graphics providing internal evidence supporting Jack Fritscher's text are located in the Jack Fritscher and Mark Hemry GLBT History collection. Out of respect for issues of copyright, model releases, permissions, and privacy, some graphics are not available for publication at this time, but can be shown by appointment.

Eyewitness Illustration: Two photographs. Jim Enger, a beau ideal behind 1970s *Drummer*, on stage (1979) winning one of his several bodybuilding champion titles. Enger was drawn by Domino and Tom of Finland (cover, *Olympus* #6, Colt Studio). Both public Enger photographs by Jack Fritscher. ©Jack Fritscher

Night Flight 1977

> Written January 6, 1978, this feature essay was published in *Drummer* 20, January 1978.
> I.   Author's Eyewitness Historical-Context Introduction written April 17, 2002
> II. The feature essay as published in *Drummer* 20, January 1978
> III. Eyewitness Illustrations

I. Author's Eyewitness Historical-Context Introduction written April 17, 2002

How the Happening Movement Became the Circuit Party

Before there was the White Party and the Black Party and the gay circuit parties, there was *Night Flight*. Into my feature essay in *Drummer* 20, I slipped the subliminal of the bittersweet sense of both *carpe diem* and *sic transit gloria mundi* that permeated life in the Titanic 70s when everything was so good we knew it couldn't last.

Drummer was always late going to press, and was always behind in the number of issues. *Drummer* was the monthly magazine that was never monthly. When *Drummer* died after twenty-four years, there should have been around 300 issues and there were barely 200 issues. Basically, one-third of *Drummer*'s monthly "energy and schedule" was eaten by the very grinding up of the talent and money and production that is part of the creative process. If only we all could have worked harder, faster, with adequate budgets and salaries paid on time by cheapskate *Drummer* publishers, and with less censorship from right-wing printers, and with no gay politics!

I tried to make each monthly issue of *Drummer* respond to gay pop culture as topically as a weekly newspaper.

I loved the pop-culture mixed-media concept of *Night Flight*. I saw it as part of what in the 1950s Claes Oldenburg, Jack Kerouac, and longtime lovers John Cage and Merce Cunningham named the "Happening Movement" wherein anti-narrative theatrics and nonconformist performances were staged in unexpected locations and required audience participation. In terms of my editing and writing the contents of *Drummer*, I saw the

Happening Movement as the art structure that gave permission to the colorful hippie be-ins and love-ins in the political 1960s, and that inspired the radical sex rituals and spontaneous creativity of nonconformist—and newly uncloseted—gay leather culture in the baths, bars, and playrooms of the sexually liberated 1970s.

I tripped out on reporting on *Night Flight*, and holding space in the next issue for it—in fact, holding the entire January 1978 issue open at the printers to add the still-hot December 31 party. I wanted *Drummer* to pop, to happen, to be "what's happening."

As a photographer, I had staged performance-art happenings on Midwest college campuses and in museums during the turbulent 1960s and 70s, and as faculty advisor for Women's Awareness Week at Western Michigan University.

In San Francisco in the early 1970s, at the request of my dear friend, the poet Ron Johnson (author of *To Do as Adam Did*, who with his partner, photographer Mario Pirami, invented and managed the No Name bar), I created three or four happenings over two-years' time at the No Name. With four or five projectors shining intersecting cones of light beamed over the heads of the crowd, my slides and Super-8 movies unspooled with the help of my lover, David Sparrow, as beefy men in uniform carried in naked bodybuilders in cages and set them on the bar, while the crowd—led by our wild Rainbow Motorcycle Club—joined in, smoking grass, drinking beer, tripping on acid, groping, sucking, picking guys up and passing them over everyone's head to throw them into the long trough of urinal.

In 1992, Ron Johnson (1935-1998) wrote a letter to galvanize the RMC who had prolonged the 1970s happenings in the legendary No Name bar at 1347 Folsom Street, between 8th and 9th:

> Dudes—
> This year marks the 20th anniversary of the club, and it's high time to throw a bash. Our Christmas party was so fine we've got to really rise (or stoop) to the occasion—no?....One of the things that made the Xmas party such a great success was Lurch as Santa on a beer-shell throne, greeting one and all, and we need again to come up with something so extraordinarily sleazy and daring they'll all talk about it after. Not many now remember the first anniversary RMC party [1973] where Jack Fritscher was the Entertainment Committee. He brought in three stand-up cages with live, sexy slaves inside. Spotlights! Crowd focus! Promiscuous flagellation! Frenzy! Plus, with his live-action cast,

Drummer 20: Night Flight

three slide projectors and two Super-8 projectors of his transparencies and leather films....Where can we go from there?...At the Lone Star [bar], of course...
— Ron Johnson

It was because of my experience with erotic bar happenings in SoMa that *Drummer* publisher John Embry asked me as editor in chief to start up and manage the first Mr. *Drummer* contest in 1979; but I refused, because editing and writing the magazine was task enough.

By the time New Yorkers such as *Night Flight* producer Wakefield Poole arrived in the orgy that was late 1970s San Francisco, I (who called 1960s Manhattan my second home) was very pleased to write about their new infusion of art-sex energy. This article introduced the new East Coast players to the City, and, as a calling card, introduced *Drummer* to them.

They were the best kind of Manhattanization as New York met San Francisco which had reservations about being "Manhattanized."

That was one of the great pleasures of being *Drummer* editor in chief. It was like the line in *Casablanca*. "Sooner or later everyone comes to Rick's." Almost immediately, after I became editor in chief of *Drummer* (March 1977), the ultimate New Yorker, Robert Mapplethorpe, showed up in my office for Halloween, and came back for *Night Flight* on New Year's Eve 1977. If my early issues of *Drummer* had not been well received in New York, Robert and I might never have met. He wanted *Drummer*; he needed *Drummer*; and I gave him his first magazine cover on *Drummer* 24 (September 1978).

See Victor Bockris' *Beat Punks* for his interview "Mapplethorpe Takes Off" recorded October 16, 1977, as Robert taxied to JFK to make pilgrimage to California where he scheduled himself to meet the editor of *Drummer*. See also my subsequent formal introduction of Mr. Mapplethorpe to the leather world in "The Robert Mapplethorpe Gallery" in my special New York art issue, *Son of Drummer* (September 1978), featuring three A-List New Yorkers: Mapplethorpe, the pointillist artist Rex, and photographer Lou Thomas of Target Studio. The issue also included Tom of Finland.

Night Flight producers and artists Steve Barnett, Ed Parente, and Paul Hatlestad, the partner of Wakefield Poole, became my good friends, and we worked together with New Yorker Michael Maletta's Creative Power Foundation on the next party, *Stars*, held on a pier under the Bay Bridge.

Night Flight was pure Warhol via Poole, and very much based in Andy's historic *Exploding Plastic Inevitable* tour and happening with Lou Reed, Gerard Malanga, Nico, and the Velvet Underground. For the subsequent art-sex party, *Stars* (1978), I was quite happy to have my photographic transparencies and Super-8 films projected over the heads of thousands of revelers onto white panels from Christo's famous "Running Fence" (1976) that so recently had famously been stretched for twenty-five miles over the coastal hills of Marin County north of the Golden Gate Bridge. No one then had a clue that the white fabric panels on which I projected our gay faces were a ghostly foreshadowing of the panels of the AIDS quilt.

The photographs for my *Night Flight* article were shot by frequent *Drummer* photographer Efren Ramirez.

The Titanic 70s was an art explosion in gay culture, and the salon around *Drummer* was epicentric to it.

To this day I own and love several Ed Parente sculptures. One is a bouquet of eighteen male fingertips with a single yellow butterfly specimen perched on the tallest finger. The other is a mask of a woman's face wrapped in white silk and creamy lace which Ed found blowing down Castro Street; I have always called the sculpture "The Dead Bride." Both are encased in Parente's signature Plexiglas boxes. In the same way, I treasure even more the large photographs that my bicoastal lover Robert Mapplethorpe signed to me.

As gay art galleries opened up, so did gay businesses. Paul Hatlestad, during the 1970s when we all wore gold chains around our necks, was nearly electrocuted when he was wiring his and Wakefield Poole's new boutique on Market Street at Castro. Because the chain was a ring, the electricity traveled around and around his neck without killing him, although his neck was permanently scarred 360 degrees every one of the twenty-five times the power surged around his neck.

It was a coincidence that the name of what became their very successful boutique was "Hot Flash" whose symbol was a lightning bolt.

II. The feature essay as published in *Drummer* 20, January 1978

The First Manhattan-izing Party in San Francisco...

Night Flight 1977
The Night Everybody Was a Star
& the Virgins Jumped into the Volcano

SAN FRANCISCO. DECEMBER 31, 1977. *NIGHT FLIGHT* was a golden New Year's Eve night in the Golden Age of San Francisco—and a shock to the old over-easy attitude of Sodom-by-the-Bay. Manhattan energy streaked into town, rented the entire three floors of the Gay Community Center, and designed out of its pits a night when everybody was a star.

NIGHT BEFORE 1978's EVE

The Boarding Pass ticket to *Night Flight* read 10 PM to 7 AM. By 2 AM, time-frame turned into time-warp. Barnum and Bailey with all the Ringlings of the Niebelungen could eat their hearts out. The Center is a Bette-Davis dump, but not after *Night Flight* worked the joint over like a [Phyllis] Diller redone at Arden's. The entire interior of the Center was wrapped with white billowing sections of the Christo Fence that had run through Marin County and then into the sea. Now Christo's fabric hung wall to wall, from the first-floor coat check to the third-floor movie dens. Three thousand men floated together inside a white parachute around circular silver ice-pools chock-full of beer, Calistoga, and The Real Thing.

CASINO ROYALE: STRIP-WRESTLING

The upper-floor Casino operated games of chance placed around the walls of the room. In the center of the Casino stood a boxing-ring-size platform. All night long, professional acts of juggling, magic, and strip-wrestling featured "The Amazing Kristavo"; "On-Off, The Wonder Robot"; and a healthy "Rick & Ron." Casino prizes came from 50 sponsors: health clubs, restaurants, bookstores, florists, gloryholes, galleries, baths, "Jaded Degenerate Man" T-shirts, photographers, artists, and manicurists for men who *need* smooth nails.

Behind the Casino on the right, where The Who was on first, "The Tommy Memorial Pinball Room" ran two lines of twenty machines with Levi's baskets pressed tight against the front of the flashing, flipping, score-chunking pinballs. Behind the Casino on the left, all night long, a single red light hung over a large brick room where the non-professional acts of juggling, magic, and strip-wrestling writhed the night away.

DISCOMANIACS: THE FORBIDDEN CITY OF OZ

Hovering over the dance floor, the light-and-sound saucer-booth flashed in time to the high-energy music. A thousand dancers filled the floor. Aroma of popper rose over their heads where a tight-rope walker balanced his way from crowded balcony to crowded balcony. Bodies heated. Shirts peeled off. Light show designs changed electronically. Special Duty Police stood straight and politely slack-jawed at every exit.

Grown men reported UFO sightings of a tower of sparklers and billowing smoke rolling through the sweaty crowd. From inside the tower, hands threw orange Popsicles out into the tangle of naked arms. Men moved, flowed, from amusement to amusement, wandering inside the wonderful white parachute.

Night Flight was a full Busby Berserkly production number. *Night Flight* was not just four walls and a crowd. *Night Flight* was premeditated design. Every detail was calculated to entertain the most jaded audience in the world. And its magic worked, because *Night Flight* was for one night only. Nothing about it was ordinary. Nothing about it did you see last week or could you get around to next week. *Night Flight* was the *Now* of that one night: a celebration of living life-in-the-fast-lane of The Forbidden City of Oz.

IMAGES: A ROMAN ORGY

As a ton of California grapes cascaded down the balcony walls, a second 20-foot high scaffold rolled to the middle of the dance floor. The crowd parted in an acid-red sea of sweat. Atop the scaffold, a man rode to the center of the crowd. He commanded six projectors like the multiple eyes of some closely encountered great iron beast. He shot surreal images of faces from its six eyes to six screens hung around the hall. Men dancing in front of the screens in white screen-like capes, became part of the abstraction.

In other rooms, floral displays toppled with bodies into the ice-pools.

TOWARD 1980: A SNEAK PREVIEW

For San Francisco, where failure of imagination often looks suspiciously like an energy outage, *Night Flight* was a Manhattanization much to be desired. Michael Maletta's production proved a New Wave is hitting San Francisco, because in among the dancing, sucking, fucking, fisting, and variously heavy free-for-all S&M numbers, a lot of San Francisco heads got blown away and lost their cherries at *Night Flight*. How ya gonna keep 'em down in imagination after they've experienced a night like *Night Flight*?

Laidback and waiting like Madame Recamier has finally passed as San Francisco's favorite posture. "Laidback" won't cut it anymore. The bitch-and-bull mating of New York energy with San Francisco attitude is already producing results. Four days after *Night Flight,* two "rogue" San

Francisco cops decided to raid a gay bath: a private place for consenting adults. Within hours, they were the laughing stock of the straight media and were censured by their chief. Public statements strong as *Night Flight*'s very existence strengthen the solidarity of the gay political front. The gay network is like Peter Finch's New York *Network:* "When you're mad as hell, you won't take interruptions of your lifestyle anymore."

Night Flight proceeds went to the Pride Foundation which fights for gay rights in the courts, in the military, in the bedroom, and in the playroom.

VIRGINS

After *Night Flight,* there are no virgins anymore. That one *Night Flight* night they all jumped into the volcano. Willingly. And the good times rolled.

Night Flight: produced by Michael Maletta; conceptual design, Robert Currie; music, Vincent Corleo; lighting, Roy Shapiro; visuals, David Meyer; spacecraft, Alan Greenspan; lighting and sound equipment, William Roderick Associates and Sound Genesis; poster design, Joseph Vincent; poster illustration, Ed Parente; slide show, Steve Barnett and Paul Hatlestad [and Wakefield Poole].

III. Eyewitness Illustrations

"Night Flight," New Year's Eve, December 31, 1977. Where Circuit Parties began. A "Tightrope Walker" crosses above the heads of the dancing crowd in the Gay Community Center, San Francisco. "Night Flight" publicity kit. Photograph by Efren Ramirez. ©Efren Ramirez

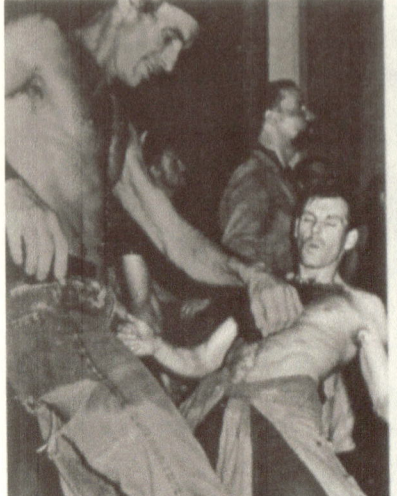

Top left and clockwise: Dancers at "Night Flight," December 31, 1977. Top right: Dancer on right is sniffing poppers. "Night Flight" publicity kit. Photographs by Efren Ramirez. ©Efren Ramirez. In the "Night Flight" article in *Drummer*, editor in chief Fritscher was the first to print the phrase "the Golden Age of San Francisco." Center: Envelope of invitation to "Stars," the party sequel to "Night Flight," May 27, 1978. Bottom: Front and back of the photo-ID Boarding Card created for each guest at "Stars."

Drummer 20: Night Flight

Top: Promotion kit for the "Stars" party published in *Drummer*. Bottom: Invitation card to "Stars" featuring Fritscher quote from *Drummer*.

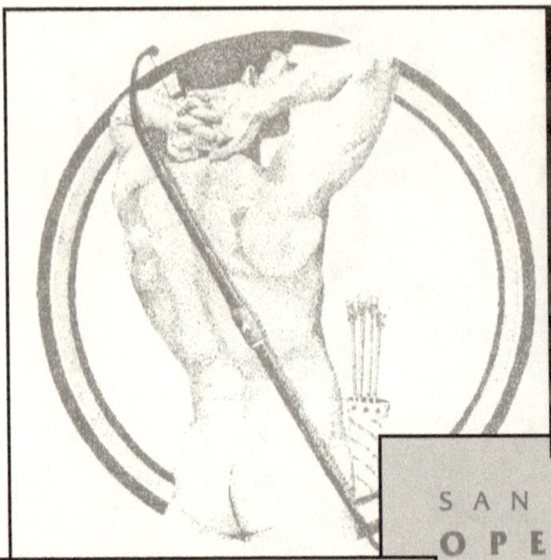

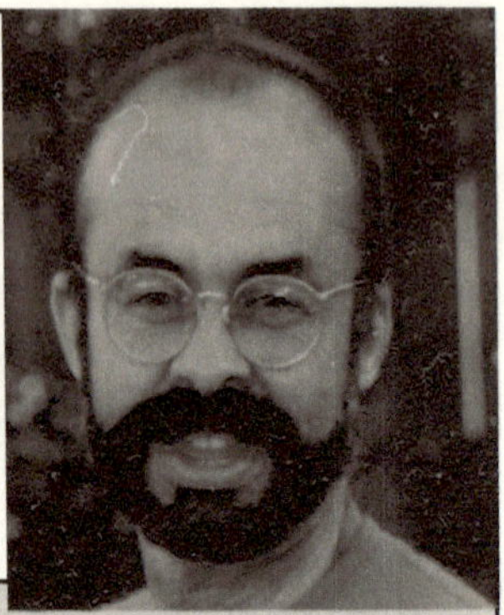

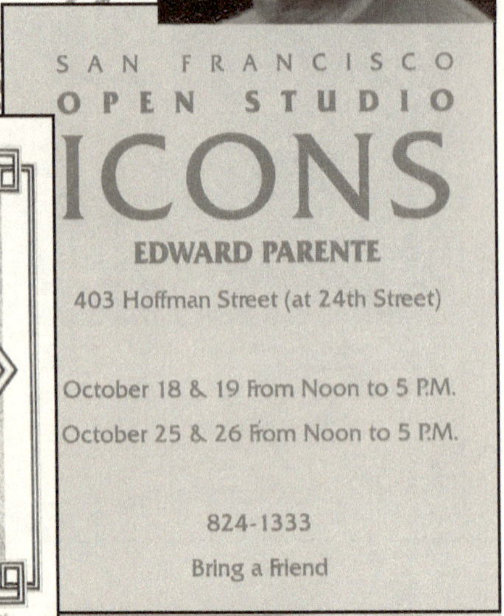

SAN FRANCISCO OPEN STUDIO
ICONS
EDWARD PARENTE

403 Hoffman Street (at 24th Street)

October 18 & 19 From Noon to 5 P.M.

October 25 & 26 From Noon to 5 P.M.

824-1333

Bring a Friend

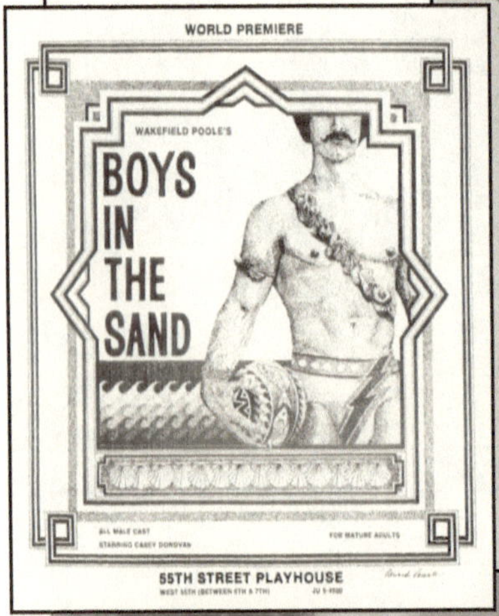

Drummer 20: Night Flight

1645 Market St.
San Francisco, CA
(415) 863-1901

MARK ON CEMENT - photo by Greg Reeder
©1977 Hot Flash of America-2351 Market-SF CA 94114

HOT FLASH OF AMERICA
presents a

**1977
Erotic Art Show**

An exhibition of contemporary works
celebrating Life, Liberty and
the Pursuit of Happiness.

June 7 - August 21, 1977
2351 Market Street, San Francisco 94114
(415) 626-4800

11:00 A.M. to 6:00 P.M. Tuesday through
Saturday. Noon to 5:00 P.M. Sunday.
Dark on Monday.

Top left-clockwise: "Steve Barnett," producer of "Night Flight," Fritscher-Hemry House, 1982. Photograph by Jack Fritscher. ©Jack Fritscher. "The Wizard's Emerald City" and "Hot Flash" were two upscale gay businesses that widened the Castro neighborhood out to Market Street. "Stare Cases" copy and "Emerald City" advertising written in 1976 within the *Drummer* salon by editor in chief Jack Fritscher for Richard Trask, star of the film *Erotic Hands*.

STARE CASES
Richard Trask:
Scorpio Rorshachs. Sensual. Erotic. Men.
Beasts. Botany. Innervisions on fabric
and leather. Tied. Dyed. Drawn.
Painted. And hung for mid-winter.
When look comes to touch.
A Premiere Showing ~ February 13, 1977
Sunday, 2:00 until 8:00 p.m.

Opposite page. Top left-clockwise: "Quiver." Drawing by Edward Parente. "Ed Parente," Fritscher-Hemry House, 1982. Photograph by and ©Jack Fritscher. "Invitation, Parente Sculpture Exhibit." Parente sculpture "Fingertips with Butterfly in Plexiglas Box," 1981, from the collection of Jack Fritscher. Photograph by and ©Jack Fritscher. Wakefield Poole's "*New York Times* Display Ad" for his film *Boys in the Sand* (1971) was a gay history first in the *NYT*, illustrated by Ed Parente. Andy Warhol famously said in the *NYT* (1972): "After Wakefield Poole's movies, mine are unnecessary and a little naive, don't you think?"

SPITTING IMAGE PRESENTS

StarMakers

Two expert cinematographers will "make you a star" in at least fifty feet of super-8 technicolor film.

Catch yourself, yourself and a friend, your friend and a pet on celluloid as you are: moving, panting, working out, posing, praying... whatever.

Cinematographers (both thirties and together) will make a movie of you, your trip, your fantasy. On location or at home.

DREAM OR DOCUMENTARIES.
Ordinary life to extraordinary trips.

FACES • PHYSIQUES • LEATHER TO GLITTER

Motion pictures give you dimension still photography can never do. Even if you don't now own a super-8 projector, prepare for the day you will. In 1984 you can screen yourself the Way You Were now.

Shooting sessions average 1 hour. You retain *all* rights and *all* copies. Your film belongs to you.

Compare: commercial film you buy of *other* guys run $25 to $45. With STARMAKERS, 50 feet of super-8 technicolor film of *you, your friend,* or *your fantasy* is lit, shot, developed, edited, and delivered. (Additional footage desired: per 50 feet, $15.)

50 ft. $50   150 ft. $80
100 ft. $65   200 ft. $95

•

"Personally, I prefer STARMAKERS."
— DORIAN GREY

Perfect for Christmas, Birthdays, and Anniversaries.
Perfect for Lovers and Others Stranger.
Practical: photograph your apartment for insurance proof in case of fire, theft, earthquake.

•

Dial 285-5329
for appointment or consultation

"StarMakers," 1975 brochure, custom filmmaking in San Francisco by David Sparrow and Jack Fritscher, domestic lovers and business partners (1969-1979), dba Spitting Image. "Faces, Physiques, Leather to Glitter....'Personally, I prefer StarMakers. —Dorian Grey'"
©Jack Fritscher

Drummer 20: Night Flight

"Previews" publicity kit. Popular culture critic Fritscher observed: "Everything in the Titanic 1970s roared up finally like the cacophonous, partially-improvised orchestral crescendo of the 24-bar extended E-major chord at the end of the Beatles' 'A Day in the Life' in the *Sgt. Pepper* album." Upping the production values of "Night Flight," the rush of high-octane parties like "Previews" starring Sylvester included a "Vinyl Record" in the "Invitation" to the concert-dance on October 9, 1982, even as Gay-Related Immune Deficiency (GRID) illnesses began to tarnish the Golden Age with whispers of HIV and AIDS. In December 1988, Sylvester (of the Hula Palace salon) died at 42, the same age at which Mapplethorpe (of the *Drummer* salon) died March 1989.

Captions: Eyewitness documentation of the existence of graphics providing internal evidence supporting Jack Fritscher's text are located in the Jack Fritscher and Mark Hemry GLBT History collection. Out of respect for issues of copyright, model releases, permissions, and privacy, some graphics are not available for publication at this time, but can be shown by appointment.

| Eyewitness Illustration | "*Drummer* Trucker Party" ad in *Drummer*. Catching the cash-cow wave of the CMC Carnival, "Night Flight," and "Stars," *Drummer* hosted its own homomasculine theme party, "Truckers," at Trocadero Transfer, 520 Fourth Street, San Francisco, November 7, 1980. This extravaganza led to the parties of the Mr. *Drummer* annual contest.

Drummer Magazine
Timeline Bibliography
The Writing and Photography of Jack Fritscher
An Accounting of Publication and Copyright

Collected and Edited by
Mark Hemry

Drummer Issues covered in this Timeline Index:
14, 15, 16, 17, 18, 19, 20, 21, 22, 23, 24, 25, 26, 27, 28, 29, 30, 31, 32, 33, 41, 81, 85, 100, 107, 115, 116, 117, 118, 119, 121, 123, 124, 126, 127, 128, 129, 130, 131, 133, 134, 135, 136, 137, 138, 139, 140, 141, 143, 144, 145, 147, 148, 155, 157, 159, 169, 170, 186, 188, 204

Drummer Special Issues covered in this Timeline Index:
Son of Drummer
Drummer Rides Again
Mr. Drummer Contest Program 1990

Drummer - Desmodus Sibling Magazine Issues covered in this Timeline Index :
Drummer Tough Customers 1, 12
Mach 20, 22, 25, 29 (35, 38)
Foreskin Quarterly 12
DungeonMaster 47

DRUMMER 14, April 1977
Jack Fritscher's first writing in *Drummer*
1 Piece of Writing by Jack Fritscher
1 Photographic Essay Produced by Fritscher
- "Men South of Market," pp. 39-46, captions for centerfold photo essay
- Centerfold Photographic Essay by Jim Stewart, pp. 39-46, produced by Fritscher

DRUMMER 15, May 1977
3 Pieces of Writing by Fritscher as Staff Ghostwriter-editor; A. Jay draws cover as Guest Artist
- "Stunning Omission," letter to the editor, p. 6
- "Cock Casting," pp. 20-21, feature
- "Durk Parker," aka Durk Dehner, p. 39-46, centerfold text produced and written by Fritscher

DRUMMER 16, June 1977
Second Anniversary Issue
2 Pieces of Writing by Fritscher and Produced by Fritscher
- "Tom Hinde Folio: Drawings 1977," pp. 39-46, feature written by Thom Hinde with Jack Fritscher, produced by Fritscher
- "Johnny Gets His Hair Cut," pp. 66-68; photo essay produced by Fritscher

DRUMMER 17, July 1977
1 Feature Article with Photographs Produced by Fritscher
- "Famous Dungeons of San Francisco," pp. 8-11, feature produced by Fritscher including photos by Gene Weber (picturing Fritscher) and text by Joe Cook

DRUMMER 18, August 1977
Masthead: Ghost-editor in chief Fritscher is not credited
Last issue of *Drummer* (4-month hiatus) until December 1977
1 Piece of Writing by Fritscher
2 Feature Articles with Photographs Produced by Fritscher
First issue of *Drummer* with byline by Jack Fritscher
- "Body Casting," pp. 66-69, feature article with photographs by Gene Weber produced by Fritscher
- "The Leatherneck," pp. 82-84, feature article written by and photo essay produced by Fritscher

   [Editor's Note: August 1977 – December 1977: Publisher John Embry, Editor in Chief Fritscher, and Art Director Al Shapiro put *Drummer* on 4-month hiatus to reinvent the LA magazine into a San Francisco magazine]

DRUMMER 19, December 1977
Masthead: Jack Fritscher, editor in chief
7 Pieces of Writing by Fritscher
- "Contents Page," one liners
- "Leather Christmas," pp. 8-10, cover feature article
- "Gifting," pp. 20-21, holiday photo feature
- "Astrologic" (Capricorn), p. 26, satire
- "*El Paso Wrecking Corp*: The Gage Brothers," pp. 62-64, film review
- "Steve Reeves' Screen Test," pp. 66-68, feature essay and captions
- "*Star Trick* Artist Dom Orejudos Is Etienne!," pp. 71-74, art review
- "Mineshaft," pp. 82-83, cover feature article

DRUMMER 20, January 1978
Masthead: Jack Fritscher, editor in chief
Theme for *Drummer* 20 Created by Fritscher: Gay Sports
10 Pieces of Writing by Fritscher
1 Photograph (Interior Editorial) by Fritscher solo
18 Photographs (Interior Editorial) by Fritscher and Sparrow dba "Photos by Sparrow"
- "Contents Page," one liners
- "Crimes Against Nature," p. 6, editorial review
- 1 Photograph (Interior Editorial): "Jockstrap Chest with *Sports Illustrated* Magazine," p. 10, by Fritscher solo
- "Gay Jock Sports: Wrestling, Boxing, Rollerballing, Soaring, Scuba, Bodybuilding, Dune Bodies, Films," cover lead feature article, pp. 8-17 and 70-71 and 83-84
- "Dune Body," p. 16, poem
- "Gifting," pp. 20-22, feature article
- "Pissing in the Wind: The Mineshaft," pp. 22-24 and 83, feature article
- "Astrologic" (Aquarius), p. 30, satire
- 1 Photograph (Interior Editorial): "David Wycoff, Soldier," p. 39, by Fritscher and Sparrow dba "Sparrow Photography"
- "*Salo*: A Review of Pasolini, Toward an Understanding of *Salo*" pp. 66-67, feature review

Drummer: Fritscher Timeline Bibliography 663

- *"Gay Source: A Catalog for Men,"* p. 72, book review by Fritscher and Bob Zygarlicki
- "CMC Carnival 1977," pp. 74-77, feature
- 17 Photographs (Interior Editorial): "CMC Carnival 1977," pp. 74-77, by Fritscher and Sparrow dba "Photos by Sparrow"
- "Night Flight: New Year's Eve Party 1977," p. 88-89, feature

DRUMMER 21, March 1978
Masthead: Jack Fritscher, editor in chief
The Most Perfectly Representative Issue of *Drummer*
Theme for *Drummer* 21 Created by Fritscher: Prison
9 Pieces of Writing by Fritscher
1 Photograph (Front Cover Portrait): "John Trowbridge as Ex-Con," designed and cast by Fritscher, and photographed by David Sparrow and Jack Fritscher dba "David Sparrow"
2 Photographs (Interior Editorial) by Fritscher solo
4 Photographs (Interior Editorial) by Fritscher and Sparrow dba "Photos by Sparrow"
1 Story ("In a Pig's Ass" by Phil Andros) edited and produced by Fritscher

- 1 Photograph (Front Cover Portrait): "John Trowbridge as Ex-Con," designed and cast by Fritscher, and photographed by David Sparrow and Jack Fritscher dba "David Sparrow"
- "Contents Page," one liners
- "Defending Your Attitude," editorial, p. 6
- "Prison Blues: Confessions of a Prison-Tour Junkie," pp. 8-11 and 70-73; cover lead feature
- 4 Photographs (Interior Editorial): "Prisoners," pp. 8-11, by Fritscher and Sparrow aka "Photos by Sparrow"
- 1 Photograph (Interior Editorial): "RCMP Mountie in Boots and Sweater," p. 27, by Fritscher solo
- "Scott Smith: Heavy Rap with a Solitary Ex-Con," feature interview, written by David Hurles and Fritscher
- "Astrologic" (Aries), p. 30, satire
- "In a Pig's Ass," short fiction by Phil Andros aka Sam Steward, edited and produced by Fritscher
- "Gay Deteriorata," p. 38, satire of "Desiderata"
- "Pumping Roger: Acts, Facts, and Fantasy, A Night at the Nob Hill Theater," pp. 45-46 and 68, feature
- 1 Photograph (Interior Editorial): "Bear on Toilet," p. 71, by Fritscher solo
- "Punk Funk: You Read This, You Deserve It," pp. 74-76, feature, with additional reporting by M. Board
- "Dr. Dick, *Drummer* Goes to the Doctor, PCP: Short Cut to Suicide," p. 77, column, written by Fritscher based on interview with Dr. Richard Hamilton, M. D.

DRUMMER 22, May 1978
Masthead: Jack Fritscher, editor in chief
Theme for *Drummer* 22 Created by Fritscher: Cigars
11 Pieces of Writing by Fritscher
2 Photographs (Interior Editorial) by Fritscher solo
1 Interview ("Tom of Finland" by Robert Opel) Produced by Fritscher

- "Contents Page," one liners
- "Attitude Begets Attitude," p. 6, editorial

- "Cigar Blues," pp. 8-12, feature, illustrated with 5 photographs from Fritscher's 1960-1970s collection but not shot by Fritscher
- 1 Photograph (Interior Editorial): "Cigar Smoker USMC," p. 8, by Fritscher solo
- 1 Photograph (Interior Editorial): "Cigar Smoker Dan Dufort," p. 14, by Fritscher solo
- "Firebomber: Cigar Sarge," p. 15, fiction
- "USMC: Strip-Shaving the Raw Recruit," pp. 20-21, feature
- "Astrologic" (Taurus), p. 30, satire
- "Corporal in Charge of Taking Care of Captain O'Malley, Part 1," pp. 32-35, erotic drama
- "*Sebastiane*," pp. 66-67, film review of Derek Jarman
- "*End Product: The First Taboo*," p. 69, book review; Fritscher pseudonym as "David Hurles"
- "Arena Slave Auction," pp. 73-77, feature
- "Tom of Finland Interview," by Robert Opel, pp. 90-91, produced by Fritscher
- "Club San Francisco, Ritch Street," pp. 92-93, feature

DRUMMER 23, July 1978
Third Anniversary Issue
Masthead: Jack Fritscher, editor in chief
Theme for *Drummer* 23 Created by Fritscher: Underground Sex: Gay Pop-Culture — The Catacombs
12 Pieces of Writing by Fritscher
12 Photographs (Interior Editorial) by Fritscher solo aka "Larry Olson"
Fritscher adds tag line: "*Drummer*: The American Review of Gay Popular Culture"

- "Contents Page," one liners
- "Gay Pop Culture in *Drummer*," p. 6, editorial
- "The Catacombs: Upstairs over a Vacant Lot," pp. 8-11, feature essay
- 12 Photographs (Interior Editorial): "The Catacombs," pp. 8-11, photographs by Fritscher solo aka "Larry Olson"
- "Redneck Biker," pp. 16-18, poem
- "Astrologic" (Leo), p. 31, satire, limerick
- "Corporal in Charge of Taking Care of Captain O'Malley, Part 2," pp. 32-35 and 73, erotic drama
- "Target Men," p. 45, captions
- "Golden Drumsticks Awards," p. 74, awards column invented this issue by Fritscher
- "Reviewing Straight Magazines: Some Babes in the Woods," pp. 78-79, captions, short essay
- "Tough Shit," p. 84, debut of feature column Fritscher created, collected, and produced for ongoing issues through *Drummer* 30.
- "How I Spent My Summer Vacation, or, Pigging It in New York," pp. 87-88, feature essay by Al Shapiro (A. Jay) with Fritscher
- "Submit to *Drummer*," p. 94, letter soliciting talent

DRUMMER 24, September 1978
Masthead: Jack Fritscher, editor in chief
Theme for *Drummer* 24 Created by Fritscher: Authenticity, Mapplethorpe, and Bondage
9 Pieces of Writing by Fritscher
2 Photographs (Interior Editorial) by Fritscher solo
47 Photographs (Interior Editorial) by Fritscher and Sparrow dba "Photos by David Sparrow"

Drummer: Fritscher Timeline Bibliography 665

1 Photograph (Front Cover Portrait) by Robert Mapplethorpe, designed, cast, and produced by Fritscher
1 Photograph (Front Cover Portrait) "The Mapplethorpe Cover: Biker for Hire," photograph by Robert Mapplethorpe; commissioned, designed, cast, and produced by Fritscher

- "Contents Page," one liners
- "Let Us Now Praise Fucking with Authentic Men," p. 8 and 72-73, editorial
- "Bondage: Blest Be the Tie That Binds," pp. 16-23 and 76, feature essay
- 13 Photographs (Interior Editorial): "Bondage," pp. 16-23, photographs by Fritscher and Sparrow dba "Photos by David Sparrow"
- "Castro Street Blues: 1978 Style," pp. 32-36, feature satire
- 11 Photographs (Interior Editorial): "Castro Street Fair 1978," pp. 34-36, photographs by Fritscher and Sparrow dba "Photos by David Sparrow"
- "In Hot Blood: Ex-Cons-We Abuse Fags, Part 1," pp. 37-44, feature interview, created by David Hurles and Fritscher
- "Jocks: Holtz and Ed Wiley," pp. 46-52, centerfold, text by Fritscher; see Holtz shot by Fritscher solo on cover of *Rainbow County and Other Stories*
- 3 Photographs (Interior Editorial): "Richard Locke," p. 38, by Fritscher and Sparrow dba "Photos by David Sparrow"
- "Tough Shit," p. 83, feature column created, collected, and produced by Fritscher
- "The Quarters: Slave Training," pp. 10-15, 70-71, essay
- 20 Photographs (Interior Editorial): "The Quarters," pp 10-15, 70-71, photographs by Fritscher and Sparrow dba "From the Desk of the D.I. Photos by David Sparrow"
- 1 Photograph (Interior Editorial): "David Sparrow in Bondage with Collar," p. 76, by Fritscher solo
- 1 Photograph (Interior Editorial): "Skip Navarette in Bondage," p. 76, by Fritscher solo
- "Men's Bar Scene: A Farewell to Larry's," p. 88, essay
- "Gay Writers/Writer's Aid," p. 86, notice of Fritscher tutorial for erotic authors

***SON OF DRUMMER*, September 1978, A *Drummer* Special Issue, Published Same Month as *Drummer* 24**
Jack Fritscher, editor in chief
Theme for *Son of Drummer* Created by Fritscher: New York Art—Mapplethorpe and Rex
8 Pieces of Writing by Fritscher
8 Photographs (Interior Editorial) by Fritscher solo
35 Photographs (Interior Editorial) by Fritscher and Sparrow dba "Sparrow Photography"

[Editor's Note: Fritscher wrote nearly the entirety of this special issue.]

- "Contents Page," one liners
- "Arab Death," pp. 8-11, feature; Fritscher bylined by pseudonym, "Denny Sargent," the protagonist in his 1969 novel *I Am Curious (Leather)* aka *Leather Blues* serialized in this issue
- "The Robert Mapplethorpe Gallery (Censored)," pp. 14-17, feature
- "Target Studio Retrospective," pp. 22-25, captions
- "Turkish Delight: Macho Wrestling with Leather, Oil, and Heavy Sweat," pp. 28-30, essay
- 35 Photographs (Interior Editorial): "Ass-Sets," p. 31, by Fritscher and Sparrow dba "Sparrow Photography"
- 4 Photographs (Interior Editorial): "Filmstrips: Candle Power," p. 34, by Fritscher solo
- 4 Photographs (Interior Editorial): "Filmstrips: Rude Rubbers," p. 35, by Fritscher solo

- "*I Am Curious (Leather)*: The Adventures of Denny Sargent," pp. 41-47, excerpt of Fritscher's 1969 novel *Leather Blues*
- "Rex Revisited," p. 48-51, feature essay
- "Chico Is the Man," pp. 52-54, poem

DRUMMER 25, December 1978
Masthead: Jack Fritscher, editor in chief
Theme for *Drummer* 25 Created by Fritscher: Leather Identity—Homomasculinity
17 Pieces of Writing by Fritscher
1 Photograph (Front Cover Portrait) "Ed Dinakos," by Fritscher and Sparrow dba "Staff Photographer David Sparrow"
33 Photographs (Interior Editorial) for Centerfold and Interior Photographs by Fritscher and Sparrow dba "Staff Photographer David Sparrow"

- 1 Photograph (Front Cover Portrait) "Ed Dinakos," by Fritscher and Sparrow dba "Staff Photographer David Sparrow"
- "Contents Page," one liners
- 1 Photograph (Interior Editorial): "Torso," contents page, by Fritscher and Sparrow dba "David Sparrow"
- "Afraid You're Not Butch Enough?" p. 6, editorial
- "*Drummer* Gift Guide," pp. 17-21, captions
- "Astrologic" (Scorpio), p. 22, satire
- "Drumbeats, Yule Recipe: Bat," p. 30, satiric essay
- "Gay Pop Culture Series: Fetishes, *Equus* (A One-Horse Open Sleigh)," pp. 31-39, review
- "Horsemaster: Come to the Stable," p. 40, fiction
- "In Hot Blood: Ex-Cons-We Abuse Fags, Part 2," pp. 37-44, feature interview, created by David Hurles and Fritscher
- "Big Mike (Ed Dinakos)," p. 49, centerfold captions
- 7 Photographs (Interior Editorial): "Big Mike Dinakos," p. 49, by Fritscher and Sparrow dba "Staff Photographer David Sparrow"
- "We're Looking for Mr. *Drummer*," p. 68, promotional text
- 2 Photographs (Interior Editorial): "Looking for Mr. *Drummer*," p. 68, by Fritscher and Sparrow dba "David Sparrow"
- "*The Norseman*," p. 70, film review
- "Tough Shit," p. 73, feature column created, collected, and produced by Fritscher
- "Tough Customers," p. 75, first appearance of feature column invented, collected, and produced by Fritscher through *Drummer* 33; this column continued for twenty years
- "Dr. Dick, *Drummer* Goes to the Doctor, Amoebiasis: Your Ass Is Falling Out," p. 80, feature, based on interview with Dr. Richard Hamilton, M. D.
- "*Drummer* Goes to Its Own Party," pp. 88-91, feature
- 15 Photographs (Interior Editorial): "*Drummer* Goes to Its Own Party," pp. 88-91, by Fritscher and Sparrow dba "David Sparrow"
- "Scottish Games: Men in Kilts," pp. 92-93, feature
- 8 Photographs (Interior Editorial): "Men in Kilts," pp. 92-93, by Fritscher and Sparrow dba "Photos by David Sparrow"
- "Sleep in Heavenly Peace," p. 102, fiction

DRUMMER 26, JANUARY 1979
Masthead: Jack Fritscher, editor in chief
Theme for *Drummer* 26 Created by Fritscher: Cowboys and Performance Art
11 Pieces of Writing by Fritscher
6 Photographs (Interior Editorial) by Fritscher solo

Drummer: Fritscher Timeline Bibliography 667

22 Photographs (Interior Editorial) by Fritscher and Sparrow dba "David Sparrow"
- "Contents Page," one liners
- "Grand National Rodeo Blues: Comes a Horseman, Cowboys and Mounties," pp. 8-17, feature
- 8 Photographs (Interior Editorial): Cowboys, pp. 10, 12-14, 16, by Fritscher and Sparrow dba "Photo Essay by David Sparrow"
- 6 Photographs (Interior Editorial): RCMP Mounties, pp. 11, 14-17, by Fritscher solo
- "High Performance: Or, Sex without a Net," pp. 18-22, review, by Fritscher using pseudonym of "David Hurles" with permission of Hurles
- 1 Photograph (Interior Editorial): "Mike (Ed Dinakos) with Blond and Ball Gag," p. 21, by Fritscher and Sparrow dba "David Sparrow"
- "Astrologic" (Sagittarius), pp. 30-31, satire
- "The Battered Lex Barker," pp. 32-36, feature article and captions
- "*Midnight Express*," pp. 68-69, review, in collaboration with John Trojanski
- "Tough Shit," p. 70, feature column created, collected, and written by Fritscher
- "Tough Customers," p. 76, feature column created, collected, and edited by Fritscher
- "CMC Carnival 1978: Seaman's Semen's End," pp. 82-85, feature
- 13 Photographs (Interior Editorial): "CMC Carnival 1978," pp. 82-85, by Fritscher and Sparrow dba "David Sparrow"
- "Gay Writers/Writer's Aid," p. 86, notice of Fritscher tutorial for erotic authors
- "Harvey Milk and Gay Courage: In Passing," p. 96, essay

DRUMMER 27, February 1979
Masthead: Jack Fritscher, editor in chief
Theme for *Drummer* 27 Created by Fritscher: Gay Film and The Society of Janus
10 Pieces of Writing by Fritscher
4 Photographs (Interior Editorial) by Fritscher and Sparrow dba "Sparrow Photography" and "Photos by David Sparrow"
- "Contents Page," one liners
- 1 Photograph (Interior Editorial): Letters to the Editor, p. 7, by Fritscher and Sparrow dba "Sparrow Photography"
- "Basic Plumbing Unplugged: LA Plays Hard with Itself," pp. 8-13, lead feature, by Fritscher with additional reporting by Terry Sabreur
- "Dirty Poole: Everything You Fantasized about Wakefield Poole," pp. 14-22, cover feature interview
- 3 Photographs (Interior Editorial): "Wakefield Poole," p. 15, by Fritscher and Sparrow dba "Photos by David Sparrow"
- "S&M: The Last Taboo, The Janus Society," pp. 32-36, feature essay, by Fritscher with additional reporting by "Eric Van Meter"
- "*Movie Movie*," p. 61, film review
- "*Superman*," pp. 61-62, film review
- "Golden Drumsticks Awards: The Pet Gloryhole," p. 64, awards column created and written by Fritscher
- "Tough Shit," p. 70, feature column collected and written by Fritscher
- "Tough Customers," p. 76-77, feature column created, collected, and edited by Fritscher
- "Men's Bar Scene: *Drummer* Goes to Boots," pp. 82-84, essay

DRUMMER 28, April 1979
Masthead: Jack Fritscher, editor in chief
Theme for *Drummer* 28 Created by Fritscher: Gyms and Prisons
6 Pieces of Writing by Fritscher

10 Photographs (Interior Editorial) by Fritscher and Sparrow dba "David Sparrow Photography"
- "Contents Page," one liners
- "Wet Stough," pp. 14-17, poem for "Swim Meet" photographs
- 10 Photographs (Interior Editorial): "Swim Meet," pp. 13-14, by Fritscher and Sparrow dba "David Sparrow Photography"
- "Bare-Ass Wrestling," p. 41, centerfold poem, caption
- "*The Deer Hunter*," pp. 53-54, movie review
- "Tough Shit," p. 62, feature column created, collected, and written by Fritscher
- "Tough Customers," pp. 64-65, feature column created, collected, and edited by Fritscher

DRUMMER 29, May 1979
Masthead: Jack Fritscher, editor in chief
Theme for *Drummer* 29 Created by Fritscher: Dangerous Sex, Boxing, and Blue-Collar Men
9 Pieces of Writing by Fritscher
3 Photographs (Interior Editorial) by Fritscher and Sparrow dba "Sparrow Photography"
1 Story (*Mr. Benson* by John Preston) edited, serialized, and produced by Fritscher
- "Contents Page," one liners
- "The Most Dangerous Game in the Whole Wide World," p. 6, editorial
- "Drawings by Domino," p. 9-11, essay in two parts, "Domino/Summer of 1978" and "An Artist's Statement," written by Fritscher with Al Shapiro from Shapiro-Fritscher interview
- "Foot Loose," p. 13, poem
- "Noodles Romanov and the Golden Gloves," pp. 14-17, feature article
- 3 Photographs (Interior Editorial): "Golden Gloves," pp. 14, 16-17, by Fritscher and Sparrow dba "Sparrow Photography"
- *Mr. Benson*, pp. 18-23, Part One of a novel written by John Preston; edited, serialized, and produced by Fritscher
- "On Target: The New American Masculinity," pp. 37, centerfold copy
- "Tough Shit," p. 62, feature column created, collected, and written by Fritscher
- "Tough Customers," p. 62, feature column created, collected, and edited by Fritscher
- "Gay Writers/Writer's Aid," p. 72, notice for Fritscher tutorial for erotic authors

DRUMMER 30, June 1979
Fourth Anniversary Issue
Masthead: Jack Fritscher, editor in chief, and contributing writer
Copyright on masthead is incorrectly marked as "1978"
Theme for *Drummer* 30 Created by Fritscher: Nipples and Arthur Tress Photography
8 Pieces of Writing by Fritscher
1 Photograph (Front Cover Portrait) by Fritscher and Sparrow dba "David Sparrow Photography"
1 Story (*Mr. Benson* by John Preston) edited, serialized, and produced by Fritscher
- 1 Photograph (Front Cover Portrait): "Val Martin and Bob Hyslop," by Fritscher and Sparrow dba "David Sparrow Photography"
- "Contents Page," one liners
- "Tit Torture Blues," pp. 10-18, feature article

Drummer: Fritscher Timeline Bibliography

- "Meditations on Arthur Tress," pp. 22-25, four poems for four Tress photographs: "Code 1: Gifts of Nature," "Code 2: Black Boy," "Code 3: Sebastiane," and "Code 4: Confession de Kafka Caca"
- *Mr. Benson*, pp. 26-31, Part Two of a novel written by John Preston; edited, serialized, and produced by Fritscher
- "Zeus Men In Bondage: Introducing a New Studio," p. 48, centerfold copy, produced and written by Fritscher
- "The Brothel Hotel," pp. 63-64, feature review
- "Tough Shit," p. 72, feature column created, collected, and produced by Fritscher included two original essays by Fritscher, "Bloody 'Marys' at Elephant Walk" and "How Relaxed Can Straights Get?"
- "Tough Customers," p. 74-75, feature column created, collected, and edited by Fritscher

DRUMMER 31, September 1979
Masthead: Fritscher, who edited *Drummer* 31, is not credited; Embry removed Fritscher credit line on masthead, but kept some Fritscher bylines; credit was assigned to "Robert Payne" aka publisher John Embry.
The 1970s *Drummer* salon exited with Fritscher on December 31, 1979
Theme for *Drummer* 31 Created by Fritscher: Spit and Other Erotic Bodily Functions
8 Pieces of Writing by Fritscher
40 Photographs (Interior Editorial) for Centerfold by Fritscher (Solo) credited wrongly by Embry to "Sparrow Photography"
1 Story (*Mr. Benson* by John Preston) edited, serialized, and produced by Fritscher
- "Contents Page," one liners
- "Martin of Holland Interview," pp. 18-19, feature interview, written by Al Shapiro (A. Jay) and Fritscher; Fritscher byline deleted by Embry
- "The First International Mr. Leather (IML)," pp. 20-24, feature
- 40 Photographs (Interior Editorial, Centerfold): "Spit, Sweat, and Piss with Val Martin and Bob Hyslop," pp. 41-48, shot by Fritscher solo——with byline changed by Embry to "Sparrow Photography"
- *Mr. Benson*, pp. 25-29, Part Three of a novel written by John Preston; edited, serialized, and produced by Fritscher
- "Tough Shit," p. 64, feature column created, collected, and produced by Fritscher
- "Tough Customers," pp. 66-67, feature column created, collected, and edited by Fritscher
- "The Macho Images of Tony Plewik: A *Drummer* Do-er's Profile," pp. 68-70, essay
- "Men's Bar Scene: Pure Trash," pp. 74-75, essay
- "In Passing, Robert Opel: His Last High Performance, His Murder," p. 86, essay, collage from original reporting by Maitland Zane, *San Francisco Chronicle*

DRUMMER 32, October 1979
Masthead: Fritscher, who edited *Drummer* 32, was not credited; credit was assigned to "Robert Payne" aka publisher John Embry; Embry removed Fritscher's credit line on masthead, leaving only the coded byline signature, "20 June 1979," Fritscher's day and month of birth, p. 19.
5 Pieces of Writing by Fritscher
1 Story (*Mr. Benson* by John Preston) edited, serialized, and produced by Fritscher
- "A Confidential *DRUMMER* Dossier," pp. 19-21, byline coded with Fritscher birth date

- *Mr. Benson*, pp. 22-27, Part Four of a novel written by John Preston; edited, serialized, and produced by Fritscher
- "The Men by Robert Opel," pp. 28-29, writing by Robert Opel researched, collected, and produced by Fritscher
- "Tough Shit," p. 66, feature column created, collected, and produced by Fritscher
- "Tough Customers," pp. 68-69, feature column created, collected, and edited by Fritscher
- "Conrap," p. 71, debut of column created, collected, and edited by Fritscher with reporting by David Hurles (Old Reliable)
- "Tough Tales," pp. 72-73, 76, debut of column created, collected, and edited by Fritscher

DRUMMER RIDES AGAIN, December 1979, A *Drummer* Special Issue, published same month as *Drummer* 33
Title of Special Issue Created by Fritscher
No masthead listed; masthead deleted because of arguments over byline representation; issue initially edited and produced by Fritscher; subsequent changes and deletions in content by "Robert Payne" with credit for editing by "Robert Payne" buried at bottom of contents page, p. 3
1 Piece of Writing by Fritscher
1 Photograph (Interior Editorial) by Fritscher solo
13 Photographs (Interior Editorial) by Fritscher and Sparrow dba "David Sparrow Photography"
2 Graphic Features (Cavelo Art; Rink Photography) Produced by Fritscher
- "Bound and Gagged: Zeus Studio." text for photo feature
- "Cavelo's Men," pp. 24-27, produced by Fritscher; new text by "Robert Payne"
- 1 Photograph (Interior Editorial): "Val Martin," p. 44, by Fritscher solo (wrongly credited to "Photo by David Sparrow")
- "A Very Private Orgy: Photos by Rink," pp. 50-52, produced by Fritscher; Fritscher text replaced with text by "Robert Payne"
- 13 Photographs (Interior Editorial): "The Quarters: How I Spent My Summer Vacation," pp. 45, 53-56, by Fritscher and Sparrow dba "David Sparrow Photography"

DRUMMER 33, December 1979
Masthead: Fritscher performed basic edit on *Drummer* 33 which was credited to "Robert Payne"; Embry completed removal of Fritscher byline and deleted two feature articles by Fritscher and five photographs by Fritscher and Sparrow
5 Pieces of Writing by Fritscher
1 Photograph (Interior Editorial) by Fritscher and Sparrow dba "David Sparrow"
1 Story (*Mr. Benson* by John Preston) edited, serialized, and produced by Fritscher
1 Photograph (Interior Editorial), contents page, by Fritscher and Sparrow dba "David Sparrow"
- 1 Photograph (Interior Editorial): "Ed Dinakos Hood and Harness," p. 19, by Fritscher and Sparrow dba "David Sparrow"
- "*Drummer* Gift Guide," pp. 19-23, captions
- *Mr. Benson*, pp. 24-29, Part Five of a novel written by John Preston; edited, serialized, and produced by Fritscher; beginning with Part Six, Embry absorbed the Fritscher edit and serialization through the ten parts of *Mr. Benson*
- "Tough Shit," p. 66, feature column created, collected, and produced by Fritscher
- "Tough Customers," pp. 68-69, feature column created, collected, and edited by Fritscher

Drummer: Fritscher Timeline Bibliography

- "Conrap," p. 71, column created, collected, and edited by Fritscher with reporting by David Hurles (Old Reliable)
- "Tough Tales," pp. 72-73, 76, debut of column created, collected, and edited by Fritscher

DRUMMER 41, December 1980
1 Piece of Writing by Fritscher (Fritscher's "Astrologic" Pirated and Reprinted without Copyright Permission and Falsely Bylined as "Aristide")
2 Photographs (Interior Editorial) by Fritscher and Sparrow dba "David Sparrow"

- "Astrologic" (Sagittarius), p. 63, written by Fritscher and pirated in a reprint by publisher Embry and editor John W. Rowberry without permission from Fritscher's copyright column "Astrologic" in *Drummer* 21 (March 1978), p. 30; Embry and Rowberry colluded in this direct violation of Fritscher's copyright; falsely assigning the byline to "Aristide," it seems they set out to deceive the readership by rearranging the order of the months in Fritscher's original in order to recycle and resell the column.
- 2 Photographs (Interior Editorial) from "The Quarters," p. 43 (inset in "Key Club Carpenters"), and p. 44, by Fritscher and Sparrow dba "David Sparrow"; both reprinted without permission.

DRUMMER 81, February 1984
1 Editorial Mention: 2 Books Reviews

- Editorial Mention: Book Review, "Drummedia Books: Men Who Say Yo," p. 81, review written by Aaron Travis (Steven Saylor) of two books collecting Fritscher's fiction first serialized or published in *Drummer*: the novel *Leather Blues* and *Corporal in Charge of Taking Care of Captain O'Malley and Other Stories* which was the first collection of *Drummer* stories published outside of *Drummer*.

DRUMMER 85, December 1985
10th Anniversary Issue
1 Piece of Writing by Fritscher

- "Smut Is Where You Find It—Erotic Writers: What They Read to Turn on," p. 86, personal essay

DRUMMER 100, October 1986
Special 100th Issue
1 Piece of Writing by Fritscher (cover lead feature)
  [Editor's Note: In 1986, Anthony F. DeBlase and Andrew Charles, Desmodus Inc., purchased *Drummer* from publisher John Embry]

- "The Lords of Leather," pp. 30-35, short fiction, featured on cover

DRUMMER 107, August 1987
2 Pieces of Writing by Fritscher

- "The Artist, A. Jay: Al Shapiro—The Passing of One of *Drummer*'s First Daddies," pp. 34-40, feature obituary
- "Obituary Sidebar: Shapiro," p. 40, book dedication of *Stand by Your Man and Other Stories*

DRUMMER 115, April 1988
1 Piece of Writing by Fritscher
2 Photographs (Interior Editorial) by Fritscher dba "Palm Drive Video"

- "Fetish Feature," p. 26, schedule of themes created by Fritscher for upcoming issues 116-121

- 2 Photographs (Interior Editorial) for Video Review: "Palm Drive Models Dan Dufort and Gino Deddino," p. 40; plus mention on pp. 26 and 40

DRUMMER 116 (incorrectly marked on masthead as issue 114), May 1988
Masthead: Jack Fritscher, Contributing Writer; Fritscher dba Palm Drive Video, Photography
1 Piece of Writing by Fritscher
2 Photographs (Interior Editorial) by Fritscher dba "Palm Drive Video"
4 Photographs (Interior Advertising) by Fritscher dba "Palm Drive Video"
- "Fetish Feature," p. 40, schedule of themes created by Fritscher for upcoming issues 118-121
- 1 Photograph (Interior Editorial): "Palm Drive Model John Muir in Uniform and Underwear," p. 48, from Fritscher video, *A Man's Man*, by Fritscher dba "Palm Drive Video"
- 2 Photographs (Interior Editorial): "In Passing: Washday at Palm Drive Video, Hanging Out to Dry" p. 98, by Fritscher dba "Palm Drive Video" from the video *Vigilante*
- 4 Photographs (Interior Advertising): "Sonny Butts, Dave Gold, Jason Steele, and Bruno," p. 39, by Fritscher dba "Palm Drive Video," display ad, one-sixth page; this is the first display ad for Palm Drive Video to be published in *Drummer*—four years after the founding of Palm Drive Video (1984)

DRUMMER 117, June 1988
Masthead: Jack Fritscher, Writer, Frequent Contributors; Palm Drive Video, Photography, Frequent Contributors
1 Piece of Writing by Fritscher
2 Photographs (Interior Editorial) by Fritscher solo
4 Photographs (Interior Advertising) by Fritscher dba "Palm Drive Video"
1 Piece of Writing (Advertising) by Fritscher dba "Palm Drive Video"
- "Fetish Feature," p. 41, schedule of themes created by Fritscher for upcoming issues 118-122
- 2 Photographs (Interior Editorial): "Video Daddies: Dave Gold," p. 45, by Fritscher
- 4 Photographs (Interior Advertising): "Sonny Butts, Dave Gold, Jason Steele, and Bruno," p. 17, by Fritscher dba "Palm Drive Video," display ad, one-sixth page
- "New S&M Fetish Videos," p. 86, classified ad copy by Fritscher for Palm Drive Video

DRUMMER 118, July 1988 (*Drummer* 118 and *Drummer* 119 were both dated July 1988)
Masthead: Jack Fritscher, Writer, Frequent Contributors; Palm Drive Video, Photography, Frequent Contributors
Theme for *Drummer* 118 Created by Fritscher: Rubber (Keith Ardent)
2 Pieces of Writing (including Lead Feature Article) by Fritscher
1 Photograph (Front Cover Portrait) by Fritscher dba "Palm Drive Video"
9 Photographs (Interior Editorial) by Fritscher dba "Palm Drive Video"
2 Photographs (Interior Editorial, Inside Back Cover) by Fritscher dba "Palm Drive Video"
7 Photographs (Interior Advertising) by Fritscher dba "Palm Drive Video"
1 Piece of Writing (Advertising) by Fritscher dba "Palm Drive Video"
- 1 Photograph (Front Cover Portrait): "Palm Drive Model Keith Ardent" by Fritscher dba "Palm Drive Video"; plus mention, p. 4, with Fritscher misspelled as "Fritcher"
- 9 Photographs (Interior Editorial): Keith Ardent in "Pec Stud in Black Rubber," pp. 2, 3, 11-18, 32, by Fritscher dba "Palm Drive Video"
- "Nine-Inch Pec Stud in Black Rubber," p. 14, photo caption

Drummer: Fritscher Timeline Bibliography   673

- "Rubberotica: Confessions of a Rubber Freak," pp. 28-32, lead feature article
- 7 Photographs (Interior Advertising) by Fritscher: "Palm Drive Models Sonny Butts, Dave Gold, Jason Steele, Bruno, Keith Ardent, Mike Welder, Redneck Cowboy," p. 80, by Fritscher dba "Palm Drive Video," display ad, half-page
- "New S&M Fetish Videos," p. 82, classified ad copy by Fritscher for Palm Drive Video
- 2 Photographs (Interior Editorial, Inside Back Cover): "Grizzly Action" and "Beards, Bears, and Barbarous Butts" by Fritscher dba "Palm Drive Video"

DRUMMER 119, July 1988 (*Drummer* 118 and *Drummer* 119 were both dated July 1988)
Masthead: Jack Fritscher, Writer, Frequent Contributors; Palm Drive Video, Photography, Frequent Contributors
Theme for *Drummer* 119 Created by Fritscher: Bears
1 Piece of Writing (Lead Feature Article) by Fritscher
21 Photographs (Interior Editorial) by Fritscher
7 Photographs (Interior Advertising) by Fritscher dba "Palm Drive Video"
1 Piece of Writing (Advertising) by Fritscher dba "Palm Drive Video"
1 Editorial Mention: Letter to the Editor

- Editorial Mention: "Fritscher/Palm Drive Video's *Mud Pillow Fight*," letter to the editor, p. 5
- "Fetish Feature," p. 19, schedule of themes created by Fritscher for upcoming issues 120-123
- "Bears! How to Hunt Buckskin Leather Mountain Men and Live Among the Bears," pp. 22-26, cover feature article, first Bear article in *Drummer*
- 21 Photographs (Interior Editorial): "Palm Drive Models John Muir, Jack Husky, and Mr. America Chuck Sipes with Mountain Men" pp. 2, 3, 18, 22-26, by Fritscher dba "Palm Drive Video"; Fritscher photo, page 18, is "Daddy's Beerbelly in Bondage"; on pages 22-26, Fritscher photos are numbered as 1-7, 9, 11-13, 15, 17-20; Fritscher photo inside front cover is "Big Bruno" in white cowboy hat, with three more photos on page 3, "Long Hair, Long Beard," "Jack Husky with Hammer," and "Mountain Man Black Hat"
- 7 Photographs (Interior Advertising): "Palm Drive Models Sonny Butts, Dave Gold, Jason Steele, Bruno, Keith Ardent, Mike Welder, Redneck Cowboy," p. 68, by Fritscher dba "Palm Drive Video," display ad, half-page
- "New S&M Fetish Videos," p. 76, classified ad copy by Fritscher for Palm Drive Video

DRUMMER 121, September 1988
Masthead: Jack Fritscher, Writer, Frequent Contributors; Palm Drive Video, Photography, Frequent Contributors
1 Photograph (Interior Editorial) by Fritscher dba "Palm Drive Video"
2 Editorial Mentions: 1 Video Review and 1 Book Review of Fritscher work
1 Piece of Writing (Advertising) by Fritscher dba "Palm Drive Video"

- 1 Photograph (Interior Editorial): "Palm Drive Model Jason Steele," p. 97, shot by Fritscher, illustrating Ken Kissoff's video and book reviews of Fritscher's Palm Drive Video feature *Tit Animal* and Fritscher's fiction anthology book *Stand by Your Man and Other Stories*
- Editorial Mention: Video Review of Fritscher's *Tit Animal*
- Editorial Mention: Book Review of Fritscher's *Stand by Your Man and Other Stories*
- "New S&M Fetish Videos," p. 80, classified ad copy by Fritscher for Palm Drive Video

DRUMMER 123, September 1988
Masthead: Jack Fritscher, Writer, Frequent Contributors; Palm Drive Video, Photography, Frequent Contributors
1 Piece of Writing (Lead Feature Article) by Fritscher
22 Photographs (Interior Editorial, including Inside Front Cover) by Fritscher dba "Palm Drive Video"
7 Photographs (Interior Advertising) by Fritscher dba "Palm Drive Video"
1 Piece of Writing (Advertising) by Fritscher dba "Palm Drive Video"
1 Editorial Mention
- 1 Photograph (Inside Front Cover): "Solo Sex: Cheesiest Uncut Cowboy in West Texas," p. 2, by Fritscher dba "Palm Drive Video"
- Editorial Mention: "Leather Pride Weekend," p. 7, listing of Fritscher as a judge of the 1988 Mr. *Drummer* Contest
- "Solo Sex, A Man's Guide," pp. 34-41, cover feature article
- 20 Photographs (Interior Editorial), "Solo Sex": 8 photographs, pp. 34 and 35; 1 photograph, top p. 36; 4 photographs, pp. 38-39; 6 photographs, p. 40; 1 photograph, bottom, p. 41, by Fritscher dba "Palm Drive Video"
- 7 Photographs (Interior Advertising), "Palm Drive Models Sonny Butts, Dave Gold, Jason Steele, Bruno, Keith Ardent, Mike Welder, Redneck Cowboy," p. 54, by Fritscher dba "Palm Drive Video," display ad, half-page
- "New S&M Fetish Videos," p. 81, classified ad copy by Fritscher for Palm Drive Video

DRUMMER 124, December 1988
Masthead: Jack Fritscher, Writer, Frequent Contributors; Palm Drive Video, Photography, Frequent Contributors
Theme for *Drummer* 124 Created by Fritscher: Bodybuilders and "the *Drummer* Novel," *Some Dance to Remember: A Memoir-Novel of San Francisco 1970-1982*
2 Pieces of Writing (Lead Feature Article and Book Excerpt) by Fritscher
5 Photographs (Interior Editorial) by Fritscher dba "Palm Drive Video"
2 Photographs (Interior Advertising) by Fritscher dba "Palm Drive Video"
2 Pieces of Writing (Advertising) by Fritscher dba "Palm Drive Video"
- "Bodybuilding: How to Judge It Inside and Out: A Sensual Critic's Eye View," pp. 7-9, lead feature
- 4 Photographs (Interior Editorial): "Bodybuilding: How to Judge It: Palm Drive Models Dick Black, Sonny Butts, and Anonymous Bodybuilder Contestant," pp. 16-17
- "*Some Dance to Remember,* Excerpts from the New Novel, *Drummer*'s Sneak Preview of a Literary Event," pp. 20-25, "The *Drummer* novel" about *Drummer*
- 1 Photograph (Interior Editorial): "Handsome, Bald Bodybuilder," p. 35, photograph by Fritscher illustrates review of a documentary video by Fritscher titled *Police Olympics Bodybuilding*
- 2 Photographs (Interior Advertising): "Handsome Bald Bodybuilder and Professional Bodybuilder Mike Sable," p. 53, Palm Drive Video display ad, half-page
- "New S&M Fetish Videos" and "Cop Jock Videos," p. 80, classified ad copy by Fritscher for Palm Drive Video

DRUMMER 126, March 1989
Masthead: Jack Fritscher, Writer, Frequent Contributors; Palm Drive Video, Photography, Frequent Contributors
1 Piece of Writing by Fritscher
1 Photograph (Interior Editorial, Inside Back Cover) by Fritscher dba "Palm Drive Video"
7 Photographs (Interior Advertising) by Fritscher dba "Palm Drive Video"

Drummer: Fritscher Timeline Bibliography

2 Pieces of Writing (Advertising) by Fritscher dba "Palm Drive Video"
2 Editorial Mentions
- "Rear-View Mirror #1: Home Is the Sailor! Home from the Sea!"; pp. 8-9, debut of Fritscher's GLBT leather history column
- 7 Photographs (Interior Advertising): "Palm Drive Models Sonny Butts, Dave Gold, Jason Steele, Bruno, Keith Ardent, Mike Welder, Redneck Cowboy," p. 87, by Fritscher dba "Palm Drive Video," display ad, half-page
- "New S&M Fetish Videos," and "Cop Jock Videos," p. 95, classified ad copy by Fritscher for Palm Drive Video
- Editorial Mention in "Tough Customers" of Palm Drive Video, p. 98
- 1 Photograph (Interior Editorial, Inside Back Cover): "Palm Drive Model J. D. Slater," p. 99
- Editorial Mention of Fritscher fiction "The Shadow Soldiers" and Fritscher photo for "J. D. Slater Is 'Dirt,'" p. 99

DRUMMER 127, April 1989
Masthead: Jack Fritscher, Writer, Frequent Contributors; Palm Drive Video, Photography, Frequent Contributors
3 Pieces of Writing (Short Fiction, History Essay, and Poem) by Fritscher
4 Photographs (Interior Editorial) by Fritscher dba "Jack Fritscher's Palm Drive Video"
7 Photographs (Interior Advertising) by Fritscher dba "Palm Drive Video"
2 Pieces of Writing (Advertising) by Fritscher dba "Palm Drive Video"
- "Rear-View Mirror #2: Bars and Bikes," pp. 15 and 97, GLBT leather history essay
- "J. D. Slater Is 'Dirt,'" pp. 16-17, poem
- 4 Photographs (Interior Editorial): "Palm Drive Model J. D. Slater," pp. 16-17, by Fritscher dba "Jack Fritscher's Palm Drive Video"
- "Shadow Soldiers," pp. 23-35, short fiction; with four drawings by Skipper produced by Fritscher; Skipper drawings © 1989 and 2007 Jack Fritscher
- 7 Photographs (Interior Advertising): "Palm Drive Models Sonny Butts, Dave Gold, Jason Steele, Bruno, Keith Ardent, Mike Welder, Redneck Cowboy," p. 85, by Fritscher dba "Palm Drive Video." display ad, half-page
- "New S&M Fetish Videos," and "Cop Jock Videos," p. 93, classified ad copy by Fritscher for Palm Drive Video

DRUMMER 128, May 1989
Masthead: Jack Fritscher, Writer, Frequent Contributors; Palm Drive Video, Photography, Frequent Contributors
7 Photographs (Interior Advertising) by Fritscher dba "Palm Drive Video"
2 Pieces of Writing (Advertising) by Fritscher dba "Palm Drive Video"
[Editor's Note: *Drummer* 128 contains a "Letter to the Editor," p. 5, re Fritscher's "Solo Sex" feature in *Drummer* 123. The editorial by Anthony F. DeBlase states that the success of *Drummer* is owed precisely to its showcasing of "real," that is, actual men, the readers, which as a concept was created and inaugurated in the 70s in the column "Tough Customers" by then editor in chief Fritscher. On p. 4, DeBlase also acknowledges that Fritscher's "Tough Customers" concept **"is obviously one of the, if not the, most popular feature in** *Drummer*."]
- 7 Photographs (Interior Advertising): "Palm Drive Models Sonny Butts, Dave Gold, Jason Steele, Bruno, Keith Ardent, Mike Welder, Redneck Cowboy," p. 65, by Fritscher dba "Palm Drive Video," display ad, half-page
- "New S&M Fetish Videos," and "Cop Jock Videos," p. 70, classified ad copy by Fritscher for Palm Drive Video

DRUMMER 129, June 1989
Masthead: Jack Fritscher, Featured Contributors; Palm Drive Video, Photography, Frequent Contributors
1 Piece of Writing by Fritscher
7 Photographs (Interior Advertising) by Fritscher dba "Palm Drive Video"
2 Pieces of Writing (Advertising) by Fritscher dba "Palm Drive Video"
- "Rear-View Mirror #3: Leather's Founding Daddies," pp. 33-34, GLBT leather history essay
- 7 Photographs (Interior Advertising): "Palm Drive Models Sonny Butts, Dave Gold, Jason Steele, Bruno, Keith Ardent, Mike Welder, Redneck Cowboy," p. 67, by Fritscher dba "Palm Drive Video," display ad, half-page "New S&M Fetish Videos," and "Cop Jock Videos," p. 72, classified ad copy by Fritscher for Palm Drive Video

DRUMMER 130, July 1989 (*Drummer* 130 and *Drummer* 131 were both dated July 1989)
Masthead: Jack Fritscher, Featured Contributors; Palm Drive Video, Photography, Frequent Contributors
1 Feature (Cirby Art) Produced by Fritscher
7 Photographs (Interior Advertising) by Fritscher dba "Palm Drive Video"
2 Pieces of Writing (Advertising) by Fritscher dba "Palm Drive Video"
1 Editorial Mention
- Editorial Mention: "Eroticizing Vietnam" in "Male Call" of Fritscher fiction, "The Shadow Soldiers," *Drummer* 127, pp. 5-6
- "Cirby: The Erotic Artist," pp. 21-23, art feature produced by Fritscher collaborating with Cirby on a Palm Drive Video; Cirby was himself a Palm Drive Video model photographed by Fritscher
- 7 Photographs (Interior Advertising): "Palm Drive Models Sonny Butts, Dave Gold, Jason Steele, Bruno, Keith Ardent, Mike Welder, Redneck Cowboy," p. 83, by Fritscher dba "Palm Drive Video," display ad, half-page "New S&M Fetish Videos," and "Cop Jock Videos," p. 90, classified ad copy by Fritscher for Palm Drive Video

DRUMMER 131, July 1989 (*Drummer* 130 and *Drummer* 131 were both dated July 1989)
Masthead: Jack Fritscher, Writer, Featured Contributors; Palm Drive Video, Photography, Frequent Contributors
2 Pieces of Writing by Fritscher
7 Photographs (Interior Advertising) by Fritscher dba "Palm Drive Video"
2 Pieces of Writing (Advertising) by Fritscher dba "Palm Drive Video"
- "Rear-View Mirror #4: Inventing the Leather Bar (Tony Tavarossi)," pp. 22-23, GLBT leather history essay
- "You're History!" p. 23, Fritscher asks readers to send in their own "Rear-View Mirror" histories to the series he produced
- 7 Photographs (Interior Advertising): "Palm Drive Models Sonny Butts, Dave Gold, Jason Steele, Bruno, Keith Ardent, Mike Welder, Redneck Cowboy," p. 83, by Fritscher dba "Palm Drive Video," display ad, half-page "New S&M Fetish Videos," and "Cop Jock Videos," p. 90, classified ad copy by Fritscher for Palm Drive Video

DRUMMER 133, September 1989
Masthead: Jack Fritscher, Writer, Featured Contributors; Palm Drive Video, Photography, Frequent Contributors
Theme for *Drummer* 133 Created by Fritscher: Mapplethorpe and Censorship
1 Piece of Writing (Cover Lead Feature) by Fritscher

Drummer: Fritscher Timeline Bibliography 677

1 Photograph (Interior Editorial, Inside Back Cover) by Fritscher dba "Palm Drive Video"
2 Pieces of Writing (Advertising) by Fritscher dba "Palm Drive Video"
6 Editorial Mentions
- Editorial Mention (Front Cover Copy): "Jack Fritscher on Robert Mapplethorpe: Intelligent People Making Intelligent Sex"
- Editorial Mention: by Anthony DeBlase of Mapplethorpe and Fritscher, p. 4
- Editorial Mention: by Paul Martin of Fritscher and drug use in *Some Dance to Remember*, p. 6
- Editorial Mention: by Paul Martin of extreme S&M in Fritscher's fiction, "The Shadow Soldiers," p. 7
- "Pentimento for Robert Mapplethorpe: Fetishes, Faces, and Flowers of Evil," pp. 8-15, cover lead feature
- Editorial Mention: by Anthony DeBlase aka Fledermaus of "Master of Sleaze" Fritscher as video-photographer of Roger Earl and Terry LeGrand's six-video series, *Bound for Europe* (1989), p. 34
- Editorial Mention: by Kevin Wolff of Fritscher as cinematographer and collaborator with Roger Earl and Terry LeGrand on the six-video series, *Bound for Europe* (1989), p. 43
- 7 Photographs (Interior Advertising): "Palm Drive Models Sonny Butts, Dave Gold, Jason Steele, Bruno, Keith Ardent, Mike Welder, Redneck Cowboy," p. 90, by Fritscher dba "Palm Drive Video," display ad, half-page "New S&M Fetish Videos," and "Cop Jock Videos," p. 92, classified ad copy by Fritscher for Palm Drive Video
- 1 Photograph (Interior Editorial, Inside Back Cover): "Palm Drive Model Bobby Stumps," inside back cover, by Fritscher dba "Palm Drive Video"

DRUMMER 134, October 1989
Masthead: Jack Fritscher, Writer, Featured Contributors; Palm Drive Video, Photography, Frequent Contributors
Theme for *Drummer* 134 Created by Fritscher: Brown Leather
1 Piece of Writing by Fritscher
7 Photographs (Interior Editorial, Centerfold) by Fritscher dba "Palm Drive Video"
11 Photographs (Interior Advertising) by Fritscher dba "Palm Drive Video"
2 Pieces of Writing (Advertising) by Fritscher dba "Palm Drive Video"
- "Rear-View Mirror #5: Artist Chuck Arnett—His Life, Our Times," pp. 32-36, GLBT leather history column
- 7 Photographs (Interior Editorial, Centerfold) "Palm Drive Model Bobby Stumps," pp. 50-55 by Fritscher dba "Palm Drive Video"
- 11 Photographs (Interior Advertising) : "Palm Drive Models Redneck Cowboy Curtis James, Mike Welder, Pro-Wrestler Chris Colt, Big Hairy Bruno, Jack Husky, Cigar Sarge, Vigilante, Jason Steele, Dave Gold, Bobby Stumps, Keith Ardent," p. 72, by Fritscher dba "Palm Drive Video," full-page display ad for Christmas
- "New S&M Fetish Videos," and "Cop Jock Videos," p. 92, classified ad copy by Fritscher for Palm Drive Video

DRUMMER 135, December 1989 (First Post-Earthquake Issue)
Masthead: Jack Fritscher, Writer, Featured Contributors; Palm Drive Video, Photography, Frequent Contributors
1 Photograph (Interior Editorial) by Fritscher dba "Palm Drive Video"
3 Photographs (Interior Advertising) by Fritscher dba "Palm Drive Video"
2 Pieces of Writing (Advertising) by Fritscher dba "Palm Drive Video"

- 1 Photograph (Interior Editorial): "Uncut Bear," p. 24, by Fritscher dba "Palm Drive Video" of Ken Wimberly in the Palm Drive Video *Bear in the Woods* illustrating Larry Townsend's "Leather Notebook"
- 3 Photographs (Interior Advertising): "Palm Drive Video Model Rick Conder," p. 82, by Fritscher dba "Palm Drive Video," display ad, "Star Search," a video casting call for grass-roots actors who are not models for roles in Palm Drive "reality TV."
- "New S&M Fetish Videos," and "Cop Jock Videos," p. 94, classified ad copy by Fritscher for Palm Drive Video

DRUMMER 136, January 1990
Masthead: Jack Fritscher, Writer, Featured Contributors; Palm Drive Video, Photography, Frequent Contributors
2 Photographs (Interior Advertising) by Fritscher dba "Palm Drive Video"
1 Photograph (Interior Advertising) by Fritscher for Roger Earl and Terry LeGrand, Marathon Films
2 Pieces of Writing (Advertising) by Fritscher dba "Palm Drive Video"
- 2 Photographs (Interior Advertising): "Palm Drive Models Sonny Butts and Goliath," p. 86, by Fritscher dba "Palm Drive Video," display ad, half-page
- 1 Photograph (Interior Advertising) for *Argos Session*, p. 99, by Fritscher for Roger Earl and Terry LeGrand, Marathon Films: one photograph designed and shot by Fritscher during videotaping of *The Argos Session* shot and composed in two Hi8 cameras by Mark Hemry and Fritscher for Marathon Films in Amsterdam, June 21, 1989
- "New S&M Fetish Videos," and "Cop Jock Videos," p. 102, classified ad copy by Fritscher for Palm Drive Video

DRUMMER 137, February 1990
Masthead: Jack Fritscher, Writer, Featured Contributors; Palm Drive Video, Photography, Frequent Contributors
1 Photograph (Interior Advertising) by Fritscher for Roger Earl and Terry LeGrand, Marathon Films
2 Photographs (Interior Advertising) by Fritscher dba "Palm Drive Video"
2 Pieces of Writing (Advertising) by Fritscher dba "Palm Drive Video"
2 Editorial Mentions
- Editorial Mention: "Letters to the Editor" regarding Fritscher's Palm Drive Video, p. 6
- Editorial Mention: (Inside Back Cover) with announcement for Fritscher's proposed satirical "topsy-turvy earthquake" special issue of *Drummer* titled "*Dummer* #1, A Desmodus Flip Publication"; see Fritscher concept incorporated into *Drummer* 138.
- 2 Photographs: "Palm Drive Models Sonny Butts and Goliath," p. 87, Palm Drive Video display ad, half-page
- 1 Photograph (Interior Advertising) for *Argos Session*, p. 99, by Fritscher for Roger Earl and Terry LeGrand, Marathon Films
- "New S&M Fetish Videos," and "Cop Jock Videos," p. 98, classified ad copy by Fritscher for Palm Drive Video

DRUMMER 138, March 1990 aka "*Dummer* [*sic*, Satire] 1: A Unique *Drummer* Semi-Publication"
Masthead: Jack Fritscher, Writer, Frequent Contributors; Palm Drive Video, Photography, Frequent Contributors
Theme for *Drummer* 138 Created by Fritscher: Satirical Upside-Down Earthquake Issue of *Drummer* titled "*Dummer*": *A Unique Drummer Semi-Publication*
1 Editorial Review
2 Photographs (Interior Advertising) by Fritscher dba "Palm Drive Video"

Drummer: Fritscher Timeline Bibliography 679

2 Pieces of Writing (Advertising) by Fritscher dba "Palm Drive Video"
- Editorial Review: "Drummedia" by Joseph W. Bean, pp. 36, 37, 38, of three Fritscher "Palm Drive Video" features: *Blond Saddle Tramp, Mud and Oil, The Hun Video Gallery #1: Rainy Night in Georgia*
- 2 Photographs: "Palm Drive Models Sonny Butts and Goliath," p. 58, by Fritscher dba "Palm Drive Video," display ad, half-page
- "New S&M Fetish Videos," and "Cop Jock Videos," p. 80, classified ad copy by Fritscher for Palm Drive Video

DRUMMER **139, May 1990**
Masthead: Jack Fritscher, Writer, Frequent Contributors; Palm Drive Video, Photography, Frequent Contributors
Theme for *Drummer* 139 Created by Fritscher: Remembrance of Sleaze Past in the Titanic 70s
1 Piece of Writing (Cover Lead Feature) by Fritscher
2 Photographs (Interior Advertising) by Fritscher dba "Palm Drive Video"
1 Photograph (Interior Advertising) by Fritscher for Roger Earl and Terry LeGrand, Marathon Films
2 Pieces of Writing (Advertising) by Fritscher dba "Palm Drive Video"
3 Editorial Mentions
- Editorial Mention: in Deblase editorial, p. 4, referencing Fritscher as source for issue's theme
- "Remembrance of Sleaze Past…and Present and Future," cover feature article, pp. 7-11
- Editorial Mention: in "Sidebar" by Gayle Rubin, p. 34, concerning her research in Fritscher's feature article, "Catacombs," *Drummer* 23, 1978
- Editorial Mention: in Deblase introduction, p. 35, "Remembrance of Sleaze Past" referencing Fritscher as source for issue's theme and for photo shoot by Jim Wigler
- 1 Photograph (Interior Advertising) for *The Argos Session*, p. 77, by Fritscher for Roger Earl and Terry LeGrand, Marathon Films
- 2 Photographs (Interior Advertising): Palm Drive Models Terry Kelly with Jack Fritscher as well as Jack Husky with Chris Colt, p. 85, by Fritscher dba "Palm Drive Video," display ad, half-page, p. 85: one photograph by Hemry and Fritscher of "Terry Kelly with Fritscher" in Hemry-Fritscher video, *Hot Lunch*, and one photograph of "Chris Colt with Jack Husky" in Fritscher's video, *Sex Aggression: Jack Husky's First Night at Chris Colt's Wrestling Academy*
- "New S&M Fetish Videos," and "Cop Jock Videos," p. 89, classified ad copy by Fritscher for Palm Drive Video

DRUMMER **140, June 1990**
Masthead: Jack Fritscher, Writer, Featured Contributors; Palm Drive Video, Photography, Frequent Contributors
1 Photograph (Front Cover Portrait) by Fritscher dba "Palm Drive Video"
4 Photographs (Interior Centerfold Editorial) by Fritscher dba "Palm Drive Video"
7 Photographs (Interior Advertising) by Fritscher dba "Palm Drive Video"
1 Photograph (Interior Advertising) by Fritscher for Roger Earl and Terry LeGrand, Marathon Films
2 Pieces of Writing (Advertising) by Fritscher dba "Palm Drive Video"
1 Editorial Mention
- 1 Photograph (Front Cover Portrait): "Palm Drive Video Star of *Daddy's Tools*" by Fritscher dba "Palm Drive Video"
- 2 Photographs (Interior Editorial): "Palm Drive Model Goliath," pp. 20 and 23, by Fritscher dba "Palm Drive Video"

- Editorial Mention: by Joseph W. Bean of Fritscher's memoir-novel, *Some Dance to Remember*, p. 28
- 4 Photographs (Centerfold): "Palm Drive Video: Randy, Carpenter Bear," pp. 55-58, by Fritscher dba "Palm Drive Video" of *Drummer* 140 cover model, Ken Horan
- 7 Photographs (Interior Advertising): "Palm Drive Video Models Sonny Butts, Dave Gold, Keith Ardent, Jason Steele, Big Bruno, Mike Welder, and Curtis James," p. 75, by Fritscher dba "Palm Drive Video," display ad, half-page
- 1 Photograph (Interior Advertising) for *Argos Session*, p. 83, by Fritscher for Roger Earl and Terry LeGrand, Marathon Films
- "New S&M Fetish Videos," and "Cop Jock Videos," p. 88, classified ad copy by Fritscher for Palm Drive Video

DRUMMER 141, August 1990
Masthead: Jack Fritscher, Writer, Featured Contributors; Palm Drive Video, Photography, Frequent Contributors
1 Photograph (Interior Editorial, including Centerfold) by Fritscher dba "Palm Drive Video"
6 Photographs (Interior Editorial) by Fritscher for Roger Earl and Terry LeGrand, Marathon Films
7 Photographs (Interior Advertising) by Fritscher dba "Palm Drive Video"
2 Pieces of Writing (Advertising) by Fritscher dba "Palm Drive Video"
3 Editorial Reviews
- Editorial Book Review by Paul Martin: review of *Some Dance to Remember*, pp. 32-33
- Editorial Video Review by Paul Martin: review of Fritscher's video, *Hot Lunch*, pp. 33-34;
- Editorial Video Review by DeBlase aka Fledermaus: review of *The Argos Session*, p. 34, a feature video shot and composed in two Hi8 cameras by Mark Hemry and Jack Fritscher for Roger Earl and Terry LeGrand, Marathon Films in Amsterdam, June 21, 1989
- 6 Photographs (Interior Editorial): "*The Argos Session*: Photo Feature and Video Review," pp. 34, 35, 36, 37, 38, shot by Fritscher for Roger Earl and Terry LeGrand, Marathon Films, in the Argos Bar, Amsterdam, June 21, 1989
- 1 Photograph (Interior Editorial): "Palm Drive Model Goliath," p. 47, by Fritscher dba "Palm Drive Video"
- 7 Photographs (Interior Advertising): "Palm Drive Models Sonny Butts, Dave Gold, Keith Ardent, Jason Steele, Big Bruno, Mike Welder, and Curtis James," p. 68, by Fritscher dba "Palm Drive Video," display ad, half page
- "New S&M Fetish Videos," and "Cop Jock Videos," p. 89, classified ad copy by Fritscher for Palm Drive Video

MR. DRUMMER CONTEST FINALS AND SHOW PROGRAM MAGAZINE, September 1990
1 Photograph (Interior Advertising) by Fritscher dba "Palm Drive Video" and David Hurles (Old Reliable)
1 Photograph (Interior Advertising) by Fritscher dba "Palm Drive Video"
- 1 Photograph (Interior Advertising): "How I Write Erotica: Thinking 'XXX' Auto-Photograph of Jack Fritscher," p. 4, by Fritscher dba "Palm Drive Video" and David Hurles (Old Reliable)
- 1 Photograph (Interior Advertising): Insert photograph of Palm Drive Video model Brutus into "How I Write Erotica: Thinking 'XXX,'" Auto-Photograph of Jack Fritscher, p. 4

Drummer: Fritscher Timeline Bibliography 681

DRUMMER 143, October 1990
Masthead: Jack Fritscher, Writer, Featured Contributors; Palm Drive Video, Photography, Frequent Contributors
1 Piece of Writing (Cover Lead Feature) by Fritscher
1 Photograph (Interior Advertising) by Fritscher dba "Palm Drive Video" and David Hurles (Old Reliable)
1 Photograph (Interior Advertising) by Fritscher dba "Palm Drive Video"
2 Pieces of Writing (Advertising) by Fritscher dba "Palm Drive Video"
1 Advertising Notice by Malibu Sales of Fritscher books
- "Radical Nipples," pp. 18-22, cover lead feature article
- 1 Photograph (Interior Advertising): "How I Write Erotica: Thinking 'XXX' Auto-Photograph of Jack Fritscher," p. 15, by Fritscher dba "Palm Drive Video" and David Hurles (Old Reliable)
- 1 Photograph (Interior Advertising): Insert photograph of Palm Drive Video model Brutus into "How I Write Erotica: Thinking 'XXX' Auto-Photograph of Jack Fritscher," p. 15
- Advertising Notice by Malibu Sales, p. 87, of two Fritscher books, *Corporal in Charge of Taking Care of Captain O'Malley and Other Stories* and *Stand by Your Man and Other Stories*
- "New S&M Fetish Videos," and "Cop Jock Videos," p. 95, classified ad copy by Fritscher for Palm Drive Video

DRUMMER 144, November 1990
Masthead: Jack Fritscher, Writer, Frequent Contributors; Palm Drive Video, Photography, Frequent Contributors
1 Piece of Writing
3 Photographs (Interior Editorial) by Fritscher
1 Photograph (Interior Advertising) by Fritscher dba "Palm Drive Video"
2 Pieces of Writing (Advertising) by Fritscher dba "Palm Drive Video"
1 Editorial Mention
- 3 Photographs (Interior Editorial): "The Training Center: The Academy," pp. 29, 30, and p. 98, by Fritscher dba "Palm Drive Video"
- "I, Brutus: Muscle-Cop Road Warrior," poem, p. 73
- 1 Photograph (Interior Advertising): "Palm Drive Model Brutus," p. 73, by Fritscher dba "Palm Drive Video." display ad, half-page
- "New S&M Fetish Videos," and "Cop Jock Videos," p. 93-94, classified ad copy by Fritscher for Palm Drive Video
- Editorial Mention: "Fritscher Takes You inside the Academy," p. 98

DRUMMER 145, December 1990
Masthead: Jack Fritscher, Writer, Frequent Contributors; Palm Drive Video, Photography, Frequent Contributors
1 Piece of Writing (Cover Lead Feature) by Fritscher
5 Photographs (Interior Editorial) by Fritscher (not as "Palm Drive Video")
1 Photograph (Interior Advertising) by Fritscher dba "Palm Drive Video"
2 Pieces of Writing (Advertising) by Fritscher dba "Palm Drive Video"
1 Editorial Mention
- Editorial Mention (Front Cover Copy): "Incarceration for Pleasure! Jack Fritscher Takes on the Academy"
- "The Academy: Incarceration for Pleasure–Real Cops and Rough Fun in Missouri," pp. 24-29, cover lead feature article

- 5 Photographs (Interior Editorial) by Fritscher solo (not as "Palm Drive Video"), pp. 24-25, 27-29
- 1 Photograph (Interior Advertising): "I, Brutus: Muscle-Cop Road Warrior," p. 70, by Fritscher dba "Palm Drive Video," display ad, half-page
- "New S&M Fetish Videos," and "Cop Jock Videos," p. 95, classified ad copy by Fritscher for Palm Drive Video

DRUMMER 147, March 1991
Masthead: Jack Fritscher, Writer, Frequent Contributors; Palm Drive Video, Photography, Frequent Contributors
1 Photograph (Interior Advertising) by Fritscher dba "Palm Drive Video"
2 Pieces of Writing (Advertising) by Fritscher dba "Palm Drive Video"
1 Editorial Review

- Editorial Review: Review by Joseph W. Bean of video series *Bound for Europe*, six S&M video features shot by Jack Fritscher and Mark Hemry for Roger Earl and Terry LeGrand, Marathon Films, p. 65; display ad, p. 77
- 1 Photograph (Interior Editorial): "Palm Drive Model Brutus," p. 88, by Fritscher dba "Palm Drive Video," display ad, half-page
- "New S&M Fetish Videos," and "Cop Jock Videos," p. 95, classified ad copy by Fritscher for Palm Drive Video

DRUMMER 148, April 1991
Masthead: Jack Fritscher, Writer, Frequent Contributors; Palm Drive Video, Photography, Frequent Contributors
7 Photographs (Interior Editorial, Including Centerfold) by Fritscher dba "Palm Drive Video"
1 Photograph (Interior Advertising) by Fritscher dba "Palm Drive Video"
1 Photography Feature (by DeBlase) Produced by Fritscher
2 Pieces of Writing (Advertising) by Fritscher dba "Palm Drive Video"
1 Editorial Mention

- Editorial Mention: Contents Page, p. 3, "Slap Happy. What Is the Sound of One Hand Slapping? Palm Drive Video Has the Answer"
- "Steve Parker Photography by Anthony DeBlase," pp. 27-30, produced by Fritscher who cast his Palm Drive Video model Steve Parker with DeBlase at DeBlase's request
- 3 Photographs (Interior Editorial, Centerfold): "Slap Happy," pp. 50-51, by Fritscher dba "Palm Drive Video"
- 4 Photographs (Interior Editorial): "Wes Decker in *Sodbuster*," p. 60-62, by Fritscher dba "Palm Drive Video"
- 1 Photograph (Interior Advertising): "Brutus," p. 92, by Fritscher dba "Palm Drive Video," display ad, half-page
- "New S&M Fetish Videos," and "Cop Jock Videos," p. 96, classified ad copy by Fritscher for Palm Drive Video

DRUMMER 155, May 1992
Masthead: Jack Fritscher, Writer, Frequent Contributors; Palm Drive Video, Photography, Frequent Contributors
10 Photographs (Interior Editorial) by Fritscher dba "Palm Drive Video"
1 Photograph (Interior Advertising) by Fritscher dba "Palm Drive Video"
2 Pieces of Writing (Advertising) by Fritscher dba "Palm Drive Video"
1 Editorial Mention
Editorial Mention: Contents Page Caption, p. 3, "Latino Attitude! Photography by Fritscher dba "Palm Drive Video"

Drummer: Fritscher Timeline Bibliography 683

10 Photographs (Interior Editorial): "Attitude Latino," pp. 18-22, cover photo essay by Fritscher dba "Jack Fritscher/Palm Drive Video"
1 Photograph (Interior Advertising): "Redneck Cowboy Curtis James," p. 73, by Fritscher dba "Palm Drive Video," display ad, half-page
"New S&M Fetish Videos," and "Cop Jock Videos," p. 81, classified ad copy by Fritscher for Palm Drive Video

DRUMMER 157, August 1992
Masthead: Jack Fritscher, Writer, Frequent Contributors; Palm Drive Video, Photography, Frequent Contributors
1 Photograph (Front Cover Portrait Insert) by Fritscher dba "Palm Drive Video"
1 Photograph (Interior Editorial) by Fritscher dba "Palm Drive Video"
1 Photograph (Interior Advertising) by Fritscher dba "Palm Drive Video"
2 Pieces of Writing (Advertising) by Fritscher dba "Palm Drive Video"
- 1 Photograph (Front Cover Portrait Insert): "Moustached Bodybuilder," by Fritscher dba "Palm Drive Video"
- 1 Photograph (Interior Editorial): "Moustached Bodybuilder: Double Biceps Pose," p. 10, by Fritscher dba "Palm Drive Video"
- 1 Photograph (Interior Advertising): "Brutus," p. 77, by Fritscher dba "Palm Drive Video," display ad, half-page
- "New S&M Fetish Videos," and "Cop Jock Videos," p. 77, classified ad copy by Fritscher for Palm Drive Video

DRUMMER 159, December 1992
Masthead: Jack Fritscher, Writer, Frequent Contributors; Palm Drive Video, Photography, Frequent Contributors
1 Photograph (Front Cover Portrait Insert) by Fritscher dba "Palm Drive Video"
8 Photographs (Interior Editorial) by Fritscher dba "Palm Drive Video"
1 Photograph (Interior Advertising) by Fritscher dba "Palm Drive Video"
2 Pieces of Writing (Advertising) by Fritscher dba "Palm Drive Video"
1 Editorial Mention
- 1 Photograph (Front Cover Portrait Insert): "Larry Perry," cover photograph by Fritscher dba "Palm Drive Video"
- Editorial Mention: Contents Page Caption, p. 3, "Barman Larry Perry"
- 8 Photographs (Interior Editorial): "Palm Drive Model Larry Perry," pp. 14-18, photo feature by Fritscher dba "Palm Drive Video"
- 1 Photograph (Interior Advertising): "Brutus," p. 60, by Fritscher dba "Palm Drive Video," display ad, half-page
- "New S&M Fetish Videos," and "Cop Jock Videos," p. 78, classified ad copy by Fritscher for Palm Drive Video

DRUMMER 169, November 1993
Masthead: Jack Fritscher, Writer, Frequent Contributors; Palm Drive Video, Photographer, Frequent Contributors
1 Photograph (Interior Editorial) by Fritscher dba "Palm Drive Video"
1 Photograph (Interior Advertising) by Fritscher dba "Palm Drive Video"
1 Piece of Writing (Advertising) by Fritscher dba "Palm Drive Video"
- 1 Photograph (Interior Advertising): "Donnie Russo," p. 67, by Fritscher dba "Palm Drive Video," display ad, quarter page
- "Cop Jock Videos," p. 78, classified ad copy by Fritscher for Palm Drive Video
- 1 Photograph (Interior Editorial): "Donnie Russo," p. 82, by Fritscher dba "Palm Drive Video"

***DRUMMER* 170, December 1993**
Masthead: Jack Fritscher, Writer, Frequent Contributors; Palm Drive Video, Photography, Frequent Contributors
Theme for *Drummer* 170 Created by Fritscher: Russomania—Shooting Porn
1 Photograph (Front Cover Portrait) by Fritscher dba "Palm Drive Video"
1 Piece of Writing (Cover Lead Feature Article) by Fritscher
13 Photographs (Interior Editorial, Centerfold) by Fritscher dba "Palm Drive Video"
1 Photograph (Interior Advertising) by Fritscher dba "Palm Drive Video"
1 Piece of Writing (Advertising) by Fritscher dba "Palm Drive Video"

- 1 Photograph (Front Cover Portrait): "Donnie Russo" by Fritscher dba "Palm Drive Video"
- "Russomania: Inside Porn Star Donnie Russo," pp. 39-46, cover lead feature article
- 13 Photographs (Interior Editorial, Centerfold): "Donnie Russo," pp. 39-46, centerfold by Fritscher dba "Palm Drive Video"
- 1 Photograph: "Donnie Russo," p. 66, by Fritscher dba "Palm Drive Video," display ad, quarter page
- "Cop Jock Videos," p. 74, classified ad copy by Fritscher for Palm Drive Video

***DRUMMER* 186, July 1995**
Masthead: Jack Fritscher, Writer; Palm Drive Video, Photography
3 Pieces of Writing (Two: Cover Fiction) by Fritscher
1 Drawing by Skipper Produced by Fritscher
2 Editorial Mentions

- Editorial Mention: Contents Page, p. 5, cover fiction, "Uncut Lust," "My Foreskin Fetish"
- Editorial Mention: Contents Page, p. 5, "'Foreskin Prison Blues,' Story and Illustration by Jack Fritscher"
- "Uncut Lust: Foreskin Fetish," pp. 19-20, cover fiction
- "Foreskin Prison Blues," pp. 26-27, feature fiction (published foreshortened in an unauthorized edit)
- Drawing: "Foreskin Mask," p. 27, by Skipper, commissioned and produced by Fritscher for "Foreskin Prison Blues"; copyright 1995 and 2007 Jack Fritscher
- "Digital Mapplethorpe," p. 59

***DRUMMER* 188, September 1995**
20th Anniversary Issue
Masthead: Jack Fritscher, Writer; Palm Drive Video, Photography
1 Piece of Writing (Historical Essay) Fritscher
1 Photograph (Interior Advertising) by Fritscher dba "Palm Drive Video"
5 Editorial Mentions

- Editorial Mention: Contents Page, p. 5, "Cover Story, '*Drummer*, The Magazine with Balls' by Jack Fritscher,"
- Editorial Mention: "Mapplethorpe cover, shot by Mapplethorpe, designed and cast by Jack Fritscher," p. 17
- Editorial Mention: Joseph W. Bean and Anthony DeBlase re Fritscher, pp. 18, 19
- Editorial Mention: Cover of *Drummer* 100, p. 21
- "20 Years of *Drummer* History: The Magazine with Balls," pp. 21-22, excerpt of a longer historical feature essay by founding San Francisco editor in chief Fritscher
- Editorial Mention: John Embry, p. 23, "What happened in 1977 could fill a book. We hired A. Jay's friend Jack Fritscher as editor in chief and bought a building on Harriet Street...."
- 1 Photograph: "Donnie Russo," p. 48, by Fritscher dba "Palm Drive Video," display ad, quarter page

Drummer: Fritscher Timeline Bibliography 685

DRUMMER 204, June 1997
Masthead: Jack Fritscher, Writer; Palm Drive Video, Photography
1 Piece of Writing (Short Story) by Fritscher dba "www.JackFritscher.com"
19 Photographs (Interior Editorial) from a Video by Fritscher dba "Palm Drive Video"
1 Photograph (Interior Editorial) by Fritscher dba "www.JackFritscher.com"
- 19 Photographs (Interior Editorial): "Gym Jock from Palm Drive Video," pp. 22-25, pictorial essay of color video frames chosen and printed as underground new-tech art by *Drummer* art director from Fritscher's video, *Dave Gold's Gym Workout*
- "Hustler Bars: Tricks of the Trade," pp. 36-37, short story, by Fritscher dba "www.JackFritscher.com"
- 1 Photograph (Interior Editorial): "Mike Welder," p. 36, by Fritscher dba "www.Jack-Fritscher.com"

   [Editor's Note: Palm Drive Video display ad and classified ad, despite trade agreement, not honored by editor Wickie Stamps, and so not inserted.]

FORESKIN QUARTERLY 12, August 1989
Masthead: Publisher Anthony F. DeBlase; Managing Editor Joseph W. Bean
6 Photographs (Interior Editorial) by Fritscher dba "Palm Drive Video"
7 Photographs (Interior Advertising) by Fritscher dba "Palm Drive Video"
- 6 Photographs (Interior Editorial): "*Cheesiest Uncut Cowboy in West Texas*," pp. 10-15, photo essay
- 7 Photographs (Interior Advertising): "Palm Drive Models Sonny Butts, Dave Gold, Keith Ardent, Jason Steele, Big Bruno, Mike Welder, and Curtis James," p. 63, by Fritscher dba "Palm Drive Video," display ad, half page

MACH 20 — A *DRUMMER SUPER PUBLICATION*, April 1990
Masthead: Publisher Anthony F. DeBlase; Managing Editor Joseph W. Bean
1 Photograph (Front Cover Portrait) by Fritscher for Roger Earl and Terry LeGrand, Marathon Films
12 Photographs (Interior Editorial, Including Inside Front Cover) by Fritscher for Roger Earl and Terry LeGrand, Marathon Films
- 1 Photograph (Front Cover Portrait): "Argos," one photograph designed and shot on set by Fritscher during videotaping of *The Argos Session* shot and composed in two Hi8 cameras by Mark Hemry and Jack Fritscher for Roger Earl and Terry LeGrand, Marathon Films in the Argos Bar, Amsterdam, June 21, 1989
- 1 Photograph (Inside Front Cover), "*Argos*," color photograph shot on set by Fritscher of *The Argos Session* for Roger Earl and Terry LeGrand, Marathon Films.
- 1 Photograph (Contents Page), "*Argos*," shot by Fritscher on set of two actors during taping of *The Argos Session* for Roger Earl and Terry LeGrand, Marathon Films.
- 10 Photographs (Interior Editorial): "*The Argos Session*, Photographic Essay," pp. 41-45, ten photographs shot by Fritscher on set during taping of *The Argos Session* for Roger Earl and Terry LeGrand, Marathon Films.

MACH 22 — A *DRUMMER* SUPER PUBLICATION, December 1990
Masthead: Publisher Anthony F. DeBlase; Managing Editor Joseph W. Bean
1 Piece of Writing by Fritscher
10 Photographs (Interior Editorial) by Fritscher dba "Palm Drive Video"
1 Photograph (Interior Advertising) by Fritscher dba "Palm Drive Video"
1 Editorial Mention
- Editorial Mention (Front Cover Copy): "A Palm Drive Boy in Bondage"
- 10 Photographs: "The Excellent Adventure of Peter Longdicker," pp. 53-59, ten color photographs shot July 5, 1989, in Germany by Fritscher dba "Palm Drive Video"

- "Muscle-Cop Road Warrior," p. 79, poem
- 1 Photograph: "Palm Drive Model Brutus," p. 79, by Fritscher dba "Palm Drive Video," display ad

MACH 25 — A *DRUMMER* SUPER PUBLICATION, April 1992
Masthead: Publisher Anthony F. DeBlase; Editor Joseph W. Bean
1 Piece of Writing by Fritscher
10 Photographs (Interior Editorial) by Fritscher dba "Palm Drive Video"
2 Photographs (Interior Advertising) by Fritscher dba "Palm Drive Video"
1 Editorial Mention
- Editorial Mention (Contents Page): p. 3, "Wes Decker in Photography by Palm Drive Video"
- 4 Photographs (Interior Editorial): "Wes Decker," pp. 56-57, by Fritscher dba "Palm Drive Video"
- 2 Photographs (Interior Advertising): "Mr. *Drummer* Contestant Larry Perry," p. 51, by Fritscher dba "Palm Drive Video," display ad, half-page

MACH 29 — A *DRUMMER* SUPER PUBLICATION, July 1993
Masthead: Publisher Anthony F. DeBlase; Editor Joseph W. Bean
1 Photograph (Front Cover Portrait) by Fritscher dba "Palm Drive Video"
1 Piece of Writing by Fritscher
11 Photographs (Interior Editorial) by Fritscher dba "Palm Drive Video"
2 Photographs (Interior Advertising) by Fritscher dba "Palm Drive Video"
   [Editor's Note: Surviving long past Embry, Fritscher's fiction continued to be published in *Mach* by managing editor Joseph W. Bean at *Drummer* rival, Brush Creek Media: *Titanic: The Novella, Mach* 35 (March 1997) and by managing editor Peter Millar: "Father and Son Tag Team," *Mach* 38 (January 1998)]
- 1 Photograph (Front Cover Portrait): "Terry Kelly," shot by Fritscher dba "Palm Drive Video"
- 11 Photographs (Interior Editorial): "Terry Kelly, The Biker Next Door, Photo Essay," pp. 5-9, by Fritscher dba "Palm Drive Video"
- 1 Photograph (Interior Advertising): "Palm Drive Model Curtis James," p. 51, by Fritscher dba "Palm Drive Video," display ad, half-page

DRUMMER: TOUGH CUSTOMERS 1, July 1990
Masthead: Publisher/Editor Anthony F. DeBlase; Managing Editor/Art Director Joseph W. Bean
1 Photograph (Front Cover Portrait) reprint of *Mach* 20 cover, p. 12, shot by Fritscher for Roger Earl and Terry LeGrand, Marathon Films
- Palm Drive Video Display Ad, "Casting Call: Document Yourself Forever!" p. 75, by Fritscher dba "Palm Drive Video," half page

DUNGEONMASTER 47 — A *DRUMMER*-DESMODUS, INC, PUBLICATION, January 1994
Masthead: Publisher Martijn Bakker, Editor Anthony F. DeBlase
1 Piece of Writing by Fritscher
1 Photograph (Front Cover) by Fritscher dba "Palm Drive Video"
2 Photographs (Interior Editorial) by Fritscher dba "Palm Drive Video"
Editorial Review of four videos produced, directed, and photographed by Fritscher dba "Palm Drive Video"
- 1 Photograph (Front Cover Portrait): *Slap Happy* by Fritscher dba "Palm Drive Video"

Drummer: Fritscher Timeline Bibliography

- Editorial Mention: Contents Page, p. 3, Fritscher and Palm Drive Video
- "USMC Slapcaptain," pp. 9-10
- 2 Photographs (Interior Editorial): "Terry Kelly" and "Gut Punchers in Action," pp. 24-25, by Fritscher dba "Palm Drive Video"
- Editorial Video Review by Tony DeBlase of four videos produced, directed, and photographed by Fritscher dba "Palm Drive Video," pp. 24-25

DRUMMER: TOUGH CUSTOMERS 12, 1996
Masthead: Publisher/Editor Anthony F. DeBlase; Managing Editor/Art Director Joseph W. Bean
4 Photographs (Interior Editorial) by Fritscher dba "Palm Drive Video"
- 4 Photographs (Interior Editorial): "Mickey Squires: How to Be a Tough Customer," pp. 6-7, by Fritscher dba "Palm Drive Video"

Index

120 Days of Sodom: 601, 617
15 Association: 636
2001: A Space Odyssey: 380
20th Century Latin American Art: 48
4436 25th Street: 271, 298
8mm: 227, 392, 409, 572

A

A. Jay (Allen Shapiro): xi, 1, 10, 23, 71, 79-80, 89, 91, 118, 122-123, 126, 128, 230, 249, 266-267, 295, 297-300, 310-311, 313, 315, 334, 341, 348, 356, 363, 367, 375, 404, 412-414, 416-417, 419, 423, 425-426, 435-441, 446, 456, 498, 511, 575, 635, 645, 661-662, 664, 668-669, 671, 684
A-List: 238, 355, 649
Aardvark Cinematheque: 184
AAU: 420, 427
ABA (See American Book Association)
ABC-TV: 399
Abzug, Bella: 6
Academy Award: 78, 109, 121, 141, 182, 264, 300, 319, 332, 401, 453, 609, 642
Academy Training Center: 59, 219, 268, 433, 681
Accu-Jac: 493, 496
Acid Test: 634
ACLU (see American Civil Liberties Union)
ACT Up: 203
Action Male: 201
Ad Rem, The: 144
Adams, Gary: 379
Adidas: 549-551
Adonis Theater: 408
Adventures of Denny Sargent: 375, 576, 666
Advocate, The: ii, 4, 12, 28, 69, 77, 90-91, 102, 104, 109, 201, 217, 254, 311, 386, 395-396, 398-399, 436, 468, 528, 532, 537, 539, 611, 625
Advocate Experience: 386
Advocate Men: 15
African-American: 67, 145, 160, 163, 167-174, 214, 494, 581, 590
Afro-cultures: 21
Age of Aquarius: 395
Agrippa: 602
AIDS Cult: 72
AIDS Quilt: 274, 650
Alan, Starlight: 514
Albee, Edward: 203, 542
Alexandre, Luc: 283
Alexandria Quartet, The: 1, 4, 84
Algonquin Club: 134, 594
Alhambra Theater: 269
Ali, Muhammed: 546, 572
Alinsky, Saul: 67, 145, 160, 163, 166-167, 171, 175, 181
All That Glitters: 544
All-American Boy: 97
All-American Hero: 546
Allen, Woody: 46, 108, 162, 543
Allison, Dorothy: 65
Alternate, The: 201
Alternate Publishing: 129, 375
Altman, Robert: 135
Alyson Publishing: 68, 202, 207-208, 238, 257, 259, 506
Amaya, Mario: 66
Amazing Kristavo: 651
Ambidextrous: The Secret Lives of Children: 65
Ambush: 23, 120, 266, 277, 284, 313, 319, 321, 356-357, 583, 591, 594, 643
America Busted: A Satirical Revue: 337
America Sings: The Anthology of College Poetry 1958: 263
American Civil Liberties Union (ACLU): 237
American Dictionary of Adult Sexual Terms: 257
American Fascists: 603
American Gigolo: 436, 635
American Men: xv, 43, 49-56, 69, 112, 254-255, 258, 260, 525, 570
American Popular Culture Association: 5, 101, 196, 215, 245, 297
American Psychiatric Association: 200, 238-239
American Review of Gay Popular Culture, The: 5, 59, 201, 250, 409, 459, 664
American Studies Association: 5, 101, 245
Americanism: 614-615
AMG Studios (Athletic Model Guild): 41, 77, 136, 197, 243, 254, 394, 409, 434, 493, 496, 540, 558, 572
Amory, Richard: 249
Amsterdam: 1, 67, 268, 474, 537, 678, 680, 685
Anderson, Roger: 517
Androgyne: 249
Andros, Phil (see Samuel Steward)
Angel Island: 594
Angel of Light: 215
Angelou, Maya: 204
Angels on the Bough: 86, 429
Anger, Kenneth: 120-121, 135, 196, 251, 270, 288, 379, 409, 412, 431, 433, 437, 448, 456, 514, 580, 588
Ann-Margret: 97, 614
Anthony, Bob: 379
Antonioni, Michelangelo: 265, 270
Antoniou, Laura: 63, 207
Anvil: 162, 197-198, 492, 510, 583
AP (see Associated Press)
Apollo Theater: 605
Apostolic Delegate: 157, 161
Aquinas, Thomas: 67, 193, 241, 257, 538
Ardent, Keith: 131, 410, 672-677, 680, 685
Arena of Masculinity, The: 539, 560
Argosy: 376
Aristide (Joseph Laurence, Joseph Laurent, P. Nutz): 395-401, 671

Index

Arnett, Chuck: xi, 23, 25, 34, 92, 107, 120, 138, 196, 273, 275, 289-290, 316, 334, 348, 356, 430, 434-436, 444, 446, 452, 479, 677
Arnold, C. D.: 504, 515, 527
Arrabal, Fernando: 604-605, 614, 624
Ars Erotica: 48, 69
Artaud, Antonin: 605
Arthur, Gavin: 269
Arts Council of Great Britain: 48
Ask Larry: 193, 201-202, 205
Ass Eaters Association: 483
Associated Press (AP): 259, 310, 419, 568
Astrologic: xvi, 395-397, 399-402, 593-595, 662-664, 666-667, 671
Athena: 414
Athletic Model Guild (see AMG Studios)
Atlanta: 217, 475, 541
Atlas, Charles: 543
Aubrey, Walter: 254, 260
Aunt Jemima: 169
Auntie Mame: 480
Austria: 415
Axe, Kevin: 162
Aziz, Sultan Abdul: 555

B

Bad Boy Books: 202
Bad Lieutenant: 606
Bag of Toys: Sex, Scandal, and the Death Mask Murder: 459
Bailey, Bob: 458
Bailey, Harry: 448
Baker, David (Thumper): 380, 503, 507, 515-517, 521, 523-525
Baker, Paul: 259
Bakker, Martijn: 1-2, 125, 128, 472, 478, 686
Baldwin, Guy: xi, 110, 373
Baldwin, James: 168, 170
Bales, Mikal: xi, 201
Ball Four: 552
Bankhead, Tallullah: 247
Banshee: 213-214
BAR (see Bay Area Reporter)
Barger, Sonny: 431
Barker, Lex: 410, 667
Barnes, Ike: 92, 262, 267, 287, 304, 431, 593
Barnett, Steve: 649, 653, 657
Barney, Jeanne: i, iii, xi, 1, 77-79, 82, 97, 119-120, 122-123, 126-127, 201, 262, 295-297, 299-300, 319, 376, 396, 398-399, 401, 423, 426, 434, 439, 443, 608
Barnum and Bailey Circus: 449, 651
Barracks Baths: 25, 106, 120, 122, 150, 211, 253, 273, 277, 340, 350, 373-374, 386-387, 454, 457, 491, 528, 581, 634, 639
Barrus, Tim (Nasdijj): iv, xi, xv, 13, 15, 17, 127, 359, 361, 459, 568
Bassi, Paesi: 606
Bast, William: 134, 137, 147

Bates, Alan: 546
Bates, Kathy: 135
Battle of Algiers, The: 300-302, 615
Bay Area Boxing Club: 554
Bay Area Reporter (BAR): i, 2, 67, 72, 77, 88, 99, 125, 211, 214, 245, 323, 514, 529, 539
BBC: 48, 219
BDSM: 91-92, 163, 252, 373, 603
Bean, Joseph W.: ii, xi, xv, 7, 11, 50, 56, 63, 94, 110, 127, 250, 252, 428, 679-680, 682, 684-687
Bear Book: 251, 254, 258
Bear Book II: 251, 254, 258
Bear Classic: 219, 226
Bear Cult, The: 49, 253
Bear Lake: 225-226
Bear Magazine: v, 53, 106, 226, 250, 253, 301
Bearotica: 253
Bears on Bears: iv, 251, 254, 257, 259
Beat Punks: 649
Beattie, Ann: 213, 229
Beausoleil, Bobby: 196
Beautiful Thing: 72
Bell, Vanessa: 516
Belleview Avenue: 558
Beltane: 91
Benson, Jared: 412
Benwell, B.: 259
Bergman, David: 213
Berkeley, Bud: 574
Berkeley Publishing Corporation: 626
Berlin: 108, 242, 506, 514, 581, 608-609, 635, 644
Berlin, Peter: 409
Berlin Stories, The: 62
Bernstein, Leonard: 429
Berserkers: 640-641
Bertman, Tom: 200
Best American Erotica: 226
Best Dirty Blond Carpenter, The: 311
Best Gay Erotica: 226, 504
Bible: 160, 165, 238, 240-241, 243, 359, 387, 588, 607
Bible, The (film): 411, 504-505
Big Mack Macker: 633
Bijou: 409, 504
Bilignin: 429, 444
Billboard: 532
Bird Cage, The: 72
Birimisa, George: 411, 503, 518
Biron, Lionel: 327, 348
Bitter Harvest: 159
Black, Karen: 135
Black and Blue Party: 451
Black Castle: 197, 425
Black House: 197, 397
Black Leather Wings: 109
Black Muslims: 175
Black Party: 647
Black Pipe: 198

Index

Blackboard Jungle: 133, 378
Blacks (see African American)
Blackstone Rangers: 166, 183
Blazek, Mark C.: 102
Blood, Dick: 559
Blood Crucifixion: 263, 304
Blood Runs Like a River Through My Dreams, The: 17
Bloomsbury: 23, 234, 395, 401, 516
Blowjob: 409
Blue, Solly: 38, 74, 348, 421
BoBo: 212
Boccaccio: 193
Bockris, Victor: 649
Body Casting: 304-305, 662
Bodybuilders: 43, 45-47, 121, 131, 164, 194, 199, 263, 316, 387, 428, 504, 513, 534, 536, 538, 543, 554, 558, 563, 565, 572, 634, 644, 648, 674, 683
Bodybuilding: 39, 45, 52-53, 122, 233, 259, 272, 494, 518, 538, 541, 553, 560, 563, 575, 646, 662, 674
Bogaos: 102
Bogarde, Dirk: 162, 398, 605
Bogart, Humphrey: 469
Bolt (bar): 317, 380, 650
Bond Street: 449, 514
Bondage: 28, 36, 46, 58, 60-61, 63, 79, 131, 155, 192, 201, 205, 241, 248, 286, 305, 322, 356, 362, 385, 451, 453, 480, 491, 495, 504, 514, 572, 580, 596, 638, 643, 664-665, 669, 673, 685
BooksToWatchOutFor.com: iii
Borg, Rick: 290, 327, 341
Born to Raise Hell: 45, 78, 409-410, 608, 613, 634-635
Boston: iv, 49, 105, 151, 157, 247, 257, 259, 433, 534, 576
Botticelli, Sandro: 554
Bound and Gagged: 63, 202, 670
Bound for Europe: 635, 644, 677, 682
Boundy, John: 411
Bourne, Matthew: 250
Bowers, Billy: 14
Bowie, David: 67
Bowling Green University: 6, 245
Bowling Green University Popular Culture Press: 245
Boy and His Dog Are Sleeping, The: 17
Boy Named Frank Mills: 263
Boy's Own Story, A: 65
Boy Scout Handbook: 199
Boys in Leather: 19, 22, 230
Boys in the Band, The: xi, 6, 235, 245, 463, 488, 509, 513
Boys in the Sand, The: 274, 409-410, 510, 634, 657
Boys of Summer, The: 552
Bradburn, Mike: 307, 394
Braddock, Stan: 412

Brand, Adolph: 392
Brando, Marlon: 110, 133, 135-136, 138, 198, 205, 251, 393, 416, 424, 437, 508-509, 546, 548-549
Brandon House: 258
Brassart, Scott: 207
Brave New World: 103
Braveheart: 10
Brecht, Berthold: 514
Brian, J.: 412
Bridge, The: 88, 303, 649
Brig (bar): 221-222, 317, 362, 374, 380, 506-507, 510, 588, 625
Brig, The (book): 221
Brig, The (play): 507, 510, 588
Brigadoon: 638
Briggs, John: 80, 417, 420, 603, 606-607
Briggs Initiative: 417, 607, 610
Bright, Susie: 226
Bright Lights Film Journal: 465
Bringing Christ to Woodlawn: 160, 167, 181
Broadway: xiii, 134, 142, 145, 184, 241, 256, 430, 479, 505, 507-509, 536, 547, 593, 608
Brokeback Mountain: 103, 105, 138, 246, 256, 569
Bromilow, Peter: 198
Bronski, Michael: iv, 62, 105, 209, 213, 229, 245, 259, 433, 533-534, 608
Bronson, Charles: 301
Brook, Peter: 507
Brooks Brothers: 583
Broshears, Ray: 77
Brown, Kenneth: 507, 510, 588
Brown, Rita Mae: 65
Brown Shirts: 607
Brown University: i
Browne, Ray: 6, 101
Bruce of LA: 197
Brush Creek Media: 50, 253, 301, 686
Bryant, Anita: 80, 337, 417, 420, 468, 550, 559, 580, 603, 606
Brynner, Yul: 141
Buckley, Tim: 362, 461, 491
Budd, Billy: 269, 514
Bughouse Square: 424
Bulger, Richard: 250, 420
Bullenhochzeit: 444
Bunuel, Luis: 270
Burning Pen, The: 69, 74, 207-208, 375
Burns, Stevie "Chazda": 76
Burroughs, William: 180
Bush, President George W.: 182, 248, 580, 610
Butch and Sundance: 544, 549
Butler, Rhett: 541
Bye Bye Birdie: 430

C

Cabaret: 88, 386, 405, 527, 556, 593, 608-609, 614, 624, 643

Index

Cadmus, Paul: 429
Caffee, Mike: 136, 273, 345
CAG (see California Action Guide)
Cage, John: 647
Calamus: 233, 241
Calamusbooks.com: iii
Califia, Pat: 90, 92, 97, 219
Califia, Patrick: xi, 63, 90-92, 532
Califia-Rice, Patrick: 207
California Action Guide (CAG): 90, 245, 250, 252, 260, 348, 411, 505, 536, 563, 572
California Cup: 553
California Highway Patrol (CHP): 577
California Motor Club (see CMC)
California Motorcycle Club: 631
California Pleasure Guide: 411
California State University: 191
California Street: 126, 296, 298, 397
Callard, Roger: 558
Calvinism: 184
Cambridge: 235
Camelot: 67, 198
Camp, Reverend Alfred E.: 144
Camp Pendleton: 585
Campus Theater: 270-271, 276, 355
Camus, Albert: 507
Canterbury Tales: 85, 200, 448, 518
Capote, Truman: 46, 521
Cardini, Leo: 359, 459
Care and Training of the Male Slave: 201, 349
Caribbean: 262, 540
Carmen: 457
Carmine, Al: 510
Carnaby Street: 67
Carnegie Hall: 236, 462
Carnegie Hall Cinema: 301, 604, 618
Carnera, Primo: 418, 421, 538, 621
Carney, William: 65, 194-196, 392, 397
Carpenter, Edward: 269
Carribean: 304, 511
Carried Away: An S&M Romance: 63
Carson, Johnny: 550
Casablanca: 205, 469, 494, 649
Case of the Naves Brothers, The: 301, 604-605, 618
Casillo, Charles: iv
Casino Night: 456-457, 491
Casino Royale: 651
Cassady, Neal: 233, 269, 432
Cassandra: 468
Castro Café: 268, 593-594
Castro Camera: 99, 307
Castro Street: 61, 80, 97-99, 112, 114-115, 208, 233, 255, 271, 310, 329, 336, 342, 355, 368-369, 371, 375, 390, 527, 529, 533, 536-537, 542, 559, 566, 573, 593-594, 607, 610, 636, 650, 665
Castro Street Blues: 61, 233, 310, 375, 533, 665
Castro Street Fair: 98-99, 114-115, 636, 665

Castro Theater: 114, 342, 399, 495, 559, 565, 594
Cat on a Hot Tin Roof: 136, 241, 542, 552
Catacombs: 59, 89-90, 97, 131, 277, 327, 387, 451, 492, 517, 548, 664, 679
Catholic Preview of Entertainment: 137, 147, 160-161, 378
Catholic Worker, The: 145
Catholicism: 60, 65, 67, 71, 85, 90, 92, 100, 116, 121, 133-134, 136-137, 145, 150-151, 155-157, 159-167, 170-173, 175, 177, 179-180, 183-184, 193, 212, 218, 220, 240, 263-264, 267, 270, 304, 311, 318-320, 378, 383, 388, 410, 414, 416, 418, 432-434, 443, 469, 611
Cato, Bob: 52, 536
Cavani, Liliana: 604-605
CBGB: 263, 319, 453, 456, 470
CBS News: 180
Cedric: 344
Censorship: ix, 19, 73, 80, 131, 151, 184-185, 212, 233, 242, 244, 255, 358, 419, 455, 463, 468-469, 477, 491, 508, 579-581, 592, 604, 611-612, 615, 647, 665, 676
Censorship: A World Encyclopedia: 358
Central Park: 236
Cey, Ron: 540
Chaikivsky, Andrew: 17
Champion, The: 311, 546
Chanel Number 5: 107
Chaney, Ed: 290
Chaney, James: 173
Changing Room, The: 507, 547
Changing Shape: 48
Chaos: 13, 92, 98
Chapters from an Autobiography: 86
Charles, Andrew: xi, 110, 118, 124-125, 476-477, 671
Charles, Sidney: 410
Charming Fred: 514
Chasing Danny Boy: 214, 219, 222, 253
Chaucer: 85, 200, 448
Chavez, Cesar: 640
Chazda (see Stevie Burns)
Checkmate Incorporating DungeonMaster: iii, 28-31, 50, 201, 219, 262, 462, 478
Chelsea: 205, 458
Cher: 135
Chester, Mark I.: xi, 13, 127, 340, 457, 527
Cheyenne: 511
Chicago (musical): xiii, 480
Chicago Archdiocesan Conservation Council: 171
Chicago Bears: 250
Chicago Film Board: 184-185
Chicago International Film Festival: 185
Chicago Public Library: ii, 19, 25, 277
Chicago Seven: 179-182, 185, 188
Chicago Sun-Times: 183
Chicago Wrestling Club: 557
Children's Hour, The: 508

Chorus Line, A: 417, 505, 507, 510, 515, 520, 544
CHP (see California Highway Patrol)
Chris LeClaire Publishing: 418
Christ: 149, 155, 160, 163, 167, 171-173, 181, 220, 241, 246, 251, 263, 323, 329, 538, 577, 611
Christ-queering: 251
Christian, M.: 74, 207-208, 375
Christianity: 149, 163, 165, 173-174, 240-241, 263, 392, 595
Christo: 274, 277, 650-651
Christopher, Kit: v
Christopher and His Kind: 608
Christopher Street: 136, 470, 573
Christopher Street Liberation Day: 236
Church of Satan: 66, 397
Cirby (Robert Kirk): 271, 676
Circle of Blood: 615
Circle of Obsessions: 615
Circle of Shit: 615
Circuit Parties: 647, 653
Citadel Press: 245
City Lights Books: 601
City of Night: 33, 135
City Slickers: 103
City University of New York: 71
Civic Center Auditorium: 39
Civil Rights Bill: 168, 170, 173
Civil Rights Movement: 43, 181, 194, 236, 580
Civil War: 29, 89, 93-95, 97, 124, 130, 256, 265, 451, 463, 528, 539, 601, 607-608
Claflin, Victoria Woodhull: 29
Clave, Tom: 316, 323
Clementina Street: 22, 25, 34, 266, 273, 275, 277, 304-305
Clementina Tales: 22, 26, 277
Cliburn, Van: 305
Clift, Montgomery: 82
Clinton, President Bill: 239
Close Encounters of the Third Kind: 582
Club Baths: 387
CMC (California Motor Club): 350, 366, 631-635, 640-643
CMC Carnival: xvi, 305, 366, 518, 521, 626, 628, 631-636, 639-642, 644-645, 659, 663, 667
CNN: 69, 157, 162, 541
Coates, Gregg: 266, 275, 283, 305
Cockettes: 67, 507
College of Marin: 324
Collins, Judy: 180, 632
Collins, William: 586
Colorado Springs: 116, 179, 187
Colosseum: 149, 218
Colt Studios: 162, 197, 230, 254, 309, 312, 314, 375, 441, 511, 513, 534, 538, 646
Coltours: 511
Come Back to the Five and Dime, Jimmy Dean, Jimmy Dean: 135

Coming Attractions: 88, 507, 510, 514, 529, 566
Coming of Age in Somoa: 592
Compton's Cafeteria: 102, 104, 107
Congdon, Kirby: 527
Continental Baths: 510
Continental Caper: 67, 518
Continuum: 72
Cooper, James Fenimore: 249
Coors: 403, 552
Corleo, Vincent: 653
Corporal in Charge of Taking Care of Captain O'Malley: 53, 59, 69, 105, 219, 223, 225, 253, 269, 359, 411, 514, 579, 591, 664, 671, 681
Cosmo: 547
Costa-Gavras, Constantin: 182, 185, 615
Cottage Grove: 67, 163, 166, 175, 181-182
Country Baths: 425
Covered Wagon: 583
Coward, Noel: 81
Cox, Harold E.: 27
Creative Power Foundation: 649
Crews, Laura Hope: 81
Crimes Against Nature: xvi, 407, 503, 510, 515-516, 520, 522-523, 525, 662
Crip Theory: Cultural Signs of Queerness and Disability: 233
Crisco: 354, 387, 483, 490
Criscomas Party: 453
Crisp, Quentin: 215, 432, 488
Croce-Spinelli: 582
Cronkite, Walter: 180
Cross, Frank (see Jim Kane)
Crowley, Aleister: 103, 335
Crowley, Mart: 235, 463, 509
Cruising: 74, 183, 199, 238, 362, 417, 424, 461, 463-465, 469, 488-489, 491, 512, 518, 564, 572, 602, 622, 626, 636, 638
Cry! The Young Hunters: 137, 378-379, 389
Crying Game, The: 217
Crystal Meth: 437
Culture War: vii, 3, 20-21, 29, 100, 213, 237, 258, 463, 499, 540, 579, 592, 601, 603, 607
Culver, Cal (see Casey Donovan)
Cummings, e e: 323
Cunningham, Blaine: 426
Cunningham, Merce: 647
Currie, Robert: 653
Curry, Tim: 420
Cycle Sluts: 79, 138, 299, 414, 575
Czar: 202
Czonka, Larry: 544

D

D'Arti, Nick (see Lou Thomas)
da Vinci, Leonardo: 308, 602
Dade County: 417, 615
Dade County Human Rights Ordinance: 606

694 Index

Dagion, John: 520
Daley, Mayor Richard: 175, 180
Dalgleish, Brian: 594
Dallesandro, Joe: 409
Dalzell, Tom: 258, 590
Damiano, Gerard: 411
Damn Yankee in Savannah, A: 76
Dancer from the Dance: 65
Dante: 193, 603
Darkling, Dusk: 101
Darling! What to Do at a Dirty Movie: 160
Dateline Colorado: 116, 162, 179-182, 188
David of Cleveland: 379
Davis, Bette: 203, 549
Davis, Brad: 399
Davis, Glenn (see Skipper)
Davis, Police Chief Ed: 78, 122-123, 201, 607, 614
Davis, Rennie: 180
Davolt, Robert: xi, 88, 128, 377, 478
Day, Dorothy: 145
Dayton, Mike: 536, 572
de Arechaga, Frederick: 397
de Sade, Marquis: 193, 222, 601, 617
de Talleyrand, Charles Maurice: xiii, 239, 460
Dean, James: xv, 133-143, 147, 160-161, 251, 268, 378, 429, 508
Dean, Mildred: 141-142
Death Mask Murder: 459
DeBlase, Anthony F. (Fledermaus): ii, xi, 1-2, 11, 28-31, 50, 54, 58, 94-95, 110, 118, 123-128, 138, 191, 213-214, 228, 251, 260, 357, 374, 398-399, 404, 426, 449-450, 469, 471-479, 498, 507, 532, 625, 671, 675, 677, 679-680, 682, 684-687
Decker, Ed: 523
Deco: 44, 379, 418, 603
Deddino, Gino: 540, 560, 672
Deer Hunter, The: 410, 668
Dehner, Durk (Durk Parker): xv, 10, 261, 309-314, 377, 427, 661
DeLaurentis, Dino: 546
Delay, David: 23, 356, 643
Deleuze, Gilles: 156
Deliverance: 410
Delivery: 292, 504, 515, 527
Delta Run: 30
DeMille, Cecil B.: 387
Democratic Convention: 166, 179-180, 183, 187, 235, 428
Denbeigh Street: 379
Denim Publications: 315
DeNiro, Robert: 553
Denneny, Michael: 213, 229
Dennis, Sandy: 135
DePaul University: 431-432
Der Eigene: 242, 392
Desai, Prime Minister Norarji: 588
Descartes, Rene: 207, 373
Detective Story: 512

Devil in Miss Jones, The: 411, 505
Dewar's Profile: 556
DiCaprio, Leonardo: 510
Diethelm, Hank: 506, 625
Different Light Bookstore: iii, 80, 219, 361, 504
Different Strokes: 359, 361, 444
Dinakos, Ed (Michael Glassman): 538, 561, 633, 666-667, 670
Dionysius: 220
Disuniting of America, The: 22
Divine: 67, 483, 612
Divisadero Street: 126, 299, 512
Dog Soldiers: 269
Doggie Diner: 274, 348
Dom (see Etienne)
Dominican Order: 149
Domino: 107, 198, 248, 254, 311, 341, 412, 426, 436-437, 646, 668
Don Levine: 593-594
Don't Think of an Elephant: 239
Donovan, Casey (Cal Culver): 510
Doors, The: 35, 385, 465
Doors of Perception, The: 385
Dore Alley Street Fair: 292, 639
Dorothy Chandler Pavilion: 119
Double Exposure: 266, 283, 305
Douglas, Jerry: 495
Douglass, Stephen: 29
Downhill Racer: 546
Dr. Caligari: 313
Drag: 27, 37, 78, 99, 102-104, 107-108, 138, 153-154, 195, 236, 255, 262, 264, 297, 299, 389, 414, 417, 455, 463, 465-466, 509-510, 527, 536, 575, 608, 643
Drew, Michael: 327, 496
Druids: 165, 240, 273, 392
Drum: 8, 89, 268
Drummer, Best of: 68, 498
Drummer, Son of: 2, 60, 97, 119, 126, 130-131, 138, 211, 265, 295, 310-311, 340, 344, 360, 375, 390, 436, 456, 575-576, 580, 611-612, 649, 661, 665
Drummer, Virtual: 31, 50, 53, 135, 260, 291, 332, 338, 360, 408, 411, 434, 443, 449, 500, 505, 563, 572, 626, 628
Drummer Salon: 1-2, 21-23, 31, 38, 52, 85, 87, 89, 110, 123, 162, 229, 253, 263, 266, 280-281, 284, 286, 290, 295, 300-301, 305, 310, 316, 331, 333, 340, 347-348, 374, 395, 397-398, 400, 425, 428, 430, 436, 443-444, 499, 501, 504, 506-507, 527, 555, 560, 591, 609, 634-635, 644, 657, 659, 669
Drummer Trucker Party: 659
Duberman, Martin: 104, 200, 469, 610
Dublin: 214, 231-232, 234, 402, 506, 532, 581, 590
DuBois, Blanche: 482, 509
Dudley, George: 454
Duffy, Chris (Bull Stanton): 45, 53, 591
Dufort, Dan: 540, 560, 634, 644, 664, 672

Index

Dumb and Dumber: 95
Dumbing of America: 269, 576, 606
Dundas, Edward: 510
DungeonMaster: 12, 28-31, 50, 54, 201, 260, 262, 462, 473, 478, 661, 686
Dungeons of Europe: 635, 644
Dungeons of San Francisco: 261, 267, 304, 662
Dunne, Don: 394
Dunne, Irene: 81
Dureau, George: 66, 69-70, 119
Durrell, Lawrence: 4
Duvall, Claude: 516-517, 526-527
Dybek, Stuart: 183
E., John: 349, 351-354

E

Eagle (bar): 324, 378, 411, 431, 452
Eagle (magazine): 51
Eagles, Allen: 163, 302, 407
Eagles, The: 19, 217, 350, 403
Earl, Roger (Roger Earl Warnix): 78, 379, 409-410, 613, 635, 644, 677-680, 682, 685-686
East of Eden: 134, 136, 142-143, 508
Easy Rider: 236
Ebert, Roger: 183
Ebonics: 237
Eccentricities of a Nightingale: 431
Editions Aubrey Walter: 260
Edmonds, Don: 605
Edward II: 514, 620
Edwards, T.: 259
Effemiphobia: 508
Egan, Monsignor John J.: 171
El Paso Wrecking Corp.: xvi, 407, 411-412, 581, 662
Elephant Walk: 513, 669
Elgin Marbles: 230
Embry, John (Robert Payne): xi, 1-2, 22, 36, 53, 56, 77, 79-82, 84-85, 121-122, 125-129, 138, 201, 252, 260, 262, 265, 275, 291, 295, 297-298, 326, 332, 342, 349, 357, 360, 367, 374, 376, 379, 395, 398, 404-405, 413, 415-416, 418-420, 425-427, 476-478, 497, 506, 527, 535, 573, 575, 580, 608, 612, 625, 635, 645, 649, 662, 669-671, 684
Emerson, Ralph Waldo: 256-257
Empty Rooms: 54, 56
End as a Man: 508
End of the Affair: 218
Enger, Jim: 46, 52, 121, 444, 504, 513-514, 634, 644, 646
Eons Gallery: 315, 438, 440
Episcopal Church: 167, 175
Eppridge, William: 130
Equus: 504, 547, 666
Erotic Authors Association: ii, 68, 76, 112
Erotic Hands: 264, 307, 409, 497, 657
Esalen Institute: 385
Essex, Bill: 271-272, 274, 278, 364

Etienne (Dom, Domingo Orejudos): 121, 136, 178, 196-197, 230, 307, 311, 314-315, 356, 394, 423-441, 444-446, 472, 662
Etienne Video Gallery: 426
Eulenspiegel Society: 448
EUR Magliana Station: 601
Euripides: 192
Euro-cultures: 21
Evans, Arthur: 255
Evansville: 544
Everard: 211, 456, 480
Evergreen Press: 196
Evergreen Review: 297
Everything You Always Wanted to Know About Sex and Were Afraid to Ask: 543
Evil That Men Do, The: 301
Ex-Cons: We Abuse Fags: 62, 411, 504
Exorcist: 65, 70, 85, 157, 267, 319, 463
Exploding Plastic Inevitable, The: 193, 507, 649
Expose: 411

F

F. S. M. C.: 479
Fag: 38, 204, 238, 241, 247, 273, 415, 469, 543, 581, 590
Faggot, The: 510
Fairmount Park Trolley: A Unique Philadelphia Experiment, The: 30
Falconhead: 409
Falstaff Brewery: 239, 528
Falwell, Jerry: 237
Fancy Free: 430
Farrell, Reverend Martin: 163, 171, 181
Fascism: 95, 98, 155, 163, 166, 179-181, 185, 392, 421, 465, 538, 601, 603-604, 607-616, 620-621, 624
Fascist America: 608
Fassbinder, Rainer Werner: 399, 470, 492, 506
Fate Magazine: 397
Father and Son: 136, 160
Father and Son Tag Team: 219, 686
Fe-Be's: 136, 195, 273, 345, 633
FeBe's: 345
Feinberg, Leslie: 469
Feinstein, Dianne: 116, 336, 530
Fellhauer, Bishop David: 149-150
Fellini, Federico: 232, 270
Female: 43, 88, 90, 92-93, 97, 180, 195, 199, 202, 219, 246, 252, 254-255, 263, 305, 317, 432, 452-453, 533, 548, 583
Feminine Mystique, The: 135
Ferber, Edna: 134, 141
Ferlinghetti, Lawrence: 378, 601
Ferrara, Abel: 606
Ferrari, John: 110, 475
Fesco, Michael: 461, 491
Fetters: 518
Fey-Way Gallery: 22-23, 26, 109, 118, 121, 123, 263-264, 275, 280-281, 290, 313, 315,

Index

317-318, 321, 325, 327, 330-331, 334-335, 337, 341, 343-344, 348, 367, 423, 435, 437-440, 453
FFA (see Fist Fuckers of America)
Fick, Reverend Leonard J.: 159-160, 164-165
Fierstein, Harvey: 510
Fight Club: 84, 554-555
Fillmore: 634
Film Associates: 558, 572
Finch, Peter: 521, 653
Firebirds, The: 512
FirstHand: 311
Firsthand Books: 495
Firth, Peter: 547
Fiske, Peter: 636
Fist Fuckers of America (FFA): 447, 454, 483
Fisting Ballet: 454-455, 491
Fitzgerald, Ella: 461
Fitzgerald, F. Scott: 209
Fitzroy Dearborn: 358
Fleck, Ludwik: 19
Fledermaus (see Tony DeBlase)
Fleet's In, The: 429
Flesh and Stone: 48
Flick, Larry: 532
Florida Citrus Commission: 559
Florida Orange Juice Commission: 606
Flowers of Evil: 612, 677
Flynt, Larry: 219
Folsom Baths: 380, 548
Folsom Prison: 374, 507, 583
Folsom Street: ii, 19, 23, 26, 88, 92, 106, 120, 126, 129, 136, 138, 194, 253, 262, 266, 270, 273, 275, 288, 293-294, 303, 305, 316, 340, 345, 347-351, 362, 367, 371, 373-374, 380-381, 386-387, 397, 404, 415, 430, 457, 473, 476, 491, 496, 506, 512, 517, 520, 527, 530, 537, 559, 572, 594, 625-626, 628, 639, 648
Folsom Street Fair: 91, 301, 476, 631, 635-636, 638-639, 644
Fonda, Jane: 182, 535, 614
For the Love of a Green-Eyed Piano Player: 221
Forbidden Tricks: 76
Ford, John: 110
Foreign Legion: 298
Foreskin: Its Past, Present and Future: 574
Foreskin Quarterly: 12, 130, 661, 685
Forest Park: 302
Foreword Magazine: i, v
Foro Italico: 418, 421, 538, 621
Forster, E. M.: 429
Forster, Robert: 548
Fortkamp, Frank E.: 160, 167, 175, 181
Fosse, Bob: 614
Foucault, Michel: 97, 193-194, 251, 253, 316, 470, 492, 606, 640
Fox News: 72
FQ (see Foreskin Quarterly)

Framing Keywords of Queer Popular Culture: 231, 234, 402, 532, 581, 590
Frampton, Peter: 547
France, David: 459
Francis, Russ: 559
Franco, Generalissimo Francisco: 603, 612, 614, 624
Frank, Anne: 614
Frankenstein: 71
Franklin, Ed: 80, 400, 407, 410, 535
Franklin Avenue: 557
Frasier: 247
Free Speech Movement: 235
French, Jim (Luger, Rip Colt): 197, 254, 309, 312, 314, 511, 513
French Connection, The: 463-464
Freud, Sigmund: 192, 209
Friedan, Betty: 135
Friedkin, William: 199, 463-465, 469, 488, 491
Friedman, Lewis: 527
Friends of Dorothy: 195, 238
Frisch, Max: 512
Frizer, Ingram: 515
Front Runner: 76, 255, 552
Frontier Bulletin Gazette: 77, 436
Frontiers: 436
Frost, Robert: 246
Fuck You, Santa Claus: 334
Fulbright grant: 359
Fundamentalism: 68, 97, 136, 165, 180, 204-205, 212, 237-239, 321, 323, 463, 469, 540, 580-581, 604, 607, 609-611
Fusion: 76

G

Gage Brothers (Joe & Sam): 254, 407-412, 495, 501, 518, 581, 662
Galeria Vandres: 277
Gallagher, Joe: 88
Galleria: 118
Gallipoli: 555
Gallucci, Ed: 319
Gardner, Gerald: 243
Garfield, John: 546
Garland, Judy: 143, 236
Garrison, Michael: 458
Gauguin, Paul: 263
Gay Agenda: 539
Gay and Lesbian Literary Heritage: 357-358, 360
Gay Bill Doll: 248
Gay Book of Astrology: 397
Gay Cancer (see GRID)
Gay Community Center: 651, 653
Gay Community News: iv, 105, 259, 433, 534
Gay Freedom Day Parade: 96, 377, 493, 538, 609
Gay Games (Gay Olympics): 495, 518, 531, 533, 560, 565, 574

Index

Gay Guerrilla Theater: 520
Gay Justice: 318, 337, 609
Gay Marriage: 121, 192, 200, 237, 259, 608, 611
Gay Men's Press (see GMP)
Gay Men's SM Activists (see GMSMA)
Gay Men's Theater Collective: 510, 520
Gay Olympics (see Gay Games)
Gay Rodeo: 4, 310, 548, 568-571
Gay Roots: iv, 20, 69, 137, 219, 225, 253, 257, 259, 428, 515
Gay Source Catalog: xvi, 625-627, 663
Gay Sunshine Press: 73, 211, 257, 303, 360, 378, 495, 515, 576, 579, 591
Gay Wrestling: 556-557
Gay-Related Immune Deficiency (see GRID)
Gayellow Pages: 626
Gayism: 414
Gaynor, Janet: 52, 536
Genesis and Development of a Scientific Fact: 19
Genet, Jean: 432, 507, 514
Genome of Bear: 219
Genome of Leather: 219
Geography of Women, The: 65, 69, 219, 225-226
George Washington University: 233
German: 56, 67, 76, 82, 160, 191, 219, 240, 242, 313, 323, 399, 444, 506, 540, 608, 610, 615, 644, 685
Geronimo's Bones: A Memoir of My Brother and Me: 17
Gerrior, Paul: 305, 511-513, 540
Gershman, Elizabeth: 15, 216, 361
Getting Off: 61, 126, 520
Ghirardelli Square Cinema: 605
Giant: 134, 136, 138, 141, 143
Gibson, Mel: 575, 611
Gide, Andre: 134
Giffney, Noreen: 232
Gifts of Nature, The: 449, 669
Gilbert Street: 633
Gilmore Art Center: 270
Ginsberg, Allen: 180, 233, 269, 375, 378-379, 576
Ginzler, Nicola: 91
Giordana, Marco Tullio: 606
Giovanni, Tina: 17
Glass Menagerie, The: 103, 136
Glassman, Michael (see Ed Dinakos)
GLBT Historical Society (see San Francisco GLBT Historical Society)
GMP (Gay Men's Press): 50, 56, 68-69, 254, 258
GMSMA (Gay Men's SM Activists): iii, 63, 94, 450, 518
Go-Between, The: 1, 3, 19
Gold Coast: 105, 196-197, 269, 275, 356, 379, 424-425, 427-428, 430, 432, 435, 441, 446, 465, 476

Golden Gai: 514
Golden Gate Bridge: 25, 66, 650
Golden Gate Park: 26, 112, 287, 293, 379, 504
Golden Girls: 72
Golden Gloves: 39, 540, 554, 560, 632, 668
Golden Showers: 449, 582-583
Goldstein, Richard: 321, 466-469
Goley, Frank: 197
Golightly, Holly: 521
Gomorrah: 237, 240
Gone with the Wind: 69, 82, 217, 528, 608
Good-Timing Pinkhams of Chowder Lane: 160
Goodbye to Berlin: 608
Goodman, Andrew: 173
Goodman Theater: 431
Goodstein, David: 90, 311, 386, 396, 399, 468
Gordon, Al: 78
Gospel according to Saint Matthew, The: 606, 611
Graham, Bill: 547
Grand Cayman: 304, 553, 572
Grand National Rodeo: 268, 667
Grant Park: 171
Great Lakes Naval Training Station: 428
Green Door, The: 78
Green Sleeves: 403
Greene, Graham: 218
Greenleaf Classics: 81
Greenleaf Press: 377
Greenspan, Alan: 653
Greenwich Village: 137, 151, 160, 181, 195, 263, 270, 388, 435, 449
Greenwood Press: 257
Greerson, Ralph: 551
Gregory, Lady: 214
Grey, Joel: 386
Grey Gardens: 198
GRID (Gay-Related Immune Deficiency): 120, 238, 511, 640, 659
Griese, Bob: 543-544
Griff's: 198, 200
Griffith Park: 46, 333
Grimaldi, Aurelio: 606
Grossman, Nancy: 492
Grumley, Michael: 319
Grymkowski, Pete: 272
Guernica: 614
Guild Press: 41, 89, 197, 307, 379-380, 392-393
Gunn, Thom: 23, 66, 233, 269, 356, 379
Gurganus, Allan: 65
Gut Punchers: 73, 540, 560, 687
Gyllenhaal, Jake: 103, 133, 138
Gymnastics: 544, 550-551

H

H. E. L. P.: 77-78, 82, 189, 200-201
Haines, Jack: 345, 349-350, 537, 633
Hair: 184
Hale, Barbara: 403

698   Index

Hale, George: 269
Hale, Nathan: 269
Hallam Street (Close/Mews): 293, 373-374, 457, 639
Halsted, Fred: xi, 10, 59, 77-78, 80, 183, 201, 230, 238, 332, 334, 379, 400-401, 409, 411-412, 425, 503-504, 574
Hamilton, Richard, M. D.: xi, 548, 663, 666
Hampton, Christopher: 430, 510
Handbook of Erotic Dominance: 12
Handkerchief Color Code: 93
Handley, John: 540, 556-557, 560-562
Hanging Tree Ranch: 495-496, 501
Hanson, Daryll (see Roger)
Happening Movement: 195, 265, 580, 647-648
Harakiri: 120, 122, 604
Hardy, Ed: 430
Haring, Bernard: 160
Harlem: 455
Harley-Davidson: 262, 432, 443, 512
Harper's Magazine: 239
Harrington Gay Men's Fiction Quarterly: 536
Harris, Julie: 548
Harris, Richard: 384, 546-547
Harrison Street: 356
Harry Bush: 493, 496
Harry Chess: 23, 89, 413, 437
Hartley, L. P.: 1, 3, 19
Hartman, Dennis: 378, 507
Harvard Gay and Lesbian Review: 219
Hastings House: 218, 258, 611
Hatlestad, Paul: 504, 649-650, 653
Hawks: 569, 634
Haworth Press, The: 216, 258-259
Hay, Harry: 243
Hayden, Tom: 180, 182
Hayn, Bob: 55
HBO: 72
Hedda Gabler: 512
Heeter, Lyle: 491
Heffron, Bob: 265, 540
Hefner, Hugh: 240, 275, 414
Heliotrope Drive: 315
Hellfire: 464
Hellman, Lillian: 65, 86, 508, 614
Hello, Dolly: 88, 145, 510
Hells Angels: 431
Helms, Senator Jesse: 3, 468, 611
Hemingway, Ernest: 149, 209, 234, 258
Hemry, Mark: vii-ix, xi, xv, 1, 4-5, 44, 46, 53, 66, 118-121, 147, 177, 206, 214, 252, 260, 289, 295, 310, 339-344, 350, 371, 389, 394, 399, 410-412, 419, 446, 450, 477, 485, 491, 495, 500-501, 516-517, 530, 563, 566, 572, 581, 592, 601, 606, 609, 621-624, 635-636, 644-646, 659, 661, 678-680, 682, 685
Hennessy, Keith: 523
Henry, George W.: 257
Hepburn, Audrey: 508
Hepburn, Katharine: 199, 467

Hephaistion: 102
Hercules: 414-415, 418, 421, 437
Hercules Unchained: 418, 421
Herlihy, James Leo: 136
Herth Realty: 371
Hinde, Thomas G.: xi, xv, 23, 261, 264, 275, 290, 315-318, 320-327, 329, 344, 348, 436, 661
Hirsch, Elroy (Crazy Legs): 544
Hirschfeld, Magnus: 242
History of Homosexuality, The: 200
History of Our Leather-S/M Fetish Sub-Culture and Communities: 63
Hitler: 138, 603, 608, 611, 614-615
Hoffman, Abbie: 180, 182
Hoffman, Bear-Dog: 301
Hoffman, Dustin: 549
Holleran, Andrew: 213, 637
Hollywood Bowl: 417
Hollywood Film Institute: 69
Holocaust: 632
Holst: 310
Holy Cross Parish: 166, 171, 181
Holy Grail: 193
Holy Mountain, The: 305, 384, 605
Homomasculinity: xv, 7, 21-22, 24, 31, 41, 43, 49, 58-59, 68, 72-73, 76, 92-93, 98, 101-106, 122, 131, 138-139, 147, 176, 178, 190, 194, 196, 199-200, 212, 230-234, 240-242, 244, 246-257, 260, 264, 268, 274, 300, 307-309, 311-314, 321, 348, 352, 356-357, 373, 379-380, 392, 394, 402, 407, 409-410, 414, 420, 424, 426, 428-429, 432, 436-437, 445, 449, 451, 467-468, 491, 498, 504-505, 508-509, 511, 514-515, 526, 530-535, 563, 572, 574, 581, 590, 604, 607, 609, 631, 634, 636, 639-640, 659, 666
Homophile Effort: 77, 82, 189, 200
Homosexual Revolution: 237
Honcho: v, 69, 80, 191, 201, 210, 411-412
Hooker: 411, 505
Hormel, James C. Gay and Lesbian Center: ii, 304
Hornack, Nicholas: 76
Horsemen: Leathersex Short Fiction: 63
Hot Flash: 479, 650, 657
Hot L Baltimore: 510
Hotel California: 19, 217, 350, 403
Hotel Quirinale: 601
House Un-American Activities (HUAC): 3, 243
Howard, Leslie: 549
Howard Street: 318, 343, 348
Howe, Delmas: 49
Howl: 269, 324
HUAC (see House Un-American Activities)
Hubbard, Ron: 240
Hubbell, John: 587
Hudson, Rock: 141, 461
Hudson River: 602
Hughes, Glenn: 253, 448

Index

Hula Palace: 271, 659
Hull, R. F. C.: 257
Hun, The: xi, 163, 254, 327, 334, 339, 341, 348, 426, 437, 679
Hunt, Larry: 23, 46, 275, 327, 333, 344, 348
Hurles, David: xi, xv, 23, 25, 33, 41-42, 89, 128, 177, 197, 274-275, 291, 296, 310, 312, 326, 348, 410-411, 493-494, 498-500, 504, 506-507, 515, 540, 555, 557, 560-561, 606, 663-667, 670-671, 680-681
Huxley, Aldous: 103, 385
Hyslop, Bob: 635, 668-669

I

I Am Curious (Leather): 8, 61, 69, 81, 100, 137-138, 196, 211, 245-246, 303, 311, 359-360, 374-375, 377, 390, 392, 423, 441, 576, 580, 665-666
I Am Curious (Yellow): 375
I Didn't Do It for the Money: 495
I Rise in Flame Cried the Phoenix: 431
I-Beam: 521, 625
Icarus: 577
Illinois Ballet Company: 430
Illinois Dental Journal: 430
Illinois Institute of Technology: 431
Ilsa: She-Wolf of the SS: 97, 605, 624
Imitation of Art: 316, 329
Imitation of Christ: 329
IML (see International Mr. Leather)
Immoralist, The: 134
Impossible Dream, The: 538
In and Out: 72, 414, 535
In Cold Blood: 46
In Hot Blood: We Abuse Fags: 62, 310, 665-666
In the Realm of the Senses: 604
In Touch: 411
Inauguration of the Pleasure Dome, The: 448
Inches: 94, 210, 216, 219, 253, 449, 494, 521, 573, 577, 583, 594
Incredibly True Adventure of Two Girls In Love, The: 72
Independent Publisher: i, 69
Indiana University: i
Industrial Revolution: 172
Inferno: 63, 196
Ingram, Cliff: 428
Inquiries of Hope: Ten Poems of Kirby Congdon: 527
Inquisition: 164
Inside Daisy Clover: 546
International Drummer: 125, 259, 475, 604
International Leatherman: 12, 53, 63, 479
International Mr. Leather: 25 Years of Champions: 12, 56, 428
International Mr. Leather (IML): iii, 12, 56, 110, 314, 427-428, 440, 540, 669
International Ms. Leather: 94

International Stud: 510
International Union of Gay Athletes: 559
Interview with the Vampire: 65, 68, 196, 208
Ireland: 5, 231-232, 234, 402, 532, 581, 590
Irish: 5, 71, 92, 171, 183, 214, 217, 219, 237, 394
Isherwood, Christopher: ii, 22, 62, 108, 190, 506, 581, 608-609, 624
Islam: 165, 240-241, 392
Isomer: 503, 510
It Came Upon a Midnight, Dear: 160
Italians: 80, 414, 421, 544, 601, 603, 605-606, 612
Ivanhoe: 536
Ixia: 85

J

J & R Studios: 503
J. Brian's Flashbacks: 412
Jac Masters: 496
Jack Fritscher's American Men: xv, 43, 49-56, 69, 112, 254-255, 258, 260, 525, 570
Jacked: The Best of Jack Fritscher: 68
Jacob, Mike: 56, 540
Jaded Degenerate Man: 593, 595, 651
Jagger, Mick: 470, 492, 547
Jaguar Bookstore: 594, 599
Jailbait: 414
James Dean, A Biography: 134, 147
James Dean (film): 135
Janus Society, The: 23, 89-90, 93-94, 116, 667
Japanese: 25, 262, 304-305, 322, 557, 572, 603-604, 638
Jarman, Derek: iii, 56, 60, 233, 410, 605, 619-620, 664
Jarry, Alfred: 516, 526
JC Penney: 438
Jebe, Walt: 99, 198, 307
Jebe's Camera: 99, 198, 307
Jenner, Bruce: 543, 597
Jeremiah Johnson: 546
Jesuits: 155, 184
Jesus: 103, 167, 241, 379, 611
Jesus Depressed: 580
Jesus-freak: 387
JFK (see President John Kennedy)
Jock Strap League: 483
Jocks Studio: 310
Jockstrap Gym: 540
Jodorowski, Alejandro: 605
John, Elton: 547
John, Tommy: 514
Johnson, Irv: 424
Johnson, Ron (Ronald): xi, 23, 316, 356, 643, 648-649
Johnson-Roehr, Catherine: i
Jones, Christopher: 548
Jones, Derek: 358
Jones, Jim: 109, 123

Jones, Robert: 541
Jonestown: 109, 123, 342, 461
Jordan, Neil: 253
Josephinum Review, The (TJR): 144, 150-151, 159-161, 167, 175-177, 181, 263
Journal of Popular Culture, The: 5-6, 24, 101, 245
Joy of Piss, The: 589
Joyce, James: 209, 222
Judaism: 90, 162, 165, 213, 237, 240-241, 392, 469, 594, 603, 608, 611, 632
Judas: 149
Judy at Carnegie Hall: 236
Juice (see O. J. Simpson)
Juicy Fruit Was Down That Day: 160
Julia: 614
Jung, Carl: 177, 192, 209, 257, 512
Just Men: 219, 253, 411
Justice Weekly: 28

K

Kabuki: 104
Kadota, Mark: 327
Kaiser Engineers: 100, 296, 356
Kalamazoo: 112, 233, 269-271, 287, 319, 347
Kander & Ebb (John Kander, Fred Ebb): xiii, 405, 480, 609
Kandy-Kolored Tangerine-Flake Streamline Baby, The: 209
Kane, Jim (Reverend James Kane, Frank Cross): 90, 92, 116, 121, 162, 179-182, 187-188, 261-262, 267, 270, 287, 304, 311, 380, 383, 416, 431-432, 443-444, 593
Kansas City Trucking Co.: 407, 409, 412
Karr, John F.: i, 2, 67, 72-73, 125, 211, 214
Karsten, David: 509
Kasak, Richard: 202
Keehnen, Owen: v
Keller's: 138, 198, 602
Kelly, Gene: 430
Kempker, Reverend George: 150
Kennedy, President John F.: 134, 167, 171-172, 310, 379, 649
Kennedy, Robert: 235
Kent State University: 186
Kerouac, Jack: 233, 269, 647
Kertbeny, Karoly: 241
Kesey, Ken: 379, 432, 634
Key West Literary Seminar: 229
Key West Writers: 213
Keyhole Studios: 19, 26, 264, 266, 271, 275, 277, 280-282, 284-285, 348, 351-355
Keystone Cops: 296, 607
Keywords: A Vocabulary of Culture and Society: 235, 258
Kiick, Jim: 544-545
Kilgallen, Rob: 458
Kimball, Roger: 258
King, Martin Luther: 4, 166, 175, 181, 235, 640

King, Steve: 412
King and I, The: 141, 430
King Must Die, The: 552
King of Sleaze: 70, 217-218
Kinsey, Alfred: 86, 429, 444
Kinsey Institute: i, 86-87, 429
Kinsey Report, The: 241
Kirk, Marshall: 94
Kirk, Robert (see Cirby)
Kirkwood, James: 510
Kitaro: 461
Kitten with a Whip: 97
Klein, Calvin: 197, 538
Knights Press: 15, 17, 259, 361, 418
Kool-Aid: 84, 123, 461, 634
Kopay, Dave: 540, 550, 572
Korea: 107
Kovalski, Sheldon: 349, 352-353
Koymasky, Andrej: 165
Kraftwerk: 461
Kramer, Larry: 65, 203, 213, 229, 469, 546
Kratzer, Larry: 553
Kriegmont, Dick: xi, 118, 404, 438, 440
Kris Photo Studio: 77, 136, 196, 243, 254, 307, 379, 394, 425, 430-431, 435, 445, 604
Kristal, Hilly: 319
Kristofferson, Kris: 547, 549
Kronengold, A. J.: 510
Kuchar Brothers (George & Mike): 270, 409
Kunstler, William: 184
Kurosawa, Akira: 3, 25
Kushner, Tony: 203, 213, 229, 469
Kustom Kar Kommandos: 409
Kweenasheba: 88, 514
KY Flats: 511

L

L. A. Tool and Die: 407-408
L. T. Publications: 202, 258, 260
L Word: 240
La Boheme: 273, 347
La Cienega: 496
LA&M (see Leather Archives & Museum)
La Mama: 448
LA Plays Itself: 78
Labonté, Richard: iii, 80, 219, 504
Lacoste: 362, 386, 466, 470
Lady Chablis: 104
Lake Michigan: 15, 184
Lakoff, George: 239
Lambda Book Report: 637
Lambda Literary Award: 3, 219, 253, 515, 637
Lane, Larry: 557
Language of Homosexuality, The: 257
Language of Sadomasochism, The: 245, 257
LAPD (see Los Angeles Police Department)
Larry's: 198
Las Vegas: 454
Lascaux: 196, 244, 356, 435-436

Index

Last Picture Show: 603, 612
Last Temptation of Christ: 611
Latin (Latino): 39, 48, 65, 149, 160, 218-219, 233, 247-249, 268, 357, 425, 430, 469, 500, 548, 553, 619, 632, 682-683
Laurence, Joseph (see Aristide)
Laurent, Joseph (see Aristide)
Lautrec, Toulouse: 273, 345, 430
LaVey, Anton: 66, 70, 397
Law, Bernard Cardinal: 145, 151, 157, 247
Law of Christ, The: 160
Lear, Norman: 544
Leary, Timothy: 180, 379
Leather! (booklet): 197, 210, 307, 379-380, 392-393, 493
Leather 'n' Things Catalog: 511, 530
Leather Archives & Museum (LA&M): ii-iv, 12, 56, 78, 90, 92, 195, 197-198, 200-201, 250, 267, 297-298, 300, 302, 305, 314, 348, 356, 383, 394, 398, 426, 428, 438, 440-441, 444-445, 448, 472-473, 478, 505, 519, 574, 604-605, 612, 614, 667
Leather Blues: 61, 65, 69, 100, 105, 137, 196, 211, 233, 303, 311, 359-361, 375, 378, 380, 390, 392, 441, 576, 580, 665-666, 671
Leather Boy, Leather Man: 315
Leather Christmas: xvi, 97, 137, 373, 379-380, 507, 516, 662
Leather David: iv, 136, 273, 345
Leather Emporium: 376, 398
Leather Fraternity: 268, 299, 508, 520, 589
Leather Heritage: 1, 83, 87, 136, 426, 493
Leather History Timeline: 473
Leather Journal, The: iv, 51, 250
Leather Liberation Brigade: 197, 434
Leather List: 194-195, 197-198
Leather Man: 69
Leather Mural Movement: 435
Leather Narcissus: 392
Leather Notebook: 80, 82, 190, 201, 678
Leather Rick: 454, 456, 491
Leather Sabbath: 634
Leather Times: ii, 12, 196, 250, 448
Leather Week: 91
Leatherfolk: Radical Sex, People, Politics, and Practice: 63, 92, 109, 257, 348, 375
LeatherLit Writers Series: 361
Leatherman's Handbook: iii, 5, 8, 61, 81, 189-192, 194-196, 199-203, 205-206, 251, 258-259, 359, 361, 392, 434
Leatherneck: xv, 9, 22-23, 26, 262-264, 266, 275, 278-279, 282, 285-286, 288, 298, 305, 355-357, 362-367, 370-371, 381, 435-436, 446, 512, 517, 572, 662
Leathers, Mike (Dane Leathers): 94
Leathersex Shadows: The Art of Joseph Bean: 12
Leaves of Grass: 134, 233, 241
Leavitt, David: 213, 229
Lebanese-American: 309

LeClaire, Chris: 418
Ledermeister: 305, 420, 511-513, 530, 540
Ledger, Heath: 103, 133, 138
Left Bank: 606
LeGrand, Terry: 78, 379, 409-410, 608, 613, 635, 644, 677-680, 682, 685-686
Lehrer, Tom: 58
Leiber, Jerry: 378
Leibowitz, Annie: 46
Lennox, Annie: 193
Leonardo da Vinci Fiumicino Airport: 602
Lesbian: ii, iv, viii, 2, 69, 87, 89-91, 93-94, 134, 212, 214, 219, 225, 248, 272, 304, 345, 357-358, 360, 508, 537, 570
Lesbian Collection: 304
Lesbian Hanky Code: 93
Lesbian Historical Society: 2, 345
Lesbian Separatism: 94
Levi's: v, 107, 312, 373, 388, 414, 451, 466, 507, 548, 583, 593-594, 651
Levin, Joan: v
Levine, Don: 593-594
Levine, Joseph E.: 414
Lewinsky, Monica: 516
Lewis, Bob: 309
Lewis, Marilyn Jaye: ii, 76, 112
Lewis, Michael: 88, 510, 529
Leyland, Winston: 69, 211, 253, 257, 360, 378, 495, 515, 576, 579
Library Journal: v
Liddy, Gordon: 534, 542
Liebermann, Craig: 559
Life: 33, 130, 193, 236, 273, 313, 435
Lifetime Achievement Award: 48, 68, 112
Lincoln, President Abraham: 241
Lincoln Art Theater: 410
Lincoln Park: 180, 183, 187, 426
Lira, Jack: 632
Little Fauss and Big Halsey: 546
Locke, Richard: 249, 273, 407, 412, 414, 495, 501, 518, 534, 665
Locke Out: The Collected Writings of Richard Locke: 495
Lockner, Clint: 52, 408, 444
Lockwood, Gary: 380
Log Cabin Republicans: 539
Loma Prieta Earthquake: 11, 124, 292, 467
Lone Mountain College: 514, 527
Loneliness of the Long Distance Runner, The: 547
Lonesome Cowboys: 409
Longest Yard: 540, 547
Look Homeward Angel: 209
Looking for Mr. Goodbar: 417, 420
Lorca, Federico Garcia: 609, 614
Lords of Leather: 218, 671
Los Angeles Police Department (LAPD): 22, 36, 52, 77-78, 104, 122-123, 126, 266-267, 296, 299, 396, 401, 410, 417, 465, 580, 607-608, 612, 614

Index

Los Angeles Times: 235
Losey, Joseph: 3
Loss Within Loss: 65
Lourdes Room: 583
Love Story: 102, 139, 217, 222, 255, 315, 452
Love with the Proper Stranger: 450
Lowery, Allan: 23, 264, 266, 316, 355-356, 362-369, 371, 381, 512
Loyola University: 66-67, 100, 164, 167, 181, 184, 431
Luc: 283
Lucie-Smith, Edward: xv, 1, 5, 43, 48-49, 66, 70, 208, 254, 258, 260
Lucifer: 192, 512
Lucifer Rising: 196
Ludlam, Charles: 507
Luger (see Jim French)
Lumiere: 23
Lure: 30, 198, 356, 462
Lurie, Dan: 411
Lyon, Lisa: 263

M

MacArthur Fellowship: 183
MacCloud, Sweat (see Chris Meyrovich)
MacDonald, Boyd: 360
Mach: 12, 14, 130, 163, 223, 260, 412, 661, 685-686
Macho Man: 253
MacLaine, Shirley: 508
Mad Max: 575
MADD (see Mothers Against Drunk Driving)
Madden, John: 541
Maddox, Bob: 197, 432
Madison Theater: 415
Madness of Lady Bright, The: 88, 514, 529
Madsen, Hunter: 94
Mafia: 76, 90, 198, 210, 381, 462, 602-603, 635
Magnum: 100
Mahler, Gustav: 190
Mailer, Norman: 76, 247
Mains, Geoff: ii
Maison Europeene de la Photographie: 69
Maitresse: 604
Majors, Lee: 575
Malanga, Gerard: 649
Male: 23, 27-28, 39, 43, 45, 47-48, 58, 60, 62-63, 66, 69, 71, 92, 95, 103, 107-108, 121, 138-139, 169, 180, 202-204, 207-208, 210, 214, 219, 233, 240, 244, 248-256, 258, 263-264, 268, 276, 305, 309, 357, 376, 379-381, 408, 412, 414, 420, 432, 451, 456, 469, 494, 507, 532-533, 535, 547, 549-550, 554-555, 558, 563, 574, 604, 614, 639, 650, 676
Male Hide Leathers: 197
Maletta, Michael: 649, 652-653
Malory, Sir Thomas: 247
Man Called Horse, A: 384, 547

Man of La Mancha: 538
Man's Country Baths: 425
Man Who Shot Liberty Valence, The: 110
Man-to-Man: 28, 35, 138, 149, 195, 233, 242, 252-253, 360, 363, 373, 382, 384, 387, 533, 556, 559-560, 584
Man2Man Quarterly: 42, 60, 63, 90, 106, 135, 211, 245, 247, 250, 252, 260, 291, 311, 348, 359-361, 411, 434, 443-444, 449, 499-500, 517-518, 540, 564, 576
Mandingo: 409, 546, 572
Manet, Edouard: 437
Maneuvers: 38, 172, 256
Manhattan: iii, 23, 63, 87, 121, 136-137, 162, 197-198, 214, 263, 309-310, 319, 344, 408, 413, 448, 451, 464-465, 468, 480, 483, 492, 506, 527, 540, 641, 649, 651
Manhattanization: 99, 307, 504, 645, 649, 652
Manhood Rituals: 1, 53, 295
Manifest Reader (MR): 1, 84-85, 124, 127-128, 130, 260, 295
Mann, Gill: 327
Manscape: 311
Manson, Charles: 236
Manson Family: 137, 196
Mapplethorpe: Assault with a Deadly Camera: 49, 65, 70-71, 81, 119, 129, 147, 165, 217-218, 258, 263, 317, 330, 344, 348, 425, 449, 453, 455-457, 469, 611
Mapplethorpe, Robert: iv-v, xi, 1, 3, 5, 23, 37, 42, 44, 46, 60, 62, 66, 69-71, 75, 79, 89, 119, 121, 123, 131, 137, 147, 166, 177, 197, 208, 213, 215, 217-218, 220, 230, 243, 246, 249, 254-255, 263, 265, 275, 290, 296, 300, 310, 313, 317-319, 327, 333, 338, 344, 348-350, 352-353, 356, 358, 374, 419, 429, 448-449, 453-457, 460, 463-464, 468-470, 478-479, 491, 499, 505-507, 514, 517, 527, 534-535, 574-575, 581, 604, 611-612, 634, 636, 649-650, 659, 664-665, 676-677, 684
Mapplethorpe Foundation: 455
Marat/Sade: 507
Marathon Man: 384
March, R. J.: 207
Marchand, Jeanne Marie: 412
Marchant, Jonni: 327
Marines (see U. S. Marines Corps)
Mark IV Bath: 465
Market Street: 13, 33-34, 264, 267, 273, 292, 348, 490, 493, 497, 605, 650, 657
Marlboro: 138, 256-257, 381, 512, 584
Marlboro Man: 138, 310, 534, 540, 548
Marlowe, Christopher: 514-515
Marlowe, Kenneth: 199, 235
Mars: 178, 307, 394, 435, 445, 639
Marseille: 479
Martin, Mary: 52, 536
Martin, Paul: 94, 677, 680
Martin, Val (Vallot Martinelli): xi, 10, 45, 78, 425, 500, 608, 634-635, 645, 668-670

Index

Martin of Holland: 436-437, 669
Martinelli, Vallot (see Val Martin)
Marxism: 68, 97-98, 198, 212, 219, 238, 386, 467-468, 537, 539, 595
Masculinist Manifesto: 255, 380, 392, 533
Masculinity: ii, iv-v, viii, 6, 21-23, 27-29, 43, 45-48, 58-59, 62-63, 68, 79-80, 93-94, 97, 102-104, 106-107, 123, 127, 130, 135-136, 138-139, 176, 193-200, 202, 209, 230, 233-234, 236, 239, 242-243, 245-246, 248-249, 251-252, 254-257, 259, 268-269, 274, 297, 300, 312-313, 357, 380, 384, 392, 401-402, 408, 420, 434, 437, 451, 467-469, 480, 507, 509, 514, 520, 527-528, 531-535, 539-540, 548-550, 552, 560, 564, 609, 668
Masculinity and Men's Lifestyle Magazines: 259
Masonic: 39, 237
Masquerade Books: 202
Master's Manual: A Handbook of Erotic Dominance (with Jack Rinella), The: 12
Master Tau: 201
Masters, Scott: 400, 410, 535
Masters, Steve: 197
Masters and Slaves Together (MasT): 63
Mattachine Society: 243
Maupin, Armistead: 38, 65, 71, 316
Maurice: 429
Mavety Corporation: 253
Max's Kansas City: 319, 470
Mayor of Castro Street: 593
Maysles, Albert and David: 198
McCabe, Christina: 327
McCarthy, Judy Tallwing: 94
McCarthy, Senator Joseph: 3, 243, 539
McClemont, Doug: 201
McCullough, C. Michael: 409
McDonald, Boyd: 545
McEachern, Steve: 89, 327, 451
McKnight, Sharon: 88
McMurtry, Larry: 103, 246
McNally, Terrence: 510
McNeill, William: 320-322
McNenny, Jack: 448-449
McPherson, Jim (Thumper): 380-381, 394, 501, 516, 558, 560
McQueen, Steve: 450
McRuer, Robert: 233
McWilliams, Bob: 399-400
MDA: 480
Mead, Margaret: 408, 592
Meaning of Gay, The: 239
Means, Joe: 558
Meat on the Hoof: 552
Meatpacking District: 449, 491
Medici: 388
Medium Cool: 180, 183
Meese Commission: 73
Mellon Fellowship: 359
Melville, Herman: 269, 514
Mendelsohn, Karen: 91

Menerth, Ed: xi, 400, 410, 535
Mentzer, Mike: 558
Merar, Paul: 540
Merrick, Don (see Domino)
Merry Pranksters: 634
Metalious, Grace: 134
Metamorphosis of the Owls: 431
Meterman, The: 511
Metropolitan Community Church: 77
Meyer, David: 653
Meyer, Richard: 233, 611
Meyrovich, Chris (Sweat MacCloud): 355-356, 365, 370
MGM: 397, 414, 616
Miami Dolphins: 544
Michaels, Dick: 77, 396, 399, 625
Michelangelo: 308-309, 345, 456, 495
Midler, Bette: 135
Midnight Cowboy: 103, 136, 235
Midnight in the Garden of Good and Evil: 104
Midnight Sun: 271
Mike Dayton Strength Show: 572
Miles, Sarah: 548
Milk, Harvey: 99-100, 123, 198, 238, 271, 307, 336-337, 342, 352, 504, 530, 593, 609-610, 631-632, 636, 640, 667
Millay, Edna St. Vincent: 430
Miller, Ann: 430
Miller, April: 91
Miller, Arthur: 75
Miller, Edmund: 357-358, 360
Miller, Stephen H.: 202
Miller's Tale: 85, 448
Milton, John: 193
Mineo, Sal: 134-135
Mineshaft: xvi, 59, 90, 198-199, 263, 267, 319, 334, 340, 359, 403, 427, 435, 447-467, 469-474, 478-488, 490-492, 499, 510, 517, 579-580, 582-583, 585, 592, 662
Mineshaft (novel): 359, 361
Mineshaft Man: 454, 481, 484
Mineshaft Manifesto: 451
Mineshaft Newsletter: 427, 447, 457, 459-460, 466, 489
Mineshaft Nights: 359, 459
Minnelli, Liza: 556
Mishima, Go: 315
Mishima, Yukio: 120, 122, 194, 604, 624
Mission Street: 274, 348
Mitchell Brothers: 410
Mizer, Bob: 41, 77, 136, 178, 197, 243-244, 254, 394, 409, 434, 445, 493, 540, 572
Mohn, Carl: 274
MOMA (see Museum of Modern Art)
Mondo Cane: 408
Monet: 437
Mongoose: 37, 499
Monroe, Marilyn: ii, 75-76, 112
Montini, Cardinal: 171
Monty Python: 193

Mooney, Mike: 554
Morales, Max: xi, 266, 275-276, 282-283, 285, 288, 304-305, 366, 370
Morali, Jacques: 448, 491
Moriarity, Dean: 269
Moritz, Bill: 332, 334
Morris, Charles: 321
Morris, Gary: 465
Morris, Mike: 412
Morrison, Don: 162, 197, 510
Morrison, Jim: 319, 385
Morrison, Thom: 116, 370
Morrisroe, Patricia: 70, 204, 217
Morte d'Arthur, Le: 247
Moscone, Mayor George: 123, 238, 337, 342, 530, 609-610, 631-632
Mothers Against Drunk Driving (MADD): 536
Mott, George: 418, 421, 538, 621
Mount Tam: 277, 350
Movements in Art Since 1945: 48
Mr. America: 420, 572, 673
Mr. America AAU: 420
Mr. Benson: 92, 105, 213, 228, 630, 668-670
Mr. California: 540, 563
Mr. Drummer: 68, 118, 124, 127-129, 191, 275, 425-426, 469, 500, 503, 540, 581, 590, 635, 645, 659, 666, 686
Mr. Drummer Contest: 118, 128, 260, 291, 426, 428, 475, 649, 659, 661, 674, 680
Mr. Eagle: 302
Mr. Iron Man: 46
Mr. Madam: 199, 235
Mr. Marcus: xi, 94
Mr. Mineshaft: 455, 458, 469, 491
Mr. Norris Changes Trains: 608
Mr. Pacific Coast: 420
Mr. Universe: 420
Mr. Western America: 420
Mr. World: 420
Mucha, Alphonse: 282
Muir cap: 458, 519
Mulligan, Robert: 450
Munekee, Peter: 304, 306
MUNI (see San Francisco Municipal Railway)
Murphy, Michael: 151
Murray, Thomas E.: 245
Murrell, Thomas R.: 245
Muscle Agonistes: 316
Muscle Beach: 415
Muscle Builder: 543
Muscle Queens: 549
Muscle Training Illustrated: 411
Muse: 70, 263-264, 317, 331, 344
Museum of Modern Art (MOMA): 409, 610
Musgrave, Charles: 400
Music Man, The: 322
Mussolini, Benito: 418, 421, 538, 581, 601, 603, 615, 621
My Hustler: 409
My Shy Bashful Sammy: 444

N

NAACP: 171, 181
Naked and the Dead: 247
Naked and the Nude: 323
Naked Civil Servant, The: 488
Naked Olympics: 537
Namath, Joe: 543, 550
NAMBLA: 13
Narrow Rooms: 68
Nasdijj (see Tim Barrus)
Nashak, Robert: 357, 359-361
Nashoba Institute: 254
National Endowment for the Arts (NEA): 19, 68, 432, 468
National Endowment for the Humanities (NEH): 432
National Film Board of Canada: 410-411
National Guard: 180, 186
National Poetry Association: 378
National Pornographics: 338
National Socialist League: 405
Native American: 21, 24, 155, 546
Natoma Gallery: 507, 515
Naugahyde: 95, 299, 377
Nautilus Fitness Center: 553
Navarette, Skip: 625, 665
Nazi: 242, 398-399, 405, 506, 538, 605, 608, 610, 614
NEA (see National Endowment for the Arts)
Neal, Brian: 14
Negro (see African-American)
NEH (see National Endowment for the Humanities)
Nelson, Chris: 49
Nero, Franco: 399
Network: 653
New Conservatory Theater: 516, 523
New England Patriots: 559
New Guard: 202-203
New Leatherman's Guide: 201
New Partridge Dictionary of Slang and Unconventional English, The: 258, 590
New York Daily News: 235
New York Eagle: 411
New York Native: iv
New York Police Department (NYPD): 187, 488, 607
New York Post: 235
New York's Gay Newspaper Connection: 458
New York Times: 235, 463, 618, 657
New York Wrestling Club (NYWC): 483, 540, 556-557, 560-562
New Yorker: 91, 98-99, 139, 218, 246, 593, 649
Newberry Library: 259, 424
Newman, Leslea: 207
Newman, Paul: 547, 553
Newsleather: 91
Newsletter of Personal Rights: 399

Index 705

NewsWest: 401
Nico: 649
Night Flight: xvi, 274, 505, 518, 521, 647-654, 657, 659, 663
Night Porter, The: 127, 398, 404, 605
Nights in Black Leather: 409
Niven, David: 109
Nixon, President Richard: 185-186, 624
No Name: 23, 316-317, 380, 512, 518, 643, 648
Nob Hill Theater: 408, 410, 505, 663
Nobody Knows What Sorrow: 160
Noebel, David A.: 237
Noh Oratorio: 517, 526-527
Noh Orchestre de Salon du Vay Say: 517
Nolte, Nick: 269
Norse Cove: 310, 594
North American Soccer League: 547
North Beach: 285, 305, 634
Norton, Ken: 531, 534, 546, 572
Numbers: 65
Nureyev, Rudolf: 420, 452, 461, 470, 492
Nutz, P. (see Aristide)
NYPD (see New York Police Department)
NYWC (see New York Wrestling Club)

O

O'Brien, David: 454-455, 469
O'Connor, Flannery: 616
O'Farrell Theater: 410
O'Grady, Camille: 25, 70, 97, 199, 219, 259, 263-264, 275, 280, 284-285, 317-321, 323, 327, 330-331, 333-334, 337, 344, 453, 456, 489, 492
O'Hara, Ryan: 392
O'Hara, Scott: 13, 51
O'Hare, Madelyn Murray: 185
O'Neal, Ryan: 546
O'Rourke, Michael: 232
Oak Street Beach: 424, 427
Oakland Raiders: 541
Obama, Barack: 160
Objectives of the Second Vatican Council: 159
Ochs, Phil: 180
Odyssey of Bobby Joad: 136, 160
Ogle, Alice: 159
Olaf: 334, 339, 493
Old Crow: 41, 348
Old Guard: iv, 202-203
Old Man's Boy Grows Older: 250
Old Reliable: xi, 33, 36-37, 41-42, 62, 73, 79, 89, 128, 177, 197, 274-275, 291, 296, 310, 348, 410-411, 493-494, 496-500, 504, 506, 515, 560-561, 606, 670-671, 680-681
Old Religion of Gay Faerie: 165, 243, 392
Old Testament: 24, 239
Oldenburg, Claes: 647
Oldest Living Confederate Widow: 65
Olive-Oil Wrestling: 555-556
Olson, Frank: 162, 197, 510

Olympia Press: 81
On the Road: 269, 299, 519, 542
On the Town: 430
On the Waterfront: 546
Onassis, Jackie Kennedy: 84, 137, 151, 198
One Arm: 147, 431, 514
One Flew Over the Cuckoo's Nest: 615
Ontkean, Michael: 553
Opel, Robert: xi, 22-23, 25-26, 70, 77-79, 109-110, 121, 123, 200-201, 264, 273, 275, 281, 290, 315, 317-320, 327, 330, 332, 334, 337-338, 340, 343-344, 348, 401, 423, 453, 609-610, 663-664, 669-670
Orange County: 607
Order of the Sixth Martyr, The: 195
Orejudos, Domingo Stephen (see Etienne)
Oscars (see Academy Award)
Oshima, Nagisa: 604
Ossana, Diana: 103, 246
Ostia Antica: 601-602, 622-623
Other Traveler: 81
Outlaw Representation: Censorship and Homosexuality in Twentieth-Century Art: 233, 611
OutWrite: 203
Owsley Acid: 634
Oxford University Press: 24, 258
Oz: 299, 615, 651-652

P

P. G. T. Club: 450
P. R. I. D. E.: 399
P.O.W.: A Definitive History of the American Prisoner-of-War Experience: 587
Pace, Dan (Daniel Pacella): 408
Pacella, Daniel (see Dan Pace)
Pacem in Terris: 172
Pacific Drill Patrol (PDP): 635
Pacino, Al: 461, 469, 488, 491
Package: 80, 332, 401
Paderski, Jerry: 23
Paglia, Camille: 199, 219, 259, 319
Palahniuk, Chuck: 84
Palimpsest: 180
Pallazzo della Civita del Lavoro: 601
Palm Drive Publishing: vii-viii, 258, 515, 570, 579, 591
Palm Drive Video: 46, 51-56, 91, 191, 254, 271, 312, 339-341, 355, 370, 410, 412, 446, 471, 474, 494-495, 516, 525, 539, 576, 636, 643, 671-687
Pan and the Firebird: 86, 431
Panic Movement: 604
Papierowicz, Robert: 161
Paradise Cove: 594
Parente, Ed: 649-650, 653, 657
Parfitt, Matthew: 358, 361
Paris: 17, 67, 69, 235, 306, 516, 581, 606
Parker, Durk (see Durk Dehner)

Pasolini, Pier Paolo: xiii, 60, 386, 410, 588, 601-606, 609-613, 615-617, 622, 624, 662
Pasolini Requiem: 606
Passage to India, A: 429
Passion of the Christ: 611
Passos, John Dos: 614
Patterson, Tico: 500
Paul Cadmus: The Male Nude: 429
Payne, Robert (see John Embry)
PDP (see Pacific Drill Patrol)
Peace Movement: 43, 194, 236, 580
Pearl Harbor: 164, 557
Pearl Street: 267
Pelosi, Pino: 601-602, 617
Penderton, Captain: 548
Pentecostal: 509, 537
Peoria: 159, 415, 606
Peoria Journal Star: 159
Pere Lachaise: 581
Peron, Evita: 476, 612
Perrottet, Tony: 537
Perry, David: ii, 4
Perry, Jay: 397
Perry, Larry: 410, 540, 683, 686
Person, Luiz Sergio: 301, 604, 618
Peter Pan: 139, 249
Peyton Place: 134
Pfleiderer, John: 92, 304
Philadelphia Gay News: v
Philadelphia Joe: 75
Photography: iii, viii, 5, 27-28, 31, 47-49, 62, 66-67, 70, 77, 81, 86-87, 121, 124, 131, 138, 166, 176, 178, 197, 210-212, 228, 230, 242, 255, 274-275, 277, 296, 298, 301, 304, 309-310, 326, 344, 347, 350, 356, 374, 379, 404, 425, 428, 441, 455, 501, 504, 509, 544, 574, 611, 625, 631, 636-638, 661-662, 665, 667-670, 672-686
Physique Pictorial: 77, 178, 197, 244, 307, 394, 421, 434, 445, 496, 558, 572
Picano, Felice: 65, 207, 637
Picasso, Pablo: 25, 66, 437
Piccadilly Circus: 234
Pinero, Miguel: 588
Pink Alley: 267
Pinter, Harold: 3, 19, 505
Pipistrelle: 95
Pirami, Mario: 648
Piss Factory: 453
Pissarro: 436
Planetout.com: i, 2, 245, 469
PlanetSoma.com: 469
Plato: 135, 215, 233, 538
Platonic Ideal: 92, 178, 215, 255-256, 270, 309, 414-415, 498, 513, 530, 534-535, 538
Platt-Lynes, George: 428, 430
Playboy: 266, 275, 414, 471, 537
Playgirl: 47, 501, 559
Plewik, Tony: 512, 669
Plimpton, George: 557

Poe, Edgar Allen: 218
Poe, Terry: 371
Pogey Bait: 411, 503
Pogue, Jim: 150
Poirot, Carl: 150
Polak, Clark: 89
Police (Cop) Olympics: 47, 494, 674
Political Correctness: 9, 21, 43, 68, 84, 95, 97-98, 124, 138, 180, 187, 202, 204, 212, 219, 238, 256, 258, 321, 386, 445, 467-468, 527, 533, 537-539, 604
Polk Street: 269, 348, 494, 573
Pollock, Gordon: 327
Pompeii: 602
Pontecorvo, Gillo: 300-301, 615
Pontifical College Josephinum: 65, 67, 144, 149-151, 156-157, 159-162, 164-165, 167, 175-177, 181, 247, 263
Pookong: 103
Poole, Wakefield: xi, 260, 274, 409-411, 414, 504-507, 510, 518, 649-650, 653, 657, 667
Pop Culture: vii, 6, 43, 66, 70, 101, 131, 133, 189-190, 192-194, 199, 201, 204, 218, 220, 234-235, 239, 244-246, 252, 259, 275, 360, 414, 417, 532, 603, 635, 647, 664, 666
Pope Paul VI: 171
Pope Pius XII: 145
Poppers: 306, 319, 437, 461, 480, 491, 496, 518, 544, 550, 559, 576, 579, 654
Popular Culture Press: 6, 245
Popular Mechanics: 306
Popular Witchcraft: Straight from the Witch's Mouth: 6, 8, 61, 65-67, 70, 100-102, 136-137, 164-165, 195-196, 208, 217, 241, 245-246, 258, 273, 345, 397
Pork: 507
Pornographic Pulsar: v, 66, 76
Port-a-Sans: 640
Porter, Bill: 256
Porter, Cole: 234
Powell, Mason: xi, 221-222
Power Exchange: 91
Powerhouse: 317, 418
Powerplay: 12, 50, 69, 253
Prague Spring: 5, 235, 624
Pravda: 144
Prelude, The: xiii, 236
Prescott, Jack (see John Preston)
Preston, John: xi, 105, 167, 181, 213, 228, 358, 434, 630, 668-670
Preview: The Family Entertainment Guide: 133, 137, 140
Priapus Unsheathed: 219
Pride Foundation: 653
Princeton University Press: 257
Priscilla, Queen of the Desert: 102
Prison Blues: 40-41, 61, 212, 233, 268, 375, 446, 663, 684
Probe Disco: 435-436, 446, 635
Probe Newsletter: 436

Index

Prokaski, Steve: 349, 354
Pronger, Brian: 539, 560
Protestant: 165, 183, 540
Proulx, Annie: 103, 105, 139, 246
Proust, Marcel: 83, 505, 513, 581
Prowler Press: 515, 579, 591
Pruzan, Robert: 515
Pryor, Richard: 417, 420, 606
Psychedelic Ron: 514
Psycho: 459
Pulse: 67, 144-146, 156, 177
Pumping Iron: 543
Pumping Roger: 212, 408, 505, 663
Purdy, James: 54, 56, 68, 432, 434
Pyramide Station: 601

Q

QQ (see Queen's Quarterly)
Quaalude: 320, 373, 383, 597
Quarters, The: 59, 665, 670-671
Queen: iv, 27, 88, 94, 102, 104, 107-108, 199, 207, 214, 222, 235, 237, 239, 247, 249, 255-258, 273, 304, 319, 398, 413, 437, 455, 463, 465-467, 469, 513, 527, 542, 549, 551, 581, 590, 608-609, 612, 620
Queen, Carol: 207
Queen's Quarterly: 249, 413-414, 437, 513, 581, 590
Queening of America, The: iv, 258, 304
Queens' Vernacular: 239
Queer as Folk: 72, 241
Queer Cinema of Derek Jarman, The: iii, 233
Queer Eye: 216, 241
Queer Keyword Conference: 402, 581, 590
Querelle: 399, 514
Quo Vadis: 149

R

R. A. Enterprises: 379
Rabe, David: 510
Race, Sex, and Gender: 48-49, 245, 258
Radical Faeries: 109
Radical Sex: 63, 109, 257, 519, 648
Radloff, Roger: 177
RAF (see Royal Air Force)
Railway Children, The: 198
Rainbow County and Other Stories: 65, 221, 226, 310, 317, 570, 665
Rainbow Motorcycle Club (RMC): 648
Rainbow Tour: 476
Rainier Creek: 643
Ramirez, Efren: xi, 118, 439, 650, 653-654
Rampling, Charlotte: 398, 605
Ramrod: 138, 512
Rand, Bill: 396, 399, 625
Random House: 15, 70, 218
Rashomon: xviii, 1, 3-4, 25, 84, 110, 250, 275, 337

Rasmussen, Mary Louise: 254
Ratched, Nurse: 615
Rather, Dan: 180
Raven, Cliff: 197, 428, 430, 432, 434
Rawhide Male, The: 307, 379, 394
Ray, Nicholas: 134
Real Thing, The: 65, 195-196, 268, 364, 392, 397, 492, 651
Rebel Without a Cause: 134-135, 142-143, 251, 268, 378, 429
Recamier, Madame: 652
Rechy, John: 33, 65, 135, 190, 194, 243, 433
Red Queen: 255
Red Star Saloon: 356
Redford, Robert: 546
Redgrave, Vanessa: 516, 614
Redman Chew: 260, 541
Rednour, Shar: 207
Reed, Lou: 67, 137, 193, 319, 649
Reed, Oliver: 546
Reeves, Steve: xvi, 410, 413-421, 437, 662
Reflections in a Golden Eye: 548
Reisz, Karel: 269
Reite, Bob: 28, 30
Religion: 90, 159, 165, 173-174, 184-185, 231, 239-241, 243, 392, 397, 539, 626
Religious Right: 239, 468, 580, 609
Renault, Alexander: v, xv, 65, 76
Renault, Mary: 552
Reno: 4, 310, 527, 548, 568-571
Reno Sweeney Cabaret: 527
Renslow, Chuck: iii, xi, 12, 56, 77, 121, 136, 178, 196-197, 230, 243, 254, 269, 275, 307, 314, 379, 394, 424-428, 430-432, 434-435, 437-438, 440-441, 444-445, 448, 465, 472, 476
Repubblica di Salo: 603
Republican Convention: 72
Republican Neocons: 580
Rex: xi, 30, 42, 60, 131, 199, 248, 254, 265, 275, 311, 334-335, 340-341, 348, 426, 436-437, 456-457, 467-469, 476-479, 484, 486-487, 491, 499, 516, 544, 649, 665-666
Rex Mundi High School: 544
Rexwerk: 457
Reynolds, Burt: 547, 588
Reynolds, Debbie: 414
RFD: 250
Rhodes, Dave: iv, 51
Riccardo, Guillermo: 412
Rice, Anne: 65, 68, 196, 208, 220
Rice, Jerry: 461, 491
Rich, Frank: 213, 229
Richardson, John: 66
Richardson, Niall: iii, 233
Richter, Daniel: 24
Ridiculous Theatrical Company: 507
Ridley, Brian: 491
Riley, Beau: 320-323
Rimbaud, Arthur: 71, 209

Rinella, Jack: 12
Ringold Alley: 19
Rink: 119, 136, 141, 559, 670
Rip Colt (see Jim French)
Ritch Street Baths: 237
Rite of Love and Death: 604
Ritual: 6, 8, 16, 61, 73, 99, 104, 120, 147, 157, 205, 251, 373, 384-385, 397, 492, 519, 547, 555, 583, 586, 613, 616, 633-634, 642
Ritz, The: 510
RMC (see Rainbow Motorcycle Club)
Robb of Amsterdam: 474
Robbins, Jerome: 429
Robert Mapplethorpe Gallery: 344, 612, 649, 665
Roche, Thomas S.: 207
Rocky (bartender): 286
Rocky (film): 540-541, 546
Rocky Horror Picture Show, The: 420
Rocky Mountains: 313
Rodeo Blues: 375, 667
Rodgers, Bruce: 239
Rofes, Eric: iv, 254
Roger (Daryll Hanson): 212, 260, 408, 410, 505, 518, 663
Rogers, Anthony: 318
Rollerball: 384, 537, 541, 559, 575, 662
Roma Sub Rosa: 420
Roma-Lido: 601
Roman Empire: 198
Roman Martyrology of the Saints, The: 149, 163, 166
Roman Poems: xiii, 601
Romans: 38, 149, 151, 155, 162-164, 166, 168, 171, 192-193, 196, 198, 218, 232, 386, 418, 421, 551, 581, 601-603, 605, 617, 619, 621, 623, 652
Romney, Mitt: 608
Roosevelt, President Franklin D.: 171, 603
Roquelaure, A N: 220
Rorschach: 196
Rose, The: 135, 226, 431, 480
Rose Tattoo: 431
Roseanne: 72
Rosetta Stone: 83, 256
Rota, Katos: 337
Rousseau, George: 241
Routledge: 258, 590
Rove, Carl: 3
Rowberry, John: v, 91, 121, 124, 127, 265, 291, 358, 395-396, 398-401, 404, 671
Roxie: 23
Royal Air Force (RAF): 48
Royale Photography: 379
Rubin, Gayle: 90-91, 97, 469, 679
Rubin, Jerry: 180
Rubyfruit Jungle: 65
Rudolph, Lou: 120, 327, 348
Rugby: 466, 547
Run Little Leather Boy: 81, 196, 201, 205

Run No More: 201
Running Fence (see Christo)
Rush Street: 424, 427
Russell, Ken: 546, 614
Russian River: 26, 527
Russo, Donnie: 44, 51, 410, 683-684
Russo, Vito: 469
Ruth, Babe: 553
Ryan's Daughter: 548
Rydell, Mark: 135

S

S&M: The Dark Side of Gay Liberation: 321, 467
Sabaean Religion: 397
Sabatino, Michelangelo: 418
Sackville-West, Vita: 83
Saigon: 467
Saint Among the Hurons: 155
Saint Francis: 611
Saint Isidore: 514
Saint Sebastian: 597, 605-606, 619
Salo: xvi, 60, 386, 410, 601, 603-606, 609-613, 615-617, 662
Salo Republic: 603
Samois: 90, 93-94
Samurai: 305
San Diego: 496, 586
San Francisco Actors Ensemble (SFAE): 512
San Francisco Art Institute: 324
San Francisco Ballet: 60, 504
San Francisco Chronicle: i, iv, 4, 88, 99-100, 115, 231, 237-238, 293, 310, 332, 342, 568-569, 639, 669
San Francisco Chronicle Pink Section: 514
San Francisco City Hall: 337, 566, 610
San Francisco Civic Center: 116
San Francisco Deputy Sheriff: 28, 100, 272, 274, 278, 288, 364
San Francisco Ferry Building: 273
San Francisco Gay and Lesbian Film Festival, The: 212
San Francisco GLBT Historical Society: i, 87, 98, 245, 263
San Francisco Historical Society: 98
San Francisco Municipal Railway (MUNI): 296
San Francisco Police Department: 107, 336, 535-537, 566-567, 607
San Francisco Public Library: ii, 304
San Francisco Review of Books: iii
San Francisco Seaman's Hall: 632-635, 640, 642, 645
San Francisco Sheriff: 75, 272, 364, 536
San Quentin: 40
Sanctuary: 356, 435, 446
Sanders, Dennis: 626
Sandinistas: 538
SandMutopia Guardian: 12

Index

Santa Monica Boulevard: 127, 135, 398, 404, 500, 573
Sarandon, Susan: 243
Sardinia: 605, 619
Sarria, Jose: 106, 640
Sartre, Jean-Paul: 507
Satanic Warrior: 595
Satanism: 66, 68, 70-71, 164, 193, 195, 208, 210, 243, 397, 463, 595
Saunders, Dick: 77, 435-436, 446, 635
Saunders, Steve: 113
Sausalito: 411
Savage, Dan: 469
Save Our Children: 606
Saylor, Steven (Aaron Travis): iii, xi, 198, 358, 420, 671
Scatology: 62, 218, 386, 480, 517, 580, 596
Schlesinger, Arthur, Jr.: 22
Schlesinger, John: 136
Schmitz, Sepp: 512
School for Lower Education: 450, 484, 489
Schroeder, Barbet: 604
Schulman, Sarah: 229, 469
Schultz, Fred: 200
Schwartz, Barth David: 606
Schwartz, Thomas: 479
Schwarzenegger, Arnold (Arnold Strong): 272, 414-415, 419, 538, 543-544, 575
Schwerner, Michael: 173
Schwirtz, Mira: iii
Scientology: 240
Scorpio Rising: 65, 120-121, 135, 196, 251, 268, 288, 379, 409, 431, 437, 588
Scorsese, Martin: 611
Scott, Donald: 535
Scott, George C.: 457
Scott, Walter: 535-536
Scott of London: 379
Scuba Diving: 553
SCUM (Society for Cutting Up Men): 255
Scum That I Am: 580
Seaman's Hall: 632-635, 640, 642, 645
Sebastiane: 60, 410, 605, 619, 664, 669
Second Coming Out: 57, 236, 373
Secret Storm, The: 162, 510
Sedgwick, Eve Kosofsky: 104
Selby Avenue: 378
Semi-Tough: 547, 549, 552, 588
Sending My Heart Back Across the Years: Tradition and Innovation in Native American Autobiography: 24
Sentinel: 318, 320-321, 323
Seven Beauties: 605, 614
Sex and Temperament in Three Primitive Societies: 408
Sex Variants: A Study of Homosexual Patterns: 257
Sextool: 78, 409-410, 634
Sexual Outlaw, The: 135, 243
Sexuality in Western Art: 48-49

Shadow Soldiers: 219, 675-677
Shakespeare: 193, 217, 241, 519, 530
Shapiro, Allen J. (see A. Jay)
Shapiro, Roy: 653
Shaw, Gary: 552
Shepard, Matthew: 210, 606
Sheppard, Simon: 207
Sheridan Square: 235
Shiites: 27
Shilts, Randy: iv, 14, 107-108, 310, 568
Shiny Boots of Leather: 193
Short Eyes: 588
Shryock, Nick: 517
Shulman, Sarah: 213
Siegal, Elliot: 44, 310
Simon, Mario: 78, 275, 425, 612
Simon, Paul: 547
Simon Lowinsky Gallery: 344
Simpson, Mark: 76
Simpson, O. J. (The Juice): 531, 534, 545
Sin: A Cardinal Deposed: 151
Sinatra, Frank: 143, 430
Sink, Virginia: v
SIR (Society for Individual Rights) Center Theater: 88
Sissy: 256, 263, 274, 468, 532-534, 548, 553
Sisters of Perpetual Indulgence: 639
Six Feet Under: 72
Six Million Dollar Man: 575
Skin: 219, 411
Skinflicks: 253, 408
Skipper (Glenn Davis): xi, 356, 426, 435, 437-438, 446, 542, 675, 684
Skulls of Akron: 454-455, 491-492
Skylstad, Bishop William: 151
Slapshot: 553
Slater, Cynthia: xi, 23, 89, 92, 97, 327, 675
Slave Auction: 36, 78, 102, 104, 106, 122, 126, 201, 267, 299, 401, 417, 465, 580, 607-608, 664
Slavery of Words: 581, 590
Slaves of the Empire: iii, 420
Slot Hotel: 23, 211, 253, 265, 272-273, 277, 316, 345, 349-354, 454, 490, 537, 633
Smith, Jack: 270, 409
Smith, Michael: 547
Smith, Patti: 263, 319, 327, 344, 448, 453
Smithee, Alan: 297
Society for Cutting Up Men (see SCUM)
Sodom-by-the-Bay: 651
Sodomite: 240
SoHo: 205
Solanas, Valerie: 235, 255
Solomon, Holly: 70
Solstice: 67, 91, 217, 524-525
SoMa (see South of Market)
SoMa Open Studio: 273
Some Dance to Remember: ii, iv, 3-6, 15, 17, 24-25, 33, 38, 41, 43, 65-66, 69, 71, 74, 81, 83, 88-90, 94-95, 100-101, 103, 116, 120,

129, 131, 164-165, 167, 208-209, 216-218, 236, 241, 246, 251, 253, 255-259, 269, 271, 290, 305, 317-318, 337, 340, 348, 359-361, 380, 392, 399, 403, 415, 418, 421, 424, 433, 444, 453, 457, 463, 471, 479, 505-506, 512, 528, 533, 536, 538-539, 545, 560, 563, 569, 582, 590, 594, 605, 608-609, 621, 632, 674, 677, 680
Somebody Up There Likes Me: 546
Something for Everyone: 363, 484, 588
Sondheim, Stephen: 212
Song of Norway: 430
Sonoma County: 274, 283
Sontag, Susan: 156, 235-236, 239, 392
Soul Kiss: 76
South China Café: 107
South of Market (SoMa): i, xv, 2, 15, 19-20, 22-26, 34, 88, 92, 109, 121, 123, 125, 129, 205, 214, 261, 263-268, 270-271, 273-277, 283, 292, 298, 303, 305, 313, 317, 321-322, 327, 333, 340, 343, 345, 347-350, 371, 387, 394, 457, 528, 591, 593, 634, 639-640, 645, 649, 661
South of Market Club: 387
South of Market Open Studio: 277
South of the Slot: 264, 273, 292-294
South Pacific: 252
Souza, John Philip: 426
Spain: 149, 249, 275, 425, 603-604, 612, 614, 624
Spanner Defense Fund: 91
Sparrow, David: xi, 23, 39, 60, 98-99, 112-114, 116, 121, 198, 264, 267, 269-271, 273, 287, 303, 307, 310, 316-317, 319, 326, 329-330, 347, 349, 355, 368, 371, 374, 390, 424-425, 428, 430-432, 477, 509, 512, 514, 544, 551, 593-594, 596, 598, 631-633, 636, 648, 658, 663-668, 670-671
Sparrow, Nellie: 269
Sparrow, Phil (see Samuel Steward)
Speeding: The Old Reliable Photos of David Hurles: 42, 499
Spelvin, Georgina: 411, 505
Spielberg, Steven: 582
Spike: 411, 452, 510
Spitting Image: 317, 658
Sports Film International: 558-559
Sports Illustrated: 540-542, 544-545, 662
SPQR: 163
Spring, Justin: iii, xi, 429, 432, 438
St. Mark's: 211
St. Mark's Theater: 604
St. Mary's College: 323-324
Stabler, Ken: 534, 540-542
Stacy, Jim: 553
Stallone, Sylvester: 546, 549
Stamp, Terence: 601
Stamps, Wickie: 478, 685
Stanford University: 545
Stanislavski, Constantin: 220

Stanton, Bull (see Chris Duffy)
Star Pharmacy: 268, 594
Starmakers: 658
Stars: 649-650, 654-655
State of Siege: 615
Steam: 51
Steel, Richard A.: 40, 503, 510
Stein, David: iii, xv, 57, 63, 518
Stein, Gertrude: 2-3, 68, 121, 196, 220, 305, 428-429, 431-433, 443-444, 581
Steinbeck, John: 134, 142
Steinem, Gloria: 235
Steptoe, Lydial: 91
Sterling, Jim: 34
Steroids: 272, 415, 517, 535
Stevenson, Adlai: 33
Steward, Samuel Morris (Phil Andros, Phil Sparrow): iii, xi, 2, 23, 66, 68, 86-87, 105, 121, 196-197, 220, 305, 316, 345, 347, 359, 361, 377, 423-424, 427-434, 438, 443-444, 517, 581, 593, 663
Stewart, Jim: ii, xi, xv, 19, 25-26, 34, 121, 261, 263-266, 268-286, 288, 290, 298, 304-305, 315, 319, 327, 347-355, 362, 365-367, 370, 661
Stewart, Jim (Fetters of London): 518
Stewart, Robert: 315, 326
Stierman, Hy: 218
Stoller, Mike: 378
Stomp: 515
Stompers Gallery: 177, 313, 315, 435, 527
Stone, Gary: 230
Stone, Oliver: 102, 208
Stone, Robert: 269
Stonehenge: 240
Stonewall Inn: 235, 428, 465, 607
Stonewall Rebellion: 27, 96, 102, 108, 135, 166, 179, 181, 187, 230, 462, 465, 536, 576
Storer, Rick: iv, xi, 448
Storey, David: 547
Story of O: 90
Strachey, Lytton: 516, 526
Strand Theater: 23, 605
Strange One, The: 508
Streaking: 332, 401, 453
Streamers: 510
Streetcar Named Desire, A: 136, 147, 219, 251, 509
Streisand, Barbra: 19, 212, 546
Streit, Samuel: i
Stripper, The: 553
Strite, Arnold: 99-100
Strogen, Tom: 458
Stroke: v, 360
Strong, Arnold (see Arnold Schwarzenegger)
Stryder, Kent: 327
Stud ($tud): 444
Studio 54: 90, 470, 491-492
Studio Rhino: 515-517, 526

Index

Suddenly Last Summer: 136, 147, 241, 386, 431, 509
Sullivan, Andrew: 251, 532
Summer and Smoke: 512
Summer of Love: 194, 379
Summers, Claude: 357-358
Sun and Steel: 120, 194
Sun Dance: 373, 547
Sundstrom, Nancy: v, 69
Sunnis: 27
Sunset Boulevard: 404, 494
Super Bowl: 541, 642
Super MR: 1, 85, 129-130, 295
Super-8: 37, 41, 52, 86, 227, 316-317, 394, 410, 506, 511-512, 516, 535, 543, 558, 572, 576, 648-650
Superman: 384, 530, 667
Suresha, Ron: iv, 251, 254, 257, 259-260
Sutherland, Joan: 457
Sweeney, Robin: 91
Sweet Bird of Youth: 136, 265, 431
Sweet Embraceable You: 65, 317, 529
Sweet Life Café: 527
Sweet Surrender: 461, 491
Swinton, Tilda: 620
Sylvester: 67, 271, 659
Sylvestri, Leonard: 493, 495, 501
Syphilis: 19

T

Tabard Inn: 448
Tales of the City: 65, 71, 208, 316
Tan, Cecilia: 207
Tangier: 581
Tap Dogs: 515
Target Studios: 162, 197, 254, 265, 308-309, 311-312, 314, 375, 390, 411, 423, 438, 441, 496, 505, 576, 649, 664-665, 668
Tavarossi, Tony: 106-107, 120, 122, 198, 316, 349-350, 425, 441, 479, 537, 633, 676
Tavern Guild: 107
Taxi Driver: 553, 594-595
Tay-Bush Inn: 107
Taylor, Elizabeth: 78, 109, 141, 548
Taylor, Lucy: 207
Taylor, Scott: 13
Taylor of San Francisco: 304-305
Television Today: 71, 100, 162, 217, 510, 573
Tellman, Bill: 273, 290, 345
Tenderloin: 23, 41, 348, 520
Tennis: 496, 553
Tennis shoes: 195
Teorema: 588, 601
Terminator: 575
The Boys in Blue: 444
Theater of Cruelty: 605
Theater Rhinoceros: 515
Theatre de Lys: 508
These Three: 508

Thewlis, David: 510
They Shoot Horses Don't They: 548
This Sporting Life: 547
Thomas, Coulter: 13
Thomas, Lou (Nick D'Arti): xi, 162, 197, 230, 254, 265, 308-314, 374-375, 377, 390, 423, 441, 576, 649
Thompson, Hunter: 200, 245
Thompson, JimEd: xi, 201
Thompson, Mark: ii, xi, 63, 92, 109-110, 348, 375
Thoreau, Henry David: 61, 128, 200, 257, 261, 550, 576
Thorne, Dyanne: 605
Thornton, Graylin: 68, 581, 590
Thrasher, Steve: 54, 56
Three Bears in a Tub: 219, 225-226
Three Days of the Condor: 546
Thrust: 53, 69
Thumper: 380-386, 388, 394, 501, 516, 558, 560
Tiber: 602
Tiffany: 521
Tiffenbach, Joe: 534-535, 540, 573-575
Tijuana Bible: 243, 359
Timothy and the Shamrocks: 160, 263
To Live and Die in LA: 463
Today: 160, 162
Toilet, The: 459, 552, 583, 588
Toilet Kiss: 264, 319, 453
Toklas, Alice B.: 2, 68, 121, 428-429, 432, 443-444
Tokyo: 305
Tom Hinde Portfolio: xv, 261, 315, 324
Tom of Finland: 59, 197, 199, 254, 304, 309-311, 313-315, 334, 356, 377, 426-427, 434-438, 440, 444, 446, 456, 527, 646, 649, 663-664
Tom of Finland Foundation: 48, 311-314, 377, 426
Tom's Bar: 446
Tom's Saloon: 356, 435
Tomlin, Lily: 417, 550
Tommy: 514, 527, 614, 651
Tomnitz, Jim: 557
Tomorrow Belongs to Me: 614
Tomorrow's Man: 307, 379, 424, 435, 445
Tool Box: 34, 107, 138, 193, 195-196, 273, 289, 356, 430, 435, 444, 446, 452, 583
Torch: 149, 152, 159-160, 168, 181, 221
Torres, Jerry: 198
Torso: v
Torture: 205, 300-301, 384, 579-580, 585-588, 604-605, 618
Total Eclipse: 430, 510
Tough Customers: 12, 59, 62, 139, 252, 661, 666-670, 675, 686-687
Townsend, Larry: iii, xi, xv, 5, 8, 61, 77, 81-82, 119, 126, 189-203, 205-206, 251, 258-259, 359, 361, 377, 379, 392, 434, 570, 678

Trading Post: 496
Trans-Europe Express: 461
Transcendentalist: 257
Trash: 65
TRASH: True Relations and Strange Happenings: 285, 520, 669
Trask, Cal: 136, 142
Trask, Richard (Dick): 264, 497, 657
Travis, Aaron (see Steven Saylor)
Tress, Arthur: 60, 131, 254, 574, 668-669
Triangle Building: 464
Triumph: 435
Triumph Gym: 196, 425, 428
Trocadero Transfer: 659
Trojan Horse: 97, 190, 300
Trojanski, John: 296, 410, 625, 667
Trowbridge, John: 593, 599, 663
Trucks: 27
Tubstrip: 510
Tuck, Alan: 419
Tuffy's Sport Shop: 495-496, 540, 553-554
Turd Bound: 517
Turd Cuckolded: 517
Turkish Delight: 556, 665
Turner, Ted: 534, 541
Turner, Tina: 364
TWA: 310
Twilight Zone: 449
Twink: Stories of Gay Young Men: 238
Twinkie Defense: 238, 337, 609
Tyrrhenian Sea: 602

U

U. S. Air Force: 191
U. S. Constitution: 165, 179, 240, 607-608, 610
U. S. Declaration of Independence: 179, 181, 192-193, 200, 255, 531
U. S. Marines Corps (USMC): 27, 59, 150, 162, 220, 362-364, 381, 467, 504, 580, 583, 585, 645, 664, 687
U. S. Navy: 586
U. S. Post Office: 243
U. S. Senate: 243, 468, 610
Ubu Cuckolded (Ubu Cocu): 517
Ubu Cycle, The: 516-517, 526
Ubu Enchained (Ubu Enchaine): 517
Ubu Rex (Ubu Roi): 516
UC Berkeley (see University of California, Berkeley)
UCLA (see University of California, Los Angeles)
Ulrichs, Karl: 241
Un Mondo d' Amore: 606
Unchained Melody: 544
Uncut: 223, 253, 411
Uncut Society of America (USA): 574
Universal Gym: 545
University College Dublin: 231-232, 234, 402, 532, 581

University of California, Berkeley: 231, 432, 545, 550-551
University of California, Davis: iv
University of California, Los Angeles (UCLA): 82, 191, 359
University of Chicago Press: 19
University of Exeter: 232
University of Southern California: 233, 545
University of Sussex: iii, 233
University of Wisconsin Press: 245, 258, 345
Untimely Death of J. Cristobal: xv, 149, 152, 160, 218
Unzipped: 210, 338
Upper Terrace: 304
Urban Aboriginals: ii, 100, 537
USA Athletic Club: 496
USA Trilogy: 614
USMC (see U. S. Marines Corps)
USMC Recruit Depot: 362

V

Vader, Darth: 438
Vagnozzi, Egidio Cardinal: 157
Valence, Liberty: 110
Valentino, Rudolph: 140, 420, 549
Valerio, Michael S.: 635
Valium: 596
Van Buskirk, Jim: ii
Van Gogh, Vincent: 263
Van Leer, David: iv, 304
Van Leer, Russell: 263, 304, 349, 351, 353-354
Van Meter, Eric: 667
Vanity Fair: 70, 217, 448
Variety: 151
Varney, Greg: 39, 540, 554, 560
Vatican: 65, 159, 166, 212
Vatican II: 160
Velvet Mafia: 76
Velvet Underground: 193, 507, 649
Venable, Sebastian: 386, 509
Venice Beach: 45, 194, 272, 415, 558, 572
Venus: 20
Vere, Captain: 269
Verite: 6, 102, 127, 133, 139, 180, 190, 208-209, 218, 227, 250, 262, 274, 300, 329, 351, 408, 491, 562, 573, 604, 618
Veronica: 149
Vesti, Eigil: 459
Vichy: 603
Vickers, Frank: 464
Victor, Terry: 258, 590
Victorian: 27, 126, 299, 506, 588
Vidal, Gore: ii, 42, 180
Vietnam War: 28, 301, 467, 624
Village People, The: 81, 87, 196, 253, 448, 491, 533
Village Voice, The: 235, 254, 321, 466-467
Vincent, Joseph: 653
Violet Quill: 87, 637

Index 713

Virginia Beach: 27
Visual Art of Sam Steward: 438
Vitamin Q (see Quaalude)
Vitruvian Man: 308-309
Vittore, Sal: 94
Viva la Muerte: 604-605, 614, 624
Vogler, Christopher: 217
Voight, John: 136, 546, 549
Voracity Beat: 76

W

Waddell, Tom: 495, 531, 560, 574
Wagner, Alex: 50
Wagstaff, Sam: 42, 499
Waiting for Mr. Goodbar: 553
Walker, Cleo: 317
Walker, Clint: 511
Walker, Gerald: 463
Walker, Robert: 316-317
Walker, Willie: i, 87
Walking Higher: Gay Men Write about the Deaths of Their Mothers: 76
Walla Walla State Penitentiary: 38
Wallace, James: 448, 460
Wallace, Kevin: 99
Wallace, Wally: 198, 319, 340, 427, 447-464, 466, 469-470, 472-479, 484-485, 487, 489, 491-492, 592
Waller, Ken: 415
Walls, Jack: 456
Ward, Bill: 8, 198
Warhol, Andy: 66-67, 193, 235, 252, 270, 319, 409, 456, 507, 511, 649, 657
Warren, Patricia Nell: 76, 255
Washer, Ben: 536
Washington Street: 447, 450-451, 485, 492
Waterboard: 587
Watergate: 542, 624
Waters, John: 42, 67, 456
Waters, Leif: v
Way We Were, The: 19, 23, 232, 249, 262, 274, 408, 462, 546, 576, 581
Wayne, John: 248
Weber, Bruce: 197
Weber, Gene: xi, 262-263, 267, 304-305, 540, 553, 572, 662
WeHo (see West Hollywood)
Weider, Joe: 414, 543
Weingarden, Louis: 315, 527
Welch, Paul: 130
Weld, Tuesday: 269
Wendell, Reverend Francis N.: 168
Werner, Bruce: 201
Wertmueller, Lina: 604-605, 614
West Hollywood (WeHo): 73, 127, 205, 378, 398, 404, 573
West Side Story: 430
West Street Gang: 510
West Village: 449, 470, 602

Western Michigan University (WMU): 186, 270, 355, 432, 509, 648
Wexler, Haskell: 180, 183
What They Did to the Kid: 65, 69, 100, 157, 162-163, 167, 218, 246, 424, 427
Wheaties: 543
When in Rome Do: 196
When Malory Met Arthur: 67
Where Angels Fear to Tread: 429
Whipcrack: 77, 99, 113, 198, 303, 307
White, Dan: 109, 317-318, 337, 530, 609-610, 632
White, Edmund: 65, 108, 213, 229, 637
White House: 241, 610
White Night Riot: 238, 318, 336, 342, 536, 566, 607, 609
White Party: 647
White Stains: 335
Whiter Shade of Pale, A: 93, 211
Whiting, Margaret: 493
Whitman, Walt: 28, 134, 209, 223, 233, 236, 241, 256, 268-269, 609
Who Killed Pasolini?: 606
Who'll Stop the Rain?: 269
Who's Afraid of Virginia Woolf?: 509
Who's Written History?: 24
Whoever Says the Truth Shall Die: 606
Wicked Witch of the West: 606
Wigler, Jim: 13, 110, 679
Wilburn, Jack: 626, 628
Wild Blue Yonder: 207, 218, 375
Wild One, The: 110, 135, 198, 251, 268, 378, 393, 416, 424, 437, 508-509, 588
Wilde, Oscar: 27, 76, 209, 470
Wilder, Thornton: 68, 581
Wilkes University: 30, 76
Will and Grace: 72
Willard, Avery: 379, 392-393
William and Mary Quarterly: 24
Williams, Raymond: 258
Williams, Tennessee: 66-67, 100-101, 103, 136, 147, 166, 241, 246, 301, 431, 482, 509, 512, 514, 542
Willingham, Calder: 508
Wilson, Doric: 510
Wilson, Lanford: 88, 510, 514, 529
Wilson, S. Clay: 290
Wilson, Scott: 558
Winnic, Charles: 71
Winnie the Pooh: 67
Winning: 547
WITCH (see Women's International Terrorist Conspiracy from Hell)
Witchcraft: 66, 75, 103, 164-165, 243-244, 345
Witkin, Joel-Peter: 46, 70
Witomski, TR: 13
Wizard's Emerald City: 264, 493, 497, 657
Wockner, Rex: 469
Wolfe, Thomas: 209
Wolfe, Tom: 209

Womack, Dr. Herman Lynn: 89
Women (Woman): 21, 29, 43, 45, 47-48, 65, 69, 78, 89, 91-97, 100, 103, 108, 126, 135, 153-154, 164, 183, 199-201, 204, 209, 214, 219, 225-226, 229, 232, 235-236, 239-240, 242-243, 246, 249, 252, 254-257, 264, 272, 319, 327, 373, 385, 410, 452-453, 470, 518, 533, 537-539, 546, 549, 551, 553, 576, 580, 604, 608, 614-615, 636, 648, 650
Women in Love: 546, 549
Women's International Terrorist Conspiracy from Hell (WITCH): 3, 6, 65, 67, 72, 100-102, 136, 165, 183, 195, 208, 217, 243, 246, 258, 273, 345, 397, 516, 539, 606, 615
Wonder Robot: 651
Wong, Hertha Dawn: 24
Wood, Natalie: 134, 450, 546
Woodlawn Organization, The: 145, 166, 171, 181, 428
Woods, Ed: 414
Woodstock: 108, 236, 428, 470
Woolf, Virginia: 234, 317, 509, 516
Wordsworth, William: xiii, 236, 408
World Trade Center: 580
World War II: 27-28, 107, 150, 193, 207, 252, 305, 379, 572, 603, 605, 610
Worlds to Conquer: An Authorized Biography of Steve Reeves: 418
Wrangler, Jack: 407, 493
WRET-TV: 541
Wright, Les: 251, 254
Wright, Richard: 170
Writer's Aid: 213-214, 228, 377, 625, 629, 665, 667-668
Writer's Journey: Mythic Structure for Storytellers and Screenwriters: 217
Wycoff, David: 594, 598, 662
Wyler, William: 508

X

X-Files: 199

Y

Yale, Joey: 10, 59, 238
Yellow Bird: 431
Yippie: 180
YMCA, Golden Gate: 237
YMCA, Lawson: 145, 427, 551
Yonkers Theater Production Company: 88, 510, 514, 529
York, Susannah: 546
Young, Ian: 72
Young, Neil: 582
Young, Wendell Richard: 586
Young Lords: 183

Z

Z: 182, 185, 301, 615
Zach of Los Angeles: 315
Zebra, Ruby: 334
Zee Hotel: 41, 348
Zelig: 46, 108
Zen, Michael: 409
Zeus Studio: 201, 469, 670
Zinnemann, Fred: 614
Zodiac (bar): 450, 583
Zorba the Greek: 551
Zulu Dance: 547
Zygarlicki, Bob: xi, 625-626, 628, 663

www.ingramcontent.com/pod-product-compliance
Lightning Source LLC
Chambersburg PA
CBHW021049080526
44587CB00010B/186